THE COMPLETE

DOG BOOK

THE COMPLETE
DOG BOOK

[*New and Revised Edition*]

THE CARE, HANDLING, AND
FEEDING OF DOGS

AND

PURE BRED DOGS: THE RECOGNIZED
BREEDS AND STANDARDS

AN OFFICIAL PUBLICATION OF

THE AMERICAN KENNEL CLUB

*With Over 100 Illustrations by R. W. Tauskey
and Others*

HALCYON HOUSE : NEW YORK

PREFACE

This book is offered to the public by The American Kennel Club in response to the many requests received by it from dog owners throughout the United States who felt there existed a need for an official publication giving the latest standards and also the origin and histories of the different recognized breeds of dogs in this country and in addition reliable information on their care, handling, and feeding. The valuable treatise thereon included in this volume was carefully prepared for the American Kennel Club by that most eminent authority, Edwin Reginald Blamey, M.R.C.V.S., and the American Kennel Club deeply appreciates his painstaking co-operation.

In the main each standard and historical article as presented, is the one drawn up by the breed club of this country or, if none existed here, the country where the breed originated or is now most popular. The American Kennel Club, beyond endeavoring to present the latest official standard of each breed, assumes no responsibility for the drawing up or forming of these standards and articles.

It was felt that each breed should be represented or pictured by illustration. Sketches of the ideal dog of each breed were suggested. After a careful deliberation of the subject, it was decided this would be unwise as it would mean presenting only the artist's conception of the ideal type, which might very possibly not conform with that of the majority interested in that particular breed.

PREFACE

Therefore, illustrations of actual photographs of dogs considered to be typical specimens of their breeds, are used. In order to obtain these, requests were made to the different breed clubs for a photograph of a dog considered to be a typical specimen. The majority of the photographs, so submitted, appear in the book. In some instances, however, the club was unable to furnish a photograph suitable for reproduction, in which case a more typical picture was selected. It however is understood that these photographs are not published as being examples of perfect dogs but only prints them as being pictures of the most typical type procurable of each breed.

For help in the preparation of this book, The American Kennel Club desires to extend its most grateful thanks to the secretaries and other officers of the various breed clubs, both in this country and abroad, and to all who have so kindly assisted in the effort and thus made the work easier of accomplishment and more valuable in result.

CONTENTS

CONTENTS

GROUP II—SPORTING DOGS (HOUNDS)

GROUP III—WORKING DOGS

CONTENTS

GROUP IV—TERRIERS

CONTENTS

LIST OF ILLUSTRATIONS

(Arranged alphabetically in order of breed)

LIST OF ILLUSTRATIONS

LIST OF ILLUSTRATIONS

[xiii]

LIST OF ILLUSTRATIONS

NOTE

Various States throughout the United States of
America have laws which forbid the cropping or
cutting of dog's ears, or the possession of dogs
whose ears have been cropped in those States
subsequent to the enactment of such laws

INTRODUCTION

In modern times there has come a fuller appreciation of the dog and his importance to man; yet the bond of companionship that links man and dog extends back to the dim beginnings of civilization. In the history of the dog lies the history of all peoples; in the development of the dog is the development of all races; and in the love of the dog is reflected the finer instincts of all human kind.

Man and dog have grown apace through the generations. Theirs is a partnership that has endured through happiness and sorrow; has persisted when cataclysmic disaster shook the earth; and has been of such force as to catch the attention of our greatest philosophers.

If there is any single service that can aid the cause of the dog and his many pure-bred varieties it is the collecting of the countless fragments of his history from the literature of the world. And this is the work that finds fruition in the publishing by the American Kennel Club of "The Complete Dog Book." This book is submitted to dog lovers with the conviction that it is the most complete and authentic work ever published on the recognized breeds of the world. It shows facts in dozens of cases where only hazy speculation has been true in the past. The men and women who have contributed to these pages —penning the histories of more breeds than are recognized by any other nation in the world—have left few ancient or modern sources unplumbed to gather material for their articles which have been edited with a constantly challenging, critical eye that demanded authentic foundation for every statement.

The dog is mentioned in some of the earliest parts of the Old Testament and in the course of some forty references to him in the Bible one learns that there was great

INTRODUCTION

differentiation in breeds and types, and of all the basic lore on the dog, the most definite has been bequeathed to us by the ancient Egyptians and Assyrians. The earliest picture showing dogs is found on the Tomb of Amten, in Egypt, which dates to the 4th Dynasty, or between 3500 and 4000 B.C. Hunting scenes are depicted showing dogs of the sight-hound type. And from later Egyptian Dynasties comes concrete evidence of three other types of dog. Monuments in Assyria before the Christian Era give us more views of the old kinds of dogs.

Like man and with man, the dog has migrated ever Westward. He has made his home wherever and however his master has been satisfied; seeking only that small measure of affection from man which is so slight when set beside what the dog has to return. And, in this second third of the twentieth century, the dog finds his greatest home in the United States of America; in a country that now recognizes more pure breeds than any other in the world.

Every year brings a broadening of the horizon of knowledge in all fields, and it is possible that in time to come we will know much more than we do today about dogs. But, until that time arrives, it is my firm belief that "The Complete Dog Book" with its valuable information on the selection, care, feeding and common diseases of the dog and with its revised and up-to-date edition of "Pure Bred Dogs" should serve as the most authoritative text-book of the dog-lover.

BOOK ONE

THE CARE, HANDLING AND
FEEDING OF DOGS

By

by Edwin Reginald Blamey,

M.R.C.V.S.

SELECTING A DOG

In selecting a dog the prospective purchaser should bear in mind the purpose for which he intends to use the dog, the surroundings in which the dog will live and the temperament of the individual purchaser. The confined area of a modern apartment in a large city is naturally not conducive to the well-being of hunting breeds or the larger breeds. The congestion of city streets and the hard pavement are not suitable surroundings for a dog requiring plenty of exercise and open country as a normal part of existence.

The city dweller, though his personal inclination may lean toward the large breeds or hunting dogs, would do well to consider a dog who in stature will best fit into his surroundings and at the same time give his owner to a certain degree those same qualities and habits which he will expect to find in the breed of his first choice. Outstanding characteristics found in some large breeds can likewise be found in smaller breeds and to a certain extent the expression and nature of the large dog duplicated in the smaller. We have but to compare the general makeup of the large breeds with certain of the terriers and toy dogs to discover that the above holds true.

At present there are over one hundred breeds of dogs recognized by the American Kennel Club and eligible for registration in the United States of America. These breeds are classified in groups, closely associating the dogs according to uses. From these groupings the prospective purchaser can select a dog best suited to his needs whether they be for work, sporting or companionship. Breed standards were drawn up for the purpose of guiding those breeding or judging and today these standards govern the type of each individual breed. By becoming familiar with the standards any one can form a picture of what each breed of dog should be and look like.

The great differentiation in breeds and types of dogs was the primary object for the classification of the numerous breeds into groups. A study of the breeds and their standards will give the person interested in selecting a dog an excellent idea of just what he is looking for.

Variety Group One, Sporting Dogs, comprises the gun dogs.

Variety Group Two, Sporting Dogs Hounds, includes dogs for sport employing the sense of smell in the hunting field and accustomed to trailing.

Variety Group Three, Working Dogs, includes the breeds for practical uses such as herding, guarding, police duties, etc.

Variety Group Four, Terriers, covers the breeds of this variety.

Variety Group Five, Toy Dogs, includes the smaller dogs used primarily as pets.

Variety Group Six, Non-sporting Dogs, includes breeds used as companions.

A fuller appreciation of the dog and his importance to man has aroused in the average dog owner a desire to posses only the best type of pure bred dog. The appellation "pure bred" means that the dog is of the purest breeding and when bred with a suitable mate, will reproduce true to type.

Selecting the best puppy from a litter with any degree of certainty is a problem. Successful breeders have been

SELECTING A DOG

known to ignore certain puppies in litters which eventually defeated more favored brothers or sisters. Nevertheless there are certain rules if applied to the selection of a puppy should assure the purchaser of securing a dog representative of the breed desired, possessing to a marked degree the character, type and balance required by the standard.

The puppy to choose is the one showing the strongest characteristics of the breed. He should be sturdy and strong. It is usually advisable to select neither the largest nor the smallest of the litter as the medium sized puppies have a better chance of maturing to the correct size in a majority of the breeds. While a puppy's coat is an uncertainty at the early stages, nevertheless, density of coat should be looked for.

In choosing a puppy always bear in mind the characteristics of the antecedents of the puppy in order to avoid selecting one which shows a tendency to inherit some family failing. A great advantage will be found in knowing the hereditary failings as well as the family virtues of different matings.

CARE AND FEEDING OF YOUNG DOGS

At the age of six weeks the young dog is still dependent on milk for the greater part of its nourishment. The digestive organs have commenced to change, and acid is making its appearance in the gastric juice in sufficient quantity to digest meat. For many years, I have made a study of the diet for young puppies. I have considered the health of the dog first, but I have attempted to simplify the list in such a way that it can be used under almost any circumstances. I have given a broad list so that it may fit any pocketbook.

Before going further with a dietary, it may be a good plan to lay down an extremely important fact. This cannot be taken too literally if the dog owner desires to raise a healthy dog. It is that all dogs are primarily carnivorous animals. This is true of Chihuahua and Great Dane, of the terriers, poodles, hounds and pugs. Meat is the essential ingredient of a successful canine diet.

There are common superstitions and legends about meat as a food for dogs. I most emphatically say that meat does not cause worms; it does not make a dog vicious; and it does not cause fits. In fact, meat nourishes young carnivora and is a perfectly balanced diet if the animal lives in a natural state.

Under the conditions imposed on our pets, meat does not contain sufficient roughage. To remedy this, it is customary to add some form of indigestible fibre to a meat diet. Vegetables supply this deficiency.

To return to the six weeks puppy. Give four or five

meals a day. Start the morning with a bowl of warm milk and dry cereal. Season it slightly with sugar. The sugar may be omitted. The amount of milk and cereal must be left to the discretion of the owner. Do not overload the stomach. If the dog is of a large breed, the inclusion of raw egg will be beneficial. Use one egg to a pint of milk. This mixture may be kept in the refrigerator and used when indicated. If the egg and milk mixture is heated, the result will be custard-like which will not be harmful. I prefer the egg and milk to be fluid.

By dry cereal, I mean any cereal food which has been treated by heat and which is ready to eat when purchased. This list includes shredded wheat, pep, corn flakes, Post toasties, puffed wheat and puffed rice. Sweetened or unsweetened zwieback, rusk, and Melba toast may be used. This last consists of thin slices of white or whole wheat bread baked in a slow oven until brown throughout.

If the puppy does not finish the meal provided for it, the bowl and remaining food should be removed in a few minutes and nothing else given until the next feeding hour. In this way, the puppy will learn to eat at regular intervals instead of picking at the plate whenever the fancy to do so comes into its mind.

The next meal should be given about noon. It should consist of raw beef which may be chopped or ground, scraped or cut into small pieces with knife or scissors. The latter are handy. The amount must be left to the dog owner. As a slight guide, I may say that a six weeks' fox terrier will take a ball of chopped meat about the size of a small hen's egg. It is better to slightly season meat with salt.

At four P.M. the puppy may be given a repetition of the morning meal of milk and dry cereal. Or the milk may be replaced by clear broth or soup stock.

About eight P.M. give a second meal of meat. This time it may be varied by using finely ground or diced, cooked meat. Slightly season with salt, as before.

If it is deemed necessary, the young puppy may be given a small quantity of warm milk or warm broth between ten P.M. and midnight. This often will induce sleep and will keep the puppy quiet until much later in the morning.

The four meal a day régime is continued until the puppy has cut its second teeth. That is, until the dog is about six months old. In large breeds, it is wise to continue it until nine or ten months because the development is relatively slower.

The amount of food to the meal is increased gradually as the puppy grows. When the animal is over teething, it often will cease to be interested in the four P.M. meal or will stop eating it voluntarily. To compensate for this, increase the amount of meat given at the last feeding.

The puppy becomes a dog at the age of twelve months. Many of the larger breeds are very immature at this age and require three meals for at least six months longer.

Stop the four P.M. meal when the average puppy is six months. From one year the dog is fed two meals a day. Since the average dog does not care to eat early in the morning, the best feeding times are about eleven A.M. and six P.M. These times may be changed to suit circumstances. It always is better to feed at regular times. If a dog does not finish a meal at once, the plate or feed pen should be removed and nothing else given until the next meal time.

When the puppy reaches the age of about four months, it will commence to change its teeth. The first or milk teeth are mere shells. As the dog grows, the spaces between them become greater. Just before they are

[6]

exfoliated, they are widely spaced and look disproportionately small.

The second or permanent teeth replace the milk teeth, there are some extra molars. Sometimes the first teeth are not shed properly. To facilitate this, the teething puppy may be allowed a large raw or cooked bone on which to gnaw. This will loosen the first teeth. If they are retained in spite of this, they must be extracted.

Good substitutes for bones are tennis balls, pure rubber balls, and strips of sole leather which have been boiled in water for several hours to remove the chemicals used in tanning.

The best simple laxative for a puppy is milk of magnesia. The dose is one to eight teaspoonfuls according to the weight and the size of the dog.

When the puppy has a simple diarrhoea, it may be checked by castor oil which should be administered plain. The dose is one to eight teaspoonfuls.

Fasting for a few hours, followed by a small dose of milk of magnesia will stop most cases of simple vomiting.

Excessive bloating of the abdomen, following a meal, is fairly good evidence of the presence of worms. It should be attended to promptly.

When a puppy is sick, it is best to seek the advice of a veterinarian who specializes in the ailments of dogs. Do not listen to the advice of some well meaning friend who has a little knowledge and is perfectly willing to "try it on your dog."

Rickets is a disease of the growing animal. It is due to the inability of the animal to fix the soluble calcium (lime) salts in the bony tissues. If such a diet, as described, is given, there is little or no danger of the puppy developing rickets. Direct sunshine, exercise, proper rest and a wholesome diet, containing sufficient milk and meat, are the best preventatives.

When raising winter puppies it is advisable to give cod liver oil, either plain or with viosterol. The dose of viosterol should be regulated carefully. Or haliver oil with or without viosterol may be used. As a general rule these additions to diet are not necessary from May to October.

FIRST AID—DISEASES AND COMMON ILLS OF DOGS

In recent years the care of small animals has enlisted the interest of an ever-increasing number of veterinarians. Small animal hospitals have sprung up in almost every community. Many of these hospitals are admirably equipped with every modern method for the relief of suffering and the care of their patients. Probably a majority of these institutions maintain a more or less efficient ambulance service.

But there are enormous areas which do not enjoy the advantages of the proximity of a hospital with ambulance and here the dog lover must call upon his own resources in time of stress.

No matter where you go with your dog you are sure to find innumerable pests who are willing to advise you on all matters pertaining to your dog. Much of this gratuitous advice is worthless. Some of it is positively dangerous.

Therefore, a few hints on emergency treatment may save some dogs from unfortunate mishandling.

WOUNDS

Wounds of all kinds are very common. Simple abrasions of the skin should be washed with any available antiseptic. Soap and water is better than nothing. All trace of contaminating material should be removed. Then apply zinc ointment, borated vaseline, plain vaseline, or carbolated vaseline. Cover with sterile gauze and apply a bandage. If gauze and bandage are not available, an old cotton or linen sheet may be torn into narrow strips and used as a substitute. Zinc ointment is apt to cause vomiting if the dog is allowed to lick it.

WOUNDS—Deep

Deeper wounds which puncture the skin require much the same kind of handling. Whenever possible it is better to eliminate the use of an ointment in these cases. After thorough cleansing, apply a wet dressing of any available antiseptic in watery solution and keep the dressing in place with a bandage. Tincture of iodine is a valuable emergency antiseptic. It may be applied to a wound with a brush or a swab of cotton. A cover should never be applied to a wound treated with a tincture of iodine. Failure to follow this advise will result in severe burning.

Wounds accompanied by severe hemorrhage require prompt attention. In some cases it is necessary to apply a tourniquet. A strong rubber band may be cut and applied on the side of the wound nearer the heart. A piece of cord or a handkerchief make good substitutes. If the patient has to be transported any distance, or if some time must elapse before professional assistance can be obtained, it will be necessary to relieve the pressure of the tourniquet for several minutes at intervals of ten to fifteen minutes.

Surface oozing of blood may be controlled by the use of a solution of peroxide of hydrogen, tincture of iron perchloride or Monsell's solution (subsulphate of iron). Often the use of a pressure bandage is sufficient. It is not advisable to use peroxide of hydrogen solution on deep wounds. Mouth washes make good emergency wet dressings.

Deep bleeding wounds on the body should be covered with a pressure bandage. If the patient is very restless it may be necessary to hold the dressing in place by hand. Usually surgical adhesive tape is sufficient to exert pressure and to hold the dressing in place.

The hair around wounds should be cut off with scissors. If hair is allowed to enter the wound, infection of more or less serious kind may ensue.

Skin wounds of any length over one inch should be sutured (sewn) as soon as possible. In order to keep the lips of such a wound in good condition a wet dressing is essential. It must be kept wet until a veterinarian is reached. As a general rule it is not a good idea for a layman to attempt to suture a wound.

Never use a poisonous solution in making a wound dressing. All dogs will attempt to lick their wounds and the use of any poison may cause unnecessary suffering or death.

BURNS AND SCALDS

Apply Carron oil (equal parts of linseed oil and lime water). If this is not available use vaseline in some form, unguentine, burn emollient, or butter. Olive oil makes a fair dressing. Burnt hair and skin should be removed as quickly as possible. If they are allowed to remain in contact with the wounds, absorption of toxic material is made possible. This materially increases the danger of shock.

BROKEN NAILS

Remove the broken portion as quickly as possible. This may be done with nail clippers. If there is bleeding it may be stopped with a solution of peroxide of hydrogen or with Monsell's solution. A pad of cotton held in place by a bandage and adhesive tape is an efficient dressing. It may be removed in from twelve to twenty-four hours. It is not necessary to replace the dressing unless the hemorrhage commences again.

The pads of hunting dogs often are cut on ice splinters. Occasionally the pads are worn through by rough going, especially when the dog is made to work without proper training. On all hunting trips, it is advisable to examine the dog's feet from time to time. It is easier to avoid trouble than to mend it. Bruised, wounded, or worn feet should be bathed with water to remove all dirt and contamination. Soap may be used. If there is any chance that the feet are frost-bitten they should be rubbed with snow or simply massaged. Then they should be bandaged. If they are very sore, the bandage should be padded with cotton or with some soft woollen material.

GUN SHOT WOUNDS

These should be treated as ordinary wounds. The animal should be placed in a quiet spot. If there is any hemorrhage it should be controlled by pressure or by the use of styptics. If the wounds are deep and there is a possible involvement of vital organs, the aid of a veterinarian should be sought immediately. In the case of superficial wounds there need be no cause for excitement.

If there is a suspicion that a bone of one of the limbs has been fractured, the leg should be made as comfortable as possible. A splint should be fashioned from a board or stick. This must be held to the leg by a bandage. The leg should be padded thoroughly. The animal should be carried in such a way that the movement of the leg is as limited as possible. Fractures are handled most successfully but professional aid is necessary if the dog is to retain the full use of the injured limb.

EYE INJURIES

These are common in all hunting breeds due to the nature of their work. They are common also in the short nosed breeds, especially the Pekingese, because of the anatomical prominence of the eyes. As a general rule it is a good plan to wash the injured eye as quickly as possible. If there are any particles of foreign matter in the conjunctival sacs, they should be removed at once. As a relief to the pain, hot compresses will be found more effective. If the cornea or clear surface of the eye is gouged or pitted by the injury, the eye should be covered and the aid of a veterinarian sought at once.

Occasionally the eye is dislocated, that is the eyeball is outside the margin of the lids. If the condition is discovered at once, it is comparatively easy to replace the eye with a wet pad of cotton and giving a quick, outward and forward pull on the lower eyelid. If the condition has existed for some time, rush the dog to a veterinarian. If there must be some delay, it is a very good plan to cover the eye with a light layer of surgical cotton saturated with castor oil or mineral oil. This prevents desicration and serious injury to the cornea. In fact, the use of castor oil or mineral oil in an injured eye is always useful, and forms a protective film until professional aid arrives.

SHOCK

Occasionally dogs are overcome from various causes. Puppies have a habit of gnawing electric wires on lamps, etc. The result is a badly burned mouth and considerable shock. Falls, collisions with motors, cycles, trains, etc., immersion in cold water, and similar conditions may cause shock characterized by collapse, and interference with the heart and respiration. The quick use of aromatic spirits of ammonia or an alcoholic stimulant may save a life. In any event, it will act beneficially especially if the doses are small and given frequently to effect. Immersion in hot water is recommended. Smelling salts applied to the nostrils is another form of rapid stimulation. Slow, rhythmic artificial respiration may be necessary. A small amount of strong coffee makes an excellent stimulant for the dog's heart.

VOMITING

Stop feeding, give white of egg beaten to a freely running fluid—a teaspoonful every fifteen to sixty minutes, either plain or with bismuth subcarbonate or subnitrate (usual dose is five to fifteen grains). Occasionally, the addition of a few drops of brandy or whisky is beneficial. Water should be withheld. If the dog is thirsty, allow it to lick a small piece of ice held in a towel or placed in a strainer. Sometimes a few drops of paregoric (opiated tincture of camphor) in a very small amount of water will stop vomiting. Sodium bromide in small doses will often overcome nervous vomiting. Lime water or small doses of bicarbonate of soda neutralize acidity of the stomach and control the condition. Milk of magnesia is useful in some cases. A hot compress or hot water bottle may be held to the region of the stomach (at the left side just behind end of ribs). This also will relieve pain. An old fashioned and valuable first aid method of controlling vomiting is the oral administration of one drop of carbolic acid in a teaspoonful of water. It should be mixed thoroughly before administration.

CONSTIPATION

Give a high colonic irrigation with a fountain syringe to which is attached a human infant rectum tube. Use a solution of salt (teaspoonful to a quart), soap, bicarbonate of soda (teaspoonful to a quart), or olive or mineral oil. Occasionally a glycerin suppository or soap suppository will give relief. As soon as relief is given, it is necessary to discover cause and to administer correct course of treatment to prevent recurrence.

DIARRHOEA

Give a dose of castor oil. This has the effect of removing the irritant from the bowel. The after effect of castor oil is constipation. When available, it is a good plan to follow the oil with several doses of bismuth subgallate or salol—2½ to 10 grains—every two to four hours.

DYSENTERY

Diarrhoea with blood. Make up a solution of common laundry starch of such a consistency that it will pour freely. Take two-thirds of a teacup full, add fifteen to twenty drops of paregoric (tincture of opium or laudanum is better) and a teaspoonful of bismuth subgallate. Draw this into an infant enema syringe. Inject very slowly into bowel. Withdraw syringe, and hold down the tail in an effort to make the patient retain the enema for ten to fifteen minutes. This may be repeated if the first treatment is expelled.

HYSTERIA

If possible, hold the dog and cover with a heavy towel or blanket. As soon as quiet, place in a darkened room or kennel away from noise and excitement. Give a dose of sodium bromide, paregoric, or luminol. Repeat if necessary. In some cases it may be necessary to anaesthetize carefully with chloroform.

CONVULSIONS or FITS

Hold dog to prevent injury. Remove to quiet place. If possible put into a tub of hot water. At the same time apply ice to head. Or massage the junction of the head and neck with the index finger and thumb. Give sedatives as for hysteria.

Vomiting, constipation, diarrhoea, dysentery, hysteria, and convulsions are usually symptoms of some disease and should not be considered as cured when the disturbance subsides. It is always necessary to make a study of each case to ascertain the cause. Sometimes this is obvious, more often it is hidden. Generally, it is a good plan to consult a veterinarian when the emergency has passed.

POISONS

Occasionally dogs are poisoned. In most cases the cause of the trouble is accidental, and the specific toxin is known. The manufacturers of rat poisons always print the antidote on the label of the container. If such poisons are used it is a good plan to observe every precaution to prevent a dog from reaching them. It is also wise to read the label carefully so that treatment may be given promptly if the necessity arises.

It is a fortunate thing that the average dog is able to vomit at will. If a dog eats or drinks anything which causes distress, it is able to disgorge voluntarily. This fact has saved many lives.

Strychnine poisoning is not uncommon in house pets. It arises in many cases from the administration of human cathartic pills. The average compound laxative for adult human use contains a certain proportion of nux vomica or its active principle—strychnine. The dog has an idiosyncrasy for this drug, and cannot stand it in any quantity. Since prevention is better than cure, do not give human cathartics to dogs unless it is certain that they do not contain strychnine. If it is given, the best antidote is morphine. This drug cannot be purchased without a prescription. Consequently it is advisable to call a veterinarian immediately. Meanwhile, the patient should be placed in a darkened room and kept as quiet as possible.

Morphine, its salts, and its derivatives generally cause vomiting in the dog. If they are acquired accidentally they provide their own first aid. The average dog is able to take relatively, enormous doses of this drug without lethal effect. It may cause profound sleep which may last twenty-four hours or longer.

In recent years various compounds containing barbituric acid derivatives have been placed on the market as sedatives. This class of drugs is useful in controlling the muscular spasm caused by overdosing with strychnine.

The best first aid remedies for almost all forms of poisoning are large forced draughts of salt solution, milk, or beaten white of egg. As soon as possible the patient should be rushed to a veterinarian.

If a dog is known to have eaten glass, bones, coal or other irritant solids it should not be given a purgative. The pain may be controlled by the use of sedatives such as paregoric or one of the barbital preparations. In many cases a good meal of oatmeal or other boiled cereal will form a homogenous mass around the foreign body and facilitate its passage through the alimentary tract. After an interval of several hours mineral oil may be given by mouth. High saline irrigations also help to remove foreign bodies. A liquid or semi solid diet should be given for several days.

HOUSING AND KENNELING

An entire volume could be written on this subject. However, there are certain essentials which should be enumerated. The owner of one or two house-broken dogs may keep them healthy in the house.

During the greater part of the year in the country typical outdoor kennels may be used. In winter a floor and plenty of bedding such as straw or fresh hay is desirable. A flap of several folds of burlap, canvas or old carpet may be nailed over the entrance so that it may be pushed aside for entrance and exit.

Kennels in buildings should be well ventilated and free from draughts. The individual dogs may be kept in boxes or cages. Or they may be provided with a small run with a sleeping platform. Young puppies may be kept together as litters in runs. Older dogs may be kept in pairs—dog and bitch. These arrangements save space. Fighting may be eliminated by careful pairing. When possible it is a good plan to have the inside kennels communicate with outdoor runs by means of slide or trap doors which can be operated from inside. Floors of kennels may be made of common flooring, hardwood, tile or concrete. In any case they should be arranged for easy cleaning and disinfection. In northern climates some kind of heating should be arranged. Dogs will not come to any harm so long as a temperature of 45° F. is maintained. Puppies and brood bitches require special protection. Older dogs will be unharmed by the most severe weather conditions provided that they are given plenty of bedding. The coat of many breeds is improved by keeping the kennel temperature at a moderate point.

An ideal kennel should contain an office and reception room, kennels with runs for litters, cages or boxes for grown dogs, whelping kennels with runs, an indoor exercising room, kitchen, and a room where grooming may be done. If possible a separate room should be provided for visiting bitches and for dogs returning from shows—this isolation ward saves much trouble.

Outdoor runs are most useful when connected with the kennels by doors or traps. They should be constructed on a slight slope to facilitate drainage. The surface of the runs may be grass, clay, gravel, ashes, flooring, tile or concrete. The most satisfactory flooring is concrete or well laid tile. These are capable of proper disinfection and help to keep down or eliminate worms. They do not hurt the feet. They should be provided with drains. They can be cleaned with a hose at regular intervals and in case of infection a disinfectant may be sprinkled on the floor before it is hosed.

Large grass runs are useful and not apt to become badly infected if enough space is provided. They should be cleaned up occasionally.

Outdoor platforms and shelters make the dogs more comfortable. Solid fences provide wind breaks and prevent much unnecessary barking.

HOUSE TRAINING

Puppies normally defecate three to five times a day and urinate very frequently. The stool is seldom formed, but it should not be watery. The color varies from a creamy yellow to medium brown. When raw beef is fed, it may be black. The urine is pale in color and is passed in amazing quantity.

When you purchase a very young puppy, it is frequently used to attending to these duties on paper. During its youth, it may be held to this habit by placing pads of newspaper where the puppy may reach them easily. If there are symptoms of uneasiness on the part of the puppy, it should be picked up and taken to one of these pads. The bath room with its tiled floor, is a good place to use as the regular situation for the paper pad.

If it is desired to train the dog to go outdoors, the secret is absolute regularity of time for the walks. Set four to six fixed times, and make it the duty of someone to attend to the dog at each of them. When the desired result is accomplished, the puppy should be praised. When mistakes occur indoors, it should be scolded or mildly punished.

It is extremely difficult to train a dog to use a box of sawdust or sand. So much confusion arises in the brain of the puppy, if this is attempted, that it frequently makes the trainer's task much more difficult when another method is tried.

SLEEPING QUARTERS

Toy dogs may be trained to sleep in baskets of which there are many shapes and sizes to accommodate any breed. The sleeping surface should be flat and reasonably soft. Most baskets are provided with a cushion of the mattress type—tufted. It may be covered with a small blanket or with a towel which may be removed easily for cleaning. The flat area should be large enough to permit the puppy to stretch out flat on its side.

Larger breeds may be provided with a stand supporting a small mattress. Or they will sleep in comfort on a small rug or carpet. There is a cold draught on the floor of almost all rooms. To avoid this, the actual bed should be raised about six inches above the floor. Grown dogs, which are allowed the freedom of the house, often will select an arm chair or couch as a suitable place. If the owner does not object, there is no reason why it should not be allowed to occupy the selected place. In the city apartment, the bath room is a convenient sleeping place for a toy dog. It has the added advantage of a tiled floor which is easy to clean until the dog is house trained.

GENERAL CARE AND FEEDING

Meat is the essential part of a normal dog's diet. A puppy may be raised on biscuits and vegetables with stock and broth. Such a dog is often strong and healthy to outward appearances, but it lacks that stamina and resistance to disease which is possessed by one that has had proper nourishment during its life.

In many parts of the country, especially in the less settled parts where game is still fairly abundant, the average man keeps one or more hounds. They are raised for hunting birds and small animals. Usually they are not of any fixed breed. They have been developed to meet the requirements of the owner and possess the instinct to seek the game of the region where they live. These dogs receive very little meat in their diet because it is difficult to obtain and it is expensive beyond the means of the owner.

The dogs are usually keen to hunt. They are willing and able workers but they cannot stand up to the hounds which are meat fed. The meat fed hound has a great store of energy in its body. It can call on that reserve when it is needed.

Of course, it is necessary to train a meat fed animal by exercise in the field. If training is neglected, the hound will be unable to perform his allotted task and will make a sorry showing even when matched with the ill-fed native dog.

When meat is used as a ration, it is almost completely digested and assimilated. The result is a small stool. If there is any facility, a meat fed dog will eat certain forms of grass which grow as weeds. This is done to provide roughage. It is instinctive to seek such indigestible material.

When eaten by a dog, the grass passes to the stomach where it forms a loose elongated bolus. From the stomach it reaches the intestine and is propelled through the enteric tube by the muscular action of the involuntary muscle fibres.

This muscular action passes in waves from the stomach to the rectum. It is known as peristalsis. The stomach and intestine are lined with a complicated epithelial membrane. This membrane is developed in the stomach and the several parts of the intestine into simple or complicated glands. The function of the glands is to secrete several digestive ferments. The digestion depends on a proper supply of these fluids.

There is a tendency in dogs and other carnivora for the lining membrane of the intestine to become covered with a coating of stagnant partly fermented ingesta (digesting food material). If rough, indigestible material is constantly withheld, the animal will develop symptoms of intoxication because the bacteria in the stagnant layer will find a good medium for their growth.

The common colon bacillus which is normally present in the intestine will produce a poison under these circumstances. The poison is absorbed with the prepared food. It reaches the blood stream and is carried to all parts of the body. The poisoning is usually very insidious and unnoticeable. If it is allowed to go on, it may reach very serious proportions. It may even result in death and this is frequently the termination.

Grass eating is the dog's instinctive method of preventing auto-intoxication. The grass passes through the intestine in an undigested mass and scrapes the lining membrane as it travels. The same result may be obtained in house pets by the occasional addition of bran to the diet. It is easy to get bran today. It is packed in sealed containers and offered for sale by all grocers.

Bran acts more efficiently if it is given about twice a week. The amount necessary to obtain the desired result is a matter of experiment. A full grown shepherd dog requires a heaped tablespoonful. The bran is best given with the food. It may be mixed with one of the regular meals. If there is a tendency to make the meal dry, a little broth or soup stock may be added to facilitate mixing.

There are other agents which will mix in the same way. The commonest is known as agar-agar. It is prepared from seaweed. Agar may be employed in the same way as bran but it is not necessary to use more than half the quantity. Agar is more useful in providing bulk to the stool than as roughage. It is dry when fed and in its passage through the bowels it absorbs moisture and swells considerably.

When it reaches the rectum, it retains this water while the other waste products give up theirs to the drying process going on in the organ. The swollen agar causes a pressure on the closing muscle at the end of the alimentary canal and provides a stimulus to defecation.

Some writers on canine dietetics advise the use of liquid petroleum or so called "Russian" oil. While this has undoubted value in many patients suffering from constipation, I am decidedly of the opinion that the employment of bran, and even agar, is infinitely preferable. This opinion is based on the fact that bran is much nearer the natural grass-eating habit than is the artificial dosing with oil.

CARE AND FEEDING

The use of Russian mineral oil for long periods of time is not recommended. This is because the animal acquires a peculiar tolerance for the oil which is manifested by leaking of almost pure oil from the anus. Mineral oil is purely mechanical in its action. It acts as a lubricant to the stool and facilitates expulsion. When the contents of the bowels reach saturation, the surplus oil is carried to the rectum and passes the sphincter muscle which guards the exit. The act is involuntary and is really in the nature of a leak.

Mineral oil leakage is specially objectionable in toy dogs which are in the habit of spending parts of their days on the laps of their owners, or on pillows, or the seats of chairs.

During recent years, yeast has been advocated very widely as a cure for constipation. The writer has used yeast in the hospital and in private patients. The result has been gratifying in many cases but in some animals it has caused vomiting. And in some, there has been no apparent benefit. Yeast is also advocated as a cure for auto-intoxication. It is of undoubted use in many cases of this kind but the writer finds it necessary to carry out a great deal of other treatment if any permanent cure is to be attained.

Yeast usually is sold in powder as desiccated brewers' yeast. Usually it is irradiated. The dose varies according to weight of the dog. A full grown St. Bernard may be given one tablespoonful, morning and evening, with the food. A shepherd may be given half a tablespoonful, morning and evening, with the food. A foxterrier should not require more than a teaspoonful, twice a day. Other breeds of dogs should receive a proportionate dose.

The most valuable vegetables, from a canine dietetic viewpoint, are carrots, spinach, string beans, onions, boiled celery, kohlrabi, fresh greens of turnips or beets and lettuce. These vegetables may be prepared by boiling, in slightly salted water, until tender; or they may be used raw. If cooked, it is better to thoroughly mash a vegetable before mixing it with meat. If a vegetable is to be used raw, it should be finely chopped. Tomatoes are sometimes the cause of vomiting, but the raw juice is good, especially for growing puppies. Spinach is not always tolerated and may cause vomiting. In such cases it is only necessary to discontinue the use of the offending food.

As a general rule, I do not recommend peas, lima beans, corn, beets, parsnips or potatoes of any variety in the canine diet.

The members of the cabbage family may be included in the dog's diet. They may be used cooked or raw. Cooked cabbage is sometimes the cause of unpleasant flatulence. In all other ways it is a good adjunct to the diet list.

Many breeders and handlers of dogs ascribe special virtue to the feeding of onions and garlic to dogs. These vegetables are supposed to keep the eater free from worms. I have been able to demonstrate worms in dogs which are fed in this way.

Frequently the question of fruit as an article of diet is brought to my attention. No harm can come to a dog from a tidbit of raw apple or pear. As a general rule the feeding of fruit to a dog is not recommended.

Cooked figs, dried figs, and cooked prunes are relished by some dogs. If they are not too sweet, a small quantity of any of these is not objectionable. They sometimes exert a healthy laxative effect on the animal.

Cereals. These may be used to increase the bulk of the food and to provide nourishment. The boiled cereals such as rice and oatmeal are not recommended. The average dog can digest them but they are often the direct cause of allergic skin reactions commonly classed as eczema. Cereals included in the breakfast food list are very useful. These include shredded wheat, pep, corn flakes and similar products.

Some of the large baking companies sell rebaked stale bread in bulk by weight. If it is clean, and, if it is well baked, it makes an excellent filler in the menu of the dog. Shredded wheat may be obtained from the manufacturer in bulk and many large kennels keep it on hand to be used as roughage and filler in the meat diet.

The manufacturers of dog biscuits, kibbled biscuits, and meals usually add some meat to the cereal content of their products. In general the biscuits may be classed as cereals. They may be used in that capacity.

Dog biscuits. In all parts of the country there are companies and individuals who manufacture dog biscuits and dog bread. Many make special foods for the different breeds, for puppies, grown dogs and delicate feeders. Some of the preparations are medicated with charcoal, cod liver oil or phosphates. Such biscuits and cakes have a varying merit.

In my opinion very few manufacturers turn out biscuits which are a balanced canine ration. In almost all cases it is necessary to add considerable meat before the correct proportion is reached. Practically all the dog biscuits are carefully prepared of wholesome ingredients.

Some biscuits may become wormy or infected with weevils. From an esthetic point of view such biscuits are objectionable, but as a matter of practical fact they will not harm dogs which eat them. If biscuits are found to be mouldy, it is not a good plan to use them. Mouldy biscuits will cause serious attacks of diarrhoea and even dysentery.

Occasionally biscuits ferment and have a sour odor. When such a condition is discovered they should not be used for food, as there has been a chemical reaction in the ingredients which will cause some form of gastro-intestinal disturbance.

Prepared meat rations have been on the market for some time. Some of these are carefully and intelligently made. They are sold in cans of various sizes.

As an emergency ration there is no objection to canned dog food. It is better than a diet consisting of dog biscuit alone. In combination with other food stuffs, it is good. But no matter how carefully the food may be prepared, it cannot possibly compete with a ration prepared from fresh ingredients.

Canned salmon or canned tuna fish, as an emergency ration, is excellent. But it should not be used as a steady diet. Fresh fish, such as cod, is a good substitute for meat. It is nourishing and easily digested. Fish has a high place in the list of good foods for a dog. Some individuals cannot be fed canned salmon because it causes an allergic eczema of more or less severe degree, with severe itching and badly injured areas due to the resultant scratching and biting.

Liver is a good article of diet. The liver is a gland which secretes bile. It is also the storehouse of the body for partially converted starch. It is composed of epithelial cells held together by fibrous tissue through which the various vessels and ducts pass. Liver is not a good steady diet and cannot be compared with flesh. An occasional meal in which liver is the chief constituent will be found beneficial. Liver is a laxative when given to a dog which is unused to it. Raw liver is more active in this respect than cooked liver.

Beef heart may be used occasionally. Heart muscle is of peculiar construction. It is half way between epithelium and ordinary muscle fibre. If it is thoroughly boiled and ground, it may be used occasionally as a change from the ordinary fare, or it may be used raw.

Tripe is an excellent food for puppies and grown dogs. It may be used as it is purchased or it may be cooked. It should be cut into small pieces.

An excellent muscle for canine feeding is beef cheek. It is not usually obtainable from markets but must be ordered from the packing house direct. It is good either raw or cooked. It has the additional advantage of being much cheaper than the usual cuts used for feeding.

Horse meat has been used as a kennel ration for many years. It is really a good wholesome flesh. The great trouble is that the horses slaughtered for feeding purposes are usually worn out and very emaciated. If the carcass is in good condition, there is no reason why it should not be used as freely as beef. When it is given as a change from beef, horse flesh often causes a relaxed condition of the bowels. This trouble is automatically corrected by continued feeding on the same diet.

Lamb or mutton may be used as freely as beef. The fat of mutton will cause vomiting in many cases. It is safer to remove as much surplus fat as possible before it is cooked. Lamb and mutton are better when cooked than when raw. When this meat is used, it is necessary to exercise care to remove all bones. Serious disturbances to the stomach and bowels have been caused by splinters of mutton bones.

Bones are absolutely unnecessary to the health of a grown dog. It is true that the average adult healthy dog is able to digest uncooked bones with comparative ease. It is able also to digest cooked bones in nearly all cases. But, the nourishment in a bone is of little consequence when compared with the danger that lies in such a diet. During the teething period a raw bone will help a puppy to remove the temporary teeth and facilitate the cutting of the permanent teeth. As soon as these teeth are all through the gums, it is better to discard bones as playthings and as diet.

The constant gnawing of bones wears down the enamel-covered crowns of the teeth. After several years of this exercise the teeth are usually so worn as to be almost useless. Such things as the bones of chicken, turkey, game birds, rabbits, coon, and other small animals are more dangerous than those of the larger animals normally used as food.

Bones of birds are high in mineral content and splinter freely when crushed by the dog's teeth. These splinters are sharp-pointed and frequently scrape, cut and even perforate the stomach or intestine. If they pass safely to the rectum, the small particles are apt to pack together and cause an impaction which is very painful to break down.

Not infrequently the after effect of an impaction of this nature is ulceration of the rectum, chronic proctitis (inflammation of the rectum), or prolapse of the rectum. It is no exaggeration that bones are frequently the cause of death. It is obvious that death from this cause is needless. The pain suffered before death ensues is wanton cruelty due to carelessness, thoughtlessness or ignorance.

Whatever there is of value in bones may be extracted by boiling them in water for a considerable time—three or four hours. In this way the animal matter is extracted and the worthless mineral matter left. Broth prepared in this manner may be used to soften dog biscuit or re-baked bread.

Large or small bones may be used if they are cooked thoroughly in a pressure cooker until they are soft enough to be crushed by the pressure of the hand. The minerals contained in them are good for growing puppies and for pregnant or nursing bitches. The amount of bone should be regulated carefully.

As a general rule it will be found better to feed dogs on a fairly dry diet. Sloppy food is difficult to digest because the excessive moisture in the food dilutes the gastric juice and retards the chemical action of the food on the ingesta. Sloppy food, such as stew, is vomited by some dogs.

A dog's food should be seasoned with salt. By this is meant that a sprinkle of salt may be added to each meal in addition to the usual seasoning used in cooking vegetables and meat. The food should not be made briny.

WATER

It is necessary to supply clean, fresh water for drinking purposes. Usually a dog is not particular about the source of its water supply and will drink anywhere if it is thirsty. Occasionally a fussy individual is encountered which will not drink unless the water is freshly drawn and cold.

Water should not be given to any dog in the habit of drinking excessively after it has been fed. The observing dog owner will notice that a dog will eat the meal provided and immediately go to the water bowl. Usually it will drink a few laps and go away. Sometimes it will continue to drink until the bowl is empty.

At first, excessive drinking may have no apparent effect on the dog's health, but if it is allowed to go on, it will gradually weaken the animal's digestion. This result is manifested by vomiting of the meal. The food will be returned in almost the same condition as it was when swallowed and with it will come most of the water.

The cause of this vomiting is excessive dilation of the stomach and dilution of the gastric juice. When a normal dog is fed, the glands of the stomach pour out a large quantity of fluid containing hydrochloric acid and pepsin. The acid and the ferment are mixed with the ingesta by a churning muscular movement of the wall of the stomach.

The amount of acid and ferment is limited to the capacity of the glands which have formed these substances and stored them since the last meal was taken. When a large quantity of water is added it makes the solution of the gastric juice so weak that it is unable to do even a part of its work. The ingested food is held in the stomach in an undigested mass which finally acts as an irritant and causes a reflex regurgitation.

In some cases excessive drinking is followed immediately by vomiting. This is due to the pressure on the nerves, caused by over-distention of the organ.

Occasionally vomiting is noticed after drinking even when the stomach is empty. In such cases it is necessary to remove the bowl and to carefully ration the water in small quantity at more or less frequent intervals. Or the owner may have to resort for a while to giving small pieces of ice to lick. Usually the vomiting habit may be overcome by resorting to rationing of water or to giving ice for a short time.

It is a well established fact that the dog has the ability to vomit at will. If it eats anything which is uncomfort-

[33]

able in the abdomen, the animal is able to expel it without much distress. If anything which is unpalatable is given forcibly, vomiting will follow usually in a very short while. Knowing this, it is easy to understand how easily the animal can empty its stomach if the food or water cause any distress. It follows, naturally, that only very slight disturbance is necessary to cause a reflex action with involuntary emptying of the stomach.

Snow eating sometimes gives rise to a severe irritation of the stomach and intestines which may assume the gravity of actual inflammation. Repeated attacks of such a condition have been observed in certain individuals and isolated attacks on many occasions. Since prevention is better than cure, the obvious thing to do is to discourage your dog from eating snow.

Most of the troubles arising from water can be eliminated by keeping a fresh supply where the dog is able to reach it at all times.

There are some trivial matters concerning the average pet dog which are overlooked in many instances. Particular reference is made to such matters of hygiene as the care of the eyes, mouth, ears and nails.

The eyes of a dog are exposed at all times to the irritation of dust and other flying particles. They are also liable to irritation from the hair of the eyelids or face. Eyes are much more frequently irritated in the dog than in humans because the animals are so much closer to the ground. It is a good plan to make a daily habit of performing some kind of a toilet for a pet dog. It requires very little time and will be repaid many times over in the improved health and appearance of the pet.

The mouth of a pet dog, especially of the toy variety, should be inspected daily. If this is started when the dog is very young and continued as the dog grows, there will be little or no resistance on the part of the animal. The mouth may be rinsed out with a weak antiseptic solution such as the usual alkaline mouth washes sold by all druggists for the use of humans. The wash may be applied with a soft, infant-size tooth brush or with swabs of cotton.

Care should be taken to remove particles of food which become lodged between the incisors (front) teeth in all breeds. In the short-nosed breeds such as Pekingese and Boston terriers, the first three permanent upper molars are so crowded that they lie side by side in the mouth and form a splendid anchorage for the retention of food particles. Any food retained between the teeth will ferment quite rapidly and will give rise to foul breath or halitosis, which is most objectionable in a pet. It also will result in sore gums, pyorrhea and loss of the teeth at a ridiculously early age.

The ears of the average dog require very little care. The ear flaps have been designed by nature as a protection to the aural orifices against the accidental invasion of anything which might be irritant. As a precaution, it is a good plan to inspect the ears at frequent intervals to avoid any disturbance. If there is an excess of wax it may be removed with a swab of cotton saturated with peroxide of hydrogen solution or with alcohol. Use as many swabs as necessary to clean the ear. Finish by dropping in a pinch of dry powdered boracic acid. Repeat the cleaning of the ear whenever necessary. When the excess of wax stops, it is unnecessary to continue the ear dressing.

Sometimes the ear flaps become thickened at the tips and at the margins. It is usually seen in cold weather and is due to the low temperature and exposure. It may be caused by shaking the ears hard enough to cause the tips to strike the crown or the lower jaws. In almost all cases it will disappear in a few days if the thickened parts are massaged once or twice a day with lanoline, white vaseline or cold cream.

At times the ears must be bandaged or held down by a cap to prevent continued bruising and more severe injury such as splitting or a swollen inflammatory condition known as haematoma. Usually these conditions require the service of a veterinarian.

Some breeds of dogs, notably poodles, have an excessive growth of hair in the ears. It grows from the skin lining the inner part of the external passage. When found in any large amount it causes considerable irritation, characterized by shaking of the head, twitching of the ears, general malaise, and by the animal carefully scratching the ear by putting the hind foot of the same side into the ear and moving it in a most gentle fashion. Inspection of the ear usually reveals a felted mass of hair which has become stained a peculiar reddish brown. Treatment consists of careful removal of the wad of matted hair by the use of forceps and scissors. Afterward the use of peroxide of hydrogen or alcohol on swabs will clear up the ear.

NAILS

Each toe on the dog's foot terminates in a nail. Under normal circumstances there are supernumerary nails on the inner side of each foreleg. These are attached to partly formed digits which correspond to the human thumbs. Occasionally there are two of these nails on each side. They are called "dew claws." Because they have no bearing on the ground they are not subjected to wear. Consequently it is necessary to clip the dew claws from time to time. Not infrequently the dew claws are inclined to grow in circles instead of being slightly curved. In such cases the nail will enter the foot, if not watched. Ingrowing nails cause considerable pain and lameness. They may be clipped off when discovered. The wound, when present may be dressed with an antiseptic solution, dried with sterile cotton or gauze, and touched with a small swab of iodine.

Dew claws also are seen on the hind feet, where they give a clumsy appearance to the dog. Many breeders remove them from the puppies at birth. When they are present in the adult they are far more likely to grow into the feet than are the nails of the fore feet. They should not be forgotten, and should be cut at frequent intervals.

Ingrowing nails are found in all breeds occasionally. Such cases are due to insufficient exercise in toy dogs. In more active breeds, such as the hounds and terriers, the owner will occasionally notice a nail growing in an abnormal way. It may be growing in a circular manner or in an odd direction. It may be due to an injury to the toe or to a congenital deformity which causes the nail to bear imperfectly on the ground. In any event it is best to clip the nail every now and then.

Dew claws are frequently torn off or broken close to the leg. Sometimes the other claws are injured accidentally. If the injury is at all severe, it is best to remove the nail at the fracture. The after treatment consists of stopping the hemorrhage with peroxide of hydrogen solution and applying a bandage for twenty-four hours. If there is not any bleeding, it is not even necessary to bandage. There is little or no danger of infection because the dog is highly resistant to the pus organisms. If the hemorrhage is severe, it may be stopped quickly by the application of a small pledget of cotton soaked in Monsell's solution, which may be bandaged in position.

Any dog, given a fair amount of exercise on city pavements or in the country, will not have much trouble with its nails or pads. Pampered pets, which are carried everywhere and which only exercise by walking indoors on carpeted floors, always will need care of feet and nails.

THE COAT

The hair on the body of a dog is called the coat. It is a special development of the skin where each hair grows from a separate hair follicle. The coat was developed as a protection from the elements such as rain and cold weather. Some breeds, such as the chow chow, Pekingese and the Pomeranian, have a double coat. The deeper layer is composed of soft woolly hair. It is known as the undercoat. The superficial layer of more or less coarse hair.

The growing of the coat depends on several factors. Good health is essential to the growth of good coat. Consequently proper diet and good housing are of prime importance. Dogs should not be kept in very hot kennels. Since the coat is provided by nature as a protective covering against the cold, it follows that a dog kept in a very warm room will not grow a coat because it is unnecessary. A moderately cold kennel causes more blood to flow through the subcutaneous vessels and brings more nourishment or building material to the cells of the hair follicles. In their turn they utilize this additional material to make more, longer and stronger hairs. This statement is especially true of the undercoat. There is no question that a somewhat damp atmosphere is better for coat growing than a very dry one.

Nature has provided that the coat, or part of it, shall be shed each year. In most cases this shedding or coating takes place twice a year. No exact time can be set for shedding, but it usually comes with the onset of warm weather in spring and the cold of the fall. Shedding varies with the individual. Often one dog of a breed will lose almost all its coat during the spring or fall, while another of the same breed, kept under the same conditions of diet and housing, will scarcely undergo any perceptible change.

When the coat commences to fall out, as the result of this physiological condition, it is better to brush and comb the dog daily. Grooming may be pursued with vigor. The sooner the old coat is out, the sooner the new coat will come in strong and healthy.

In many breeds "plucking" is necessary. This is the removal of dead or superfluous coat forcefully. Plucking combs and knives are on the market. Plucking charts may be purchased showing the correct appearance of the individual breeds needing this attention. In most cases it is advisable to obtain expert instruction in plucking or to employ a professional handler to get the right effect.

GROOMING

Grooming the coat is necessary the year round for many reasons. Combing prevents tangling and matting. It is specially necessary in long-coated breeds. Brushing assists combing in separating the hairs. It also burnishes the hairs and gives the coat a healthy appearance or "bloom." In cities at all times and in the country during rainy seasons, a dog's coat is apt to become soiled. The dirt accumulation is almost always on the surface. If the coat is parted, the skin will be seen to be quite clean. In these cases a vigorous rubbing with a damp cloth will remove most of the surface dirt. It is followed by a good brushing with a clean long-bristled brush.

The skin of the dog is peculiar. There are no sweat glands. It is quite rich in grease glands which secrete an oily material. This oil keeps the skin soft and pliable. It also protects the coat.

When a dog is bathed too frequently, the result is to remove the natural oil from the skin and to make the skin and coat unnaturally dry. The result is poor coat, presenting an unthrifty appearance. The drying of the skin causes the appearance of minute cracks which, in turn, often become infected. Sometimes the cracks cause an irritation which causes the dog to scratch or bite itself with more or less disastrous results for the skin and to the coat which is pulled out in patches.

BATHING

A normal, healthy dog should be bathed as infrequently as possible. The reason for this has been stated in a preceding paragraph. This point cannot be made too strongly. It is really essential to the general growth of the coat and to the good health of the dog.

When a bath is necessary, the dog should be bathed in warm water. The temperature of the water should be about 105° F. To those who do not use a thermometer, this means that the water should be comfortably warm to the hand. There are many dog soaps on the market. Many of them are of inferior quality, but some are good. Any good laundry soap which does not contain too much free alkali may be used.

A good soap consists of tincture of green soap to which five per cent. of creolin is added. Care should be taken to rinse out all trace of soap before the dog is removed from the bath. When soap is left in the coat, it becomes sticky and quickly collects dirt. It also causes an irritation of the skin. Rinsing should be done with warm water followed by tepid or almost cold water.

The animal should be dried with towels as thoroughly as possible. This may be followed with hand massage and brushing. Finally the dog may be encouraged to run outdoors for a while unless the weather is very cold. Electric hot air dryers are useful.

Small breeds may be washed in an ordinary wash basin, laundry tub, or small sink provided with a stopper. Larger breeds may be put in an ordinary bath tub. The very large breeds may be readily washed on a stand such as is used for horses. In the latter case a hose, with hot and cold water connection, is a great asset. In any case a hose, with a spray nozzle, will be found of great assistance in removing the soap.

There is not much danger of a dog "catching cold" after a bath. This is accounted for by the fact that a dog's skin presents the peculiarity mentioned before. There are some individuals who claim that a cold always follows a bath. In most of these cases the nasal and ocular irritation was caused by the soap, which is indicated by the fact that the symptoms were developed while the dog was in the bath or immediately after removal from the bath. If it were a cold as a result of the bath the symptoms would not develop for an appreciable period of hours or even days.

CARE OF THE ADULT MALE

The following are a few pointers which may help the owner of a dog. Quite frequently a dog has a discharge from the prepuce or sheath. It may be watery, mucus, or purulent in character. The cause is a non-specific infection due to the moist sheath coming in contact with the floor or ground when the dog is in repose. It is rather stubborn, but in almost all cases the unpleasant condition may be cured by persistent treatment. This consists of daily use of an antiseptic solution with a syringe.

A soft rubber ear syringe, of one fluid ounce capacity, is the most useful instrument for the purpose. Any syringe with a small nozzle will suffice.

Some good antiseptic solutions are permanganate of potash or of zinc, 1%; argyrol, 10%; creolin, 5%; salt, teaspoonful to a pint of water; Dobell's solution; and carbolic acid, 1 to 1000 of water. Zonite which is an active chlorine solution, will be found useful in weak solution.

The method of administration is to stand the dog on a table or platform. Hold the free end of the sheath with the index finger and thumb of one hand and introduce the end of the syringe into the orifice of the prepuce. Fill the sheath with the antiseptic solution and withdraw the nozzle, at the same time compressing the skin to prevent the expulsion of the fluid. The lotion should be retained for about a minute. Then the pressure may be released and the elasticity of the skin will empty the sheath automatically. All that remains is to wipe the organ with a pledget of gauze or cotton.

The male does not exhibit the same periodic phenomenon of sex that is seen in the female. Puberty is reached at a varying age. The average age is about eight months. There are instances of precocity and numerous cases when puberty is delayed until a year or more. The larger dogs develop more slowly in this respect.

If the owner of a dog is interested in allowing his dog

to attain full growth, he will be wise to refrain from using the animal at stud too early. Early sexual intercourse is apt to arrest growth. It is much better not to use a house pet for stud. Stud dogs often develop unpleasant and embarrassing habits. They are rarely fully house-broken and even when clean they have a tendency to lapse from their habits of training.

If a dog is kept as a pet and shows symptoms of sexual excitement, it can be calmed down by reducing the pro-tein (meat) part of the diet and by giving more exercise. Dogs which are not used at stud sometimes become uncer-tain in temper during middle age. There are harmless ways of overcoming this tendency and a visit to any veterinarian specializing in dogs will obtain relief.

As the dog grows older he develops the usual signs of senility, such as loss of weight, loss of coat, grayness of the muzzle and extremities, loss of teeth and dimness of vision. Old dogs often become deaf.

The tendency of the male to fight others of the same sex is a characteristic. In many cases it is quite impossi-ble to train a dog not to fight. If a dog is controlled properly, the danger of serious fighting is reduced to a minimum. It is very seldom that a male will attack a female. This fact is made use of in kennels. It is cus-tomary to place animals of opposite sex in runs or cages together, thereby conserving valuable space.

BREEDING—PRINCIPLES OF

This should be a matter for careful thought. The modern owner of thoroughbred dogs cannot breed successfully unless he considers several vital factors. These include the general conformation of the bitch, the pedigree, and the condition of the bitch. In selecting the sire conformation, condition, and pedigree are extremely important. Minor factors are the time of year, proper handling, housing and correct feeding. There are many other things which bear on the subject but which can be overcome by the use of common sense. Line breeding and inbreeding may be adopted with caution.

OESTRUM

This is the period during which the ovaries are most active in the reproduction function. In most breeds it appears first at eight to ten months. From the time of the first period of "heat" it recurs regularly every six months. There may be some variation from this rule, such as every four months, every eight months, or even a year in certain individuals.

The period usually lasts for eighteen to twenty-four days. It may be divided into two distinct phases. The change from one to the other is gradual. The ninth or tenth day usually marks the point at which the second phase is well developed.

Often oestrum is preceded by an indefinite period during which there is a slight discharge from the vulva. The period proper commences with a rather dark colored discharge from the vulva (external female organ). After a day or two the discharge becomes more normal in blood color and more copious. It rarely reaches the proportion of a hemorrhage. The flow continues for about ten days. During the latter part, it often becomes lighter in color and might be described as a blood-tinged serum. This latter fluid may continue to flow until the end of the period. Frequently it practically ceases at ten days.

The second phase is that part of the oestrum when the flow is light in color and the external genital organ swells to three or four times its average size. During this part of the heat the bitch is receptive and will draw up the vulva in a characteristic manner. It is during this period that she should be bred, if the owner intends her to have puppies.

During the earlier part of oestrum a bitch will rarely allow a dog to pay her any attention. As a general rule she will turn on a dog and drive him away in a savage manner. This behavior will continue until the second phase is well developed.

It is during the second or receptive phase that the bitch is ready to mate. Because mating is an instinctive desire on the part of the female, it is during this stage that she must be guarded carefully. If an opportunity occurs, the average bitch will find her way to a dog. She is not at all particular as to the breed of the chosen mate. The result of such a mating is disastrous for the time being.

The act of breeding is instinctive and under normal circumstances does not require special knowledge on the part of the handler. It is safest to hold the bitch's head during the act and afterward, until the mating is completed and the animals have separated.

[45]

CARE AND FEEDING

If the bitch is a maiden, she will be rather fractious and require more patience than the experienced matron.

Occasionally a bitch is found which rebels at breeding during her whole life. In such cases, it is necessary to muzzle her and adopt other means of restraint which suggest themselves to the person or persons superintending the mating. In any event it is better to have an experienced person to handle the mating because it insures the safety to both dog and bitch. It also makes the result more certain.

Oestrum is rarely accompanied by any manifestation of pain either before or during the period. There may be symptoms of a slight disturbance of the nervous system which is made evident by hyperaesthesia. Occasionally a perfectly house-broken bitch will forget her manners during the period. This laxness applies to the control of the bladder. More rarely it is seen in the control of the bowels.

If it is not intended to breed the bitch she should be shut up and carefully guarded until the external genital organ has become normal in size and the discharge has stopped. The bitch then may be bathed to remove any trace of odor which would attract dogs to her. When this is done, she may be returned to her place in the home or kennel. And she may be treated as a normal dog.

Generally it is not recommended to an owner to allow his bitch to be mated until the second or third period. When a young and immature bitch is allowed to raise a litter too early the strain and drain on her system will arrest her full growth and development. This is made use of in cases where the animal shows signs of becoming too large or when her legs are too long. Many a good show prospect has been ruined by an early mating.

No special care of the breasts is necessary during

oestrum. During the first period the breasts fill out and the teats usually enlarge a trifle, but the whole enlargement gradually recedes until the only sign of puberty is that the teats are more prominent than formerly.

Bathing during the period is not advisable. Some bitches swim during the period. I have known a number of cases where an over-hygienic owner has put her dog in the bath while she was in heat. In both cases no harm has occurred, but it was due to luck and not to good judgment.

Whether a bitch is to be kept as a house pet or to be shown, it is much better for her health if she is allowed to raise one litter of puppies. It is not necessary to continue breeding at any subsequent heat, but the successful mating will have a tendency to ward off many unpleasant and serious disturbances in later life. These troubles do not necessarily follow in every bitch which goes through life as a maiden, but one or more commonly do make their appearance in late middle age.

The normal female in old age behaves very much like the old male. The rounded, well-kept appearance of maturity gradually changes to the lean, drawn and gray of advancing years. The dog loses her playfulness and shows an increasing tendency to rest and sleep. The appetite often becomes less, but this is not a constant feature. Gray or white hairs appear around the muzzle and on the feet. The coat becomes shorter and thinner. The eyes frequently take on an increasing blue appearance.

With advancing years the periods of oestrum often become irregular in their appearance and sometimes stop. When they appear the symptoms are considerably modified, especially in the character of the discharge, which is usually a pink-tinted serum instead of the normal blood.

The procreative function is often lost or, if puppies are

[47]

born, as the result of mating, they will be few in number and usually weak in general formation. Oestropause is not a constant feature of aged bitches, but it is usual in most cases. It is not marked by nervous pathological or psychological phenomena.

It is rather dangerous to breed bitches in middle age if they have not had a litter of puppies during their earlier life. The bones of the pelvic girdle are held together during the first few years by strong, short ligaments and cartilaginous joints. During parturition or expulsion of the puppies these ligaments stretch. There is also a cartilaginous union which acts as a hinge at the floor of the pelvis and permits enlargement of the bony ring. If these are used in early life to allow the passage of puppies, they never quite return to their previous positions and this fact lessens the danger if the bitch is again bred later.

When the stretching is not accomplished in youth, there is a marked tendency for these limited movements to become impossible because the ligaments and cartilage are replaced by bony structure. This condition is known as fusion or anchylosis. When it is complete the pelvis is a hard, bony ring which cannot stretch. The result is that only very small foeti can pass out. If large, the puppies must be removed by the Caesarian operation, or by forceps. In either event, the lives of both puppies and mother are placed in danger.

If you are going to breed, make up your mind while the bitch is young. Then there will be little trouble and practically no danger. These remarks on the pelvis of older dogs apply to all breeds, but they are of the utmost importance in those possessing large heads and short muzzles.

They apply to our American production, the Boston

terrier, because this favorite breed has a bulldog type of head and a terrier type of pelvis. This curious combination is the cause of so much of the trouble in whelping and can often be overcome by breeding not later than the third heat.

It is essential to success that both the sire and the dam be free from worms. In fact hook worm can cause so much harm in a kennel that it is impossible to raise puppies. In extreme cases it is not possible to get the bitches in whelp in spite of apparently good matings.

The actual details of mating are so simple and natural that they need not be described in this article. Mating will usually be facilitated if an experienced stud dog is chosen as the mate for a bitch which is to be covered for the first time. Similarly, in breaking in a stud dog, it will be easier to breed him to several experienced bitches before he is tried with a virgin female.

Occasionally, it will be noticed that a proper union cannot be established. In most cases, this is due to a constriction or stricture of the wall of the vagina. It can be detected by digital examination. The treatment is simple. A local anaesthetic is applied to the part and the ringlike stricture is dilated with a specially made instrument. It should be done by an experienced man or there may be danger of a rupture of the vaginal wall. The attendant bleeding will soon stop.

Douche the bitch with warm water and common salt (teaspoonful to a quart). Wait four or five hours. Then attempt breeding again. Simple strictures may be broken down with the fingers, starting with the little finger and gradually changing to larger fingers. A lubricant should be used. The hands should be scrubbed before attempting this method to avoid danger of infection.

There is no apparent effect from coition in the male.

Neither is there any immediate change in the female. Some breeders like to mate a bitch twice with an interval of one or two days between the matings. This is unnecessary in most cases, and it is usually done only as a safeguard that the mating will produce results.

It is safer and better that all matings are superintended by an experienced handler because the physiological act of coition involves a chance of physical injury to the dog or the bitch if they are not attended. This is especially the case when a small stud is used to a larger bitch.

The normal period of pregnancy is known as gestation. In the dog it is stated as nine weeks. As a matter of actual fact, it is usually one or two days short of the full-time.

If the bitch is normal in every way, no alarm need be felt if the puppies are carried several days over full term. It is a well established fact that the act of coition and conception or fertilization of the ova by the male element are not coincident. Pregnancy actually starts with conception and if that is delayed, birth of the litter will be correspondingly later.

Pregnancy in the early stages is not marked by any unusual change in the bitch. There is hardly ever any trace of vomiting. The appetite may gradually become abnormal. There is a gradual increase in girth. In the early stages, this is more apparent in the horizontal diameter. The bitch shows a desire to sleep more than usual. The nipples enlarge and become rather congested. The breasts show indistinct outline and gradually enlarge.

The diet during pregnancy should be fairly concentrated and free from anything which is likely to cause a serious disturbance of the digestive organs. Meat, raw eggs, fish, milk, broth, fresh vegetables—except peas, lima beans, corn and potatoes—dry breakfast foods manufactured for human consumption, puppy biscuit and zwieback (unsweetened). During the last ten days of pregnancy, it is recommended that the diet be reduced to meat or fish which may be given with or without a small quantity of bran. Season food with salt.

Special attention should be paid to the condition of the dog's bowels, which should be kept active. If necessary, it is a good plan to give laxative doses of milk of magnesia or other mild purgative from time to time. The activity of the kidneys should be observed also. If the kidneys are not normally active, poisons are accumulated in the mother's blood stream and endanger the lives of both dam and puppies. Any abnormality of this nature is best handled by a canine veterinarian. Allow water at all times.

Exercise during pregnancy is very important. In the first weeks normal activities may be allowed without harm. Later it may be necessary to give road work, on a leash, because the bitch may develop a lazy attitude which is prejudicial to healthy normal puppies.

Violent running and jumping may not cause any disturbance during early pregnancy but they may be dangerous in the later stages and may lead to injury to the puppies in the uterus and premature parturition with loss of the litter or the bitch or both.

THE STUD DOG

He should be selected carefully. The dog reaches puberty at about seven months in the smaller breeds and somewhat later in the larger breeds. There are cases of precocity, therefore it is not always safe to allow a young dog to remain with a bitch in heat unless it is desirable that they mate. The testicles appear in the scrotum early in life and continue to develop until the animal is one year or more according to the breed. The young dog should not be used too early. Large well developed specimens may be used occasionally after reaching nine months. Regular service at stud should be delayed until one and a half to two years. The male should have two sound testicles properly placed in the scrotum and the penis should be free in the prepuce and in healthy condition. It should be free from discharge, especially from any trace of blood which should suggest a pathological condition with danger of contagion. The diet of the stud dog should be rich in protein, such as meat, fish and eggs.

Probably the use of wheat germ oil in small, carefully regulated doses will increase the potency of the stud dog. There is no doubt that it will help greatly in the female, both before, during and after oestrum, and during pregnancy and the nursing period.

The stud dog should be given plenty of exercise and should be in hard condition during his active service period. Obesity in male or female is undesirable and should be avoided.

The number of puppies in a litter is governed by the number of ova released by the ovaries during oestrum. The male has nothing whatever to do with the size of the litter. If the stud is potent the live male elements probably will fertilize all the ova set free at that period.

TELEGONY (mismating)

There was an old belief that a bitch was spoiled for further breeding if she became pregnant to a stud of another breed. This is not true. If mongrel puppies are produced by a bitch, her uterus is emptied completely at parturition. She may be bred to a correct sire at the next period and will produce thoroughbred puppies. There will not be any trace of the sire of the previous litter.

ATAVISM

Occasionally in a litter there will appear a puppy which is untrue to type. The variations may be in color, type, coat, or conformation. This is due to the influence of some more or less remote ancestor on one side or the other. It must be remembered that most standard breeds are the result of selective breeding and crossing. In other words they are synthetic. Therefore it is natural to find occasional "sports" which throw back to a forgotten ancestor.

WHELPING

In most cases the bitch requires no assistance at whelping. If there seems to be difficulty call in a veterinarian immediately. The puppies are delivered in an individual sack which the bitch removes. She also severs the navel cord and licks the puppy until dry. At times delivery is accomplished very rapidly and in some cases is prolonged over a period of hours.

Do not handle newly born puppies too much. There is more danger in overhandling than from the mother lying on them. The quarters in which the mother and puppies are to be confined should be comfortable and warm, free from draughts.

Frequently bitches do not remove the after birth or sever the cord. In these cases the attendant must do it at once. The cord should not be cut too near the puppy.

Whelping Table based on 63 days.

Service Date	Jan																														
January (Service)	1	2	3	4	5	6	7	8	9	10	11	12	13	14	15	16	17	18	19	20	21	22	23	24	25	26	27	28	29	30	31
March (Whelp)	5	6	7	8	9	10	11	12	13	14	15	16	17	18	19	20	21	22	23	24	25	26	27	28	29	30	31	April 1	2	3	4
February (Service)	1	2	3	4	5	6	7	8	9	10	11	12	13	14	15	16	17	18	19	20	21	22	23	24	25	26	27	28			
April (Whelp)	5	6	7	8	9	10	11	12	13	14	15	16	17	18	19	20	21	22	23	24	25	26	27	28	29	30	May 1	2			
March (Service)	1	2	3	4	5	6	7	8	9	10	11	12	13	14	15	16	17	18	19	20	21	22	23	24	25	26	27	28	29	30	31
May (Whelp)	3	4	5	6	7	8	9	10	11	12	13	14	15	16	17	18	19	20	21	22	23	24	25	26	27	28	29	30	31	June 1	2
April (Service)	1	2	3	4	5	6	7	8	9	10	11	12	13	14	15	16	17	18	19	20	21	22	23	24	25	26	27	28	29	30	
June (Whelp)	3	4	5	6	7	8	9	10	11	12	13	14	15	16	17	18	19	20	21	22	23	24	25	26	27	28	29	30	July 1	2	
May (Service)	1	2	3	4	5	6	7	8	9	10	11	12	13	14	15	16	17	18	19	20	21	22	23	24	25	26	27	28	29	30	31
July (Whelp)	3	4	5	6	7	8	9	10	11	12	13	14	15	16	17	18	19	20	21	22	23	24	25	26	27	28	29	30	31	August 1	2
June (Service)	1	2	3	4	5	6	7	8	9	10	11	12	13	14	15	16	17	18	19	20	21	22	23	24	25	26	27	28	29	30	
August (Whelp)	3	4	5	6	7	8	9	10	11	12	13	14	15	16	17	18	19	20	21	22	23	24	25	26	27	28	29	30	31	September 1	
July (Service)	1	2	3	4	5	6	7	8	9	10	11	12	13	14	15	16	17	18	19	20	21	22	23	24	25	26	27	28	29	30	31
September (Whelp)	2	3	4	5	6	7	8	9	10	11	12	13	14	15	16	17	18	19	20	21	22	23	24	25	26	27	28	29	30	October 1	2
August (Service)	1	2	3	4	5	6	7	8	9	10	11	12	13	14	15	16	17	18	19	20	21	22	23	24	25	26	27	28	29	30	31
October (Whelp)	3	4	5	6	7	8	9	10	11	12	13	14	15	16	17	18	19	20	21	22	23	24	25	26	27	28	29	30	31	November 1	2
September (Service)	1	2	3	4	5	6	7	8	9	10	11	12	13	14	15	16	17	18	19	20	21	22	23	24	25	26	27	28	29	30	
November (Whelp)	3	4	5	6	7	8	9	10	11	12	13	14	15	16	17	18	19	20	21	22	23	24	25	26	27	28	29	30	December 1	2	
October (Service)	1	2	3	4	5	6	7	8	9	10	11	12	13	14	15	16	17	18	19	20	21	22	23	24	25	26	27	28	29	30	31
December (Whelp)	3	4	5	6	7	8	9	10	11	12	13	14	15	16	17	18	19	20	21	22	23	24	25	26	27	28	29	30	31	January 1	2
November (Service)	1	2	3	4	5	6	7	8	9	10	11	12	13	14	15	16	17	18	19	20	21	22	23	24	25	26	27	28	29	30	
January (Whelp)	3	4	5	6	7	8	9	10	11	12	13	14	15	16	17	18	19	20	21	22	23	24	25	26	27	28	29	30	31	February 1	
December (Service)	1	2	3	4	5	6	7	8	9	10	11	12	13	14	15	16	17	18	19	20	21	22	23	24	25	26	27	28	29	30	31
February (Whelp)	2	3	4	5	6	7	8	9	10	11	12	13	14	15	16	17	18	19	20	21	22	23	24	25	26	27	28	March 1	2	3	4

WEANING

The eyes of puppies are closed when born and remain so for nine or ten days. After two weeks, if they are not then open, it is advisable to wash them carefully with warm water or a saturated solution of boracic acid.

The puppies usually nurse until a month or more old. About this time the secretions of milk in the bitch begin to dry and she leaves her puppies at longer intervals. Puppies can be weaned very easily. The usual procedure is to dip their noses into a dish of warm milk. When about six or seven weeks old they can be fed a little meat scraped raw, free from fat. A good rule in feeding puppies is little and often as there is danger of their overeating. Feeding dishes should be scalded and kept scrupulously clean.

WORMS

Dogs and puppies harbor four common varieties of worms. They are round worms, hook worms, tape worms, and whip worms. These are found in the stomach occasionally and in the intestine usually. As a rule the stomach location is due to the worms being forced there by reverse intestinal peristalsis or in the case of the round worms by their own motion.

Round worms—common in puppies and found in dogs of all ages. Sometimes called puppy or stomach worms. Two varieties—*toxascaris limbata* and *belaccaris marginata*. Reproduce by production of ova by the female. These eggs are of characteristic shape and form. They are diagnostic when found in the stool. The worms vary from two to four or more inches long and may be one-eighth inch thick, pointed at each end, sometimes straight or coiled.

Treatment consists of fasting and administration of a vermicide in correct dose. It should be repeated in seven to fourteen days. Santonin, oil of chenopodunis, pelletierine tannate, carbon tetrachloride (chemically pure), tetrachlorethylene and hexylresorcinol have been used. The most recent research has shown that tetrachlorethylene, in capsule with or without a purgative included, is efficient. The dose is about o.1 c.c. per pound of body weight. The only precaution necessary is to avoid feeding fat or oil of any kind (milk included) for a day before and after administration. Tetrachlorethylene is not purgative therefore a milk saline purgative must be given with or after treatment. Epsom salts or milk of magnesia is effective. A high saline enema sometimes renders treatment more efficient.

Oil of chenopodunis or worm seed oil may be used in doses of about one minim per pound of body weight. Hexylresorcinol in crystals in hard gelatin capsules is available. Santonin was used a great deal but has been superseded by more recently discovered methods.

HOOK WORM

Formerly found in dogs in the southern states it now has spread widely throughout the country. The worms are called *uncinaria stenocephala* or *anchylostoma cannium*. The male is about one-third of an inch long, the female about one-half an inch. Both are slender. They live in the small intestine where they attach themselves to the mucosa by means of small hooks and suck blood. The female produces large numbers of characteristically shaped ova which pass out with the feces of the host.

[56]

There they hatch out and pass through several molts. They can live in the soil for a considerable time. They gain access to the dog by boring through the skin of the feet and possibly by ingestion with contaminated food or water. They pass by way of the blood stream to the lung, then to the air passages, going up to the mouth, being swallowed and eventually gaining the small intestine.

The attack of these worms is insidious. Nursing puppies cease to feed, appear to fade rapidly, and die. Older puppies are markedly anaemic. Infected brood bitches often fail to become pregnant or produce full term puppies which die soon after birth as described already. Stud dogs may be sterile. All infested animals usually have an unthrifty appearance but adults may appear normal and in good condition—for this reason the presence of the worms is not suspected. Positive diagnosis is made by microscopical examination of the feces. Stools are often loose and contain blood and mucus.

TREATMENT

The administration of tetrachlorethylene or hexylresorcinol as recommended for round worms is efficient. Several treatments at intervals of seven to ten days must be given. Since the parasites may spend some time outside the host's body kennels, runs, etc., must be sterilized. For this purpose the runs may be treated with a solution of salt—one and a half pounds to the gallon of water. It should be sprinkled liberally over the ground—about a gallon per square yard. All kennels and inside floors must be sterilized.

WHIP WORMS

Once this worm was comparatively rare—now it is found all over the country. It is very common in the east. The worm is named because the short thick body resembles a handle and the long fine neck looks like a lash. Male and female are alike. The female produces ova which are lemon shaped with a flattened knob at each end. The scientific name is *trichuris depressiuscula* or *trichuris vulpis*. The adult worms are found in the caecum or blind pouch of the large intestine, and in the upper colon. They are not active.

As a rule they do not cause much disturbance of health. Sometimes they cause a persistent foetid diarrhoea. They have been known to cause nervous symptoms similar to "running fits," in young animals. Occasionally they appear to aid in producing general unthriftiness with symptoms of skin irritations.

TREATMENT

I have had most success by giving small doses of santonin and thymol in enteric capsules. As the worms live in the caecum and are not accessible directly I find it better to give a series of doses morning and evening for seven to ten days. The dose varies from one-eighth to one-half grain of thymol and one-half to two grains of santonin according to the weight and condition of the patient. The patient is fasted after the last dose and given the usual dose of tetrachlorethylene and Epsom salt—or milk of magnesia as recommended for round worms. It may be necessary to repeat.

Some cases are exceedingly stubborn. These may be treated by a surgical operation involving opening the

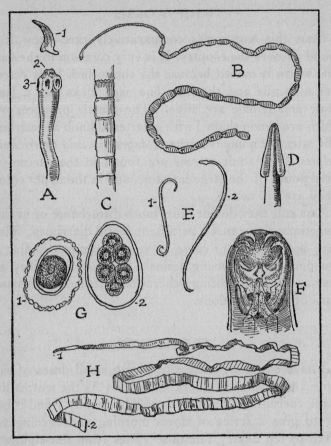

The intestinal parasites of dogs. The tape worms are:
H, *taenia serrata* and B, *taenia cucummerina*. The heads are
minute and the segments increase in size. G, six connected
segments passed in feces, natural size. A, head of *taenia serrata,* magnified; figure 1 single hook, figure 2 circle of hooks
on the head, figure 3 suckers. E, common round worm, *ascaris
marginata,* natural size; the male is twice the size of the
female. D, head of round worm, magnified. It is slightly
flattened with wing shaped borders. F, hook worm, *uncinaria,*
greatly enlarged. The mouth is bellshaped with six hooks like
teeth. G, figure 1 round worm eggs, figure 2 hookworm eggs.

abdomen and removal of the caecum—caecectemy. A method has been described whereby a tube is passed per rectum into the caecum and worm medicine injected directly to the seat of infectation. In almost all cases which are treated with thymol and santonin the worms may be eliminated or reduced to the point where they cease to cause trouble.

TAPE WORM

The dog is the host of several tape worms which are characterized by flat segmented bodies from which the rearmost segments become detached. These segments often appear on the stool as small maggotlike individuals. They also may appear to creep out of the anus and are called rectal, "seat," or pin worms. The dried segments may be found adhering to the coat around the anus or on the underside of the tail. They then look like dried buff color seeds.

Tape worms may cause anal irritation, poor coat, emaciation (rare), extreme nervousness even to convulsions, skin irritation, and occasionally diarrhoea and other evidence of intestinal irritation. The common tape worm of the dog is the *dipylidium cannium*. All tape worms must pass through a bladder state of development and require a separate host for that stage. The flea and louse are the hosts of the bladder form of *dipylidium cannium*. Other dog worms have the secondary stage in the liver of rats and mice, in the cranium of the sheep (causing a disease called gid), and in the bodies in various parts of man, horses, cattle, etc., *(taenia echinococcus)*. Usually diagnosis is based on finding living or dried segments of the worms. Occasionally the ova may be detected but they are not by any means constant.

BREEDING—PRINCIPLES OF

TREATMENT

Several drugs are useful in the removal of tape worms. I prefer to fast the patient for twenty-four hours. Then give the correct dose of oleoresin of male fern and kamala. This is followed in several hours with a saline purgative such as Epsom salts. Finally the patient is given a high colonic irrigation with salt and water.

The expelled worms should be examined for heads. If the heads are not removed the worms will develop again. If the heads are found there is not any need for further treatment.

Reinfection must be guarded against—especially as regards fleas.

The dose of male fern extract is about (1) minim to each two pounds of body weight and of kamala (1) gram to each two pounds. Arecoline hydrobromide is another drug used for expulsion of tape worm. It is a violent purgative which acts very quickly—the dose is about one-eighth grain for small dogs, one-fourth grain for medium, and half grain or slightly more for large dogs.

Worming indiscriminately with many of the nostrums on the market is to be condemned as dangerous. The drugs employed may kill worms but they shorten the lives of dogs by causing serious disturbances of the structure of the liver and kidneys.

EXERCISE

The question of exercise must be regulated by many influences such as location, breed, age, and sanitary laws. In cities and large towns it is almost impossible to give the larger breeds enough exercise to keep them in good hard condition. Few owners of big dogs are willing to walk for miles, on city pavements, with a dog on a leash. Traffic in our cities is so heavy that a leash is a necessity as a protection to the animal's life. The exercise which city dogs get is extremely limited in most cases.

Lack of exercise makes the average dog soft. Frequently the food is not cut down to the proper amount to suit the requirements of the body. As a result, the dog becomes obese and short of breath. The improper oxygenation of the blood lays the animal open to the infections which abound in large communities, because it lessens the ability of the body to overcome such invasions.

This gloomy picture is not always seen, in reality, but there are enough of these cases to make the dog lover take more interest in the welfare of his voluntary charge. The task of keeping a dog is almost always self-imposed. This being the case, the owner can find no legitimate excuse for constantly neglecting to give the required amount of time for proper exercise.

The small and medium-sized breeds will do well under the adverse conditions of city dwelling. The distance required by them is not excessive. It is within the power of most people to walk these animals enough to keep them in good shape.

EXERCISE

One of the best types of dog for city dwellers is included in the class known as toys. There are many breeds which may be chosen from. These are chosen because they can be quite properly exercised by a few blocks of walking each day. They are readily house broken to paper. And they usually are active while indoors and make up for the lack of outdoor walks by running to doors and telephone signals. They are small enough in most cases to be carried when the weather is inclement. Consequently there is no need for them to be soiled with the city slush during rain and snow storms.

The distance which should be covered by the larger dogs depends very much on the athletic ability of the owner. They can hardly be given too much daily walking to keep them fit. The average terrier will do well on two miles a day. Smaller dogs require less.

It is not considered a good plan to exercise puppies on the streets. Living conditions are crowded even for canines and it is so easy for a puppy to pick up the infection of distemper or any other contagious disease. As a dog grows older, there is less danger of its dying from distemper, but the possibility of infection remains the same.

In the city the smaller dogs get a great deal of exercise by being encouraged to chase and retrieve such objects as tennis balls. This may be done indoors. If the thrower refrains from boisterousness, no harm will be done to the home and much good will accrue to the dog.

All dogs should be exercised on a leash. If the sanitary code of the locality requires that the dog be muzzled, it is a good plan to train the dog to wear one. This is rather easily accomplished by making the young animal wear its muzzle indoors for a short period every day.

The period may be lengthened as the puppy learns not to fear the contrivance.

In a similar way puppies may be taught to become accustomed to the collar and leash. Start with the collar. Then add the leader after two or three weeks. Finally add the muzzle. Some dogs learn much more quickly than others. Occasionally a specimen is met with who refuses to wear a muzzle. This is very rare. It would not exist if the training were started sooner.

Some owners find a collar irritates the pet's throat, causing coughing or shortness of breath. It is usual in such cases, to find that the dog pulls constantly on the leash. Train a dog to walk at the side of the person holding the leader and pulling will not cause any irritation. When this training proves difficult, the owner may resort to punishment. The use of a choke or running noose collar very often is effective in checking a puller.

There is a collar with spikes lining the inside. It is strapped on the neck loosely and does not cause pain until the dog pulls. It is effective as a training measure. If such a device is used, it should be resorted to only in extreme cases. Patience, in training, will produce good results in almost all cases.

Dog owners often complain that a dog suffers unnecessarily when it is forced to exercise in a muzzle while on a leash. Most well-trained dogs do not seem to suffer any inconvenience when the muzzle is well made and properly fitted. Many muzzles are cheap and ill fitting. They undoubtedly do work a hardship. The only way to overcome objectionable legislation against the dog—such as the clause which causes the owner to muzzle a dog even when it is controlled by a leader—is to get all dog owners to combine in each locality and bring pressure to bear on the responsible legislative body.

EXERCISE

When a muzzle is purchased it should be examined for sharp projections, such as points of wire and imperfectly clamped rivets. These chafe and cause painful wounds. In some cases a judiciously placed pad or binding will make a muzzle tolerable, if not comfortable. Collars and leaders should be as light as possible. But they should be strong enough to meet the strain which is put on them when an emergency arises.

Chains are an absolute necessity to fasten dogs to kennels or for traveling on railroad trains. It is too easy for an average dog to gnaw through a leather leash. There is a good leader which combines a leather hand end with a short chain part running to the spring clasp. This prevents the dog from wearing out its end by playing with the leather and cutting it. Another good lead is made by sewing leather over a thin flexible piece of braided or twisted cable. This is not heavy and has great strength.

In the country the problem of exercise is comparatively simple. Here walking becomes a pleasure which is enhanced when a doggy companion is added. Hounds, setters, pointers and spaniels will pay for the trouble of exercising them by providing almost endless moments of interest. Terriers will provide amusement as they scurry about and enjoy the country, even if they require little or no straight-forward walking. All dogs enjoy the sunshine and fresh air. Sunshine is really essential to the full and proper growth of puppies. It will go a long way toward avoiding such diseases as rickets and anaemia.

SWIMMING

Swimming is a wonderful exercise for dogs. All dogs are able to swim, but some of them prefer to keep out of the water. If a dog is taught carefully to approach the water without force, it will often wade and retrieve small floating objects at an early age. Once this is accomplished, it is a matter of patience and easy stages to actual swimming. Both fresh and sea water seem to cause little or no disturbance of the skin. Several cases of skin disease, resembling eczema, have been reported to be caused by excessive swimming in salt water. In these it is reasonable to assume that the eczema existed already, and the constant wetting aggravated the condition.

JUMPING

In some breeds jumping is a good form of exercise. Many dogs take naturally to it and may be trained to jump almost incredible heights. It should not be encouraged in the young, because the bones are soft and easily injured.

CLOTHING

There may be some amusement at this caption, but when it is considered from the utilitarian standpoint, as against the esthetic, there is no real cause for laughter. But coats, sweaters and even raincoats are useful and often necessary.

In the Northern States, short-haired breeds suffer considerably during the winter from rigors of the climate. There is no better example of this than our native breed, the Boston terrier. This dog has a comparatively thin skin and short, fine coat, which provides poor protection to the winter winds and low temperatures.

The best protection for short-haired dogs is a well-fitting, closely-knit sweater. If a lighter garment is needed, a coat of cloth is recommended. The coat should be cut in such a manner that the chest is fully covered. It should be long enough to reach to the root of the tail and deep in girth to cover the ribs. A coat is usually held in place by a strap similar to a circingle for a horse.

A raincoat for a dog is useful especially for long-haired toys. It is made of rubberized material and fitted the same way as the ordinary coat. When a dog returns from a walk in the rain, it should be dried carefully. This saves the dog from the effects of a thorough wetting and goes a long way toward saving clothing, carpets and furniture for the owner.

DISTEMPER

True distemper is a disease of dogs caused by a filterable virus. It attacks dogs, foxes and ferrets. The work of Laidlaw and Dunkin confirmed the work done earlier by Carré. The disease is complicated by the fact that it breaks down the normal resistance of the dog's defensive armament to other pathological organisms such as the *bacillus paratyphosus, salmonella enteriditis, bacillus bronchisepticus* and certain *staphylococci* and *streptococci*. It is the active disease caused by one or more of these bacteria following an attack of virus distemper which gives rise to the symptoms commonly associated with the disease in the mind of the layman.

The widely diversified symptoms are due also to the fact that several organisms may be involved.

Symptoms of distemper may be produced by infection with one of the organisms already named without previous infection with virus. Apparently the virulence of the secondary invaders may be stepped up by passage through several susceptible animals and become strong enough to cause disease.

These paragraphs should be sufficient to make it clear that diagnosis is a matter of considerable difficulty and frequently involves the use of a first class laboratory before any definite conclusion can be reached.

The fairly constant symptoms of canine distemper include a preliminary sudden rise of temperature with more or less dullness and loss of appetite. The temperature varies from 104° to 106° F. It is followed quickly (twenty-four to forty-eight hours) by a rapid drop almost to normal. Then it rises again slowly to 103.5 or 104° where it has a tendency to remain rather steady. With this second rise the dog develops conjunctivitis characterized by photophobia, serious discharge, purulent discharge and itching of eyelids. In some cases ulcerations of the cornea and pus in the anterior chamber of the eye.

This may be accompanied by respiratory or gastro-intestinal inflammatory symptoms or by both at once.

The respiratory symptoms include tonsillitis which is a common early symptom, laryngitis, bronchitis and lobar pneumonia. A hard irritating cough is a common feature.

The gastro-intestinal symptoms include vomiting, constipation followed by diarrhoea and later turning to dysentery. Evacuation is accompanied by considerable straining. Not infrequently the liver becomes involved.

The urinary system usually is injured in a well developed attack of distemper. It may not show during the acute attack. If it does become involved the patient often dies quickly as the result. Chronic nephritis or chronic interstitial nephritis is very apt to be left as a sequel to virus distemper and its complications. These diseases of the kidneys cause serious trouble later and curtail the length of the patient's life.

The pustules often seen on the abdomen and inside the thighs are not serious and usually resolve without treatment.

Nervous complications are not uncommon. They are caused by a streptococcus infection and vary much in intensity. The brain and the cord may be involved. Usually they follow a mild but long drawn out case. Some time may elapse between the recognized attack of distemper and the onset of nervous symptoms. Sometimes the nervous symptoms develop early while recognized symptoms are present. Usually the earliest symptom is rapid champing of the jaws and salivation. These attacks may occur at more or less frequent intervals. Convulsions may intervene and there may be considerable disturbance of the vital functions of the heart and respiration. There is usually considerable depression. Posterior paralysis may develop and this may spread forward to include the whole muscular structure. Sometimes rhythmic twitching may start in certain sets of muscles—so called "chorea." Some cases lapse into coma and death ensues. In chronic chorea the muscles involved usually atrophy. Paralysis of the muscles of mastication and of the tongue is not uncommon. Blindness and deafness may develop slowly or rapidly. The temperature usually rises at the onset of nervous symptoms and remains high throughout the acute stage of the attack.

The prognosis in all cases of distemper in the second stage should be extremely guarded. In the nervous involvement it is grave.

TREATMENT

When distemper is diagnosed in the earliest stages the most satisfactory treatment is the use of massive doses of homologous canine anti distemper serum. This should come from a recognized biological laboratory. It should be handled carefully and protected from heat and light. The date on the bottle should be correct—it should not be stale or outdated. One to two c.c. per pound of body weight is not too much to use in a single dose. It is administered subcutaneously with a regular hypodermic syringe under aseptic conditions. It may be repeated several times at intervals of twelve to twenty-four hours if necessary.

Careful nursing, housing, and feeding are absolutely necessary. In many cases it is advisable to put on a pneumonia jacket, especially if there is danger of chilling in winter.

When secondary symptoms appear they should be treated in orthodox manner. It is often wise to give a dose of castor oil or milk of magnesia as soon as possible. I incline to the former as it cleans the intestine thoroughly and has a tendency to constipate afterward checking the diarrhoea so often seen with the disease. The patient should be isolated and kept quiet. In good weather exposure to direct sunlight for short periods is beneficial. Some practitioners recommend the use of mixed bacterius in the secondary stage.

There are many "cures" on the market. Most of them are of very little value. Many are positively harmful. The best plan is to seek the advice of a veterinarian specializing in the diseases of dogs. Follow this advice. And place the patient in a hospital with a competent staff if such an institution is available.

If the dog will eat provide small easily digestible meals. Feed every four hours during the day. Raw, broiled, or roast meat, chicken, fish, oatmeal or barley gruel, raw eggs, pabulum, buttered toast, milk, buttermilk, acidophilus milk, and store cheese may be given. Dry cereals and some carefully prepared dog biscuits and foods may be included in the list.

Sudden temperature changes and wetting or dampness should be avoided.

CARE AND FEEDING

PROPHYLAXIS

The prevention of canine distemper has been given considerable attention. It has been highly successful when administered by competent technicians who use high class laboratory products and observe every precaution in selecting the candidates to be treated. In my opinion it is better to give young puppies between the ages of six weeks and four and a half months a correct dose of anti-distemper homologous serum every two to four weeks. After teething is complete the puppies should be tested for worms and should be treated if necessary. Each dog coming up for permanent inoculation should be examined carefully for rickets, skin diseases, malnutrition, and anaemia in addition to worms. It should not have been exposed to distemper infection. The temperature should be normal. In other words puppies presented for permanent distemper prophylaxis should be absolutely normal and well nourished.

There are several recognized methods of inoculation in giving permanent immunity from virus distemper. In every case the use of living virus must be involved. The reputable biological laboratories producing serum, bacteria, vaccine, and virus for prophylaxis and treatment of canine distemper do not allow their products to get into the hands of the layman. The only way to obtain reliable material is through your local veterinarian. Therefore it is best to consult him and to follow his instructions. Use the method which has been most successful in his locality. If the vaccine-virus method is employed it is better to give two injections of vaccine before the virus. If the virus-serum or virus-concentrated serum methods are used it is better to follow with a second injection of serum or concentrated serum in ten to fourteen days. Temperature

[72]

charts should be kept with A.M. and P.M. recordings from time of virus injection to about two weeks later. A sudden rise of temperature may be expected about seven to ten days after the virus—usually it subsides in a day. If it remains up the veterinarian should be notified at once.

Some veterinarians prepare the candidates and place them in distemper wards of hospitals instead of administering virus. There is much to be said in favor of this if there is absolute certainty that virus distemper is present and that the preparation has been carried out efficiently.

Modern distemper prophylaxis is not dangerous and is extremely efficient. It is humane. And it is inexpensive compared with the cost of treatment, nursing, and feeding sick dogs. Also the increased income accruing from strong healthy puppies more than offsets the fee for prophylaxis.

RABIES

In the past few years, the question of rabies has occupied a prominent place in the daily papers and in the minds of all those interested in the welfare of the dog. It is of particular interest because the disease has appeared as an endemic condition in centers where there are many kennels and where dog shows are held.

To anyone who has experience there cannot be any doubt as to the existence of a specific disease known as rabies in dogs, and more commonly as hydrophobia in humans.

Rabies is defined by Doctor O. B. Brumley of Ohio State College of Veterinary Medicine as "an acute infectious disease fatal in the majority of cases, and characterized clinically by disturbance of consciousness, marked irritability, and later by symptoms of paralysis."

The disease apparently is caused by a filterable virus. It is infective by direct inoculation, as by the bite of an animal in the saliva of which there is virus. If there is not a break in the continuity of the skin there is not any danger of infection. In most cases of natural infection, the disease is spread by the victim being bitten by a dog. In addition to dogs and humans, the disease may attack horses, cattle, sheep, pigs, cats, wolves, foxes, and most of the warm blooded animals. Birds are said to be infected by inoculation. Rabies is as common in winter as in summer.

The period of incubation varies very much and differs from most acute infective diseases because it is much longer. Usually it averages from twenty (20) to fifty (50) days. A dog bitten in the head or neck usually develops the disease more quickly than one bitten on the extremities. Cases have been recorded where the acute symptoms of infection have not developed for six to twelve months after the patient was bitten. On the other hand, cases are cited in which the period of incubation is as brief as ten days.

The virus passes by way of the nerves to the central nervous system, and to some extent the period of incubation corresponds with the position of the infective wound. In other words, the closer the wound is to the head of the victim the shorter the period of incubation, and similarly the greater the distance of the wound from the head the longer the period of incubation.

It is interesting to note that all animals vary in resistance to the infection. While some have practically no resistance, others have a natural resistance which amounts to immunity. This, too, aids in causing a widely varying period of incubation. This apparent immunity may be due to the fact that the virus does not reach the nerve trunk when it is introduced into a wound by the teeth. Incidentally, there is less danger when a victim is bitten through clothing or shoes or gloves, but this should not cause a human to neglect taking every possible precaution against infection.

There are described, generally, two forms of the disease—furious and dumb rabies.

Furious rabies is characterized by three stages of development which blend into one another. The first stage is one of melancholy. There is a marked change in the dog's character. Usually there is a tendency to creep away into a darkened place. Sullenness, irritability, and disobedience may be noticed. The animal is restless. There may be a change in the voice with a higher pitch to the bark. Occasionally, there is a tendency to snap at quickly moving objects, especially if they shine. There may be some salivation. The expression of the eyes is altered, and a fixed stare replaces the usual appearance.

The second stage is that in which the animal becomes very excitable. It may walk or run aimlessly, paying little or no attention to anything or snapping furiously at any quickly moving object which crosses its path. There is seldom any tendency to hang on, but to bite again and again. The dog does not have any symptoms of hydrophobia as is common in man. In fact, an infected dog will wade or swim streams or lakes if they are encountered in its wanderings.

There is a marked change in the voice in this stage. It is high pitched and peculiarly "cracked." It is practically characteristic and almost anyone with experience can recognize it. There is a more or less curious desire to eat foreign bodies such as sticks, stones and other foreign bodies. There may be a desire to bite the feet, legs, or site of original infection.

As the furious stage passes into the final paralytic stage there is a commencing paralysis of the lower jaw. The interior of the mouth becomes dry. The tongue hangs out. If there is any saliva, it hangs in strings of mucus. The tongue is dry and discolored. The dog often appears to have something in its throat.

As the paralysis develops, the patient is unable to swallow. The lust of wandering is changed to deep depression. There is increasingly difficult breathing. And there is a noticeable paralysis commencing with the hind legs and spreading forward to the loins, fore legs, neck, and head. This slips into coma and death.

The symptoms of the three stages blend together and each stage varies in duration in each case. The time of the attack from inception to death varies usually from five to eight (5-8) days.

RABIES

Dumb rabies is practically the same as the third stage of furious rabies—the change of voice, change of expression, paralysis of mandible, and paralysis commencing in the hind quarters and spreading forward more or less rapidly to be succeeded by coma, and death are the common sequence of symptoms. Sometimes there is a tendency to attempt to bite if the victim is irritated.

In both forms of rabies the saliva is virulent for a period of three to five days before any symptoms appear. Consequently it is the height of folly to neglect the bite of a strange dog. In all cases when humans are bitten by an unknown or stray dog, it is extremely advisable to go at once to a clinic or private practitioner for cauterization and advice. If the biting dog is known to be free from the disease, there is absolutely no danger in a bite except the danger of common infection which may arise in any other wound.

Rabies is almost invariably fatal if the symptoms are allowed to develop before prophylaxis is administered. Therefore, if prophylaxis is to be used it should be commenced as soon as possible after the biting has taken place. The best available vaccine should be used, and treatment for dogs should be in the hands of a veterinarian or competent health authority specializing in the disease.

In this respect there are several methods of prophylaxis applicable, and the choice should be discussed with the local authority.

Much has been written about the "one shot" method of immunization recommended by local and state health authorities where endemics occur. I am of the opinion that the use of vaccine as a yearly inoculation for the eradication of rabies has some value as proven by statistics, but I do not believe that it should be relied upon solely as the method for combating the disease.

It is very doubtful in my mind whether the passive immunity derived from a single injection of vaccine will last even six months, and the degree of protection must vary even at the time of inoculation.

It is stated that only from 20 to 40 percent of all bites of rabid dogs are infective to the victims, but the vulnerable animals merit whatever protection we can offer. The use of the single injection method is employed, and the maximum value is present during the greatest emergency.

On the other hand, the public should not be lulled into a feeling of false security because the dogs of an infected area are given one inoculation vaccination. The health authority of the district should enforce such measures as rigid licensing, muzzle and leash rules, catching of all stray and unowned dogs with a 48 hour detention period in the pound before final disposition of individual cases, and a quarantine whenever it is practicable. Such measures, if carried out generally, should go far toward wiping out rabies.

There does not appear any need to stop dog shows in communities under quarantine. The dogs exhibited at shows are mainly raised and handled in the seclusion of carefully guarded kennels. They can be admitted under a blanket permit issued to the show superintendent, confined to the show premises, and removed in crates or cars immediately after the show is finished. The disease is not kept alive in the pure-bred show specimens. The stray is the carrier in almost all cases. The regularly designated agent, functioning properly and backed by local and state health authorities, can function to remove the menace and stamp out the disease if the dog owners will cooperate.

BOOK TWO

PURE-BRED DOGS

Compiled by Charles T. Inglee

EXECUTIVE VICE-PRESIDENT
AMERICAN KENNEL CLUB

GRIFFONS (WIRE-HAIRED POINTING)
(Illustration facing page 82)

The origin of the dog known in America as the Wire-haired Pointing Griffon came in the great period of biological awakening—the last quarter of the nineteenth century. Just a few years before, the Austrian abbot, Mendel, had published his experiments on inheritance; and the youth of Western Europe were anxious to try their skill at breeding.

Thus it was that E. K. Korthals, the son of a wealthy banker at Schooten, near Haarlem, in Holland, began to assemble the dogs from which he was to establish a new sporting breed. His first purchase was Mouche, described as a griffon bitch, grey and brown. She was bought in April of 1874, from M. G. Armand of Amsterdam, for 60 florins or about $25, and was thought to be about seven years old. It is said of her that she was equally excellent in the woods or in the open. There is considerable doubt regarding her ancestry.

Korthals acquired five other dogs during the next three years, these being named Janus, Hector, Satan, Junon, and Banco. Janus had woolly hair, Junon was short-haired, and the others were rough-coated. The first mating was between Mouche and Janus. The result was a puppy named Huzaar—apparently the only one in the litter. The next mating was between Mouche and Hector, and this produced a bitch puppy, Madame Augot. The dog Satan was later bred to Madame Augot, resulting in Zampa.

The first breeding of importance was that of Huzaar, son of the rough-coated Mouche and the woolly-coated

[81]

Janus, to the short-haired bitch, Junon. From this mating came Trouvee, a bitch with a harder coat than any of the others. Trouvee then was bred to Banco, and she whelped Moustache I, Querida, and Lina—three specimens from which, it is agreed, springs the best line in the breed.

Although the origin of the Wire-haired Pointing Griffon is undoubtedly Dutch, it is regarded principally as a French breed, for it was in France that the major portion of its development took place. This is due, in measure, to the fact that Korthals did not remain in Holland. It seemed that the elder Korthals, who was a successful breeder of cattle, could not understand his son's interest in "insignificant animals," as he termed dogs. They evidently had a number of heated discussions of the matter. Finally, rather than give up his interest in dogs, the son left the parental house.

Young Korthals went to Biebesheim, Germany, and soon resumed his breeding activities, again. Yet Korthals was a man of wide acquaintance among the sporting fraternity of Europe; and he invariably was present at any major field activity connected with dogs. Later he followed the bench shows very closely, seeking to popularize the type of griffon—for there had been, for several centuries, dogs called griffons—that he had originated.

Perhaps, though, if any single factor can be credited with the spread of interest in the Wire-haired Pointing Griffon, or Korthals griffon as it is known in France—it was the travelling done by the young breeder during the years he spent as the advance agent of the French nobleman, the Duke of Penthievre. Korthals never forgot his great hobby, and whenever he found congenial company he extolled the virtues of the new breed. Admitting that it was a deliberate, even slow, worker, his enthusiasm over

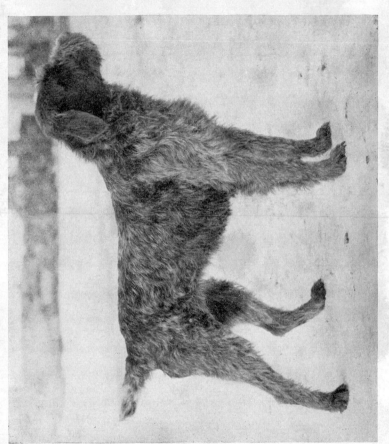

GRIFFON (*Wire-haired Pointing*)

POINTER

its keen nose and its ability to point and retrieve game was infectious. Undoubtedly Korthals had sound reasons, even at that early date, for praising this breed, for it has since gained a wide reputation. It is particularly adapted for swampy country, where its harsh coat—unique in a sporting breed—is a great protection. It also is a strong swimmer, and serves as an excellent water retriever. But adherents of the breed claim it can be trained and entered to any game.

When Korthals left Holland for Germany, he disposed of the greater portion of his dogs, and as a consequence found it necessary to replenish his stock to some extent. His first new brood matron in Germany was Donna, which he purchased from Heinrich Freytag in February, 1879. She was of the boulet type, which meant that her coat was rather long. Donna was mated twice to Moustache I, and left two daughters, Augot, and Clairette, both of which showed the characteristics desired. Six years later, Korthals effected a lease for the bitch Vesta, and the breeding from her provided another very successful line in the breed. Vesta had rough hair; and all her descendants were typical species that carried the right sort of coat.

While there remains some doubt as to the various crosses in the background of the dogs known as the "Korthals patriarchs," it has been suggested by a wide number of authorities that they carried setter, spaniel, and otterhound blood. It is known that certain specimens, described in *Livre des Origines du Griffon a poil dur,* as true griffons, trace their ancestry back to the ancient breed called the griffon hound; and it also is known that at least one cross with a pointer—no doubt the German shorthair—was effected.

The Wire-haired Pointing Griffon was exhibited in

England shortly after it was developed, and it attracted considerable attention. Still, classes were not provided until some years later, the first record of these being at the Barn Elms show in the Jubilee year, 1888. The breed came across the Atlantic twelve years later. The first specimen registered by The American Kennel Club was Pocahontas, 64,232, by Medard, ex Flora. The registration appears in Vol. 18, published in 1901. The dam, Flora, was a direct descendant of Vesta. So started the American fancy.

DESCRIPTION AND STANDARD OF POINTS

(Furnished by Société Centrale Canine pour l'amelioration des Races de Chiens en France)

The Wire-Haired Griffon is a dog of medium size, fairly short-backed, rather a little low on his legs, he is strongly limbed, everything about him indicating strength and vigor.

His coat is harsh like the bristles of a wild boar and his appearance, notwithstanding his short coat, is as unkempt as that of the long-haired Griffon, but on the other hand he has a very intelligent air.

DESCRIPTION

Head.—Long, furnished with a harsh coat, forming a mustache and eyebrows, skull long and narrow, muzzle square.

Eyes.—Large, open, full of expression, iris yellow or light brown.

Ears.—Of medium size, flat or sometimes slightly curled, set rather high, very lightly furnished with hair.

Nose.—Always brown.

Neck.—Rather long, no dewlap.

Shoulders.—Long, sloping.

Ribs.—Slightly rounded.

Forelegs.—Very straight, muscular, furnished with rather short wire hairs.

Hindlegs.—Furnished with rather short stiff hair, the thighs long and well developed.

Feet.—Round, firm and well formed.

Tail.—Carried straight or gaily, furnished with a hard coat without plume, generally cut to a third of its length.

Coat.—Hard, dry, stiff, never curly, the undercoat downy.

Color.—Steel grey with chestnut splashes, grey white with chestnut splashes, chestnut, dirty white mixed with chestnut, never black.

Height.—21½ to 23½ inches for males, and 19½ to 21½ inches for females.

POINTERS

(Illustration facing page 83)

The Pointer comes by his name honestly. He was the first dog, so far as we know, that was used to stand game in the sense in which we use the term today, and was developed as a distinct breed much earlier than any of the setters. For years it was believed the first Pointers used in England were importations from Spain and Portugal, but that theory has been pretty thoroughly disproved and it seems far more likely that Pointers came into general use in Spain, Portugal, throughout eastern Europe and in the British Isles at approximately the same time. Whether or no the dogs from which they sprung were native to all these places no one can say, but it can be stated with confidence that the *development* of the English pointer took place within the confines of Great Britain, most probably in England itself. Later on Spanish pointers were brought in, but, from the first they were considered as a different strain, if not a different breed, from the English dogs.

The first Pointers of which there is any dependable record appeared in England about 1650, some years before the era of wing-shooting with guns, and the use to which they were put is interesting. Coursing with greyhounds was a favorite sport of those times and the earliest accounts of Pointers reveal that they were taken afield to locate and point hares. When the hare had been found, the greyhounds were brought up and unleashed, the game was kicked from cover and the fun began. But early in the eighteenth century, at least by 1711, wing-shooting had come into vogue and, from that day on, the "shorthair" has been considered by the majority of sportsmen the equal, if not the superior, of any of the gun dogs.

As to the Pointer's lineage, as usual we find it something of an enigma, but there is no question that the foxhound, greyhound and very possibly the bloodhound, all had a share in his making. Individuals of all three breeds were probably crossed with the inevitable "setting spaniel," which played such a prominent part in the creation of all our modern bird-dogs.

The adherents of the foxhound cross were especially persistent and active. Even as late as 1868 many English breeders were using it, or at least strongly advocating it as a means to improve the Pointer. A well known authority who wrote over the *nom de plume* of "Sixty-one," came out with the statement that "as far as my experience goes, I consider the foxhound cross with the pointer most valuable," and we find Idstone expressing himself as follows: "If the pointer must be crossed, would it not be advisable to combine foxhound, bulldog and greyhound?" While it is doubtful if any such radical measures were actually used, it was not until the stud book and dog show era that the idea was definitely discarded. The importance of our official record of breeding and the value of bench shows in establishing and maintaining the correct standards can hardly be over-estimated. Without these two institutions it is terrifying to consider the chaos that might well have resulted, not only in Pointers, but practically every breed recognized today.

During the first years of the eighteenth century the Spanish pointer began to appear in England, and he, too, was used for a cross, but as he was exceedingly heavy and very slow in comparison with the English, French and

German pointers, subsequent breeding operations not only left him out but definitely attempted to correct the faults he had introduced. It appears that his real value was not to improve type but to fix and intensify the pointing instinct, in which, we are told, he was peculiarly strong.

If this was the purpose it seems to have been exceedingly successful. Remarkable (and incidentally quite unbelievable) stories are to be found in British sporting papers of the early nineteenth century, relating the prodigies performed by certain English pointers of a former day. Col. Thornton's Pluto and Juno, for example, are said to have held a point on a covey of partridges for an hour and a quarter by the watch. But when we find so solid an authority as Stonhenge telling as gospel truth the now famous yarn of the sportsman who lost his Pointer on the moors, and returning a year later, discovered the skeleton of the dog pointing a skeleton bird, we realize that the statements of these pre-Victorian worthies must be taken with considerably more than a pinch of salt.

During the nineteenth century the English pointer was repeatedly crossed with the various setters as they came into existence and favor. This, it seems, was partly to improve his disposition, for an old-time writer, commenting on the breed says: "They have a ferocity of temper which will not submit to correction or discipline, unless taken in hand very young." While the Pointer of today is anything but ferocious, it may be that this characteristic, tempered by judicious breeding and in combination with the natural independence that made him object to correction and discipline, has made him the superlative field-trial dog he is today. He certainly possesses the competitive spirit to a greater degree than is usually found in the other bird-dogs, a quality that makes him especially suited to public performance.

The modern Pointer is a specialist and looks the part. He is every inch a gun-dog. Clean-limbed, lithe and muscular without being coarse, full to the brim of nervous energy and "hunt," put together for speed and endurance, courageous and with the ability to concentrate on his job, he is the ideal dog for the man or woman who is looking for results when afield. Then, too, he has other and equally important virtues. His short hair makes him neat and clean around the house and his disposition makes him perfect for the kennel. Affectionate as he is, he has hardly the "softness" of the setters in that respect. As a result he requires less personal attention than the latter and is more willing to work satisfactorily for someone other than his own master and handler.

In addition to all this, he has another characteristic— one that has had much to do with his brilliant successes as a field trial dog. This is his faculty for early development. As a breed, Pointers seem to acquire the hunting instinct at an exceedingly tender age, puppies of two months frequently pointing and even backing. For this reason they are especially suited for derby and puppy stakes and therefore favorites with professional field trial handlers.

For show purposes, while hardly as attractive in some ways as the Irish Setter, the Pointer is in many respects quite satisfactory. His short coat makes his outline, conformation, and quality easily seen at a glance and he is a superb poser. His color, usually white with rich liver markings is striking and decidedly showy and, like the Irishman, he has an ideal bench temperament. Lemon and white, orange and white, black and white and sometimes solid black are other colorings. Daniel Lambert, an English sportsman, developed a strain of solid blacks as long ago as 1820 and self-colored dogs are still seen in

POINTER (*German Shorthaired*)

CHESAPEAKE BAY RETRIEVER

the shows today. But, as already said, the liver and white, lemon and white or black and white specimens are most popular in the ring.

The Pointer is peculiarly fortunate in one all-important respect. He has always been bred for type as well as field ability, and as a natural result, we have in this case no divergence between the two insofar as appearance goes. The Pointers being shown and winning today are, almost without exception, dogs that look and in many cases are, practical and thoroughly trained bird-dogs. From the very beginning, type has been carefully developed and intelligently preserved. An illustration for Col. Thornton's book, "A Tour Through Scotland," shows Captain Fleming of Barochan out hawking. This picture was drawn or painted about 1786, yet a Pointer, which is among the dogs shown, would pass muster today as a really excellent specimen of the breed. A reprint of this illustration is to be seen in James Watson's excellent work, "The Dog Book," and deserves your attention. It would be well for the other sporting breeds if their sponsors had taken the care and used the good judgment in their breeding operations that have made the modern Pointer, not only a prime utility dog, but a consistently typy one as well.

DESCRIPTION AND STANDARD OF POINTS

Head.—Skull long, moderately wide with forehead rising well at brows, showing marked stop. Full development of the occipital protuberance with slight furrow between eyes. Muzzle long, square and straight with widely opened nostrils, cleanly chiseled under the eyes. Nose black or dark brown except in the white and orange and white and lemon where deep flesh shades are permissible. The ears should be thin and silky and of such length as to reach just below the throat, that is, when hanging in usual position. They should set on just below the square of the skull and hang flat to the cheeks. Eyes soft and of medium size, color black, in the white and black, hazel in the white and liver, black or deep hazel in the white and orange, brown varying in shade with that of coat in the white and lemon. In all colors of dogs the darker the eyes the more desirable. Lips well developed but not flewlike.

Neck.—Long, clean and firm, arched toward the head without suggestion of dewlap or throatiness.

Shoulders and chest.—Shoulders should be long, oblique and free from excessive width with top of blades close. Chest, deep and as wide as a proper shoulder will permit. Ribs deep and well sprung, not narrowing too abruptly at the brisket.

Body.—Back should be strong with slight rise to top of shoulders. Loin of moderate length slightly arched. Hips wide which should fall slightly to the tail. Tail should be straight, strong, tapered and carried level with or slightly above the line of the back. Quarters very muscular.

Legs and Feet.—Stifles moderately bent. Legs should be moderately short rather than long, with plenty of bone. Front legs straight but with no tendency to knuckle. Elbows should be well down and straight. Hocks should be square with the body and well bent. Both front and back pasterns should be short, strong and nearly upright. Feet should be round, closely set, deep, well padded, and toes well arched. Coat should be short, flat and firm.

Symmetry and Quality is most essential. A dog well balanced in all points is preferable to one with outstanding good qualities and defects. A smooth frictionless movement with high head carriage is required and will always receive preference.

POINTERS (GERMAN SHORTHAIRED)

(Illustration facing page 90)

(By Courtesy of National German Shorthaired Pointer Dog Club)

Copy writers have told us of products "as new as tomorrow" in their design. And now among Sporting Dogs there is a breed which may be classified "as new as tomorrow" in its ability to supply a rapidly growing demand for greater adaptability. This breed is known as the German Shorthaired Pointer. It combines in field dog requirements all of those sterling qualities which for centuries has so popularized the various breeds of hunting dogs. This coupled with the modern version as laid down by the most exacting and sophisticated present day sportsman; whether his quest be fur or feather.

So successfully has keen scenting powers, linked with high intelligence been fused into this outstanding breed through judicious crossing of the old Spanish Pointer, English Foxhound and Bloodhound, and so varied his field accomplishments, that his adaptability has earned him the reputation of being the All-Purpose dog—a term which incidentally was given him by the Germans before sportsmen in the United States started to import them to any extent which was in the early twenties. But in the brief ten years we have known him in the United States he has more than amply demonstrated his worthiness of the title All-Purpose dog.

For in no other breed do we find "wrapped up in one package" 1. A staunchly pointing bird dog. 2. A keen nosed night trailer. 3. A proven duck dog. 4. A natural retriever, on land or water. 5. Pleasing conformation and markings, with great powers of endurance. 6. An alert and intelligent family watch dog and companion.

A brief history of the breed is as follows. During the seventeenth century the Germans imported from Spain, individuals of the old Spanish Pointer breed. So far as we know, this breed was mainly hound, but he was used primarily as a pointing bird dog, and imported for that purpose by the Germans.

While the German sportsmen liked the old Spanish Pointer as a bird dog, they later determined that what they needed was a dog which would point birds and rabbits during the day and trail four footed animals at night. So they crossed the Spanish Pointer with the Bloodhound. They got what they wanted. The results of this crossing was a heavy dog that pointed upland game during the day and did a splendid job of trailing at night. For many years they were well satisfied with this dog—known as the German Pointer.

Then about fifty years ago when field trials first reached popularity in the United States, German and Austrian sportsmen looked with envy on the speed and dash of our American Pointers. Taking a tip from us they straightway started to cross their heavy German Pointer with our American or English Pointer. Results were very gratifying. They developed a smaller and faster dog than they had in the old German Pointer, but one which retained all the stanchness and keen scenting powers which had made the old German Pointer such a favorite. By selective breeding they bred to type, producing a dog with more pleasing conformation, and one with astonishing powers of endurance; for land or water hunting. This dog, a breed but little over a half century old, is known as the German Shorthaired Pointer.

Our American or English Pointer is a cross between the old Spanish Pointer and the English Foxhound. The old German Pointer was a cross between the old Spanish Pointer and the Bloodhound. Now the German Shorthaired Pointer is a cross between the American Pointer and the old German Pointer. Hence in this breed we have a double cross, or 50% old Spanish Pointer, 25% English Foxhound, and 25% Bloodhound. Thus his exceptionally keen nose is accounted for.

In this country as well as abroad, the German Shorthaired Pointer has proven himself an outstanding bird dog, (it is recommended that he be broken on birds first) an A-1 trailing dog for night hunting, and a duck dog of a high order. He has a webbed foot, a water resilient coat, and retrieves with passion from rough terrain or icy waters.

Indicative of the great versatility of this breed are the following traits. They are enthusiastic and successful workers on pheasants, quail, grouse, partridge, jacksnipe, woodcock, duck, rabbits, 'coon, 'possum, and are used to trail and point deer. But as mentioned in the foregoing, it is recommended that they first be broken on birds.

It is not the thought or aim to disparage in any way the good work which has and will continue to be done, by other pointing, trailing and retrieving breeds. The writer has owned many of them, and many good ones. But when adaptability as well as excellence of performance is considered, then the German Shorthaired Pointer is without a peer. For he will do and do well, the many field duties which hitherto were considered possible only through the use of individuals of different hunting breeds. A host unto himself, he will gladden the heart of the sportsman who chooses dog and gun for his recreation.

DESCRIPTION AND STANDARD OF POINTS

(Adopted March, 1935, by National German Shorthaired Pointer Dog Club, and Approved by The American Kennel Club, April 9, 1935)

Head.—Skull long and broad, slightly rounded, with well defined stop. Slight furrow between eyes, not quite so deep as that of the English Pointer, nor is the occiput and the beginning of the neck as distinct as in the English Pointer. Muzzle sufficiently long to enable the dog to pick up and carry game for a long distance. Muzzle should not be snipy, but should be square. Jaws should be of equal length, teeth evenly matched. Nose solid brown. Ears placed rather high, have short soft coat, medium long, and not too thin or too thick in leather; hung close to the cheeks, slightly folded and should somewhat resemble the hound's in appearance. Eyes, soft and of medium size, varying in shades of brown or olive to harmonize with coat, not protruding nor too deep set. Lips well developed and slightly pendulous.

Neck.—Moderately long, muscular and slightly arched, and larger toward the shoulders. Moderate hound-like throatiness permitted.

Shoulders and Chest.—Shoulders should be muscular, oblique, moderately wide, with top of blades close. Chest deep and wide. Ribs deep and well sprung.

Body.—Back should be short and strong with slight rise to top of shoulders. Loin of moderate length, slightly arched. Body well tucked. Hips rather wide, which should fall slightly toward tail in graceful curve. Tail should be docked, leaving two-fifths of length. Quarters should denote strength and field stamina with agility.

Legs and Feet.—Legs should be straight in front, muscular and well boned. Elbows well let down and should turn neither in nor out. Hind legs strongly muscled with stifles well bent. Hocks

[96]

square with the body and slightly bent. Both front and back pasterns should be strong and nearly upright. Feet should be round, turn neither in nor out, close, deep, well padded, and toes well arched and heavily nailed.

Coat.—Should be short, flat and firm.

Weight and Height.—Dogs fifty-five to seventy pounds and bitches forty-five to sixty pounds. Height; dogs twenty-three to twenty-five inches and bitches twenty-one to twenty-three inches at the shoulders.—Symmetry and field quality is most essential. A dog well balanced in all points is preferable to one with outstanding good qualities and defects. A smooth, lithe gait is most desirable.

Color.—Solid liver, liver and white spotted, liver and white spotted and ticked, liver and white ticked. Any colors other than liver and white not permitted.

Faults.—Bone structure too clumsy or too light. Head too large. Too many wrinkles in forehead. Dish-faced. Snipy muzzle. Ears too long, pointy or fleshy. Flesh colored nose. Eyes too light, too round, or too closely set together. Cowhocks. Feet or elbows turned inward or outward. Down on pasterns. Loose shoulders, swayback. Black coat or tri-colored. Any colors except liver or some combination of liver and white.

RETRIEVERS (CHESAPEAKE BAY)

(Illustration facing page 91)

(By Courtesy of The American Chesapeake Club)

There is no complete and authentic record of the Chesapeake Bay dog's development. The theory which follows, as to the origin of the breed, is probably correct and at present is the one most generally accepted. Theories as to the later developments are entirely supposition and as yet have no definite proof.

While the Chesapeake Bay Retriever originated in this country, and is the only native American sporting dog, he came from parents who were destined to sail from England.

In the year 1807 an English brig was wrecked off the coast of Maryland. The crew and cargo of this brig were rescued by the American ship *Canton*. They also rescued two Newfoundland puppies, a dog and a bitch. The dog was named "Sailor," and the bitch was named after the rescuing boat "Canton." These two dogs were given to the gentlemen who gave hospitality to the sailors of the wrecked brig, and were soon found to possess wonderful qualities as retrievers. The dog was a dingy red in color, and the bitch was black. These dogs earned a great reputation as retrievers, and many of the common nondescript dogs then used for retrieving were bred to "Sailor" and "Canton." We do not know whether the two dogs themselves were ever mated together. Eventually other out-crosses were used, and among others the English otter hound has been claimed as one of the most

[99]

influential crosses. Such a cross would probably have produced much different results as the Chesapeake shows no trace of the hound. It is much more likely that the flat-coated and curly-coated retrievers were the most influential out-crosses, if any were ever purposely made.

By 1885 a very definite type of dog was developed, and this breed became known far and wide for its prowess in the icy and rough waters of Chesapeake Bay, where they were often called upon to retrieve 200 or 300 ducks in a day. During the War further developments arose, including the deadgrass color which has become so popular in the middle-west. The Chesapeake of today has improved in looks and is still without peer in the water.

DESCRIPTION AND STANDARD OF POINTS

(Adopted by The American Chesapeake Club, July 1, 1933, and Approved by The American Kennel Club, September 12, 1933)

GENERAL DISQUALIFICATIONS

1. Black or liver colored.
2. White on any part of body, except breast, belly or spots on feet.
3. Feathering on tail or legs over 1¾ inches long.
4. Dewclaws, undershot, overshot or any deformity.
5. Coat curly or tendency to curl all over body.
6. Specimens unworthy or lacking in breed characteristics.

Head.—Skull broad and round with medium stop, nose medium short-muzzle pointed but not sharp. Lips thin, not pendulous. Ears small, set well up on head, hanging loosely and of medium leather. Eyes medium large, very clear of yellowish color and wide apart.

Neck.—Of medium length with a strong muscular appearance, tapering to shoulders.

Shoulders, Chest and Body.—Shoulders, sloping and should have full liberty of action with plenty of power without any restrictions of movement. Chest strong, deep and wide. Barrel round and deep. Body of medium length, neither cobby nor roached, but rather approaching hollowness, flanks well tucked up.

Back Quarters and Stifles.—Back quarters should be as high or a trifle higher than the shoulders. They should show fully as much power as the forequarters. There should be no tendency to weakness in either fore or hind quarters. Hind quarters should be especially powerful to supply the driving power for swimming. Back should be short, well-coupled and powerful. Good hind quarters are essential.

Legs, Elbows, Hocks and Feet.—Legs should be medium length and straight, showing good bone and muscle, with well webbed hare feet of good size. The toes well rounded and close pasterns slightly bent and both pasterns and hocks medium length—the straighter the legs the better.

Stern.—Tail should be medium length—varying from: Males 12 inches to 15 inches, and females from 11 inches to 14 inches; medium heavy at base, moderate, feathering on stern and tail permissible.

Coat and Texture.—Coat should be thick and short, nowhere over one and one-half inches long, with a dense fine woolly undercoat. Hair on face and legs should be very short and straight with tendency to wave on the shoulders, neck, back and loins only. The curly coat or coat with a tendency to curl not permissible.

Color.—Any color varying from a dark brown to a faded tan or deadgrass. Deadgrass takes in any shade of deadgrass, varying from a tan to a dull straw color. White spot on breast and toes permissible, but the smaller the spot the better, solid color being preferred.

Weight—Males, 65 to 75 pounds; females 55 to 65 pounds.

Height—Males, 23 inches to 26 inches; females, 21 inches to 24 inches.

Symmetry and Quality.—The Chesapeake dog should show a bright and happy disposition and an intelligent expression, with general outlines impressive and denoting a good worker. The dog should be well proportioned, a dog with a good coat and well balanced in other points being preferable to the dog excelling in some but weak in others.

SPORTING DOGS

The texture of the dog's coat is very important as the dog is used for hunting under all sorts of adverse weather conditions, often working in ice and snow. The oil in the harsh outer coat and wooly undercoat is of extreme value in preventing the cold water from reaching the dog's skin and aids in quick drying. A Chesapeake's coat should resist the water in the same way that a duck's feathers do. When he leaves the water and shakes himself, his coat should not hold the water at all, being merely moist.

Color and coat are extremely important as the dog is used for duck hunting. The color must be as nearly that of his surroundings as possible and with the fact that dogs are exposed to all kinds of adverse weather conditions, often working in ice and snow, the color of coat and its texture must be given every consideration when judging on the bench or in the ring.

Courage, willingness to work, alertness, nose, intelligence, love of water, general quality, and, most of all, disposition should be given primary consideration in the selection and breeding of the Chesapeake Bay Dog.

Positive Scale of Points

Points

Head, including lips, ears and eyes	16
Neck	4
Shoulders and body	12
Back quarters and stifles	12
Elbows, legs and feet	12
Color	4
Stern and tail	10
Coat and texture	18
General conformation	12
Total	100

Note:—The question of coat and general type of balance takes precedence over any scoring table which could be drawn up.

Approximate Measurements

Length head, nose to occiput	9½ to 10
Girth at ears	20 to 21
Muzzle below eyes	10 to 10½

RETRIEVERS (CHESAPEAKE BAY)

Length of ears	4½ to 5
Width between eyes	2½ to 2¾
Girth neck close to shoulder	20 to 22
Girth of chest to elbows	35 to 36
Girth at flank	24 to 25
Length from occiput to tail base	34 to 35
Girth forearms at shoulders	10 to 10½
Girth upper thigh	19 to 20
From root to root of ear, over skull	5 to 6
Occiput to top shoulder blades	9 to 9½
From elbow to elbow over the shoulders	25 to 26

RETRIEVERS (CURLY-COATED)

(Illustration facing page 114)

(By Courtesy of The Curly Retriever Club, England)

The origin of the Curly Retriever is one of doubt, but he is popularly believed to be descended from the old English Water Spaniel, which breed was known to have existed at the beginning of the sixteenth century, and from the retrieving setter. Some maintain the Irish Water Spaniel was his ancestor and it is more than probable that a cross has been taken with this Spaniel from time to time, the liver color being a recognized color for the Curly as well as the black.

Whichever Spaniel was his progenitor, it is certain that added to the mixture of Water Spaniel and Retrieving Setter was the small, or St. John's Newfoundland, which, according to records, first arrived in England in 1835 as a ship's dog on board the boats that brought salted cod from Newfoundland. The St. John's dog, curiously enough, is sometimes called a Labrador by early writers, a fact which has given rise to some confusion with respect to the modern Labrador.

In the early eighties the Curly is said to have been crossed again with the Poodle (the one-time Retriever of France), this cross was taken with the object of giving his coat the tight curl, so much admired. In the absence of very early records, the correct origin of the Curly must, however, always remain a matter of conjecture, but there appears very little doubt that he is by far the oldest of all breeds now classified as Retrievers.

The Curly was the popular Gun Dog following the old English Water Spaniel and was first shown at the Birmingham Dog Show, England, in 1859. Field Trials for Retrievers were started in 1899. Curlies were exported to New Zealand in 1889 and are still to be found there, where they are used for retrieving duck and Californian quail. Their performance is so good that they are used by many in preference to any other kind of Retriever. In Australia also they are used in the swamps and lagoons of the Murray River, duck being the chief quarry, and here again they are spoken of by their admirers as being the best workers and stayers of any form of Gun Dog, the steadiest, the most tender mouthed, and quite unsurpassed in water. A dog and a bitch were exported to the United States of America about 1907, both were trained to the gun and were also successfully exhibited at shows. Curlies have recently taken part in Field Trials in England, open to all types of Retrievers and have more than held their own.

Many assert that the Curly Retriever is temperamentally easier to train than other varieties of Gun Dogs. He is very affectionate, possesses phenomenal staying powers, is hardy and will practically live in water, his wonderfully thick coat also enabling him to face the most punishing covert, and in this capacity he excels, and has many a time "wiped the eye" of other Retrievers less well equipped by nature. He is a charming and faithful companion, an excellent guard, and, it is said, is used as such and carefully bred among the gypsies in the South West of England.

A Club was formed in the British Isles in 1896, known as the "Curly-coated Retriever Club," but ceased to exist some years before the founding in England of the present Curly Retriever Club in February 1933, which has as its object—"to promote breeding of Pure Curly Retrievers and to foster the interests of the breed, particularly as a working Gun Dog, while preserving the correct type for the dual purpose of the Field and the Show Bench"— (extract from Rule 1, The Curly Retriever Club).

A Special Committee was selected to carefully consider and possibly revise the Standard of Points as drawn up by the former Club. The Committee met in March 1933 and after considerable deliberation, the standard that appears herewith was presented and approved by a General Meeting shortly after. The Club is most fortunate in having as its President, (1935) Lord Ashburton, an enthusiast of the breed and one who has owned and shot over Curlies for some time, and who has most generously presented a magnificent Silver Cup to be competed for at the Field Trials organized by the Club for Curly Retrievers. Two of such meetings have already been held, the first in November 1933, at Idsworth, Horndene, Hants, by kind permission of Lorna, Countess Howe, the honors of the All-aged Stake being divided between Brig. General F. F. Lance's Pycombe Sable and Captain C. A. Monson's Calgary Grizzly. The second, in January 1935 near Hungerford, Wilts, by kind permission of Sir Earnest Wells and Mr. W. E. Rootes when the first place in the All-aged Stake, and the Ashburton Cup, was won by Captain C. A. Monson's Calgary Grizzly with Brig. General F. F. Lance's Pycombe Sable a close second.

DESCRIPTION AND STANDARD OF POINTS
(By Courtesy of The Curly Retriever Club, England)

Head.—Long and well proportioned, skull not too flat, jaws long and strong but not inclined to snipiness, nose black, in the black coated variety, with wide nostrils. Teeth strong and level.

Eyes.—Black or brown, but not yellow, rather large but not too prominent.

Ears.—Rather small, set on low, lying close to the head, and covered with short curls.

Coat.—Should be one mass of crisp curls all over. A slightly more open coat not to be severely penalised, but a saddle back or patch of uncurled hair behind the shoulder should be penalised, and a prominent white patch on breast is undesirable, but a few white hairs allowed in an otherwise good dog. Color, black or liver.

Shoulders, Chest, Body and Loins.—Shoulders should be very deep, muscular and obliquely placed. Chest, not too wide, but decidedly deep. Body, rather short, muscular and well ribbed up. Loin, powerful, deep and firm to the grasp.

Legs and Feet.—Legs should be of moderate length, forelegs straight and set well under the body. Quarters strong and muscular, hocks low to the ground with moderate bend to stifle and hock. Feet round and compact with well arched toes.

Tail.—Should be moderately short, carried fairly straight and covered with curls, slightly tapering towards the point.

General Appearance.—A strong smart upstanding dog, showing activity, endurance and intelligence.

RETRIEVERS (FLAT-COATED)
(Illustration facing page 115)

The Flat-Coated Retriever presents something of a paradox, as far as the United States is concerned, for this breed traces its ancestry back to two breeds that are indigenous to the North American continent—yet it is one of the least known species of pure-bred dog in America. Its actual origin and almost its entire development was in England, cradle of so many different varieties of the dog.

The earliest known specimen that approximated the present standard of the flat-coated retriever appeared at the Birmingham show (England) in 1860. This was a dog named Wyndham, and it was owned and exhibited by R. Braisford. The dog excited no little comment, for retrievers of any kind were a rarity in those days. All the sportsmen at the show inspected it closely, and they put all sorts of questions to its owner. The answers were not very satisfactory in regard to its breeding; yet among those who saw this first flat-coated—or wavy-coated, as it was then called—were some experienced authorities who later set their opinions to paper.

Wyndham was very much on the type of the Labrador retriever, with the exception of coat. Almost wholly black in color, his conformation also followed that of the Labrador. But there the resemblance ended, for Wyndham carried a much heavier coat. Due to his coat, it was reasoned that half of his inheritance came from the St. John's Newfoundland, which then was enjoying great popularity in England. This cross also accounted for Wyndham's size, which was slightly larger than that of the Labrador.

SPORTING DOGS

It is impossible to say just how long various sporting dog men had been experimenting with various crosses before the first specimen called the wavy-coated retriever was taken to a bench show; but it probably had been at least half a decade. Formal shows were in their infancy, and the greater interest was in work afield. So it is quite probable that a fairly long and varied history lay behind Wyndham. Also, he had many contemporary specimens, some of which carried the same strains and some that were of slightly different type and consequently different ancestors.

The real proof of this breed that since has come to be known as the Flat-Coated Retriever was to be found in the efficiency of its work. It proved a natural water dog, marking, retrieving, and delivering with a style that always elicited favorable comment. Others found the dog equally satisfactory for upland shooting, and it was only a few years before it was used in great numbers on pheasant and other kinds of feather.

The early rapid progress of the breed may be imagined from the fact that it was only four years after its show debut that it had classes at the regular shows. The first exhibition where classes were provided was at the big all-breed event at Ashburnham Hall, Chelsea, in April of 1864. By then there was considerable discussion of type, and the leading breeders were beginning to be rather set in their ideas.

Perhaps the one man who deserves most credit for the pure development of the most desirable type was Dr. Bond Moore of Wolverhampton. He was convinced that the new breed should follow the Labrador in both color and conformation. It is said that he was such a stickler for the solid black that he destroyed all puppies that had any traces of other colors on them.

RETRIEVERS (FLAT-COATED)

Dr. Moore's strictness in regard to color and type was inspired by the large number of crosses that had been tried by other breeders, with a consequent confusion in size, type, and color. His aims proved a stabilizing factor at a time when it seemed that no very definite breed would result.

Aside from the Labrador retriever, and the St. John's Newfoundland—the original cross—there is evidence that both the Gordon setter, and the Irish setter were used to advantage. There also is believed to have been an infusion of blood from the Russian tracker, the breed that later was refined into the golden retriever. Some talk of a cross with the collie is prevalent in the history of the Flat-Coated Retriever, but this is doubtful.

The Flat-Coated Retriever of today is a sturdily made dog of 60 to 70 lbs., with a close-lying, somewhat dense coat that is a splendid protection in the water. The great majority of specimens are wholly black, but occasionally there is found a bit of other color—usually white—on the chest.

While the breed was introduced to the United States many years ago, it never has mustered sufficient supporters to have a specialty club. As a consequence, specimens of the flat-coated retriever are not plentiful, although they may be found scattered through the shooting country.

DESCRIPTION AND STANDARD OF POINTS
(By Courtesy of The Flat-Coated Retriever Association, England)

GENERAL APPEARANCE

A bright active dog of medium size (weighing from 60 lbs. to 70 lbs.) with an intelligent expression, showing power without lumber and raciness without weediness.

[111]

SPORTING DOGS

DETAILED DESCRIPTION

Head.—This should be long and nicely molded. The skull flat and moderately broad. There should be a depression or stop between the eyes, slight and in no way accentuated so as to avoid giving either a down or a dish-faced appearance. The nose of good size with open nostrils. The eyes, of medium size, should be dark brown or hazel, with a very intelligent expression (a round prominent eye is a disfigurement), and they should not be obliquely placed. The jaws should be long and strong, with a capacity of carrying a hare or pheasant. The ears small and well set on close to the side of the head.

Neck, Shoulders and Chest.—The head should be well set in the neck, which latter should be long and free from throatiness, symmetrically set and obliquely placed in shoulders running well into the back to allow of easily seeking for the trail. The chest should be deep and fairly broad, with a well-defined brisket, on which the elbows should work cleanly and evenly. The fore ribs should be fairly flat showing a gradual spring and well arched in the center of the body but rather lighter towards the quarters. Open couplings are to be ruthlessly condemned.

Back and Quarters.—The back should be short, square and well ribbed up, with muscular quarters. The stern short, straight and well set on, carried gaily but never much above the level of the back.

Legs and Feet.—These are of the greatest importance. The forelegs should be perfectly straight, with bone of good quality carried right down to the feet which should be round and strong. The stifle should not be too straight or too bent and the dog must neither be cowhocked nor move too wide behind, in fact he must stand and move true all round on legs and feet, with toes close and well arched, the soles being thick and strong and when the dog is in full coat the limbs should be well feathered.

Coat.—Should be dense, of fine quality and texture, flat as possible. Color: Black or Liver.

RETRIEVERS (GOLDEN)
(Illustration facing page 122)

There probably is less doubt about the origin of the Golden Retriever than there is concerning that of many other breeds. This sporting breed, in the form we know it today, dates back to 1860, for it was in that year Sir Dudley Marjoribanks visited a circus at Brighton, England and saw the immediate ancestors of the golden.

The circus was featuring a troupe of Russian performing dogs, that were doing a rather elaborate routine under the direction of their Russian trainer. The feats accomplished by the dogs impressed Sir Dudley, and after the show he made an effort to purchase a pair of them. He reasoned that the intelligence evinced in performing could be put to great use in the field.

The Russian trainer, however, proved a problem. He refused to sell a pair on the grounds that it would ruin his act. Perhaps it is just as well that he refused, for Sir Dudley—who was later to become the first Lord Tweedmouth—countered by making an offer for the entire troupe of eight dogs. The deal was accomplished.

This proved a fortunate purchase, for instead of acquiring two dogs that he probably would have used merely for sport afield, Sir Dudley received enough stock, and enough variety of blood lines to try some extensive breeding experiments.

These dogs were called Russian trackers, and they came from a very old breed that had served the usual variety of purposes in its original home in Asiatic Russia. One of the chief uses of the Russian tracker was as a guardian of the flocks of sheep, and he was admirably adapted to withstand the rigors of the severe winters of the Caucasus Mountains where he made his habitat.

The Russian tracker was a much larger dog than his descendant, the Golden Retriever, for the original breed measured about 30 inches at the shoulder and often weighed as much as 100 lbs. Today the males weigh from 65 to 68 lbs., the bitches from 55 to 60 lbs. The old breed was well protected from cold, and also from the attacks of wild animals, by a thick, double coat. This coat, incidentally, was almost taffy colored.

The story is told that the Russian tracker was possessed of such intelligence, and was so admirably adapted to stand the long, hard winters, that the shepherd often left the dog in sole charge of the sheep for months. The man would build a shelter, provide a big cache of food, and then would return to his home. When spring came, the shepherd would set forth again, and find the flock just as he had left it.

Of such ancestry were the dogs that Lord Tweedmouth established at his Scottish seat in the Guisachan deer forest in Invernessshire; and these dogs were bred without out-crossing for ten years. The big breed continued to prove intelligent, but there was no game in Scotland suitable to the size of the tracker. Many British sportsmen who saw them working were of the opinion that the breed was too cumbersome.

About 1870, Lord Tweedmouth abandoned his efforts to establish the breed in its original form. The records do not reveal whether or no he tried a number of crosses, but it is established that in 1870 he crossed the Russian tracker with the bloodhound. As far as known, this is the only cross perpetuated, and it was done only once.

Crossing with the bloodhound caused a reduction in the

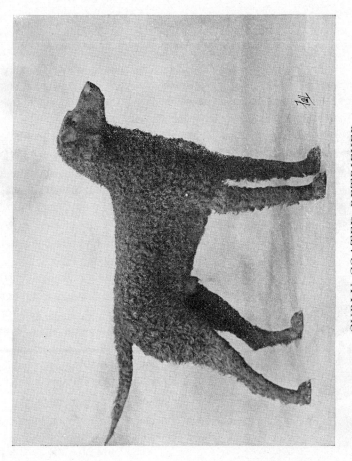

CURLY COATED RETRIEVER

FLAT COATED RETRIEVER

size of the breed; an intensification of scenting powers that already were considered a little better than average; a refinement in the texture of the coat; and a slight darkening in the color of the coat.

The Golden Retriever of today is very close in appearance to the dogs of 60 years ago. In fact, the pictorial history of the breed is complete from its early days at Guisachan. Two photographs are still in existence of Nous, regarded as the best of the group of dogs purchased at Brighton. There is another of a dog bred at Guisachan about 1871, and one of a group of goldens owned by Col. W. le Poer Trench in 1908.

Regarded by many in America as simply a retriever, the golden has been used frequently as a combined setter and retriever. Its forte, of course, is retrieving, and it is equally at home on land or in the water.

The Golden Retriever made its first appearance in the United States just before the World War, but interest in him rather flagged until half a dozen years ago when several breeders began importing some of the leading specimens from England. Still one of the rare breeds, it is likely that within the next decade the Golden Retriever will make appreciable progress.

DESCRIPTION AND STANDARD OF POINTS
(By Courtesy of The Golden Retriever Club, England)

General Appearance.—Should be of a symmetrical, active powerful dog, a good level mover, sound and well put together, with a kindly expression, not clumsy or long in the leg.

Head.—Broad in skull, well set on a clean and muscular neck, muzzle powerful and wide, not weak jawed, good stop. Eyes— Dark and set well apart, very kindly in expression with dark rims. Teeth—even, neither under nor overshot.

Color.—Rich golden, must not be as dark as an Irish Red Setter or cream color. The presence of a few white hairs on chest permissible, but white collar, feet, toes or blaze to be penalized.

Coat.—Must be flat or wavy, good undercoat, dense and water resisting.

Ears.—Small and well set on.

Feet.—Round and cat-like, must not open or splay.

Forelegs.—Straight, with good bone.

Hindlegs.—Strong and muscular, well-bent stifles.

Hocks.—Well let down, not cowhocked.

Nose.—Should be black, but a light-colored nose should not debar a dog from honors who is good in all other respects.

Tail.—Should be straight, not curled at tip or carried over the back.

Body.—Well balanced, short coupled, and deep through the heart. Loins must be strong, back ribs must be deep and strong with good second thighs; shoulders must be well laid back and long in the blade.

Note.—The ideal weights for adult dogs and bitches in good, hard condition should be: Dogs, 65-68 lbs.; Bitches, 55-60 lbs.: and heights at shoulder: Dogs, 23-24 inches; Bitches, 20½-22 inches.

	Points
Head	20
Color	10
Coat	5
Ears	5
Feet	10
Forelegs	10
Hindlegs	10
Hocks	10
Nose	5
Tail	5
Body	25
Total	115

RETRIEVERS (LABRADOR)

(Illustration facing page 123)

(By Courtesy of The Labrador Retriever Club, Inc.)

The Labrador Retriever did not, as his name implies, come from Labrador, but from Newfoundland. They were carried to England by fishermen, and the 2nd Earl of Malmesbury happened to see one of these dogs on a fishing boat and early in the nineteenth century arranged to have some imported. There is no indication of how these dogs originally got to Newfoundland, but in 1822 a traveler in that region reported a number of what he called "small water dogs" and said: "The dogs are admirably trained as retrievers in fowling, and are otherwise useful. . . . The smooth or short-haired dog is preferred because in frosty weather the long-haired kind become encumbered with ice on coming out of the water."

The dogs were not at first generally known in England as Labradors.

Colonel Hawker, a noted British sportsman, in 1830 referred to the ordinary Newfoundland and what he called the St. John's breed of water dog, and mentions the former "which is very large, strong of limb, rough hair, and carries his tail high." Referring to what is now known as the Labrador, he said they were "by far the best for any kind of shooting. He is generally black and no bigger than a pointer, very fine in legs, with short smooth hair and does not carry his tail so much curled as the other; is extremely quick, running, swimming and fighting. . . . Their sense of smell is hardly to be credited: in finding wounded game there is not a living equal in the canine race."

The origin of the name Labrador is shown in a letter written in 1887 by the 3rd Earl of Malmesbury two years before his death in which he said: "We always call mine Labrador dogs, and I have kept the breed as pure as I could from the first I had from Poole, at that time carrying on a brisk trade with Newfoundland. The real breed may be known by their having a close coat which turns the water off like oil, and, above all, a tail like an otter."

An account of a cruise to Naples made in 1839 by the Duke of Buccleuch in his yacht states that he and Lord Home took their Labradors with them.

The Labrador gradually died out in Newfoundland on account of a heavy dog tax and this, with the English quarantine law, practically stopped the importation of Labradors into England. Thereafter a great many Labradors were interbred with other types of retrievers. Fortunately, however, owing to the fact that the Earl of Malmesbury had kept the breed as pure as he could, and that it was a very old breed, the Labrador characteristics predominated.

Later, Labrador fanciers, desiring to stop this interbreeding, so drew the standard as to discourage crossing with other retrievers.

There is printed a stud book of the Duke of Buccleuch's Labrador retrievers which made it possible to work out pedigrees of the two dogs that did most to produce the modern Labrador, Mr. A. C. Butter's Peter of Faskally, and Major Portal's Flapper. These pedigrees go back as far as 1878.

The Labrador was first recognized by the English Kennel Club as a separate breed in 1903 and has since frequently won the Kennel Club's cup for best in show.

RETRIEVERS (LABRADOR)

The Labrador's chief characteristic is his desire to please his owner or handler, for in almost every case if the dog understands what is wanted of him he will do it.

Mr. Leslie Sprake's book "The Labrador Retriever" (published in 1933 by H. F. & G. Witherby, 326 High Holborn, London W. C. 1), deals very fully with the breed and its history. He quotes therein from an article written in 1923 by the Hon. A. Holland Hibbert (the late Lord Knutsford) who, in commenting on the two most important points of the Labrador, the eye and the tail, said:

"Tail.—The nearer the level carriage and the closer resemblance to an otter tail the better, i.e., short and thick at stump with the hair underneath divided almost as if parted. Otter tails are very rare and straight tails are not common—the more usual carriage being like a foxhound, except when hunting, and then the tail is almost invariably carried level.

*   *   *   *   *

"Eye.—The color of the eye, about which much has been written; when Labradors first came into general notice, the dark eye, which was a great point with the flat coat, was supposed to be necessary also for the Labrador. This was nothing but a show ring opinion, and entirely wrong. Although the very light eye has a startled, and I think disagreeable look, yet the dark eye to my mind is lacking in expression, and looks sulky, hence I welcome what is now generally considered the best color, i.e., light brown, the color of burnt sugar."

In England no Labrador can become a bench show champion unless he has received a working certificate. In other words, he must qualify in the field as well as on the bench, so that in looking at an English pedigree if a dog is designated as a champion you know that he must have qualified in the field as well as on the bench. The initials "F.T.CH." indicate that the dog is a Field Trial champion as distinguished from a Bench Show champion.

[119]

There have been, however, dogs that have won dual championships and they are listed below:

Lady Howe's Dual Champions Banchory Bolo, Bramshaw Bob and Banchory Painter.

The Hon. J. A. Joicey's Dual Champion Flute of Flodden.

Major Twyford's Dual Champion Titus of Whitmore.

DESCRIPTION AND STANDARD OF POINTS
(By Courtesy of The Labrador Retriever Club, Inc.)
GENERAL APPEARANCE

The general appearance of the Labrador should be that of a strongly built, short-coupled, very active dog. Compared with the Wavy or Flat-Coated Retriever he should be wider in the head, wider through the chest and ribs, wider and stronger over the loins and hind quarters. The coat should be close, short, dense, and free from feather.

DETAILED DESCRIPTION

Head.—The skull should be wide, giving brain room; there should be a slight "stop," i.e., the brow should be slightly pronounced, so that the skull is not absolutely in a straight line with the nose. The head should be clean-cut and free from fleshy cheeks. The jaws should be long and powerful, and quite free from snipiness or exaggeration in length; the nose should be wide and the nostrils well developed.

The ears should hang moderately close to the head, rather far back, should be set somewhat low and not be large and heavy. The eyes should be of a medium size, expressing great intelligence and good temper, and can be brown, yellow or black.

Neck and Chest.—The neck should be long and powerful, and the shoulders long and sloping.

The chest must be of a good width and depth, the ribs well sprung and the loins wide and strong, stifles well turned, and the hind quarters well developed and of great power.

[120]

RETRIEVERS (LABRADOR)

Legs and Feet.—The legs must be straight from the shoulder to ground, and the feet compact with toes well arched and pads well developed; the hocks should be well bent, and the dog must neither be cowhocked nor move too wide behind; in fact, he must stand and move true all round on legs and feet.

Tail.—The tail is a distinctive feature of the breed; it should be very thick towards the base, gradually tapering towards the tip, of medium length, should be practically free from any feathering, but should be clothed thickly all round with the Labrador's short, thick, dense coat, thus giving that peculiar "rounded" appearance which has been described as the "otter" tail. The tail may be carried gaily, but should not curl too far over the back.

Coat.—The coat is another very distinctive feature; it should be short, very dense and without wave, and should give a fairly hard feeling to the hand.

Color.—The color is generally black, free from any rustiness and any white marking except possibly a small spot on the chest. Other whole colors are permissible.

GOLDEN RETRIEVER

LABRADOR RETRIEVER

SETTERS (ENGLISH)

(Illustration facing page 126)

(By Courtesy of The English Setter Association)

From the best authorities on the subject, it appears that the English Setter was a trained bird dog in England approximately four hundred years ago. A perusal of some of the old writings leads us to believe that the English Setter had its origin in some of the older of the land spaniels that originated in Spain. We are indebted, however, to Hans Bols, who, in "Partridge Shooting and Partridge Hawking" written in 1582, presents quite definite pictorial evidence that the setter and the spaniel breeds were quite different in appearance and even at that time the tails of the spaniels appeared to have been docked as they are today and the tails of setters left as nature intended them. There is some evidence in the earlier writings of sportsmen that the old English Setter was originally produced from crosses of the Spanish pointer, the large water spaniel, and the springer spaniel, and by careful cultivation attained a high degree of proficiency in finding and pointing game in open country. We can see from examination of the sketches in many of the old writings that this setter-spaniel was an extremely handsome dog, many having a head much longer and with a more classical cut than that of the spaniel, while others had the short spaniel like head, lacking the well defined profile of the skull and foreface of the modern dogs. Also most of these older setters had coats which were quite curly, particularly at the thighs. It can be seen from this brief review of the origin of the English Setter that even our oldest authorities were not entirely in accord as to the origin of this breed.

There is little doubt that the major credit for the development of the modern setter should go to Mr. Edward Laverack, who about 1825 obtained from the Rev. A. Harrison, "Ponto" and "Old Moll." The Rev. Harrison had apparently kept this breed pure for thirty-five years or more. From these two setters Mr. Laverack through a remarkable process of inbreeding, produced Prince, Countess, Nellie, and Fairy, who were marvelous specimens of English Setters. Along about 1874 Mr. Laverack sold a pair of dogs to Charles H. Raymond of Morris Plains, N. J. During the next ten years the English Setter became more and more popular and it was around this time that many setters bred by Mr. Llewellin were imported into this country and Canada.

In considering the so-called Llewellin strain it is recorded in the writings of Dr. William A. Bruette that about the time the Laverack strain of setters was at its zenith in England, Mr. R. L. Purcell Llewellin purchased a number of Mr. Laverack's best show dogs of the pure Dash-Moll and Dash-Hill Laverack blood. The Laveracks he crossed with some entirely new blood which he obtained in the north of England, represented by Mr. Statter's and Sir Vincent Corbet's strain, since referred to as the Duke-Rhoebes, the latter being the two most prominent members of the blood. The result of these crosses was eminently successful, particularly at field trials, and swept everything before them. Their reputation spread to America and many were purchased by sportsmen in different sections of the United States and Canada, so that this line of breeding soon became firmly established in this country.

SETTERS (ENGLISH)

Probably the name that stands out most conspicuously in the foundation of the field-trial setter in America is Count Noble. This dog was purchased from Mr. Llewellin by Dave Sanborn of Dowling, Michigan, who, after trying him out on the prairies was upon the point of returning him to England, but was persuaded not to do so by the late B. F. Wilson of Pittsburgh. On the death of Mr. Sanborn, Count passed into the hands of Mr. Wilson who gave him an opportunity to demonstrate his sterling qualities from coast to coast. The body of this famous dog was mounted at his death and is now in the Carnegie Museum at Pittsburgh where it is visited annually by many sportsmen.

Dr. Walsh in 1878 stated that Mr. Llewellin's dogs were Dan-Laveracks, because according to him they were all either by Dan out of Laverack bitches or by a Laverack dog out of a sister of Dan. It is quite difficult to give a proper definition of a straight-bred Llewellin, but it is generally accepted that all setters may be called Llewellins which trace back in all lines to Duke-Rhoebe-Laverack. This, however, would shut out everything that had Dash II blood and this the Llewellin enthusiast does not wish to do for under such definition it would eliminate a great number of the best known names that appear in the so-called Llewellin pedigrees. R. L. Purcell Llewellin is given credit for making the Duke-Rhoebe-Laverack cross, but in justice to him according to Mr. A. F. Hochwalt, one of our noted authorities on gun dogs, he is not responsible for the breed being named for him. The name was originated in America by breeders who imported dogs from Mr. Llewellin's kennels and, being great admirers of the man and the dogs he bred, they naturally gave them the name of him from whom they were purchased.

The first show for setters was held at Newcastle on

Tyne on January 28, 1859, and from this time on dog shows flourished throughout England, gradually increasing in popularity and to their present high state of perfection. English Setters became increasingly popular and it is of interest in passing to note that in 1930 for the first time an American was invited abroad to judge English Setters. The expert so honored was none other than the late Benj. F. Lewis of Lansdowne, Pa., who had been associated with English Setters since his boyhood. His father, B. F. Lewis, born in South Wales, for many years was unquestionably the outstanding handler of all sporting show dogs in America, and it is believed that no one will dissent from the opinion that his son, the late Benny, was without an equal as a handler of sporting dogs.

The English Setter has retained its popularity since its introduction to this country primarily because of its usefulness and beauty. There is little doubt that its usefulness has been a prime factor in this respect, and as a result of intelligent breeding it has been brought to a high state of perfection and there is always to be found a representative entry at all bench shows and field trials.

The mild, sweet disposition characteristic of this breed along with the beauty, intelligence, and aristocratic appearance it makes in the field and in the home has endeared it both to the sportsman as well as all lovers of a beautiful, active, and rugged outdoor dog. The lovable disposition of the English Setter makes it an ideal companion for children; it is, however, a dog that requires considerable exercise and therefore is better suited to ownership in the suburbs than in the city.

ENGLISH SETTER

GORDON SETTER

SETTERS (ENGLISH)

DESCRIPTION AND STANDARD OF POINTS
(By Courtesy of The English Setter Association)

Head.—Long and lean, with a well-defined stop. The skull oval from ear to ear, of medium width, giving brain room but with no suggestion of coarseness, with but little difference between the width at base of skull and at brows and with a moderately defined occipital protuberance. Brows should be at a sharp angle from the muzzle. Muzzle should be long and square, of width in harmony with the skull, without any fullness under the eyes and straight from eyes to tip of the nose. A dish face or Roman nose objectionable. The lips square and fairly pendant. Nose should be black or dark liver in color, except in white, lemon and white, orange and white, or liver and white dogs, when it may be of lighter color. Nostrils should be wide apart and large in the openings. Jaws should be of equal length. Overshot or undershot jaw objectionable. Ears should be carried close to the head, well back and set low, of moderate length, slightly rounded at the ends, and covered with silky hair. Eyes should be bright, mild, intelligent and dark brown in color.

Neck.—The neck should be long and lean, arched at the crest, and not too throaty.

Shoulders.—Shoulders should be formed to permit perfect freedom of action to the forelegs. Shoulder blades should be long, wide, sloping moderately well back and standing fairly close together at the top.

Chest.—Chest between shoulder blades should be of good depth but not of excessive width.

Ribs.—Ribs, back of the shoulders, should spring gradually to the middle of the body and then taper to the back ribs, which should be of good depth.

Back.—Back should be strong at its junction with the loin and should be straight or sloping upward very slightly to the top of the shoulder, the whole forming a graceful outline of medium length, without sway or drop. Loins should be strong, moderate in length, slightly arched, but not to the extent of being roached or wheel backed. Hip bones should be wide apart without too sudden drop to the root of the tail.

[127]

Forelegs.—The arms should be flat and muscular, with bone fully developed and muscles hard and devoid of flabbiness; of good length from the point of the shoulder to the elbow, and set at such an angle as will bring the legs fairly under the dog. Elbows should have no tendency to turn either in or out. The pastern should be short, strong and nearly round with the slope from the pastern joint to the foot deviating very slightly forward from the perpendicular.

Hindlegs.—The hindlegs should have wide, muscular thighs with well developed lower thighs. Stifles should be well bent and strong. Hocks should be wide and flat. The pastern should be short, strong and nearly round, with the slope from the pastern joint to the foot deviating very slightly forward from the perpendicular.

Feet.—Feet should be closely set and strong, pads well developed and tough, toes well arched and protected with short, thick hair.

Tail.—Tail should be straight, set low and taper to a fine point, with only sufficient length to reach the hocks, or less. The feather must be straight and silky, falling loosely in a fringe and tapering to the point when the tail is raised. There must be no bushiness. The tail should not curl sideways or above the level of the back.

Coat.—Coat should be flat and of good length, without curl; not soft or woolly. The feather on the legs should be moderately thin and regular.

Weight.—Dogs, about 55 to 70 pounds; bitches, 50 to 65 pounds.

Height.—Dogs, about 23 to 25 inches; bitches, 22 to 24 inches.

Colors.—Black, white and tan; black and white; blue belton, lemon and white; lemon belton, orange and white; orange belton; liver and white; liver belton; and solid white.

Markings.—Dogs without heavy patches of color on the body, but flecked all over preferred.

Symmetry.—The harmony of all parts to be considered. Symmetrical dogs will have level backs or be very slightly higher at the shoulders than at the hips. Balance, harmony of proportion, and an appearance of breeding and quality to be looked for, and coarseness avoided.

SETTERS (ENGLISH)

Movement and Carriage.—An easy, free and graceful movement, suggesting rapidity and endurance. A lively tail and a high carriage of head. Stiltiness, clumsiness or a lumbering gait are objectionable.

	Head	*Points*	
Skull		5	
Ears		5	
Eyes		5	
Muzzle		5	20

	Body		
Neck		5	
Chest and Shoulders		12	
Back, Loin and Ribs		10	27

	Running Gear		
Forelegs		5	
Hips, Thighs and Hindlegs		12	
Feet		6	23

	Coat		
Length and Texture		5	
Color and Marking		3	8

	Tail		
Length and Carriage		5	5

	General Appearance and Action		
Symmetry, Style and Movement		12	
Weight and Size		5	17

Total		100	100

SETTERS (GORDON)

(Illustration facing page 127)

(By Courtesy of The Gordon Setter Club of America)

The Gordon, or Black and Tan Setter, although one of the brainiest and by no means least handsome of the bird-dog family, is undeniably least known here in America, and, as a natural consequence, is also least understood and appreciated. Comparatively few are seen at the shows for the simple reason that comparatively few are bred and sold, and while a considerable number are used here for field work, the sum total, in comparison with the other setter breeds, is small. Yet the owners of Black and Tans are almost invariably enthusiastic in their praise of the breed and exceedingly jealous of its good name. It is a situation so contradictory as to be almost uncanny, and as such, deserves a brief analysis here.

Certainly the Gordon's ancestry is not at fault; his genealogy is no more clouded than that of any of the other setters. Although the breed originated in Scotland and probably became known before the Irish Setter appeared in Ireland, it is extremely doubtful that it came into existence, as its name would imply, at the Castle Kennels of the Duke of Gordon. That His Grace was partial to black and tan setters, or, more accurately, black, tan and white ones, and bred them extensively in the latter part of the eighteenth century is an established fact; but it is also known that half a score of wealthy Scotch sportsmen were doing the same thing at the same time, and even earlier than that. So the prominence and social standing of the Duke reasonably explains the choice of his name to identify the breed.

It may be assumed that the forebears of the Black and Tan were much the same as those of the other setters, the distinctive color combination having been obtained, perhaps, by breeding from the black and tan setting spaniels by no means rare in Great Britain at that time and which had been popular with sportsmen ever since 1575 or thereabouts. Of course there must have been many and varying outcrosses during all those years. Even the Duke of Gordon himself is said to have used in his breeding an exceptionally intelligent and birdy Collie bitch named Maddy. It is significant that this bitch was a black and tan, had a remarkable nose and was adept at locating grouse in the heather. She did not actually point her birds, but, according to the legend, stood and "watched" them, whatever that may mean. The reference to her keen nose would seem to indicate that her "watching" was done after the game had been scented and located in the orthodox bird-dog way. As a possible confirmation of the Maddy story it should be said that for many years thereafter an occasional Gordon was whelped that carried a characteristic collie tail. The modern Gordon, on the contrary, almost invariably has an unusually fine bird-dog stern, short, straight, well carried and nicely tapered. Summing up his vital statistics, then, we find them fully as legitimate as those of his setter cousins. Incidentally, it is interesting to note that the finest individuals imported into the United States during the last decade have come from Denmark, Norway, and Sweden.

In general appearance the Gordon loses little, if anything, by comparison with his rivals in the bird-dog field. Of course there is no argument in matters of taste, but surely the glossy black coat of a well-bred Gordon, set off as it is by rich mahogany tan, must appeal to an artistic eye as an attractive color scheme. Granted that it is not as flashy as the solid red of the Irishman nor as conspicuous as the varying colors of the English dog, few will deny that it is equally classy. It is difficult to believe that his coat alone has kept the Scotch dog in the background.

In conformation the Gordon is thoroughly individual and has, in the main, kept pretty consistently to type. He never was and is not today an Irish or English setter with a black and tan jacket. Idstone described Lord Bolingbroke's Argyle as having "a grand frame, powerful hocks and loin, with neck and shoulders so long, well-poised and muscular that he would have taken high rank anywhere. He was," continues this writer, "a narrow, deep-made, racing-looking dog."

In a general description of the breed as commonly seen at the shows of his day, Idstone writes: "He has not so finely formed a head; it inclines occasionally to the heavy and bloodhound type. His ears are frequently too large and weighted with coat, as well as leather. He is far too heavy—I am writing of the common type observed at our shows—and he must be refined at any cost. In spite of his wide chest and loaded fore quarters, he is free, active and lithe in his gallop, and a good specimen (I mean a narrow, deep-chested, long and low Gordon setter) will more than hold his own. I have seen better setters of the black and tan than of any other breed."

The above is both interesting and illuminating. It shows that, even in the early dawn of the breed, there were Gordons and good Gordons of the light, racy type and refutes the charge sometimes made, that the standard of the breed adopted by the Gordon Setter Club of America, which appears below, is written along radically modernistic lines at variance with true Gordon traditions.

Other writers of Idstone's day confirm this. As a result we may conclude that the so-called "modern Gordons" and the best of the "old timers" were built along almost identical lines. The extremely heavy head, loaded shoulders, wide front, curly coat and other faults frequently met with today were apparently considered quite as undesirable then as now.

As a bird-dog the Black and Tan's status seems to be a moot question. His defenders claim that for cover shooting he has no superior; that his tendency to cover his ground slowly and thoroughly is a distinct asset. It is certainly true that he is peculiarly adapted to woodcock and handles that sporty little bird exceptionally well. At the same time a number of the faster and lighter type Gordons have performed exceedingly well in field trials when pitted against other setters and pointers. In other words it has been demonstrated that, if bred and trained along field-trial lines, he has flattering possibilities.

Why, then, should he occupy the obscure corner in the bird-dog world that has been assigned him? His disposition may be one of the answers. He is almost invariably a one-man dog. While this is a virtue in one way, it is a handicap in another. Ideal in the home and family, he is by no means suited to spend his days in a large kennel of dogs or to be simply one of a professional handler's "string." He seeks and requires the personal attention of his master; given affection and companionship he will return them in full measure and prove himself a loyal friend in the household and a dependable and valuable servant in the field. At the same time, it is easy to see why the field-trial handler does not take kindly to the Black and Tan. He wants a dog that develops early, has natural speed and independence and can be trained easily to handle kindly for anyone capable of working a dog in public competition. Not only that; he also prefers a dog which will be perfectly satisfied to spend his leisure hours in a kennel and does not particularly require the close companionship of his handler and trainer. Such being the case, the Gordon fails to fill his bill, and as a result, has had but little opportunity to show his wares in public. And, after all, it is as true in the dog game as elsewhere that "it pays to advertise."

All this suggests an interesting angle to the Gordon situation in this country. There have always been, and there are now a large number of men and women who have a flair for owning "something different," who like to be apart from "the common herd" in their fads and fancies. They collect rare objects of art, fine old furniture, raise new and unusual varieties of flowers or fruits, gather a collection of ancient coins—in short, go in for the unusual and the little known. When these collectors choose as a hobby articles that are utterly useless and of no real value, there is little to be said in their favor; but when, as is frequently the case, their taste turns to the truly fine and historically interesting, they perform a distinct service to society.

For the latter class of dog-lover the Gordon should have a strong and compelling appeal. He is not only a rarity, he has in addition sterling merits, beauty, real practical value and an interesting history. He is no freak, no newly developed upstart with no pride of ancestry nor hope of posterity—he is an old and long-established member of bird-dog aristocracy. He deserves every advantage he can get and will repay every bit of intelligent effort in his behalf. Some day he will come into his own. It is inconceivable that so grand a dog should do otherwise.

DESCRIPTION AND STANDARD OF POINTS
(By Courtesy of The Gordon Setter Club of America)

General Impression.—A stylish, rather racy built, medium size, muscular dog of clean setter type, usual length legs and of symmetrical conformation throughout. Strong fairly short back and short tail, a fine head, clearly lined, intelligent expression, clear colors and straight or slightly waved coat.

Size.—Shoulder height for males 22 inches to 25 inches; for females, 21 inches to 24 inches.

Head.—Deep rather than broad with plenty of brain room, nicely rounded good-size skull, broadest between the ears. The head should have a clearly indicated stop. Below and above the eyes should be lean and the cheek as narrow as the leanness of the head allows. The muzzle fairly long with almost parallel lines and not pointed either as seen from above or from the side. The flews not pendulous but with clearly indicated lips. The nose big, broad with open nostrils and of black color.

Eyes.—Of fair size, neither too deep set nor too bulging, dark brown, bright and wise.

Ears.—Set low on the head, fairly large and thin.

Neck.—Long, lean, arched to the head and without throatiness.

Shoulders.—Long shoulder blades, lying close to the chest and not going above the back line of the neck.

Chest.—Deep and not too broad in front; the ribs well sprung leaving plenty of lung room.

Forelegs.—Big boned, straight not bowed either in or out with elbows free, well let down and not inclined either in or out.

Hindlegs.—The hindlegs from hip to hock should be long, flat and muscular, from hock to heel short and strong. The stifle and hock joints well bent, and not inclined either in or out.

Feet.—Both fore and hind feet should have close knit, well-arched toes with plenty of hair between with full toe pads and deep heel cushions.

Tail.—Short and should not reach below the hocks, carried horizontal or nearly so, thick at the root and finishing in a fine point.

The feather, which starts near the root of tail should be straight, have a three-square appearance, growing shorter uniformly toward the end.

Coat.—Should be soft and shining, resembling silk, straight or slightly waved but not curly, with long hair on ears, under the stomach and on chest, on back of the fore and hindlegs down to the feet.

Color and Markings.—Deep, shining, coal black with tan markings, either of rich chestnut or mahogany red color. The tan should be shining and not dull, yellowish nor straw color and not mixed with black hairs. Black penciling allowed on toes. The border lines between black and tan colors should be clearly defined. There should not be any tan hairs mixed in the black.

TAN MARKINGS

1. Two clear spots over the eyes not over three-quarters of an inch in diameter.

2. On the sides of the muzzle, the tan should not reach above the base of nose resembling a stripe around the end of the muzzle from one side to the other.

3. On the throat.

4. Two large, clear spots on the chest.

5. On the inside of the hindlegs and inside of thighs showing down the front of the stifle and broadening out to the outside of the hindlegs from the hock to the toes. It must, however, not completely eliminate the black on the back of hindlegs.

6. On the forelegs from the knees or a little above downward to the toes.

7. Around the vent.

A white spot on chest is allowed, but the smaller the better.

GORDON SETTER FAULTS

General Impression.—Unintelligent appearance. The bloodhound type with heavy and big head and ears and clumsy body; as well as the Collie type with its pointed muzzle and curved tail.

The Head.—Pointed, snipy, dropping or upturned muzzle, too small or large mouth.

The Eyes.—Too light in color, too deep set or too prominent.

The Ears.—Set too high or unusually broad or heavy.

The Neck.—Thick and short.

Shoulders and Back.—Irregularly formed.

The Chest.—Too broad.

The Legs and Feet.—Crooked legs. Outturned elbows. The toes scattered, flat footed.

The Tail.—Too long, badly carried or hooked at the end.

The Coat.—Curly like wool, not shining.

The Color.—Yellow or straw colored tan or without clearly defined lines between the different colors. White feet. Too much white on the chest. In the black there must be no tan hairs. It appears often around the eyes.

SETTERS (IRISH)
(Illustration facing page 142)

(By Courtesy of The Irish Setter Club of America)

The Irish Setter first came into popular notice early in
the eighteenth century and less than a hundred years later
his reputation was firmly established, not only in his
native Ireland but throughout the British Isles. Specula-
tions as to his origin are little more than guesswork, various breeds having been named as his progenitors, but
none that can boast a clear title to the honor. Among
the conjectures is that he was developed from an Irish
Water Spaniel—Irish Terrier cross, but it is far more
believable that an English setter-spaniel-pointer combination, with a dash of Gordon thrown in, was the true
formula. But, whatever his family tree may have been,
its fruit has ripened into one of the handsomest as well
as most companionable and useful of dogs. Add to these
virtues the fact that he is exceptionally hardy, vigorous
and long-lived, and the list of his good qualities is an impressive one. It is no wonder, then, that he apparently
made good from the start. Many years ago no less an
authority than Idstone wrote of him: "No better breed
exists," and the same writer describes an ideal specimen
of that day as having "a narrow front, a capital forehead,
a fine lean head and a long tapering neck, together with
the broad back, ragged hips, strong hind quarters, firm,
small feet and long muscular thighs suitable for the rough
sporting of his native Ireland, or the Scotch mountains
and granite boulders," and adds that "you have in the

Irish Setter the quality, the pace, the endurance and style which are to be obtained in few others of what I consider the best dogs for moor and gun."

This eulogy of the Irish Setter as originally developed overseas applies equally well to the modern Irish Red Setter, the latter being the name officially chosen by the Irish Setter Club of America to designate the breed in this country. His earliest ancestors in the Emerald Isle, on the contrary, were rarely self-colored dogs. By far the larger number were red and white, the white frequently predominating over the red, and even today many individuals across the water are parti-colored. In America, however, solid reds or reds with small and inconspicuous white markings are the only ones accepted as typical, and any large and noticeable white patches are considered blemishes. The Irishman's rich mahogany coat is thoroughly distinctive and has done much to make its wearer the bench show favorite he is today.

The solid red setter, as distinguished from the red and white, first appeared in Ireland early in the nineteenth century. Mr. Jason Hazzard of Timaskea, County Fermanagh, Sir St. George Gore and the Earl of Enniskillen all bred self-colored dogs, and it is a matter of record that in 1812 the Earl would have nothing else in his kennels. A few years later Stonehenge wrote: "The blood red, or rich chestnut or mahogany color is the color of an Irish Setter of high mark. This color must be unmixed with black; and studied in a strong light, there must not be black shadows or waves, much less black fringes to the ears, or to the profile of the form." The mention of black in the above is significant as indicating the possibility of the Gordon cross already mentioned. Today this color is absolutely taboo and even a few black hairs are considered enough to disqualify at the shows.

SETTERS (IRISH)

So much for the external appearance of the Irish Setter; now for more important, if less obvious characteristics. The breed is essentially a sporting one, and it is as a gun-dog, after all, that this flashy red fellow must stand or fall. The first individuals imported into this country were brought over for use on game and, in spite of the fact that our ruffed grouse, quail and prairie-chicken were new and strange to them, they made good immediately and emphatically. Elcho, imported in 1875 and one of the first of his breed to make a reputation for himself and his progeny in the United States, was not only a sensational success on the bench but a thoroughly trained and capable shooting dog, and used as such. As proof of his field quality it is only necessary to say that he was the sire of seven field-trial winners which ran in open stakes against the top-notch English setters, Gordon setters and pointers of that period. To quote Mr. A. F. Hochwalt, in his book, "The Modern Setter," "All through the early field-trial records we find the Irish setter holding his own with the 'fashionable blue bloods.' Had the Irish setter fanciers continued on—their favorite breed would no doubt now be occupying a place as high in field trials as the other two breeds"; by which he means, of course, the English setter and pointer.

But the Irish Setter men didn't continue on, in so far as field trials were concerned, with the result that the Llewellin setter and pointer have practically cornered the market in public competition in that field. Yet, in spite of this handicap, the red dog from Erin has lost none of the attributes of the perfect hunting companion, and given a fair chance, can and does demonstrate his quality as a high-class gun dog on all kinds of game. A half century ago he was fully as popular for this purpose as was the English setter, Gordon or pointer, and certain strains of the breed are as good or better today. Strange as it may seem, his good looks have been his undoing in a way. His fatal gift of beauty, together with his natural gaiety, courage and outstanding personality, have made him an ideal show-dog. For this reason many fanciers have yielded to the temptation to breed for the bench only and to sacrifice to this most worth-while object, field ability equally worth while and in no way incompatible with proper color, good size and correct breed type.

But, fortunately for the Irishman, the last few years have seen a widespread revival of interest in his future as a field dog. Fanciers are realizing that here is one breed in which strict adherence to type and practical utility are still in the cards and many of the best and most far-seeing of the fraternity are working to that end. With this in mind, the Irish Setter Club of America is now sponsoring both spring and fall trials for Irish Setters exclusively and it is by no means unusual to see red-coats returned winners in stakes open to all bird-dog breeds. More encouraging still is the fact that in many cases these good bird-dogs are bench champions as well, thus proving that the dual-type Irishman is not only a possibility, he is actually here.

Just a word *in re* the characteristic personality of the red dog. First and foremost, he is typically Irish, with a devil-may-care something about him that not only makes him tremendously likable but also adds to his value as a bird-dog in rough country and briers. He is bold as a lion and at the same time wonderfully gentle and lovable and loyal. He is tough—good and tough. He can stand continued work in the brush remarkably well, is almost never stiff or sore, has the very best of feet and running gear and almost never gets "sour" when corrected in his work. He is not an early developer and frequently re-

IRISH SETTER

SPANIEL (*Brittany*)

quires more training than some other breeds, but, in spite of certain critics, he is not as a rule headstrong in the sense that he is hard to handle in the brush. In fact, quite the opposite is usually the case. His outstanding fault as a field-trial performer is that he is not independent enough and pays too much attention to his handler. In reply to the criticism that he develops slowly, it is only fair to say that, once trained on birds, he is trained for the rest of his natural life and does not require a repetition of the process every fall. And a crowning argument in his favor is his long life and hale and hearty old age. When you own a good Irishman, you own him for many years, every day of which you can be proud of his appearance, his personality and his performance.

DESCRIPTION AND STANDARD OF POINTS
(By Courtesy of The Irish Setter Club of America)

Head.—Should be long and lean. The skull oval (from ear to ear) having plenty of brain room and with well-defined occipital protuberance. Brows raised, showing stop. The muzzle moderately deep and fairly square at end. From the stop to the point of the nose should be long, the nostrils wide and the jaws of nearly equal length, flews not to be pendulous. The color of the nose dark mahogany or dark chocolate and that of the eyes (which ought not to be too large) rich hazel or brown. The ears to be of moderate size, fine in texture, set on low, well back and hanging in a neat fold close to the head.

Neck.—Should be moderately long, very muscular but not too thick, slightly arched, free from all tendency to throatiness.

Body.—Should be proportionately long, shoulders fine at the points, deep and sloping well back. The chest deep, rather narrow in front. The ribs well sprung, leaving plenty of lung room. The loins muscular and slightly arched. The hind quarter wide and powerful.

[143]

Legs and Feet.—The hindlegs from hip to hock should be long and muscular, from hock to heel short and strong. The stifle and hock joints well bent, and not inclined either in or out. The forelegs should be strong and sinewy, having plenty of bone, with elbows free, well let down and like the hock not inclined either out or in. The feet rather small, very firm, toes strong, close together and arched.

Tail.—Should be of moderate length, set on rather low, strong at root and tapering to a fine point; to be carried in a slight scimitar-like curve or straight, nearly level with the back.

Coat.—On the head, front of legs and tips of ears should be short and fine, but on all other parts of the body it should be of moderate length, flat and as free as possible from curl or wave.

Feathering.—The feather on the upper portion of the ears should be long and silky, on the back of fore and hindlegs long and fine, a fair amount of hair on belly, forming a nice fringe, which may extend on chest and throat. Feet to be well feathered between the toes. Tail to have a nice fringe of moderately long hair, decreasing in length as it approaches the point. All feathering to be as straight and as flat as possible.

Color and Markings.—The color should be a rich golden chestnut or mahogany red, with no trace whatever of black; white on chest, throat or toes, or a small star on the forehead, or a narrow streak, or blaze on the nose or face not to disqualify.

	Points
Head	10
Eyes	5
Ears	5
Neck	5
Body	15
Shoulders, forelegs and feet	12
Hindlegs	10
Tail	8
Coat and feather	8
Color	8
Size, style and general appearance	14
Total	100

SPANIELS (BRITTANY)
(Illustration facing page 143)

During the past few years American sportsmen have begun to realize the qualities of a French breed that has been known on the Continent for many centuries. This dog is known officially in the United States as the Brittany Spaniel, but from his size and the manner of his working he might, properly, be called a setter. He stands 18 to 20 inches at the shoulder, is liver and white, or, preferably, orange and white, and is either without a tail or has one of only a few inches.

The basic stock for all the spaniels, pointers, and setters came originally from Spain, but the migration of these dogs took place so long ago that it is impossible for anyone to say with certainty just when it occurred. The greatest development of these breeds took place in England, Ireland, and Scotland, but many of them spread through various parts of the Continent, and today there are many varieties—particularly in France—that trace back to the old Spanish strains.

The Brittany Spaniel is one of the oldest of them all, and he was bred up from the original spaniel size in much the same manner as the British, using similar stock, produced the setters. In fact, there is reason to believe that he had attained his present size long before his cousins across the channel had attained to recognizable type.

It is believed by some that the Brittany Spaniel was related to the red and white setter which preceded the golden red setter in Ireland. There is a strong possibility that some of the Irish chieftains, who invaded Gaul

[145]

—or what is now France—during the first third of the Fifth Century A.D., carried their hunting dogs with them. These dogs, left in France may have contributed something to the development of the Brittany Spaniel. The Irish influence also is seen in the orange and white Epagneul Ecossais, or Scotch spaniel—especially if it is remembered that at the time of these invasions the Irish were known as Scoti.

The first tailless ancestor of the modern Brittany Spaniel was bred, about a century ago, at Pontou, a little town situated in the Valley of Douron. It was the result of a cross between a white and mahogany bitch, owned by an old hunter of the region, and a lemon and white dog brought to Brittany by an English sportsman for the woodcock shooting. Of two tailless specimens produced in this litter, only one was considered worth keeping. He grew into a splendid dog. His work in the field has been described as wonderful, and because of this he became a popular stud. All his litters contained puppies either without tails or with short stubs.

The modern history of the Brittany Spaniel dates back only to the beginning of the present century. At that time the breed had degenerated badly, principally because it had been closely inbred, but also because it had not been regarded as a show specimen. Eventually it caught the attention of Arthur Enaud, a French sportsman with a biological turn of mind. He admired the all-around working qualities of the breed so highly that he undertook to improve its appearance.

M. Enaud went about his work very thoroughly, and he did not try to accomplish too much in too short a time. He was forced to use certain crosses, but after each cross he returned immediately to the old breed. Unfortunately, like many breeders who have done the same thing

SPANIEL (*Clumber*)

COCKER SPANIEL

with other breeds, he left no clear record of the different dogs that entered into this restoration. In fact, it is only through a study of the other breeds available that it is possible to follow this period in the history of the Brittany Spaniel.

The intensification of the desired orange and white color was one of the chief aims of M. Enaud, and for this he found two breeds that had not only the colors but keen scenting ability. One was the Italian Bracco, or pointer, and the other was the Braque de Bourbonnais, also a pointer. This second breed was the more suitable for his purposes, for besides its other points it was possessed of a very short tail.

The only drawback to the use of pointers was that the coat of the Brittany Spaniel might be affected, but as sparing use was made of crosses and the rest was a matter of selective breeding after improving the blood lines, the modern dog was still the counterpart of his ancient Breton ancestors. By 1907 the breed had been restored to all its former glory.

The first specimens of the Brittany Spaniel were imported to America in 1931, and they have been exhibited at many of our shows since that time. The breed has proved a capable gun dog, and like most of the Continental-bred setters and pointers it can be trained very easily as a retriever. The original use of the breed in France was for woodcock hunting, but it is far from a specialist. And it has proved already that it can hold its own in field trials, for, the first time in competition in America, a Brittany Spaniel carried off a prize against a field of more experienced dogs from other breeds.

SPORTING DOGS

DESCRIPTION AND STANDARD OF POINTS
(Adopted by The American Kennel Club, March 12, 1935)

GENERAL APPEARANCE

Height.—17 inches minimum; 19¾ maximum, with toleration of ¾ inch more for males, back short; head rounded; muzzle rather pointed; with lips close fitting; ears short rather than long and placed high, relatively but little fringed; hair close on body; fringes wavy, never curly, a compact cob type; tail always naturally short, about 4 inches. (See note at end.)

Nose.—Nostrils well open; color brown or rose according to whether the dog is white and liver, or white and orange.

Faults.—Black and shiny; tight or snipy.

Muzzle.—Medium length narrowing toward nose; straight or very slightly curved.

Faults.—Too short or too long.

Lips.—Fine, close fitting, the upper lip overlapping the under lip by very little.

Faults.—Thick or too overlapping.

Crown of Head.—Medium length, rounded; each side of the depression well marked and rounded; well defined stop though sloping gently and not too abrupt.

Faults.—Square; narrow; apple-headed; stop too abrupt.

Eyes.—Deep amber, bright and expressive.

Faults.—Too light, mean look.

Ears.—Placed high, short rather than long, slightly rounded, but little fringe, though the ear should be well covered with wavy hair.

Faults.—Placed low; falling; large; curly.

Neck.—Medium length, well placed on shoulders; without dewlap.

Faults.—Too long; too thin; too short or too heavy.

Shoulders.—Slightly oblique and muscular.

Faults.—Straight or too oblique.

[148]

Arm.—Muscular and bony.

Faults.—Fatty or too fine.

Chest.—Deep, reaching quite to level of elbow; sides rounded enough and quite large.

Faults.—Chest narrow; not deep, sides flat.

Back.—Short, withers well marked; never hollow or saddle backed.

Faults.—Long or hollow.

Loin.—Short and strong.

Faults.—Long; narrow or weak.

Flanks.—Well tucked up but not to excess.

Faults.—Fat; falling.

Hind Quarters.—Broad—strong and muscular.

Croup.—Slightly sloping.

Faults.—Too narrow; too straight; too sloping.

Tail.—(See note at end)—Straight and carried low; always short naturally; about 4 inches long, often screw tail ending in a mesh of hair, or "anoure."

Front Legs.—Very straight; forearm slightly oblique, fine and muscular; fringes not heavy but wavy.

Faults.—Forearm too straight or too oblique; without fringes or too heavily fringed.

Hindlegs.—Thighs large, well muscled, well fringed and wavy half down thigh, canon well set with hock and not too angular.

Faults.—Straight thighs, without fringes or too oblique.

Feet.—Toes close with a little hair between them.

Faults.—Large; long, fat, too round or open.

Skin.—Fine and fairly loose.

Faults.—Thick or too loose.

Coat.—Hair flat on body, fine but not to excess and quite smooth or slightly wavy.

Faults.—Long, curly or too silky.

Color.—Liver and white preferably with roan ticking, or orange and white preferably with roan ticking.

SPORTING DOGS

As a Whole.—A small dog, closely knit and strong though elegant, very vigorous; energetic of movement; intelligent expression; presenting the aspect of a thoroughbred cob.

Note:—The question of Brittany Spaniels born with tails being admitted to the Show Ring, was voted on in the General Assembly of 1933 and it was decided that a cut tail was no disqualification either in the Show Ring or the Field Trials.

SPANIELS (CLUMBER)

(Illustration facing page 146)

(By Courtesy of The American Spaniel Club)

One of the longest established breeds of Spaniels is the Clumber. He is very distinctive in type from any of the others and a good specimen is a dog of great beauty and an impressive picture. A partial explanation of the individuality of the breed was the introduction very early in its history of Basset Hound blood. 1859 saw the first class for Clumbers in England and from then on in that country they have enjoyed considerable popularity. Due to abundance of game there is not the need of a bustling, fast-moving Spaniel that we have here and therefore the Clumber is better suited to foreign shooting conditions than he is to our own.

The Clumber is a dignified, rather slow-moving dog but a sure finder and splendid retriever when trained. His most outstanding identifying external characteristic is his color as noted in the standard.

DESCRIPTION AND STANDARD OF POINTS
(By Courtesy of The American Spaniel Club)

General Appearance and Size.—General appearance, a long, low, heavy-looking dog, of a very thoughtful expression, betokening great intelligence. Should have the appearance of great power. Sedate in all movements, but not clumsy. Weight of dogs averaging between 55 and 65 pounds; bitches from 35 to 50 pounds.

Head.—Head large and massive in all its dimensions; round above eyes, flat on top, with a furrow running from between the eyes upon the center. A marked stop and large occipital protuberance. Jaw long, broad and deep. Lips of upper jaw overhung. Muzzle not square, but at the same time powerful looking. Nostrils large, open and flesh-colored, sometimes cherry-colored.

Eyes.—Eyes large, soft, deep set and showing haw. Hazel in color, not too pale, with dignified and intelligent expression.

Ears.—Ears long and broad at the top, turned over on the front edge; vine-shaped: close to the head; set on low and feathered only on the front edge, and there but slightly. Hair short and silky, without the slightest approach to wave or curl.

Neck and Shoulders.—Neck long, thick and powerful, free from dewlap, with a large ruff. Shoulders immensely strong and muscular, giving a heavy appearance in front.

Body and Quarters.—Body very long and low, well ribbed up and long in the coupling. Chest of great depth and volume. Loin powerful and not too much arched. Back long, broad and straight, free from droop or bow. Length an important characteristic; the nearer the dog is in length to being two and one-half times his height at shoulder the better. Quarters shapely and very muscular, neither drooping nor stilty.

Legs and Feet.—Forelegs short, straight and immensely heavy in bone. Well in at elbows. Hindlegs heavy in bone, but not as heavy as forelegs. No feather above hocks, but thick hair on back of legs just above foot. Feet large, compact and plentifully filled with hair between toes.

Coat and Feathers.—Coat silky and straight, not too long, extremely dense; feather long and abundant.

Color and Markings.—Color, lemon and white, and orange and white. Fewer markings on body the better. Perfection of markings, solid lemon or orange ears, evenly marked head and eyes, muzzle and legs ticked.

Stern.—Stern set on a level and carried low.

	Points
General appearance and size	10
Head	15
Eyes	5

SPANIELS (CLUMBER)

Ears	10
Neck and shoulders	15
Body and quarters	20
Legs and feet	10
Coat and feather	10
Color and marking	5
Total	100

COCKER SPANIEL (*English Type*)

SPANIEL (*English Springer*)

SPANIELS (COCKER)
(Illustration facing page 147)

(By Courtesy of The American Spaniel Club)

The Cocker Spaniel is the smallest of the sporting Spaniel family and by reason of his versatility in the field in addition to his sterling worth as a companion in the house to adults and children alike is a very popular breed. The variations in color add to the interest in the breed among which are the solid colors, consisting of black, red, the various shades of cream or buff and liver, and the parti-colors among which you will find black and white, black and tan and combinations of black, tan and white known as tricolors; also a few liver and whites.

The Spaniel family is a large one and one of considerable antiquity. As far back as 1386, we find mention of the Spanyell which in the next century was divided into two groups; the land and the water Spaniel. Later a further division of the large Spaniels and the small ones, cut the toy Spaniels from the sporting ones and eventually as various localities developed individualistic strains, the classification became a definite one of which, numerically the Cocker Spaniels have held the lead both in England and the United States. Like most breeds, however, they have had their phases of long legs and short; long back and short, etc., but are at the time of the publication of this volume, being bred with a closer adherence to the standard and with more regard for their natural vocation as hunters than at any time in the history of the breed in this country.

The Cocker is a great lover of his human family and his home. He is trustworthy with children and contented to adapt himself to the mood of his master or mistress. If permitted to indulge his inherent love of hunting and through judicious training, his capabilities are developed, he will give great sport, and when well taught, makes a most desirable retriever.

Like all of the Spaniel group the method of hunting with the Cocker is to let him quarter the ground ahead of the gun, covering all territory within gun range, which he should do at a fast, snappy pace. Upon flushing game he should immediately stop or preferably drop to a sitting position so as not to interfere with the shot, after which, he should retrieve on command only. He should be so trained that he will be under control at all times as there is nothing that can spoil so many shots as an uncontrollable dog. All Spaniels, speaking of them as a unit, are valuable for occasional water retrieving, as most of them take to water readily. There is at this time a vast difference in the type of Cocker bred in America and in Great Britain. The English Cocker does not conform either in type or in size with the American Cocker and is therefore seldom seen at our shows.

Field Trials for Cockers were started in the United States by the Cocker Spaniel Field Trial Club in 1924 and are being held in increasing numbers each year.

DESCRIPTION AND STANDARD OF POINTS
(By Courtesy of The American Spaniel Club)

Skull.—Not so heavy as in other Sporting Spaniels, with smooth forehead and clearly defined eyebrows and stop, the median line distinctly marked and gradually disappearing until lost rather more than halfway up, a well developed, rounded and comparatively wide skull showing no prominence in the cheeks, which, like the side of the muzzle, should present a smooth, clean-cut appearance.

Muzzle.—Proportionately shorter and lighter than in the Field Spaniel, showing no fullness under the eyes, the jaws even and approaching squareness. Teeth sound and regular, the front ones meeting. Lips cut off square, preventing any appearance of snipiness. Nose well developed in all directions and black in color excepting in the reds, livers, parti-colors of these shades and in the roans of the lighter lines, when it may be brown or black.

Eyes.—Comparatively large, round, rather full, yet never goggled nor weak, as in the Toy Spaniel kind. They should be dark in the blacks, black and tans, the darker shades of parti-colors and roans. In the reds and livers and in the parti-colors and roans of these colors they should be brown, but of a shade not lighter than hazel.

Ears.—Lobular, set low, leather fine and not extending beyond the nose; well clothed with long, silky hair, which should be straight or wavy.

Neck and Shoulders.—Neck sufficiently long to allow the nose to reach the ground easily, muscular, free from throatiness and running into clean-cut, sloping shoulders, which should not be wide at the points.

Body.—Comparatively short, compact and firmly knit together, giving the impression of a concentration of power and untiring activity. Chest deep rather than wide, not narrow fronted nor yet so wide as to interfere with free action of the forelegs. Ribs well sprung, deep and carried far back, short in the couplings and flank, free from any tucked appearance. Back and loin immensely strong and compact in proportion to the size of the dog, the former level and the latter slightly arched. Hips wide, with quarters considerably rounded and very muscular.

Legs and Feet.—Forelegs short and straight, though proportionately longer than in any of the other breeds of short-legged Spaniels; strongly boned and muscled, with elbows well let down and straight, short, strong pasterns. Hindlegs proportionately short. Stifles well bent, strong thighs, clearly defined. Hocks clean, strong, well let down, presenting an impressive combination of propelling power. Feet neither small nor large, round, firm, not spreading and with deep, strong, horny pads and plenty of hair between the toes. They should turn neither in nor out.

Stern.—Should be set on and carried level with the back, and when at work its action should be incessant in this, the brightest and merriest of the whole Spaniel family.

Coat.—Flat or slightly waved, silky and very dense, with ample Setter-like feather.

Color and Markings.—Blacks should be jet black, and reds, livers, etc., should never be faded or "washy" shades, but of good, sound colors. White on the chest of self-colors, while objectionable, should not disqualify.

Weight.—Not under 18 nor exceeding 24 pounds.

General Description.—Embodying the foregoing, i.e., a neat headed, wide-awake, serviceable-looking little dog, with an expression of great intelligence; short in body when viewed from above, yet standing over considerable ground for one of his inches upon strong, straight front legs, with wide, muscular quarters suggestive of immense power, especially when viewed from behind. A downward tendency in front he ought not to possess, but should stand well up at the shoulders, like the clever little sporting dog that he is. Massive in appearance by reason of his sturdy body, powerful quarters and strong, well-boned limbs, he should, nevertheless, impress one as being a dog capable of considerable speed combined with great powers of endurance and in all his movements he should be quick and merry, with an air of alertness and a carriage of head and stern suggestive of an inclination to work.

	Points
Skull	8
Muzzle	10
Eyes	7
Ears	4
Neck and shoulders	15
Body	18
Legs and feet	18
Stern	5
Coat	10
Color and marking	5
Total	100

SPANIEL (*Field*)

IRISH WATER SPANIEL

SPANIELS (COCKER)
(English Type)
(Illustration facing page 154)

DESCRIPTION AND STANDARD OF POINTS FOR ENGLISH TYPE COCKER SPANIELS

(As Adopted by the Cocker Spaniel Club, England, and Approved by the Board of Directors of The American Kennel Club, May 12, 1936)

Head.—A nicely-developed square muzzle and jaw, with distinct stop. Skull and forehead should be well developed, with plenty of room for brain power, cleanly chiselled and not cheeky.

Eyes.—Full, but not prominent, hazel or brown colored, harmonizing with color of coat, with a general expression of intelligence and gentleness, decidedly wide-awake, bright, and merry.

Ears.—Lobular, set on low, leather fine and not extending beyond the nose, well clothed with long silky hair, which should be straight—no positive curls or ringlets.

Neck.—Long, strong and muscular, and neatly set on to fine sloping shoulders.

Body.—(Including Size and Symmetry.) Compact and firmly knit together, giving the impression of a concentration of power and untiring activity; the total weight should be about 25 lb. to 28 lb.

Nose.—Sufficiently wide and well-developed to insure the exquisite scenting power of this breed.

Shoulders and Chest.—The former sloping and fine, chest deep and well developed, but not too wide and round to interfere with the free action of the forelegs.

Back and Loin.—Short in back. Immensely strong and compact in proportion to the size and weight of the dog; slightly drooping towards the tail.

[159]

Hind Quarters.—Wide, well rounded, and very muscular.

Stern.—That most characteristic of blue blood in all the Spaniel family may, in the lighter and more active Cocker, although set low down, be allowed a slighter higher carriage than in the other breeds, but never cocked up over, but rather in a line with the back, although the lower the carriage and action the better, and when at work its action should be incessant in this, the brightest and merriest of the whole Spaniel family. Not docked too short.

Feet and Legs.—The legs must be well boned, feathered and straight, for the tremendous exertions expected from this grand little sporting dog, and should be sufficiently short for concentrated power, but not too short as to interfere with its full activity. Feet firm, round, and cat-like, not too large or spreading or loose jointed.

Coat.—Flat and silky in texture, never wiry nor wavy, with sufficient feather; but not too profuse, and never curly.

Color.—Various; in self colors; a white shirt frill is most undesirable; white feet should not be allowed in any specimen of self-color.

General Appearance.—That of an active, merry sporting dog. The Cocker Spaniel does not follow on the lines of the larger Field Spaniel, either in lengthiness, lowness, or otherwise, but is shorter in back, and rather higher on the legs.

SCALE OF POINTS FOR JUDGING COCKER SPANIELS (ENGLISH)

Positive Points

Head and Jaws	10
Eyes	5
Ears	5
Neck	10
Body	20
Forelegs	10
Hindlegs	10
Feet	10
Stern	10
Coat and Feather	10
Total Positive Points	100

SPANIELS (COCKER)

Negative Points

Light Eyes 10
Light Nose 15
Hair Curled on Ears (very undesirable) 15
Coat (curly, woolly, or wiry) 20
Carriage of Stern 20
Top Knot 20
                                               ———

Total Negative Points 100

SPANIELS (ENGLISH SPRINGER)

(Illustration facing page 155)

(By Courtesy of The English Springer Spaniel Field Trial Association)

The name "Springing Spaniel" was originally occupational in its nomenclature and generic in its application, and included in one brood classification the ancestral stock from which most, if not all, of our present day land spaniels emanated. In 1902 the Kennel Club of England recognized the English Springer Spaniel as a distinct breed.

Though several individuals in America had these spaniels for their shooting, it was not until 1924 when the English Springer Spaniel Field Trial Association was formed that they became better known. Field Trials were inaugurated and three years later (1927) the English Springer Spaniel Field Trial Association became the parent club of the breed.

It has been the idea of this Association to further the English Springer Spaniels, both on the bench and in the field. A Standard was approved when the Association was formed and later, in 1932, a committee representing the entire breed drew up a new standard, which was better. It was adopted by the English Springer Spaniel Field Trial Association and approved by the American Kennel Club. This Standard was made as near as possible to take care of the natural ability of the Springer Spaniel. As this breed was strictly a hunting dog, it was felt that the Standard should be such that it would keep the breed in such conformity that, with training, he would have the physical make-up to do his required work.

The Association also has conducted Field Trials every year and has endeavored to demonstrate to the public at large just how good these dogs are as shooting dogs. Field Trials are to show to what a degree of excellence a Spaniel can be trained. As competition becomes greater, they must of necessity be able to cover their ground fast, and, if well trained, to obey any signals or orders given them. Unquestionably the new standard has helped to make the breed more uniform and the Spaniels have now come to be much more standardized both on the bench and in the field trials. Being a great sporting dog, they should be kept as they are at this date and not allowed to lose any of their characteristics by breeding a heavy boned and stocky type that would make them lose their usefulness in the field. Their purpose alone is to hunt and find game. If more Springer Spaniels were put into field training at an early age and this training kept up until they had reached their full physical development, they would then be far better dogs to put on the bench.

DESCRIPTION AND STANDARD OF POINTS

(As adopted by The English Springer Spaniel Field Trial Association and approved by the Board of Directors of the American Kennel Club, July 12, 1932)

Foreface.—Nostrils well developed, soft, liver color or black, according to color of coat. Muzzle deep, with plenty of upper lip and flew. Jaws good length, straight, fairly square, neither under nor overshot. Nicely chiseled below eyes.

Skull.—Should rise from foreface without a pronounced stop. Skull of medium length and fairly broad. From the stop the median line, or groove, continues backward to the front of the sagittal crest (forehead) forming two slightly rounded halves above the eyes. Eyebrows and temples well developed, not thick in cheeks. Top of skull flat from forehead to occiput and slightly rounded on sides and back; occiput not domed; the top of occiput bone should be rounded, not pointed or angular in contour.

The resulting appearance is a head of medium length, fairly broad and slightly rounded, with a well defined stop effect—well chiseled under the eyes and free of cheekiness—with a strong, lean fairly square jaw and well muzzled with plenty of lip, but not too thick or pendulous as in the hound, even set teeth, and well developed nostrils—an impressive head without being heavy. A ponderous head is objectionable.

Faults.—Oval skull—cheekiness—too much stop which gives Clumber expression. Too heavy appearing head.

Eyes.—Neither too full nor too small—medium size—not prominent or sunken but well set in, not showing haw, of an alert and kindly expression. In color dark hazel, brown or nearly black, harmonizing with the coat.

Note: Seldom darker than dark hazel in the liver and white.

Faults.—Light yellow eyes, or eyes showing much haw, should be penalized.

Ears.—Lobular, long and wide, set on not higher than in line with level of eye, flaps hanging close to cheeks, well covered both inside and outside with fine feather, which should not be curly. The leather should not be longer than to reach to the tip of the nose.

Faults.—Ears off line of level of eyes, or set too far back on head.

Neck.—Moderately long, strong and muscular coming out of shoulders rather full and tapering to the head, slightly arched and free from throatiness. "A springer grasps with the teeth, but weight is bourne by the neck."

Faults.—Too short, or ewe-like; set into head too heavily, causing throatiness.

Brisket.—Not too wide so as to interfere with the free action of the forelegs, but well developed and nicely rounded.

Shoulders.—The blades wide, strong and sloping, well set back forming a strong and powerful upper arm, muscular without being mutton shouldered.

[165]

Faults.—Straight shoulders or mutton shoulders, which cause the dog to be paddle gaited.

Body.—The chest deep and well developed, with plenty of heart and lung room, but not too round or wide. Walls of chest deep with well sprung ribs. Back from withers to root of tail equal height at shoulder. Back should be strong, straight—never sway-backed. Strong loins, with hips nicely rounded, slight arch over loin and hip joints, thighs broad; well developed and muscular. The hind quarters giving the appearance of great driving power. Rump slightly sloping to base of tail, belly nicely curved from chest to flank, but not in any way "tucked up."

Faults.—Sway back. Ribs too round, too flat or too shallow. Too long body, or loosely coupled body. Too high rump.

Legs.—Forelegs—elbows well let down, setting close to the body, with free action from the shoulder. Forearm straight, with the same degree of size to toes, with slightly flattened bone and muscle. Wrist, sometimes called the "knee," straight and almost flat. Pastern short and strong. Feet strong and compact, with good strong round pads, well feathered between toes. Wavy feathering of moderate heaviness down to pastern.

Note:—When viewed from the front, Springer should be straight from shoulder to foot, elbow close to body and knee bending neither in nor out.

Faults.—Crooked legs. Too light bones. Splay or hare feet.

Hindlegs.—From hip to hock, long and sinewy; hock to heel, short and strong. Stifles and hock moderately bent and not inclining either in or out, firm on feet, feet round and not too small, with strong, thick close pads. Well feathered between toes. Moderately feathered down to hock. Profuse feathering objectionable.

Stern.—Set on low, well fringed with wavy feather. Preferably never carried above the level of the back. Of lively motion when dog is excited.

Coat.—On head, front of forelegs and below hock on front of hindlegs, short and fine; on other parts of body, flat or wavy (never curly) of medium length but of sufficient density to be waterproof, weatherproof and thornproof, glossy and refined in texture. A nice fringe of wavy hair on throat, brisket, chest and belly.

SPANIELS (ENGLISH SPRINGER)

(Close trimming or treatment of coat to give artificial appearance should be severely penalized.)

Height.—Dogs—18½ inches at shoulder. Should not vary more than ½-inch either way therefrom. Bitches—18 inches at shoulder. Should not vary more than ½-inch either way therefrom.

Weight.—Dogs about 45 lbs.—should not exceed 50 lbs. Bitches about 42 lbs.—should not exceed 47 lbs.

Note:—It is desirable that proper balance and proportion shall always be considered more important than mere weight, and the dog or bitch possessing true Springer type which is balanced in both vertical and horizontal dimensions and possesses bone and substance in keeping with its size, should, even though under or over the weight and dimension limits set down, always be considered preferable to one which is ill proportioned and attains the weight limit through excess or lack of height, length, width or substance.

Color.—Liver and white; black and white; liver and tan; black and tan; tan and white; black, white and tan; liver; black; roan, etc., anything except red and white, and lemon and white, which should be penalized.

Gait.—The Springer gait is strictly his own. His forelegs should swing straight forward from the shoulder, throwing the foot well forward in an easy and free manner, not a paddle or with a choppy or Terrier stride. In the rear his hocks must drive well under his body following on a line with the forelegs.

Note:—At slow movement many Springers have a pacing stride which is also acceptable for Springer gait.

General Appearance and Type.—The Springer Spaniel is a hunting dog of all work. His qualities, stated in this standard, will give him speed, agility and endurance to cope with the most difficult field trial and hunting conditions. He is a medium size variety of Spaniel, active, symmetrical, upstanding, strong, built for endurance, but not in any way coarse or ponderous. A well balanced sporting dog of distinct Spaniel character, combining beauty and utility. Excessive lowness or length should be penalized as interfering with the dog's activity.

SPORTING DOGS

The following table of positive and negative points is attached simply as a guide to the relative importance of perfect or defective features.

Note:—The question of "type" and "balance," however, takes precedence over any scoring table which could be drawn up.

Positive Points

	Points
Head and Jaw	15
Eyes	5
Ears	5
Neck	5
Body	10
Forelegs	10
Hindlegs	10
Feet	10
Stern	5
Coat and Feather	10
General Appearance	15
Total	100

Negative Points

	Points
Light Eyes	5
Light Nose	10
Poor Ears	5
Bad Neck	5
Curly Coat	10
Weak or Uneven Jaw	15
Bad Carriage of Tail	5
Crooked Legs	15
Poor Gait	15
Excessive Lowness or Length	15
Total	100

SPANIELS (FIELD)

(Illustration facing page 158)

(By Courtesy of The American Spaniel Club)

More than any variety of the Spaniel group has this breed been taken over the hurdles of man's fancy for exaggerations of type and for a number of years the breed suffered greatly from this treatment. To Mr. Phineas Bullock of England can be given the credit of perpetuating this variety which in his day was a dog of tremendous length and lowness to the ground. The type was established by repeated crosses of the "Welch Cocker" with the Sussex Spaniel. A phenomenal amount of bone was desired resulting in a grotesque caricature of a Spaniel. Within the last ten years, largely through the tireless efforts of Mr. Mortimer Smith the breed has made amazing strides in settling into a type which all who like sporting Spaniels can admire. Usually black in color, the Field Spaniel by wise and careful breeding has been brought to a useful and handsome breed. Sound and straight in his front legs, upstanding and with good balance of height for length he unquestionably ranks with the handsomest of his cousins. When built along these lines, he is a dog with endurance, speed and agility. Level-headed and intelligent this breed should be, and a dog with great perseverance.

There has been considerable difficulty in establishing the "Modern" Field Spaniel in the United States due to the necessity of introducing Springer and Cocker blood in order to eliminate the aforementioned gross exaggerations, which have made many of them ineligible for registration in the American Kennel Club. At the time of the introduction of Cocker Spaniels to America and for several years afterwards the distinction for the purposes of showing of Cockers and Field Spaniels was solely one of size.

DESCRIPTION AND STANDARD OF POINTS

(By Courtesy of The Field Spaniel Society, England, and The American Spaniel Club)

Head.—Should be quite characteristic of this grand sporting dog, as that of the Bulldog, or the Bloodhound; its very stamp and countenance should at once convey the conviction of high breeding, character and nobility; skull well developed, with a distinctly elevated occipital tuberosity, which, above all, gives the character alluded to; not too wide across the muzzle, long and lean, never snipy nor squarely cut, and in profile curving gradually from nose to throat; lean beneath the eyes, a thickness here gives coarseness to the whole head. The great length of muzzle gives surface for the free development of the olfactory nerve, and thus secures the highest possible scenting powers.

Eyes.—Not too full, but not small, receding or overhung, color dark hazel or brown, or nearly black, according to the color of the dog. Grave in expression and showing no haw.

Ears.—Moderately long and wide, sufficiently clad with nice Setter-like feather and set low. They should fall in graceful folds, the lower parts curling inwards and backwards.

Neck.—Long, strong and muscular, so as to enable the dog to retrieve his game without undue fatigue.

Body.—Should be of moderate length, well-ribbed up to a good strong loin, straight or slightly arched, never slack.

Nose.—Well developed, with good open nostrils.

Shoulders and Chest.—Former long, sloping and well set back, thus giving great activity and speed; latter deep and well developed, but not too round and wide.

SPANIELS (FIELD)

Back and Loin.—Very strong and muscular.

Hind Quarters.—Strong and muscular. The stifles should be moderately bent, and not twisted either in or out.

Stern.—Well set on and carried low, if possible below the level of the back, in a straight line or with a slight downward inclination, never elevated above the back, and in action always kept low, nicely fringed with wavy feather of silky texture.

Forelegs.—Should be of fairly good length, with straight, clean, flat bone, and nicely feathered. Immense bone is no longer desirable.

Feet.—Not too small; round, with short soft hair between the toes; good, strong pads.

Coat.—Flat or slightly waved, and never curled. Sufficiently dense to resist the weather, and not too short. Silky in texture, glossy and refined in nature, with neither duffleness on the one hand, nor curl or wiriness on the other. On the chest, under belly and behind the legs, there should be abundant feather, but never too much, especially below the hocks, and that of the right sort, viz., Setter-like. The hind quarters should be similarly adorned.

Color.—This Society maintains that the Field Spaniel should be a self-colored Dog, viz., a Black (as he was originally some 60 years ago), or a "Sport" from Black, i.e., Liver, Golden Liver, Mahogany Red, Roan; or any one of the colors with Tan over the eyes, on the Cheeks, Feet and Pasterns. Other colors, such as Black and White, Liver and White, Red or Orange and White, etc., while not disqualifying a Dog (provided the architecture is correct), will not be considered so desirable, since it is the aim of the Society to make a clear distinction between the Field and the Springer Spaniel.

Height.—About 18 inches to shoulder.

Weight.—From about 35 pounds to 50 pounds.

General Appearance.—That of a well-balanced, noble, upstanding sporting dog; built for activity and endurance. A grand combination of beauty and utility, and bespeaking of unusual docility and instinct.

[171]

SPORTING DOGS

	Points
Head and jaw	15
Eyes	5
Ears	5
Neck	5
Body	10
Forelegs	10
Hindlegs	10
Feet	10
Stern	10
Coat and feather	10
General appearance	10
Total	100

SPANIELS (IRISH WATER)

(Illustration facing page 159)

(By Courtesy of The American Spaniel Club)

In appearance the Irish Water Spaniel is the clown of
the Spaniel family. He is by far the tallest of the Spaniels. In coat, texture and color there should be no variance. He is a dog with a peculiar temperament. Loyal
to those he knows but forbidding to the stranger. He is
a grand water dog both by reason of his liking for it and
the quality of his coat which is water shedding. He is
therefore used in some parts of the country quite extensively as a duck retriever but has not been found so practical for upland work as this coat, so good for water,
catches in briars, etc.

As the name implies, he was developed in Ireland
where there were two distinct strains prior to 1859, "The
South Country Water Spaniel" and "The North Country
Water Spaniel." The South Country of more distinctive
color and shape would seem to have been most largely
used for perpetuating the breed as we see it today. The
first special class for Irish Water Spaniels was offered in
1859.

DESCRIPTION AND STANDARD OF POINTS
(By Courtesy of The American Spaniel Club)

Head.—Is by no means long, with very little brow but moderately wide. It is covered with curls, rather long and more open
than those of the body, nearly to the eyes, but not so as to be
wigged like the poodle.

[173]

Face and Eyes.—Are very peculiar. Face very long and quite bare of curl, the hair being short and smooth, though not glossy; nose broad and nostrils well developed; teeth strong and level; eyes small and set almost flush, without eyebrows.

Topknot.—Is a characteristic of the true breed and is estimated accordingly. It should fall between and over the eyes in a peaked form.

Ears.—Are long, the leather extending when drawn forward a little beyond the nose, and the curls with which they are clothed two or three inches beyond. The whole of the ears is thickly covered with curls, which gradually lengthen towards the tips.

Chest and Shoulders.—There is nothing remarkable about these points, which must, nevertheless, be of sufficient dimensions and muscularity. The chest is small compared with most breeds of similar substances.

The Back and Quarters.—Also having no peculiarity, but the stifles are almost always straight, giving an appearance of legginess.

Legs and Feet.—The legs should be straight and the feet large and strong; the toes are somewhat open and covered with short, crisp curls. In all dogs of this breed the legs are thickly clothed with short curls, slightly pendant behind and at the sides, and some have them all around, hanging in ringlets for some time before the annual shedding. No feather like that of the setter should be shown. The front of the hindlegs below the hocks is always bare.

Tail.—Is very thick at the root, where it is clothed with very short hair. Beyond the root, however, the hair is perfectly short, so as to look as if the tail had been clipped, which it sometimes fraudulently is at shows, but the natural bareness of the tail is a true characteristic of the breed.

Coat.—Is composed of short curls of hair, not woolly, which betrays the poodle cross. A soft, flossy coat is objected to as indicative of an admixture with some of the land spaniels.

Color.—Must be deep, pure liver without white; but, as in other breeds, a white toe will occasionally appear with the best bred litter.

SUSSEX SPANIEL

WELSH SPRINGER SPANIEL

SPANIELS (IRISH WATER)

Symmetry of this dog is not very great.

	Points
Head	10
Face and eyes	10
Topknot	10
Ears	10
Chest and shoulders	7½
Back and quarters	7½
Legs and feet	10
Tail	10
Coat	10
Color	10
Symmetry	5
Total	100

SPANIELS (SUSSEX)

(Illustration facing page 174)

(By Courtesy of The American Spaniel Club)

The first and most important kennel of Sussex Spaniels belonged to Mr. Fuller of Brightling in England, and it was he who developed the rather peculiar color of golden tinge to what might be known as a liver colored coat. Mr. Phineas Bullock also did notable work on the Sussex.

This breed is inclined to give tongue on scent. The Sussex Spaniel has an extremely good nose, lacking the speed of the Springer and Cocker but a determined hunter and valuable for all forms of upland shooting. This breed was allotted its support in a class at the Crystal Palace Show in 1862. They have not been imported very heavily to this country due probably to the fact that they have not sufficient speed for the average sportsman. In this respect they somewhat resemble the Clumber; their whole conformation pointing towards a slow-moving dog, good for certain types of rough shooting in England and also for birds.

In disposition he is a very normal, attractive dog, not too hard to train and when properly taught an excellent retriever.

DESCRIPTION AND STANDARD OF POINTS

(By Courtesy of The American Spaniel Club)

Head.—The skull should be moderately long and also wide, with an indention in the middle and a full stop, brows fairly heavy; occiput full, but not pointed, the whole giving an appearance of heaviness without dullness.

Eyes.—Hazel color, fairly large, soft and languishing, not showing the haw overmuch.

Nose.—The muzzle should be about three inches long, square, and the lips somewhat pendulous. The nostrils well developed and liver color.

Ears.—Thick, fairly large and lobe shaped; set moderately low, but relatively not so low as in the black Field Spaniel; carried close to the head and furnished with soft, wavy hair.

Neck.—Is rather short, strong and slightly arched, but not carrying the head much above the level of the back. There should not be much throatiness about the skin, but well-marked frill in the coat.

Chest and Shoulders.—The chest is round, especially behind the shoulders, deep and wide giving a good girth. The shoulders should be oblique.

Back and Back Rib.—The back and loin is long and should be very muscular, both in width and depth; for this development the back ribs must be deep. The whole body is characterized as low, long and level.

Legs and Feet.—The arms and thighs must be bony as well as muscular, knees and hocks large and strong; pasterns very short and bony, feet large and round, and with short hair between the toes. The legs should be very short and strong, with great bone, and may show a slight bend in the forearm, and be moderately well feathered. The hindlegs should not apparently be shorter than the forelegs, or be too much bent at the hocks, so as to give a settery appearance, which is so objectionable. The hindlegs should be well feathered above the hocks, but should not have much hair below that point. The hocks should be short and wide apart. (The hock is the joint itself and cannot be short. What is meant is that from the hock to the ground should be short, or that the hind pasterns should be short.—Ed.)

Tail.—Should be docked from five to seven inches, set low, and not carried above the level of the back, thickly covered with moderately long feather.

Coat.—Body coat abundant, flat or slightly waved, with no tendency to curl, moderately well feathered on legs and stern, but clean below the hocks.

SPANIELS (SUSSEX)

Color.—Rich golden liver; this is a certain sign of the purity of the breed, dark liver or puce denoting unmistakably a recent cross with the black or other variety of Field Spaniel.

General Appearance.—Rather massive and muscular, but with free movements and nice tail action, denoting a cheerful and tractable disposition. Weight from 35 pounds to 45 pounds.

POSITIVE POINTS

Head	10
Eyes	5
Nose	5
Ears	10
Neck	5
Chest and shoulders	5
Back and back ribs	10
Legs and feet	10
Tail	5
Coat	5
Color	15
General appearance	15
Total	**100**

NEGATIVE POINTS

Light eyes	5
Narrow head	10
Weak muzzle	10
Curled ears or set on high	5
Curled coat	15
Carriage of stern	5
Topknot	10
White on chest	5
Color, too light or too dark	15
Legginess or light of bone	5
Shortness of body or flat sided	5
General appearance—sour or crouching	10
Total	**100**

SPANIELS (WELSH SPRINGER)

(Illustration facing page 175)

(By Courtesy of The Welsh Springer Spaniel Club, England)

There does not appear to be any authentic information as to the approximate date when the above Spaniel appeared; but if we examine old writings and old pictures and prints, we find that when our ancestors took up shooting over dogs they undoubtedly used a medium sized spaniel more like the Welsh Springer Spaniel of today than any other variety. It is strange to note that the color of these dogs of old was always red and white—the one and only color of the Welsh Springer. In this respect he differs from English Springers—Cockers and Field—as they may be most any color. The Welsh Springer is principally found in Wales and the West of England where he has been known for several hundred years and lately he is finding his way to Scotland and England while a large number have been exported from England to India, America, Australia and Siam. The reason for this is that as a breed it is a "tough" proposition, standing extremes of heat and cold better than most dogs. The Welshman's coat helps him. Naturally it is a flat even coat with a soft undercoat which prevents the skin from injury, thorns or water. By the way, he is an excellent water dog. A very keen hard working dog—no day is too long and no country too rough. If well trained, there is no better gun dog, and he can be used on any kind of game. We have stated above "if well trained"—we stress this point as the Welshman has one fault—and what dog or man if it comes to that is faultless? He has the best of noses and if not well trained is inclined to become a lone hunter and is then difficult to handle. Do not run away with the idea that he is a difficult dog to train— far from it—if a dog is taken young, say about 6 months and first of all taught obedience and retrieving, that dog will never forget his early lessons, because it is inherent with the breed to always do all they can to help you. It is the strong desire of the breed at all times and in all circumstances to be a faithful and willing worker for man. As a companion there is no more delightful dog, a true pal in every sense of the word—an excellent guard, yet always gentle and kind with children and young animals. A dog of very handy size,—he does not take up too much room in a motor car when this form of transport is used. He is stronger and bigger than the Cocker, but smaller than the English Springer. He is easy to keep and is very free from skin disease and most of the ills to which dogs seem prone. He can live in towns and be happy, but of course to have him at his best he should be used as a gun dog in the country.

DESCRIPTION AND STANDARD OF POINTS

(By Courtesy of The Welsh Springer Spaniel Club, England)

The "Welsh Spaniel" or "Springer" is also known and referred to in Wales as a "Starter." He is of very ancient and pure origin, and is a distinct variety which has been bred and preserved purely for working purposes.

Head—Skull.—Proportionate, of moderate length, slightly domed, clearly defined stop, well chiselled below the eyes.

Muzzle.—Medium length, straight, fairly square; the nostrils well developed and flesh colored or dark.

Jaw.—Strong, neither under nor overshot.

[182]

Eyes.—Hazel or dark, medium size, not prominent, nor sunken, nor showing haw.

Ears.—Set moderately low and hanging close to the cheeks, comparatively small and gradually narrowing towards the tip, covered with nice setter-like feathering.

A short chubby head is objectionable.

Neck and Shoulders—Neck.—Long and muscular, clean in throat, neatly set into long and sloping shoulders.

Forelegs.—Medium length, straight well boned, moderately feathered.

Body.—Not long; strong and muscular with deep brisket, well sprung ribs; length of body should be proportionate to length of leg, and very well balanced; with muscular loin slightly arched and well coupled up.

Quarters.—Strong and muscular, wide and fully developed with deep second thighs.

Hindlegs.—Hocks well let down; stifles moderately bent (neither twisted in nor out), moderately feathered.

Feet.—Round with thick pads.

Stern.—Well set on and low, never carried above the level of the back; lightly feathered and with lively action.

Coat.—Straight or flat and thick, of a nice silky texture, never wiry nor wavy. A curly coat is most objectionable.

Color.—Dark rich red and white.

General Appearance.—A symmetrical, compact, strong, merry, very active dog; not stilty, obviously built for endurance and activity.

Group II—SPORTING DOGS (HOUNDS)

AFGHAN HOUNDS
(Illustration facing page 190)

It was near Jebel Musa, or the Mountain of Moses, on that small peninsula called Sinai, between the Gulf of Suez and the Gulf of Akaba, that the breed now known as the Afghan Hound first became a recognizable type of dog. This spot, long held sacred by Hebrew and Christian alike—where Jehovah delivered to Moses the tables of the Ten Commandments—was a part of Ancient Egypt at the time when the Afghan's existence was first mentioned on a papyrus.

The document that thus forms the cornerstone of the history of the Afghan Hound has been attributed to the period, 3,000 to 4,000 B.C., and it mentions the dog so many times that there can be little doubt. According to Major H. Blackstone, an English authority on antiquities, who made the translation, the dog is referred to as "cynocephalus," which may be literally translated as "baboon" or freely translated as "monkey-faced hound." This is the meaning that Major Blackstone ascribes to it, for illustrations of the dog found on the tombs of the time offer convincing proof that even then the Afghan Hound's head was suggestive of the baboon.

The fact that the Afghan Hound was the subject of mention in a valuable document of the times is tantamount to saying that he was accepted among royalty, and that his value as a hunting dog of rare ability had been noted. His development must have progressed systematically under the desert Sheikhs, and although they have left us no stud books, there can be little doubt of the purity of his line for several thousand years. In the beginning it probably was a matter of selective breeding—of breeding that was as successful as its most modern, scientific counterpart.

The tombs on which the Afghan is portrayed are in the Valley of the Nile, so it must be inferred that in the beginning the hound was sent as a regal present to Memphis, or came in the entourage of a Sheikh. His first appearance at the palace must have occasioned some little stir; and there is no doubt that an Egyptian princess claimed him as her pet and applied to him the nickname, "monkey-face."

Considering the turbulent history of Egypt, and the nature of the Afghan Hound, it is not unusual that the archeologists could find no trace of the dog itself when they unearthed the evidence that he had existed in Egypt and that he came from Sinai. He is not a dog that would have prospered in urban surroundings; indeed, only the royal and the wealthy in a land such as Egypt would have been able to maintain him.

Just when the breed became established in the Hill country of the northern part of Afghanistan may remain a mystery for a long time. Likewise the question as to why no traces of the hound were found in Arabia or Persia,—across which it would have had to travel—may never be answered.

The modern history of the Afghan Hound dates from the World War. It was taken to England by returning British Army officers after the war, and since then it has become quite the rage across the Atlantic. Also, the British officers were responsible, in great measure, for the spread of the dog into India, Persia, and Arabia, where, today, it is found in increasing numbers. It is the dog

most favored for hunting the leopard, and in coursing gazelle and jack rabbits.

While the Egyptian origin of the breed is well founded,
there is little doubt that Afghanistan has made the greatest contributions to the development of the Afghan
Hound. Bred in mountainous country, and living throughout the ages at high elevations, where the winters are
especially severe, the Afghan Hound has defied any
change in its distinguishing characteristics. Its coat is of
silky, thick hair of very fine texture, that stands off the
body. The quarters, flanks, ribs, and fore quarters are
well covered. The pendulous ears and the four legs are
well feathered—the hair on the legs being quite full on
the sides and extending right down to the feet. It has a
topknot of long, silky hair.

While the tail is set low, the tail carriage is high. This
high tail carriage is emphasized in Afghanistan, for the
hounds hunt so much in thickets that it is only by watching the tails that the movement of the dogs can be detected. Another most distinguishing point in the Afghan
is the assembly of his hip bones. These are considerably
higher than in the ordinary dog, and set much wider
apart. These unique hip bones make it possible for him
to negotiate hilly country and uneven ground with ease,
and give him a motion like that of a monkey. Built in
this manner, he turns easily and gets tremendous power
into his leaps.

The Afghan hunts by sight, and while he is possessed
of great speed, it is doubtful if he is as fast, on the flat,
as some of the other hound varieties. However, the
Afghan knows no equal as a hurdle racer. Used for
countless centuries in a country where leaping over obstacles was even more essential than speed, he has developed this specialty to the ultimate degree. Another

heritage he brings to his new abodes in Europe and America is the ability to withstand any temperature—either hot or cold. Summers in Afghanistan are terrifically hot, and winters severely cold.

It was ten years ago that the Afghan Hound first made its appearance in the United States, but for some reason or other the breed did not catch popular fancy at that time. Now it is enjoying a rebirth of interest, with a number of kennels that formerly were outstanding in other breeds endeavoring to spread knowledge of it. Gradually it is becoming known as a splendid all-around dog; quite aside from any ability it may have in the hunting field.

DESCRIPTION AND STANDARD OF POINTS
(By Courtesy of The Afghan Hound Club, England)

Head.—Narrow, conforming to that of a greyhound but more powerful; skull oval, with prominent occiput; jaws long and punishing; mouth, level, not overshot nor undershot; ears long; eyes dark, little or no stop.

Neck.—Long, strong, arched, and running in a curve to shoulders, which should be long and sloping, and well laid back.

Body.—Strong powerful loin, and slightly arched, falling away towards stern; well ribbed and tucked up underloins; should be that of a hound and have ample length; the tail set not too high on body similar to greyhound, having a curve at the end, but on no account a bushy tail.

Legs.—Forelegs straight and strong, great length between elbow and ankle, elbows well tucked in; forefeet very large both in length and breadth, toes well arched and the feet covered with long thick hair, fine in texture; pasterns long and pads well down on ground.

Brisket.—Deep and not too narrow.

Hind Quarters.—Powerful, well muscled, great length between hip and hock, this is one of the main features of the hound; fair bend in stifle.

Hindfeet.—Broad but not so long as forefeet; toes arched; feet covered in long, thick hair.

Coat.—Hind quarters, flanks, ribs and fore quarters well covered with silky, thick hair, very fine in texture; ears and all four feet well feathered; head surmounted with topknot of long, silky hair.

General Appearance.—Strong, alert, and active; looking a combination of speed and power, with a graceful outline.

Height.—Dogs about 27 inches; bitches, 25 inches.

Weight.—About 60 pounds.

AFGHAN HOUND

BASSET HOUND

BASSET HOUNDS

(Illustration on opposite page)

(By Courtesy of The Basset Hound Club of America)

The Basset Hound, as the dog is called in the United States and in England, is an old, aristocratic breed. It is of ancient lineage, and has flourished for centuries upon the continent, chiefly in France and in Belgium, where it was raised by royalty, principally for moderately slow trailing of deer, hares, rabbits, and kindred game. Its traditional origin is in France, where it was called the basset, and its ancestry was the old French bloodhound and the St. Hubert hounds.

In the United States, the Basset Hound is used for hunting foxes, rabbits, and pheasants. Also he is trained, quickly, to be of great value in raccoon hunting, and for trailing, flushing, and securing wounded pheasants and other game birds. As most sportsmen can follow them easily while on the scent and be ready when the bird rises, Basset Hounds are unexcelled for trailing and flushing pheasants.

They are steady, accurate trailers, give plenty of tongue, and with their extremely short legs are particularly valuable in hunting in dense cover. With the exception of the pure bloodhound, no breed can lay claim to greater scenting ability.

Being bred for centuries as a strictly sporting dog— well disciplined for hunting either in packs or singly— the Basset is both intelligent and docile; and with a kindly disposition that makes him a loyal hunting pal. While at work, he will do his best to bring the game around to the waiting hunter. If trained and handled by his master only, the Basset is strictly a one-man dog. He cannot be coaxed away by any stranger, even if the latter has a gun. If kindly raised and trained, a Basset puppy will turn into the most loyal, enjoyable, and satisfactory hunting pal any man would want to own. He is easy to control, and as a rule very affectionate, if treated kindly by his master.

In appearance the Basset Hound is low, from 11 to 15 inches at the shoulder; of long body and heavy bone; weighing from 25 to 40 pounds. In America, the most popular Basset is the crooked or half-crooked front leg type. There is a straight leg type that is a little rangier, and somewhat faster as a rule. The front leg is broad. The foot likewise. The shoulders heavy and well muscled. The chest deep. The hindlegs are likewise heavy and well muscled, on the hip.

The head is long. The nose is long, also, and well developed clear to the muzzle. The flews are heavy. The dewlap is commonly pendant. In the English type, which has a more recent infusion of the original bloodhound, the eye is deep-set, with wrinkle above and haw beneath. The ears are long, soft, and pendant. In fact, they are so long that, sometimes, they may be tied in a knot above the head. The nose usually is black, well developed, and of great scenting power. French Bassets are of the same general lines as the English dog, except that they are of a smaller type, lighter weight, and are more agile.

In recent years, there were two types of smooth Basset Hounds in France, and two strains: the Le Contealx, and the Lane; named after the two largest breeders in France: Comte le Contealx, and Mons Lane of Francquevilli, near Boos. These hounds differ mostly in the head and eye. The Lane hound has a big, prominent eye like a beagle, and with a much broader skull. The Le Contealx hound has that down-faced look, giving it a sad expression; a brown eye, deeply sunken, showing a prominent haw; a domed head of considerable length, and narrow in comparison to the Lane hound, which is inclined to cheek bumps or apple headedness.

It is the Le Contealx type that is most favored in America. Lord Galway was the first to import hounds of this type into England. In 1866, the Comte de Tournow sent Lord Galway a pair of hounds that the latter called Basset and Belle. In 1867, Lord Galway bred a litter of puppies from the pair. In 1872, he sold them to the late Lord Onslow, the 4th Earl. Lord Onslow augmented his pack from the kennels of Comte Canteleu le Contealx; and about 1882, he sold them—some 14 or 15 pairs—to the late George Krehl, and the late Sir Everett Millais, the latter being the son of Sir John Millais. From these hounds, all the best Bassets in England and America are descended.

Until recent years, the French short-legged hound has never been popular in America. The late Sir Everett Millais, who was the first to introduce the dog into England, and also a bloodhound cross, wrote a description of the breed. So far as it goes, the description is excellent. But Sir Everett made no attempt to go into the history of the breed.

Buffon describes it, and named two varieties: the crooked, and the straight-legged types. But Millais made the mistake of saying that the latter were the *petit cheins courant,* or small running hound. The probability is that these dogs were descendants from the old breed of greffiers—dogs bred from the white St. Hubert hounds and the hounds of Italy—or else from the St. Hubert hounds direct.

These dogs were used on the liam. And it is easy to

understand that a dog, which held its nose low to the ground because of its short legs, would be preferred to one which had to make an effort to get his nose equally as low. Undoubtedly, the Basset is the dog most entitled to be considered a direct descendant of the dogs which the Abbots of St. Hubert had to contribute, annually, to the Kings' kennels, and which were used mainly for tracking on the liam.

It was in 1875, that Sir Everett introduced the Basset to English dog shows. But it was not until 1880, at the Wolverhampton show, that the breed really got its start. At that show, Sir Everett made a large entry, and the breed attracted great attention. The late George R. Krehl then took up the breed, and it became slightly popular on account of its "quaintness." But the difficulty of breeding good dogs, caused many, in England, to give them up; and, except at the larger shows, the Basset was relegated to the variety classes.

DESCRIPTION AND STANDARD OF POINTS

Head.—The head should be large, the skull narrow and of good length, the peak being very fully developed, a very characteristic point of the head, which should be free from any appearance of, or inclination to, cheek bumps. It is most perfect when it closest resembles the head of a bloodhound, with heavy flews and forehead wrinkled to the eyes. The expression when sitting or when still should be very sad, full of reposeful dignity. The whole of the head should be covered with loose skin, so loose in fact, that when the hound brings its nose to the ground the skin over the head and cheeks should fall forward and wrinkle perceptably.

Jaws.—The nose itself should be strong and free from snipiness, while the teeth of the upper and lower jaws should meet, a pig-jawed hound, or one that is underhung, being distinctly objectionable.

[194]

BASSET HOUNDS

Ears.—The ears are very long, and when drawn forward folding well over the nose. They are set on the head as low as is possible and hang loose in folds like drapery, the ends curling inward, in texture thin and velvety.

Eyes.—The eyes should be deeply sunken, showing a prominent haw, and in color they should be a deep brown.

Neck and Shoulder.—The neck should be powerful with heavy dewlaps set on sloping shoulders.

Forelegs.—The forelegs should be short, very powerful, very heavy in bone, close fitting to the chest with a crook'd knee and wrinkled ankle, ending in a massive paw. A hound must *not* be "out at *elbows*" which is a bad fault. *Feet.*—He must stand perfectly sound and true on his feet which should be thick and massive, and the weight of the forepart of the body should be borne equally by each toe of the fore feet so far as it is compatible with the crook of the legs. *Unsoundness in legs or feet should absolutely disqualify a hound from taking a prize.*

Chest and Body.—The chest should be deep and full. The body should be long and low and well ribbed up. Slackness of loin, flatsidedness and a roach or razor back are all bad faults.

Hocks.—A hound should not be straight on his hocks, nor should he measure more over his quarters than he does at his shoulder. Cowhocks, straight hocks, or weak hocks, are all bad faults.

Quarters.—The quarters should be full of muscle, which stands out so that when one looks at the dog from behind, it gives him a round, barrel-like effect, with quarters "round as an apple." He should be what is known as "a good dog to follow," and when trotting away from you, his hocks should bend well and he should move true all round.

Stern.—The stern is coarse underneath, and carried "gaily" in hound fashion.

Coat.—The coat should be similar to that of the fox-hound, not too fine and not too coarse, but yet of sufficient strength to be of use in bad weather. The skin loose and elastic.

Color.—No good hound is a bad color, so that any recognized fox-hound color should be acceptable to the judge's eye, and only in the very closest competition should the color of a hound have any weight with a judge's decision.

SPORTING DOGS (HOUNDS)

Points of Basset Hound (Smooth)

Head, skull, eyes, muzzle, flews	14
Ears	10
Neck, dewlap, chest and shoulders	18
Forelegs and feet	18
Back, loins, hocks and hind quarters	18
Stern	5
Coat and skin	5
Color and markings	5
Basset hound character and symmetry	7
Total	100

BEAGLES

(Illustration facing page 206)

(By Courtesy of The National Beagle Club of America)

The actual origin of the Beagle is lost amongst the dim mists of ancient days and no research can ever bring the true history to light. Several well-known beaglers who have devoted their lives to this sport have written their opinions on the origin of the breed and the following remarks are by Captain Otho Paget of Melton Mowbray, England, who was, perhaps, the Dean of all Beaglers in the last generation.

"According to Xenophon there were hounds that hunted by scent in his day and the Romans acquired many of the sports of ancient Greece. There were, however, in England, packs of hounds before the time of the Romans and it is on record that Pwyll, Prince of Wales, a contemporary of King Arthur, had a special breed of white hounds of great excellence. Wales, to this day is still celebrated for its hounds, generally of a light color. Admirers of shooting dogs, setters, spaniels and other breeds, have asserted that these animals were used in building up the hound. By exercise of a little thought it will seem that this must be wrong and that in fact it is the other way about. The hound was the original progenitor of all sporting dogs, and the two distinct breeds would be the "Gaze" or "Greyhound" that hunted by sight alone, and the hound, probably the bloodhound, that relied entirely on its nose. By the time of good Queen Bess, nearly every country gentleman in England kept a pack of hounds of some sort and hunted the animal of his choice. The fox was not at that time an honored beast of the chase. Hounds in those days seem to have been divided into two classes, the large and the small. The large sort were called "Buck Hounds" and hunted the deer, and the smaller variety were called "Beagles" from the French "Begle" and were hunted on hare.

Coming down to the middle of the eighteenth century we find fox hunting becoming popular with the younger generations of men who wanted something quicker and more exhilarating than watching hounds puzzling out the intricate windings of a hare. The fox hound was undoubtedly evolved from a mixture of buck hound and Beagle. By this time the vagaries of breeders had produced two distinct types of hare-hunting hounds, one of which was called the Southern hound and the other the North Country Beagle. The former was slow and ponderous, with long ears and deep voice, whilst the other was the exact opposite. According to a writer of that day the "North Country Beagle" is nimble and vigorous and does his business as furiously as Jehu himself can wish him.

I think we may accept it as a fact that by the middle of the eighteenth century there were Beagles varying in size from 22″ to 5″ and in spite of this difference all descended from the same stock.

In the middle of the nineteenth century Parson Honeywood got together a very good pack and showed some excellent sport in Essex. His pack dates as the beginning of the modern Beagle and nearly every well-known pack of subsequent date owed its origin to that blood. The colored engraving "THE MERRY BEAGLERS" is as familiar to American sportsmen as it is to anyone in England and will preserve for all time the name of the Rev. Philip Honeywood.

BEAGLES

We can accept it as true that the Beagle is one of the oldest breeds in history and with the bloodhound and perhaps the otter hound is closest to the original breed of hounds.

Previous to about 1870 in the United States, the little hunting hounds of the Southern States, then called Beagles, were more of the type of straight-legged Bassets or Dachshunde with weaker heads than the Bassets and were mostly white with a few dark markings. They were said to be snappy, tireless hunters, full of vim and quick at a turn, but not handsome in outline. The importations of the late General Rowett of Carlinsville, Illinois in the sixties marks the turning point in the history of the American strain or strains of Beagles and brought to this country an acquisition of canine beauty little thought of by those who hitherto had hunted with Beagles. From what packs in England General Rowett obtained his hounds is not known.

About 1880 Mr. Arnold of Providence, R. I., imported a pack from the Royal Rock Beagles in the North of England, and this also has had a good deal of influence on the development of American Beagles.

In 1896 Mr. James L. Kernochan imported a pack from England and from then on a great many high class hounds have been brought over every year.

Among the first sportsmen of note in the Beagle world whose importations have helped to create the modern Beagle in America, may be mentioned, Mr. Harry Peters of Islip, L. I., Mr. George Post of Bernardsville, N. J., Mr. James W. Appleton of Ipswich, Mass., Mr. Eugene Reynal of Millbrook, N. Y., Mr. H. C. Phipps of Westbury, L. I., and many others.

In 1888 The National Beagle Club was formed and held the first field trial. From that time on Field Trial

Clubs have sprung up very rapidly all over the United States, until at present there are some forty Clubs licensed by the American Kennel Club to conduct field trials carrying championship points and as many more Clubs and Associations sanctioned by the Kennel Club to hold informal trials. At all these Field Trials packs are run in single classes for hounds 13 to 15 inches in height, and classes for those under 13 inches and at the National Trials the pack classes are an important feature. There are single classes for young hounds called "Derbies" and all age classes for large and small dogs and bitches.

At the National, there are in addition to these single classes, four pack classes divided as follows:

A class for 13″ 2 couple packs;
A class for 15″ 2 couple packs;
A class for 4 couple packs; and
A class for 8 couple packs.

These packs, of course, cannot be run against each other at the same time as are the hounds in the single classes. Each pack is hunted separately and scored by the Judges.

All the Dog Shows throughout the United States have classes for Beagles, and the entries are generally very large.

In addition to the regular All Breed American Kennel Club shows, almost all the Field Trial Clubs conduct Specialty Shows in connection with their fields trials and in addition to this again, there are two or three Hound Shows each year, limited to the various breeds of hounds, the most important ones being the Bryn Mawr Hound Show in September and the Riding Club Hound Show in New York City in February.

Those who are interested in hunting Beagles as a pack, generally enjoy hunting the larger hares, rather than cot-

ton tail rabbits. Hares do not go to ground and spoil a
hunt, and they give much longer, straighter and faster
runs. Kansas Jack rabbits have, therefore, been brought
to many parts of the East and have bred extensively in
each community in which they have been placed. They
are only fairly satisfactory, however, for two reasons,—
in the first place they have a tendency to lie very close
and not get up until the pack is all around them. This
means either a sudden "chop" or a wild sight chase at the
start, which is very demoralizing to the pack. The other,
and more serious characteristic, is their tendency to run
all roads and paths. They will find the nearest macadam
road and run it for miles, dodging around motor cars
with the greatest indifference. This, of course, is disastrous for good sport.

Several experiments have been made in importing English hares but they have not been very successful. It is
probably due to the fact that the climate and feed in this
part of the world do not suit them. Hares have been
imported from Germany, however, with great success.
Duchess County in New York and Somerset County in
New Jersey are now well stocked with these. They show
splendid sport and thrive in this country.

The white hare, or snow-shoe rabbit, is found in
Northern swamps and provides excellent sport for a pack
but these hares will not do well when imported to other
communities and disappear immediately.

There are thousands of men all over the United States
who keep a few Beagles and hunt them individually. They
take great pride in their hounds and show them or run
them in the Field Trials frequently. The Beagle is today
one of the most popular of sporting dogs in the United
States. In addition to the great number of hounds kept
for individual hunting there are today about twenty packs

of Beagles of twelve couples or more in the United States recorded with the National Beagle Club. They are all hunted in the legitimate manner with a regular hunt staff, in hunt liveries, with their own distinctive colored collar, etc.

In conclusion, a few remarks as to the modern standard for type may be of interest. The limit of height of a Beagle in the United States is 15 inches and in England 16 inches. Hounds above this height cannot be entered in Field Trials or Shows. The head should be strong and well proportioned, with a fairly long, clean neck. Sloping shoulders are very important for speed and endurance. The body should be close-coupled and well ribbed up. The front legs should be very straight with as much bone as possible and small, round cat feet. The quarters should be strong and powerful and the hocks set low to the ground. The stern should be set moderately high with a good brush, but a proud or curly stern is most undesirable. Any true hound color is suitable.

DESCRIPTION AND STANDARD OF POINTS

(As Adopted by The National Beagle Club of America and Approved by the American Kennel Club, February 13, 1935)

Head.—The skull should be fairly long, slightly domed at occiput, with cranium broad and full.

Ears.—Ears set on moderately low, long, reaching when drawn out nearly, if not quite, to the end of the nose; fine in texture, fairly broad—with almost entire absence of erectile power—setting close to the head, with the forward edge slightly inturning to the cheek—rounded at tip.

Eyes.—Eyes large, set well apart—soft and houndlike—expression gentle and pleading; of a brown or hazel color.

Muzzle.—Muzzle of medium length—straight and square cut —the stop moderately defined.

[202]

BEAGLES

Jaws.—Level. Lips free from flews; nostrils large and open.

Defects.—A very flat skull, narrow across the top; excess of dome, eyes small, sharp and terrier like, or prominent and protuding; muzzle long, snipy or cut away decidedly below the eyes, or very short. Roman nosed, or upturned, giving a dish-face expression. Ears short, set on high or with a tendency to rise above the point of origin.

Body—Neck and Throat.—Neck rising free and light from the shoulders, strong in substance yet not loaded, of medium length. The throat clean and free from folds of skin; a slight wrinkle below the angle of the jaw, however, may be allowable.

Defects.—A thick, short, cloddy neck carried on a line with the top of the shoulders. Throat showing dewlap and folds of skin to a degree termed "throatiness."

Shoulders and Chest.—Shoulders sloping—clean, muscular, not heavy or loaded—conveying the idea of freedom of action with activity and strength. Chest deep and broad, but not broad enough to interfere with the free play of the shoulders.

Defects.—Straight, upright shoulders. Chest disproportionately wide or with lack of depth.

Back, Loin and Ribs.—Back short, muscular and strong. Loin broad and slightly arched, and the ribs well sprung, giving abundance of lung room.

Defects.—Very long or swayed or roached back. Flat, narrow loin. Flat ribs.

Forelegs and Feet—Forelegs.—Straight, with plenty of bone in proportion to size of the hound. Pasterns short and straight.

Feet.—Close, round and firm. Pad full and hard.

Defects.—Out at elbows. Knees knuckled over forward, or bent backward. Forelegs crooked or Dachshundlike. Feet long, open or spreading.

Hips, Thighs, Hindlegs and Feet—Hips and Thighs.—Strong and well muscled, giving abundance of propelling power. Stifles strong and well let down. Hocks firm, symmetrical and moderately bent. Feet close and firm.

Defects.—Cowhocks, or straight hocks. Lack of muscle and propelling power. Open feet.

SPORTING DOGS (HOUNDS)

Tail.—Set moderately high; carried gaily, but not turned forward over the back; with slight curve; short as compared with size of the hound; with brush.

Defects.—A long tail. Teapot curve or inclined forward from the root. Rat tail with absence of brush.

Coat.—A close, hard, hound coat of medium length.

Defects.—A short, thin coat, or of a soft quality.

Height.—Height not to exceed 15 inches, measured across the shoulders at the highest point, the hound standing in a natural position with his feet well under him.

Color.—Any true hound color.

General Appearance.—A miniature fox-hound, solid and big for his inches, with the wear-and-tear look of the hound that can last in the chase and follow his quarry to the death.

		Points
Skull	5	
Ears	10	
Eyes	5	
Muzzle	5	
Head		25
Neck	5	
Chest and shoulders	15	
Back, loin and ribs	15	
Body		35
Forelegs	10	
Hips, thighs and hindlegs	10	
Feet	10	
Running Gear		30
Coat	5	
Stern	5	
		10
Total	100	

BEAGLES

Packs of Beagles

Score of Points for Judging

Hounds.—General levelness of pack....	40%
Individual merit of hounds	30%
	—— 70%
Manners	20%
Appointments	10%
	——
Total	100%

Levelness of Pack.—The first thing in a pack to be considered is that they present a unified appearance. The hounds must be as near of the same height, weight, conformation and color as possible.

Individual Merit of the Hounds.—Is the individual bench show quality of the hounds. A very level and sporty pack can be gotten together and not a single hound be a good Beagle. This is to be avoided.

Manners.—The hounds must all work gaily and cheerfully, with flags up—obeying all commands cheerfully. They should be broken to heel up, kennel up, follow promptly and stand. Cringing, sulking, lying down to be avoided. Also a pack must not work as though in terror of master and whips. In Beagle packs it is recommended that the whip be used as little as possible.

Appointments.—Master and whips should be dressed alike, the master or huntsman to carry horn—the whips and master to carry light thong whips. One whip should carry extra couplings on shoulder strap.

RECOMMENDATIONS FOR SHOW LIVERY

Black velvet cap, white stock, green coat, white breeches or knickerbockers, green or black stockings, white spats, black or dark brown shoes. Vest and gloves optional.

Ladies should turn out exactly the same except for a white skirt instead of white breeches.

BEAGLE

BLOODHOUND

BLOODHOUNDS
(Illustration on opposite page)

When Claudius Aelianus, or "Aelian," wrote his famous "Historia Animalium" in the 3rd Century A.D. he mentioned in especially glowing terms a breed of hound that was unrivalled for its scenting powers and which was possessed of such great determination that it would not leave the trail until the quarry was located. Thus the early Italian scholar gives us a picture of the dog that is known today as the Bloodhound, a breed that has improved considerably in appearance but which still retains its peculiarly intensified ability to follow the faintest scent.

There has been little evidence to prove how far back the origin of the Bloodhound extends, but it is believed by many authorities that it was known throughout the Mediterranean countries long before the Christian Era. It is called the modern representative of the oldest race of hounds that hunt by scent, indicating, of course, that selective breeding over many centuries has made it outwardly changed from the breed the ancients extolled. Yet, its characteristics are so distinctive that cynologists have traced it throughout dog history.

The Bloodhound made its appearance in Europe long before the Crusades, the first specimens being brought from Constantinople. There were two strains, black and white. The blacks were the famed St. Huberts of the 8th Century, while the whites later became known as the Southern hounds. It was from the black stock that importations were made to England. Both varieties have played big parts in the development of other hounds and hound-type dogs.

In the 12th Century, when even Bishops rode to hounds, dignitaries of the Church were among the foremost in fostering the development of the Bloodhound. A number of high ecclesiastics maintained packs, and the kennel was an important part of every monastery. To them goes a great deal of the credit for keeping clean the strain. In fact, so much care was taken in the breeding of this hound that it came to be called the "blooded hound," meaning aristocratic.

Several centuries later that noted English physician and dog lover, Dr. Johannes Caius, gives a different explanation of the name, but his description of the breed is interesting. It follows:

". . . The larger class remain to be mentioned; these too have drooping lips and ears, and it is well known that they follow their prey not only while alive but also after death when they have caught the scent of blood. For whether the beasts are wounded alive and slip out of the hunter's hands, or are taken dead out of the warren (but with a profusion of blood in either case), these hounds perceive it at once by smell and follow the trail. For that reason they are properly called Sanguinarii.

"Frequently, however, an animal is stolen, and owing to the cleverness of the thieves there is no effusion of blood; but even so they are clever enough to follow dry human footsteps for a huge distance, and can pick a man out of a crowd however large, pressing on through the densest thickets, and they will still go on even though they have to swim across a river. When they arrive at the opposite bank, by a circular movement, they find out which way a man has gone, even if at first they do not hit on the track of the thief. Thus they supplement good luck by artifice and deserve what Aelian says of them in his 'Historia Animalium'. . ."

Although the Bloodhound reached approximately its modern form in England, the breed has perhaps reached its greatest development in the United States, as far as usefulness is concerned. The breed has been known in America for at least a century. "Abolitionists" once drew touching pictures of poor fugitive slaves pursued by the Bloodhounds, but it is doubted if many of the breed— then fairly numerous in the South—were so employed. Mongrels were frequently called "bloodhounds" and no doubt some of these did harass the slaves.

The pure-bred Bloodhound is one of the most docile of all breeds. His trailing is more for his own sport than for anything else. Unlike police-trained dogs, he does not attack the man he is trailing. The Bloodhound's task ends once he has followed the trail to its termination. But so accurate is the Bloodhound in following a trail that he is the only dog whose evidence is accepted in a court of law.

Some of the great Bloodhounds of the United States have brought about more convictions for police departments than the best human detectives. One dog was credited with more than 600 actual convictions. The famous dog, Nick Carter, picked up a trail that was 105 hours old, and followed it to a subsequent conviction. The breed's stamina and determination are apparent in the great distances it will travel. Several specimens have followed human quarry for more than 50 miles, and one led the detectives 138 miles—all with success.

Bloodhounds have been exhibited in the United States almost from the beginning of organized dog shows in America, but, until very recent years, interest in the show-type dog has been falling off. Now the breeders of the

Bloodhound are organizing a specialty club, and much wider popularity for this ancient breed should follow.

DESCRIPTION AND STANDARD OF POINTS
(By Courtesy of the Association of Bloodhound Breeders, England)

General Character.—The Bloodhound possesses, in a most marked degree, every point and characteristic of those dogs which hunt together by scent (Sagaces). He is very powerful, and stands over more ground than is usual with hounds of other breeds. The skin is thin to the touch and extremely loose, this being more especially noticeable about the head and neck, where it hangs in deep folds.

Height.—The mean average height of adult dogs is 26 inches, and of adult bitches 24 inches. Dogs usually vary from 25 inches to 27 inches, and bitches from 23 inches to 25 inches; but, in either case, the greater height is to be preferred, provided that character and quality are also combined.

Weight.—The mean average weight of adult dogs, in fair condition, is 90 pounds, and of adult bitches 80 pounds. Dogs attain the weight of 110 pounds, bitches 100 pounds. The greater weights are to be preferred, provided (as in the case of height) that quality and proportion are also combined.

Expression.—The expression is noble and dignified, and characterized by solemnity, wisdom, and power.

Temperament.—In temperament he is extremely affectionate, neither quarrelsome with companions nor with other dogs. His nature is somewhat shy, and equally sensitive to kindness or correction by his master.

Head.—The head is narrow in proportion to its length, and long in proportion to the body, tapering but slightly from the temples to the end of the muzzle, thus (when viewed from above and in front) having the appearance of being flattened at the sides and of being nearly equal in width throughout its entire length. In profile the upper outline of the skull is nearly in the same plane as that of the foreface. The length from end of nose to stop (midway between the eyes) should be not less than that

[210]

from stop to back of occipital protuberance (peak). The entire length of head from the posterior part of the occipital protuberance to the end of the muzzle should be 12 inches, or more, in dogs, and 11 inches, or more, in bitches.

Skull.—The skull is long and narrow, with the occipital peak very pronounced. The brows are not prominent, although, owing to the deep-set eyes, they may have that appearance.

Foreface.—The foreface is long, deep, and of even width throughout, with square outline when seen in profile.

Eyes.—The eyes are deeply sunk in the orbits, the lids assuming a lozenge or diamond shape, in consequence of the lower lids being dragged down and everted by the heavy flews. The eyes correspond with the general tone of color of the animal, varying from deep hazel to yellow. The hazel color is, however, to be preferred, although very seldom seen in red-and-tan hounds.

Ears.—The ears are thin and soft to the touch, extremely long, set very low, and fall in graceful folds, the lower parts curling inwards and backwards.

Wrinkle.—The head is furnished with an amount of loose skin, which in nearly every position appears superabundant, but more particularly so when the head is carried low; the skin then falls into loose, pendulous ridges and folds, especially over the forehead and sides of the face.

Nostrils.—The nostrils are large and open.

Lips, Flews, and Dewlap.—In front the lips fall squarely, making a right angle with the upper line of the foreface; whilst behind they form deep, hanging flews, and, being continued into the pendent folds of loose skin about the neck, constitute the dewlap, which is very pronounced. These characters are found, though in a less degree, in the bitch.

Neck, Shoulders and Chest.—The neck is long, the shoulders muscular and well sloped backwards; the ribs are well sprung; and the chest well let down between the forelegs, forming a deep keel.

Legs and Feet.—The forelegs are straight and large in bone, with elbows squarely set; the feet strong and well knuckled up; the thighs and second thighs (gaskins) are very muscular; the hocks well bent and let down and squarely set.

Back and Loin.—The back and loins are strong, the latter deep and slightly arched.

Stern.—The stern is long and tapering, and set on rather high, with a moderate amount of hair underneath.

Gait.—The gait is elastic, swinging and free, the stern being carried high, but not too much curled over the back.

Color.—The colors are black-and-tan, red-and-tan, and tawny; the darker colors being sometimes interspersed with lighter or badger-colored hair, and sometimes flecked with white. A small amount of white is permissible on chest, feet, and tip of stern.

BORZOI

(Formerly Russian Wolfhounds)

For description and Standard of Points see page 283.

DACHSHUNDE

(Illustrations facing pages 222 and 223)

(By Courtesy of The Dachshund Club of America, Inc.)

The name Dachshund (*dachs*-badger, *hund*-dog) at once reveals and conceals the origin of the breed. In Mediaeval European books on hunting, dogs similar only in possessing the tracking ability of hounds and the proportions and temperament of terriers, because they were used to follow badger to earth, were called badger-dogs or *dachs-hunde*. A parallel is suggested by the current use of the name "rabbit dog" in various parts of this country for dogs of informal breeding, used to hunt rabbits.

Illustrations dating from the fifteenth, sixteenth, and seventeenth centuries show badgers hunted by dogs with elongated bodies, short legs, and hound-type ears,—some with the bent front legs of the basset, some with the heads of terriers, and some with indications of rough and long coats. It is well to consider that these illustrations were made before the days of photography, that artists capable of depicting dogs with anatomical fidelity have always been rare, and that wood cuts do not lend themselves to fine reproductions of coat distinctions. At best, the pictures and descriptive words can be interpreted with certainty, only as defining the functions of the dogs used on badger.

Whether the wirehaired and longhaired coats were purposely developed after the general characteristics of the smooth Dachshund became fixed: the wirehaired during the early part of the nineteenth century by out-cross-

[215]

ing with terrier types for a wire coat protective against brush and bramble, and the longhaired still earlier by out-crossing with spaniel types for a long coat protective against cold water, (and diligently breeding out any re-sulting "foreign" characteristics except the desired coats), —or whether these coats survive from a still earlier period before coat separation was accomplished in the original fixation of Dachshund breed characteristics,—is a subject of controversy obscured by ambiguous termi-nology, and evidence of inter-breeding.

The evidence neither traces the process of combination and fixation of early characteristics, nor establishes the date prior to the beginning of preserved breeding records, at which the transition was completed, and the name Dachshund became the designation of a pure breed with three coat-variations.

The badger was a stout adversary. Strength and stamina, as well as keenness and courage above and be-low ground, were required of the badger dog. Weights of 30 and 35 pounds were not uncommon, and such a Dachshund was also serviceable against wild boar. With this start, the breed has been adapted to the hunting of other game. A smaller-sized Dachshund proved effective against foxes, and for tracking wounded deer; a still smaller, for stoat and hare. By the beginning of the twentieth century, for bolting rabbits, miniatures had been produced having adult weights down to four and five pounds, with chest circumferences less than twelve inches.

Before the German Dachshund or *Teckel* Club was founded in 1888, "racial characteristics" or standards for the breed had been set up in 1879; and German registra-tion of Dachshunde was included (not always with com-plete generation data or systematic coat notations) in a general all-breed stud book, the *Deutsches Hunde-Stamm-buch,* whose first volume, in 1840, recorded 54 Dachshunde and the names of several subsequently prominent breeders, and whose publication continued until officially terminated in 1935. The *Gebrauchsteckel-Klubs* or hunting Dachshund association kept separate stud books, in which were recorded only dogs of demonstrated hunting accomplishment, with scant attention to coat or conformation. From early volumes of the *Techelklub* stud book, first published in 1890, despite meagre correlation with older records, pedigrees have been extended back as far as 1860 and 1859. Stud books maintained by clubs devoted to wirehairs, longhairs, and miniatures have waxed and waned. Not until 1915 did the coat-identifying initials "K" for *Kurzhaar* or smooth, "R" for *Rauhhaar* or wirehair, and "L" for *Langhaar* or longhair, become integral components of the *Teckelklub* registration numbers, and later "Z" was added to distinguish *Zwergh* and *Kaninchenteckel* or miniatures.

The management of the breed, as well as the stud books, has been divided. The *Teckelklub* managed the bench shows, while the *Gebrauchsteckel-Klubs* conducted organized hunting activities. Of the ability-tests organized by the bench-show club as alternatives to the hunting association's natural hunting field trials *(Jagdgebrauch),* the artificial-burrow "dig" test *(Schliefen)* was by law abolished in 1933, and the artificially-laid-scent "drag" test *(Schweiss-Suchen)* has lost favor, since training for this test impairs capacity for real hunting, and *vice versa.* In 1935, the federalized consolidation of all German Dachshund clubs as the *Fachschaft Dachshunde im Reichsverband für das Deutsche Hundewesen (FD-RDH)* has unified the breed stud books, and coordinated the conduct of bench shows with natural hunting field trials.

Thus the breed in Germany encompasses the remarkable diversification of field and show representation in a size-range from 5 to 35 pounds, and in three coat-types. The wires, longs, and miniatures reflect their functional development by not having as long a record of accomplishment on the bench as the smooths, with the result that more data are preserved and available on the history and characteristics of smooth bloodlines and strains, as well as more definite fixation. In the German Standard four weight divisions are recognized and at the larger German dog shows, classes are now offered in all three coats, in four weight divisions:

Weight Division	Sex	Kilo-grams	Pounds Avoirdupois	
Heavy weight	dogs	7	15.4	minimum
	bitches	6.5	14.3	
Light weight	dogs	7	15.4	maximum
	bitches	6.5	14.3	
Zwerg * (dwarf)	dogs	4	8.8	maximum
	bitches	3.5	7.7	

Miniature

Zwerg * (dwarf)
(with maximum chest circumference 35 centimeters—13.8 in.)

Kaninchen * (rabbit) dogs 3.5 7.7 maximum
                      bitches 3.5 7.7
(with maximum chest circumference 30 centimeters—11.8 in.)
* Both measured at a minimum age of twelve months. These data must be certified, to register *Zwerg-* or *Kaninchen-teckel* in Germany.

Prior to 1912, the present "heavy weight" class was called "medium," and there was a heavy weight class over 10 kilograms (22 pounds) for dogs and bitches, but this class has disappeared from German standards and premium lists, suggesting perhaps that the pursuit of the badger is no longer the principal purpose of the breed.

Importation of Dachshunde into this country antedates the earliest American dog shows or stud books. Our dogs have found little employment in organized hunting, as we lack the badger and wild boar, and do not hunt deer with dogs, nor foxes with pick-and-shovel. The true character and conformation of the breed has been maintained by constant importation of German hunting strains. Now that natural hunting field trials suitable to American conditions have come to the fore in Germany, rules have been formulated and Dachshund field trials instituted, carrying American Kennel Club championship point rating, to encourage hunting capacity here, as well as exemplary conformation.

The advance of the breed in this country has not been without reverses. Fostered since 1895 by The Dachshund Club of America, it had by 1913 and 1914 gained a place among the ten most numerous breeds at the Westminster Kennel Club shows,—to fall in the post-war years to a mere dozen and temporarily translate its name to "badger-dog." Since 1930, when breeding stock had been replenished, the gain has been spectacular,—reaching eleventh position in 1934 American Kennel Club registrations, sixth position in 1934 dog show entries in the United States, and leading the breeds at the two largest shows of 1935. During 1934 separate championship ratings were established for wirehaired and longhaired Dachshunde, and classes set up for miniatures, simplified to a nine-pound maximum, as both sexes are advantageously combined when classes are small.

Specialized characteristics of the breed for its purposes include a long head and well-developed nose; properly angulated shoulder, pelvis, and leg bones; close elbows, and free straight gait of fore and hindlegs; large chest for ample lung and heart room; supple and elastic skin for free action in restricted quarters under ground; a remarkably long, powerful jaw with well-fitted teeth; a long, strong neck capable as a fencer's wrist; powerful legs and sound feet for digging, a well-muscled back for sustained effort; and above all, that fine high courage which enables it to measure up to every demand of attack or defense without being quarrelsome or undesirably aggressive.

The medium-sized smooth-haired Dachshund, which predominates in this country, is small enough to live in house or apartment, yet large enough for street, suburb, or country. Its short legs insure maximum exercise per mile. Its odorless, sleek, dark, short, coat leaves no hair on clothes or furniture; requires no plucking, trimming, brushing, combing, oiling, and no bathing except to remove accidental dirt. Outdoors the Dachshund is hardy, vigorous, and tireless; indoors he is affectionate and responsive, companionable in restful mood, hilarious in play, alert in announcing strangers. He is capable of learning much.

The American Standard, adapted literally from the German standard, may be too detailed for amateur or novice. The summary fulfils all but professional requirements.

SUMMARY OF DACHSHUND STANDARD

General Appearance. — Short-legged, long-bodied, low-to-ground; sturdy, well-muscled, neither clumsy nor slim, with audacious carriage and intelligent expression; conformation pre-eminently fitted for following game into burrows.

Head.—Long, uniformly-tapered, clean-cut; teeth well fitted, with scissor bite; eyes medium oval; ears broad, long, rounded, set on high and well back; neck long, muscular.

Fore Quarters.—Muscular, compact. Chest deep, long, full and oval; breastbone prominent. Broad, long shoulder, and oblique humerus forming right angle; heavy, set close; forearm short, inclined slightly in. Foreleg straight and vertical in profile, covering deepest point of chest. Feet broad, firm, compact, turned slightly out.

Hind Quarters.—Well-muscled and rounded. Pelvis, femur and tibia oblique, forming right angles; tarsus inclined forward. Hip should be level with shoulder, back strong, neither sagged nor more than very slightly arched. Tail strong, tapered, well-covered with hair, not carried gaily.

Varieties.—Three coat types: *Smooth* or Shorthaired, short and dense, shining, glossy. *Wirehaired,* like German Spiky-Haired Pointer, hard, with good undercoat. *Longhaired,* like Irish Setter. *Miniature,* symmetrical rather slender body conformation below maximum limits of 11.8 and 13.8 inches chest girth, 7.7 and 8.8 pounds weight at minimum age of 12 months.

Color.—Solid red (tan) of various shades, and black with tan points, should have black noses and nails, and narrow black line edging lips and eyelids; chocolate with tan points permits brown nose. Eyes of all, lustrous, the darker the better.

Faults.—Over- or under-shot, knuckling over, loose shoulders; high on legs, clumsy gait, long, splayed or twisted feet, sagged or roached back, high croup, small, narrow or short chest, faulty angulation of fore or hind quarters, weak loins, narrow hind quarters, bowed legs, cowhocks; weak or dish-faced muzzle, dewlaps, uneven or scanty coat.

DESCRIPTION AND STANDARD OF POINTS

Translated from the Dachshund Standard of the *Fachschaft Dachshunde im Reichsverband für das Deutsche Hundewesen*—a consolidation of all the Dachshund Clubs in Germany.

(Adopted by The Dachshund Club of America, Inc., and approved by the Board of Directors of The American Kennel Club, July 9, 1935)

GENERAL FEATURES

General Appearance.—Low to ground, short-legged, long-bodied, but with compact figure and robust muscular development; with bold and confident carriage of the head and intelligent facial expression. In spite of his shortness of leg, in comparison with his length of trunk, he should appear neither crippled, awkward, cramped in his capacity for movement, nor slim and weasel-like.

Qualities.—He should be clever, lively, and courageous to the point of rashness, persevering in his work both above and below ground; with all the senses well developed. His build and disposition qualify him especially for hunting game below ground. Added to this, his hunting spirit, good nose, loud tongue, and small size, render him especially suited for beating the bush. His figure and his fine nose give him an especial advantage over most other breeds of sporting dogs for trailing.

Conformation of Body—Head.—Viewed from above or from the side, it should taper uniformly to the tip of the nose, and should be clean cut. The skull is only slightly arched, and should slope gradually without stop (the less stop the more typical) into the finely-formed slightly-arched muzzle (ram's nose). The bridge bones over the eyes should be strongly prominent. The nasal cartilage and tip of the nose are long and narrow; lips tightly stretched, well covering the lower jaw, but neither deep nor pointed; corner of the mouth not very marked. Nostrils well open. Jaws opening wide and hinged well back of the eyes, with strongly developed bones and teeth.

Teeth: Powerful canine teeth should fit closely together, and the outer side of the lower incisors should tightly touch the inner side of the upper. (Scissors bite.)

Eyes: Medium size, oval, situated at the sides, with a clear, energetic, though pleasant expression; not piercing. Color, lustrous dark reddish-brown to brownish-black for all coats and colors. Wall (fish or pearl) eyes in the case of grey or dapple-colored dogs are not a very bad fault, but are also not desirable.

Ears: Should be set near the top of the head, and not too far forward, long but not too long, beautifully rounded, not narrow, pointed, or folded. Their carriage should be animated, and the forward edge should just touch the cheek.

Neck: Fairly long, muscular, clean-cut, not showing any dewlap on the throat, slightly arched in the nape, extending in a graceful line into the shoulders, carried proudly but not stiffly.

Front.—To endure the arduous exertion underground, the front must be correspondingly muscular, compact, deep, long and broad. Fore quarters in detail:

DACHSHUND (*Smooth*)

DACHSHUND (*Longhaired*)

DACHSHUND (*Wirehaired*)

DACHSHUNDE

(a) Shoulder Blade: Long, broad, obliquely and firmly placed upon the fully-developed thorax, furnished with hard and plastic muscles.

(b) Upper Arm: Of the same length as the shoulder blade, and at right angles to the latter, strong of bone and hard of muscle, lying close to the ribs, capable of free movement.

(c) Forearm: This is short in comparison to other breeds, slightly turned inwards; supplied with hard but plastic muscles on the front and outside, with tightly-stretched tendons on the inside and at the back.

(d) Joint between Forearm and Foot (wrists): These are closer together than the shoulder joints, so that the front does not appear absolutely straight.

(e) Paws: Full, broad in front, and a trifle inclined outwards; compact, with well-arched toes and tough pads.

(f) Toes: There are five of these, though only four are in use. They should be close together, with a pronounced arch; provided on top with strong nails, and underneath with tough toe-pads.

Trunk.—The whole trunk should in general be long and fully muscled. The back, with sloping shoulders, and short rigid pelvis, should lie in the straightest possible line between the withers and the very slightly arched loins, these latter being short, rigid, and broad.

(a) Chest: The breast bone should be strong, and so prominent in front that on either side a depression (dimple) appears. When viewed from the front, the thorax should appear oval, and should extend downward to the mid-point of the forearm. The enclosing structure of ribs should appear full and oval, and when viewed from above or from the side, full-volumed, so as to allow by its ample capacity, complete development of heart and lungs. Well ribbed up, and gradually merging into the line of the abdomen. If the length is correct, and also the anatomy of the shoulder and upper arm, the front leg when viewed in profile should cover the lowest point of the breast line.

(b) Abdomen: Slightly drawn up.

Hind Quarters.—The hind quarters viewed from behind should be of completely equal width.

(a) Croup. Long, round, full, robustly muscled, but plastic, only slightly sinking toward the tail.

[223]

(b) Pelvic Bones: Not too short, rather strongly developed, and moderately sloping.

(c) Thigh Bone: Robust and of good length, set at right angles to the pelvic bones.

(d) Hindlegs: Robust and well-muscled, with well-rounded buttocks.

(e) Knee Joint: Broad and strong.

(f) Calf Bone: In comparison with other breeds, short; it should be perpendicular to the thigh bone, and firmly muscled.

(g) The bones at the base of the foot *(tarsus)* should present a flat appearance, with a strongly prominent hock and a broad tendon of Achilles.

(h) The central foot bones *(metatarsus)* should be long, movable towards the calf bone, slightly bent toward the front, but perpendicular (as viewed from behind).

(i) Hind Paws: Four compactly-closed and beautifully-arched toes, as in the case of the front paws. The whole foot should be posed equally on the ball and not merely on the toes; nails short.

Tail.—Set in continuation of the spine, extending without very pronounced curvature, and should not be carried too gaily.

Note:—Inasmuch as the Dachshund is a hunting dog, scars from honorable wounds shall not be considered a fault.

SPECIAL CHARACTERISTICS OF THE THREE COAT-VARIETIES OF DACHSHUNDE

The Dachshund is bred with three varieties of coat: (A) Short-haired *(or Smooth)*; (B) Wirehaired; (C) Longhaired. All three varieties should conform to the characteristics already specified. The longhaired and shorthaired are old, well-fixed varieties, but into the wirehaired Dachshund, the blood of other breeds has been purposely introduced; nevertheless, in breeding him, the greatest stress must be placed upon conformity to the general Dachshund type.

The following specifications are applicable separately to the three coat-varieties, respectively:

(A) *Shorthaired (or smooth) Dachshund.*—Hair: Short, thick, smooth and shining; no bald patches. Special faults are: Too fine or thin hair, leathery ears, bald patches, too coarse or too thick hair in general.

Tail: Gradually tapered to a point, well but not too richly haired; long, sleek bristles on the underside are considered a patch of strong-growing hair, not a fault. A brush tail is a fault, as is also a partly- or wholly-hairless tail.

Color of Hair, Nose and Nails: (a) One-Colored Dachshund: This group includes red (often called tan), red-yellow, and yellow, with or without a shading of interspersed black hairs. Nevertheless a clean color is preferable, and red is to be considered more desirable than red-yellow or yellow. Dogs strongly shaded with interspersed black hairs belong to this class, and not to the other color groups. No white is desirable, but a solitary small spot is not exactly disqualifying.

Nose and Nails: Black; red is admissible, but not desirable.

(b) Two-Colored Dachshund: These comprise deep black, chocolate, grey, and white; each with rust-brown or yellow marks over the eyes, on the sides of the jaw and underlip, on the inner edge of the ear, front, breast, inside and behind the front leg, on the paws and around the anus, and from there to about one-third to one-half of the length of the tail on the under side. (The most common two-colored Dachshund is usually called black-and-tan.) Except on white dogs, no white is desirable, but a solitary small spot is not exactly disqualifying. Absence, or undue prominence of tan markings is undesirable.

Nose and Nails: In the case of black dogs, black; for chocolate, brown or black; for grey, grey or even flesh color, but the last named color is not desirable; in the case of white dogs, black nose and nails are to be preferred.

(c) Dappled and Striped Dachshund: The color of the dappled (or tiger) Dachshund is a clear brownish or greyish color, or even a white ground, with dark irregular patches of dark-grey, brown, red-yellow or black (large areas of one color not desirable). It is desirable that neither the light nor the dark color should predominate. The color of the striped (brindle) Dachshund is red or yellow with a darker streaking.

Nose and Nails: As for One- and Two-Colored Dachshunde.

(B) *Wirehaired Dachshund.*—The general appearance is the same as that of the shorthaired, but without being long in the legs, it is permissible for the body to be somewhat higher off the ground.

Hair: With the exception of jaw, eyebrows, and ears, the whole body is covered with a perfectly uniform tight, short, thick, rough, hard coat, but with finer, shorter hairs (undercoat) everywhere distributed between the coarser hairs, resembling the coat of the German spiky-haired pointer. There should be a beard on the chin. The eyebrows are bushy. On the ears the hair is shorter than on the body; almost smooth, but in any case conforming to the rest of the coat. The general arrangement of the hair should be such that the wirehaired Dachshund, when seen from a distance should resemble the smooth-haired. Any sort of soft hair in the coat is faulty, whether short or long, or wherever found on the body; the same is true of long, curly, or wavy hair, or hair that sticks out irregularly in all directions; a flag tail is also objectionable.

Tail: Robust, as thickly haired as possible, gradually coming to a point, and without a tuft.

Color of Hair, Nose and Nails: All colors are admissible. White patches on the chest, though allowable, are not desirable.

(C) *Longhaired Dachshund.*—The distinctive characteristic differentiating this coat from the short- or smooth-haired Dachshund is alone the rather long silky hair.

Hair: The soft, sleek, glistening, often slightly-wavy hair should be longer under the neck, on the underside of the body, and especially on the ears and behind the legs, becoming there a pronounced feather; the hair should attain its greatest length on the underside of the tail. The hair should fall beyond the lower edge of the ear. Short hair on the ear, so-called "leather" ears, is not desirable. Too luxurious a coat causes the longhaired Dachshund to seem coarse, and masks the type. The coat should remind one of the Irish setter, and should give the dog an elegant appearance. Too thick hair on the paws, so-called "mops," is inelegant, and renders the animal unfit for use. It is faulty for the dog to have equally long hair over all the body, if the coat is too curly, or too scrubby, or if a flag tail or overhanging hair on the ears are lacking; or if there is a very pronounced parting on the back, or a vigorous growth between the toes.

Tail: Carried gracefully in prolongation of the spine; the hair attains here its greatest length and forms a veritable flag.

Color of Hair, Nose and Nails: Exactly as for the smooth-haired Dachshund.

DACHSHUNDE

Miniature Dachshund—Note.—Miniature Dachshunde are bred in all three coats. They are not under-sized or undeveloped specimens of full-sized Dachshunde, but have been purposely produced to work in burrows smaller than light- and heavy-weight Dachshunde can enter. The limits set upon their weight and chest circumference have inevitably resulted in a more slender body structure. Depth of chest and shortness of leg proportionate to the regular conformation, would in these diminutive animals, prove impractical for their active hunting purposes.

The German specifications limit Zwergteckel (dwarf dachshunde) to a chest circumference of 13.8 inches (35 centimeters) and to weights for males of 8.8 pounds avoirdupois (4 kilograms, 8 pfunde) and for females of 7.7 pounds (3.5 kg., 7 pfd.), and limit Kaninchenteckel (rabbit dachshunde) to a chest circumference of 11.8 inches (30 cm.) and to weights for both sexes of 7.7 pounds, certified at a minimum age of twelve months. Rather than the ideal, these sizes represent instead the upper limit for miniature registration; and thus in pedigrees provide an index to purity of miniature breeding. For hunting, where Kaninchenteckel originated, in order to move freely through rabbit holes, weights from 6 to below 5 pounds are preferred. In the show ring, weights well below the above maxima, far from being penalized, represent the desired type.

Miniature Dachshunde have not been given separate classification in the United States. A class for "under nine pounds" at American shows permits Zwerg- and Kaninchenteckel to compete as miniatures according to the German specifications. Within the limits imposed, symmetrical adherence to the general Dachshund conformation, combined with smallness, and mental and physical vitality should be the outstanding characteristics of the miniature Dachshund.

GENERAL FAULTS

Serious Faults (which may prevent a dog from receiving any show rating) : Over- or under-shot jaws, knuckling over, very loose shoulders.

Secondary Faults (which may prevent a dog from receiving a high show rating) : A weak, long-legged, or dragging figure; body hanging between the shoulders; sluggish, clumsy, or waddling gait; toes turned inwards or too obliquely outwards; splayed paws, sunken back, roach (or carp) back; croup higher than withers; short-ribbed or too-weak chest; excessively drawn up flanks like those of a greyhound; narrow, poorly-muscled hind quarters; weak loins; bad angulation in front or hind quarters; cowhocks; bowed legs; "glass" eyes, except for grey or dappled dogs; a bad coat.

Minor Faults (which may prevent a dog from receiving the highest rating in championship competition): Ears wrongly set, sticking out, narrow or folded; too marked a stop; too pointed or weak a jaw; pincer teeth, distemper teeth; too wide or too short a head; goggle eyes, "glass" eyes in the case of grey and dappled dogs, insufficiently dark eyes in the case of all other coat-colors; dewlaps; short neck; swan neck; too fine or too thin hair.

DEERHOUNDS (SCOTTISH)

(Illustration facing page 238)

(By Courtesy of The Scottish Deerhound Club of America)

The origin of the Deerhound breed is of such antiquity and the earliest descriptive names bestowed on it so inextricably mixed that no sound conclusion can be arrived at as to whether the Deerhound was at one time identical with the ancient Irish Wolfdog and, in the course of centuries bred to a type better suited to hunt deer, or whether, as some writers claim, he is the descendant of the hounds of the Picts. Very early descriptive names were used to identify the purpose of the dog rather than to identify species. We find such names as "Irish Wolf Dog," "Scotch Greyhound," "Rough Greyhound," "Highland Deerhound." Dr. Caius, in his book "Englische Dogges" (1576) speaking of greyhounds, relates: "Some are of a greater sorte, some of a lesser; some are smoothe skynned and some curled, the bigger therefore are appointed to hunt the bigger beastes, the buck, the hart, the doe."

All this is relatively unimportant when we can definitely identify the breed as Deerhounds as early as the sixteenth and seventeenth centuries. From there on the term Deerhound has been applied to the breed, which of all dogs has been found best suited for the pursuit and killing of the deer.

At all times great value has been set on the Deerhound. The history of the breed teems with romance increasing

[229]

in splendor right down through the Age of Chivalry when no one of lower rank than an earl might possess these dogs. A leash of Deerhounds was held the fine whereby a noble lord condemned to death might purchase his reprieve. Records of the Middle Ages allude repeatedly to the delightful attributes of this charming hound, his tremendous courage in the chase, his gentle dignity in the home.

So highly has the Deerhound been esteemed that the desire for exclusive ownership has at many times endangered the continuance of the breed. As the larger beasts of the chase became extinct, or rare, in England and southern Scotland, the more delicate smooth greyhound took the place of the larger Deerhound. The Highlands of Scotland, the last territory wherein the stag remained numerous in a wild state, became as might be expected, the last stronghold of this breed. Here again the Highland Chieftains assumed exclusive proprietorship to such an extent that it was rare to find a good specimen south of the River Forth. So severely was this policy pursued that in 1769 the breed physically and numerically ran very low. This, of course, must be attributed in a great measure to the collapse of the clan system after Culloden 1745. It was not until about 1825, when the restoration of the breed was undertaken very successfully by Archibald and Duncan McNeill (the latter afterwards Lord Colonsay), that the Deerhound regained his place of pre-eminence and former perfection. The Great War, in later times, had considerable effect on the breed when so many of the large estates in Scotland and England were broken up. Although this "Royal Dog of Scotland" is represented at English shows in good numbers and to a considerable extent at shows in the Eastern States of this country, the Deerhound remains a rare dog of such historical interest and wonderful character that ownership should give anyone great pride of possession.

The high valuation of the Deerhound is not the result of rarity so much as the fact that as a hunter he is par excellence, with a very high aggregate of desirable characteristics. He has a keen scent which may be used in tracking but it is that combination of strength and speed necessary to cope with the large Scottish deer (often weighing 250 pounds) that is most valued. The hounds are usually hunted singly or in pairs. Centuries of hunting as the companions and guards of Highland Chieftains have given the Deerhound an insatiable desire for human companionship. For this reason the best Deerhounds are seldom raised as kennel dogs. In character the Deerhound is quiet and dignified, keen and alert, and although not aggressive has great persistence and indomitable courage when necessary. While it might savor of boasting to claim that the Deerhound of today is identical with the dog of early history, descriptions of which are mostly legendary, it is nevertheless a well established fact that in type, size and character he closely conforms to authentic records of the eighteenth and nineteenth centuries.

The hunting of antlered game with dogs is not permitted in the United States but the Deerhound has been used very successfully on wolves, coyotes, rabbits and is keen to match his speed with anything that runs. As a companion the Deerhound is ideal, being tractable and easy to train and possessing the most dependable loyalty and utmost devotion to his master. The most authentic and complete work on the breed is "Scotch Deerhounds and their Masters" written by George Cupples. Much has also been written about the Deerhound by Scrope in "Days of Deerstalking" and other works. The best descriptions of the breed are found in nineteenth century

British dog books. Unfortunately some of our more modern publications have been handicapped by a lack of intimate acquaintance with the Deerhound or influenced by nationalistic prejudices.

The grace, dignity and beauty of the Deerhound have been faithfully depicted in many of Landseer's paintings and drawings and Sir Walter Scott, who owned the famous Deerhound "Maida," makes many enthusiastic allusions to the breed which he describes as "The most perfect creature of Heaven."

The following description, which closely follows the standard of the Deerhound Club of England, was approved by the Scottish Deerhound Club of America.

DESCRIPTION AND STANDARD OF POINTS

(Adopted by The Scottish Deerhound Club of America and Approved by The American Kennel Club, March, 1935)

Head.—Should be broadest at the ears, narrowing slightly to the eyes, with the muzzle tapering more decidedly to the nose. The muzzle should be pointed, but the teeth and lips level. The head should be long, the skull flat rather than round with a very slight rise over the eyes but nothing approaching a stop. The hair on the skull should be moderately long and softer than the rest of the coat. The nose should be black (in some blue fawns—blue) and slightly aquiline. In lighter colored dogs the black muzzle is preferable. There should be a good moustache of rather silky hair and a fair beard.

Ears.—Should be set on high; in repose, folded back like a greyhound's, though raised above the head in excitement without losing the fold, and even in some cases semi-erect. A prick ear is bad. Big thick ears hanging flat to the head or heavily coated with long hair are bad faults. The ears should be soft, glossy, like a mouse's coat to the touch and the smaller the better. There should be no long coat or long fringe, but there is sometimes a silky, silvery coat on the body of the ear and the tip. On all Deerhounds, irrespective of color of coat, the ears should be black or dark colored.

Neck and Shoulders.—The neck should be long—of a length befitting the greyhound character of the dog. Extreme length is neither necessary nor desirable. Deerhounds do not stoop to their work like the greyhounds. The mane, which every good specimen should have, sometimes detracts from the apparent length of the neck. The neck, however, must be strong as is necessary to hold a stag. The nape of the neck should be very prominent where the head is set on, and the throat clean cut at the angle and prominent. Shoulders should be well sloped; blades well back and not too much width between them. Loaded and straight shoulders are very bad faults.

Tail.—Should be tolerably long, tapering and reaching to within 1½ inches off the ground and about 1½ inches below the hocks. Dropped perfectly down or curved when the Deerhound is still, when in motion or excited—curved, but in no instance lifted out of line of the back. It should be well covered with hair, on the inside, thick and wiry, underside longer and towards the end a slight fringe is not objectionable. A curl or ring tail is undesirable.

Eyes.—Should be dark—generally dark brown, brown or hazel. A very light eye is not liked. The eye should be moderately full, with a soft look in repose, but a keen, far-away look when the deerhound is roused. Rims of eyelids should be black.

Body.—General formation is that of a greyhound of larger size and bone. Chest deep rather than broad but not too narrow or slab-sided. Good girth of chest is indicative of great lung power. The loin well arched and drooping to the tail. A straight back is not desirable, this formation being unsuited for uphill work, and very unsightly.

Legs and Feet.—Legs should be broad and flat, and good broad forearms and elbows are desirable. Forelegs must, of course, be as straight as possible. Feet close and compact, with well-arranged toes. The hind quarters drooping, and as broad and powerful as possible, the hips being set wide apart. A narrow rear denotes lack of power. The stifles should be well bent, with great length from hip to hock, which should be broad and flat. Cowhocks, weak pasterns, straight stifles and splay feet are very bad faults.

[233]

Coat.—The hair on the body, neck and quarters should be harsh and wiry, about 3 or 4 inches long; that on the head, breast and belly much softer. There should be a slight fringe on the inside of the fore and hindlegs but nothing approaching the "feather" of a collie. A woolly coat is bad. Some good strains have a mixture of silky coat with the hard which is preferable to a woolly coat. The climate of United States tends to produce the mixed coat. The ideal coat is a thick, closelying ragged coat, harsh or crisp to the touch.

Color is a matter of fancy but the dark blue-grey is most preferred. Next come the darker and lighter greys or brindles, the darkest being generally preferred. Yellow and sandy red or red fawn, especially with black ears and muzzles, are equally high in estimation. This was the color of the oldest known strains—the McNeil and Chesthill Menzies. White is condemned by all authorities, but a white chest and white toes, occurring as they do in many of the darkest colored dogs are not objected to, although the less the better for the Deerhound is a self-colored dog. A white blaze on the head, or a white collar, should entirely disqualify. The less white the better but a slight white tip to the stern occurs in some of the best strains.

Height of Dogs.—From 30 to 32 inches, or even more if there be symmetry without coarseness, which is rare.

Height of Bitches.—From 28 inches upwards. There is no objection to a bitch being large, unless too coarse, as even at her greatest height she does not approach that of the dog, and therefore could not be too big for work as overbig dogs are.

Weight.—From 85 to 110 pounds in dogs and from 75 to 95 pounds in bitches.

Points of the Deerhound
ARRANGED IN ORDER OF IMPORTANCE

1. *Typical.*—A Deerhound should resemble a rough-coated greyhound of larger size and bone.

2. *Movements.*—Easy, active and true.

3. As tall as possible consistent with quality.

4. *Head.*—Long, level, well balanced, carried high.

5. *Body.*—Long, very deep in brisket, well sprung ribs and great breadth across hips.

6. *Forelegs.*—Strong and quite straight, with elbows neither in nor out.

7. *Thighs.*—Long and muscular, second thighs well muscled, stifles well bent.

8. *Loins.*—Well arched, and belly well drawn up.

9. *Coat.*—Rough and hard with softer beard and brows.

10. *Feet.*—Close, compact, with well knuckled toes.

11. *Ears.*—Small (dark) with greyhound-like carriage.

12. *Eyes.*—Dark, moderately full.

13. *Neck.*—Long, well arched, very strong with prominent nape.

14. *Shoulders.*—Clean, set sloping.

15. *Chest.*—Very deep but not too narow.

16. *Tail.*—Long and curved slightly, carried low.

17. *Teeth.*—Strong and level.

18. *Nails.*—Strong and curved.

FOXHOUNDS (AMERICAN)

(Illustration facing page 239)

(By Courtesy of The American Foxhound Club)

According to well known authorities on the American Hound the first mention that we have of hound importations to America appears in a diary of one of De Soto's retainers. It is further mentioned that hounds were utilized to hunt Indians instead of foxes and hare.

From this same good authority we learn that in 1650 Robert Brooke sailed for the Crown Colony in America, taking his pack of hounds with him, which according to this authority were the tap-root of several strains of American hounds and remained in the family for nearly three hundred years. Then Mr. Thomas Walker of Albemarle County, Virginia, imported hounds from England in 1742, and in 1770 George Washington subscribed to the importation of hounds from England, and in 1785 received some French hounds from Lafayette, their voices being "like the bells of Moscow." These importations formed the foundation from which have developed some of the strains of the present day Virginia hounds. In 1808 the Gloucester Foxhunting Club imported some of the "best English Hounds," and the Baltimore Hunt Club made many importations from England. Then followed the Rosseau importations from France, and the Irish importations of 1830. The latter are the tap-root of the Henry-Birdsong and Trigg strains. Around 1857 General Maupin got from east Tennessee the dog, Tennessee Lead, which crossed on English importations produced the "Maupin dog" now known as the Walker hound, another well known strain of American hound.

The Foxhound in this country is used for four purposes, all of them quite different from each other, and thus calling for hounds of a different characteristic.

1. The field trial hound which is run competitively at field trials where speed and a rather jealous nature are important.

2. To hunt a fox with a gun. Here a slow trailing hound with a good voice is needed.

3. "Trail" hounds or drag hounds which are raced or hunted on a drag, speed alone counting.

4. Hounds to hunt in large numbers (say 15 to 20 or more) in a pack. This latter class is, of course, the type used by the hunt clubs and hunting farmers.

The types of American hounds have varied widely in different localities, but in the last few years the American Foxhound Club and the hunts which are members of the Masters of Foxhounds Association have made great strides in developing a more standard type.

DESCRIPTION AND STANDARD OF POINTS

(By Courtesy of The American Foxhound Club)

Head—Skull.—Should be fairly long, slightly domed at occiput, with cranium broad and full.

Ears.—Ears set on moderately low, long, reaching when drawn out nearly, if not quite, to the tip of the nose; fine in texture, fairly broad, with almost entire absence of erectile power—setting close to the head with the forward edge slightly inturning to the cheek —round at tip.

Eyes.—Eyes large, set well apart—soft and houndlike—expression gentle and pleading; of a brown or hazel color.

Muzzle.—Muzzle of fair length—straight and square cut—the top moderately defined.

[238]

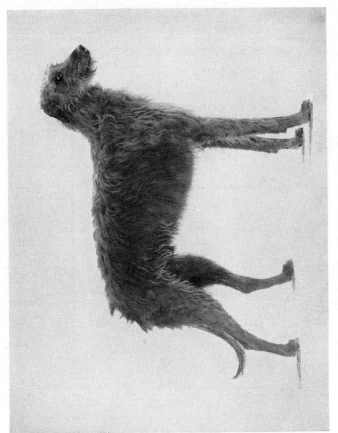

SCOTTISH DEERHOUND

AMERICAN FOXHOUND

FOXHOUNDS (AMERICAN)

Defects.—A very flat skull, narrow across the top; excess of dome; eyes small, sharp and terrier like, or prominent and protruding; muzzle long and snipy, cut away decidedly below the eyes, or very short. Roman nosed, or upturned, giving a dish-face expression. Ears short, set on high, or with a tendency to rise above the point of origin.

Body—Neck and Throat.—Neck rising free and light from the shoulders, strong in substance yet not loaded, of medium length. The throat clean and free from folds of skin, a slight wrinkle below the angle of the jaw, however, is allowable.

Defects.—A thick, short, cloddy neck carried on a line with the top of the shoulders. Throat showing dewlap and folds of skin to a degree termed "throatiness."

Shoulders, Chest and Ribs.—Shoulders sloping—clean, muscular, not heavy or loaded—conveying the idea of freedom of action with activity and strength. Chest should be deep for lung space, narrower in proportion to depth than the English hound—28 inches *(girth)* in a 23-inch hound being good. Well sprung ribs—back ribs should extend well back—a three-inch flank allowing springiness.

Back and Loins.—Back moderately long, muscular and strong. Loins broad and slightly arched.

Defects.—Very long or swayed or roached back. Flat, narrow loins.

Forelegs and Feet—Forelegs.—Straight, with fair amount of bone. Pasterns short and straight.

Feet.—Fox like. Pad full and hard. Well arched toes. Strong nails.

Defects.—Straight, upright shoulders, chest disproportionately wide or with lack of depth. Flat ribs.

Defects.—Out at elbow. Knees knuckled over forward, or bent backward. Fore legs crooked. Feet long, open or spreading.

Hips, Thighs, Hindlegs and Feet—Hips and Thighs.—Strong and muscled, giving abundance of propelling power. Stifles strong and well let down. Hocks firm, symmetrical and moderately bent. Feet close and firm.

Defects.—Cowhocks, or straight hocks. Lack of muscle and propelling power. Open feet.

SPORTING DOGS (HOUNDS)

Tail.—Set moderately high; carried gaily, but not turned forward over the back; with slight curve; with very slight brush.

Defects.—A long tail. Teapot curve or inclined forward from the root. Rat tail, entire absence of brush.

Coat.—A close, hard, hound coat of medium length.

Defects.—A short thin coat, or of a soft quality.

Height.—Dogs should not be under 22 or over 25 inches. Bitches should not be under 21 or over 24 inches measured across the back at the point of the withers, the hound standing in a natural position with his feet well under him.

Color.—Any color.

SCALE OF POINTS

Head

Skull	5
Ears	5
Eyes	5
Muzzle	5
	20

Body

Neck	5
Chest and shoulders	15
Back, loins and ribs	15
	35

Running Gear

Forelegs	10
Hips, thighs and hindlegs	10
Feet	15
	35

Coat and Tail

Coat	5
Tail	5
	10

Total	100

FOXHOUNDS (ENGLISH)

(Illustration facing page 242)

(By Courtesy of The Masters of Foxhounds Association of America)

Foxhunting in the United States is almost contemporaneous with the sport in Great Britain. The Foxhound with which we are dealing, is known in the United States in dog shows and elsewhere as the *English* Foxhound, though why it should be designated by that name any more than a fox terrier should be called an *English* fox terrier, is hard to understand. The English Foxhound has been bred along careful lines for over one hundred and fifty years, the stud books now published by the Masters of Foxhounds Association (of England) date back before 1800, and it is an easy matter for any owner of an English Foxhound to trace its pedigree back. The breeding of foxhounds in England has always been in the hands of Masters of Hounds who kept the most careful records of their breeding operations.

For the benefit of those who may be interested in knowing how long the English Foxhound in his pure state has been in the United States we find that there are records which established the fact that the first Lord Fairfax imported hounds from England in 1738, and there are unauthenticated records of even earlier importations. The English Foxhound Stud Book of America published by the Masters of Foxhounds Association of America dates its earliest entries back to 1890, but there are earlier records which would incline one to the belief that there

[241]

were many earlier importations and certainly the blood of the Genesee Valley pack must date at least twenty years before that time, records having been kept of it with fair accuracy ever since.

In England, as in America these hounds have been always used for foxhunting as followed in the English fashion of riding to hounds. There are today over 250 packs of hounds in Great Britain all of which use English hounds, while in America, we have over a hundred packs of which not over 10% use hounds which would be eligible for the English Foxhound Stud Book, although the blood has been freely mixed with the American Foxhound.

In appearance the English hound is far stouter than his American cousin, and perhaps no better description of his general appearance can be given than to quote a passage from Mr. Cuthbert Bradley's "Reminiscences of Frank Gillard" in which he describes Belvoir Gambler '85, one of the greatest foxhounds that was ever bred. He says: "Although Belvoir Gambler cannot be bred from rule of thumb, the proportions of this remarkable foxhound are worth preserving as an example of what symmetry should be. Standing twenty-three inches at the shoulder, from the extreme point of his shapely shoulders to the outer curve of his well-turned quarters, he measured twenty-seven and a half inches in length whilst from elbow to ground his height was only twelve inches. Possessing great depth of rib and room round the heart, he girthed thirty-one inches, and his arm below was eight and a quarter inches round. Below the knee he measured eight and a quarter inches of solid bone, while round the thigh he spanned full nine and a quarter inches. The extended neck was ten inches from cranium to shoulder and the head ten inches and a half long. His color was of the

ENGLISH FOXHOUND

GREYHOUND

richest, displaying all of the beautiful 'Belvoir tan,' and his head had that brainy appearance expressive of the highest intelligence. Gambler might have inspired that earnest poet, Cannon Kingsley, when he described the modern foxhound, 'The result of nature not limited, but developed by high civilization. Next to an old Greek statue there are few such combinations of grace and strength as in a fine foxhound.' "

Although the tendency today is to breed hounds a little bigger, the above description cannot be equalled.

DESCRIPTION AND STANDARD OF POINTS
(By Courtesy of The Masters of Foxhounds Association of America)

The *Head* should be of full size, but by no means heavy. Brow pronounced, but not high or sharp. There should be a good length and breadth, sufficient to give in a dog hound a girth in front of the ears of fully 16 inches. The nose should be long (4½ inches) and wide, with open nostrils. Ears set on low and lying close to the cheeks. Most English hounds are "rounded" which means that about 1½ inches is taken off the end of the ear. The teeth must meet squarely, either a *pig-mouth* (overshot) or undershot being a disqualification.

The *Neck* must be long and clean, without the slightest throatiness, not less than ten inches from cranium to shoulder. It should taper nicely from shoulders to head, and the upper outline should be slightly convex.

The *Shoulders* should be long and well clothed with muscle, without being heavy, especially at the points. They must be well sloped, and the true arm between the front and the elbow must be long and muscular, but free from fat or lumber.

Chest and Back Ribs.—The chest should girth over 31 inches in a 24-inch hound, and the back ribs must be very deep.

The *Back* and *Loin* must both be very muscular, running into each other without any contraction between them. The couples must be wide, even to raggedness, and the top line of the back should be absolutely level, the *Stern* well set on and carried gaily but not in any case curved *over* the back like a squirrel's tail.

[243]

The end should taper to a point and there should be a fringe of hair below.

The *Hind Quarters* or propellers are required to be very strong, and as endurance is of even greater consequence than speed, straight stifles are preferred to those much bent as in a greyhound.

Elbows set quite straight, and neither turned in or out are a *sine qua non*. They must be well let down by means of the long true arm above mentioned.

Legs and Feet.—Every Master of Foxhounds insists on legs as straight as a post, and as strong; size of bone at the ankle being especially regarded as all important. The desire for straightness had a tendency to produce knuckling-over, which at one time was countenanced, but in recent years this defect has been eradicated by careful breeding and intelligent adjudication, and one sees very little of this trouble in the best modern foxhounds. The bone cannot be too large, and the feet in all cases should be round and cat-like, with well-developed knuckles and strong horn, which last is of the greatest importance.

The *Color* and *Coat* are not regarded as very important, so long as the former is a good "hound color," and the latter is short, dense, hard, and glossy. Hound colors are black, tan, and white, or any combination of these three, also the various "pies" compounded of white and the color of the hare and badger, or yellow, or tan.

The *Symmetry* of the foxhound is of the greatest importance, and what is known as "quality" is highly regarded by all good judges.

	Points
Head	5
Neck	10
Shoulders	10
Chest and back ribs	10
Back and loin	15
Hind quarters	10
Elbows	5
Legs and feet	20
Color and coat	5
Stern	5
Symmetry	5
Total	100

GREYHOUNDS

(Illustration facing page 243)

Swift as a ray of light; graceful as a swallow; and wise as a Solomon, there is some basis for the prediction that the Greyhound is a breed that will never die. His fame, first written in the hot sands of Egypt, can be traced in the varying terrains of almost every country, on every continent on the globe. His was the type the ancients knew, and from time immemorial he has been a symbol of the aristocracy. Yet, the Greyhound is a dog that needs no fanfare to herald his approach, no panoply to keep him in the public eye. His innate qualities give him admittance to any circles, high or low.

The first knowledge of the Greyhound comes from the Tomb of Amten, in the Valley of the Nile, regarded by Eygptologists as belonging to the 4th Dynasty, which in modern chronology would be between 3,500 and 4,000 B.C. The carvings in this old tomb show dogs of unmistakable Greyhound type in three separate scenes. In two they are attacking a deer, while in the other an animal with horns, somewhat similar to the American mountain goat. The dogs have ring tails.

The origin of the name "Greyhound" is somewhat open to dispute, and a number of suppositions have been advanced. One is that it is derived from "Graius" meaning Grecian, because the dog was in high esteem among the ancient Greeks. Another conjecture is that it derives from the old British "grech" or "greg," meaning a dog. Also, some say that it came to use because grey was once the prevailing color in the breed.

While the old Egyptian scenes establish the Greyhound as a recognizable type at a very early date, it is from a Grecian source that there has come the first complete description of the breed. This was written by Ovid, who lived from 63 B.C. to A.D. 17. Reading this, one can have little doubt that the dog of ancient times is the same as the one of today. With certain allowances, it fits perfectly.

The Greyhound always has had a cultural and aristocratic background. He was the favorite of royalty in Egypt, and he was bred and raised in such luxurious surroundings that there was every reason why the oppressed races and the common people of those times hated this dog. Yet the disposition of the dog was just as lovable and tractable then as it is today. Had the common people been allowed to own specimens of this dog, the story would have been entirely different, but his ownership was restricted to the ruling classes.

The ancient traditions connected with the Greyhound have come down throughout history. He is found in England at a very early date. In fact, a manuscript from the ninth Century, A.D., is illustrated with a picture of Elfric, Duke of Mercia; and beside this old Saxon chieftain stands his huntsman with a brace of Greyhounds. Just how many centuries before the time Elfric, the Greyhound was known in England is not known, but there is every reason to suppose that the breed had been there a long time.

The famous Canute Laws, written in Danish—for at that time the Danes had conquered much of what is now England—and enacted in a Parliament held at Winchester in 1016, give further evidence as to the status of the Greyhound. No. 31 of these Canute Laws states:

"No meane person may keepe any greihounds, but

freemen may keepe greihounds, so that their knees may be cut before the verderons of the forest, and without cutting of their knees also, if he does not abide 10 miles from the bounds of the forest. But if they doe come any nearer to the forest, they shall pay 12 pence for every mile; but if the greihound be found within the forest, the master or owner of the dog shall forfeit the dog and ten shillings to the King."

The Greyhound has been used on practically all kinds of small game from time to time, including deer, stags, foxes, and so forth, but the hare is his natural quarry, and coursing, the sport with which he has been associated for centuries. In fact, coursing has been done on an organized basis in England for nearly two centuries.

The famous Waterloo Cup Meet was instituted in England in 1836, and it has been held continuously ever since—with the exception of the war years, 1917 and 1918. On the other hand, two meetings were held in 1887, so actually the 1936 event will be the 100th. At the beginning this was an eight-dog stake, but in 1837 the number was double, and the next year it was double again to 32 dogs. In 1857 it became a 64-dog stake, and it has remained that way ever since.

More than half a century before the Waterloo Cup event, there was organized one of the most colorful clubs in the sporting history of England. This was known as the Swaffham Coursing Society, and it came into being in 1776, being organized by the Earl of Orford. It was limited to 25 members, using all but one letter of the alphabet, each member being assigned a letter and colors. Still, coursing did not assume uniformity until the Duke of Norfolk drew up a set of rules, some years later, that have been accepted as the standard procedure ever since.

SPORTING DOGS (HOUNDS)

In recent years the Greyhound has added another laurel to his crown. This is his use as a racing dog. This was brought about, a decade ago, by the invention of a mechanical "rabbit" that could be used on circular or oval tracks. The first successful tracks were in England, but it is now a growing sport in the United States where phenominally fast times are being recorded continually.

DESCRIPTION AND STANDARD OF POINTS
(Courtesy of The Greyhound Club of America)

Head.—Long and narrow, fairly wide between the ears, scarcely perceptible stop, little or no development of nasal sinuses, good length of muzzle, which should be powerful without coarseness. Teeth very strong and even in front.

Ears.—Small and fine in texture, thrown back and folded, except when excited, when they are semi-pricked.

Eyes.—Dark, bright, intelligent, indicating spirit.

Neck.—Long, muscular, without throatiness, slightly arched, and widening gradually into the shoulder.

Shoulders.—Placed as obliquely as possible, muscular without being loaded.

Forelegs.—Perfectly straight, set well into the shoulder, neither turned in nor out, pasterns strong.

Chest.—Deep, and as wide as consistent with speed, fairly well-sprung ribs.

Back.—Muscular and broad, well arched.

Loins.—Good depth of muscle, well cut up in the flanks.

Hind Quarters.—Long, very muscular and powerful, wide and well let down, well-bent stifles. Hocks well bent and rather close to ground, wide but straight fore and aft.

Feet.—Hard and close, rather more hare than cat feet, well knuckled up with good strong claws.

Tail.—Long, fine and tapering with a slight upward curve.

[248]

GREYHOUNDS

Coat.—Short, smooth and firm in texture.
Color.—Immaterial.
Weight.—Dogs, 65 to 70 pounds; bitches, 60 to 65 pounds.

SCALE OF POINTS

General symmetry and quality	10
Head and neck	20
Chest and shoulders	20
Back	10
Quarters	20
Legs and feet	20
Total	100

HARRIER

NORWEGIAN ELKHOUND

HARRIERS

(Illustration facing page 250)

Probably the oldest work on hare hunting is the famous essay penned by the ancient Greek historian, Xenophon about 400 B.C., and with that as a basis, the subject has been a favorite subject of the greatest authorities on the dog for the past 2,300 years. Regardless of that, there is a striking unanimity of doubt concerning the direct ancestors of this old breed of scent hound.

The Harrier, as he exists today, was unknown in Xenophon's time, although he describes two types of hound that were used with equal success in the early hunting of the hare. One he calls "the Castorean," which was reputed to be the favorite of the demi-god, Castor. The other is designated as "the fox-breed," which is explained as a product of the fox and the dog. On the other hand, Xenophon has listed the qualities of a hound suitable for the purposes, and they bear amazing similarity to the desirable points of modern times.

This early treatise on hunting is no fragmentary remnant of a scholarly mind, but one of the most definite and minute portrayals of a sport that ever has been written. Perhaps the only real difference between the way the Greeks hunted the hare and the manner accepted in England and other countries is that in 400 B.C. the hares were driven into nets. This practice would bring great censure on hunters of today. Still, sportsmanship was given some consideration in ancient times, for Xenophon says:

"In tracking the hare, no delay should be made, for it is sportsmanlike, as well as a proof of fondness for exertion, to use every means to capture the animal speedily."

Even the great English authority on all breeds, Stonehenge, was a little mystified by the origin of the Harrier. The theory he advances rather cautiously is that it springs from the old Southern hound, with an infusion of a little greyhound blood.

Undoubtedly the Southern hound has played a great part in the development of all scent hound breeds in the British Isles, yet there is little or no mention of the origin of this basic breed. The most logical supposition appears to be that it was brought to England by the Normans, for hunting is of great antiquity on the Continent.

The first pack of Harriers in England was the Penistone, which was established by Sir Elias de Midhope in 1260. These Harriers were held together for at least five centuries, and it is recorded that in the fourteenth, the seventeenth, and the eighteenth Centuries, the masters were supplied by the Wilsons of Broomhead Hall. Hunting the hare has always had great popularity throughout the British Isles, and in some ways enjoyed greater favor than foxhunting. One great cause of its popularity was that a pack of Harriers could be followed on foot. This enlisted the interest of many, and among the hundred odd packs that hunted regularly in England half a century ago, many were scratch packs. A scratch pack was made up of hounds owned by various individuals—thus bringing the sport down to the level of the poorer man. However, horses are used in most cases today.

In support of the Norman origin of this and other hound breeds, there has been an interesting bit of information supplied by Wynn in regard to the name, "harrier." He shows that this may have come from the

HARRIERS

Norman word, "harier," denoting Saxon raches or hounds. Further, "harier" was used down to 1750 for all hounds, not necessarily hare-hounds. And back in 1570, Dr. Caius mentioned stag- and fox-harriers.

Despite all stories of the ancient origin of Harriers, it is the general belief that the dog of today is merely a smaller edition of the foxhound, and that he has been bred down from the larger hound by selective breeding. Save in size, the Harrier is the external replica of the foxhound. Some specimens of the Harrier bear a unique, blue mottle color, which is not recognized in English Foxhounds, but in the majority of cases their colors are the same. It also is said that some Harriers are somewhat heavier in the head, in proportion, than is the foxhound.

Harriers have been known in the United States as long as any of the scent hound breeds, and they have been used for hunting since Colonial times. In later times, the Harrier proved a great favorite of the drag-hunt, in which his slower pace is no detriment.

DESCRIPTION AND STANDARD OF POINTS

The points of the modern Harrier are very similar to those of the English Foxhound. The Harrier, however, is smaller than the English Foxhound and the most popular size is 19 to 21 inches.

They should be active, well balanced and full of strength and quality, with shoulders sloping into the muscles of the back, clean and not loaded on the withers or point.

The back level and muscular, and not dipping behind the withers or arching over the loin.

The elbow's point set well away from the ribs, running parallel with the body and not turning outwards.

Deep, well-sprung ribs running well back, with plenty of heart room, and a deep chest.

Good straight legs with plenty of bone running well down to

the toes, but not overburdened, inclined to knuckle over very slightly but not exaggerated in the slightest degree.

Round cat-like feet, and close toes turning inwards.

Hindlegs and hocks stand square, with a good sweep and muscular thigh to take the weight off the body.

The head should be of a medium size with good bold forehead, and plenty of expression; head must be well set up on a neck of ample length, and not heavy; stern should be set well up, long and well controlled.

NORWEGIAN ELKHOUNDS

(Illustration facing page 251)

(By Courtesy of The Norwegian Elkhound Association of America)

Comrade to the vikings, guardian of lonely farms and *saeters,* herder of flocks and defender from wolves and bear, a hunter always and a roamer with hardy men, the Norwegian Elkhound comes down to us through more than six millenia with all his Nordic traits untainted, a fearless dog and friendly, devoted to man and the chase. We read of him in sagas, we find his remains by the side of his viking-master along with the viking's weapons—sure proof of the esteem in which he was held; and in the Viste Cave at Jaeren, in western Norway, his skeleton was uncovered among the stone implements in a stratum dating from 4,000 to 5,000 B.C.

Selected and bred for his ability to accomplish a definite purpose, the Elkhound achieved his distinctive type by natural methods. No form was imposed upon him; he was not squeezed into a pre-conceived standard: his structure and rare beauty, like those of the thoroughbred horse, were evolved from the tests of performance. Every physical characteristic is the expression of a need. His compactness, his muscled robustness, his squareness, his width and depth are a true expression of nature's requirements for a dog that would hunt day after day and all day long in rugged country, where stamina rather than extreme speed is called for.

For, though the Elkhound in foreign countries has become known and loved chiefly, perhaps, for his engaging and sensitive qualities as a comrade of man, for his un-impeachable reliability and his quickness to learn and adapt himself to any circumstances and conditions, it should never be forgotten that, from first to last, he has been at all times the peerless hunter of big game.

Thirty years ago, bear were still common in Norway, but today they are almost extinct, and the native dog's main use is the hunting of elk. ("Elk" is incorrectly used in the United States for the Wapiti, *Cervus Canadensis,* and our "moose" is a true elk.) A century ago, Capt. Lloyd, an English sportsman, a mighty hunter, and a fascinating writer, devoted his leisure to the description of bear hunting in Norway; and from that time on, everyone that has seen the Elkhound work in the forests of his native land has added to his praise. Space forbids adequate treatment of the subject here; but those who wish to pursue the matter further and who cannot obtain a copy of Capt. Lloyd's books, now long out of print, will find an excellent substitute in Frantz Rosenberg's "Big Game Shooting," published in England in 1928.

The Elkhound's highly developed senses amount almost to intuition, and it is common to read or, if one is fortunate, experience, such incidents as seeing a seasoned dog take body scent at from two to three miles or to hear him indicating to his master by a slight whimpering that the elk has become alarmed and has begun to run, at a time when no human senses can apprehend any sign by which the hound ascertains this fact. Equally subtle is his method of engaging a bull. Knowing well that an elk can outfoot him, he holds the animal by just enough barking to attract his attention. Even with a skillful dog, however, the elk often moves on before the hunter can get up over the steep countryside; and in that case, the dog, aware that the bull, if not excited by sound or scent, will soon pause, works silently and very carefully up wind until he is once more with his quarry.

After a while, the bull, becoming angry at the small beast annoying him, begins to attack with a wide sweeping movement of the great antlers and by striking with his deadly forefeet; but now, the Elkhound, short-backed so that he can, to use Herr Aarflot's apt expression, bounce like a rubber ball, jumps nimbly in and out, while giving full and furious tongue so that his high-pitched voice will reach his master.

The Elkhound is well adapted to the hunting of any other four-footed game and soon becomes expert on lynx, mountain lion, and raccoon; and Sir Henry Pottinger declares that he is also an excellent tracker of fox. The same authority states: "There is no more deadly way of approaching capercailzie, black game, and other forest birds than with a dog of the breed under discussion held or fastened to the belt by a long leash and allowed to precede the hunter."

The Elkhound, then, is an exceedingly versatile dog developed through constant contact with man in pursuit of game. It was not until 1877 that he began to be considered from an exhibition point of view. In that year the Norwegian Hunters' Association held its first show, and shortly thereafter pedigrees, which had been handed down, were checked and traced as far back as feasible, a stud book (Norsk Hundestambok) was published and a standard drawn up. Before that time, there had been some confusion of type owing to different developments in different parts of the country; but if we study the photograph of such a grand dog as that pillar of the Stud Book, known to fame as Gamle Bamse Gram (Old Bamse that belonged to Consul Gram), we shall see that all the essential elements of the modern show dog were already there, needing only a little refinement, a little emphasis. At any rate, by the turn of the century, the breed was making very rapid progress, and, though there were few or no really large kennels, there were many expert breeders devoted to the Elkhound's improvement; and when the Norwegian Kennel Club (Norsk Kennelklub) inaugurated its annual shows at Oslo, the Elkhound came into his own as Norway's great contribution to dogdom. Since then, he has been exported in ever-increasing numbers; and his friendly disposition, his intelligence, his staunchness, his absolute dependability and trustworthiness, his eagerness to praise, his sensitivity and his fearless confidence have gained for him everywhere a popularity based even more on his comradely character than on his unsurpassed abilities as a sporting hound.

DESCRIPTION AND STANDARD OF POINTS

(This Standard, adopted May 25, 1925 by the Norwegian Elkhound Association of America, is, as nearly as possible, a literal translation of the Standard of the Norsk Dyrehundklub of Norway.)

(Approved November, 12, 1935, by The American Kennel Club)

General Description.—The Norwegian Elkhound is a typical northern dog, of medium size, with a compact, proportionately short body, with a thick and rich, but not bristling, grey coat, with prick ears, and with a tail that is curled and carried over the back. His temperament is bold and energetic.

Head.—"Dry" (without any loose skin), broad at the ears; the forehead and back of the head only slightly arched; the stop not large, yet clearly defined. The muzzle is of medium length, thickest at the base and, seen from above or from the side, tapers evenly without being pointed. The bridge of the nose is straight; the lips are tightly closed.

Ears.—Set high, firm and erect, are higher than they are wide at the base, pointed (not rounded) and very mobile. When the dog is listening, the orifices are turned forward.

Eyes.—Not protruding, brown in color, preferably dark, lively, with a fearless energetic expression.

Neck.—Of medium length, "dry" (without any loose skin), strong, and well set up.

Body.—Powerful, *compact,* and short, with broad deep chest, well-sprung ribs, straight back, well-developed loins, and stomach very little drawn up.

Legs.—Firm, straight and strong; elbows closely set on; hind-legs with little angulation at knees and hocks. Seen from behind, they are straight.

Feet.—Comparatively small, somewhat oblong, with tightly closed toes, not turned out. There should be no dewclaws on hindlegs.

Tail.—Set high, short, thickly and closely haired, but without brush; tightly curled, not carried too much to one side.

Coat.—Thick, rich and hard, but rather smooth-lying. On head and front of legs, short and even; longest on neck and chest, on buttocks, on hindside of forelegs and on underside of tail. It is made up of longer and harder covering hairs, dark at the tips, and of a light, soft, woolly undercoat.

Color.—Grey, with black tips to the long covering hairs; somewhat lighter on chest, stomach, legs, underside of tail, and around anus. The color may be lighter or darker, with a slight shading towards yellow; but a pronounced variation from the grey color disqualifies. Too dark or too light individuals should be avoided; also, yellow markings or uneven coloring. There should be no pronounced white markings.

Height at Shoulder.—For dogs about 20.5 inches; for bitches about 18 inches.

OTTERHOUNDS

(Illustration facing page 262)

While there are allusions to otterhunting and Otterhounds in the time of King John, who reigned in England from 1199 to 1216, it is not until Edward II, 1307-1327, that there is any sort of a description of the kind of dogs that made up a pack of Otterhounds. This record has been left, fortunately, by William Twici, the huntsman. He makes mention of them as a "rough sort of dog, between a hound and a terrier."

The hunting of the otter never was a so-called major sport in England, but it appears to have existed from very early times. It first was practiced because the otters were preying on the fish in the rivers and streams to an annoying extent. Later it enjoyed a considerable vogue, because it was the only kind of hunting possible from April to September.

The undoubted heyday of the Otterhound in England extended from the middle to the end of the nineteenth century. During many of those years there were 18 to 20 packs hunting regularly through the season. Most famous, for its record of killing otters, was the Hawkstone pack of the Hon. Geoffrey Hill. From 1870 to 1890 this pack disposed of 704 otters, in 1881, alone, killing 62.

Still all authorities agree that the best trained pack of Otterhounds ever hunted in England was that of Squire Lomax of Clitheroe. This was at the peek of its perfection about 1868. The Squire was a stickler for the fine points of the game, and, while results interested him, his major concern was the manner in which his pack worked. It is said that they were trained so well that his signals could be given with the most casual wave of the hand. But then, Squire Lomax had spent the greater part of his life developing this pack. And when the majority of them died in one season, he did not attempt to replace them, believing that enough years did not remain for him to train a new pack as well as the first.

The origin of the Otterhound is shrouded in mystery, but the earliest writers advance a number of logical opinions as to its origin. According to Stonehenge, its ancestors are the Southern hound and the Welsh harrier. This is supported by the fact that there were large numbers of Otterhounds to be found in Devonshire, the chief stronghold of the Southern hound, and in Wales.

A somewhat less acceptable opinion is that of E. Buckley, who ascribes the coat of the Otterhound to the water spaniel—a somewhat different type from the breed known today—and credits the hardiness to the bulldog. Other writers mention the bloodhound, supporting this by the domed shape of the skull, and the length of the ears. In fact, writing as early as 1575, Turberville makes no distinction between the bloodhound and the Otterhound in describing the hunting of the otter.

The French origin of the Otterhound appears to be one of the most reasonable. This is the opinion of Marples, who, describing the Otterhound, says it is the almost exact duplicate of the old Vendee hound of France. The two breeds are alike in both coat and bodily formation.

The Otterhound is a big dog, standing 24 to 26 inches, and weighing up to 65 pounds. He has a hard, crisp and close coat of an oily nature that can stand any amount of immersion in water. The most desired combination of colors always has been the blue and white, but the

OTTERHOUND

breed ranges through many shades to black and tan. It is a peer among swimmers, its progress through the water being aided greatly by its webbed feet.

The working qualities of the Otterhound always have been emphasized to such an extent that it never has been popularly known as a bench show specimen in England. Still, it usually was the custom for some of the great packs to send a few couple apiece to the major shows. The Carlisle and Kendal packs were noted for their show dogs.

Otterhounds first made their appearance in the United States more than 30 years ago, and they made their bench show debut in 1907 at shows in Claremont, Okla., and Seattle, Wash. Yet it was three years before the first registrations are recorded. These are of Hartland Mosstrooper, 135,335, and Hartland Statesman, 135,334, both owned by H. S. Wardner of New York City. Incidentally, Mr Wardner was one of the two exhibitors of 1907, and he undoubtedly was America's first breeder.

While the Otterhound never has grown to wide popularity in the United States, its sagacity and character have retained for it many steadfast friends. What it lacks in smartness of appearance is compensated by its working qualities and its unfailing devotion to its master.

DESCRIPTION AND STANDARD OF POINTS

In general appearance—always excepting the coat—he much resembles the bloodhound; he should be perfect in symmetry, strongly built, hard and enduring, with unfailing powers of scent, and a natural antipathy to the game he is bred to pursue. The head should be large, broader in proportion than the bloodhound's, the forehead high, the muzzle a fair length and the nostrils wide. The ears are long, thin and pendulous, fringed with hair. The neck is not naturally long, and looks shorter than it really is from the abundance of hair on it; the shoulders should slope well, the legs be straight and the feet a good size, but compact; the back strong and wide, the ribs, and particularly the back ribs, well let down; the thighs should be big and firm, and the hocks well let down; the stern well and thickly covered with hair and carried well up, but not curled; the colors are generally grizzle or sandy, with black and tan more or less clearly defined.

	Points
Skull	10
Jaws	10
Eyes	5
Ears	10
Chest and shoulders	15
Body and loin	15
Legs and feet	10
Coat	10
Stern	5
Symmetry and strength	10
Total	100

SALUKIS

(Illustration facing page 270)

(By Courtesy of The Saluki Club of America)

The Saluki, the Royal Dog of Egypt, is, perhaps, the
oldest known breed of domesticated dog, "a distinct
breed and type as long ago as 329 B.C. when Alexander
the Great invaded India." The Saluki is claimed to be
as old as the earliest known civilization, the claim being
based on the fact that the hounds shown on the earliest
carvings look more like Salukis than any other breed:
(a greyhound body with feathered ears, tail and legs).

Exactly the same hound appears on the Egyptian tombs
2100 B.C. and more recent excavations of the still older
Sumarian empire, estimated at 7000-6000 B.C. have produced carvings of striking resemblance to the Saluki.

"Whenever one sees the word 'dog' in the Bible it
means the Saluki." As the Mohammedan religion
classes the dog as unclean, the Moslem declared the
Saluki sacred and called him "The Noble One" given
them by Allah for their amusement and benefit. This
permitted them to eat of the meat brought down in the
chase. The Saluki was the only dog of the time allowed
to sleep on the carpet of the Sheikh's tent.

So great was the esteem in which the Saluki was held,
that his body was often mummified like the bodies of the
Pharaohs themselves.

The remains of numerous Salukis have thus been found
in the ancient tombs of the Upper Nile region.

As the Saluki was considered sacred he was never sold
or allowed to go out of his native haunts. The Arab

chiefs attached as much importance to their breeding as they did to the pedigrees of their famous horses.

They did, however, trade among themselves and placed their values in terms of mares, female camels and gennets, according to the Saluki's ability in the chase. It is said that the native women often nurse the Saluki pups in order to increase their sustenance.

As the desert tribes are nomadic, the habitat of the Saluki comprised all the region stretching from the Caspian Sea to the Sahara, including Egypt, Arabia, Palestine, Syria, Mesopotamia, Anatolia and Persia. Naturally, the types varied somewhat in this widely scattered area. However, this difference was mostly in size and coat. Thus the Arabian bred Saluki, we find of a smaller type with less feathering on the legs and ears than the Persian variety.

Salukis were first brought into England in 1840: a bitch owned by Sir Hamilton Smith, a dog in Regents Park Zoological Gardens and one owned by the Duke of Devonshire at Chatsworth. They were then known as Persian Greyhound, as these three dogs came from Persia.

Evidently there was no real interest, however, in Salukis until the Hon. Florence Amherst imported the first Arabian Salukis in 1895. These were from the kennels of Prince Abdulla in Transjordania. It is greatly to her credit that the breed has made such headway among European countries.

England later learned more about the Saluki from her army officers stationed in the East during the Great War. Other specimens either as prizes of war or the gifts of friendly tribes were brought home. Mr. Mervyn Herbert brought back several fine specimens from Egypt and Mr. Vereker-Cowley imported Malik-el-Zobair and Zo-

beida-el-Zobair. These with Ch. Sarona Kelb and Sa-
rona-Sarona, imported from Mesopotamia by Brigadier
General Lance in 1920, figure prominently in the pedigrees of most of our present day Salukis.

The Saluki, having tremendous speed, was used by the
Arabs principally in bringing down the Gazelle, that fastest of antelopes. It is recorded that the Pharaohs rode
to the chase with their hawks on their wrists and Salukis
on the lead.

We also believe the Saluki was used on jackals, foxes
and hares. A cut published in 1852 shows a wild boar
hunt in Algeria with Salukis tackling the boar.

In England, the Saluki is used largely on hares and regular Coursing Meets are held. The judging is based on
ability to turn quickly and overtake the hare in the best
possible time. The Saluki hunts largely by sight although
he has a fair nose.

The sport of racing Salukis is much enjoyed in England and on the Continent. A special track with mechanical rabbit and hurdles at intervals is used. It is hoped
that we may shortly see this popularized in this country.

The sight of the Saluki is remarkable and his hereditary traits often crop out. He loves to lie on the sand
and watch an eagle soaring for his prey, while paying
no attention to the gull.

Sarona Dhole, a son of Sarona Kalb, soon after his
arrival in America chased a fox and registered a kill
within a few seconds after sighting the quarry.

On his native heath the Saluki gets no pampering. He
lives hard and it is a case of survival of the fittest; one
reason for his strong constitution and sturdy frame, enabling him to stand any climate in unheated kennels.

The feet of the Saluki are hard and firm and the hair
between the toes is a great protection. In all his running

and dodging over the roughest kind of ground and rocky country he never damages pads or toes.

The beauty of the Saluki is that of the throughbred horse—grace and symmetry of form—clean cut and graceful—short silky hair with the exception of the ears, legs and tail—slender well muscled neck, shoulders and thighs—arched loins—long tail carried naturally in a curve with silky hair hanging from the underside—the arched toes—the rather long head with deep far seeing eyes—an expression of dignity mixed with gentleness.

In color, the Saluki can meet the demands of the most fastidious, as while cream and fawn seem to predominate, there is red, grizzle and tan, white and chestnut, tricolor (black, white and tan), as well as solid black.

In disposition the Saluki shows great attachment to his master and is most gentle with children. He is affectionate without being demonstrative. They are good watch dogs but not aggressive.

In England they are fast becoming one of the most popular of breeds. Today one finds many Salukis in London and Paris promenading in the parks with their owners.

The Saluki was a well established breed in England for a number of years before he began to come into his own in this country. It was not until November 1927, that the breed was officially recognized by the American Kennel Club.

In July 1927, the Saluki Club of America was formed with only seven or eight fanciers among its members. Since that time, interest in the Saluki has been steadily growing. Several people have imported Salukis from England and the East. Most of the Saluki Kennels are located in the Atlantic States, although there are several breeders in California.

SALUKIS

At the Westminster Show of 1927, there were two Salukis entered in the Miscellaneous Class. The following year regular classes were provided, and there were ten Salukis. In 1929 there was a further increase in entries with much more interest shown by the public.

Since the breed was officially recognized by the American Kennel Club, there have been regular classes at all the principal shows. So now instead of being looked upon as something of a curiosity, the Saluki is a familiar sight in the dog world, and is becoming more popular year by year.

DESCRIPTION AND STANDARD OF POINTS
(By Courtesy of The Saluki Club of America)

Head.—Long and narrow, skull moderately wide between the ears, not domed, stop not pronounced, the whole showing great quality. Nose black or liver.

Ears.—Long and covered with long silky hair hanging close to the skull and mobile.

Eyes.—Dark to hazel and bright; large and oval, but not prominent.

Teeth.—Strong and level.

Neck.—Long, supple and well muscled.

Chest.—Deep and moderately narrow.

Fore Quarters.—Shoulders sloping and set well back, well muscled without being coarse.

Forelegs.—Straight and long from the elbow to the knee.

Hind Quarters.—Strong, hip bones set well apart and stifle moderately bent, hocks low to the ground, showing galloping and jumping power.

Loin and Back.—Back fairly broad, muscles slightly arched over loin.

Feet.—Of moderate length, toes long and well arched, not

splayed out, but at the same time not cat footed; the whole being strong and supple and well feathered between the toes.

Tail.—Long, set on low and carried naturally in a curve, well feathered on the underside with long silky hair, not bushy.

Coat.—Smooth and of a soft silky texture, slight feather on the legs, feather at the back of the thighs and sometimes with slight woolly feather on the thigh and shoulder.

Colors.—White, cream, fawn, golden, red, grizzle and tan tricolor (white, black and tan) and black and tan.

General Appearance.—The whole appearance of this breed should give an impression of grace and symmetry and of great speed and endurance coupled with strength and activity to enable it to kill gazelle or other quarry over deep sand or rocky mountains. The expression should be dignified and gentle with deep, faithful far-seeing eyes. Dogs should average in height from 23 to 28 inches and bitches may be considerably smaller, this being very typical of the breed.

The Smooth Variety.—In this variety the points should be the same with the exception of the coat which has no feathering.

SALUKI

WHIPPET

WHIPPETS

(By Courtesy of The American Whippet Club)

The Whippet, an English Greyhound in miniature, is a sporting dog of the first flight as well as a very charming, affectionate and intelligent pet. He is the fastest domesticated animal of his weight living and is capable of speeds up to 35 miles per hour. Though his main forte is as a race-dog, he is a courser of rabbits of great ability. His rat killing feats too are nearly equal to those of the most hard-bitten terriers. As an animal of sheer beauty, grace of outline and smoothness of action, he stands near the top in the realm of dogdom.

He is extraordinarily keen when racing or on game though in the living room he is quiet, dignified, unobtrusive and above all, highly decorative. His intelligence, when treated as a member of the family, compares favorably with most terriers. He is never snappy nor "barky" though as a watch dog he is excellent. Contrary to external appearances he is by no means delicate and difficult to care for. All in all he makes an ideal dual-purpose small dog for an owner of discrimination.

As a breed the Whippet is not one of our oldest, having been evolved in England between seventy-five and a hundred years ago, though it was not until 1891 that official recognition was given by the English Kennel Club.

It is said that when such barbaric pastimes as bull and bear baiting and dog fighting began to lose favor, the sporting gentry of that period originated the Whippet for the milder (to them) entertainment of coursing rabbits in an enclosure. The early specimens differed a great deal from our best present day dogs. These were crosses of small English Greyhounds and various terriers, both smooth and rough coated. It was not until a much later date that fanciers added an infusion of Italian Greyhound blood which aided so materially in improving type.

At first the breed was known as "snap-dogs" and the socalled sport was termed "snap-dog coursing." This was because the dog that caught or snapped-up the greatest number of rabbits during a match was declared winner. It will be noted that this ignoble pastime, in which the rabbit had absolutely no chance of escape, differed greatly from legitimate coursing in the open with Greyhounds and was purely a gambling proposition.

Later the Whippet was used primarily for straight racing. This sport had its inception, and still flourishes for that matter, in Lancashire and Yorkshire. Here the colliers nicknamed the Whippet, "the poor man's race horse," a term that even today is occasionally heard.

The standard course is 200 yards straightaway and the method of racing unique. Each dog has two attendants —a slipper and a handler. All dogs are held on their handicap marks by their slippers while their handlers trot up the track and across the finish line, all the while yelling encouragement and frantically waving towels or rags (which the Whippets are trained from puppy-hood to run to) to their charges. At the "get-set" command of the starter each slipper picks his dog up by the tail and the skin of the neck and when the pistol cracks the animals are literally thrown into their stride. They then race at top speed up the track and grab the waving rags of their handlers, who are some twenty yards behind the actual finish. Different colored wool collars are worn to distinguish the entries.

WHIPPETS

As Whippets vary in weight, from ten to twenty-eight pounds, a rather elaborate system of handicapping was evolved. This is based upon the fact that the heavier the dog, everything else being equal, the faster he should be. Times as fast as eleven and a half seconds have been recorded but any dog that can do twelve flat from his handicap mark is considered excellent. Generally speaking bitches are slightly faster than males and are usually handicapped accordingly.

Whippets appear first to have been brought to America by English mill operatives of Massachusetts. Lawrence and Lowell, for many years, were the center of Whippet racing in this country. Lately, however, the sport has moved South and at present Maryland, particularly in the neighborhod of Baltimore, holds the spotlight. Many refinements have been made that have improved racing immensely. Electric starting boxes are used, steeplechases inaugurated and the entire establishments patterned after the best of horse tracks. Now the very latest thing in Maryland is a circular track with electric hare, built especially for the "little longtails."

From the standpoint of the fancier Whippets make an ideal exhibition dog. With their small size (around 20 pounds) and smooth coat they are neither difficult to transport nor keep in condition. Their quiet deportment in the ring makes them comparatively easy to show, as is attested by the winnings of numerous novices who handle their own entries. To the expert breeder they are still a challenge for very few specimens so far have approached the perfection of the best Greyhounds.

The breed, as has already been stated, is extremely charming and versatile and anyone thinking of going into them should have few regrets.

SPORTING DOGS (HOUNDS)

DESCRIPTION AND STANDARD OF POINTS

(Adopted by The American Whippet Club, June 2, 1934, and Approved by The American Kennel Club, July 10, 1934)

Head.—Long and lean, fairly wide between the ears, scarcely perceptible stop, good length of muzzle, which should be powerful without being coarse.

Ears.—Small, fine in texture, thrown back and folded. Semipricked when at attention. Gay ears incorrect.

Eyes.—Bright, intelligent and dark.

Teeth.—White, strong and even. Upper jaw should fit nicely over lower.

Neck.—Long and muscular, well arched with no suggestion of throatiness, widening gradually into the shoulders.

Shoulders.—Oblique and muscular, without being loaded.

Chest.—Deep and capacious, as wide as consistent with speed. Ribs fairly well sprung.

Forelegs.—Straight and rather long, held in line with shoulders. Elbows neither in nor out, moving freely with point of shoulder. Pasterns strong. Fair amount of bone.

Feet.—Either cat or hare foot is permissible, must be well formed, with strong pads and claws well knuckled up.

Hind Quarters.—Long and powerful, stifles well bent, thighs broad and muscular, hocks well let down.

Back.—Broad and square, rather long and well arched over the loin, which should be strong and powerful.

Tail.—Long and tapering.

Coat.—Close, smooth and firm in texture.

Color.—Immaterial.

Height.—Dogs from 18 to 20 inches. Bitches from 17 to 19 inches.

WOLFHOUNDS (IRISH)

(Illustration facing page 286)

(By Courtesy of The Irish Wolfhound Club of America)

The Irish Wolfhound is the tallest of all dogs. He is built on greyhound lines, but more robust, with a harsh wiry coat and a short but dense undercoat; the eyes well-browed, the muzzle feathered, the underjaw evenly bearded and a well-covered stern.

The lines of strength are major points in an Irish Wolfhound, but they must be compatible with lines of swiftness; a muscular, graceful dog that is large and active.

His colors are interesting and the standard recognizes light cream or fawn brindles, various greys and the tawny grey shades down to the darkest brindles, some almost black. Color is not a point but a matter of personal preference.

The Irish Wolfhound as we know him today, a large rough coated hound, with piercing eyes, shaggy brows, and built on galloping lines, fits exactly into the picture of the feudal life of the Middle Ages. Yet, beneath this fierce looking exterior there beats the gentlest of hearts.

An ancient and romantic aura clothes the origin of the great hound from Ireland. Arrian, writing in the second century A.D. mentions the swift hounds brought to Greece during the invasion of the Celts, who sacked Delphi in 273 B.C. Evidences of this is borne out by some of the statues, jewelry and paintings described and some of which have been recovered.

The breed was well known in Roman days. The first

[275]

authentic record, however, was in 391 A.D., when the Roman Consul, Quintus Aurelius Symmachus, mentions them in a letter to his brother, Flavianus, in thanking him for the gift of seven Irish Wolfhounds which he had contributed for their circus combats and of which he said, "All Rome viewed them with wonder."

The early literature of Ireland abounds in references to these large dogs, and their ancient laws show they were held in great esteem.

They were the most valued hunting dogs of the early centuries, renowned for their hunting prowess, and their wisdom; and were much sought after by foreign monarchs, being considered a fit and pleasing gift to royalty.

In the fourth century, Cormac, a King of Ireland, had a great kennel of hounds and the Master of Hounds was the famous Finn. Early Celtic literature is richly endowed with the stories of Finn and his hounds.

In the tenth century, Olaf, a Norwegian, son of an Irish Princess, says to his friend Gunnar, as we find in the Saga of the Burnt Njal: "I will give thee a hound that was given to me in Ireland; he is big, and no worse than a stout man. Besides, it is part of his nature that he has a man's wit, and he will bay at every man whom he knows to be thy foe, but never at thy friends. He can see, too, in any man's face whether he means thee well or ill, and he will lay down his life to be true to thee. This hound's name is 'Sam'." After that he spoke to the hound: "Now shalt thou follow Gunnar, and do him all the service thou canst." The hound went at once to Gunnar, and laid down at his feet. Later, history relates, when Gunnar's enemies plotted to kill him, they killed the Irish hound first.

A curious old manuscript, of the twelfth century, mentions a certain Mesrodia, King of Leinsternien. who had a wolfhound named Aibe, whose fame filled all Ireland. For this hound six thousand cows and other things were offered by the King of Connacht. At the same time the King of Ulster offered approximately the same sum. Feeling ran so high over the dog that the kings and their retainers betook themselves to their swords and a mighty battle ensued. History does not relate who won the dog.

In 1596 the great Spanish poet, Lope de Vega, wrote a sonnet on the Irish Wolfhound.

In 1790, Bewick says: "The Irish greyhound is the largest of the dog kind, and its appearance the most beautiful. He is about three feet high, somewhat like a greyhound, but more robust. His aspect is mild, his disposition peaceable, his strength so great that in combat the mastiff or bulldog is far from being equal to him. He mostly seizes his antagonist by the back and shakes him to death, which his great strength enables him to do."

These powerful dogs were used not only in hunting the Irish wolf, but also the gigantic Irish elk, which stood six feet at the shoulder.

They are referred to as "Irish dogs," "big dogs of Ireland," "greyhounds of Ireland," "wolfdogs of Ireland," the "great hounds of Ireland," and the more modern appellative, "the Irish Wolfhounds."

But with the disappearance of the wolves and elk, and the steady depletion caused from excessive exportation from now dwindling ranks, the breed was allowed to become almost extinct. It was left to Captain G. A. Graham, of Dursley, a Scotchman, and an officer in the British army, to collect some of the remaining specimens and by judicious outcrosses, rehabilitate the breed. Captain Graham deserves unlimited credit for his work, which was begun in 1862. He worked for twenty years before his ideal was attained, and the present standard, to which the modern breeder subscribes, was drafted under Graham's supervision in 1885. Its continued existence is justified, inasmuch as it was drawn up after an exhaustive study of all old prints and historical references to this hound and the findings carefully sifted—and all this by gentlemen who had at some time been on intimate terms with some of the "last remaining specimens," and were fully qualified both from the standpoint of integrity and experience to do this work. This standard describes the ancient hound and the present day effort is to breed the old hound in fullest perfection. The List of Points in Order of Merit was added some time after the standard was written and be it noted that there is a note at the end of this list which calls attention to the fact that this list in no way alters the standard and if in any case it appears at variance, it is the standard which is correct. So, wisely, the standard is preserved and affirmed in its true form and by this precedent is protected from modern imaginations.

The sporting afflatus of the Irish Wolfhound cannot be questioned, they are pre-eminent in the field whenever tried. On the Continent they are used successfully in various hunts. For wild-boar, the larger animals, and even in lion hunts in the Kenya Colony, favorable reports are forthcoming. In America they are frequently used in running and killing coyotes, or brush wolves (a work at which some other breeds can also qualify), but the Irish Wolfhound is at his best when tried on the big timber wolf. When in good hard condition, he is capable of overtaking a wolf and dispatching him singly. He has the speed to get on terms with him and the power to finish him off afterwards.

But they are more rarely used now for this work, as

the better specimens quite consistently find their way into the private home, where they supplement the family life and deport themselves with credit in the home, being quiet mannered and dignified.

Their wonderful gift for attaching themselves to humankind, coming so close to that understanding which exists between humans, makes of them the greatest of companions. But this loyalty to man has been dominant in them for over two thousand years. They are reliable with children and smaller dogs, being kind and patient. They are capable guards, but never a nuisance in this respect. Fearless and powerful, they are not sharp mannered nor aggressive to well-meaning strangers, but do nicely distinguish between them and trespassers. They are knowing hounds!

Because the standard to which these hounds are bred describes a hound that will make a mighty hunter, it is not surprising to see this breed so often winning in the Sporting Hound Group at dog shows, and occasionally receiving the coveted best in show award. This hound will maintain indefinitely his dual-purpose. Civilization will claim him for his remarkable companionship, his spectacular appearance, his sense of devination, his reliability! And he must always be a sporting hound, if he is bred to meet the requirements of the standard. Though his usefulness in the field is not so broad as it once was, it is sufficient the world over to make a decent present-day field record.

The Irish Wolfhound of today still bears witness to the ancient proverb regarding them,—"Gentle when stroked, fierce when provoked," and yet another, written in the sixteenth century, "And all their manners do confess that courage dwells in gentleness."

SPORTING DOGS (HOUNDS)

"The Grey Hound! The Great Hound!
    The Graceful of limb!
Rough Fellow! Tall Fellow!
    Swift Fellow and Slim."

"Let them sound through the earth,
    Let them sail over the Sea,
They will light on none
    More ancient than thee."

DESCRIPTION AND STANDARD OF POINTS

(By Courtsey of The Irish Wolfhound Club of America)

1. *General Appearance.*—The Irish Wolfhound should not be quite so heavy or massive as the Great Dane, but more so than the Deerhound, which in general type he should otherwise resemble. Of great size and commanding appearance, very muscular, strongly though gracefully built, movements easy and active; head and neck carried high; the tail carried with an upward sweep with a slight curve towards the extremity.

The minimum height and weight of dogs should be 31 inches and 120 pounds; of bitches, 28 inches and 90 pounds. Anything below this should be debarred from competition. Great size, including height at shoulder and proportionate length of body, is the desideratum to be aimed at, and it is desired to firmly establish a race that shall average from 32 to 34 inches in dogs, showing the requisite power, activity, courage and symmetry.

2. *Head.*—Long, the frontal bones of the forehead very slightly raised and very little indentation between the eyes. Skull, not too broad. Muzzle, long and moderately pointed. Ears, small and Greyhound-like in carriage.

3. *Neck.*—Rather long, very strong and muscular, well arched, without dewlap or loose skin about the throat.

4. *Chest.*—Very deep. Breast, wide.

5. *Back.*—Rather long than short. Loins arched.

6. *Tail.*—Long and slightly curved, of moderate thickness, and well covered with hair.

7. *Belly.*—Well drawn up.

WOLFHOUNDS (IRISH)

8. *Fore Quarters.*—Shoulders, muscular, giving breadth of chest, set sloping. Elbows well under, neither turned inwards nor outwards. *Leg.*—Forearm muscular, and the whole leg strong and quite straight.

9. *Hind Quarters.*—Muscular thighs and second thigh long and strong as in the Greyhound, and hocks well let down and turning neither in nor out.

10. *Feet.*—Moderately large and round, neither turned inwards nor outwards. Toes, well arched and closed. Nails, very strong and curved.

11. *Hair.*—Rough and hard on body, legs and head; especially wiry and long over eyes and under jaw.

12. *Color and Markings.*—The recognized colors are grey, brindle, red, black, pure white, fawn, or any other color that appears in the Deerhound.

13. *Faults.*—Too light or heavy a head, too highly arched frontal bone; large ears and hanging flat to the face; short neck; full dewlap; too narrow or too broad a chest; sunken or hollow or quite straight back; bent forelegs; overbent fetlocks; twisted feet; spreading toes, too curly a tail; weak hind quarters and a general want of muscle; too short in body.

List of Points in Order of Merit

1. *Typical.* The Irish Wolfhound should not be quite so heavy or massive as the Great Dane, but more so than the Deerhound, which in general type he should otherwise resemble.
2. *Great* size and commanding appearance.
3. Movements easy and active.
4. Head, long and level, carried high.
5. Forelegs, heavily boned, quite straight; elbows well set under.
6. Thighs long and muscular; second thighs, well muscled, stifles nicely bent.
7. Coat, rough and hard, specially wiry and long over eyes and under jaw.
8. Body, long, well ribbed up, with ribs well sprung, and great breadth across hips.
9. Loins arched, belly well drawn up.

[281]

10. Ears, small, with greyhound-like carriage.
11. Feet, moderately large and round; toes, close, well arched.
12. Neck, long, well arched and very strong.
13. Chest, very deep, moderately broad.
14. Shoulders, muscular, set sloping.
15. Tail, long and slightly curved.
16. Eyes, dark.

Note.—The above in no way alters the "Standard of Excellence," which must in all cases be rigidly adhered to; they simply give the various points in order of merit. If in any case they appear at variance with Standard of Excellence, it is the latter which is correct.

BORZOI
(Formerly Russian Wolfhounds)
(Illustration facing page 287)

(By Courtesy of The Borzoi Club of America)

The breed name of Russian Wolfhound was officially changed to "BORZOI" by the Board of Directors of the American Kennel Club at its meeting held November 10, 1936.

The change was made at the request of the Parent Club of the breed, which Club has changed its name to "Borzoi Club of America."

The Borzoi or Russian Wolfhound has been used in Russia since the early part of the Seventeenth Century, for hunting wolves, coursing hare, and other game, as were also used the "Sloughi" or greyhounds of Egypt many centuries B.C. as depicted on tombs and monuments of that country.

It is noted from old books all over the world that coursing has been conducted for many hundreds of years, it may be for thousands, originally probably with the sole motive of procuring food and then later for sport.

There are many accounts of hunting expeditions of the several Mongol rulers from the time of the conqueror Genghis Khan, in the thirteenth century, in which long hounds or greyhounds were mentioned as the principal coursing dogs. All breeds of coursing hounds resemble each other in general conformation, all of them having been bred for speed.

SPORTING DOGS (HOUNDS)

The Russian Wolfhound, "Borzoi," "Psovoi," "Gustopsovoy," and several other Borzois, had many varieties, but they all conformed to the following general characteristics. Ears: short and pointed, when quiet, lying back on the neck and touching each other at the tips. The ribs: extending down to the elbow or below. Back: that of the male rising in a graceful curve from the shoulders to hips: the female more often had a straight back, although sometimes also showed a slight curve. Feet: long hare-shape, never round like the English hound. Coat: dense, soft, silky and fairly long, being longest and heaviest on the neck and inclined to be curly. Color: of the true type, was grey or yellow, also these two mixed, but the color could not be too deep nor the same all over the dog (straw or maize color preferred). The muzzle, throat, chest, hip edges and underside of tail considerably lighter in color, becoming white at the tips, as with the Arabian Greyhound, "Gazelle Hound."

In respect to the special features of all the different varieties of the Russian Borzoi or Russian Wolfhound, the authorities do not differ very much. If occasionally someone defends some particular deviation, it is usually due to private reasons or opinions, and though such a person's dogs may be of pure blood and breed, their deviation from the established type cannot be approved. For instance the ribs of the Russian Borzoi, or Russian Wolfhound, are not barrel-shaped as are those of the Crimean Borzoi; they are longer and extend further down, and the hips are never so large as are those of the Caucasian Borzoi or of the English greyhound. It seems certain that all breeds of Russian Borzois, or Russian Wolfhounds, come from one common source, namely from the crossing of the Asiatic or Eastern Borzoi, which penetrated into Russia several hundred years ago, with the Northern wolf-like dogs. This is indicated by the ears and by the long hair on the neck. The Courland or Kurland Borzoi seems also to have added its blood to the breed and given to it the long curly coat. Doubtless one will be interested in knowing how it came about that the ancient type of Russian Wolfhound has become so difficult to obtain or to breed. So much is heard, and so much is said about it, that this should be explained. It so happened in the early part of the eighteenth century, after many wars, that with subsequent revival of sporting activities in Russia, there arose a great craze to cross Russian Wolfhounds with foreign dogs of the same general type, such as Asiatic greyhounds, Crimean greyhounds and gazelle hounds with flapping ears. This crossing was practiced to such an extent that about the middle of the eighteenth century there were few pure-blooded wolfhounds left in the whole of Russia. At this time a large number of the nobility left their estates and repaired to different cities and to sojourn in various places in Europe and in many cases their kennels were given up entirely. Thus it will be seen that first from the mixing of other blood with the breed and later from the decrease in the number of hounds, the ancient type became almost extinct, so that when the first exportations of Russian Wolfhounds were made from Russia, practically none of the real ancient type hound ever left the country. Of course in some cases an occasional good specimen may have come out of Russia, but usually any such hounds were duly sent out to individuals as presents.

As far as is known, the first Russian Wolfhound which came to America was brought over from England by Mr. William Wade, of Hulton, Pa., in 1889, this hound being purchased from Mr. Freeman Lloyd. This was a bitch, named Elsie, and described in "The English Stock-keeper" as "Nothing much to look at, being small, light, and weedy, with no bone, straight back, very curly tail and too much bent in stifles."   Mr. C. Stedman Hanks in the early or middle nineties imported several Russian Wolfhounds and the records show that some of them were considered very good ones.   Mr. Hanks appears to be the only extensive American importer of these hounds who ever visited Russia, until 1903, when Mr. Joseph B. Thomas went there, with the exception of Mr. E. L. Krauss of Pennsylvania, whose importations were of German origin, and as somebody writes, many of them were very weedy, although very pretty to look at, with good heads and coats, but they had evidently been kennel raised for many generations and seemed to show it in disposition and lack of stamina.

Mr. Joseph B. Thomas' importations were made directly from Russia, from the Perchina Kennels, owned by the Grand Duke Nicholas of Romanoff and from the Woronzova Kennels of Mr. Arten Balderoff.   In these kennels, Mr. Thomas found the good ancient type of hound that everyone interested in the breed was looking for and is still looking for and about which so much is said.   It seems that from some of Mr. Thomas' memoirs the reason these two gentlemen, the Grand Duke and Mr. Balderoff, had the ancient type of the breed well preserved in their kennels was due to the fact that during the period of the degeneration of the breed, their places and places from whence they got their stock were so far out of the way that the craze of crossing did not reach that far.

As you visit different kennels and dog shows and observe Russian Wolfhounds, you will see the well-knit, well proportioned animal with perfect conformation, that

IRISH WOLFHOUND

BORZOI OR WOLFHOUND (*Russian*)

will move elegantly, with great poise, and remind you in the whole of the great superiority of a true aristocrat. Then you will also see the hound that apparently does not look just right to the eye, and to the novice this particular dog is a sort of puzzle. He or she will realize that there is something radically wrong but will be unable to say what it is. This is the type of hound that everyone should try to eliminate. It is either too long for its height, with too small or too large a head for the rest of its body, fox- or Roman-headed, with improper carriage of tail which is sometimes too short, in whole, all out of proportion, not typical or of good conformation, being unable to move properly and lacking the grace and appearance the breed should have. This type is mostly found in the larger sized hound where it has been raised in confinement and did not have the chance to exercise properly, and as a rule it will be found to be unsound.

Latest research into the much discussed origin of the Borzoi (Russian Wolfhound) brings out the very interesting discovery, that in the very early part of the seventeenth century a certain Russian Duke, who liked very fast dogs for hunting, imported a number of Arabian Greyhounds—probably of the breed known as the Gazelle Hound. These hounds were very speedy runners, but it seems that having thin coats they were unable to stand the severe weather and cold winters of Russia and soon died.

The gentleman in question, undaunted by his first failure, later sent for more of these hounds, and carefully crossed them with a native Russian breed somewhat similar to the Collie of today, but slightly different in build, having longer legs, longer gracefully curved tail, neck slightly longer and more powerful, very heavy furred ears and a carriage more like the wolfhound of today. This dog's coat was very heavy, wavy or curly and with tendency to be woolly. In color he was sable red or grey. He was a powerful dog able to stand great hardship and from all accounts was a real working dog.

The result of this crossing was the graceful elegant and aristocratic dog we know as the Russian Wolfhound in America and as the Borzoi in most other countries.

The above mentioned crossing produced a coat that only the Russian Wolfhound has. He also has speed and endurance surpassing that of his ancestors; the heart and courage of a lion; yet withal he is as gentle as a kitten in the home.

DESCRIPTION AND STANDARD OF POINTS
(By Courtesy of The Borzoi Club of America)

Head.—Skull slightly domed, long and narrow, with scarcely any perceptible stop, rather inclined to be Roman-nosed; jaws long, powerful and deep; teeth strong, clean and even, neither pig-jawed nor undershot; nose large and black.

Ears.—Small and fine in quality, lying back on the neck when in repose with the tips when thrown back almost touching behind occiput; raised when at attention.

Eyes.—Set somewhat obliquely, dark in color, intelligent, but rather soft in expression, never full nor staring, nor light in color, eyelids dark.

Neck.—Clean, free from throatiness, somewhat shorter than in the greyhound, slightly arched, very powerful and well set on.

Shoulders.—Sloping, should be fine at the withers and free from coarseness or lumber.

Chest.—Rather narrow, with great depth of brisket.

Ribs.—Only slightly sprung, but very deep, giving room for heart and lung play.

Back.—Rising a little at the loins in a graceful curve.

BORZOI

Loins.—Extremely muscular, but rather tucked up, owing to the great depth of chest and comparative shortness of back and ribs.

Forelegs.—Bone flat, straight, giving free play for the elbows, which should be neither turned in nor out; pasterns strong.

Feet.—Hare shaped, with well-arched knuckles, toes close and well padded.

Hindquarters.—Long, very muscular and powerful, with well bent stifles and strong second thighs, hocks broad, clean and well let down.

This ideal has been reached by a study of dozens of photographs of celebrated dogs all over the world, in many cases by a personal inspection of the same, and by the criticism and assistance of many members of the Borzoi Club. The Club places this picture before fanciers in the hope that it may thereby assist in fixing the proper type in the minds of breeders and judges.

Tail.—Long, set on and carried low in a graceful curve.

Coat.—Long, silky (not woolly), either flat, wavy or rather curly. On the head, ears and front of legs it should be short and smooth; on the neck the frill should be profuse and rather curly. Feather on hindquarters and tail, long and profuse, less so on the chest and back of forelegs.

Color.—Any color, white usually predominating, more or less marked with lemon, tan, brindle, grey or black. Whole colored specimens of these tints occasionally appear. Solid black or black marked with tan to be considered a disqualification.

General Appearance.—Should be that of an elegant, graceful aristocrat among dogs, possessing courage and combining great muscular power with extreme speed.

Size.—Dogs, average height at shoulder from 28 to 31 inches; average weight from 75 to 105 pounds. Larger dogs are often seen, extra size being no disadvantage when it is not acquired at the expense of symmetry, speed and staying quality.

Bitches are invariably smaller than dogs, and two inches less in height, and from 15 to 20 pounds less in weight is a fair average.

	Points
Head	15
Ears	5
Eyes	5
Neck	5
Shoulders and chest	15
Ribs, back and loins	15
Hindquarters, stifles and hocks	15
Legs and feet	10
Coat and feather	10
Tail	5
Total	100

ALASKAN MALAMUTE

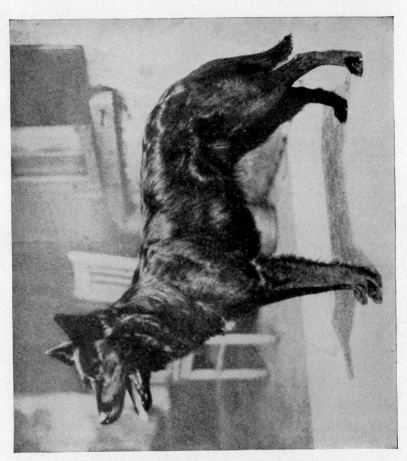

BELGIAN SHEEPDOG (*Groenendael*)

Group III—WORKING DOGS

ALASKAN MALAMUTE
(Illustration facing page 290)

(By Courtesy of The Alaskan Malamute Club)

The Alaskan Malamute is one of the oldest breed of Arctic sled-dogs known. It was named after the native Innuit tribe called Mahlemuts, who settled along the shores of Kotzebue Sound, which is in the upper western part of Alaska. Long before Alaska became a possession of the United States, this Arctic region was called by the Russians, who were the discoverers, "Alashak" or "Alyeska," meaning in the Russian tongue "Vast Country." Native people were already living in Alyeska land when these Asiatic sailors visited the shores, having been forced by storms when whaling in Bering Strait to land in this North country opposite Siberia. They returned to their homelands and told stories about seeing "native people using dogs to haul sledges, which were heavily loaded." The origin of these people and also of the dogs has never been ascertained. We do know that they had been in Alaska for generations, and from whence they come, is as indefinite as it is with any of the other Arctic natives, either of Greenland in the east of North America or the Samoyede tribe of Russia. Likewise the same is true about the origin of all Arctic dogs. Some theories hold that the pure bred Arctic sled-dog was a cross of the Arctic wolf and dog, generations back, and this seems to make a colorful background for these animals. Others do not attempt to argue but are satisfied that no wolf blood has been crossed with Arctic dogs for generations so that the characteristics or any wolf traits are far removed. Nature has provided the Arctic breeds of dogs with thick double coats, tough feet, well furred tails to protect the faces against the cold, when sleeping, powerful bodies and an appearence of "wolflike" expression around the eyes, due to their slantwise position. The Malamute breed has all these characteristics and has always been used for draught purposes in the North.

The tribe of Mahlemuts, now spelled Malamutes, were called "high type" Innuits. Many writers of Alaska, translations from Russian explorers, and records left by Englishmen who traveled the Alaskan coast, all give similar accounts about these fine Innuits. "Innuit" means "people" in the Orarian language. Never are the Mahlemuts mentioned without their dogs also being referred to. One writer, who went to Alaska in the early days of exploration after it had become a possession of the United States, gives many interesting references about the Innuits and especially about the Mahlemuts. He uses the original spelling so that we know the records were taken at an early date. "Upon arriving at Unalakleet, I found that a party of Mahlemuts had arrived the day before by dog teams. They had carried mail from Point Barrow down along the coast wherever White Men were living. They had also been runners for the Russian Muscovy Whaling Company when they had landed in this Arctic region. These Mahlemuts were wonderful looking natives and were taller than their Greenland cousins. They were industrious, skilled in hunting and fishing, made perfect sledges and had dogs of remarkable beauty and endurance. These dogs had traveled many hundreds of miles and being better cared for by their drivers than is the usual lot of Arctic dogs, these animals were affectionate and seemed tireless in energy." This description is quite different from many of the tales told by peo-

ple who have seen other native dogs in the Arctic. The
dispositions of these sledge dogs perhaps was the result
of the environment in which they lived as the usual treatment of sledge dogs in the North has been harsh, owing
to the uncivilized tribes who wandered from place to
place until White Men invaded their villages.

Another Alaskan traveler, a Missionary, who was well
known among all the Innuits and journeyed thousands
of miles by dog team writes the following: "These Malamutes, now spelled MALAMUTE, a corruption of the
original word Mahlemut, "Mahle" meaning name of the
Innuit tribe and "Mut" meaning "Village" in Orarian
vocabulary of the Mahlemut dialect, are a "high type"
people. They are peaceful, happy, hard workers, believe in "one wife," are able guides and have wonderful
dogs. Even though uncivilized, they have realized that
it is important to have fine animals to pull sledges and
that without them, means of travel in this sort of country would be impossible at times. The dogs are powerful looking, have thick dense double coats (outer coat of
thick coarse fur and inner coat a fuzzy down laying
close to skin) called weather coats, erect ears, magnificent bushy tails carried over their backs like waving
plumes, tough feet, colors varying but mostly wolf grey
or black and white. The dogs have remarkable endurance and fortitude. The Malamute people and their
dogs are much respected among other Innuits."

A book entitled "Researches of Alaska" includes
several references about these Malamute dogs, being
called the native dogs of Alaska. "Natives recognized
in their crude way the importance of the dogs, as
they were considered indispensable for transportation in
the North"——later another reference says: "Dogs were
two and two, side by side (gang hitch), leader in front,

harnessed to a sledge, colors varying from grey to black and white, and carrying a heavy load. The dogs were powerful looking animals and did not appear vicious. The natives, called Malamutes, were not Indians but perhaps related to the Asiatic Arctic natives of the Chukchis. (This is a suggestion of their ancestry but not confirmed.) The Mahlemut dialect is simple to understand and the natives themselves a happy tribe. They are fond of their children and their dogs. The dogs work hard and have wonderful endurance."

A Russian translation gives another reference about the "Mahlemuts found over the sea in the Vast Land" called the "Stopping Off" place by the Russian sailors. This writer referred to the workmanship of the Mahlemuts and the sledges, and admitted the "Mahlemut dogs and sledges were better than those of the Russians for interior travel."

It is confirmed that these Alaskan Malamute sledge dogs were used as draught animals and they have never lost their identity. When Alaska became settled by White Men, it is true that the Arctic breed was mingled with that of outside dogs just as they have been in Greenland, Labrador, Siberia or any of the other Arctic countries. During the Alaskan Sweepstakes, the lure of racing became so popular that many drivers tried all sorts of experiments in mixing the Arctic breed with some outside strain and this period from 1909 to 1918 was the age of "decay of the Arctic sledge dog." Fortunately, the sport of sled-dog racing became popular in the United States and interest to develop the pure strain of the native Alaskan Malamute started in 1926, after a careful study of all types of Northern breeds had been made. Malamutes still hold many racing records. During the World War, several Malamutes were among the dogs sent across

ALASKAN MALAMUTES

by A. A. Allen who assembled 150 dogs for this purpose
—100 coming from Alaska. These Malamutes again made
remarkable records for hauling and were distinctive in
their appearence. The two recent Byrd Antarctic Expeditions have used Malamutes as well as other Arctic
breeds and again the records have been outstanding.

Some Alaskans today call the Malamute the "personality dog" and several are now owned in the United States
and are also called by this term rather than "wolf dogs."
The question of the "wolf" ancestry in any of the Arctic
breeds is merely a supposition and for generations no
"wolf blood" has been successfully introduced, even
though some of the Alaskan breeders still maintain this
is true. One modern dog fancier brings out a most important point about the difference of Arctic pure bred
dogs and Wolf dogs. "The Arctic breeds stand erect,
have a 'proud appearance' and carry their tails up—while
a wolf has a slinking movement and carries his tail
down."

The Alaskan Malamute although quite rare is increasing in popularity and becoming more extensively bred in
the United States from dogs originally from Alaska.
The word "husky" as sometimes applied to the Malamute is a misnomer and was originally a term of disre-
spect used by the Indians or Aleuts who invaded Alaska
and were hostile to the Innuits, calling them "huskies."
This word has gradually been used in the North to describe working dogs of mixed breeds used to pull sledges.
No pure breed of Arctic dogs is called "husky" except
the Siberian Huskie. The Alaskan Malamute is the native Alaskan Arctic breed and is cousin to the Samoyede
of Russia, Siberian Huskie of Siberia (Kolyma River
Region), and the Eskimo breeds of Greenland and
Labrador. The origin of any of these breeds is only sup-

position. Well informed Arctic writers who have made a research study of Arctic formations seem to disagree about the origin of the Arctic peoples. Some believe that during the Glacier Age, there was land connecting Asia and Alaska, and also Greenland and Labrador. Perhaps our Alaskan natives and Labrador Eskimos came into these countries by dog power. Others claim immigration spread from the Hudson Bay Country, east and west; others that Greenland was originated by Norwegians who went "native" and likewise, Alaska by Asiatic people. This all happened so many generations ago that all we know today is that Arctic breeds were found and the Alaskan Arctic sledge dog native to that country, is the breed now called the Malamute. In the United States, the Alaskan Malamute is recognized and is being shown on the bench. They differ from the Samoyede, Siberian Huskie and Eskimo, yet are maintaining all the Arctic characteristics of their ancestors, having thick dense coats, tough feet, well furred "plumed" tails, wolf-like appearance around eyes, are mostly wolfish grey or black and white in color and have distinctive markings. They are being used as pets and have become a popular sled-dog among sportspeople who enjoy this winter recreation. They are very fond of humans and especially children, who enjoy driving them to sleds.

DESCRIPTION AND STANDARD OF POINTS

(As Adopted by The Alaskan Malamute Club, April 17, 1935 and Approved by The American Kennel Club)

Origin.—The Alaskan Malamute is a native sled-dog of Alaska and is the oldest native dog known to that country. It was originally named "Mahlemut" after a native Innuit (Mahlemut) Tribe.

ALASKAN MALAMUTES

General Appearance and Characteristics.—A large size dog with a strong, compact body, not too short coupled; thick dense, coarse coat and not too long; stands well over pads and has appearance of much activity; broad head, ears erect and wedge shaped; muzzle not too pointed and long, but not too stubby (other extreme); deep chest, proud carriage, head erect and eyes alert—Face markings are a distinguishing feature and the eyes are well set off by these markings which consist of either cap over head and rest of face solid color, (usually greyish white) or face marked with appearance of a mask, thus setting off eyes; tail is plumed and carried over back when not working, but not too tightly curled, more like a plume waving. Malamutes are of various colors, but usually wolfish grey or black and white. Their feet are of the "snow-shoe" type with well cushioned pads giving firm and compact appearance; front legs straight and with big bone; hind legs well bent at stifles and without cowhocks; straight back gently sloping from shoulders to hips; endurance and intelligence are shown in body and eyes; the eyes have a "wolf-like" appearance by position of eyes, but expression is soft; quick in action, but no loss of energy in moving; affectionate dispositions.

Head.—The head should indicate a high degree of intelligence —it should be in proportion to the size of the dog so as to not make the dog appear clumsy or coarse. Skull—Broad between ears, gradually narrowing to eyes; moderately rounded between ears, flattening on top as it approaches eyes, rounding off to cheeks, which should be moderately flat; there should be a slight furrow between the eyes; the top line of skull and top line of muzzle showing but little break downward from a straight line as they join.

Muzzle.—Large and bulky in proportion to size of skull— diminishing but little in width or depth from junction with skull to nose—lips close fitting—nose black—upper and lower jaws broad with large teeth—the front teeth meeting with a scissors grip, but never "overshot."

Eyes.—Almond shaped—dark in color—moderately large for this shape of eye—set obliquely in skull.

Ears.—Medium—upper half of ear triangular in shape— slightly rounded at tips—set wide apart on outside back edges of top of skull with lower part of ear joining the skull on a line with the upper corner of eye; giving the tips of the ears the appearance when erect of standing off from the skull; when erect, ears are pointed slightly forward, but when at work the ears are usually folded back on the skull.

Body.—Chest should be strong and deep; body should be strong and compactly built, but not too short coupled; the back should be straight and gently sloping from shoulders to hips. Loins well muscled, but no surplus weight.

Shoulders, Legs and Feet.—Shoulders moderately sloping; fore-legs heavily boned and muscled—straight to pasterns, which should be short and strong and almost vertical as viewed from the side; feet large and compact, toes well arched, pads thick and tough; toe nails short and strong; protective growth of hair between toes. Hindlegs must be broad and powerfully muscled through thighs; stifles moderately bent; hock joints broad and strong and moderately bent and well let down—as viewed from behind the hindlegs should not appear bowed in bone, but stand and move true and not too close or too wide. The legs of the Malamute must indicate unusual strength and powerful propelling power—any definite indication of unsoundness in legs and feet, standing or moving constitutes practically disqualification in the show ring.

Coat.—Thick, dense, coarse coat, but not long; undercoat is thick, oily and woolly, while outer coat is rather coarse and stands out. Thick fur around neck. (This allows for protection against weather.)

Color and Markings.—The usual colors are wolfish grey or black and white. Markings should be either cap-like or mask-like on face. A variation of color and markings is occasionally found.

Tail.—Well furred and carried over back when not working, but not too tightly curled to rest on back, a "waving plume" appearance instead.

Height.—Of male dog averaging from 22 to 25 inches; of bitch averaging from 20 to 23 inches.

Weight.—Of male dog averaging from 65 to 85 pounds; of bitch averaging from 50 to 70 pounds.

BELGIAN SHEEPDOG (*Malinois*)

BERNESE

ALASKAN MALAMUTES

BELGIAN SHEEPDOGS

(Illustrations facing pages 291 and 298)

The Belgian varieties of the sheepdog are not dissimilar to the breeds used for herding sheep the world over, and there seems little doubt of their distant relationship to a number of dogs bred for this purpose in Central Europe. These breeds all are descended of the oldest known strains of the dog, going back, particularly to the Moorland dog.

Most popular of all the six varieties of Belgian Sheepdog now known in Belgium is the Groenendael, or long-coated black. This is one of the two breeds recognized in the United States. The other is the Malinois, which is short-coated and usually a brindle fawn in color.

While the Groenendael has come to occupy a foremost place among the varieties of the Belgian Sheepdog, it is one of the youngest of the six. Its development was a matter of selective breeding in the latter part of the nineteenth century. The name is that of a village in Belgium where M. Rose had maintained a kennel of sheepdogs for some years. In one of his litters there happened to be a long-coated, black bitch. Rose was immediately caught by the beauty of this dog. He determined to preserve the strain.

Blacks were very rare in those days, but finally after searching for almost a year, Rose discovered a black male that was almost identical with this black female. It was owned by M. Bernaert, who resided in Feluy-Arquenes. M. Rose bought this dog and mated it to his black bitch. This variety made its show debut in

1898, when a dog named Tomy received high praise from M. Reul, who was judging, and who was a great authority on the breed. Indeed, Reul is credited with being the founder of the short-haired breeds.

The variety known as the Malinois takes its name from a town called Malines, although it also is known as Mechlin. This short-haired dog bears the closest resemblance of any of the varieties to the German shepherd, although the resemblance is only a casual one. Close inspection reveals many structural differences.

Two other varieties take their names from the towns of their origin. One is the Tervueren, which is a long-coated, fawn colored dog. The other is the de Laeken, which is short-coated but other than fawn-colored. The two wire-haired varieties are not known by special names.

The Groenendael made its appearance in the United States about a decade and a half ago, and for some years it enjoyed considerable popularity. The Malinois came to America somewhat later, but it never came to any great prominence. Some specimens of the Groenendael bred in the United States have approximated very closely the ideals of the breed as promulgated in Belgium.

Few breeds of dogs have been the inspiration of so many tributes from noted writers as the Belgian Sheepdog. Ouida's "Dog of Flanders" stands as a famous chronicle of the breed. Since Ouida, or Marie Louise Ramee, was born and raised in England, and spent much of her early career in that country, there is strong reason to believe that the Belgian Sheepdog's fame had spread far and beyond his native Belgium. Then the great Belgian poet, philosopher, and dramatist, Maeterlinck, chose this breed as his subject in "Our Friend the Dog."

All those who have had contact with any of the varieties of the Belgian Sheepdog are rich in praise of its many qualities, particularly of its devotion and its ability to fit in with the moods of its masters. But scientific dog breeders are equally enthusiastic concerning the searching intelligence of the breed, and its value as a worker. It is one of the breeds most used for police work in Europe. In fact, some authorities credit the Belgian Sheepdog with being the first breed to be thoroughly trained as a police dog. During the World War, thousands of these dogs were trained for a variety of duties. They were particularly useful for carrying messages between outflung sectors, where human messengers would have met certain death. Many of these dogs gave their lives.

It was following the World War that the Belgian Sheepdog really began to make headway in the United States, and within a few years it had become one of the popular working dogs. Entries at shows were steadily mounting until the depression. Since then the breed has been marking time, but its return to favor is predicted shortly by its followers.

DESCRIPTION AND STANDARD OF POINTS

(As Adopted by The Belgian Sheepdog Club of America, Inc., and Approved by The American Kennel Club)

General Appearance—(a) *Size.*—The height of the Belgian Sheepdog should be at least 60 centimeters (about 23½ inches) for dogs and 58 centimeters (about 22½ inches) for bitches, measured at the shoulder. The length, measured from breast bone to tip of hind quarters, should equal the height. Their weight should be at least 24 kilograms (approximately 53 pounds).

(b) *Position.*—He should stand squarely on all fours, the legs perfectly straight, viewed from all sides.

(c) *Qualities.*—The Belgian Sheepdog should reflect the qualities of intelligence, courage, alertness and devotion to his master. His native environment has fortified him with marvelous powers

[303]

of endurance, enabling him to resist the inclemency of the seasons and the vicissitudes of the weather, so characteristic of the Belgian climate.

To his inbred aptitude as a guardian of flocks he adds the valuable qualities of the best guardian of property. In emergencies he is, without any hesitation, the stubborn and spirited defender of his master.

He is watchful, attentive and always in motion; he is seemingly tireless.

He shows a marked tendency to move in a circle rather than in a straight line.

The Skull.—Flattened rather than rounded; not so wide to appear clumsy nor narrow as a whippet's.

Stop.—Moderate.

Head and Muzzle.—The head should be in proportion to the body: long, with a moderately pointed muzzle (not shorter than the skull), avoiding any tendency to snipiness. Jaws strong and powerful. Lips tight.

Eyes.—Brown, preferably dark brown, of medium size, not set too obliquely and not protruding; the gaze questioning and denoting intelligence.

Ears.—Triangular in shape, stiff, erect, well placed and not too long. Dogs whose ears are not erect are not to be considered.

Neck.—Round and rather outstretched.

Top Line.—Back, loins and hips horizontal, large and powerful, of medium length.

Tail.—Strong at the base, of medium length, differing somewhat according to the variety. At rest, the dog holds it low, the tip bent straight back level with the hock. When in action he raises it and gives it a curl, which is strongest toward the tip, without forming a hook.

Defects.—Carrying the tail too high, turning it to the right or to the left instead of carrying it in line with the center of the body.

A dog without a tail or with a stump, whether naturally or by docking, cannot take a prize at any show.

Breast.—Narrow rather than broad.

BELGIAN SHEEPDOGS

Chest.—Not broad, but deep and well let down, as in all animals with rapid gait.

Abdomen.—Of moderate development, not flagging and not like a greyhound.

Shoulders.—Long and oblique, forming a sharp angle with the upper arm.

Arms.—Governed exactly by the length of the body.

Forearms.—Long, strong and moderately heavy from elbow to pastern.

Hind Quarters and Thighs.—Strong and well muscled.

Legs.—Long and strong.

Feet.—Round and compact (cat-footed); well padded and straight in line with the body and forearm.

Hair.—Always abundant and close, forming an excellent protective covering. Undercoat dense.

Teeth.—Strong, regular and even. Neither undershot nor overshot.

Dewclaws.—Not at all desirable.

Varieties

There being a great difference in the hair of the Belgian Sheepdogs, as to its length, appearance, growth and color, this point has been adopted as the distinguishing mark of the varieties of the breed.

Distinctive Characteristics Groenendael

Long-haired—(a) *Color.*—Black. Some white hairs on the chest and hind feet are allowed. Long, smooth, straight and flat over the entire surface of the body, except on the head, the outside of the ears and the lower part of the legs, where it is short. The opening of the ear is protected by tufts of hair. The neck is adorned with long and abundant hair, like a collarette. The back of the forearm is ornamented with a fringe of long hair from the elbow to the level of the knee. The hind quarters are trimmed with long, abundant hair forming what is known as the breeches. The tail is heavily plumed.

[305]

Wavy or curly hair are faults.
(b) Fawn.
(c) Any other color.

MALINOIS

Short-haired—(a) *Color.*—Brindled fawn with black mask.
Besides the general characteristics of the breed, this variety is recognized by the hair, which appears short over the entire body, notably on the head and lower part of the limbs; half length elsewhere and more furred around the neck and tail. The back of the hindlegs is fringed with long hair.

Defects.—Hair too short. Harsh hairs scattered through the short hair. Coat too light.

(b) Fawn.
(c) Any other color.

	Points
General appearance and expression	25
Back	15
Hind quarters	15
Chest and fore quarters	15
Head and muzzle	15
Coat	15
Total	100

BERNESE MOUNTAIN DOGS

(Illustration facing page 299)

Aristrocratic in appearance, ancient in lineage, the Bernese Mountain Dog, one of the four varieties of Swiss Mountain Dogs, is a worthy addition to the American Kennel Club Stud-Book. Long-haired and distinctive in coloring, they have never been used to herd sheep as are the other varieties, but instead were used as draught dogs by the weavers of the Canton of Berne, where it was once a common sight to see them drawing to the market place, small wagons loaded with baskets.

These dogs were brought into Switzerland over two thousand years ago by the invading Roman soldiers. However, until a few years before the World War they had been almost forgotten by all save the oldest inhabitants of Berne. They were still used by the weavers but the breed had degenerated to such a marked extent as to be practically unrecognizable, and when in 1892, a Swiss fancier attempted to find good specimens to be used as breeding stock, his search was a long one. However, he was successful and several other fanciers became interested as well. A few good examples were unearthed and the rehabilitation of this worthy dog was started. In 1907, a specialty club was formed and the breed found favor with many wealthy Swiss who have developed them as house pets and companions; their old life in harness being a thing of the past.

The popularity of these Bernese Mountain Dogs has increased so greatly that they are now to be found all over Switzerland in ever-increasing numbers and the breed entries at dog shows are numerous.

A handsome, long-haired dog about the size of a collie and not unlike him in appearance, the Bernese is jet-black in color, with russet brown or rich tan markings on his forelegs, spots over each eye, on either side of the snowy white chest markings and just above the forelegs. It is highly desirable that these dogs have white feet, white tail-tip, and a pure white blaze on the foreface, as well as white star-shaped markings on the chest. However, it is not disqualifying if these white marks are missing. The coat is long and silky with a slight wave but it must not be curly. An impressive looking dog, 23 to 27½ inches in height for dogs, with bitches slightly smaller, the Bernese is characterized by fiery eyes of dark hazel, V-shaped ears hanging close to the head in repose, but brought slightly forward and raised at the base when alert. His short-backed, compact and well-ribbed up body with broad chest, deep brisket and strong muscular loins show that he is well suited to draught work.

The Bernese is an extremely hardy dog, thriving in an unheated kennel in all weather and needing only a small amount of grooming to look well kept. They are exceptionally faithful animals and once having centered their affection on an individual, they do not fawn upon or make friends with strangers.

A few of these Swiss dogs have been imported into the United States and they and their progeny are expected to be a feature of the bench shows of the future.

DESCRIPTION AND STANDARD OF POINTS
(Adopted by The American Kennel Club, April 13, 1937)

General Appearance.—A well-balanced dog, active and alert; a combination of sagacity, fidelity and utility.

BERNESE MOUNTAIN DOGS

Height.—Dogs, 23 inches to 27½ inches; bitches, 21 inches to 26 inches at shoulder.

Head.—Skull flat, defined stop and strong muzzle. Dewlaps very slightly developed, flews not too pendulous, jaw strong with good, strong teeth. Eyes dark, hazel-brown, full of fire. Ears V-shaped, set on high, not too pointed at tips and rather short. When in repose, hanging close to head; when alert, brought slightly forward and raised at base.

Body.—Rather short than too long in back, compact and well ribbed up. Chest broad with good depth of brisket. Loins strong and muscular.

Legs and Feet.—Forelegs perfectly straight and muscular, thighs well developed and stifles well bent. Feet round and compact. Dewclaws should be removed.

Tail.—Of fair thickness and well covered with long hair, but not to form a flag; moderate length. When in repose, should be carried low, upward swirl permissible; when alert, may be carried gaily, but may never curl or be carried over back.

Coat.—Soft and silky with bright, natural sheen; long and slightly wavy but may never curl.

Color and Markings.—Jet-black with russet-brown or deep tan markings on all four legs, a spot just above forelegs, each side of white chest markings and spots over eyes, which may never be missing. The brown on the forelegs must always be between the black and white.

Preferable, but not a condition, are.—White feet, tip of tail, pure white blaze up foreface, a few white hairs on back of neck, and white star-shaped markings on chest. When the latter markings are missing, it is not a disqualification.

Faults.—Too massive in head, light or staring eyes, too heavy or long ears, too narrow or snipy muzzle, under or overshot mouth, pendulous dewlaps, too long or Setter-like body, splay or hare feet, tail curled or carried over back, cowhocks and white legs.

SCALE OF POINTS

General Appearance 15
Size and Height 5

Head	15
Body	15
Legs and Feet	15
Tail	10
Coat	10
Color and Markings	15
Total	100

BOUVIERS DE FLANDRE

(Illustration facing page 318)

(By Courtesy of Club National du Bouvier des Flandres, Belgium)

Dr. Keul of the Veterinary School of Brussels was the man who first called the attention of the breeders to the many good qualities of the Bouvier. At that time, the Bouvier, was a dog of great size (about 26 inches high at the shoulder), with a heavy cylindrical body, rough grey, dark hair and a rough appearance. It was found in South West Flanders and on the French Northern hills. As a rule, it was owned by people who occupied themselves with cattle, for the chief aptitude of this dog seems to be cattle driving.

Most of the early Bouvier breeders were farmers, butchers, or cattle merchants. They were not particularly interested in breeding pure pedigree dogs. All they wanted was to have useful help in their work, so one will not be surprised that the first Bouviers were not absolutely uniform as to size, weight and color. Nevertheless, they all had enough characteristics in common to be recognized as a Bouvier. They had different names and were known as Vuilbaard (dirty beard) koe hond (cow dog) toucheur de boeuf or pic (cattle driver).

The Societe Royale St. Hubert took cognizance of the breed when it appeared on the show benches at the International Dog Show of May 1910 in Brussels. The two Bouviers shown there were Nelly and Even, belonging to a Mr. Poiret of Ghent, but a standard of the Bouviers type was not adopted until 1912. That was accomplished by a Frenchman, Mr. Fontaine, vice-president of the Club St. Hubert du Nord. At that time a society of Bouvier breeders was founded in Roulers (West) Flanders. This new society invited at that time many of the most famous Belgian experts to a meeting in August 1912. Among those who attended were M. de Hautvert of Levita, Baron van Zeiglen of Weymons, M. Van Herreweghe, Veterinary of Scharlaken and others who promulgated a Standard of Perfection which was the first official standard to be recognized by the Societe Royale St. Hubert.

From that time, the Bouviers de Flandre grew to be more and more appreciated and several dogs such as Ch. Nella, Ch. Picard, Ch. Zola of Mr. Re Rycker (Roulers), Pickzwaurt of Mr. Van Herreweghe, Jim and Maerten de lu Wornaffe Domicent, Anna de l'Yperlei and Amic of Mr. Lapierre (Ypres), were enlisted in the French Book of Origins Volume 4 (Stud Book of the Societe Royale St. Hubert).

The breed was making rapid progress, when the war broke out. Those parts of the country where the Bouvier was most largely bred, and where it was becoming more and more popular, were as you know, entirely destroyed. The population left the country and most of the dogs were lost. Many were abandoned and died, others were acquired by the Germans. Nevertheless, a few men succeeded in keeping their dogs all through the war so Sultan of Mr. Van der Vennet, Picko Carlo of Mr. Perret, Bella and Kit de Ramillies, escaped. The dog whose progeny afterwards did much to revive the Bouvier in Belgium, lived in the Belgian army and was the property of Veterinary Captain Darby. That dog was Ch. Nic de Sottegem, and was shown in 1920 at the Olympic show in Antwerp. In this relation, the judge, M. Charles

Hugo said of him—"Nic is the ideal type of the Bouvier. He has a short body, with well developed ribs, short flanks, strong legs, good feet, long and oblique shoulders. His head is of a good shape with somber eyes and an ideal courageous expression. His hair is dry and dark. The tail should not have been cut so short. I hope that dog will have numerous progeny."

Mr. Hugo's wishes were realized, and when Nic died in 1926, he left a great many descendants whose names one will still find in almost every pedigree. Among those worthy of mention are Prince D'or, Ch. Droya, Corshe de Sottegem, Goliath de le Lyt, Lyda Nefte de la Paix, Norah, Siske de Sottegem, Ch. Dragon de la Lys, etc. It was from these dogs gathered together one day at Ghent, that a group of experts including Mr. Charles Hugo Vbenret, V. Raymons, Count de Hemptenne, Captain Renon a Gevaert, after examining and measuring carefully every dog, established a more comprehensive standard of the Bouvier. It is that very standard you will find at the end of these lines.

Since then the Bouviers have attained more and more success abroad, especially in Holland and in Belgium. The average number of them at the shows is 30, which is relatively large, but so popular have Bouviers become that often this number is exceeded.

The breeders do not forget that the Bouvier is first of all a work dog, and although they try to standardize its type, they do not want it to lose the early qualities which first called attention to its desirability. For that reason, in Belgium a Bouvier cannot win the title of Champion unless he has also won a prize in a work competition as a police dog, a defense dog, or as an army dog.

WORKING DOGS

DESCRIPTION AND STANDARD OF POINTS
(By Courtesy of Club National du Bouvier des Flandres, Belgium)

General Appearance.—A dog with a coat rough to the touch, rugged, noticeable, showing by the brightness of his eye action, vigor and energy.

Head.—Of medium length in proportion to the figure and the length of the body.

Skull.—Flat, not too wide between the ears, sloping gently toward the muzzle and slightly exceeding it in length. The silky coat on the head should be tousled.

Stop.—Hardly noticeable, more apparent by the growth of the coat than actual. The superciliary arches pronounced and covered by a tousled coat.

Cheeks.—Not prominent.

Muzzle.—Large and bony, well covered with a coat not silky and not flat.

Lips.—Dry and tight, well covered with a fairly long but not silky coat.

Ears.—Cropped to a triangle, covered with a short coat, carried very straight and set high on the head, but not too far back. The opening should be well protected by the coat.

Nose.—Black, well developed, not flat on top nor pinched at the nostrils.

Eyes.—The eyes should be clear, of medium size, dark, not prominent, neither too round nor too oval, nor should they be set too far forward but slightly slanting. Light or staring eyes should be disqualified.

Teeth.—Strong and well set. The canines should be set well apart.

Neck.—Well rounded at the shoulders, of moderate length and thickness, growing gradually larger toward the shoulders.

Shoulders.—Long, sloping and rough-coated.

Brisket.—It should be deep, reaching at least to the level of the elbow. The chest should not be too wide. The fore ribs should be well arched and the hind ones well sprung.

BOUVIER DES FLANDRES

Body, Back and Loins.—They should be short, strong, straight, muscled and followed by broad, square hind quarters.

Tail.—Cropped to about 4 inches, set high and carried gaily.

Fore Quarters.—The legs from the elbows to the feet should be dead straight, on all sides.

Hind Quarters.—The hocks fairly large, but at the same time not much bent. The hams broad and well muscled.

The front and hindlegs should be parallel as seen from the front and rear.

Feet.—Round, firm, the toes close and arched, furnished with dark, well-set nails. Tough pads.

Coat.—Slightly tousled, harsh to the touch, neither silky nor long like that of the Briard. It should not be woolly, but a characteristic is seemingly badly groomed. The coat on the head is shorter, except over the eyes, on each side of the muzzle and under the chin, where it is more developed, forming thus eyebrows, a mustache and a beard, which are features very characteristic of the breed.

Color.—From fawn to black, through pepper and salt, grey and brindle. Chocolate brown and too much white are not permissible. A white star on the chest is allowed.

Height.—Dogs, from 23½ to 27½ inches; bitches, a minimum of 22¾ inches.

EXPLANATION OF THE STANDARD

In order to make our handsome national breed, the "Bouvier," better known and especially to render the standard more explicit, the Committee of the National Bouvier des Flandres Club has thought it to be its duty to amplify and to detail point by point the official standard definitely adopted at the meeting on the 3rd of June, 1923. This amplification has been made also for the purpose of enabling young fanciers to be more able to understand the points of judging and especially to familiarize them with the characteristic points and exterior anatomy required in the Bouvier de Flandres.

General Appearance.—The Bouvier is a dog of powerful build, cobby in shape, noticeable, showing, however, no heaviness, rugged looking because of the roughness of his coat, showing by the intelli-

[315]

gence and brightness of the eye, alertness, energy, spirit and courage. With his compactly built body and his rough coat, he is capable of withstanding the hardest work and most inclement weather.

The breed was for many years an unrivaled aid to the Shepherd and an excellent farm dog, but changes in customs as well as its instinctive qualities have made it appreciated by a great number of fanciers, who have made a watch and police dog of it, work in which it is able to employ all its intelligence and energy or it has been used as an ambulance dog and messenger, functions which several members of the breed filled with the greatest success during the Great War.

Head.—The head should be of medium length in proportion to the build and the length of the body, more massive than that of the Belgian Shepherd with a rough coat. In a well-proportioned head the skull should be slightly longer than the muzzle. A head with the muzzle longer than the skull lacks strength, as a head with the eyes set too high in the skull lacks all the expression of the Bouvier and gives it a strange appearance.

Skull.—The top line of the skull should be nearly flat and sloping slightly toward the muzzle. There must not be a too great or too small width between the ears. Dogs should have wider skulls than bitches, the skulls of the latter nevertheless should not be narrow to the point that they seem to be squeezed in a vise. For the rest the cheeks should be flat, not so prominent that they make the skull appear round. The muzzle should be pinched and the foreface short.

Stop.—The stop is the break between the skull and the muzzle. It should be slight, more indicated than real by reason of the growth of the coat, the arch of the brows should be pronounced and covered with a tousled coat.

Muzzle.—The foreface should be wide and bony, narrowing gradually toward the nostrils without hollows under the eye sockets. It should be well filled out. The upper and lower jaws should be powerful and deep, furnished with round, white teeth fitting like a vise. A well-proportioned muzzle gives an expression of strength while a narrow muzzle gives a look of weakness.

Lips.—The lips should be dry and compressed, not hanging, furnished with a fairly long and rough coat, an important point which renders this breed typical, from which is derived the popular name in Flanders "Vuilbaard."

Teeth.—The teeth should be strong and fitting well together like a pair of scissors, the incisors overshot almost imperceptibly, the space between the canines should be very pronounced, a quality which denotes a good muzzle.

Ears.—The ears should be cropped to triangles of proportioned size, covered with a rough coat, carried well up, neither too near together nor too far apart, very alert, giving the Bouvier a watchful and wide-awake appearance. The interior should be protected by the coat.

Nose.—The nose should be black, well developed, not flattened on top and not pinched at the nostrils.

Eyes.—The eyes should be open in expression, of medium size, dark, not prominent nor sunken, neither too round nor too oval, set in the sides of the head, without being too far apart. The color of the eye may be dark nut-brown, black giving a sad expression is not a fault, while a light eye (yellow, fawn) and wild in expression should be disqualified.

Neck.—The neck should be well rounded to the shoulders—that is to say it should not show any thickness at the throat nor at the dewlap. It should be of moderate thickness, gradually growing larger to the shoulders, from which it should spring in a good line.

Shoulders.—The shoulders should be long, sloping from points, that is to say from the joint of the leg (humerus) with the shoulder-bone to the shoulders, which should be clean cut. Seen from the front, they should slope rapidly without being straight from the base of the neck to the shoulder-blades, thus giving a look that the body is well set on the legs and not between them.

Brisket.—The brisket should be deep, reaching at least to the level of the elbow, it should not be too wide nor too narrow, for these are both faults which interfere with the proper functioning of the shoulders.

Body.—The back should be short, strong and straight, without any impression of weakness, the loins well muscled and short, slightly arched. This gives much freedom to the dog for jumping and running. The hind quarters, that is, the hind parts formed by the haunches and the rump, should be broad and square, not sloping or flabby. The chest should not be too wide, the foreribs should be hidden under the shoulders and fairly arched, the hind ribs deep and well sprung, the flanks short and slightly rising. Bitches may be a little longer in the loins than dogs. This is a great advantage for breeding purposes.

Seen from the side the dog presents great symmetry, a long head clean cut, and well set on a proportionate neck, springing gracefully from long sloping shoulders, between which is a deep brisket which slopes up gradually to the short and well-fleshed flanks. From the extremity of the neck to the base of the tail, which should be cropped to about 4 inches, set high and carried up, the dog offers an attractive outline.

Fore Quarters.—The strongly muscled legs should be dead straight seen from any angle, the elbows turned neither in nor out.

Hind Quarters.—The hind quarters should be firm and well muscled, well let down, rather than straight with large and powerful hams. The stifles turned neither in nor out, the hocks well let down, wide and not much bent, absolutely parallel, supported by straight legs, seen from any angle.

Feet.—The feet should be round, compact with rough pads, the toes close and arched, the nails dark. The feet should be dead straight, neither turned in nor out.

Coat.—The coat should be harsh, that is, rough, hard and wiry, neither silky nor long like that of the Briard, so thick that if it is separated with the hand the skin is hardly visible; it should be slightly tousled,—without, at the same time, being woolly or fleecy,—to the point of appearing badly groomed. At the base of the coat there is a finer coat of softer texture, the undercoat which is thicker in winter as with fur-bearing animals. The coat on the skull should be shorter and almost smooth, on the brows longer and tousled without falling over the eyes. On each side of the muzzle and on the chin, it should be rough and just long enough to give the characteristic look of the breed and the appearance of strength. The coat on the legs should be equally thick and rough, but on the feet it must not be as long as the Briards.

Color.—The color may be from fawn to black, passing through pepper and salt, grey and brindle; chocolate brown and white spots are not admissible. A white star on the chest is allowed if at the same time it is not too marked.

BOUVIER DES FLANDRES

BOXER

BOUVIER DES FLANDRES

Bearing.—The bearing should be alert and bold without a sign of fear or weakness. The walk and trot are the ordinary gaits of the Bouvier, although certain ambling gaits have been met with. In order that the gait should be correct, the legs of the dog must move forward in a perpendicular plane, freely and parallel to the sides of the body, the feet setting squarely on the ground in touching it—that is, the dog should not be supported on his heels. When the dog advances toward you, the forelegs should form the continuation of the straight line of the front (neck—shoulder—brisket), the feet being apart and at an equal distance from the elbows. When the dog is standing still it is difficult to see if the elbows are slightly loose, but on movement, the fault at once becomes apparent; if the dog has a tendency to cross the legs he is loose in the shoulder, while if he has the tendency to spread the legs, he is tight in the shoulder. A gait in which the foreleg moves parallel to the body or the trunk throws itself sideways in the rear or interferes. With this breed the action of the hind quarters is very often neglected and nevertheless it is the hind quarters which are the principal means of locomotion, of which perfection is achieved by the strong and capable hindlegs, the motion of which comes from the haunches, furnished by the muscular hams well rounded to the stifles, which should be set straight, neither turned in nor out, which allows the hocks to put the legs parallel. If the hocks are drawn up (the hindlegs crooked), the feet, while in motion should be turned outward. If, on the contrary, the hocks are turned in (cowhocks) the feet have a tendency to cross each other and the dog interferes. A dog whose legs are too close together, that is, whose hindlegs are not absolutely straight when looked at from the side proves that his hind quarters are bad. The gait is the logical demonstration of build.

Points of Disqualification

Nose.—Brown or pink or spotted to any extent with either of these colors.

Ears.—Not erect or falling on the sides of the head.

Jaws.—The upper or lower too pronounced, that is, if the incisors of the upper are too overshot over the incisors of the lower, when one closes the mouth, or the opposite, if the lower is undershot.

Coat.—Soft, silky or too short to permit the judge to pass an opinion on the real texture of the coat.

	Points
Coat	20
Head (eyes, ears, skull, foreface)	20
Shoulders and style	10
Hind quarters (hams and legs)	10
Back, loin, brisket, belly	15
Feet and legs	10
Symmetry, size and character	15
Total	100

BOXERS

(Illustration facing page 319)

Although it has reached its greatest perfection in Germany during the past 100 years, the Boxer springs of a line of dogs that has been known throughout the whole of Europe since the 16th Century. Prior to that time, the ancestors of this breed would hardly be recognized as the Boxer could they be placed beside modern specimens. Still, there is evidence that points to the Boxer as one of the many descendants of the old fighting dog of the high valleys of Tibet.

The Boxer is cousin to practically all recognized breeds of the bulldog type, and these all go back to the basic Molossus blood. Few other strains can claim such courage and stamina, and it is from this line that there has been handed down the attractive fawn color that recurs throughout the centuries.

Flemish tapestries of the 16th and 17th Centuries give scenes of stag and boar hunting, and the dogs in these splendid works of art are the same as the Spanish Alano, found in great numbers in Andalusia and Estramadura, and the Matin de Terceira or Perro do Presa, from the Azores. The Alano and the Matin have been regarded as the same breed, and they are either ancestors of the Boxer or trace back to a common ancestor.

In France, there is a breed known as the Dogue de Bordeaux that is very close, both in appearance and size to the old Tibetan mastiff, and it is from this massive dog that the Bouldogue du Mida was developed. The Bouldogue du Mida, found principally in the South of France, possesses many of the points of the Boxer.

While all the European breeds mentioned are related to the Boxer, this favorite of Germany has been developed along scientific lines that not only have succeeded in retaining all his old qualities but have produced a much more attractive appearance. Besides bulldog blood he carries a certain heritage from a terrier strain. There also is some reason to believe that English bulldogs were at one time imported into Germany Indeed, Reinagle's noted bulldog, done in 1803, is not unlike the Boxer, and pictures of some English specimens of 1850 are almost identical with the German dog.

Until dog fighting and bull-baiting were outlawed by most civilized peoples in the middle of the 19th Century, the Boxer, like all dogs of his type was used for this purpose. Today, he has become an accredited member of society, but he still carries his old qualities, courage, defense mechanism, and aggressiveness when needed. Withal, he is devoted to his master.

The quality of the Boxer is best emphasized, perhaps, when it is mentioned that this breed was one of the first selected in Germany for police training. This work demands great intelligence, in addition to fearlessness, agility, and strength.

Considering that the entire modern history of the Boxer is wrapped up with Germany, it seems rather curious to many that he bears a name that obviously is English. Yet the name is one that fits him. It arises from his manner of fighting, for invariably a specimen of this breed begins a fight with his front paws, somewhat like a man boxing.

The Boxer has been bred and exhibited, sporadically, in the United States for more than three decades, but it was not until recent years that the general public began to take an interest in the breed. This came about because of the consistent winning in the variety groups of certain outstanding specimens.

It is not generally known that the first Boxer was registered in The American Kennel Club Stud Book in 1904, and that the first championship by a specimen of this breed was finished in 1915. Still, the breed did not come to the front until recently, and it was not until last year that a specialty club was formed. Today more and more successful breeders are starting to feature the Boxer, and the club is spreading knowledge of his many sterling qualities.

DESCRIPTION AND STANDARD OF POINTS

(Adopted by The American Boxer Club, February 15, 1938, and Approved by The American Kennel Club, April 12, 1938)

General Appearance.—The Boxer is a medium sized, smooth-haired, sturdy dog of short, square figure and strong limbs. The musculation is very clean and powerfully developed, standing out plastically from under the skin. His movements are alive with energy, the gait although firm is elastic, the stride free and roomy, the carriage proud and noble. As a service and guard dog, he must combine with substance and ample power that considerable degree of elegance absolutely essential to his further duties; those of an enduring escort dog with horse, bicycle or carriage, and as a splendid jumper. Only a body whose individual limbs are built to withstand the most strenuous mechanical effort, assembled as a complete and harmonious whole, can respond to such combined demands. Therefore, to be at his highest developed efficiency, he must never be plump or heavy, and while equipped for great speed, he must not be racy.

The head imparts to the Boxer a unique individual stamp peculiar to him alone. It must be in perfect proportion to his body, and above all, it must never be too light. His muzzle is his most distinctive feature and the greatest value is to be placed on its being of correct form and in absolutely proper proportion to the skull.

In judging the Boxer, the first thing to be considered is general appearance and the relation of substance to elegance and of the desired proportions of the individual parts of the body to each other. Consideration is to be given to an attractive color. After which, the individual parts are to be examined for their correct constructions and their functions. Special attention is to be devoted to the head.

Faults.—Head, not typical, plump bull-doggy appearance, light bone, lack of proportion, bad condition, deficiency in nobility.

Head.—The beauty of the head depends upon the harmonious proportion between the muzzle and the skull. From whatever direction you view the head, whether from the front, from the top, or from the side, the muzzle must always appear in correct relationship to the skull. That means, it must never appear too small. The head should be clean neither showing deep wrinkles nor dewlap. Normally folds will spring up on the top of the skull when the ears are held erect. And they are always indicated from the root of the nose running downward on both sides of the muzzle. The dark mask confines itself to the muzzle and must be in distinct relief to the color of the head so that the face will not have a somber expression. The muzzle must be powerfully developed in length, breadth and height. It must not be pointed or narrow, short or shallow. Its shape is influenced first through the formation of both jaw-bones, second through the placement of teeth in same, and third through the quality of the lips.

The two jaw-bones do not terminate in a normal perpendicular level in the front, but the lower jaw protrudes beyond the upper and bends slightly upward. The Boxer is normally undershot. The upper jaw is broad where attached to the skull, and maintains this breadth except for a very slight tapering to the front. The canine teeth should be as widely separated from each other as possible. The incisors (6) are all in one row, the middle teeth not projecting; in the upper jaw they are slightly concave, in the lower they are in a straight line. Thus both jaws are very wide in front. The bite is powerful and sound, the teeth set in the most normal possible arrangement. The lips complete the formation of the muzzle. The upper lip is thick and padded, it fills out the hollow space in front formed by the projection of the lower jaw and is supported by the fangs of the same. Therefore, these fangs must stand as far apart as possible and be of good length so that the front surface of the muzzle shall become broad and almost square, and form an obtuse (rounded) angle with the top line of the muzzle. The lower edge of the upper lip rests on the edge of the lower lip. The repandous (bent upward) part of the under-jaw with the lower lip (sometimes called the chin) must not rise above the front of the upper lip, but much less may it disappear under it. It must, however, be plainly perceptible when viewed from the front as well as the side, without protruding and bending upward in the manner of the English Bulldog. The teeth of the under-jaw must not be seen when the mouth is closed; neither may the Boxer show his tongue when his mouth is closed.

The top of the skull is slightly arched. It must not be so short that it is rotund, nor too flat, nor too broad, and the occiput must not be too pronounced. The forehead forms a distinct stop with the top line of the muzzle, which must not be forced back into the forehead like that of a Bulldog, but neither should it slope away (appear downfaced). The tip of the nose lies somewhat higher than the root of the muzzle. The forehead shows a suggestion of furrow which, however, must never be too deep especially between the eyes. Corresponding with the powerful set of teeth, the cheeks are accordingly well developed without protruding from the head with too bulgy an appearance. Preferably they should taper into the muzzle in a slight graceful curve. The ears are set high, clipped to a point, and are fairly long, the shell not too broad, and are carried perpendicularly. The dark, brown eyes, not too small nor protruding nor deep set, disclose an expression of energy and intelligence, but must never appear gloomy, threatening, or piercing. The eye must have a dark rim. The nose is broad and black, very slightly turned up; the nostrils are broad with the naso-labial line running between them.

Faults.—Lack of nobility and expression, somber face, unserviceable bite whether due to disease or to faulty tooth placement. Pinscher or Bulldog head, driveling, badly trimmed ears, visible conjunctive (Haw). Showing teeth or tongue, light so-called "bird of prey" eye. Sloping top line of muzzle. Too pointed or too light a bite (snipey).

Neck.—Round, not too thick and short but of ample length, yet strong and muscular and clean cut throughout, without dewlap, running with a distinctly marked nape in an elegant arch down to the back.

Faults.—Dewlap.

Body.—Build is square, that is to say, of the profile lines, one is horizontal over the back; this, with two vertical lines, one touching the shoulder tip in the front, the other the hip protuberance in the rear, form with the ground level a square. The torso rests on trunk-like straight legs with strong bones.

Chest and Front Leg Measurements.—The Chest is deep, reaching down to the elbows; the depth of the chest amounts to half of the height of the dog at the withers. The ribs are well arched, but are not barrel shaped, extending far to the rear. The loins are short, close and taut and lightly tucked up. The lower stomach line blends into an elegant curve to the rear. The shoulders are long and sloping, close lying but not excessively covered with muscle. The upper arm is long, forming a right angle to the shoulder blade. The forelegs when seen from the front must be straight, stand parallel to each other and have strong, firmly articulated (joined) bones. The elbows must not press too closely to the chest well nor stand off too far. The underarm is perpendicular, long and firmly muscled. The pastern joint of the foreleg is clearly defined, but not distended. The pastern is short, slightly slanting but standing almost perpendicular to the ground. Feet, small with tightly arched toes and hard soles (cat's paws).

Faults.—Too broad and low in front, loose shoulders, chest hanging between the shoulders, hare's feet, hollow flanks, hanging stomach, turned legs and toes.

Back.—The withers should be clearly defined, the whole back short, straight, broad and very muscular.

Faults.—Carp (roach) back, sway back, thin lean back, long narrow, sharp sunken in loins. Weak union with the coup.

Hind Quarters.—Strongly muscled, the musculation hard as a board and standing out very plastically through the skin. The thighs are not narrow and flat but are broad and curved, the breech musculation is also strongly developed. The coup slightly sloped, flat arched, broad. Tail attachment high rather than too deep. Tail clipped, carried upward. The pelvis should be long

BOXERS

and especially broad in females. Upper and lower thigh long, hip and knee joint with as much angle as possible. In standing position the knee should reach so far forward that it would meet a vertical line drawn from the hip protuberance to the floor. The hock angle should be about 140 degrees, the lower part of the foot at a slight slope of about 95 to 100 degrees from the hock joint to the floor; that is, not completely vertical. Seen from behind the hind legs are straight. The hocks clean, not distended, supported by powerful rear pads, the rear toes just a little longer than the front toes, but similar in all other respects.

Faults.—Falling off or too arched or narrow coup. Low set tail, higher in back than in front, steep, stiff, or too little angulated hind quarters, light thighs, cow hocks, bow legs and crooked legs, dewclaws, soft hocks, narrow heel, tottering, waddling gait, hare's feet, hind quarters too far under or too far behind.

Height.—Males—22 inches to 24 inches at the withers. Females—21 inches to 23 inches at the withers. Males should not go under and females should not go over.

Weight.—Males around 23 inches should weigh over 66 lbs., and females of about 22 inches should weigh around 62 lbs.

Coat.—Short, shiny, lying smooth and tight to the body.

Color.—The colors are fawn and brindle, fawn in various shades from light yellow to dark deer red. The brindle variety should have black stripes on a golden yellow or red brown background. The stripes should be clearly defined and above all must not be grey or dirty. Stripes that do not cover the whole top of the body are not desirable. White markings in fawn and brindle dogs are not to be rejected; in fact, they are often very attractive in appearance.

The black mask is absolutely required. When white stretches over the muzzle, naturally that portion of the black mask disappears. By the same token it is not possible to get black toe nails with white feet. It is desirable to have an even distribution of head markings.

Disqualifications.—Boxers with white or black ground color, or entirely white or black or any other color than fawn or brindle. (White markings are allowed but must not exceed one third (1/3) of the ground color.)

[327]

The character of the Boxer is of the greatest importance and demands the most solicitous attention. He is renowned from olden times for his great love and faithfulness to his master and household, his alertness and fearless courage as a defender and protector. He is harmless in the family, but distrustful of strangers, bright and friendly of temperament at play, but brave and determined when aroused. His intelligence and willing tractability, his modesty and cleanliness make him a highly desirable family dog and cheerful companion. He is the soul of honesty and loyalty, and is never false or treacherous even in his old age.

Faults.—Viciousness, treachery, unreliability, lack of temperament, and cowardice.

BRIARDS

(Illustration facing page 334)

(By Courtesy of The Briard Club of America)

The Briard or Chien Berger de Brie is descended from a very old race of French dogs. The breed is mentioned in records as far back as the twelfth century in France and is accurately described in accounts of dogs in the fourteenth and sixteenth centuries. In the tapestries and monuments of those times there are dogs closely corresponding in size and appearance to the Briard of today. They were used then especially to defend their charges against wolves and robbers but the dividing up of the land and the increase of the population that followed the French Revolution gradually transformed their work into the more peaceful task of herding and guiding their flocks and keeping them from the unfenced fields of the French countryside, and of guarding the farm property. In an article written in 1809 these dogs are definitely referred to as Sheep Dogs of Brie (Berger de Brie) and they were entered in dog shows in the latter part of that century as a distinct species. The society called Les Amis du Briard, formed in France some forty years ago, established a definite standard of size and form which with slight modifications still prevails and has been adopted by the Briard Club of America. Briards do not come necessarily from the Province of Brie for they are found all over France and are at present the sheepdog par excellence of that country. Everywhere in the north or the south they guard the small farms and herd the sheep and cattle and take care of the property and animals and are useful hard working members of the community.

In build the Briard is a square dog though a little extra length of back may be allowed to bitches. The bushy eyebrows, which are useful in protecting the eyes when the dog is working in rough brushy country, should not be so heavy as to interfere with their vision. The tail which is well feathered and has a small curl at the end called the "crochet," is carried down under ordinary circumstances and only raised to the level of the back in moments of excitement or very active movement. The coat, hard and wavy and of moderate length, a real "goat's coat," not only sheds water very successfully but caked mud will drop off as it dries. In France the ears are cropped enough to make them be carried semi-erect. This tends to prevent canker ear and is characteristic of all the earliest pictures and standards of the breed but it lengthens and narrows the look of the head and the imported cropped eared dogs have a different appearance from those bred in this country. The range of color is very wide and in France the dogs are shown in two classes, the black and the colored. The latter class includes the tawny and the grey with or without black shading on ears and tail. The rule against any white except a small spot on the chest and that against the lack of dewclaws are strictly enforced as these defects are considered to signify cross breeding or degeneracy. The action of the Briard is light and supple and he takes naturally a short trot or the regular amble of a sheepdog circling his flock. He turns readily and quickly, has himself well in hand, and can show great speed at times if necessary.

In training the Briard learns slowly but has an extremely retentive memory and enjoys his lessons and work. The French trainers believe that the dog should have no punishment but a reproof and that he does best when given responsibility and left as far as possible to his own initiative. Though they have been used primarily for sheepdogs and guard dogs they have splendid records as police dogs and especially as war dogs. In the last war they did liaison work and acted as watchers at advance posts where their astonishingly acute hearing was invaluable. They accompanied patrols and carried up food and supplies and even munitions to the front line. So many of them died in the service that the race was greatly reduced in numbers and in quality and did not recover for some years after the war. Briards are used for dragging carts but this is not their natural occupation and their ambition and eagerness makes them apt to overwork and strain themselves in such labor.

Briards are not difficult dogs to raise or breed. The bitches usually have litters of from eight to ten and are careful and sensible mothers. As tawny and grey are racial colors a litter of pups is likely to be varied even thought both parents are black.

The Briard in repose has an air of calm authority; he is a guardian and presides over his domain, awake and alert, but quiet. He does not wander, seldom barks unless it is necessary to give warning and is essentially well mannered, an excellent family dog adapting himself to life inside as well as outside the house. He is neither quarrelsome nor jealous and is particularly safe and companionable with children for his temperament is gay and affectionate and he is remarkably playful for a large dog. His feeling toward the general public of men and of dogs both large and small is courteous and friendly but he is a one man dog in that he gives deep affection and loyalty to his master only.

WORKING DOGS

DESCRIPTION AND STANDARD OF POINTS
(By Courtesy of The Briard Club of America)

General Appearance.—A strong and substantially built dog, fitted for field work, lithe, muscular, and well proportioned, alert and active.

Size.—Height at shoulders: Dogs, 23 to 27 inches. Bitches, 22 to 25½ inches. Young dogs may be below the minimum.

Head.—Large and rather long. Stop well marked and placed at equal distance from top of head and tip of nose. Forehead very slightly rounded. Line from stop to tip of nose straight. Teeth strong, white, and meeting exactly even. Muzzle neither narrow nor pointed. Nose rather square than rounded, always black. Hair heavy and long on top of head, the ears, and around the muzzle, forming eyebrows standing out and not veiling the eyes too much. Eyes horizontal, well opened, dark in color and rather large; intelligent and gentle in expression. Ears placed high, not too large and not carried too flat. In France the tips of the ears are generally cropped, causing the ear to be semi-erect.

Conformation.—Neck muscular and distinct from the shoulders. Chest broad and deep. Back straight. Rump slightly sloped. Legs muscular with heavy bones. Hock not too near the ground, making a well marked angle, the leg below the hock being not quite vertical.

Tail.—Well feathered, carried low and twisted neither to the right nor to the left, curled at the end, tip when straightened reaching to point of hock.

Feet.—Strong, round, with toes close together and hard pads; nails black.

Coat.—Long, slightly wavy, stiff and strong.

Color.—All solid colors are allowed except white. Dark colors are preferable. Usual colors. Black, and black with some white hairs, dark and light grey, tawny, and combinations of two of these colors, provided there are no marked spots and the transition from one to the other takes place gradually and symmetrically.

Dewclaws.—Two dewclaws on each hindleg are required. A dog with only one cannot be given a prize.

BRIARDS

Faults.—Muzzle pointed. Eyes small, almond-shaped or light in color. Rump straight or too sloped. White spot on the breast (a large white spot is very bad). Tail too short or carried over the back. White nails.

Disqualifications.—Size below the limit. Absence of dewclaws. Short hair on the head, face or feet. Tail lacking or cut. Nose light in color or spotted. Eyes spotted. Hair curled. White hair on feet. Spotted colors of the coat.

BULL-MASTIFFS

(Illustration facing page 335)

(By Courtesy of The Bull-Mastiff Club of America)

The known history of the Bull-Mastiff begins some 70 or 80 years ago in England. It is probable that the story of the breed is really centuries old but the proof of this point is difficult and takes much reference to ancient authors, and arguments pro and con on the difference between breeds as they existed over a hundred years ago.

In the latter part of the nineteenth century in England, the problem of keeping the large estates and game preserves free from the depredations of poachers was an acute one. Penalties were severe and yet poaching, being after all a form of gambling, seemed impossible to eradicate by mere laws. The result was that the gamekeeper's life was anything but a safe one. Poachers would often prefer to shoot it out with the keeper on the chance of escape than accept the heavy penalties which they would incur upon apprehension. It is not surprising, therefore, that the gamekeepers decided to enlist the aid of the greatest protector nature has given to man— the dog. It should be obvious that these men cared nothing for the looks of a dog as long as he served them well. Numerous breeds were therefore tried out for this purpose. The mastiff was tried and it was found that, while he was sufficiently courageous and powerful, he was not fast or active enough and not sufficiently aggressive for this type of work. The bulldog was tried, and let it here be stated that the bulldog of these times and the bulldog that was used in the formation of this breed, was a very different animal from today's bench-show type.

BRIARD

BULL-MASTIFF

He was actually used to bait bulls, and he was big, strong and active. He was found by the gamekeepers, however, to be, perhaps, a trifle too ferocious and not big enough for their needs. These men wanted dogs that would remain silent at the approach of poachers, lest the position of the keeper be divulged and he be shot. They needed dogs that would attack on command, being utterly fearless. They wanted the poachers thrown and held, but not mauled. For these needs, they crossed the mastiff and the bulldog, and the dog they wanted and needed was produced.

From this utilitarian birth, then, the breed was founded. Inevitably, came the rivalry between keepers as to the quality of their dogs. Inevitably, also, came the breeding to and from the oustanding performers of their time—a true survival of the fittest. For many years, then, after the birth of the breed, its history was wholly an utilitarian one. The only contests in which Bull-Mastiffs engaged were against man, either on the moor or in demonstrations when they were muzzled and the man was allowed a club, restricted in size to certain measurements and weights. In these contests no man was ever able to hold his feet against a dog of proven worth. In those days, the Bull-Mastiff was known sometimes by his present name but more usually as the "Gamekeeper's Night-Dog."

During the early years of the existence of the breed, we find many interesting references to it by contemporary canine commentaries. One of these references is made in General William Hutchinson's book, "Dog Breaking," published in London in 1885. He says:

"Bulldogs have good noses. I have known of the cross between them and the mastiff being taught to follow the scent of a man almost as truly as a bloodhound."

In the year 1901, from "Sporting Life," we find the following commentary on a show of Keepers' Night-Dogs:

"The chief interest was centered in the Keepers' Night-Dogs. This being the Old English Bull-Mastiff and in order to give the public some idea of the duties which they are taught to perform, Mr. W. Burton of Thorneywood fame, Nottingham, gave demonstrations, designed to show the measures taken by the aid of dogs for the suppression of poaching."

In 1900, the Westminster Gazette reports that Major Crowe of the War Office visited an exhibition of these dogs with a view to reporting on their possible usefulness as an aid to sentries.

In "The Field," August 20, 1901, we find the following:

"Mr. Burton of Thorneywood Kennels brought to the show one Night-Dog (not for competition) and offered any person one pound, who could escape from it while securely muzzled. One of the spectators who had had experience with dogs volunteered and amused a large assembly of sportsmen and keepers who had gathered there. The man was given a long start and the muzzled dog slipped after him. The animal caught him immediately and knocked down his man the first spring. The latter bravely tried to hold his own, but was floored every time he got on his feet, ultimately being kept to the ground until the owner of the dog released him. The man had three rounds with the powerful canine, but was beaten each time and was unable to escape."

For this type of work, dogs of a dark brindle color were naturally preferred owing to their lack of visibility. It was inevitable, however, that as the breed gained in popularity and the true mastiff blood was used, a large number of light fawns should appear. With the gradual disappearance of poaching and the continued demand for Bull-Mastiffs as guards and watch-dogs, this latter color became highly popular. From the mastiff was often inherited the black mask and densely colored ears which added to the striking appearance of these powerful animals.

Finally, owing to the increasing popularity of this breed, a number of pioneers started, on a scientific basis, to breed for a type conformation in an effort to set, once and for all, a goal which pure-bred dog breeders might seek. After much work and care, this type finally became sufficiently evolved for the English Kennel Club to grant recognition of the Bull-Mastiff as a pure-bred dog in 1924. At this time the Kennel Club differentiated between the Bull-Mastiff, cross-bred, and the Bull-Mastiff, pure-bred, the latter being, of necessity, the descendant of three generations of dogs which were neither pure mastiff nor pure bulldog. Classes were then given at a few shows for this breed and, inasmuch as their popularity increased rapidly, they were finally awarded Challenge Certificates in 1928.

From that time forward, the story of the breed has been one of continued success and growing popularity. It has filled the need which dog owners and dog lovers have long felt, being a superlative guardian with an amazingly even disposition. In time the breed became known in many countries, having been exported from England to Siam, India, the Federated Malay States, Africa, and America. The short coat has proved convenient in warm climates, and yet they can live in the open in the harshest kind of weather. Their utilitarian background has proved to be a blessing to breeders for, through the survival of the fittest, they thrive upon a minimum of care and afford little worry to their owners.

In October, 1933, the American Kennel Club granted recognition to the Bull-Mastiff. Since that time, the breed has made numerous friends in this country, and is forging ahead, strictly on its merits, as a splendid watch-dog of even disposition and as the possessor of an enormous amount of affection for children and grown-ups alike.

DESCRIPTION AND STANDARD OF POINTS

(As Adopted 1935 by The Bull-Mastiff Club of America and Approved by The American Kennel Club)

General Appearance of the Bull-Mastiff is that of a symmetrical animal, showing great strength, powerfully built but active. He is fearless, yet docile, and has endurance and alertness. He is 60% Mastiff and 40% Bulldog.

Size.—Dogs should be 25 to 27 inches at shoulder, and about 115 pounds in weight. Bitches, 24 to 26 inches at shoulder, and about 100 pounds in weight.

Head—Skull.—Large and square with fair wrinkle, and in circumference may measure almost the height of the dog; it should be broad with cheeks well developed. Forehead flat.

Muzzle.—Should not be more than 3½ inches long, deep and broad. Nose, black, with nostrils large and broad. Flews not too pendulous, stop moderate, mouth preferably level, or may be slightly undershot. Canine teeth large and set wide. A dark mask is preferable.

Eyes.—Dark and of medium size, set apart, the width of the muzzle with furrow between.

Ears.—Should be V-shaped and carried close to cheek or folded back, set on wide and high, level with occiput and cheek, giving a square appearance to the skull. They should be denser in color than the body, and of medium size.

Body—Neck.—Should be slightly arched, of moderate length, very muscular, and almost equal in circumference to skull.

Chest.—Wide and deep, with ribs well sprung, well set down between forelegs. Girth may be up to a third more than dog's height.

Fore Quarters.—Shoulders should be muscular and slightly sloping. Forelegs straight, well boned and set wide apart, elbows square. Pasterns straight, feet medium, with round toes well arched, pads hard.

Back.—Short, giving compact carriage.

Loins.—Wide and muscular, slightly arched, with fair depth of flank.

Hindlegs.—Broad and muscular, with well-developed second thigh denoting power, but not cumbersome. Hocks bent, cow-hocks or splay feet are most undesirable.

Tail.—Set high up, strong at root and tapering, reaching to the hocks. Straight or curved, but never carried hound-fashion.

Coat.—Short and dense, giving good weather protection.

Color.—Any shade of fawn or brindle.

A scale of points is not given, for in the last analysis, a dog is judged on his breed characteristics, and his soundness which is so essential in working breeds. Great harm can be done by breeding for certain characteristics, because of heavy point score, to the detriment of soundness. This, we wish to avoid.

Due to the relatively recent origin of this breed as a pure-bred type, it was thought well to explain in detail certain aims of the breeders of Bull-Mastiffs with which the standard should not be burdened.

Relative to the mouth, it is unreasonable to expect nothing but level mouths in a breed whose blood is made up of bulldogs and mastiffs. It is the desire of Bull-Mastiff breeders to produce, in time and by selective breeding, dogs with level mouths. This, however, must be considered as secondary in importance to the production of sound dogs. The same is true of the dark mask and denseness of color of ears. The aim should be to produce sound dogs and then, by selective breeding, breed for black masks and ears. As to the size, there are dogs with ears which are "sloppy," and there are those who show too much of the bulldog ear. Here we want the happy medium and here, again, it is a refinement which must come after soundness and general type conformation. There is also the question of white tips, which has been debated at some length in the English canine press. It is maintained by some that this is from the bulldog, and by others that it is bull-terrier blood, which certain unscrupulous breeders have used. Whatever it comes from, it should be eliminated as it has no part in the color scheme of our breed. White on the head or body is not tolerated.

As to the size of the breed, the reason for the creation of the Bull-Mastiff was the desire for a dog smaller than the old English mastiff and more active, but one still big enough to throw and hold a man. Therefore, a dog of 100 pounds who is sound and active is greatly to be preferred to a dog of 125 pounds who looks like a weedy mastiff. It is only in the case that these two animals are equal in all other respects, that the larger may be preferred. Again, if we see a dog weighing 140 or 150 pounds, even though sound and active, we then approach too much the mastiff and the breed is losing identity.

To sum up, let us say that we want sound, active dogs, capable of protecting life and property, of throwing and holding a man. We want dogs conforming to breed-type, and refinements will increase in importance in direct proportion to the attainment of the primary ideals.

COLLIES (ROUGH)
(Illustration facing page 350)

The Rough-coated Collie of modern times goes back to the rough-coated shepherd's dog which Thomas Bewick depicted in those historic wood-cuts made prior to 1800, and it is probable that this breed was known in Scotland for more than a century before that time. The dog lacked today's beauty and majesty in olden times, but there has been no serious divergence from the essential type and the outstanding characteristics.

Sheep herding is one of the oldest occupations in the world, and on this basis, alone, we may assume that the Collie's ancestors go far back in the history of dogs. It may be reasoned, also, that the same conditions that promoted production of the best types of wool also contributed to the rough coat of the shepherd's dog. Except in rare instances, rough coated dogs always have been associated with sheep. The Smooth-coated Collie, answering to the same standard except in coat, was principally a drover's dog—used for guiding cattle and sheep to market, not for standing watch over them while at pasture.

Inability to give definite dates for the origin of the Collie is due to the fact that until fairly recent times the breed was solely a working dog. It was kept pure in strain, but usually without written pedigree; indeed, his untutored masters saw no need of this, even had they been capable of maintaining stud books.

When first the Collie came to the notice of dog fanciers, shortly after the start of the 19th Century, the breed was found principally in the Northern parts of

Scotland. Its form was nearly the same, but it had a broader and shorter head, and measured only 14 inches at the shoulder. The breed progressed rapidly up to 1859, when the first organized dog show was held in England, and it was one of the first breeds for which classes were provided. This was at the show of the Birmingham Dog Society in 1860.

Early writers on the dogs of the British Isles mention a number of crosses, such as the Gordon setter, and the Newfoundland, that went toward the development of the modern Collie, but these may be discounted. They are no more credible than the tale told by old Scotchmen of a century ago that the Collie, the deerhound, and the Scottish terrier all descended from a common ancestor.

From the most authentic sources comes the knowledge that the beautiful rough Collie of modern days has been developed by a careful process of selective breeding. It had reached its present height and weight as long ago as 1886, and breeding since then has been a matter of refinement.

When Queen Victoria paid her first visit to Balmoral in the early '60s, she saw specimens of the Rough-coated Collie and took an instant liking to the breed. Of course, her opinions became widely known, and suddenly the Scotch breeders found an instant market. But this stimulation was little beside that of American dog fanciers.

It is probable that working Collies were imported to America as early as Colonial days, but these dogs were scattered, and they received little or no attention except from the neighbors of their masters. The start of Collie popularity in the United States dates from about 1880. The first registrations of the breed appear in Vol. 2 of The American Kennel Club Stud Book, published in 1885, and, even at that time, a great number of these were

American-breds. In the late '8os, Collies were extremely popular at American bench shows, and there were a number of famous kennels specializing in this breed. The development on both sides of the Atlantic has continued at the same rate, and due to the need for fresh blood in a constantly growing breed there has been a considerable international traffic in Collies.

There have been occasions, during the past two decades, when the rough Collie has been outstripped by other dogs, but its popularity always has been rather consistent. Today it perhaps is the most popular of all the working variety group, and it has been among or close to the first ten breeds for a long time.

DESCRIPTION AND STANDARD OF POINTS
(By Courtesy of The Collie Club of America)

Head.—Skull flat, moderately wide between the ears and gradually tapering to the eyes. There should be but a very slight prominence of the eyebrows and a very slight depression at the stop. The proper width of skull necessarily depends on the combined length of skull and muzzle, for what would be a thick or too broad a skull in one dog is not necessarily so in another of the same actual girth, but better supported by length of muzzle. It must also be considered in conjunction with the size of the dog and should incline to lightness accompanied by cleanness of outline of cheeks and jaws. A heavy-headed dog lacks the bright, alert and full-of-sense look so much to be desired. On the other hand, the attenuated head is most frequently seen with small terrier eyes, which show no character. Muzzle should be of fair length and tapering to the nose, which should be black; it must not show weakness or appear snipy. The teeth of good size and even. English standard says, "mouth the least bit overshot," but this is by no means desirable, and if at all exaggerated, should be treated as a malformation.

Eyes.—There being no "brow" in which to set the eyes, they are necessarily placed obliquely, the upper portion of the muzzle being dropped or chiseled to give them the necessary forward look out. They should be of medium size, never showing too light in comparison with color of coat nor with a yellow ring. Expression full of intelligence, with a bright and "What is it?" look when on the alert or listening to orders; this is, of course, largely contributed to by throwing up of the ears which accompanies the "qui vive" attitude.

Ears.—The ears can hardly be too small if carried properly; if too small, they are apt to be thrown quite erect or prick-eared; if too large, they either cannot be properly lifted off the head, or if lifted, they show out of proportion. When in repose the ears are folded lengthwise and thrown back into the frill; on the alert they are thrown up and drawn close together on the top of the skull. They should be carried about three-quarters erect. A prick-eared dog should be penalized. So much attention having of late been given to securing very high carriage of ears, it has resulted in reaching the other extreme in some cases, and that is now necessary to guard against.

Neck.—Should be muscular and of sufficient length to give the dog a fine standing appearance and show the frill, which should be very full.

Body.—Rather long, ribs well rounded, chest deep, but of fair breadth behind the shoulders, which should have good slope. Loin slightly arched, showing power.

Legs.—Forelegs straight and muscular, with a fair amount of bone, the forearms moderately fleshy; pastern showing flexibility without weakness; the hindlegs less fleshy, very sinewy, and hocks and stifles well bent. Feet oval in shape, soles well padded and the toes arched close together.

Tail.—Moderately long, carried low when the dog is quiet, the end having an upward twist or "swirl"; gaily when excited, but not carried over the back.

Coat.—This is a very important point. The coat, except on the head and legs, should be abundant, the outer coat harsh to the touch, the inner soft and furry and very close, so close that it is difficult when parting the hair to see the skin. The mane and frill should be very abundant. The mask or face smooth, the forelegs slightly feathered, the hindlegs below the hocks smooth. Hair on tail very profuse and on the hips long and bushy.

COLLIES (ROUGH)

Color.—Immaterial, though a richly or nicely marked dog has undoubtedly a considerable amount of weight with judges. The black and tan with white frill and collar, or the still more showy sable with perfect white markings will generally win, other things being equal.

Size.—Dogs, about 24 inches at the shoulder; bitches, about 22 inches. Weight, dogs, about 60 pounds; bitches, about 50 pounds.

Expression.—This is one of the most important points in considering the relative value of Collies. "Expression," like the term "character," is difficult to define in words. It is not a fixed point as in color, weight or height, and is something the uninitiated can only properly understand by optical illustration. It is the combined product of the shape of the skull and muzzle, the set, size, shape and color of the eyes, and the position and carriage of the ears.

General Character.—A lithe, active dog with no useless timber about him, his chest deep, showing strength, his sloping shoulders and well-bent hocks indicating speed, and his face, high intelligence. As a whole, he should present an elegant and pleasing outline, quite distinct from any other breed, and show great strength and activity.

Faults.—Domed skull, high-peaked occipital bone, heavy pendulous ears or the other extreme, prick ears; short tail or tail curled over the back.

COLLIES (SMOOTH)

(Illustration facing page 351)

The origin of the Collies, the rough and the smooth, is buried deep in the fastnesses of the Border country, both in Scotland and in England. As working dogs they were extremely valuable to the sheep and cattle men, but they did not become known, generally, until some time after the organization of dog affairs in England. Of the two coats, the smooth was the cattle driving dog.

The earliest illustration of a Smooth Collie is the woodcut made by Thomas Bewick, about 1800, and it shows the dog as having a short tail. This tail may have been docked, for in almost all other respects the dog is similar to the specimens of today. Bewick describes the breed as larger, stronger, and fiercer than the shepherd's dog, also illustrated in his "History of Quadrupeds." Another authority contributes the information that the shepherd's dog, or Rough Collie, was about 14 inches at the shoulder in 1800, so that the smooth may not have been very large.

The immediate ancestor of the Smooth Collie probably was the dog that Bewick calls the "ban-dog," which, in turn, was a descendant of the mastiff, or Canis Molossus, which is regarded as one of the basic breeds of the world.

The earliest known specimens of the Smooth Collie carried a great deal of black in their coats, and likewise the roughs were either dark or black. Both varieties were known as the "coally dogs," and from this, undoubtedly, has sprung the modern name of Collie. In 1867, Stonehenge mentions the breed as the "Scotch Colley" or "Highland sheepdog."

[346]

COLLIES (SMOOTH)

There is a striking unanimity of opinion among the older authorities, that the smooth variety of the Collie owes its origin and development to the North of England, although it was known on both sides of the Border. The county of Northumberland was a big center of the smooth, and the black and white, mottled, strain was distinctly Northumbrian.

The Rough and Smooth Collies have been identical in form, aside from coat, for almost three quarters of a century, but there are many reasons for believing that in early days they were two separate breeds. Few types of dog have been more developed and improved—in appearance—than the Collies, and it is difficult to say just how breeders undertook this task. But it is a matter of record that by 1885, when the first specialty show was held for the breed in England, roughs and smooths often were found in the same litter.

The first organized dog show took place in England in 1859, and within a year or two the Collie was to be seen regularly on the benches. The breed, as a whole received its first great impetus in the early 60's when England's great arbiter of fashions and customs, Queen Victoria, saw and expressed her admiration for this dog. At that time the rough and the smooth competed in the same classes. It was not until the Darlington show of 1870 that separate classes were provided for Smooth Collies, although even then the name "collie" was not commonly applied to the breed.

The Collie was one of the first pure-bred dogs imported to the United States when dog lovers in America began to take an organized interest in the sport of exhibiting. It also is quite probable that scattering specimens of the Collie had come to this country many years before, purely as working dogs. This is rather difficult to place, definitely, as records of such importations have not been kept. But it is certain that the Collies, both smooth and rough, were exhibited at some of the earliest bench shows in America.

The development of the Collie in the United States has kept pace with that of England, and the strength of the breed here, is evinced by the drop in the number of importations today. However, the Smooth Collie has receded in popular favor, in recent years, and on both sides of the Atlantic it is in some need of stimulation.

DESCRIPTION AND STANDARD OF POINTS
(By Courtesy of The Smooth Collie Club, England)

Head.—Should be in proportion to dog's size; skull moderately wide between the ears, and flat, tapering to the end of the muzzle, which ought to be of a fair length but not too snipy, with only a slight stop.

Teeth.—Strong and white. The top jaw fitting nicely over the lower, and where much over or at all undershot, it should count against the dog.

Eyes.—Of almond shape, set obliquely in the head, and the shade consistent with the color of the dog. A full or staring eye is very objectionable.

Ears.—Small, and when the dog's attention is attracted, carried semi-erect; but when in repose it is natural for them to be laid back.

Neck.—Long and well arched, and shoulders muscular and sloping.

Back.—Rather long, strong, and straight, the loin slightly arched, and the chest fairly deep, but not too wide.

Forelegs.—Straight and muscular, with a fair amount of bone. The hindlegs should be rather wide apart, with stifle well bent, forming sicklehocks.

Feet.—Compact, knuckles well sprung, claws strong and close together, pads cannot be too hard.

[348]

COLLIES (SMOOTH)

Coat.—Short, dense flat coat, with good texture, with an abundance of undercoat.

Symmetry.—The dog should be of fair length on the leg, and his movements active and graceful.

Height.—Dogs, twenty-two to twenty-four inches; bitches, twenty to twenty-two inches.

Tail.—Of medium length, and when the dog is standing quietly, should be slightly raised, but more so when excited.

DOBERMAN PINSCHERS

(Illustration facing page 366)

(By Courtesy of The Doberman Pinscher Club of America)

With its racial roots somewhat obscure, the Doberman Pinscher has become, in the short space of forty-five years, a dog of definitely fixed type, whose characteristics both of body and of spirit have extended its popularity in many lands. Originating in Apolda, in Thueringen, Germany, around 1890, the breed was officially recognized in 1900. Since that date, the Doberman Pinscher has made fast friends in Europe, in the Orient and the Americas.

Of medium size and extremely clean-cut appearance, the dog, at first glance, does not give evidence of the great muscular power which it possesses. The adult male, in the pink of condition, weighs 65 to 75 pounds. So compact is its structure, so dense the laying on of muscle under the short coat and so elegant and well chiseled the outline, the novice would probably underestimate this weight by fifteen to twenty pounds. Weight is the only particular, however, in which the Doberman is deceptive. Its qualities of alertness, agility, muscular and temperamental fire stand patent for any eye to see. It is an honest dog, uncamouflaged by superfluous coat or the wiles of the artful conditioner. One gains at once the impression of sinewy nimbleness; of the quick coordination of the well-trained athlete.

There is about the Doberman Pinscher, also, an air of nobility which is part of its birthright. More than most

COLLIE

COLLIE (*Smooth*)

other breeds of dogs, it gives the immediate impression of a blue-blooded animal, of an aristocrat. From the strong muzzle and wedge-shaped head to the long clearly defined stifle, the dog's outline is definite, sharply etched, unblurred. The alert, fearless and inquisitive expression of the dark eye is in harmony with the bodily characteristics. The Doberman looks upon the stranger boldly and judges him with unerring instinct. He is ready, if need be, not merely to give prompt alarm but to back his warning with prompt defense of his master and his master's goods. Yet, he is affectionate, obedient and loyal.

Traditionally compounded of the old short-haired shepherd dog stock with admixtures of the Rottweiler, the Black and Tan Terrier and the smooth haired German Pinscher, the Doberman, which takes its name from Louis Dobermann, of Apolda, has been fortunate, with the aid of selective breeding which has been applied with consummate skill in its home land and more recently in the United States, to have absorbed the good qualities of the races which have gone to make up its bloodstream. It has been from the beginning a working dog devoted to the service of mankind.

At first, the Doberman was used almost exclusively as a guard and home watch-dog. As it developed, its qualities of ready intelligence and ability to absorb and retain training brought it into demand as a police and war dog. In this service its exceptional body agility and unswerving courage soon made it highly prized. The possession of an excellent nose made the dog highly adaptable for trailing the malefactor or the criminal and also has led to its use as a hunting dog.

Most of all, perhaps, among the endearing qualities of the Doberman has come to be its devotion to its own hearth and home and its discriminating service as the friend and guardian of the whole family and especially of children. The properly bred and trained Doberman Pinscher has a sane mind and a sound body; the heart and spirit of a gentleman.

In the United States the breed has been fostered and seen its popularity reach out into every State through The Doberman Pinscher Club of America, which was founded in February 1921. Through the efforts of this organization, keen interest has been maintained in the breed, further evidenced by the steady increase of both breeders and exhibitors. An achievement in itself was the record established at The Doberman Pinscher Club's Annual Specialty Show held in conjunction with the World's Fair in Chicago, October 1933, when the entry of this breed exceeded that of any other breed for the year.

DESCRIPTION AND STANDARD OF POINTS

(Adopted by The Doberman Pinscher Club of America and Approved by The American Kennel Club, August, 1935)

Conformation and General Appearance. — The Doberman Pinscher is a dog of good medium size, square in proportion as viewed from the side. The height, measured on a perpendicular line from the top of the withers to the ground, should equal the length, measured horizontally from the forechest, or sternum, to the outer edge of the upper thigh. Permissable height at shoulder, dogs, 24 to 27 inches; bitches, 23 to 25 inches. Compactly built, muscular and powerful, denoting great endurance and speed. Elegant in appearance, of proud carriage and great nobility, manifesting by its bearing a wide-awake vivacious personality. Temperament energetic, watchful, determined and alert; loyal and obedient, fearless and aggressive.

Faults. — Coarseness. Fineness or greyhound build. Undersize or oversize. Commonness, sluggishness, lack of nobility, fail-

DOBERMAN PINSCHERS

ure to manifest any of the temperament characteristics. *Shyness,* bad temper.

Head.—Long and clean cut, resembling a blunt wedge. Top of skull flat, with slight stop; top line of muzzle as nearly parallel as possible with top of skull. Cheeks flat; well filled under the eyes. Jaws full and powerful. Lips cleanly fitted to jaw.

Faults.—*Ramshead,* too great width between ears, occipital bone too prominent, rounded skull or apple head. Prominent growth of bone above eyes, hollowness under eyes, dish-faced, too short or snipy muzzle. Heavy cheeks. Lippiness.

Eyes.—Dark and of medium size, almond-shaped, with vigorous and alert expression. In reds, slightly lighter eye permissible.

Faults—Light eyes (sulphur color). Too small or too large. Of sinister expression.

Teeth.—Strongly developed and snow-white. Scissors bite, i.e. with upper edge of lower incisors, which should be as nearly upright as possible touching inner surface of upper incisors.

Faults.—*Missing,* poor or black-brown teeth; *Undershot or overshot.* Absence of scissors bite.

Ears.—Cropped to a point and carried erect. If uncropped, ears should be set on high, not too far apart and of medium size, drooping forward close to cheek. The top line of folded ear being slightly above the level of the skull.

Faults.—Ears badly carried or placed too low.

Neck.—Sufficiently long and clean cut, well muscled and slightly arched.

Faults.—Short or thick. Throatiness.

Body.—Backline firm, with slope to croup desirable. Must at least be level. Withers clearly defined. Back short, firm and muscular. Chest well developed and deep, reaching at least to the elbow. Noticeable spring of rib. Brisket full but not too broad. Abdomen well tucked up, continuing curved line of the chest. Loins well muscled, hips sufficiently broad. Tail docked.

Faults.—Back long, roached or swayed. *Greater height at hind quarters than at withers.* Diagonally slanting or low rounding croup. Low tail placement. Narrow, shallow or barrel-shaped chest. Lack of forechest development. Wasp-waisted. Lack of muscular development. Hips too narrow.

Fore Quarters.—Shoulders well muscled, lying close to the body. Upper arms forming as nearly as may be, a right angle with the shoulder blades. Legs straight to the pasterns. Pasterns firm. Paws compact.

Faults.—Loose or stiff shoulders. *French or "fiddle" front.* Feet turning in or out. Front narrow. Weakness of pasterns. Steepness of shoulder, (too short upper-arm or shoulder blade). Insufficient forechest. Paws long, flat or splayed.

Hind Quarters.—Broad, with upper thigh forming as nearly as may be a right angle with hip bone. Well muscled, with clearly defined stifle. Lower thigh of good length. Legs, when viewed from behind, straight, turning neither in nor out. Paws compact.

Faults.—Fine or lightly muscled hindlegs. Steepness due to insufficient angulation. Excessive angulation. *Cowhocks.* Sloping or excessively rounded croup. Low tail placement. Failure to balance with fore quarters. Feet turning in or out. Flat feet.

Gait.—Free, balanced, vigorous and true. Back firm, indicating the lasting qualities of a working dog.

Faults.—Lack of drive, stiffness, looseness, excessive back motion. Paddling. Throwing front or hind legs.

Coat, Color and Markings.—Coat short, hard and close-lying. Color, black, brown or blue, with rust-red, sharply defined markings. White hairs on chest permissible, but not desirable.

Faults.—Long or wavy hair, grey undercoat showing through. White on chest exceeding half-inch square. Straw-colored, mixed, missing or too large markings. *Light fawn coat (known as Isabella) prohibited.*

Note:—Faults printed in italics are MAJOR FAULTS indicating degeneration of the breed.

SCALE OF POINTS

General Conformation and Appearance

Proportions	8
Substance, muscle and bone	8
Temperament, expression and nobility	8
Condition	5	29

DOBERMAN PINSCHERS

Head

Shape	6	
Eyes	3	
Teeth	5	
Ears	1	15
Neck		3

Body

Backline, withers, loins, tail placement	8	
Chest, brisket, rib spring, tuck-up	8	
Shape and proportions	4	20

Fore Quarters

Shoulders, upperarms, legs and pasterns ..	5	
Angulation	4	
Paws	2	11

Hind Quarters

Upper thigh, stifle and hocks	5	
Angulation	4	
Paws	2	11
Gait		6
Coat, color and markings		5
Total		100

Note:—It is recommended that the Scale of Points be confined to use in Match Shows and Judging Classes.

ESKIMOS

(Illustration facing page 367)

(By Courtesy of The Eskimo Dog Club of America)

The Eskimo dog, claimed by his admirers as the best-footed, toughest and strongest for his size of all breeds, is a native of the Arctic. Originating, in all probability, in Eastern Siberia he has since been taken by his Eskimo owners to Alaska, Northern Canada, Baffin Island, Labrador and Greenland. In all these sections he is still fairly plentiful though at present there is considerable danger of his type being lost by indiscriminate cross-breeding.

As a member of the so-called "Spitz Group" he is closely related to Alaskan Malamutes, Siberian Huskies, Samoyedes and Chows and more distantly to many others, including Norwegian Elkhounds, German Shepherds, Belgian Sheepdogs, Finnish Spitz, Keeshonden, Schipperkes and Pomeranians.

A product of the "survival of the fittest" over a period of at least 2,000 years in the most rigorous localities, he stands supreme in his field. As an all-around canine assistant of the North he is without a peer. Not only is he the most feasible means of transportation in winter but likewise is much used as a pack animal in summer. During the warm months, too, he is frequently employed to pull boats along the shore. He is indispensable as a hunting assistant for his nose is exceptionally keen and his courage of a high order.

Since his employment by explorers some thirty or forty years ago more rapid strides have been made in

Arctic and Antarctic exploration than in the two preceding centuries. With his aid the poles of the earth were reached and both Admiral Peary and Raold Amundsen, their discoverers, give him full credit as an invaluable assistant. The recent advent of the airplane in polar work will alter his usefulness in only a minor way. Dog teams will still be essential in hauling supplies, as a means of rescue when motors fail and for detailed exploration at the frozen ends of the globe.

Besides his great usefulness, the Eskimo dog is one of the most beautiful members of the canine race. With his erect ears, keen expression, slanting eyes, tightly curled tail, massive build and glorious coat he is indeed an animal of rare good looks. Although leading the toughest sort of life, generally underfed, mistreated and often over-worked, he enjoys an excellent reputation in his association with mankind.

He is extremely affectionate and perfectly safe even with small children when fairly treated, though he is rather pugnacious and is not always to be trusted with other dogs and animals. When raised by a kind and intelligent owner he makes a good pet but it is generally unwise to allow him unrestricted liberty. Most of his coat is shed early each Spring and he is able to stand hot weather as well as any other long-haired breed. Similar to other Northern dogs he is free from the usual "doggy odor."

His coat, which consists of long guard hair and a "woolly" undercoat, is so dense that he can sleep comfortably out in the open at 60 to 70 degrees below zero and is impregnable to the heaviest rains. Eskimo dogs are found in two coats—the regular and the long-haired —and nearly every known dog coloration. Two colors, however, seem peculiar to the breed. These are white bodies with coal-black heads and all whites with double spinal markings of silver grey. Both are very beautiful, particularly when seen in perfectly matched teams.

The feet of the Eskimo dog—probably the most important point in any working breed—have reached a state of perfection that would preclude improvement. They are large, long and "flattish," though never "splayed," with strong nails, thick pads and an abundance of hair to cushion between the toes. In the long-haired variety the foot-feathering is profuse.

The Eskimo dog, when well kenneled, adequately fed and properly exercised, is a very quiet breed. Generally speaking he is incapable of barking. Instead, he either yelps or howls like a wolf, though he rarely gives vent to these weird sounds in civilization. Contrary to popular opinion, although his superficial resemblance and cries would tend to make one believe otherwise, he is not closely related to the wolf, nor has he been cross-bred with it recently, except in one or two isolated cases.

He is keenly alert, highly suspicious and extraordinarily intelligent, particularly in hunting, trail and ice sense. He is easy to train for sled work and after the commands have been mastered never forgets them. His memory for routes, once travelled, is phenomenal. As a hunting assistant he is an indispensable aid in ferreting out breathing holes of seal in the ice which are hidden by snow. He can "wind" a herd of musk-oxen several miles away and in short order have them rounded up for his owner to shoot. On polar bear, too, he is unusually good and in hunting this game furnishes probably the most thrilling of all doggy sports. The big white bruin is coursed by dog team, with the hunter hanging on as best he can the madly careening and speeding komatic (Eskimo sled). When the team nears its quarry all traces are cut and the dogs quickly bring the bear to bay. The hunter then furnishes the "coup de grace."

As a work dog he acknowledges no superior. He can pull heavier loads greater distances and on less food than almost any other living animal. The weight of the load, mileage travelled and speed made depend upon several factors, such as physical condition, size, weather and, above all, snow and ice surfaces.

On good trails, for very fast going when averages of 10 miles an hour or better are wanted, the load should not exceed half the total weight of the dogs in the team. For fairly swift going, with averages of 6 to 8 miles an hour, not more than the total weight of the team should be carried and for heavy freight work, with averages of 2 to 4 miles an hour, a good team will draw from one and a half to double its bodyweight.

On long trips, 20 to 30 miles is a good daily average, though in emergencies far greater distances may be covered. Upon one occasion, for instance, Commander Donald B. MacMillan, the famed explorer, drove his team of Eskimo dogs 100 miles in 18 hours. The regular pace is usually a fast steady trot though at times they will break into a gallop and exceed 20 miles per hour.

Eskimo dogs are ready breeders and have large litters. The puppies are easy to raise and once weaned can stand unlimited cold. Upon reaching six months of age, when they are usually broken to harness, it is best never to kennel more than two dogs together. Any good commercial dog food, with additions of raw fatty beef and codliver oil, will keep them in splendid health. When working hard, however, nothing will sustain them like a steady diet of raw meat, either walrus, seal or beef, and raw fat in approximately equal parts. In summer plenty of fresh water is needed but in winter snow is sufficient.

Dog driving is one of the most fascinating sports in the realm of winter and is becoming increasingly popular with both men and women in the United States. Those wishing to secure a team will make no mistake in choosing the Eskimo dog.

DESCRIPTION AND STANDARD OF POINTS

(By Courtesy of The Eskimo Dog Club of America)

General Impression.—The Eskimo dog is one of the best known breeds of work dogs in the world and should not be confused with smaller breeds of dogs that have borrowed his name. The real Eskimo dogs originating from Greenland, Labrador and the northeastern part of the continent are Nature's product for sled dog work. Being a draft animal for centuries in the Arctic regions, he has developed a powerful body and heavy coat. Although large-boned and of rugged build, many specimens are very beautiful, and as attractive as show types in any other breed. Eskimo dogs are good-natured and very intelligent.

Size and Weight.—Shoulder height for males, 22 to 25 inches; females, 20 to 23 inches. Weight for males, 65 to 85 pounds; females, 50 to 70 pounds.

Head.—Well proportioned, broad and wedge-shaped. Strong flat skull and powerful jaws. Large black or brown nose. Lips black or brown. Muzzle medium length.

Eyes.—Small and deep set.

Ears.—Short and firm, carried erect and turned forward.

Neck.—Short, heavy and very muscular.

Fore Quarters.—Broad, big-boned and muscular. Forelegs straight.

Chest.—Deep and broad with ribs well sprung.

Tail.—Large and bushy, and carried up or curled over the back.

Hind Quarters.—Medium length, heavy and very muscular. Stifles well bent.

ESKIMOS

Paws.—Large with thick pads and well protected with hair, so that these Eskimo dogs can haul heavy loads for miles over rough ice and crusted snow without getting footsore.

Coat.—Should be a heavy covering of master hair varying from 3 to 6 inches in length. Some specimens are found in Northern Labrador with a long, shaggy coat of master hair averaging 6 inches in length. There is also a dense undercoat of wool varying from 1 to 2 inches in length.

Color and Markings.—Genuine Eskimo dogs may be found in all known dog colors: black, white, black and white, wolf grey, blue grey, and all shades of tan or buff; and in all combinations of these colors.

GERMAN SHEPHERD DOGS

(Illustration facing page 382)

(By Courtesy of The German Shepherd Dog Club of America, Inc.)

Derived from the old breeds of herding and farm dogs and associated for centuries with man, as his servant and companion, the German Shepherd dog has been subject to intensive development during the last 45 years. Sponsored by the Verein für Deutsche Schäferhunde, the parent club of the breed, which was founded in 1899 in Germany, the cult of the Shepherd spread rapidly from about 1914 onward in many parts of the world. Interest in the breed has been fostered by specialty clubs in many lands as it has been in the United States by the German Shepherd Dog Club of America.

First, last and all the time a working dog, the German Shepherd has been developed both temperamentally and structurally through selective breeding, through judging which, on the whole, has been of a very constructive character, and through specialized training.

Considering first the more important side of the dog —its character—the Shepherd is distinguished for loyalty, courage, and the ability to assimilate and retain training for a number of special services.

He should be of equable disposition, poised, unexcitable, and with well-controlled nerves. For his typical work as a herding sheepdog, he must not be gun shy and must have courage to protect his flock from attacks, either animal or human. For his work as a police dog, a development which followed upon the natural aptitude which he showed to be trained, he must have this courage also, but, in addition, must be able to make use of the excellent nose which he usually possesses. In his work as a leader of the blind, at once the most spectacular and the most appealing of his services to man, the Shepherd must and does exhibit a very high order of intelligence and discrimination involving the qualities of observation, patience, faithful watchfulness and even, to a certain degree, the exercise of judgment.

These qualities of mind and of heart, which have endeared the German Shepherd dog to a wide public in practically every country of the globe, are those of the faithful companion, the alert protector, the unswerving friend. The German Shepherd is not a pugnacious brawler, but is a bold and punishing fighter if need be. In his relation to man, he does not give affection lightly nor make immediate advances toward indiscriminate and perhaps frivolous friendship. He has plenty of dignity and some suspicion of strangers, but his friendship, once given, is for life.

On the physical side, the German Shepherd has been developed to a point of almost ideal fitness for the work which he is called upon to do. He is a dog of middle size with enough weight to be effective as a herder or a patrolman, but not enough to be cumbersome or unwieldy. He is muscular, firmly knit, with strong bone, tough sinew, and clean cut joints.

The body is relatively long, and the length from the prominent sternum to the back of the well-muscled thigh should always be noticeably more than the height of the dog taken at the top of the withers. A desirable proportion of these measurements runs from ten to nine to ten to eight and a half. The body is capacious, without being barrel ribbed, and is marked by great depth of chest and by ribbing carried well back, giving abundant room to the vital organs. The under line of the dog is relatively level and in marked contrast to the tucked-up body of the running hounds. The back is strong and straight, the withers high, the clean-cut neck moderately long and carried rather forward than up. The tail is set on low and carried low when the dog is at rest.

The head is cleanly chiseled, strong without coarseness, but above all not fine. The muzzle is strong squarely carried out and level and the underjaw well developed. The teeth are powerfully developed and the incisors meet in a scissors bite; that is to say, with the inner surfaces of the upper incisors just engaging the upper and outer edge of the lower incisors. The eye is of medium size, set somewhat oblique, preferably dark and of a fearless and alert expression. The ears, of medium size, open to the front and are held erect when the dog is at attention.

By careful selective breeding, the naturally easy trot of the German Shepherd dog has been brought to a high pitch of nearly effortless motion. Essentially a trotting animal, his structure has been modified so as to increase the power, elasticity and length of his gait. Other things being equal, the best moving Shepherd dog is the one which covers the maximum amount of ground with the minimum expenditure of energy. To attain this end, three things are essential: an iron strong back, a hind quarter of deep and clean cut angulation and a sloping shoulder with sufficient angulation between the shoulder blade and the upper arm to take up and compensate for the stride of the hind quarter. The hind quarter assembly presents a moderately sloping croup to which is attached a long, wide and powerfully-muscled stifle and, at a sharp angle, a short, strong hock.

At a trot, the hind leg reaches far under the dog, often

well past a line perpendicular to the shoulder, the well-arched foot, with thick pad, takes a strong grip on the ground and, with the hock as a fulcrum and the leverage provided by the long stifle, propels the dog far forward. At the same time the opposite front foot is stretched far ahead of the animal by means of the opening of the well-angulated shoulder and a strong, but springy pastern takes up the shock of the step.

So well coordinated, so rhythmic and harmonious is this gait when properly exemplified that the dog seems to glide forward without visible effort, suspended, one might almost think, from the firm beam which is his back. Few animals in motion give so completely the impression of controlled and coordinated power, like the movement of a well-oiled machine.

The German Shepherd dog has a double coat to protect him in all weathers; a harsh outer coat of medium length, of which the hairs are usually straight, though sometimes somewhat crimped and wavy, and a dense woolly undercoat beneath. In color he may run from jet black to rather light grey with all sorts of variations in between. Black and tan, brindle, iron grey, grey with sable markings, and other strong colors predominate. Pale or washed-out tones are considered a sign of degeneration and are not wanted.

The impression of the dog as a whole is one of ruggedness combined with nobility, of power combined with agility. There should be a sense of balance, fore quarter and hind quarter compensating each other in their development. The outline should be smooth and flowing and the top line of the dog, from ear to the tip of the full tail, a single sweeping succession of unbroken curves. The German Shepherd is a natural dog, unmutilated for any whim of show ring. His beauty is that of high character, clothed in harmonious bodily form.

DESCRIPTION AND STANDARD OF POINTS

(By Courtesy of The German Shepherd Dog Club of America, Inc.)

General Appearance—(a) *Structure.*—The Shepherd Dog is a dog above the middle size. He is long, strong and well muscled, full of life and at attention nothing escapes his sharp senses.

The average height for dogs is 60 centimeters (24 inches) and for bitches between 55 and 58 centimeters (22 to 23½ inches). This height is established by taking a perpendicular line from the top of the shoulder-blade to the ground with the coat parted or so pushed down that the measurement will show only the actual height of the frame or structure of the dog.

The most desirable height for the Shepherd Dog, as a working dog, is between 55 to 64 or 65 centimeters (22 to 26 inches). The working value of dogs above or below these heights is lessened.

Note:—Height above the average should not be considered a fault, however, provided the proportion of length to height is correct, and the weight of bone is also in proportion and not so great as to make the dog clumsy or readily fatigued. In all cases the proportion of length to height should not be less than as ten is to nine, preferably as ten is to eight.

(b) *Characteristics.*—The traits and special characteristics of the Shepherd are watchfulness, loyalty, honesty and an aristocratic bearing, forming a combination which makes the pure-bred Shepherd Dog an ideal guard and companion. It is desirable to try to improve his appearance, but nothing must be done which in any way detracts from his usefulness.

Head.—The size of the head should be in proportion to the body, without being clumsy. It should be clean cut and of medium width between the ears. The forehead, seen from the front, only moderately arched, lacking or with very slight, center furrow. The skull slopes in a slanting line without abrupt stop, continuing into the wedge-shaped long muzzle; the muzzle is strong, the lips tight and dry, firmly fitting together; the cheeks slightly rounded toward the front, but without undue prominence as seen from the

DOBERMAN PINSCHER

ESKIMO

front. The bridge of the nose is straight and in parallel line with an imaginary elongation of the line of the forehead. Jaws and teeth are very strong, teeth meeting in a scissors grip, but not overshot.

Note:—The correct mouth is one in which part of the inner surface of the upper teeth meet and engage part of the outer surface of the lower teeth. This mouth gives a more powerful grip and sharper bite than one in which the edges of the teeth meet directly. If there is space between the upper and lower teeth, however, when the mouth is closed, the dog is overshot or undershot, and faulty in this particular.

Ears.—Medium in size, set high on the head, relatively broad at the base and pointed at the tops, opening toward the front and carried erect when at attention, though not necessarily at all times. Cropped and hanging ears are to be discarded.

Note:—A firm, erect carriage is desirable especially for breeding animals. The ideal carriage is one in which center lines of the ears, viewed from the front, are parallel to each other and perpendicular to the ground. Slight outward divergencies are permissible. In young dogs slight pliancy or lack of complete firmness is permissible. Pups usually do not straighten their ears before the fourth or sixth month and frequently not until later.

Eyes.—Medium size, almond-shaped, set a little oblique and not protruding, color dark brown. The expression should be lively, intelligent and show distrust of strangers.

Note:—In light-colored dogs eyes of light color are frequently found. If they harmonize with the coloration of the dog they should not be considered a serious fault, but the dark eye is always to be preferred.

Neck.—Strong and muscular, clean cut, proportionate to head and back and without loose folds of skin.

Note:—When the dog is excited the head is raised and the neck carried high, otherwise the head is carried but little higher than the top of the shoulder.

Body.—Chest deep, but not too wide, ribs flat rather than barrel-shaped, with the breast bone reaching to the elbow. Abdomen moderately tucked up. Back straight and very strongly developed. Short-coupled and long-legged dogs are to be discarded. The agility and elasticity required of a herding dog are attained by proper angulation at the fore and hind quarters, broad, powerful loin and long, gradually sloping croup.

Tail.—Bushy, reaching to the hock and often forming a slight hook turned to one side. At rest the tail hangs in a slight curve like a saber. When the dog is excited or in motion the curve is accentuated and the tail is raised, but it should never be lifted beyond a line at right angles with the line of the back. The tail, therefore, should never be laid over the back either straight or curved. Docked tails are to be discarded.

Note:—Bobbed tails and too short tails appear, but dogs having this fault should be discarded for breeding. The end of the last vertebra of the tail should reach fully to the hock when the tail is held against the dog's hindleg.

Fore Quarters.—The shoulders should be long and sloping, well muscled and set on flat against the body. The forearm straight viewed from all angles. The pastern long and combining springiness with strength.

Note:—The angulation of the shoulder is extremely important to the proper gait of the dog. The angle at the point of the shoulder where the shoulder-blade joins the upper arm should be very nearly a right angle. The construction of the chest, as outlined under the heading "Body" above, should permit of free play of the foreleg backward and forward. This is impossible with a round-ribbed dog.

Hind Quarters.—The thigh broad and powerfully muscled. The upper thigh long and sharply angled with the long stifle. The hock strong and comparatively short.

Note:—The hind quarters of the correctly constructed Shepherd Dog present a study in sharp angulations. This enables the dog to step far under his body with the hindleg, to take firm hold upon the ground and propel himself forward with a powerful stride. It is not sufficient that the stifle itself should be long; to secure the correct movement it must present a sharp angle with the upper thigh as well as with the hock. Great strength of hock is necessary to provide the power required in the lifting and forward-driving step. Cowhocks are a serious fault.

Feet.—Round, short, compact, and the toes well arched. Pads very hard, nails short, strong and usually dark in color. Dew-claws frequently appear on the hindleg. They are not faults in themselves, but as they usually cause a spread action and sometimes injuries they should be removed immediately after pups are whelped.

Note:—The feet of the Shepherd Dog are an important part of the working equipment. The so-called cat foot or terrier foot is not desired. On the other hand, the thin, spread or bare foot is still more undesirable. The ideal foot is compact and extremely strong with good gripping power and plenty of depth of pad.

Color.—All colors are permissible from solid black to solid white, including many variations of brown, greys and mixed wolf colorings, also brindles. White markings on chest and legs are allowed. The undercoat, except in black dogs, is always light in color. The color of a pup can only be ascertained after his outer coat comes in.

Note:—While the permissible range of color is extremely wide, the white and very pale or washed-out colors are not deemed so desirable, while albinos, white with red eyes, are to be discarded. The skin of the nose in all cases should be black.

Coat.—While there are three varieties of the Shepherd Dog recognized, namely, the smooth-coated, the rough-coated or wire-haired and the long-coated, the first of these, i.e., the smooth-coated Shepherd Dog, is the only one found in any appreciable number and the only variety here discussed.

In this variety the outer coat should be as dense as possible, each single hair straight, harsh and lying close to the body. Slightly wavy outer coat is permissible. The head, including the inner ear, front quarters and paws covered with short hair and the neck with longer and thicker hair. The fore and hindlegs have a short feather extending to the pasterns and hock, respectively.

Note:—Length of coat varies. Too short a coat is a fault; the smooth coat which is too long collects dirt and indicates either a poor or absent undercoat.

The undercoat should always be present and should be dense and form a real protection to the body.

Note:—The amount of undercoat present will, of course, vary somewhat with the season and the proportion of his time which the dog spends outdoors.

[369]

Faults.—(a) All physical defects which tend to lessen utility and endurance, especially a combination of short back and legginess.

(b) Too clumsy or too fine a build.

(c) Soft or sway back.

(d) Steep positions of the fore quarter or hind quarter assemblages or anything which would adversely affect the length or elasticity of the stride or the endurance of the running gear.

(e) The coat too short or too soft or undercoat lacking.

(f) Skull clumsy or too shallow.

(g) Muzzle too short and stumpy or too weak and pointed.

(h) Mouth overshot or undershot.

(i) Splay feet and long-coated paws.

(j) Hanging ears.

(k) Rolling, ring or badly-carried tails.

(l) Cropped ears and docked tails.

GREAT DANES
(Illustration facing page 383)

(By Courtesy of The Great Dane Club of America)

The Great Dane of today, in appearance and nature, is one of the most elegant and distinguished varieties of the giant-type of dog.

Accurate canine history is limited to but little longer than the last half century.

The first dog show was held as recently as 1859 at Birmingham, England. There the dog game was born. Before that time over a period of more than three thousand years there are occasional records of different sorts of dogs. But the items are so few, incomplete and inaccurate that a student of the dogs of antiquity can "prove" almost anything he cares to imagine.

This ignorance of the distant past is not important in the sport of breeding to a fixed standard. We are interested in the present to some extent but most of all we dream of the *future*—we dream of that day to come when we shall breed a more perfect Great Dane than we have ever seen! As sportsmen we look forward always, backward occasionally.

The reader of these lines is presumed to be one who is pondering on what breed he would fancy if he took up the sport. To him we are pleased and proud to tell all we know of the Great Dane's past in a plain, unvarnished way. If we should choose to dramatize the Great Dane or write fairy tales, no other breed could offer juicier material. But we shall stoop to nothing like that. His human admirers must try to be as dignified as the Dane himself.

The very name of our breed (in the English language) shows that absence of seriousness with which all dogs were regarded, even among fanciers, two generations ago. It is a translation of an old French designation, grand Danois, meaning "big Danish." This was only one of half a dozen names which had been used for centuries in France for our breed. Why the English adopted the name "Great Dane," from the French, is a mystery. At the same time the French were also calling it, among others, by the name *dogue allemand* or "German Mastiff." "Mastiff" in English, *dogge* in the Germanic, *dogue* or *dogo* in the Latin languages, all meant the same thing: a giant dog with heavy head for fighting or hunting purposes. It was one of the dozen varieties of canine recognized as distinctive enough at that time to have a name of its own. The organization of dog shows and kennel clubs in recent times has made dogs a complicated body of more than 100 distinct breeds, each with an Official Standard of Perfection, and stud book to keep the family trees in order.

In the good old days before 1859 things were rough and ready. It was much simpler than now!

There is no known reason for connecting Denmark with either the origin or development of our breed. In the first instance it was "made in Germany" and up to now it is German fanciers who lead the world in breeding most of the finest specimens. Probably more than half the Great Danes whelped each year are German.

If the reader is susceptible to the charms of antiquity, he will be interested in Cassel's claim that on Egyptian monuments of about 3000 B.C. there are drawings of dogs much like our Great Dane. Also, the earliest written description of a dog like our breed may be found in Chinese literature of 1121 B.C. (article by Dr. G. Ciaburri, Great Dane Club of Italy publication, 1929).

From such early times forward one might list quite a collection of art relics and literary references proving the existence of huge fighting or hunting dogs belonging to the Mastiff group. There are even more numerous amazing tales of what certain famous dogs did to attract historical notice. But this material would fill a large volume. And, after all what could it prove? What value has it for the one who is considering taking up Great Danes as a hobby today? There have been nearly 40 dog-generations since the first dog show was held. That is a long enough past to be useful and we have a huge amount of detailed information about that period, if anyone wishes to use it. Forty *human* generations in 1,200 years!

Eminent zoologists like Keller and Kraemer believe that the Mastiff Group of breeds originated in Asia. They think the modern Tibetan Mastiff, occasionally shown in England, is the most direct descendant of the prototype.

The great naturalist Buffon (1707-1788) claimed the Irish Wolfhound as the principal ancestor of our Great Dane. The comparative anatomist Cuvier (1769-1832) found more evidence in favor of the Old English Mastiff as the root from which it sprang. Both Irish and English breeds are known to have been carefully bred for 1,300 years and more. Today most students favor the idea that the Great Dane or Deutsche Dogge resulted from a mixture of both these ancient types.

This is not to say that the German Mastiff or Great Dane is a new breed. It is, indeed, a very old one and has been cultivated as a distinct type probably 400 years if not longer. Like all the old varieties of dog, it was developed for a serious, useful purpose. The Germans made the Great Dane to be a boar hound. There remain today, few wild boars in Europe to be hunted, but we all know that it is regarded as one of the most savage, swiftest, most powerful and well-armed of all the big game on the Continent. To tackle the wild boar requires a super-dog—and that is precisely what the Germans developed. We who fancy him speak of him as the King of Dogs!

In common with all other breeds of dog, the Great Dane's history and development of a modern standard type really began about 60 years ago. In 1880 at Berlin, Germany, Dr. Bodinus called a meeting of Great Dane judges which officially declared the breed should be known as *deutsche dogge* and that all other designations, especially the term "Great Dane," should be abolished from that time forward. So far as the German people are concerned, this declaration has been observed. But English-speaking people have paid no heed. The Italians, who have a large Great Dane fancy, have also failed to give Germany credit in the name selected: *Alano*. This word means "a mastiff" consequently the name of their organization means "Mastiff Club of Italy." But this has not prevented closest cooperation between fanciers of the two countries. The leading Italian breeders base their operation on nothing but German imported stock or its descendants.

In 1891 the Great Dane Club of Germany adopted a precise standard or Official Description of the ideal specimen.

In 1885 there was a Great Dane Club in England and in 1889 at Chicago was founded the German Mastiff or Great Dane Club of America, member of The American

Kennel Club with the late G. Muss-Arnoldt as first Delegate. Two years later our Club reorganized as The Great Dane Club of America with a membership mostly of Eastern fanciers and headquarters since that time has been in New York City.

But the American Standard of the Great Dane from the earliest has been based upon the German Standard as adopted by Deutsche Doggen Club. In fact all nations have recognized the authority of the Fatherland in this matter. The English, French, Italian, Indian and Dutch Standards are almost exact translations from the German. The world over there is a single ideal of excellence in Great Danes. If a Dane rates high in Germany, he will rate high anywhere. This is not true of several popular breeds which have seen local fads take hold of judges so that we have a diversity of types in the same breed: "English," "American," "Swiss" or "German." This causes confusion in judging and breeding, since a "flyer" in one country will be considered quite undesirable in another country. There is nothing like this in Great Danes.

To enlarge upon the Standard printed in this volume seems unnecessary. We think it is a very plain and also a very complete description. We have tried to cover everything you could want to know about the appearance of an ideal Great Dane. It will reward anyone who is sufficiently interested to study it carefully. At dog shows all over the world Great Danes are judged against this standard.

The Great Dane has developed more steadily in popularity than almost any breed of dog. He has never been the rage, outside of Germany in Bismarck's day. But year after year all over the world he has slowly increased in numbers until he is today perhaps the most numerous and popular of the big breeds.

The Germans have kept before them the stern business the boar-hound must engage in. A merely "pretty" dog has not been enough. He must have size and weight, nobility and courage and speed and endurance.

What more can one ask for in a dog?

If "Man's best friend" is a dog, we are convinced, that the chap who first thought so must have loved a Great Dane!

DESCRIPTION AND STANDARD OF POINTS
(Adopted by The Great Dane Club of America, 1935, and Approved by The American Kennel Club, May 14, 1935)

1. *General Appearance and Character.*—The Great Dane combines, in its distinguished appearance, dignity, strength and elegance with great size, and a powerful, well-formed body. It is the Apollo of dogs. The Great Dane attracts one by its unusually impressive head; even under the greatest excitement it does not show any nervousness and reminds one of a noble statue. He is friendly, affectionate and loyal to his owners and especially, to children; reserved and distrustful toward outsiders.

2. *Head.*—Long, narrow, distinguished, expressive, finely chiselled (especially the part below the eyes) with strongly pronounced stop. Seen from the side, the forehead must be sharply set off from the bridge of the nose. The forehead and the bridge of the nose must be straight and parallel to one another. Seen from the front, the head should appear narrow; the bridge of the nose should be as broad as possible; the cheek muscles must show slightly and must under no circumstances be very pronounced. The muzzle part must have full flews and must be as vertically blunt as possible in front; the angles of the lip must be quite pronounced. The front part of the head, from the tip of the nose up to the stop, should, as far as possible, be as long as the rear part of the head, from the stop to the only slightly developed occiput. The head should be angular from all sides and should have definite contours, but at the same time its dimensions should be absolutely in pro-

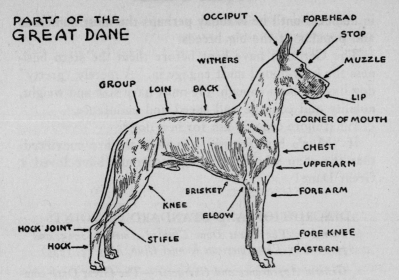

PARTS OF THE GREAT DANE

OCCIPUT

FOREHEAD

STOP

MUZZLE

WITHERS

LIP

GROUP

LOIN

BACK

CORNER OF MOUTH

CHEST

UPPERARM

FOREARM

BRISKET

KNEE

ELBOW

HOCK JOINT

STIFLE

FORE KNEE

HOCK

PASTERN

FNNOMEYER

portion to the general appearance of the Dane. Faults: A line of forehead which drops toward the back or which rises steeply; bridge of nose which rises toward the front or drops or is bent in; too small a stop or none at all; too narrow a nose bridge, and the rear of the head spreading laterally in a wedge-like manner (wedge head); furthermore, an excessively round upper head (apple head); moreover, excessively pronounced cheek musculature; pointed muzzle but also loose lips hanging over the lower jaw, so-called "fluttering lips" which create an illusion of a full, deep muzzle part. The head should rather be shorter and distinguished than long, vapid and expressionless.

3. *Eyes* (general).—Medium size, as dark as possible, with lively intelligent expression; almond shaped eyelids, well developed eyebrows. Faults: Light colored, piercing, amber colored, light blue to a watery blue or eyes of different colors; furthermore, eyes too far apart; mongolian eyes; eyelids which hang down too far with pronounced haw and excessively reddened conjunctive. (With regard to the color of the eyes, see also Art. 17.)

[377]

4. *Ears.*—Ears should be high set not too far apart, medium in size of moderate thickness, drooping forward close to the cheek. Top line of folded ear should be about level with the skull. Faults: Hanging on the side as on a fox hound, *or*

Cropped ears. High set, not set too far apart; well pointed but always in proportion to the shape of the head and carried uniformly erect.

5. *Nose.*—The nose must be large and, in case of brindled and "single-colored" Danes, it must always be black; in connection with Harlequins see Art. 17e. Faults: Split noses should be disqualified.

6. *Teeth.*—Strong developed, the incisors of the lower jaws must touch very lightly the bottoms of the inner-surface of the upper incisors. If front teeth of both jaws bite on top of each other, this bite wears the teeth too rapidly. Faults: Undershot and overshot incisors out of line, black or brown teeth.

7. *Neck.*—High set, long, muscular and sinewy, without strong pronounced pendulous throat folds and especially with no dewlaps; from the chest to the head, slightly tapering, beautifully formed, with well developed nape. Faults: Short, heavy neck, loose folds or dewlaps.

8. *Shoulders.*—The shoulder blades must be long and sloping and must be connected as nearly at a right angle as possible with the humerus, in the shoulder joint, in order to give a long stride. Faults: Steep or loose shoulders. The former occur if the shoulder blade is not sufficiently sloping; the latter if the elbow is turned toward the outside.

9. *Chest.*—Quite broad; the thorax deep in front, extending down to the elbow joint. Faults: Narrow and flat breast; shallow thorax and a strongly protruding sternum (pigeon breast).

10. *Trunk.*—The withers form the highest part of the strong back. The back drops slightly toward the rear, in an approximately straight line; it is short and tensely set. In the ratio between length and height it should appear as square as possible; in case of bitches a somewhat longer back is permitted. The loins must be slightly arched and strong. The croup must be full, slightly drooping and must continue imperceptibly to the tail root. The rear part of the belly should be well shaped and together with the lower part of the thorax should be swung in a pleasing curve.

Faults: Receding back (sway back), camel back; the height of the hindleg must not exceed the height of the fore quarters. Also an excessively long back is a fault, for this will detrimentally affect the stride (pitching walk), croup which hangs down slantingly.

11. *Tail.*—Of medium length, reaching only to the hock joint; starting high and broad but terminating slender and thin. At rest position it should fall straight. When excited or when running it should be slightly curved (saber-like); it should not be carried too high above the back. Faults: Tails which are too long or too short, or set too low; bent too far over the back and in particular, tails which are curled, twisted sidewise, turned too far up or cropped (the cropping of the tail in order to obtain the length prescribed is forbidden); brush tail (if the hair on the lower side is too long) is not desirable. The shaving of the tail is forbidden.

12. *Forelegs.*—The upper arms should be strong and muscular. The elbow joint should not be turned toward the inside or the outside but must lie along the same plane as the shoulder joint. The strong lower arms run from the elbow joint—seen from the front and also from the side absolutely straight down to the pasterns. The pastern root runs, viewed from the front, in the same straight line, to the paws, and, seen from the side, only slightly forward. Faults: Elbows turned toward the inside or toward the outside. The former position caused mostly by too narrow or too shallow a chest, brings the frontlegs too closely together and at the same time turns the entire lower part of the legs outward. The outward turned elbows turn contrary to this, the pastern and the toes inward. A considerable bend in the pastern indicates weakness and is in most cases connected with stretched and spread toes (splay foot). Just as undesirable is any deflection from the straight line of the frontlegs from the pastern joint towards the inside or towards the outside. The bending of the pastern toward the front is, of course, also a fault. Swelling above the joint of the pastern root is mostly due to diseases of the bone (rickets).

13. *Hindlegs.*—The thighs are broad and muscular. The second thighs are strong and long. The desired angular position of the hindlegs results if the thigh forms in the hip joint with the pelvis and in the knee joint with the second thigh and the latter in the hock joint with the pastern root, angles which are not too blunt. Seen from the rear the hock joints appear to be perfectly

[379]

straight, turned neither towards the inside nor towards the outside. Faults: In case of knee joints turned decidedly toward the outside, the second thighs bring the hock joints toward the inside and the result is the so-called "cow position" of the dog. The legs then turn outward again. The opposite position is that of the hock joints being too far apart (barrel legged). The faulty steep hind thighs are the result of the above-mentioned joint angles becoming too blunt or forming almost a straight line. Also exaggerated angles are ugly, if the hindlegs are too long as compared with the forelegs.

14. *Paws.*—Round and turned neither towards the inside nor towards the outside. Toes short, highly arched and well closed. Nails short, strong and as dark as possible. Faults: Spreading toes (splay foot), bent, long toes, (rabbit paws); toes turned toward the outside or toward the inside. Furthermore, the fifth toe on the hindlegs appearing at a higher position and called wolf's claw or spur. Excessively long nails.

15. *Stride.*—Long, easy, springy stride. Faults: Short steps, forced or pitching stride. Pacing not desirable.

16. *Coat (Hair).*—Very short and thick, smooth and glossy. Faults: Excessively long hair (stand-off coat), dull hair (indicating malnutrition, worms and negligent care).

17. *Color.*—(a) Brindled Danes. Base color ranging from light golden yellow to deep golden yellow, always brindled with black, strong cross stripes. The more intensive the base color and the more intensive the brindling, the more attractive will be the color. Small white marks at the chest and toes and also light colored eyes and nails are not desirable. Faults: Silver blue or greyish blue base color; dull (faded) brindling; white forehead line; white collar; white stockings and white tail tip. Danes with such white marks should be excluded from showing.

(b) Fawn Danes. Golden yellow up to deep golden yellow color; black mask is desirable and also black nails. The deep golden yellow color must always be given the preference. Faults: Yellowish grey, bluish yellow, greyish blue and dirty yellow color (drab color) must be given lower rating. With regard to white markings, what has been stated above under (a) also applies here.

(c) Blue Danes. The color must be a pure steel blue as far as possible without any tinge of yellow or black. In connection with blue Danes, lighter colored eyes are permissible. Faults: Yellow or deep blue color, very light, piercing or glassy eyes. What has been stated under (a) above applies here also with regard to white markings.

(d) Black Danes. Color black, glossy, black nose, dark eyes. Faults: Yellow black, brown black or blue black; light colored eyes. Danes with striking white markings must be given a lower rating in shows. White markings, such as stripes on the chest, speckled chest and markings on the paw are permitted here, but Danes with deep white collar and high stockings and white belly should be excluded from shows.

(e) Harlequins. Base color: pure white, if possible, without any pointings, with black spots irregularly and well distributed over the entire body, pure white neck preferred. (Eligible but less desirable are a few small grey spots.) The eyes should be dark but light colored eyes or two eyes of different color are permitted but not desirable. Black nose; black spotted or pink colored noses are permitted. Faults: White base color with a few large spots, bluish grey pointed background and water colored, red or bleary eyes.

18. Males should not be less than 30 inches at the shoulders nor females less than 28 inches.

19. Ideal conformation of an ideal Great Dane is seen in the Porcelain Statue by Rosenthal "Deutsche Dogge" No. 960-1, 2046-1.

SCALE OF POINTS

General appearance	10
Head	12
Eyes	4
Teeth	4
Neck	6
Color and markings	8
Chest and ribs	8
Trunk (croup and back)	8
Legs and feet	10
Tail	4
Size	5
Condition of coat	4
Bone and muscle	7
Movement	10
Total	100

GREAT PYRENEES
(Illustration facing page 398)

(By Courtesy of The Great Pyrenees Club of America)

Perhaps no other breed can boast such a glowing and colorful history of intimate association with and service to mankind through as many centuries as can the Great Pyrenees, Le Grand Chien des Montagnes, Le Chien des Pyrenees, or, as he is known in England and on the Continent, the Pyrenean Mountain Dog, the dog of French royalty and nobility and the working associate of the peasant shepherds high on the slopes of the Pyrenees Mountains. His remains are found in the fossil deposits of the Age of Bronze, which roughly dates his appearance in Europe between 1800 and 1000 B.C. although it is believed that he came originally from Central Asia or Siberia and followed the Aryan migration into Europe. It is also now generally accepted that they are descendants of the Mastiff type, whose remains are found in the kitchen-middens of the Baltic and North Sea coasts in the oldest strata containing evidence of the domestic dog and who appear in Babylonian art at about the close of the third millennium B.C. to be of a size and general appearance strongly resembling the Great Pyrenees. "The Pyrenean breed in itself is very ancient and is depicted in Roman works of art, being especially frequent in the Alpine districts."

Once in Europe, the Great Dog of the Mountains developed under climatic conditions similar to those of his native habitat and there remained pretty well isolated in the high mountainous areas until medieval times, when

GERMAN SHEPHERD DOG

GREAT DANE

we find him gracing bas-reliefs at Carcassone bearing the royal arms of France approximately some five hundred years before his adoption as the Court Dog in the seventeenth century in the days of Louis XIV. As early as 1407 the historian, Mons. Bourdet, describes the regular guard of Pyrenees dogs owned by the Chateau of Lourdes. These dogs were given a special place in the sentry boxes along with the armed guards and also accompanied the gaolers on their daily rounds. Their use for these purposes became very general and each large Chateau boasted its band of Great Pyrenees. It was not until the young Dauphin, accompanied by Mme. de Maintenon in 1675 on a visit to Barreges, fell in love with a Beautiful "Patou" (a generic name for the breed meaning Shepherd) and insisted on taking it back to the Louvre with him; and not until the Marquis de Louvois also succumbed, some two years later, to their charm, that the Dog of the Shepherd of the Pyrenees became King and the companion and pet of nobility. Once accepted at Court, however, and his favor was assured—every noble immediately wanted one and the breed gained great prominence.

It was, however, in the isolation of the lonely mountain pastures that the Pyrenean Mountain Dog developed his now inherent traits of devotion, fidelity, a high sense of guardianship, and intelligent understanding of mankind; for here he lived through the centuries in close proximity with his shepherd master utilizing such opportunities as few other breeds have enjoyed. Here, in the days when packs of wild animals roamed the mountain slopes freely, he was the official guardian of the flocks. Having a precocious sense of smell and an exceptionally keen sense of sight, he was an invaluable companion of every shepherd, his worth being counted equal to that of two men. Armed by nature with a long heavy coat which rendered him invulnerable against attack except for the point of the chin and the base of the brain, and armed by mankind with a broad iron collar from which protruded spikes an inch and a half long, the Pyrenees Dog was an almost unbeatable foe who won such glory and fame as a vanquisher of wolves and bears that he became known quite generally as The Pyrenean Wolf Dog or Hound and The Pyrenean Bearhound. Thus, for generations, he has been bred for guard work and today the result is a dog whose prowess in this field is unexcelled, who takes his responsibilities very seriously, and is eager and anxious to give even his life for his master or his flocks. The Great Pyrenees is a family dog, gentle and devoted to those he loves, and ever craving their affection and encouragement in return; the ideal companion for children or for man.

By disposition and profession, no more perfect dog could have been chosen to assume the role of protector and friend of the early settlements of the Biscay fisherfolk on Newfoundland Island. Hence, we are not surprized to learn that by 1662, when their first permanent colony at Rougnoust was made, that it was the Great Pyrenees dog who became the companion of the people. Here it was that he was crossed with the black English Retriever, brought over by the English settlers, and from which cross resulted the Newfoundland dog. The old Landseer type, with its black and white coat, showed the cross far more markedly because of his coloring than the black Newfoundland, although the resemblance in general type is quite noticeable in both.

With the diminution of the wild beasts in the Pyrenees, the breed for awhile seemed destined for extinction, aided by the fact that it was eagerly sought after by breeders in Continental Europe and great numbers were exported from France. However, thanks to the efforts of some gentlemen sportsmen, and the fact that the dogs were of great use about the peasants' farms in winter, when their services were not required on the mountain slopes, they were bred in increasing numbers until today the breed is very numerous and well established once again in its native habitat. They are not infrequently referred to as "Mat-Dogs," because of their habit of lying outside the cottage doors when not busying themselves with some of the menial chores, such as pulling carts—a task they are admirably suited to and fond of.

The Great Pyrenees has been so generally looked upon as a new breed in America within the last few years, and has only come into general prominence since its recognition by the American Kennel Club in February 1933, that it seems hard to realize that the first pair were brought over by General Lafayette for his friend, Mr. J. S. Skinner, in 1824, being "recommended by him from personal experience as of inestimable value to wool-growers in all regions exposed to the depredations of wolves and sheepkilling dogs." Thus writes Mr. Skinner in his book, *The Dog and the Sportsman*. Since that date a few scattered specimens have been imported, but not until 1933 was the actual breeding of the dogs launched in America. The dogs have gained immediate favor and popularity and seem destined to become one of the most sought after of the large working breeds. (It might be of interest in this connection to note that in French classifications they are still grouped as Chiens de Garde or Guard Dogs.) In the few years that have elapsed since their recognition in America, several champions have been crowned, litters raised and distributed throughout the country, and new dogs imported, until today the breed is well established. Owing to the fact that its perpetuation has been due to natural selection, the Great Pyrenees is a very hardy and strong dog and one readily adaptable to American climatic conditions.

Preeminently a watch-dog and companion, the Great Pyrenees holds promise also as a dog suited for the sportsman. His love of pulling carts makes him very amenable to sled work in winter, and his natural instincts for feeling out soft places in the snow, make him ideal for pack and guide work on ski trips. He was used during the World War for pack service; and for many years for running contraband goods over the Franco-Spanish border by similar methods. Taking dangerous by-ways impossible for man to travel, they ran the circuit regularly, very successfully avoiding the customs officials. Their beauty and regal majesty also recommend them for use in the Moving Picture Industry, especially as they have already been used with success for this purpose in France. Certainly no more picturesque animal could be found, and he has indeed been aptly called, "An animated snowdrift of the Pyrenees Mountains." The nearer his appearance approaches that of the brown bear, except for the color and the ears drooping, the closer he is to the perfect type.

To summarize, let it be said, that he possesses to an uncanny degree the understanding of man's every whim and action, that he is devoted to the point of giving his all in service and love for his master, that he is faithful to the last degree, that he is one of the most intelligent dogs in the world, and that, combined with it all, he is one of the most picturesque and beautiful of animals. Lithe and quick of action, he can keep up with a horse with ease; and of unlimited stamina and strength, he can withstand any amount of hardship, exercise, and exposure. To those who really know and love the Great Pyrenees it seems that he leaves nothing to be desired and that he combines within himself to a degree attainable in perhaps no other breed, the every attribute man looks for and admires.

DESCRIPTION AND STANDARD OF POINTS

(Adopted by The Great Pyrenees Club of America, January 1935 and Approved by The American Kennel Club, February 13, 1935)

1. *General Appearance.*—A dog of immense size, great majesty, keen intelligence, and kindly expression; of unsurpassed beauty and a certain elegance, all white or principally white with markings of badger, grey, or varying shades of tan. In the rolling, ambling gait it shows unmistakably the purpose for which it has been bred, the strenuous work of guarding the flocks in all kinds of weather on the steep mountain slopes of the Pyrenees. Hence soundness is of the greatest importance and absolutely necessary for the proper fulfilment of his centuries' old task.

2. *Size.*—The average height at the shoulder is 27 inches to 32 inches for dogs and 25 inches to 29 inches for bitches.

The average length from shoulder blades to root of tail should be the same as the height in any given specimen.

The average girth is 36 inches to 42 inches for dogs and 32 inches to 36 inches for bitches.

The weight for dogs runs 100 to 125 pounds and 90 to 115 pounds for bitches.

A dog heavily boned; with close cupped feet; double dewclaws behind and single dewclaws in front.

3. *Head.*—Large and wedge shaped, measuring 10 inches to 11 inches from dome to point of nose, with rounding crown, furrow only slightly developed and with no apparent stop.

Cheeks.—Flat.

Ears.—V shaped, but rounded at the tips, of medium size, set parallel with the eyes, carried low and close to the head except when raised at attention.

[387]

Eyes.—Of medium size set slightly obliquely, dark rich brown in color with close eyelids, well pigmented.

Lips.—Close fitting, edged with black.

Dewlaps.—Developed but little.

The head is in brief that of a brown bear, but with the ears falling down.

4. *Neck.*—Short, stout and strongly muscular.

5. *Body.*—Well placed shoulders set obliquely, close to the body.

Back and Loin.—Well coupled, straight and broad.

Haunches.—Fairly prominent.

Rump.—Sloping slightly.

Ribs.—Flat-sided.

Chest.—Deep.

Tail.—Of sufficient length to hang below the hocks, well plumed, carried low in repose, and curled high over the back "making the wheel" when alert.

6. *Coat.*—Created to withstand severe weather, with heavy fine white undercoat and long flat thick outercoat of coarser hair, straight or slightly undulating.

7. *Qualities.*—In addition to his original age old position in the scheme of pastoral life as protector of the shepherd and his flock the Great Pyrenees has been used for centuries as a guard and watch dog on the large estates of his native France, and for this he has proven ideal. He is as serious in play as he is in work, adapting and moulding himself to the moods, desires and even the very life of his human companions, through fair weather and foul, through leisure hours and hours fraught with danger, responsibility, and extreme exertion; he is the exemplification of gentleness and docility with those he knows, of faithfulness and devotion for his master even to the point of self-sacrifice; and of courage in the protection of the flock placed in his care and of the ones he loves.

8. *Scale of Points.*—(a) Head: 25 points comprised as follows:

Shape of skull 5
Ears 5
Eyes 5
Muzzle 5
Teeth 5

GREAT PYRENEES

(b) General Conformation: 25 points comprised as follows:

Neck	5
Chest	5
Back	5
Loins	5
Feet	5

(c) Coat: 10 points. (d) Size and Soundness: 25 points. (e) Expression and General Appearance: 15 points. Total number of points 100.

Adopted and accepted as the Standard for The Great Pyrenees by The Great Pyrenees Club of America, January, 1935.

KOMONDOROCK

(Illustration on opposite page)

Of the three breeds of working dog native for ten centuries to the sheep and cattle countries of Hungary there seems little doubt that the king of them all is the Komondor. This heavily coated breed is an almost direct descendant of the Aftscharka, which the Huns found on the southern steppes when they passed through Russia. Many of today's Komondorock (plural) bear striking resemblance to the massive, long-legged Russian herdsman's dog, but the breed generally has become more compact.

The Komondor is a mighty fellow, with strong bones, and he stands at least 28 to 30 inches at the shoulder. His head is impressive in its generous formation, and his general appearance is commanding. At first sight this breed is likely to create fear. As a guard of herds or as a house guard he is unexcelled. Strangers of evil intent have reason to be fearful, but he is a devoted companion to his master and readily mingles with friends of the master.

One often sees pictures of the Komondor that show him with a heavily matted coat and with his head covered all over with long hair. The dog thus seems unkempt, and this is the way he is found in his natural habitat where he lives in the open practically all the time. Under such circumstances it would be impossible for the Komondor to give a well-groomed appearance, but the breed responds very well to care. When reared in kennels and prepared for shows it is one of the handsomest dogs.

KOMONDOROCK

KOMONDOROCK

The Komondor is the chief of the herdsman's dogs, but he is not often utilized for rounding up the herds. He only accompanies the flocks and herds in exceptional cases, and then more in the capacity of a protector than as a herder. His vigilance and his courage have earned him a rather enviable position of trust, and much of the routine work is left to the smaller dogs.

The Magyars who have bred the Komondor for more than a thousand years attend principally to their herds and flocks, and do not concern themselves very greatly with keeping the pedigrees of their dogs. But there is, to them, no need of pedigrees, as these dogs are not permitted to mate outside their own race.

It is doubtful if any dogs with pedigrees could be found in the so-called "Puszta," for the shepherds and herdsmen do not look upon dog-breeding as a commercial venture, or as a hobby. Still, the crossing of a Komondor and a Kuvasz would be unimaginable, and also nearly impossible. The Komondor still resides in the Puszta, while the Kuvasz has become, in recent times, more and more the watch dog of the village.

The history of pure-bred dog breeding in Hungary is not unlike that of any other country in the world. Definite records go back hardly a century, but those in existence are soundly attested by reliable parties. The Hungarian Kennel Club, and the Hungarian Komondor Club maintain a strong control over the interests of the Komondor. These organizations have accepted the standard of the breed as drawn up by a committee made up of members of the two clubs. The American Kennel Club's standard of the breed is a translation of the Hungarian.

In reading the standard, it should be noted that its salient points denote the strength and the protective points that have been bred into the Komondor for centuries and which should be maintained. There is perhaps, today, not as pressing a need for such a self-reliant dog, as there was in the past. In times of old he had to be ready at any moment to fight all manner of beasts of prey, many of which were his superior in size and weight. When the odds were against him, he could depend to some extent on that heavy coat to cover his most vulnerable points, and could call, too, upon an intelligence far superior to that of his wild adversaries.

DESCRIPTION AND STANDARD OF POINTS
(As adopted by the American Kennel Club, November 9, 1937)

General Appearance.—The Komondor is characterized by imposing strength, courageous demeanor and pleasing conformation. In general he is a big muscular dog with plenty of bone and substance.

Nature and Characteristics.—As a houseguard as well as a guardian of herds he is, when grown up, an earnest, courageous, and very faithful dog. The young dog, however, is just as playful as any other puppy. He is much devoted to his master and will defend him against attack by any stranger. On account of this trait he is not used for driving the herds, but only for guarding them. His special task is to protect the animals, and he lives during the greater part of the year in the open air without protection against strange dogs and all kinds of beasts of prey.

Head.—The head of the Komondor is covered all over with long hair, and thus the head looks somewhat short, in comparison to the seemingly wide forehead. If the hair is smoothed it will be seen that the skull is somewhat arched if viewed from the side; the forehead is not wide, but appears, however, wider through the rich growth of hair. The stop is moderate, it is the starting point of the muzzle which is somewhat shorter than the length of the skull. The top line of the muzzle is straight and about parallel with the line of the top of the skull. The muzzle should be fairly square.

[392]

KOMONDOROCK

The lips cover the teeth closely and are black. The muzzle is mostly covered by long hair. The edges of the muzzle are black or steel-bluegrey. The jaws are powerful, and the teeth are level and close together evenly.

Ears.—The ears are rather low set and hang along the side of the head. They are medium-sized, and their surface is covered with long hair.

Eyes.—The eyes express fidelity. They are medium-sized and almond shaped, not too deeply set and surrounded by rough, unkempt hair. The iris of the eyes is of coffee or darker brown color, light color is not desirable. Blue-white eyes are disqualifying. The edges of the eyelids are slate-grey.

Muzzle.—In comparison to the length given in the head description, the muzzle is wide, coarse and not pointed. The nostrils are wide. The color of the nose is black. Komondors with flesh-colored noses must absolutely be excluded from breeding. A slate-colored or dark brown nose is undesirable but may, however, be accepted for breeding purposes.

Neck.—The neck is covered with long hair, is muscular, of medium length, moderately arched. The head erect. No dewlap is allowed.

Body.—The body is characterized chiefly by the powerful, deep chest which is muscular and proportionately wide. The height at the top of shoulders is 23½ inches to 31½ inches, the higher, the better. The shoulders slope into the neck without apparent protrusion. The body is moderately long and level. Back and loins are wide. The rump is wide, muscular, moderately sloping towards the root of the tail. The body should be somewhat drawn up at the rear, but not greyhound-like.

Tail.—The tail is as a straight continuation of the rump-line, and reaches down to the hocks slightly curved upwards at its end. It is covered in its full length with long hair, which when the dog is at ease almost touches the ground. When the dog is excited the tail is raised up to the level of the back. The tail should not be docked. Komondors born with short tails must be excluded even for breeding purposes.

Forelegs.—The forelegs should be straight, well boned and muscular. Viewed from any side, the legs are like vertical columns. The upper arm joins the body closely, without loose elbows. The legs are covered all around by long, evenly hanging hair.

Hind Quarters and Legs.—The steely, strong bone-structure is covered with highly developed muscles, and the legs are evenly covered with long hair, hanging down in matted clods. The legs should be straight as viewed from the rear. Stifles well bent. Dewclaws must be removed. The body and the legs should about form a rectangle.

Feet.—The feet should be strong, rather large and with close, well arched toes. The hind feet are stronger, and all are covered with long hair. The nails are black or slate-grey. The pads are hard, elastic and black.

Coat.—The entire body of the Komondor is covered with a long, soft woolly, dense hair, of different length on the different parts of the body, with inclination to entanglement and shagginess. If the dog is not taken care of, the hair becomes shaggy on the forelegs, chest, belly, rump and on the sides of the thigh and the tail. The longer and the more ragged, the better, though, as above stated, the length of the hair varies on the different parts of the body. The longer hair begins on the head and ears and lengthens gradually on the body, being longest on the thighs and the tail. A somewhat shorter, but still long hair is found on the legs, the muzzle and the cheeks. Too curly hair is undesirable.

Color.—The color of the hair is white. Any other color is disqualifying.

Size.—The bigger the Komondor, the better, a minimum height of 25½ inches at top of shoulders for males and 23½ inches for females is required.

Faults.—Light or flesh-colored nose, albino or blue eyes, highly set and small ears. Short, smooth hair, on the head and legs, strongly curled tail, color:—other than white.

KUVASZ

(Illustration facing page 399)

From Tibet, that strange, high-flung domain of the lamas, came the ancestors of the breed that today is known as the Kuvasz. Yet this is not a new name for the breed. It merely is a corrupted spelling of Turkish and Arabian words that signified the unexcelled guarding instincts of this big dog.

The Turkish word is kawasz, which means "armed guard of the nobility." In the Arabian this appears as kawwasz, which signifies "archer," an expression that probably was merely a figure of speech to denote the high esteem in which the dog was held, for many centuries ago an archer was regarded with great respect. Words with nearly the same spelling and meaning are found throughout all the countries whose languages originate in Tibet.

There is little doubt of the part that the Kuvasz played in the history of the kingdoms and empires that flourished throughout Europe five to eight centuries ago. This breed was the constant companion of many a ruler of a turbulent country. Indeed, none but those within the favor of the royal circles were permitted to own specimens of the Kuvasz.

Known in many countries, it was in Hungary that the Kuvasz developed into the form in which he is seen today. He still is a big dog, but he is not the giant of ancient times. At the present, he measures approximately 26 inches at the shoulder, but there is every reason to believe that the dog which issued from Tibet stood considerably higher than that. He was a dog of which the common people stood in awe; indeed, his appearance alone was enough to discourage attacks on noblemen by the populace.

The first great period in the Hungarian history of the Kuvasz seemed to reach a climax during the second half of the fifteenth century. His renown became known far and wide. There were numerous big estates that bred the dog and kept their own stud books. Many were trained for hunting, and they proved very successful on the big game of those times.

King Matthias I, who reigned from 1458 to 1490, had at least one of these dogs with him whenever he travelled and there were numerous specimens about his palace and the surrounding grounds. Few other rulers have had to strive so hard to hold their domains together. Plots and political intrigue were the rule rather than the exception. Assassinations were a not uncommon thing. It is said that King Matthias was reluctant to place any great trust in even the members of his own household, and his court was filled with ambitious noblemen.

It is no wonder that King Matthias relied more upon his dogs than upon his human guards. He knew that in this big, sturdy breed he had, perhaps, the only true security that was possible. Often, when the tumultuous day was over—and he waged wars almost continually—the king would retire to his study and spend half the night poring over his books and his maps and preparing his orders for the following day. And, while the king worked, a big, white Kuvasz sprawled just inside the door.

King Matthias became so impressed with the Kuvasz that he developed a large pack to be used for hunting purposes. His kennels on his large estates in Siebenbuer-

KUVASZ

gen were among the most impressive in Europe, and the scope of the king's breeding did a great deal toward perpetuating a splendid strain of the breed. Surplus puppies were presented only to the noblemen and to visiting dignitaries.

Eventually, many specimens of the breed got into the hands of the commoners, but this was long after the time of King Matthias I. The herders found them suitable for work with sheep and cattle. It was in this later period that the name of the breed was corrupted to its present spelling. Incidentally, this spelling is rather unfortunate, because it changes the meaning rather ridiculously to that of "mongrel."

According to von Stephanitz, the great German authority on all Central European breeds, the Kuvasz is related to the Kommondor, which had been brought from the Russian steppes by the Huns. He ventures the opinion that the kawasz or kawwasz was crossed with the indigenous country dog of Hungary. While this is something of a conjecture, there is strong evidence that points to it being true. At any rate, the original type has proved dominant, and the Kuvasz of today—perhaps a little smaller—is very similar to his earliest progenitors.

DESCRIPTION AND STANDARD OF POINTS
(As Adopted by The American Kennel Club, August 13, 1935)

General Appearance.—Being a working dog of the larger size, the Kuvasz should be sturdily built and impress the eye with its strength and activity combined with light footedness. He should move freely on strong legs and any tendency to a weak or hollow back is a decided fault.

Head.—Should be in proportion to the body, skull broad and flat with not too decided a stop.

[397]

Muzzle.—Should be clean cut, rather square in shape and covered with short, fine hair.

Ears.—Rather small, set well back folded over level with the top of skull and lying close to the head. They should be covered with fine, short hair but no fringe.

Eyes.—Should be of medium size, set slightly obliquely and rather wide apart. They should be as dark as possible.

Nose.—Nostrils well developed. The nose together with the flews should be black.

Color.—Pure white. Occasionally specimens appear with a yellow saddle but this is a decided fault and such dogs are not to be recommended for breeding purposes.

Coat.—Rather long on neck and croup becoming a little shorter and slightly wavy on sides.

Body.—Should be well ribbed up with a fairly broad back, neck is fairly short, strong, well set on sloping shoulders with strong muscular loins.

Forelegs.—Should have strong bone, be perfectly straight and well muscled, elbows should be in but well let down. Hair short on front and sides of legs. Slightly feathered on back of legs.

Hind Quarters.—Should be strong, legs should have great freedom of action, lightness of loins and cowhocks are a great defect.

Chest.—Should be deep and fairly broad.

Feet.—Should be strong and well shaped; splay or turned out feet are objectionable.

Tail.—Should be of moderate length reaching a little below the hocks and covered with thick, fairly long hair.

Height.—Dogs about 26 inches at shoulder, bitches somewhat less.

GREAT PYRENEES

KUVASZ

MASTIFFS

(Illustration facing page 402)

(By Courtesy of The Mastiff Club of America, Inc.)

The breed which is commonly called "Mastiff" in English speaking countries is more properly described as the *Old English* Mastiff. It is a giant, short-haired dog, with heavy head and short muzzle, which has been bred in England for over 2,000 years as a watch dog.

The term "Mastiff" describes a group of giant varieties of dog rather than a single breed. It is supposed to have originated in Asia; and the modern Tibetan Mastiff, seen today at dog shows in England, is thought to be the most direct descendant of the prototype. Next in purity is said to be the Old English Mastiff, which is regarded by some students as the main root from whence came many of the others of the Mastiff group.

So little is known about dogs of any sort prior to 60 years ago that almost all theories of ancestry are of small importance. Every partisan would like to claim the greatest antiquity for his particular sort of Mastiff as well as to say that the other sorts sprang from it. There is very little proof one way or the other.

Cassel finds drawings on Egyptian Monuments of typical Mastiffs dating about 3000 B.C. In literature, the earliest reference is in Chinese about 1121 B.C. So much for the undoubted antiquity of the Mastiff Group's ancestry.

So far as our breed, the Old English Mastiff, is concerned, it has a longer history than most. Caeser decribes them in his account of invading Britain in 55 B.C.

They fought beside their masters against the Roman legions with such courage and power as to make a great impression. Soon after we find several different accounts of the huge British fighting dogs brought back to Rome where they defeated all other varieties in combats at the Circus. They were also matched against human gladiators as well as against bulls, bears, lions and tigers.

Today we are likely to think of such cruel spectacles as belonging to only the dim ages of the past. But this is not true. Dog fights and bull-baiting and bear-baiting were respectable and popular forms of amusement in England and America little more than a century ago. Such brutalizing events were patronized by nobility and clergy in England and public-spirited citizens left legacies so that the common folk might be entertained in this way on holidays.

Dog fighting and animal-baiting were made illegal in England in 1835, due to Queen Victoria's insistence, but for 20 years longer the law was little obeyed. American dog fanciers are interested in the word "fancier" which was synonymous with "bettor"—meaning especially a bettor on a dog—or prize-fight, and are interested also in the name of one of the most fashionable sporting establishments in London, over 100 years ago, called the "Westminster Pit" with 300 seats. "Westminster" meant *dogs* even then—but fighting dogs!

While the Mastiff was always in front rank as a fighting dog this does not account for his great popularity in England for 2,000 years. It was as "ban-dogs" or "tie-dogs" (tied by day but loose at night) that they were found everywhere. In fact, long ago, keeping of these Mastiffs was compulsory for the peasants. During Anglo-Saxon times there must be kept at least one Mastiff for each two villains.

By this means wolves and other savage game were kept under control. They were also used in hunting packs by the nobility. But it was as protectors of the home they were most used and probably as a result of centuries of such service the Mastiff has acquired the unique traits as a family dog.

That the Mastiff has long been most numerous is indicated by the development of the English language itself.

The ancient word in Anglo-Saxon and in over a score of kindred languages for a member of the canine race is "hound" or something very similar.

A rather modern word coming from the Latin languages is like "dog" but it means one certain *type* of dog in all languages but English. In all but English it means a *Mastiff* sort.

So we can believe that when the Normans conquered the Anglo-Saxons in 1066 and made Norman-French the official language of England, "dogues" (or Mastiffs) were so plentiful that people forgot eventually there was any other name for a canine creature. This is the only explanation a dog-man can offer for such a peculiar change in a language.

Anecdotes which extol the power and agility of Mastiffs as well as their devotion to their masters would fill a large volume of marvels.

Herodotus tells of Cyrus the Great, founder of the Persian Empire about 550 B.C. who received, as a most rare and precious gift, a Mastiff, from the King of Albania. Cyrus matched the dog against another and also sent it against a bull. But the Mastiff acted like a pacifist. So Cyrus in disgust had it killed. News of this reception of his gift came back to the King of Albania. He sent messengers with another Mastiff—a bitch—to Cyrus, telling him that a Mastiff was no ordinary cur and that it scorned to notice such common creatures as a Persian dog or a bull. He urged him to select a worthy opponent such as a lion or even an elephant. The King of Albania concluded by saying Mastiffs were rare and royal gifts and that he would not send Cyrus another. Whereupon, says Herodotus, the Mastiff bitch was set to attack an elephant and did so with such fury and efficiency that she worried the elephant down to the ground and would have killed it.

That is one of the oldest and probably the tallest Mastiff tale on record!

However, it gives proof of the reputation of Mastiffs as powerful, agile and courageous dogs. It is even more interesting to know that Albania was the land of the people known as Alani, an Asiatic race. Also that similar names stand for "Mastiffs," e.g., *Alano, Alan* and *Alaunt.*

The story of Sir Peers Legh, Knight of Lyme Hall, (near Stockport, Cheshire) at the Battle of Agincourt, October 25, 1415 is well-known. He had brought his favorite Mastiff—also a bitch—to France and when he fell she stood over and defended him many hours until he was picked up by English soldiers and carried to Paris, where he died of his wounds. The faithful Mastiff was returned to England and from her is descended the famous Lyme Hall strain which the family has bred to this day—a period of over five centuries. In the drawing room of the Castle is still to be seen an old stained glass window portraying the gallant Sir Peers and his devoted Mastiff.

The present day English Mastiff is based upon the

MASTIFF

NEWFOUNDLAND

strains of Lyme Hall and that of the Duke of Devonshire's Kennels at Chatsworth. Chaucer wrote in Middle English (a mongrel language resulting from a cross between old Anglo-Saxon and Norman-French) 300 years after the Norman Conquest, describing the Old English Mastiff in his "Knight's Tale." He tried to use the Italian-French word for Mastiff: *Alan* which is still used in English heraldry to describe the figure of "a Mastiff with cropped ears" on a coat of arms.

Chaucer wrote sometime before his death in 1400:

> "Aboute his char ther wenten white *Alaunts*
> Twenty and mo, as gret as any stere
> To hunten at the leon or the dere."

So here is proof that 600 years ago Mastiffs were hunted in packs in England on such different game as lion or deer. Chaucer says they were as large as a steer! Even though cattle were much smaller in those days this is hard to credit. The white color is authentic. We have plenty of pictures and descriptions of white and piebald Mastiffs—often with long coats—of about a century ago.

The illustration shows a typical modern specimen and we hope the Official Standard completes your conception of an ideal Old English Mastiff.

DESCRIPTION AND STANDARD OF POINTS

(As Adopted September 7, 1929, by The Mastiff Club of America, Inc. and Approved by The American Kennel Club)

General Character and Symmetry.—Large, massive, powerful, symmetrical and well-knit frame. A combination of grandeur and good nature, courage and docility.

General Description of Head.—In general outline, giving a square appearance when viewed from any point. Breadth greatly to be desired, and should be in ratio to length of the whole head and face as 2 to 3.

General Description of Body (Height and Substance).—Massive, broad, deep, long, powerfully built, on legs wide apart and squarely set. Muscles sharply defined. Size a great desideratum, if combined with quality. Height and substance important if both points are proportionately combined.

Skull.—Broad between the ears, forehead flat, but wrinkled when attention is excited. Brows (superciliary ridges) slightly raised. Muscles of the temples and cheeks (temporal and masseter) well developed. Arch across the skull of a rounded, flattened curve, with a depression up the center of the forehead from the medium line between the eyes, to halfway up the sagittal suture.

Face or Muzzle.—Short, broad under the eyes, and keeping nearly parallel in width to the end of the nose; truncated, i.e., blunt and cut off square, thus forming a right angle with the upper line of the face, of great depth from the point of the nose to under jaw. Under jaw broad to the end; canine teeth healthy, powerful and wide apart; incisors level, or the lower projecting beyond the upper, but never sufficiently so as to become visible when the mouth is closed. Nose broad, with widely spreading nostrils when viewed from the front, flat (not pointed or turned up) in profile. Lips diverging at obtuse angles with the septum, and slightly pendulous so as to show a square profile. Length of muzzle to whole head and face as 1 to 3. Circumference of muzzle (measured midway between the eyes and nose) to that of the head (measured before the ears) as 3 to 5.

Ears.—Small, thin to the touch, wide apart, set on at the highest points of the sides of the skull, so as to continue the outline across the summit, and lying flat and close to the cheeks when in repose.

Eyes.—Small, wide apart, divided by at least the space of two eyes. The stop between the eyes well marked, but not too abrupt. Color hazel-brown, the darker the better, showing no haw.

Chest and Ribs—(Neck).—Slightly arched, moderately long, very muscular, and measuring in circumference about 1 or 2 inches less than the skull before the ears.

(Chest).—Wide, deep, and well let down between the forelegs.

MASTIFFS

Ribs arched and well rounded. False ribs deep and well set back to the hips. Girth should be one-third more than the height at the shoulder.

(Shoulder and Arm).—Slightly sloping, heavy and muscular.

Forelegs and Feet.—Legs straight, strong, and set wide apart; bones very large. Elbows square. Pasterns upright. Feet large and round. Toes well arched up. Nails black.

Back, Loins and Flanks.—Back and loins wide and muscular; flat and very wide in a bitch, slightly arched in a dog. Great depth of flanks.

Hindlegs and Feet.—Hind quarters broad, wide and muscular, with well developed second thighs, hocks bent, wide apart, and quite squarely set when standing or walking. Feet round.

Tail.—Put on high up, and reaching to the hocks, or a little below them, wide at its root and tapering to the end, hanging straight in repose, but forming a curve, but with the end pointing upwards, but not over the back, when the dog is excited.

Coat.—Coat short and close lying, but not too fine over the shoulders, neck and back.

Color.—Apricot or silver-fawn, or dark fawn-brindle. In any case, muzzle, ears, and nose should be black, with black round the orbits, and extending upwards between them.

	Points
General character and symmetry	10
Height and substance	10
Skull	12
Face or muzzle	18
Ears	4
Eyes	6
Chest and ribs	8
Forelegs and feet	6
Back, loins and flanks	8
Hindlegs and feet	10
Tail	3
Coat and color	5
Total	100

NEWFOUNDLAND DOGS

(Illustration facing page 403)

(By Courtesy of The Newfoundland Club of America)

There is so much uncertainty about the origin of the Newfoundland dog that I will speak of it most briefly. Some say that his ancestors are the white Great Pyrenees, dogs brought to the coast of Newfoundland by the Basque fishermen; others that he is descended from a "French hound" (probably the Boarhound); but all agree that he originated in Newfoundland and that his ancestors were undoubtedly brought there by fishermen from the European Continent. Many of the old prints of Newfoundlands show unmistakable evidence of a Husky ancestor and other traits can be traced to other breeds. At any rate a dog evolved which was particularly suited to the island of its origin. He was a large dog with size and strength to perform the tasks required of him; he had a heavy coat to protect him from the long winters and the icy waters surrounding his native island. His feet were large, strong and webbed so that he might easily travel over the wet marshes and shores. This dog was admired for his physical powers and attractive disposition and was taken to England where he was extensively bred until most of the Newfoundlands of pedigree, even in Newfoundland, today are descended from forebears born in England.

At the present time, while not numerous anywhere, the Newfoundland is admired and bred in many different countries including besides their native land, England,

France, Holland, Germany, Switzerland, Italy, Canada and the United States.

The standard of the breed was written from the point of view that the dog is a working dog and essentially a dog that is as much at home in the water as on dry land. Canine literature tells many stories of brave Newfoundland dogs who have rescued men and women from watery graves; stories of shipwrecks made less terrible by dogs who carried life-lines to the stricken vessels; of children who have fallen into deep water and have been brought safely ashore by their protector, the Newfoundland dog; and of dogs whose work was less spectacular but equally valuable as they helped their fishermen owners with their heavy nets and other tasks necessary to their occupations. Although he is a superior water dog the Newfoundland has been used and still is used in Newfoundland and Labrador as a true working dog, dragging carts or more often carrying burdens as a pack horse. In order to perform these duties to mankind the Newfoundland must be a large dog—large enough to bring ashore a drowning man—; he must have the powerful hind quarters and lung capacity which enable him to swim tirelessly for great distances; he must have the heavy coat which protects him from the icy waters; he must be strong, muscular, and absolutely sound so that he may do the work for which he has become justly famous.

Above all things the Newfoundland must have the intelligence, the loyalty and the sweetness of disposition which are his best known traits. He must be able and willing to learn to help his master perform his necessary tasks at command and also have the intelligence to act on his own responsibility when his rescue work demands it.

In this country where the Newfoundland is kept, not

as an active worker but as a companion, guard and friend, we appreciate particularly the sterling traits of the true Newfoundland disposition. In this dog we have the great size and strength which makes him an effective guard and watch dog combined with the gentleness which makes him a safe companion for the smallest child. For generations he has been the traditional children's protector and playmate. He is not easily hurt by small tugging fingers (as is a smaller dog) and he seems to undertake the duties of nursemaid of his own accord without training. We know of no better description of the character of the Newfoundland dog than the famous epitaph which reads:

Beneath this spot
Are deposited the remains of a being
Who was possessed of beauty without vanity,
Strength without insolence,
Courage without ferocity,
And all the virtues of man without his vices.

This praise would be but empty flattery
Were it inscribed upon the ashes of a human being,
And yet it is only what is due to the memory
Of the dog BOATSWAIN:
Born in Newfoundland, May, 1801
Died at Windsor, 18th November, 1815.

DESCRIPTION AND STANDARD OF POINTS
(By Courtesy of The Newfoundland Club of America)

Symmetry and General Appearance.—The dog should impress the eye with strength and great activity. He should move freely on his legs with the body swung loosely between them, so that a slight roll in gait should not be objectionable; but at the same time a weak or hollow back, slackness of the loins or cowhocks should be a decided fault.

Head.—Should be broad and massive, the occipital bone well developed, there should be no decided stop, and the muzzle should be short, clean cut, and rather square in shape, and covered with short fine hair.

Coat.—Should be flat and dense, of a coarsish texture and oily nature, and capable of resisting the water. If brushed the wrong way it should fall back into its place naturally.

Body.—Should be well ribbed up with a broad back. A neck, strong, well set on to the shoulders and back, with strong muscular loins.

Forelegs.—Should be perfectly straight, well covered with muscle, elbows in but well let down and feathered all down.

Hind Quarters and Legs.—Should be very strong; the legs should have great freedom of action, and a little feather. Slackness of loins and cowhock are a great defect; dewclaws are objectionable, and should be removed.

Chest.—Should be deep and fairly broad and well covered with hair, but not to such an extent as to form a frill.

Bone.—Massive throughout, but not to give a heavy inactive appearance.

Feet.—Should be large and well shaped. Splayed or turned out feet are objectionable.

Tail.—Should be of moderate length, reaching down a little below the hocks, it should be of fair thickness, and well covered with long hair, but not to form a flag. When the dog is standing still, and not excited, it should hang downwards with a slight curve at the end; but when the dog is in motion it should be carried a trifle up, and when he is excited straight out with a slight curve at the end Tails with a kink in them, or curled over the back, are very objectionable.

Ears.—Should be small, set well back, square with the skull, lie close to the head, and covered with short hair, and no fringe.

Eyes.—Should be small, of a dark brown color, rather deeply set but not showing any haw, and they should be rather widely apart.

Color.—Dull jet black. A slight tinge of bronze, or a splash of white on chest and toes is not objectionable.

OLD ENGLISH SHEEPDOG

PULI

NEWFOUNDLANDS

Height and Weight.—Size and weight are very desirable so long as symmetry is maintained. A fair average height at the shoulders is 28 inches for a dog, and 26 inches for a bitch, and a fair average weight is, respectively:

Dogs .... 140 to 150 pounds
Bitches .... 110 to 120 pounds

Other Than Black (Landseers).—Should in all respects follow the black except in color, which may be almost any, so long as it disqualifies for the black class, but the colors most to be encouraged are white and black or bronze. Beauty in markings to be taken greatly into consideration.

Black dogs that have only white toes and white breasts and white tip to tail, should be exhibited in the classes provided for "black."

SCALE OF POINTS

Head

Shape of skull	8	
Ears	10	
Eyes	8	
Muzzle	8	
Points for head	——	34

Body

Neck	4	
Chest	6	
Shoulders	4	
Loin and back	12	
Hind quarters and tail	10	
Legs and feet	10	
Coat	12	
Size, height and general appearance	8	
Body points	——	66
Total points		100

Markings of White and Black Dogs

	Points
Head	3
Saddle	5
Rump	2
Total	—— 10

"Definition for Preference"

Black head marked with narrow blaze.

Even marked saddle.

Black rump, extending on to tail.

The ten points above are to be considered in differentiating between "Landseers" not added to Standard.

OLD ENGLISH SHEEPDOGS

(Illustration facing page 410)

(By Courtesy of The Old English Sheepdog Club of America)

While this breed, as compared with some others, cannot boast of the same antiquity, there is nevertheless ample evidence to prove that it can trace its origin to the early nineteenth century, or at least one hundred and fifty years back, thus proving that among dogs of recognized breeds, it is no mere "upstart." As to its real origin, there exist conflicting ideas based upon premises obscured by the passage of years. A painting by Gainsborough of a Duke of Buccleugh, from which excellent engravings were struck off in 1771, shows the peer with his arms clasped about the neck of what appears to be a fairly good specimen of the breed, as known today. Incidentally this is the earliest picture known that in any way depicts the breed. What however, the dog in the picture was supposed to be at that time is not a matter of knowledge. From studies and researches made, there would seem to be little doubt that the breed as known today was first developed in the West of England, in the Counties of Devon and Somerset, and the Duchy of Cornwall. From what breeds it was produced is a matter of conjecture. Some hold that the Scotch bearded Collie had a large part in its manufacture; others have gone so far afield as to claim for one of its progenitors, the Russian Owtchah, which seems a trifle far-fetched. At all events, in the beginning of the eighteenth century, we begin to read of a "drover's dog," which was largely used for driving herds of cattle and sheep into the markets in the County towns and into the great markets of the Metropolis. We also learn that these "drover's dogs" were exempt from taxes, and to prove their occupation, the practice was adopted of docking or removing their tails. Some hold that the name, or appellation of "Bobtail" or "Bob" by which the breed is affectionately and intimately known today, is due to this custom on the part of those who used these dogs in their business or vocation. While it may be true that dogs used for such purposes were given the names of Bobtails or Bobs, it is not true that the practice of removing the tail has produced a breed of dogs that is naturally bobtailed or tailless. Very few of the breed are whelped without the caudal appendage, either long, or comparatively short. When a tail is present, according to the standard, it should always be removed at the first joint from the body, at about three to four days of age, and it should never be longer than one and a half to two inches in length, when the dog is grown. The practice of removing any existing tail as close to the body as possible, has resulted in the fact that seldom is an Old English Sheepdog seen in the show ring today, with anything more than a mere thickening of the skin where the tail has been removed, and which is not discernible except to the touch. For the reason that the breed seems to have been more frequently used for driving rather than herding, the lack of tail as a rudder, so to speak, has in no wise affected its ability for work with the heavier breeds of sheep and cattle. For a number of years after its introduction into this country breeders and exhibitors unconsciously did the breed considerable harm by misinterpreting "profuseness" of coat into "excessiveness." This had the effect of making the public believe that by reason of tremendous coat, dogs of this breed were very difficult to care for and keep in shape. As a matter of fact, an Old English Sheepdog with a typical coat of the right texture is no harder to keep in shape than is any other long haired dog. By reason of the fact that the breed for years has been used to the close companionship of man, it is home loving, not given to roaming or to fighting. Notwithstanding its appearance of size and weight, it is extremely agile, and because of its intelligence and affection and lack of boisterousness, makes an ideal house-dog, being an excellent watch dog, without ferociousness. Apart from the work the breed was originally intended for, it is most adaptable towards rendering service in other ways. It has a tender mouth and can be readily trained as a retriever, it makes a first class sledge dog, and is ideal as a companion for young children. It is even-tempered, possessed of a keen sense of humor and is equally at home in apartment, large house, in a drawing room, in the car or upon a train. In seeking a good representative of the breed the points to look for are a body practically square, good bone, a deep brisket, chest and spring of ribs sufficiently capacious to give plenty of room for heart and lungs, a strong foreface and jaw, with no snipyness (a weak underjaw is strongly to be avoided), dark or wall eyes, level teeth, dead straight forelegs, and well let down hocks. A coat of hard texture with a good underjacket. Markings are not important, except as being a matter of personal taste. These dogs are very easily trained, and do well under almost any climatic conditions; their heavy coats acting as insulation, keeping out both extreme heat and cold, as well as dampness. A marked characteristic of the breed is its gait; very much like the shuffle of a bear, moving the hindlegs from the stifle joint, thus producing a rolling movement, affecting the entire hind quarters of the dog.

DESCRIPTION AND STANDARD OF POINTS

(By Courtesy of The Old English Sheepdog Club of America)

Skull.—Capacious and rather squarely formed, giving plenty of room for brain power. The parts over the eyes should be well arched and the whole well covered with hair.

Jaw.—Fairly long, strong, square and truncated. The top should be well defined to avoid a deerhound face. *(The attention of judges is particularly called to the above properties, as a long, narrow head is a deformity.)*

Eyes.—Vary according to the color of the dog. Very dark preferred, but in the glaucous or blue dogs a pearl, wall or china eye is considered typical. *(A light eye is most objectionable.)*

Nose.—Always black, large and capacious.

Teeth.—Strong and large, evenly placed and level in opposition.

Ears.—Medium sized, and carried flat to side of head, coated moderately.

Legs.—The forelegs should be dead straight, with plenty of bone, removing the body a medium height from the ground, without approaching legginess, and well coated all around.

Feet.—Small, round; toes well arched, and pads thick and hard.

Tail.—It is preferable that there should be none. Should never, however, exceed one and a half or two inches in grown dogs. When not natural-born bobtails however, puppies should be docked at the first joint from the body and the operation performed when they are from three to four days old.

Neck and Shoulders.—The neck should be fairly long, arched gracefully and well coated with hair. The shoulders sloping and narrow at the points, the dog standing lower at the shoulder than at the loin.

Body.—Rather short and very compact, ribs well sprung and brisket deep and capacious. *Slabsidedness highly undesirable.* The loin should be very stout and gently arched, while the hind quarters should be round and muscular and with well-let-down hocks, and the hams densely coated with a thick, long jacket in excess of any other part.

Coat.—Profuse, but not so excessive as to give the impression of the dog being over-fat, and of a good hard texture; not straight, but shaggy and free from curl. *Quality and texture of coat to be considered above mere profuseness.* Softness or flatness of coat to be considered a fault. The undercoat should be a waterproof pile, when not removed by grooming or season.

Color.—Any shade of grey, grizzle, blue or blue-merled with or without white markings or in reverse. *Any shade of brown or fawn to be considered distinctly objectionable and not to be encouraged.*

Size.—Twenty-two inches and upwards for dogs and slightly less for bitches. *A height of twenty-six inches or over for dogs or bitches to be considered objectionable and not to be encouraged.* Type, character and symmetry are of the greatest importance and are on no account to be sacrificed to size alone.

General Appearance and Characteristics.—A strong, compact-looking dog of great symmetry, practically the same in measurement from shoulder to stern as in height, absolutely free from legginess or weaselness, very elastic in his gallop, but in walking or trotting he has a characteristic ambling or pacing movement, and his bark should be loud, with a peculiar "pot-casse" ring in it. Taking him all round, he is a profusely, but not *excessively* coated, thick-set, muscular, able-bodied dog with a most intelligent expression, free from all Poodle or Deerhound character. *Soundness should be considered of greatest importance.*

	Points
Skull	5
Eyes	5
Ears	5
Teeth	5
Nose	5
Jaw	5
Foreface	5
Neck and shoulders	5
Body and loins	10
Hind quarters	10
Legs	10
Coat (texture, quality and condition)	15
General appearance and movement	15
Total	100

[417]

PULIS

(Illustration facing page 411)

According to the tradition of the breed, the Puli made his first European appearance eleven hundred years ago when Central Eastern Europe was invaded by Asiatic Warriors. From that time on, these shaggy-haired canines have been an integral part of the lives of the Hungarian shepherds. Mehely, translator of Brahm's "Tierleben" in which the Puli is discussed, has, through research and study of the breed's characteristics, come to the conclusion that dogs native to Iceland and Lapland are closely related to the Puli and that this Hungarian dog is of Nordic origin.

All writers on the subject and all breeders of Pulis are, however, agreed that this dog is one of the most versatile and easily trained of all breeds. He is at his best as a herder of sheep which he often controls in his own unique fashion, by running over their backs. Runaways, he stops by jumping on their backs and digging his claws into their wool until the sheep stops from sheer fatigue; then he gently herds it back to the flock. Those who have seen the Puli actively engaged in this work are amazed by its dazzling footwork.

Faithful and intelligent, they make ideal guardians for children and are excellent companions and watch dogs. In a book written in 1751, Heppe, the German expert, mentions the "Hungarian Water Dog" and his ability at rabbit hunting as well as retrieving water fowl. The description which follows this statement practically describes the present day Puli. At the present time, the

WORKING DOGS

United States Department of Agriculture is experimenting with these dogs at a training school in Maryland, and it is to be hoped that they will try the breed out as hunting dogs as well as testing them for their ability and suitability for farm dogs in this country.

A medium-sized dog, about seventeen inches in height, his long, profuse, fine-textured coat may be any color but it is preferred in white, black and shades of cream or grey with darker ears. His deep set, medium large dark eyes reflect great intelligence and courage. He is inclined to be a "one-man dog" and is usually distrustful of strangers.

The Puli is a newcomer to American dogdom and has only recently made his debut at the bench shows, but his fanciers are most loyal and enthusiastic about his possibilities as a useful and faithful companion and are making every effort to increase his popularity.

DESCRIPTION AND STANDARD OF POINTS
(Adopted by the American Kennel Club, September 15, 1936)

General Appearance and Characteristics.—Medium size, very alert, courageous, intelligent, and extremely active. The Puli is a dog accustomed to but one person and is aggressive with and suspicious of strangers. The coat is long, of fine hair which often mats, giving his coat a somewhat corded appearance. He looks larger than he really is, due to the profuse coat on head, neck and quarters.

Head.—Should be in proportion to the body, not coarse, skull rather narrow and somewhat domed. Distinct stop, neither dished nor down-faced and strong muzzle of medium length ending in a nose of good size. Teeth are strong and large for the size of the dog. Flews should be tight and color black, as should the nose on white dogs. On dogs of other colors, flews and nose should be harmonious with the color of the coat.

Ears.—Profusely coated, medium large, V-shaped, carried flat to the side of the head. On some dogs the upper part of the ear extends out somewhat, with main ear flat to the side of the head.

Eyes.—Deep set, close together and medium large in size. Eyelids should be black or harmonizing with the color of the nose. Dark brown eyes preferred, but lighter color is not a serious fault.

Neck and Shoulders.—Neck should be free from throatiness, strong, muscular and of medium length running into clean-cut sloping shoulders with elbows set close to the chest.

Chest.—Should be fairly broad and deep, not so wide as to interfere with free action of front legs nor yet narrow. Ribs well sprung and deep.

Body.—Back not broad, straight, long and muscular, moderately broad loin and well tucked up. Rump is slightly sloping and rather long.

Tail.—Of medium length or occasionally natural bob-tails. The tail is carried low with the end curling up. When excited tail may even curl over the back to some extent.

Forelegs.—Strong and muscular, very straight when viewed from any angle, with strong, round compact feet with hard pads and strong nails. Dewclaws sometimes occur and are not a serious fault.

Hind Quarters.—Well developed, moderately broad through the stifle, which is well bent and muscular. Hocks well developed.

Coat.—Definitely long, profuse and of rather fine hair. Coat mats easily, giving a somewhat corded appearance in some dogs. The coat is especially profuse on head and face, stifles and tail. Hair may be straight, wavy or curly, medium length to long. Short hair is a bad fault.

Color.—Solid colors. Black, shades of grey, or white.

Height.—Seventeen inches. Females may be slightly smaller.

Faults.—Either over or under-shot mouth. Parti-colored nose. Short or thin coat.

ROTTWEILERS
(Illustration facing page 430)

To the Rottweiler must go considerable credit for helping to change the map and the races of Europe. Of course, the Rottweiler's part in these changes was purely involuntary; nevertheless, had it not been for him the Roman armies would not have been able to negotiate the mighty Alps and pour down into Central Europe.

Some 20 to 25 centuries ago a military expedition was a huge undertaking; far more so than it is today. Modern invention has removed many of the problems that confronted generals of old. Today we can move troops in a few days distances that occupied weeks and months of tortuous travel. And the feeding of a large body of men is now only a matter of purchasing the proper quantities of food.

The ancient Romans had to assemble vast quantities of food—along with all the other necessary supplies—and its transportation was a matter of major consideration. Perhaps the greatest problem centered around the supply of meat for the soldiers. Today we have rolling refrigeration that obviates difficulty, but even canning was unknown to the Romans. Therefore, meat had to be carried on the hoof. It is no wonder that today we use the word "impediment" to denote obstruction and hindrance, for the old Roman officers referred to the many-footed supply train as "impedimenta."

The movement of large herds of cattle meant work for many cattle dogs. These were recruited from among the three types then known in Rome; one very heavy and long-haired, the second short-haired and wolf-like and used, even then with sheep, and the third also short-haired, but of somewhat different build that was then used almost solely for herding cattle. It is this cattle dog that was the ancestor of the Rottweiler. Many dogs of this type accompanied the various Roman expeditions. They both guided and guarded the army's cattle.

In ancient days, the principal route of the Romans over the Alps was the historic St. Gotthard Pass. From this point, various passages lead downward, and each passage leads to a province that gave a dog breed a home and a name. As the size of the herd grew smaller, fewer dogs were needed and the Romans found no need of keeping them further. Thus we find, today, that at least four distinct breeds have evolved from this one type of cattle dog.

The Rottweiler has developed from Roman cattle dogs that travelled much further afield than their brothers; for their name comes from the township of Rottweil, in the county of that name, which lies on a hill on the left bank of the Neckar River, in Wurttemberg, which is in the South of Germany. This lies considerably to the west and north of the noted pass, for from St. Gotthard the armies followed over the Furkapass, through Haslital toward the flow of the Aar, to Berne, and from there towards the North into Emmental. Here are found two other descendants of the original cattle dog. But the Romans followed this old military road further North, through Aargu, Schaffhausen, Donaueschingen, and finally came to Rottweil.

Wurttemberg was conquered by the Romans in the first century, so there is assurance that the breed now called the Rottweiler is some 1,900 years old in its present form. The town of Rottweil is in the center of the livestock country. It lies 68 miles south by west of Stuttgart, and is favorably close to the borders of France and Hungary. Many things combined to make Rottweil a suitable market place, especially for grain, cattle, and other livestock, and for centuries the buyers and sellers from all over Central Europe flocked there to trade their wares.

The butchers and cattle merchants who settled in Rottweil in increasing numbers adopted a working dog because of necessity, and the Roman cattle dog was bred with a view to obtaining a dog capable of hard work. Not only did the butcher-master of Rottweil need a good worker, he needed a trusted companion and a reliable guard. Hold-ups were the rule rather than the exception, and it was especially dangerous to set forth on a buying expedition. It became the custom for the master to tie his purse around the dog's neck; and few bandits or highwaymen cared to molest one of these sturdy Rottweilers.

Aside from guard work, the principal uses of the Rottweiler always have been driving cattle, oxen, sheep, and pigs, and pulling carts. The smaller dogs were used with cattle, being able to keep up the constant trotting more easily. The larger specimens were considered unsuitable for driving and chasing cattle—some of the heavy dogs being able to knock over a cow by springing against it—and were reserved for draft work.

A few decades ago the Rottweiler was the leader and chaser of the herds on their way to market, and often stayed at his task for days. But after the driving of cattle by dogs was forbidden by law, gradually more and more were shipped by rail. The larger type Rottweiler also came to be replaced by the donkey for pulling carts; and for a time it seemed that the breed would be lost.

In fact, in 1905, the town of Rottweil had only one female member of the breed.

There came a renaissance for the Rottweiler in 1910 when it was chosen as a desirable type for police training. It joined the Airedale terrier, the German shepherd, and its own descendant, the Doberman pinscher, which were then the only breeds known for their police work. Always unfailingly faithful, and affectionate, the Rottweiler has developed more character through police work. It has served to emphasize his diligence, understanding, courage, modesty, and self-reliance.

DESCRIPTION AND STANDARD OF POINTS

(By Courtesy of Reichsverband für das Deutsche Hundewesen. Adopted by The American Kennel Club, April 9, 1935)

General Appearance and Character.—The Rottweiler is a good sized strongly built active dog. He is affectionate, intelligent, easily trained to work, naturally obedient and extremely faithful. While not quarrelsome, he possesses great courage and makes a splendid guard. His demeanor is dignified and he is not excitable.

Head.—Is of medium length, the skull broad between the ears. Stop well pronounced as is also the occiput. Muzzle is not very long. It should not be longer than the distance from the stop to the occiput. Nose is well developed, with relatively large nostrils and is always black. Flews which should not be too pronounced are also black. Jaws should be strong and muscular; teeth strong —incisors of lower jaw must touch the inner surface of the upper incisors. Eyes are of medium size, dark brown in color and should express faithfulness, good humor and confidence. The ears are comparatively small, set high and wide and hang over about on a level with top of head. The skin on head should not be loose. The neck should be of fair length, strong, round and very muscular, slightly arched and free from throatiness.

Fore Quarters.—Shoulders should be well placed, long and sloping, elbows well let down, but not loose. Legs muscular and with plenty of bone and substance, pasterns straight and strong. Feet strong, round and close, with toes well arched. Soles very hard, toe nails dark, short and strong.

Body.—The chest is roomy, broad and deep. Ribs well sprung. Back straight, strong and rather short. Loins strong and deep, and flanks should not be tucked up. Croup short, broad, but not sloping.

Hind Quarters.—Upper thigh is short, broad and very muscular. Lower thigh very muscular at top and strong and sinewy at the bottom. Stifles fairly well bent, hocks strong. The hind-feet are somewhat longer than the front ones, but should be close and strong with toes well arched. There should be no dew-claws. Tail should be short, placed high (on level with back) and carried horizontally. Dogs are frequently born with a short stump tail and when tail is too long it must be docked close to body.

Coat.—Hair should be short, coarse and flat. The under coat which is absolutely required on neck and thighs should not show through outer coat. The hair should be a little longer on the back of front and hindlegs and on tail.

Color.—Black, with clearly defined markings on cheeks, muzzle, chest and legs, as well as over both eyes. Color of markings: Tan to mahogany brown. A small spot of white on chest and belly is permissible but not desirable.

Height.—Shoulder height for males is 23¾ to 27 inches, for females 21¾ to 25 ¾ inches, but height should always be considered in relation to the general appearance and conformation of the dog.

Faults.—Too lightly built or too heavily built, sway back, roach back, too long body, lack of spring of ribs. Head too long and narrow or too short and plump. Lack of occiput, snipy muzzle, cheekiness, top line of muzzle not straight, light or flesh colored nose, hanging flews, overshot or undershot, loose skin on head, ears set too low, or ears too heavy, long or narrow or rose ear, or ears uneven in size. Light, small or slanting eyes, or lack of expression, neck too long, thin or weak, or very noticeable throatiness. Lack of bone and muscle, short or straight shoulders, frontlegs too close together or not straight, weak pasterns, splay feet, light nails, weak toes. Flat ribs, sloping croup. Too heavy or plump body. Flanks drawn up. Flat thighs, cowhocks or weak hocks, dew-

claws. Tail set too high or too low or that is too long or too thin.
Soft, too short, too long or too open coat, wavy coat or lack of
undercoat. White markings on toes, legs, or other parts of body,
markings not well defined or smudgy. The one-color tan Rottweiler with either black or light mask or with black streak on back
as well as other colors such as brown or blue are not recognized
and are believed to be cross bred, as is also a long-haired Rottweiler.
Timid or stupid appearing animals are to be positively rejected.

SAMOYEDES

(Illustration facing page 431)

(By Courtesy of The Samoyede Club of America)

Dog of the ages—with a history and tradition as fascinating as the breed itself! The legend runs that, from the Plateau of Iran, man's first earthly habitat, as the sons of man multiplied, the mightier tribes drove the lesser ones, with their families, their herds and their dogs, farther and farther away in order that the natural food there found might be ample for those remaining. Onward and still farther northward through Mongolia, then the center of the world's culture, on and on, went the lesser tribes, until eventually the Samoyede peoples, primitives of the family of Sayantsi most reliably described as a race in the "transition stages between the Mongol pure and the Finn," found themselves safely entrenched behind bulwarks of snow and ice in the vast stretches of tundra reaching from the White Sea to the Yenesei River. Here for generations untold they have lived a nomadic life, dependent for very life upon their reindeer herd, and upon their dogs as reindeer shepherds, sledge dogs and household companions.

Here through the centuries the Samoyede has bred true. Of all modern breeds, the Samoyede is most nearly akin to the primitive dog. No admixture of wolf or fox runs in the Samoyede strain. The Arctic suns and snows have bleached the harsh stand-off coat and tipped the hairs with an icy sheen. The constant companionship with man through the years has given an almost uncanny "human" understanding, and the generations of guard-

[429]

ing reindeer, requiring always a protector, never a killer, has developed through the ages in the breed a disposition unique in the canine world. Something of the happy childlike air of these primitive peoples is found as well in every Samoyede.

Nor has the long human association made of the stalwart Samoyede a pampered pet. As a work dog the Samoyedes of the great Arctic and Antarctic expeditions have a record of achievement unexcelled in the canine world. The sledge dogs of Nansen, secured from their native masters by a laughable yet pathetic ruse, averaging 45 pounds each, working day after day under conditions of the utmost hardship, drew one and a half times their own weight of supplies, and worked with that joyous abandon and carefree air typical of the breed. Used by Shackleton, Borchgrevinck, Scott, Jackson-Harmsworth, the Duc d'Abruzzi, Fiala, and others, each expedition has added to the unusual history of the breed a new lustre. The dogs of necessity deserted by the explorers amid Antarctic wastes have proven their ability to exist by themselves and have multiplied, still true to type, on the ice fields of the Antarctic Circle.

Introduced into England less than a hundred years ago, every show sees the Samoyedes in the forefront. The late Queen Mother Alexandra was an ardent fancier and the descendants of her dogs are found today in many English and American kennels. In every clime the dog is found; Samoyedes born in northern Siberia have safely crossed the equator and remained in healthy condition to work in Antarctic snows. Dogs from Antarctic expeditions have survived the suns of Australia to return to England and start great kennels there.

Beautiful; eye-arresting; perhaps the most beautiful breed in existence; gentle and companionable; an excel-

ROTTWEILER

SAMOYEDE

lent watchdog; modern in that there is no doggy odor; safe with children and never a trouble maker, yet able to hold its own when forced into a fight; with an independence born of the unusual intelligence, yet marked with a loyalty to a loved owner which wins hearts, the big, white dog with the smiling face and the dark, intelligent eyes, and the strong, sturdy, muscular body, with legs built for speed—that is the Samoyede.

As puppies, "little white teddy bears," the Samoyede characteristics are strongly shown—guardians always, gentle, kindly, of brilliant mentality, sturdy, adaptable— the promise of the grown dog which is to be is easily seen—the "big white dog which carries in its face and heart the spirit of Christmas the whole year through"— The Samoyede!

DESCRIPTION AND STANDARD OF POINTS
(By Courtesy of The Samoyede Club of America)

General Appearance.—The Samoyede being essentially a working dog should be strong and active and graceful, and as his work lies in cold climates his coat should be heavy and weather resisting. He should not be long in back, as a weak back would make him practically useless for his legitimate work; but at the same time a cobby body, such as the Chow's, would also place him at a great disadvantage as a draught dog. Breeders should aim for the happy medium, viz., a body not long, but muscular, allowing liberty, with a deep chest and well-sprung ribs, strong neck, straight front and exceptionally strong loins. A full-grown dog should stand about 21 inches at shoulder. On account of the depth of chest required the legs should be moderately long, a very short-legged dog is to be depreciated. Hind quarters should be particularly well developed, stifles well bent, and any suggestion of unsound stifles or cowhocks severely penalized.

Disposition.—Intelligent, alert, full of action, but above all displaying marked affection towards all mankind.

[431]

Coat.—The body should be well covered with a thick, close, soft and short undercoat, with harsh hair growing through it, forming the outer coat, which should stand straight away from the body and be quite free from curl.

Head.—Powerful and wedge-shaped with broad flat skull, muzzle of medium length, a tapering foreface, not too sharply defined, ears not too long and slightly rounded at tips, set well apart, and well covered inside with hair. Eyes dark, set well apart and deep, with alert, intelligent expression. Lips black. Hair short and smooth before the ears. Nose and eye-rims black for preference, but may be brown or flesh-colored. Strong jaws with level teeth.

Back.—Medium in length, broad, and very muscular.

Chest and Ribs.—Chest broad and deep. Ribs well sprung, giving plenty of heart and lung room.

Hind Quarters.—Very muscular, stifles well let down, cowhocks or straight stifles very objectionable.

Legs.—Straight and muscular. Good bone.

Feet.—Long, flattish and slightly spread out. Soles well padded with hair.

Tail.—Long and profuse, carried over back or side when alert, sometimes dropped down when at rest, tight curl or double hook is a fault.

Size and Weight.—Dogs, 20 to 22 inches at shoulder, 45 to 55 pounds; bitches, 18 to 20 inches, 36 to 45 pounds.

Color.—Pure white, white and biscuit, cream. Black or black spots to disqualify.

	Points
General appearance	20
Head	15
Coat	10
Size	10
Chest and ribs	10
Hind quarters	10
Back	10
Feet	5
Legs	5
Tail	5
Total	100

SCHNAUZERS (GIANT)

(Illustration facing page 446)

Few races have been more prolific in their development of new breeds of dog than the Germanic peoples. Not only have they evinced rare patience in tracing ancestries, but they have proved, undoubtedly, their ability to fix type and hold it. One of the most notable examples of their breeding skill is the Schnauzer, for here is a dog not only brought to a splendid physical conformation, and a keen mental development, but also reproduced in three distinct sizes. The one under consideration here is the riesenschnauzer—the giant. The others are treated more fully elsewhere.

The remarkable phase of the breeding of the Schnauzers is that all three dogs appear to have been developed up toward one standard of perfection from various sources that intermingled—if at all—only in rare instances. Of them all, the dog now known in America as the standard Schnauzer, which is the medium sized specimen, is without doubt the oldest. He is the one apparently portrayed in paintings by Durer, dated 1492 and he is also the one of the "Nachtwachter-Brunnen," the statue of a night watchman and his dog erected in a square in Stuttgart, Wurttemberg in 1620. These instances are important only as they indicate the antiquity of the type of dog perfected at those dates and still retained, today.

In unearthing the history of this breed it must be remembered that occupations of men had a great deal to do with all development in dogs. There were no bench

[433]

shows in those days, and when a new breed of dog was produced, it was aimed at a specific work. Its characteristics also were governed to large extent by weather and living conditions.

All Schnauzers had their origin in the neighboring kingdoms of Wurttemberg, and Bavaria, both of which are in the southern part of what is now the German Republic. These are agricultural sections, and the raising of sheep and cattle and other livestock has been a major occupation there for years. And since railroads were not known, sheep and cattle had to be driven to market. This meant that dogs were necessary to help the shepherds.

There is little doubt that when Bavarian cattle men went to Stuttgart they came across the medium sized Schnauzer. It was a dog to catch anyone's attention, for even then it was absolutely sound, while it showed power throughout its trim lines. The Bavarains liked the dog, but they were not satisfied with its size. The sheep men could use this size of dog, but the drovers needed a larger specimen for cattle.

The first attempts to produce a drover's dog on terrier lines, with a wiry coat, were no doubt by crossings between the medium sized Schnauzer and some of the smooth-coated driving and dairymen's dogs then in existence. Later there were crossings with the rough-haired sheepdogs; and much later, with the black Great Dane. There also is reason to believe that the Giant Schnauzer is closely related to the Bouvier de Flandres, which was the driving dog of Flanders.

For many years the Giant Schnauzer was called the Munchener, and it was widely known, by reputation, as a great cattle and driving dog. Von Stephanitz definitely places its origin as Swabia—in the south of Bavaria

—and it was found in a splendid state of perfection in the region between Munich and Augsburg.

The Giant Schnauzer was practically unknown outside of Bavaria until near the end of the first decade of this century. Cattle driving was then a thing of the past, but the breed was still found in the hands of butchers, at stockyards, and at breweries. The breweries maintained the dogs as guards, at which duty they are preeminently successful.

It was not until just before the World War that the Giant Schnauzer began to come to nationwide attention in Germany. This was the result of his acceptance as a suitable subject to receive police training at the schools in Berlin and other principal cities. He proved such an intelligent pupil that police work has been his main occupation since that time.

The Giant Schnauzer was introduced into the United States a dozen years ago, but his progress has been very slow. Making his appearance here at the time when the German shepherd was reaching its peak, the Bavarian dog had little chance to make headway against such well established, direct competition. But the very soundness, and the intelligence of the Giant Schnauzer indicate that some day it is bound to become very popular.

DESCRIPTION AND STANDARD OF POINTS

(By Courtesy of Reichsverband für das Deutsche Hundewesen)

General Impression.—The Giant Schnauzer is a robust, sinewy, more heavy set than slender dog, of somewhat rectangular build. His nature combines high-spirited temperament with extreme reliability.

Head.—Strong and elongated, gradually narrowing from the ears to the eyes and thence towards the tip of the nose, in proportion to the size of the body. Its total length (tip of nose to occiput) should compare approximately to one-third the length of the back (withers—first dorsal vertebra—to the beginning of the tail). Upper part of the head (occiput to the base of the forehead) broad between the ears—its width should not be more than two-thirds of the length—with flat, creaseless forehead and well-muscled but not too strongly developed cheeks. Ears, small and V-shaped of moderate thickness, set well on the head and dropping forward closely to the cheek, or cropped, with ears evenly cut, placed high and carried erect in excitement. Eyes medium-sized, dark, oval, turned forward, brows arched and wiry.

The powerful ferreting snout formed by the upper and lower jaw (base of forehead to the tip of nose) should be in proportion to the upper head and should end in a moderately blunt manner, with heavy stubby whiskers. Ridge of the nose straight and running almost parallel to the extension of the forehead. The tip of the nose is black and full. Lips tight and not overlapping, with strongly developed fangs, healthy and pure white.

Neck.—Not too short with skin close-fitting at the throat. Nape strong and slightly arched.

Fore Quarters.—Shoulders slanting and flat, but strongly muscled. Forelegs (upper and under arm) seen from all sides are vertical without any curve.

Chest.—Moderately broad with visible strong breast bone and reaching at least to the height of the elbow and slowly extending backwards. Back strong and straight with well-developed short thighs. The length of back equal to shoulder height (from withers vertical to floor) built squarely, belly well drawn up towards the back.

Tail.—Carried high and cut down to three joints.

Hind Quarters.—Thighs slanting and flat, but strongly muscled. Hindlegs (upper and lower thighs) at first vertical to the knee, from knee to hock in line with the extension of the upper neckline, from hock vertical to ground.

Paws.—Short, round, extremely compact paws, with close arched toes (cat's paws) dark nails and hard soles.

Hair.—Close, strong, hard and wiry, on the back seen against the grain—unruly—that is, neither short nor smooth; shorter on ears, forehead, legs and paws.

SCHNAUZERS (GIANT)

Height.—From 21½ to 25½ inches shoulder height.

Color.—All pepper and salt colored or similar equal mixtures, pure black or black with tan.

Faults.—Too plump, or too light, low or high-legged build, too heavy around head, creased forehead, sticking-out or badly carried ears, light eye (with yellow or light-grey rings) strongly protruding cheek bones, flabby throat skin; undershot or overshot jaw. Teeth too pointed, too small or too long, sunken or roached back, chest with barrel ribs (tubby) slanting crupper, elbows turned out, heels turned in, hind part overbuilt, too steep, spread open toes, long and flat (hare) paws, too short, sleek, too long, soft, silky, curled, rolled, shaggy hair, all white, spotty, tigered, red and reddish colors.

Small white breast spot, or marking on the breast is not a fault.

SHETLAND SHEEPDOGS

(Illustration facing page 447)

(By Courtesy of The American Shetland Sheepdog Association)

The Shetland Sheepdog is, as its name implies, a working collie in minature still in the process of being transformed into a more refined show type of Sheltie, keeping forever in mind its fundamental working traits of character and structure. There is little doubt that the small working collie from which came the modern show collie evolving on larger lines, was likewise the progenitor of the Shetland Sheepdog evolving on smaller ones, assisted in the process both by the environment of the Islands which produced diminutiveness in all its stock and by crosses with other small breeds, residing in if not indigenous to the Islands.

The Shetland Islands themselves are not conducive to abundance of either fodder or flocks, made up as they are of rugged rocks on which only the most meager vegetation can survive and surrounded by the sea which brews frequent and severe storms; what wonder that only the hardiest of both man and beast and the smallest could find sufficient subsistence or have sufficient foothold there. The actual origin of the breed cannot be traced by reference to records as none were ever written. Tradition makes the dogs as old as the working collies of Scotland which frequently came to Shetland as the breed's forbears and as old as the Islands themselves.

As the Islands were isolated from the trend of travel so were the little dogs a long time coming to the ken of dog-loving folk. Thus it was that the breed did not take its place on the show-bench until well along in the present century. The year 1909 marked the initial recognition of the Sheltie by the English Kennel Club. Not until 1914 did the breed obtain separate classification as Shetland Sheepdogs and not Shetland Collies because of pressure brought to bear by the collie breeders. The first Challenge certificate was awarded to the breed in 1915 after which the war put a stop to all progress for the next few years.

The history of the several Clubs catering to the breed has been one of ups and downs centering around the variations in size and type which still linger in a refined form today. The Shetland Sheepdog Club in the Islands founded in 1908 was of course the oldest. They asked for a rough collie in miniature, height not exceeding 15 inches. The Scottish Shetland Sheepdog Club, a year later, asked for first an "ordinary collie in miniature" and finally a "modern show collie in miniature," ideal height 12 inches, and eventually 13½. The English Shetland Sheepdog Club founded in 1914 was an offshoot of the Scottish requiring "approximately a show collie in miniature," height (ideal) first 12 inches and finally from 12 to 15, the ideal being 13½. The British Breeders' Association came into being for a time as the offspring of the English Club and asked for a "show collie in miniature," maintaining the same heights. In 1930 the Scottish and English Clubs revised their standards jointly to read "should resemble a Collie (Rough) in miniature." The American Shetland Sheepdog Association, youngest in years, tried to profit by the experience of its predecessors, by combining the best of each in its standard, asking for the "ideal collie in miniature," height from 12 to 15 inches.

The Club controversy was reflected by the struggle of breeders to fix and perpetuate the proper type and size. The smaller breeds intermingling with the working collies brought in many faults quite contradictory to true collie type. Small spaniels were undoubtedly responsible for contributing undesirable wavy coats, low ears, large round eyes, gay tails, long bodies, and desirable calm, devoted dispositions. Little yellow Iceland dogs with smutty muzzles and pricked ears made their mark on the breed.

To offset these influences, crosses with modern collies were resorted to which introduced in their train a new set of faults along with an undeniable set of virtues derived from long generations of breeding for perfection in collie points. The chief drawbacks, whose results we are reaping today, were legginess, loss of substance, excess size and unbalance. At the same time, the breed was given a great impetus in the improvement of head properties, especially in type, skull, and expression. While the breed is still suffering somewhat from this inescapable method of its improvement, it is likewise reaping the reward of now having within the breed all the points inseparable from the correct collie, enabling breeders to bring forth substantial beautifully balanced little dogs, with weather resisting collie coats, collie type and expression, and Sheltie size, charm, and character.

The breed characteristics common to all Shelties can be used for two purposes pertaining to their working propensities or their companionship qualities. It is their nature to obey, willingly and naturally with few or no lessons needed, an instinct coming no doubt from the many generations of obediently trained dogs behind them. The instinct to guard property or places and to give watchdog warning makes them invaluable for work as farm helpers or home protectors, a heritage of the constant vigilance required to protect the crofters cottages, flocks and herds from invaders of all varieties. Their ability to run swiftly and gracefully, and jump with agility over obstacles makes them a delight in fields and woods as well as in farm work. But what most endears them to everybody is their sweet, devoted, docile natures and their keen and all but human intelligence and understanding.

DESCRIPTION AND STANDARD OF POINTS
(By Courtesy of The American Shetland Sheepdog Association)

General Appearance.—The general appearance of the Shetland Sheepdog is that of the ideal Collie in miniature.

Symmetry.—The outline of the Shetland Sheepdog should be so symmetrical that no part appears out of proportion to the whole.

Size.—The height of the Shetland Sheepdog should be no less than twelve inches nor more than fifteen inches measured at the shoulder. The ideal height being 13½ inches.

Coat.—The coat should be double, the outer coat consisting of long, harsh hair, the under coat short, soft and close, like fur. The mane and frill should be abundant, the forelegs well feathered, the hindlegs above the hocks and the brush, profusely so. The face and tips of ears should be smooth, the hindlegs below the hocks fairly so. Smooth-coated specimens are barred.

Color.—Any color except brindle or solid white is permissible, the usual colors being sable, black, and blue merle marked with varying amounts of white and tan.

Head—Skull.—The skull should be flat, moderately wide between the ears, gradually tapering towards the eyes with a slight depression at the stop; the cheeks should not be full or prominent.

Muzzle.—The muzzle should be of fair length tapering to the nose and must not show weakness or be snipy or lippy. The jaws should be clean cut and powerful. The teeth should be of good size, sound and level; very slight unevenness is permissible. The nose must be black, whatever the color of the dog may be.

Eyes.—The eyes should be of medium size, set somewhat obliquely, of almond shape, and of a brown color, except in the case of merles when one or both are frequently blue and white or china. They should be full of intelligence and expression.

Ears.—The ears should be small, moderately wide at the base, placed fairly close together on top of the skull. When in repose they should be folded back into the frill; when on the alert, they should be brought up and carried semi-erect, with the tips drooping forward.

Body—Neck.—The neck should be of fair length, muscular and somewhat arched.

Fore Quarters.—The fore quarters should be deep in the chest and fairly broad behind the shoulders, which should be sloped.

Forelegs.—The forelegs should be straight and muscular, with a fair amount of bone, neither in nor out at the elbows.

Body.—The body should be moderately long, with level back and well-sprung ribs.

Hind Quarters.—The hind quarters should be muscular at the thighs, with loin slightly arched and powerful.

Hindlegs.—The hindlegs should be clean and sinewy below the hocks, with well-bent stifles and hocks well let down.

Feet.—The feet should be oval in shape, soles well padded and the toes arched and close together.

Tail.—The tail should be moderately long, carried low when the dog is quiet, with a slight upward swirl at the end; carried gaily when the dog is excited, but not over the back.

Faults.—Domed skull, large drooping ears, weak jaws, snipy muzzle, full eyes, or light eyes except in blue merles, crooked forelegs, cowhocks, tail carried over the back, curly coat, over or undershot mouth.

General Appearance

	Points
Size	10
Symmetry	10
Coat	10

WORKING DOGS

Head

Ears	10
Eyes and expression	10
Skull	5
Muzzle	5

Body

Neck	5
Fore quarters and forelegs	10
Back	5
Hind quarters and hindlegs	10
Feet	5
Tail	5
Total	**100**

SIBERIAN HUSKIES

(Illustration facing page 448)

The Siberian Husky comes from the northeastern part of Siberia, where he has been used for hundreds of years as a sled dog. He has the physical characteristics common to the dogs of the other Northern breeds. The Siberian Husky as he exists today has been bred true to type in northeastern Siberia and used in teams as the only means of winter transportation since the time of the earliest known inhabitants of that vast country.

The first Siberian Huskies were brought from Siberia to Alaska in 1909 to be entered in the All Alaska Sweepstakes, a non-stop race of 408 miles. Each year for ten years this grueling race was run from Nome to Candle and return. Five times it was won by Siberian Huskies and the record of 74 hours and 17 minutes was made by John Johnson with his famous team of Siberian Huskies. For more than twenty years there has been an interesting race at Nome, Alaska, known as the Borden Cup Race. It is really a Marathon, the distance being 26 miles 385 yards. The record for this race is held by Leonard Seppala with his team of Siberian Huskies, the time being 1 hour 50 minutes and 25 seconds. The Siberian Huskies have proven themselves to be not only one of the fastest of team dogs but also one of the most enduring.

Naturally, the Siberian Husky has acquired certain characteristics which distinguish him from the dogs of any other breed. It comes just as natural to the Siberian Husky to work in a team of sled dogs as it does to a setter or pointer to hunt for birds. The severe weather conditions under which he has existed, together with the kind of work which he was required to do, have resulted in producing wonderfully strong, active, and enduring animals. In Siberia it has been the custom for many years to castrate all of the male dogs used in the teams, except the very best which were selected for breeding purposes. The reason for this is the same as with horses and the practice has been followed to some extent with the work dogs in Alaska. The result has been a continued improvement in the breed.

The Siberian Husky is not a large dog, the average male weighing from fifty to sixty-five pounds and the female from forty to fifty-five pounds. A Siberian may be either white or black, but most of them are grey with white and black markings. The greater number of them have brown eyes, but the blue eyed Siberian Husky is not uncommon. The hair is not especially long, but there is a very soft under fur next to the skin, which keeps the dog warm in the coldest weather. During the summer he sheds this under fur and so is not uncomfortable during the long and hot days of the northern summer. The ears are erect and he often carries his tail curled over his back. The pads of the feet are very tough and seldom, if ever, is it necessary to moccasin a Siberian even on the iciest of trails. The Siberian Husky is exceptionally intelligent and easy to train. He is friendly and not inclined to fight with the other dogs of the team, but has little use for a dog of another breed. If a Siberian is attacked by another dog, rest assured that he will give a good account of himself, as gameness and courage are two of his outstanding characteristics. He is affectionate, but does not care for strangers. In Alaska the Siberian is known as a one man dog. He is devoted to those who

SCHNAUZER (*Giant*)

SHETLAND SHEEPDOG

care for him, but does not fawn. The Siberian Husky respects his master and seems to expect respect from his master in return. One of these dogs trained only to the harness will become a good house dog in a very short time. A puppy can be house broken with a minimum of effort. They love children.

The Siberian Husky is beginning to gain deserved recognition in the show ring. The first champion of the breed, Northern Light Kobuk, 775815, was bred and raised at Fairbanks, Alaska, and is now owned by a resident of New Hampshire.

DESCRIPTION AND STANDARD OF POINTS

General Appearance.—For hundreds of years the Siberian Husky has been used as a sled dog in northeastern Asia. He should be exceptionally active, quick and light on his feet, able to run in harness with a load, at a speed of twenty miles an hour for short distances. He should be strong, courageous and tireless on the trail. He should have a deep strong chest, heavy bone, strong legs and feet, straight powerful back and well muscled hind quarters. A grown dog should stand about 23 inches at the shoulders and weigh about 60 pounds. A bitch should be smaller and weigh about 10 or 12 pounds less.

Head.—The size of the head should be in proportion to the body, but not clumsy or too large. It should be of medium width between the ears. The ears should be erect, set high on the head, medium in size, pointed at the tops and well covered with hair on the inside. It should be of medium length and slightly wedge shaped. The jaws and teeth are very strong, and should be neither overshot nor undershot. The eyes may be either blue or brown, with a keen, friendly, and intelligent expression. Eye rims dark. The nose may be either light brown or black. The muzzle should be strong, the lips dark and firmly fitting together.

Chest and Ribs.—Chest should be deep and strong, but not too broad. The ribs should be well arched and deep.

Back, Quarters, and Stifles.—The loins should be slightly arched and especially well muscled. The stifles should be well let down and very muscular. The back should be straight, not too long, and strongly developed.

Legs.—Straight, of good length, well muscled and good bone.

Feet.—Strong, not too compact, with exceptionally tough pads protected with hair.

Tail.—Long, and usually carried curled over back but sometimes dropped down especially when tired. Should be well protected with fur and hair, but bushy tails not desirable.

Size and Weight.—Dogs, 22 to 23½ inches at shoulder, 54 to 64 pounds; bitches, 21 to 22½ inches, 44 to 54 pounds.

Color.—All colors permissible from white to black including many variations of greys and mixed wolf colorings.

Coat.—Should be thick with a very soft and warm under fur next to the skin. The guard hairs should not be too long, and should be straight, not too coarse, and fairly close to the body so that the graceful lines of the dogs are not obscured. A bushy or shaggy coat is not desirable.

	Points
Size and general appearance	25
Head and neck	10
Coat and color	10
Chest and ribs	10
Quarters and stifles	15
Back	10
Legs	10
Feet	5
Tail	5
Total	100

SIBERIAN HUSKY

ST. BERNARD

ST. BERNARDS

(By Courtesy of The St. Bernard Club of America)

Many hypotheses have been advanced to account for the origin of the St. Bernard dog, but definite proof to substantiate any one of them seems to be lacking. When one has gathered all available information on the subject, however, he is led to the following probability: That the breed originated from the heavy Molosser type that was brought back from Asia by conquering Roman armies, and which, later, in the dawn of the Christian era, was introduced into Helvetia (Switzerland) during two different invasions.

When St. Bernard de Menthon founded his famous Hospice in the Swiss Alps, in the year 980, it is probable that the *Talhund,* a descendant of the Roman Molosser, was by that time a well-established breed in the Alpine valleys. Just when dogs first were brought to the Hospice is another debatable question, as, unfortunately, in the sixteenth century the Hospice was destroyed by fire, and, later, a large part of the Hospice archives again was lost. In what remains there is nothing to be found of when, whither or whence the dogs first were brought to the Great St. Bernard pass. The prior, Erw. Ch. Lugon, asserts that according to his examination of the archives, the Hospice was still without dogs in the first part of the sixteenth century. Earlier records mention nothing about such animals, and it was not until 1707 that the first notation concerning them was made. This, however, was merely a casual reference to dogs at the Hospice and carried with it the implication that their rescue work at the St. Bernard pass was a fact then well known. An English traveler and painter, writing in 1774, also tells about the life-saving work of the dogs kept at Great St. Bernard, but he, too, mentions it in similar vein as information at that time so widely and commonly known that it needed little comment. From a digest of these early references, it appears probable that dogs were first brought to the Hospice between 1660 and 1670 as watch dogs, that they were recruited from the valleys below and were descendants of the old Roman Molosser. The lonely monks took the dogs along with them on their trips of mercy and soon discovered that not only were they excellent pathfinders in the snow but that their uncanny sense of smell made them invaluable in finding helpless persons overcome during storms. Thus it began, this working together of monk and dog that made many of the world's most romantic pages of canine history. During the last almost three centuries that St. Bernards have been used in rescue work at the Hospice, it is estimated they have been responsible for the saving of approximately 2,500 human lives. Building of railroad tunnels through the Alps in recent times greatly has lessened foot and vehicle travel across the St. Bernard pass, and consequently has reduced to a minimum the work of the dogs. Fewer dogs are now kept at the Hospice, but their work is no less important than it was centuries ago. Hardly a season goes by that some rescues from the Great White Death are not attributed to the heroic dogs of St. Bernard. A new Hospice recently has been established in the Tibet, and in this far outpost of civilization as well as in the frozen Alps the saintly dogs still ply their century-old trade of saving human lives.

St. Bernards require no training for their work, as

generations of service in this capacity seem to have stamped the rescuing instinct indelibly upon their characters. The only schooling they receive at the Hospice is being permitted as young dogs to run with the older dogs on the latter's patrol tours. Formerly, the dogs, running in packs of three or four, used to make lone patrols during and following storms in search of possible traveler casualities. When they came upon a victim, two of the animals would lie down on the snow beside him to warm him with their bodies, and one of them would lick the person's face to restore consciousness. In the meantime, one of the other dogs in the pack would be on his way back to the Hospice to give the alarm to the monks and lead them to the scene. Around their necks the dogs carried small barrels of liquid restoratives, to the contents of which the victim could help himself if he revived sufficiently. As soon as the rescue party of monks arrived, the dogs would retire at a respectful distance and apparently take no further interest in the doings, their part of it being finished. Today the dogs no longer wear the barrels attached to their collars and seldom go on patrols alone. They accompany the monks who go out when warned by telephone that a party of tourists is attempting to go through the pass. Their work on such occasions is invaluable, as the monks themselves with safety could not go more than a few feet from their Hospice door, were it not for the unerring sense of direction possessed by their dogs who can lead them back in the event of a sudden Alpine blizzard that obliterated all familiar landmarks.

In addition to their pathfinding capabilities and their sense of smell which enables them to locate human beings buried under the snow, the dogs are reputed to possess an uncanny sixth sense which warns them of approaching avalanches. Several instances have been reported wherein a dog quickly would change his position for no apparent reason and that a few seconds or minutes later an avalanche would come hurtling down across the spot where he formerly stood, burying it under tons of snow and ice.

Although by 1800 it was well known that a special type of dog did rescue work at the Hospice, the breed at that time had been given no name. Between 1800 and 1810, Barry, perhaps the most celebrated dog in history, lived at the Hospice, and for fully a half century after his demise, the Hospice dogs in certain parts of Switzerland were called "Barry hounds" after him. Barry is credited with having saved 40 lives. Legend has it that he was killed by the 41st person he attempted to rescue who mistook his huge bulk for that of a wolf, but this tale appears to be only a pretty story. As a matter of fact, Barry was given a painless death in Berne, in 1814, after he had attained a ripe, old age. His likeness in mounted form is now preserved in the Natural History museum in Berne.

The English who as early as 1810 imported some of the Hospice dogs to replenish their mastiff blood referred to the breed for a number of years as "Sacred dogs." In Germany, around 1828, the name of "Alpendog" was proposed. In 1823, a writer, Daniel Wilson, first spoke of the so-called St. Bernard dog, but it was not until 1865 that this name definitely appeared, and only since 1880 has it been recognized as the official designation of the breed. The years 1816 to 1818 were seasons of uncommon snows and rigorous weather at the Hospice, and as a result many of the leading Hospice strains perished. It was easy at that time, however, to get good animals of like breed from the underlying valleys, and a few years later the dog situation at the Hospice was again satisfactory.

Confronted by a similar problem in 1830, and also by the fact that their breed was weakened considerably by inbreeding and disease, the monks resorted to an outcross to give added size and new vigor to their dogs. The Newfoundland, which at that time was larger than the St. Bernard, was the breed decided upon to give the new blood. Results of this crossing showed all of the desired objectives and at the same time did not destroy the St. Bernard type and characteristics. Due to this crossing, however, the first long-haired St. Bernards appeared; previous to 1830 all St. Bernards were short-haired. Followed years of breeding of many St. Bernards in the valleys of Switzerland, in Germany and in other Continental European countries and England.

In 1887, an International Congress was held in Zurich. Swiss St. Bernard authorities present included Drs. Sigmund, Künzli and Max Siber. At this Congress an International Standard of Perfection for the breed was promulgated.

The St. Bernard Club of America was organized in 1888, the year following the Zurich congress, and the International standard was adopted by it. This club still continues to function for the interests of the St. Bernard and is one of the oldest Specialty Clubs in the United States.

DESCRIPTION AND STANDARD OF POINTS
(By Courtesy of The St. Bernard Club of America)

General Character.—Powerful, tall (upstanding), figure erect, strong and muscular in every part, with powerful head and most intelligent expression. In dogs with a black mask the expression appears more stern, but never ill-natured.

Head.—Like the whole body, very powerful and imposing. The massive skull is wide, slightly arched and sloping at the sides, with a gentle curve into the very well-developed cheek bones.

Occiput only slightly developed. The supra-orbital ridge is strongly developed and forms nearly a right angle with the horizontal axis of his head. Between the two supra-orbital arches, and starting at the root of the muzzle, runs a furrow over the whole skull; it is very deep between the supra-orbital arches and strongly defined up the forehead, becoming gradually more shallow toward the base of the occiput. The lines at the sides, from the outer corner of the eyes, diverge considerably toward the back of the head. The skin on the forehead forms somewhat deep wrinkles, more or less distinct, and converging from the supra-orbital arches toward the furrow over the forehead; especially in action they are more visible without in the least causing the expression to become dark. The slope from the skull to the muzzle (stop) is sudden and rather steep.

Muzzle.—The muzzle is short, not snipy, and the depth, taken at the root (at the stop), must be greater than the length of the muzzle. The bridge of the muzzle is not arched, but straight, and in some good dogs slightly broken. From the stop over the entire bridge of the muzzle to the nose runs a rather wide, well-marked, shallow furrow. The flews of the upper jaw are strongly developed, not cut at right angles, but turning with a graceful curve into the lower edge, and are slightly overhanging. The flews of the lower jaw must not be pendant. The teeth, in proportion to the conformation of the head, are only of moderately strong development. A black roof to the mouth is desirable.

The *nose* is very substantial and broad, with well-dilated nostrils, and, like the lips, always black.

Ears.—Are of medium size, set on rather high, with very strongly developed burr, they stand slightly outward at the base, then drop with a sharp bend to the side and lie closely to the head without a fold. The flap is thin and forms a rounded triangle, slightly elongated toward the point, the front edge lying closely to the head, whereas the back edge may stand away from the head somewhat, especially when the dog is listening. Ears lightly set on, which at the base lie close to the head, give it an oval and too slightly marked appearance, whereas a strongly developed base gives the skull a squarer, broader and much more expressive appearance.

Eyes.—Set more to the front than the sides, are of moderate size, brown or nut brown, with a sagacious and good-natured expression, set moderately deep. The lower eyelids do not, as a rule, fit close to the eyeballs, and form toward the inner corner an angular wrinkle. Eyelids which are too pendant, and showing conspicuously the lachrymal glands, or a red thick haw, are objectionable.

Neck.—The neck is set on high, very strong, and in action is carried erect, otherwise horizontally or slightly downward. The junction of head and neck is distinctly marked by a line. Neck very muscular and rounded at the sides, which makes it appear rather short. Clearly noticeable dewlaps, but too much development of the same is not desirable.

Shoulders.—Sloping and broad, very muscular and powerful, withers strongly defined.

Chest.—Well arched, moderately deep, not reaching below the elbows.

Back.—Very broad, slightly arched in the loin only, otherwise perfectly straight as far as the haunches, sloping gently from the haunches to the rump, and merging imperceptibly into the root of the tail.

Hind Quarters.—Well developed. Thighs very muscular.

Belly.—Showing distinctly where it joins the very powerful loins, only slightly drawn up.

Tail.—Starting broad and powerful directly from the rump, is long, very heavy, ending in a blunt tip. In repose it hangs straight down, turning gently upward in the lower third. In a great many specimens the tail is carried with the end slightly turned to one side (as in all former Hospice dogs, according to old pictures), and therefore hangs down in the shape of an *f*. In action all dogs carry the tail more or less turned upward. But it dare not be carried too erect, or by any means rolled over the back. A slight curling over of the tip is sooner admissible.

Forearms.—Very powerful and extraordinarily muscular.

Forelegs.—Straight, strong.

Hindlegs.—Slightly bent in the hocks, and, according to the presence of single or double dewclaws, the feet turn outward more or less, which, however, must not be understood to mean cow-hocked.

Feet.—Broad, with strong toes moderately well closed up, and knuckles rather high. The single or double dewclaws set on low, so as to be almost on a level with the pad of the foot, giving a greater surface, and preventing the dog from breaking so easily through the snow.

There are dogs which have on their hind feet a regular developed fifth toe (thumb). The so-called dewclaws (Wolfsklauen) which sometimes occur on the hindlegs, are imperfectly developed toes; they are of no use to the dog, and are not taken into consideration in judging.

Coat.—Is very dense, broken-haired (stock-haarig) lying smooth (flat), tough, without feeling rough to the touch. Thighs slightly bushy. The tail at the root is covered with longer and more dense hair, which gradually becomes shorter toward the tip. The tail appears bushy, not forming a flag.

Color and Markings.—White with red, or red with white, the red in all its various shades; white with light to dark barred brindle patches, or these colors with white markings. The colors, red or light brindle and dark brindle, are of entirely equal value. The following white markings are absolutely necessary: nose-band (white muzzle), blaze, chests, legs and tip of tail. A collar or a spot on the nape are very desirable. Never self-colored or without any white. Faulty are all other colors, except the very favorite black shadings on the face (mask) and ears.

Height at Shoulder.—Of the dog (measured with the Hound measure) ought to be 70 centimeters minimum (27.56 inches); of the bitch, 65 centimeters (25.59 inches). The bitches are throughout of a more delicate and finer build.

As faulty are to be considered all variations not in accordance with these points.

THE LONG-HAIRED (ROUGH) ST. BERNARD

The long-haired dog is perfectly similar, with the exception of the coat, which is not "stock-haarig" (broken-haired) but moderately long, flat to slightly wavy, but which ought never to be either rolled or curly, neither ought it to be shaggy. On the back, especially from the region of the haunches to the rump, the hair is generally more wavy; this is, moreover, also slightly noticeable in the short-haired dogs, even in those from the Hospice.

The tail is bushy, well covered with moderately long hair. Rolled or locky hair on the tail is not desirable. A tail with parted hair or feathered is faulty. Face and ears are covered with short and soft hair; longer silky hair is allowable at the base of the ears, in fact, this is nearly always the case. Forelegs only slightly feathered; thighs very bushy.

Faults are especially all such formations as indicate a Newfoundland cross, such as sway-back, disproportionately long back, hocks too much bent and spaces between the toes with upward growing hair.

No scale of points has been adopted.

WELSH CORGIS (CARDIGAN)

(Illustration facing page 460)

Although among the latest of breeds to be recognized in the United States, the Cardigan Welsh Corgi is one of the oldest breeds in the British Isles. Yet, even in England the breed has come to be a show specimen only in very recent times. The apparent mystery surrounding its origin has been due to the previous absence of any written history and the simple fact that the poor hillmen of Wales saw no reason to publicize the dogs that had been so useful to them for so many centuries.

The data upon which this summarized history of the breed is written was collected over a period of 20 years by W. Lloyd-Thomas of Mabws Hall, Llanrhystyd, Cardiganshire, South Wales, and is treated to greater extent in his recently completed, fulsome article.

In the beginning, the Corgi came to the high country now known as Cardiganshire with the tall, tawny-headed Celts from Central Europe. The migration of this warrior tribe to Wales is placed, roughly, at about 1200 B.C., which means that the Corgi has been known in the land whence comes its name for more than 3,000 years. The dog was a member of the same family that has produced the dachshund.

The village of Bronant, in Mid-Cardiganshire, became the especial stronghold of those early Celts, for the place is rich in remains of the old fortifications. Indeed, Bronant is ringed round with them. The inhabitants, too, give evidence of that early settlement, for considerable numbers of them are tall and auburn-haired. They are said to be the direct descendants of the hard-pressed, fiery race that threw up these mounds.

The vigilance and intelligence of the Corgi must have been a great asset to the Celts from earliest times, and tales, handed down from father to son for countless generations identify him always as a most valued member of the family circle. His uses were many and varied, not the least of which were his guardianship of the children, and his aid in beating out game—in those times of more than ordinary importance.

Still, the occupation that made the Corgi worth his weight in gold to those Welsh hillmen came at a much later period, but still many hundreds of years ago. This was when the Crown owned practically all land, and the tenant farmers, or crofters—as they were known—were permitted to fence off only a few acres surrounding their dooryards. The rest was open country, known as Common Land. On this the crofter was permitted to graze his cattle, one of the chief sources of his meagre income.

It can be imagined that there was great competition among the crofters to secure as much as possible of this pasture land for their own uses. This task would have been a most difficult one had it not been for the Corgi. The little dog that had been with this Celtic people so long, and which had come to be of almost human intelligence, was trained to perform a service that was the opposite of that done by the herding dog.

Instead of herding the cattle, the Corgi would nip at their heels and drive them as far afield as desired. Often the crofter called upon his dog to clear "his" ground of the cattle of the neighbors. The dog worked the same way in either case. The crofter would stand by his gate and give a soft whistle of two notes, one high, one low. Many times the dog could not see the cattle he was to

WELSH CORGI (*Cardigan*)

WELSH CORGI (*Pembroke*)

chase, but he would keep going as long as he could hear that whistle. His speed was remarkable, considering his short legs with their out-turned feet, but the length of his back gave him added spring. When the dog had scattered the cattle by biting their hocks—avoiding death only by ducking close to the ground when they kicked— the crofter would give the recall signal, a shrill, long drawn out whistle made by placing the fingers in the mouth. The dog would return at once.

The division of the Crown Lands, their subsequent sale to the crofters, and the appearance of fences, removed the usefulness of the Corgi. He was still retained as a guard and a companion by some of the hillmen, but to most he was a luxury they could not afford. In many instances he was succeeded by the red herder and by the brindle herder. The original type of Corgi known in Bronant since time immemorial became very scarce, and it is only due to the greatest care on the part of modern breeders that the old strains have been preserved.

Needless to say, stud books were unknown to the Celts and to the early Welsh farmer descendants of the old warrior tribe. But if there were no records, there was a rigid policy of selective breeding that is unsurpassed in this present day. The original Corgis had to be proficient workers, and no mating was consummated without due consideration.

After the breaking up of the Crown Lands, and the introduction of the new breeds, there was a certain amount of experimentation with crosses. The ancient dog of Bronant was crossed with the red herder, but it did not prove very successful and was not attempted many times. The brindle herder, however, made a rather fortuitous cross. The progeny followed the dominant characteristics of the Corgi, and gained a little through the finer coat and the color of the brindle herder. Crossed later with the collie, there was produced the breed known as the heeler.

The principal strains of the Cardigan Welsh Corgi of today go back to the old Bronant Corgi with a slight infusion of brindle herder blood. This dog approximates, as nearly as possible, the dog that enjoyed his greatest popularity in Cardiganshire a century and more ago.

DESCRIPTION AND STANDARD OF POINTS
(By Courtesy of The Cardigan Welsh Corgi Club)

Head.—To be foxy in shape and appearance. Skull to be fairly wide between the ears and flat, tapering towards the eyes. Muzzle to measure about three inches in length (or in proportion to skull as 3 to 5) and to taper towards the snout. Nose to be rather pointed. Teeth—strong, level and sound.

Eyes.—To be of medium size, but giving a sharp and watchful expression, preferably dark in color but clear. Silver eyes permissible in blue merles.

Ears.—Proportionate to size of dog and prominent; preferably pointed at the tips; moderately wide at the base; carried erect and set about 3½ inches apart and well back so that they can be laid flat along neck, sloping forward slightly when erect.

Neck.—To be fairly long and without throatiness, fitting into well sloped and strong muscular shoulders.

Front.—To be slightly bowed, with strong bone; Chest to be moderately broad with prominent breast bone.

Body.—To be fairly long and strong, with deep brisket, well sprung ribs and clearly defined waist. Hind quarters to be strong with muscular thighs.

Feet.—To be round and well-padded. Legs—short and strong (front forelegs slightly bowed or straight). Dew claws removed.

Tail.—To be moderately long and set in line with body (not curled over back) and resembling that of a fox.

[462]

Coat.—Short or medium, of hard texture. Any color except pure white. Other points being equal, preference to be given in following order: Red (Sable, fawn or golden); brindle; black and tan; black and white; blue merles. (White markings are considered to enhance the general appearance.)

Height.—To be as near as possible to 12 inches at shoulder.

Weight.—Dogs 18 to 25 pounds. Bitches, 15 to 22 pounds.

General Appearance, and Expression.—To be as foxy as possible; alertness essential, the body to measure about 34 to 36 inches from point of nose to tip of tail.

Faults.—(Examples.) Over or under-shot mouth; high peaked occiput; prominent cheeks, low flat forehead; expressionless eyes, crooked forearms; splayed feet; tail curled over back; silky coat, etc., etc.

Standard of Points

	Points
Head	15
Eyes	5
Ears	10
Neck	5
Front	10
Body	10
Feet	10
Tail	5
Coat	10
Height	10
General appearance and expression	10
Total	100

WELSH CORGIS (PEMBROKE)

(Illustration facing page 461)

Although all the evidence seems to point to the fact that the Pembroke Welsh Corgi is a much younger dog than the Cardigan Welsh Corgi, it is still true that the Corgi from Pembrokeshire is a breed of great antiquity. No breed that traces its origin back to A.D. 1107 can be regarded as an especially new type of dog.

In modern times there has been an effort to link the two types of Corgi under the heading of a single breed. This is far from the truth, according to W. Lloyd-Thomas, the Welsh authority who has spent so many years digging out the history of these small cattle dogs. He has given some very interesting information, that, while it tends to definitely divorce the two Corgis, gives the Pembroke a colorful past.

The direct ancestors of the Pembroke were brought across the Channel by the Flemish weavers who were induced by Henry I of England to take up their abode in Wales. This occurred in 1107, and it stands as a sturdy cornerstone upon which the development of a breed has been builded.

While weaving was one of their occupations, these Flemish people were also of an agrarian nature, and they soon had transferred to the southwest corner of Wales, at Haverfordwest, the replicas of their model homes and farms in their native land. The dog fitted into this scheme.

This early progenitor of the Pembroke Welsh Corgi of today has been described as having a noticeable resemblance to the older schipperkes. It sprang from the same family that includes the Keeshonden, the Pomeranian, the Samoyede, the chow chow, the Norwegian elkhound, and the Finnish spitz. It has little or nothing of the dachshund characteristics.

In relation to the Cardigan, the Pembroke is higher of body and less lengthy, the legs are straighter and lighter of bone, the coat is more finely textured. Two of the most noticeable differences are in the ears and the tail. Cardigan ears are rounded, while the Pembroke's are pointed at the tip and stand erect. The Cardigan has a long tail, and the Pembroke a short one. In disposition, the Pembroke is more restless, and more easily excited.

If one could see specimens of the early members of both breeds at the same time, the differences would be very marked. In modern times they have become more similar. The whole development of the Pembroke evinces a desire on the part of its breeders to produce a lower and stockier dog. It also may be noted that the head has grown stronger, while, in these times, good sized, round-tipped ears are not unusual.

The manner in which the Pembroke and the Cardigan have approached each other in appearance is not merely a matter of chance or of selective breeding. It is known, rather definitely, that the two were crossed before the middle of the nineteenth century.

The story comes direct from one of the old crofters, a man now nearly 90 years of age, who has spent his whole lifetime in Bronant. It seemed that in his youth, many of the young people in that village found a manner of increasing their pocket money. There were always plenty of the Cardigan puppies. In fact, the majority were a burden on the poor tenant farmers. If these puppies were retained, they would cost money to feed.

WELSH CORGIS—PEMBROKE

One day an enterprising young man tucked a couple of the Corgi puppies under his arm and set forth into a neighboring shire. When he returned there was the jingle of coins in his pocket. Thereafter, other young men followed the example. The old hillman who relates this incident says that he sold puppies to the farmers in Carmarthenshire and in Pembrokeshire.

It is not known whether or not any Cardigan Corgis had gone into Pembrokeshire at an earlier date, but it is quite possible. And it is only logical that if the two breeds were in the same section they would be bred together at some time. So far as known, the Pembroke was not taken into Cardiganshire up to the time of the World War, although since then there have been many instances of inter-matings.

The two breeds of Corgi were mated together frequently at the time when these dogs first came to the consciousness of the bench show fanciers. Little was known about either dog, and crossings were a quite common thing. This practice has been stopped, or practically so, since more information has become available, and all breeders of today are determined to keep the Pembroke distinct from the Cardigan.

The Pembroke is one of the most agreeable of small house dogs. It has an affectionate nature, but it does not force its attentions upon those who are unwilling to accept them. Its intelligence is undoubted, and it is a remarkably alert, ever-vigilant guard of the fireside.

DESCRIPTION AND STANDARD OF POINTS
(By Courtesy of The Welsh Corgi Club, England)

Head.—Like a fox, and wide between the ears.
Jaw.—Medium, inclined to be snipy.

Nose.—Black.

Teeth.—Level and square, large for size of dog.

Eyes.—Well set, round, of medium size and of hazel color.

Ears.—Pricked, medium size.

Neck.—Fairly long.

Chest.—Broad and deep, well let down between the forelegs.

Body.—Of medium length.

Tail.—Natural, preferably short or may be docked.

Ribs.—Well sprung.

Hind Quarters.—Strong and flexible.

Legs and Feet.—The legs short and straight as possible; feet like a collie.

Coat.—Of medium length; dense.

Color.—Any other than pure white.

Weight.—Dog, preferably 20 to 24 pounds. Bitch, preferably 18 pounds to 22 pounds.

Height.—Not exceeding 12 inches at shoulder.

AIREDALE TERRIERS

(Illustration facing page 478)

(By Courtesy of The Airedale Terrier Club of America)

The origin of the Airedale Terrier is enveloped in the same veil of theory and conjecture which shrouds the origin of all species in man's attempt to retrace the stages in evolution. Antique art records the existence of English dogs having a distinct resemblance to the terriers of later days and from which undoubtedly sprang the Broken-haired or Old English Terrier. This extinct Black and Tan tyke is thought by some authorities to have been the common progenitor of the Irish, Fox, Welsh and Airedale Terrier. At all events an admixture of his varying types and sizes from 17 to 30 pounds in weight formed the roots, so to speak, of the genealogical tree of the breed fostered by sporting Yorkshiremen for hunting the fox, badger, weasel, foumart, otter, water rat and small game in the valleys of the rivers Colne, Calder, Warfe and Aire. These constant companions and guardians, while excelling in agility, eyesight, hearing and untiring courage, lacked the keen nose and swimming ability of the rough coated Otter Hound with which they competed in the chase and was the wise reason for crossing the two breeds in the constructive attempt to embody the virtues of both in a better breed of larger and stronger terriers.

From 1864 on, the earlier whelps were called Working, Waterside and Bingley Terriers. They were shown in increasing numbers at local agricultural shows at the time dog shows were in their early growth.

[469]

TERRIERS

In 1879 classes were first provided for Airedale Terriers at the Airedale Agricultural Society's show held at Bingley, Yorkshire. Welsh Terriers received classification at shows in 1883, and the smooth Fox Terrier received separate classifications at Birmingham in 1862.

The towns of Skipton, Bradford, Keighley and Otley followed Bingley with classifications and some years later the competition for the Otley gold medal became the premier win in the breed.

Champion Master Briar (1897-1906) is conceded to be the patriarch of the breed. He may be likened to the trunk of the family tree whose branches grew in many directions.

His great sons, Ch. Clonmel Monarch and Crompton Marvel, carried on his prepotency. The former was exported to Philadelphia, where ardent fanciers moulded the breed in this hemisphere.

Present day winners in most of the countries which breed, exhibit and support the breed with Airedale Terrier Clubs all now trace to the founders of the Modern King of Terriers. This honor goes to Ch. Warland Ditto (1919-1927), the Cragsman King family and the celebrated Warland Kennels, which bred their foundation bitches to Ch. Rhosddu Royalist. His daughter, the International Champion, Warland Strategy, produced the key sire, who when bred to her sister Warland Sprite, produced the great sire Ch. Warland Whatnot. He, in turn sired Clonmel Monarque, whose sons Ch. Clee Courtier and Clee Brigand are responsible for the greater number of today's (1928-1935) champions when bred to bitches by the record sire of Champions, Ch. Flornell Mixer—a Warland Ditto grandson by Moorehead Marquis, whose grandam also owned Ch. Rhosddu Royalist as sire. Warland Ditto, his sire Cragsman Dictator, his dam Ch. Warland Strategy, and her sire Ch. Rhosddu Royalist, were all exported to the U. S. A.

Nearly all of the male lines of former families here and in Great Britian have disappeared, leaving few collateral sires for an out-cross. We still have a few in descendants of Ch. Ridgewood Rocket, Ch. Geelong Cadet and Ch. Briarcroft Perfection—dogs who held their own in competition with imported champions at the large shows.

The degree of perfection of type attained in the breed by those breeders who have carried on the idea of their standard is attested by the frequency with which Airedales have been judged Best of All Breeds in the most important All-Breed shows of England and America. They shine, however, greatest in the minds of their many fond owners who value the faithful attachment, companionship and protection of their families as a priceless possession.

Airedale Terriers are used on great game in Africa, India, Canada and our game lands They were among the first breeds used for police duty in Germany and Great Britain. They have also been used in several wars as dependable dispatch bearers due to their fortitude to stand wounds without faltering at the next order for duty. Their sweet disposition, possibly inherited from the hound blood, has endeared them to many of the best breeders and owners of leading Kennels, many of whom are women who take a pride in showing their own stock. The correct temperament in puppyhood is one of discretion, and when mature, a certain dignified aloofness both with strangers and their kind. Their dispositions can be moulded by the patience of their masters in any environment, but when trained for defense and attack are usually unbeatable for their weight.

TERRIERS

DESCRIPTION AND STANDARD OF POINTS
(By Courtesy of the Airedale Terrier Club of America)

Head.—Long, with flat skull, not too broad between the ears and narrowing slightly to the eyes, free from wrinkle. Stop hardly visible, and cheeks free from fullness. Jaw deep and powerful, well filled up before the eyes, lips tight. Ears V-shaped with a side carriage, small but not out of proportion to the size of the dog. The nose black. The eyes small and dark in color, not prominent, but full of Terrier expression. The teeth strong and level.

Neck.—Should be of moderate length and thickness, gradually widening toward the shoulders and free from throatiness.

Shoulders and Chest.—Shoulders long and sloping well into the back, shoulder-blades flat. Chest deep, but not broad.

Body.—Back short, strong and straight. Ribs well sprung.

Hind Quarters.—Strong and muscular, with no droop. Hocks well let down. The tail set on high and carried gaily, but not curled over the back.

Legs and Feet.—Legs perfectly straight, with plenty of bone. Feet small and round, with a good depth of pad.

Coat.—Hard and wiry, and not so long as to appear ragged; it should also lie straight and close, covering the dog well all over the body and legs.

Color.—The head and ears, with the exception of dark markings on each side of skull, should be tan, the ears being of a darker shade than the rest, the legs up to the thighs and elbows being also tan, the body black or dark grizzle.

Size.—Dogs, 40 to 45 pounds weight. Bitches slightly less.

It is the unanimous opinion of the club that the size of the Airedale Terrier as given in the above standard is one of, if not the most important, characteristics of the breed; all judges who shall henceforth adjudicate on the merits of the Airedale Terrier shall consider the undersized specimens of the breed severely handicapped when competing with dogs of the standard weight.

AIREDALE TERRIERS

	Points
Heads, ears, eyes, mouth	20
Neck, shoulders and chest	10
Body	10
Hind quarters and stern	5
Legs and feet	15
Coat	15
Color	10
General character, expression	15
Total	100

BEDLINGTON TERRIERS

(Illustration facing page 479)

(By Courtesy of The National Bedlington Terrier Club, England)

This unique terrier, known as the Bedlington Terrier takes his name from the mining Shire of that name, in the County of Northumberland, England. He is purely a Northumbrian production and first came to be known as the Rothbury Terrier having originated in the Hannys hills, where the sporting squires loved a game terrier.

The origin of the breed remains shrouded in mystery, but we may go back to 1820, when we find that a Joseph Ainsley of Bedlington acquired a bitch "Phoebe" from a friend at Alnwick.

This bitch was known as Coates Phoebe, owing to the fact, that she found her home at the Vicarage, where young Coates, the Vicar's son had sporting proclivities.

In 1825 Phoebe was mated to a Rothbury dog "Andersons Piper" also acquired by Ainsley of Bedlington and the fruit of this union was the Bedlington Terrier in question.

About this time a colony of Nailers flourished in Bedlington, who took to the breed and became noted for their plucky breed of terriers.

Of his gameness there is not the slightest doubt, he never shirked at any kind of vermin and could more than hold his own at drawing a Badger or at ratting in or out of Wales.

Although many crosses were introduced, there was always a band of enthusiastic admirers who kept to the

[475]

original breed, and it was not until 1877 that the National Bedlington Terrier Club (England) was formed by a few influential fanciers, who made themselves responsible for bringing him to the notice of the public, by exhibiting him fearlessly on the show bench.

Since then he has made vast improvement in type. Whereas in the old days a man who owned a Bedlington was certainly sure to be known as a fighter, such a reputation had this game and courageous terrier. Many tales have been told by the older generation, of matches made, by the miners and Nailers of that period, where large sums were at stake on the result of a fight between terriers of their respective fancies. The Bedlington was never a mischief seeker, but once started fighting, it was to the death. He neither gave nor asked quarter.

As time went on, he found his way into the homes of the elite, who found him tractable and a first class companion. Becoming more domesticated, he was not long in developing into a pet, his great heart and lovable nature endearing him to all who are fortunate enough to own him.

There are two distinct colors, viz: Liver and Blue, and it is only a question of fancy which is preferred, while some fanciers swore by the liver, others were just as emphatic in adhering to the blue.

In the early days the liver was much in evidence and some great dogs were of that color, and in fact the liver dog was preferred to the blue which is now so fashionable.

Whether the former shade has become rarer from a change of tastes on the part of Bedlington breeders, or whether it is merely a coincidence that so few good liver-colored specimens happen to be shown at the present time, we are unable to say, but the fact remains that of late, high class Blue Bedlingtons outnumber the good liver ones in a very large proportion.

It is all a matter of fancy, the principal breeders and exhibitors would just as soon have a Liver as a Blue so long as he is a good one.

There were and have been many good specimens of both colors, and it is noticeable that the mother of the celebrated "Piper" was a blue-black bitch, but possessing a light colored top-knot which characteristic has been religiously preserved.

Both Piper and his mother, Phoebe, were considerably lighter in weight and smaller in stature than the dogs of the present day, and it may be said that it is on record that Piper was set on a Badger at eight months old, and was constantly at work, more or less on badgers, foxes, otters and other vermin. He drew a badger after he was fourteen years old, when he was toothless and nearly blind, after several other Terriers had failed.

There are not many today that would face a badger, owing no doubt to the fact that many ladies have adopted him and he is becoming more and more of a pet, although the old fire is latent within him, for when his jealous nature is aroused, will fight for his place in one's affection.

One reason why this desirable terrier became less numerous was the trimming necessary for the show bench, this trimming being only known to a few so-called experts, but most owners now trim their own, and find it quite easy. After once seeing it done by someone who knows, with a little practice, the novice soon becomes expert.

He is not difficult to rear, being of a hardy nature, and his feeding is the same as other terriers of a like weight.

DESCRIPTION AND STANDARD OF POINTS

(Adopted by the Bedlington Terrier Club of America and Approved by The American Kennel Club, February 17, 1937)

Skull.—Narrow, but deep and rounded, high at the occiput, wedge-shaped, covered with profuse top-knot, which should be nearly white, and, when trimmed, should give a Roman nose appearance.

Jaws.—Long and tapering. There must be no "stop" and the line from occiput to nose end straight and unbroken. Well filled up beneath the eye. Close fitting lips, no flew.

Teeth.—Level or pincer-jawed. The teeth should be large and strong.

Nose.—The nostrils must be large and well defined. Blues and blue and tans have black noses; livers, sandies, etc., have brown noses.

Eyes.—Small, bright and well sunk. The ideal eyes have the appearance of being triangular. Blue should have a dark eye; blue and tans have light eyes with amber lights; liver and sandies have a light hazel eye.

Ears.—Moderate sized, filbert shaped; set on low and hanging flat to the cheek. They should be covered with short, fine hair, with a fringe of silky hair at the tip.

Legs and Feet.—Muscular and moderate length. The hindlegs, by reason of the roach back and arched loin, have the appearance of being longer than the forelegs. The forelegs should be straight, with a moderately wide chest and hare feet.

Body.—Muscular, yet markedly flexible. Flat ribbed and deep through the brisket, well ribbed up. The chest should be deep and fairly broad. The back should be roached and the loin markedly arched. Light, muscular, galloping quarters, which are also fine and graceful.

Neck.—Long, tapering arched neck, deep at the base. The neck should spring well from the shoulders, which should be flat, and head should be carried high.

[478]

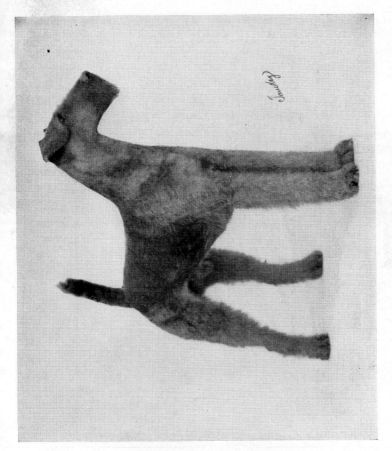

AIREDALE

BEDLINGTON TERRIER

BEDLINGTON TERRIERS

Coat.—The coat is very distinctive and unlike that of any other terrier, in that it should be thick and linty (not wiry), and when in show condition should not exceed one inch in length. It should be brushed on the body and back from the root of the tail toward the head, and should not lie flat against the body. There should be an absence of hair on the ears except at the tip, where the *fringe* should be from one-half to one inch long. The hair on the legs should be slightly longer and straighter than that of the body. The top-knot should be highest at the occiput and taper gradually to just in back of the nose. It (the top-knot) should be rounded from side to side from an imaginary line drawn from the outer corner of the eye to the top of the ear on one side to a like line on the opposite side.

Tail.—Of moderate length, thick at the root, tapering to a point and gracefully curved, slightly feathered, nine to eleven inches long, scimitar shaped, carried elevated but not over the back.

Color.—Blue, blue and tan, liver, liver and tan, sandy, sandy and tan.

Height.—About 15 or 16 inches.

Weight.—Dogs, about 24 pounds; bitches, about 22 pounds.

Action.—Very distinctive. Rather mincing, light and springy, must gallop like a greyhound, with the whole body.

General.—A graceful, lithe but not shelly, muscular dog, with no sign of coarseness or weakness. The whole head should be pear-shaped or wedge-shaped. The expression in repose is mild and gentle. When roused, the eyes should sparkle, and the dog look full of temper and courage.

Value of Points

Head	20
Size	10
Teeth	10
Color	5
Legs and Feet	10
Ears	5
Eyes	5
Nose	5

TERRIERS

Body	....	15
Coat	....	10
Tail	....	5
Total	....	100

BORDER TERRIERS

(Illustration facing page 494)

(By Courtesy of The Border Terrier Club, England)

As the name conveys, the Border Terrier had its origin on either side of the Cheviot Hills which form the Border country, and may be regarded as one of the very oldest breeds of terriers in Great Britain.

It is purely a "working terrier" and it is known to many that for generations Border farmers, shepherds and sportsmen carefully preserved a particular strain of terrier which could be found in almost every Border homestead.

With the hills at their disposal and miles from habitation, stock were subjected to the ravages of the big and powerful hill foxes, and the Border farmer and shepherd required a dead game terrier to hunt and kill them, with length of leg sufficient to follow a horse, yet small enough to follow a fox to ground.

These terriers had naturally to be active, strong and tireless, and to have sound weather-resisting coats in order to withstand prolonged exposure to drenching rains and mists in the hills. The Border Terrier is the most tireless hard-worker for his size and is full of pluck; there is no wall he cannot get over or wire entanglement he is unable to scramble through; should the fox run to earth he will bolt him every time, or stay the night in the earth until the matter is settled from his point of view.

It may therefore be gathered that in order to meet these requirements the Border Terrier, as now known, was evolved by a process of judicious selection from the native hill terriers.

Until the English Kennel Club recognition was given, the Border Terrier was, to the great majority, unknown, but was always exhibited and in considerable numbers at most of the Agricultural Societies' shows in the Border country. Following recognition by the English Kennel Club and the formation of The Border Terrier Club in 1920, the breed is catered to at most of the important shows in the British Isles, but very few are as yet seen at the shows in the United States. Much has been accomplished in the improvement of the breed, and no departure has been made from its natural vocation, or from the real Border Terrier characteristics, which are the primary objects of The Border Terrier Club in England in order to preserve this ancient and popular breed of sporting terrier.

DESCRIPTION AND STANDARD OF POINTS
(By Courtesy of The Border Terrier Club, England)

The Border Terrier is essentially a working terrier, and it being necessary that it should be able to follow a horse, must combine activity with gameness.

Weight.—Dogs between 13 and 15½ pounds; bitches between 11½ and 14 pounds.

Head.—Like that of an otter, moderately broad in the skull with a short, strong muzzle, level teeth, a black nose is preferred but a liver or flesh colored one is not a disqualification.

Eye.—Dark with keen expression.

Ears.—Small V-shaped of moderate thickness and dropping forward close to the cheek.

Loin.—Strong.

Body.—Deep and narrow and fairly long; ribs carried well back, but not over-sprung as a terrier should be capable of being

BORDER TERRIERS

spanned by both hands behind the shoulder; forelegs straight and not too heavy in bone; feet small with thick pads; stern moderately short and fairly thick at the base then tapering, set high and carried gaily but not curled over the back, hind quarters racing.

Coat.—Harsh and dense with close undercoat.

Skin.—Thick.

Color.—Red, Wheaten, Grizzle and Tan or Blue and Tan.

	Points
Head, ears, neck and teeth	20
Legs and feet	15
Coat and skin	10
Shoulders and chest	10
Eyes and expression	10
Back and loin	10
Hind quarters	10
Tail	5
General appearance	10
Total	100

BULLTERRIERS

(Illustrations facing pages 495 and 496)

(By Courtesy of The Bullterrier Club of America)

The Bullterrier dates back about 100 years. It is almost unanimously admitted that the breed was established by breeding a bull dog to a white English terrier, which breed is now extinct. The results were known as the bull and terrier. Some few years later, to gain size, the bull and terrier was crossed with the Spanish pointer and even to this day, occasionally is seen evidence of the pointer inheritance.

In those early days, the sporting writer gave much time and space writing about the new breed. Then about 75 years ago the fancy decided that an entirely white dog would be more attractive, and James Hinks produced the white dog, which was immediately taken up most enthusiastically by the young bloods of the day, as the most fashionable dog.

It was a dog for sportsmen. We must remember "other times, other customs"—and in those days, life in general was more strenuous, of rougher, coarser fibre, and dog fights were allowed and attended by all.

The Bullterrier was called the gladiator of the canine world. As such a dog he had to be of great strength, greater agility and the greatest courage. Withal, he was bred by gentlemen, for gentlemen, for those who had a great sense of fair play, who scorned the liar and the deceiver in any game. The dog was taught and trained to be a courageous dog, able to defend himself and his master, yet he was not to seek or provoke a dog fight—

and so the white variety became known as "The White Cavalier" a title which he bears with distinction to this day.

Contrary to the opinion of those who do not know him, he is an exceedingly friendly dog, and thrives upon affection, yet he is always ready for a fight and frolic. The standard calls for a dog 12 to 60 pounds but today, there are but very few 12 pound dogs. A few 20 to 30 pounds, more 35 and most above that weight. The general opinion here in this country demands a male dog about 50 pounds, a female about 45 pounds, yet the dog should be a well balanced specimen, not at all freaky in any particular but a clear, well put together, well balanced, active, agile athlete—a Gladiator of perfect form.

DESCRIPTION AND STANDARD OF POINTS FOR THE WHITE BULLTERRIER

(As Amended by the Bullterrier Club of America, February 10, 1936, and Approved by The American Kennel Club, March 14, 1936)

General Appearance is that of a symmetrical animal, an embodiment of agility, grace, strength, and determination, and in whose formation there should be an entire absence of exaggeration of any kind.

Head.—Should be long, but type should not be sacrificed to length. Skull flat and widest at the ears. Viewed from above, it should taper gradually and merge into the muzzle without break in the line. Foreface, filled right up to the eyes, should have a perceptible "downness" without "stop" and without noticeable brow. Eyes very small, black, set close together and obliquely. They should be triangular. Muzzle wide and tapering, but without such tapering as to make the nose appear pinched or snipey. Nose broad, wholly black and with wide open nostrils. Under jaw strong and well defined. Lips should fit tightly and evenly and should not run too far back. There must be an entire absence

BULLTERRIERS

of "lippiness." Teeth sound, strong, clean, regular and meeting evenly. Any deviation, such as "undershot" or "overshot," is a bad fault. Ears, when standing erect, should not cause conspicuous wrinkling of the skin on the head. Ears should be comparatively small, carried erect, of moderate length, either cropped or uncropped. It is important that there be as little cheek as possible; but, where it is present, it should not be bunchy nor prominent but should merge gradually into the lines of the muzzle and neck.

Neck.—Slightly arched, neither long nor short, tapering from shoulders to head and free from looseness of skin.

Shoulders.—Strong and muscular, but without any appearance of heaviness or "loading." Shoulder blades wide, flat and sloping well back.

Back.—Short, strong, and muscular. Should be higher at withers than at hips. There should be no slackness nor falling away back of the withers. Back should be only slightly arched at loin; loins well developed; flanks only slightly tucked. Ribs well sprung, with no falling away back of the shoulders. Ribs close together and intercostal muscles well developed; back ribs deep. Chest deep from withers to brisket, and wide from front to back ribs, and broad as viewed facing the dog.

Tail.—Short, straight, set on low, thicker where it joins the body. Should not reach below the hocks; should not be carried above the level of the back.

Legs.—Should be big boned. Forelegs straight with strong and upright pasterns, but without the stiltedness of the foxterrier. The elbows should not turn outward. Thighs, thick and wide; upper thighs, long, with muscle well developed, but without "loading." Hocks well let down. Hindlegs should turn neither in nor out as viewed from behind and carried back. Hind pasterns, short and upright.

Feet.—Compact with the toes well arched; resembling those of the cat. Pads thick and tough. Nails short and strong.

Coat.—Dense, short, flat, stiff to the touch and with fine gloss. Skin should fit the dog tightly.

Gait.—Springy, and swinging, without roll or pace.

Color.—White.

TERRIERS

Weight.—From 25 to 60 pounds, inclusive, for standard variety. Under 25 pounds shall be classed as miniatures.

Faults.—Markings; ticked coat; light bone; legginess; round eyes; badly placed eyes; domed skull; butterfly nose; pronounced cheekiness; dished faced; lippiness; throatiness; teeth not meeting evenly; long or slack back; long, thick or "gay" tail; loose shoulders; crooked elbows; loaded shoulders or thighs; weak pasterns; big feet; splay feet; toes turning in or out; soft coat; narrow chest; ewe neck.

Disqualifications.—Markings behind the set on of head; deafness; wall eye; pig jaw; tail carried over the back; wholly flesh-colored nose.

DESCRIPTION AND STANDARD OF POINTS FOR THE COLORED BULLTERRIER

(Approved by the Board of Directors of The American Kennel Club, May 12, 1936)

General Appearance is that of a symmetrical animal, an embodiment of agility, grace, strength, and determination, and in whose formation there should be an entire absence of exaggeration of any kind.

Head.—Should be long, but type should not be sacrificed to length. Skull flat and widest at the ears. Viewed from above, it should taper gradually and merge into the muzzle without break in the line. Foreface, filled right up to the eyes, should have a perceptible "downness" without "stop" and without noticeable brow. Eyes very small, black, set close together and obliquely. They should be triangular. Muzzle wide and tapering, but without such tapering as to make the nose appear pinched or snipey. Nose broad, wholly black and with wide open nostrils. Under jaw strong and well defined. Lips should fit tightly and evenly and should not run too far back. There must be an entire absence of "lippiness." Teeth sound, strong, clean, regular and meeting evenly. Any deviation, such as "undershot" or "overshot," is a bad fault. Ears, when standing erect, should not cause conspicuous wrinkling of the skin on the head. Ears should be compara-

[488]

tively small, carried erect, of moderate length, either cropped or uncropped. It is important that there be as little cheek as possible, but, where it is present, it should not be bunchy nor prominent, but should merge gradually into the lines of the muzzle and neck.

Neck.—Slightly arched, neither long nor short, tapering from shoulders to head and free from looseness of skin.

Shoulders.—Strong and muscular, but without any appearance of heaviness or "loading." Shoulder blades wide, flat and sloping well back.

Back.—Short, strong, and muscular. Should be higher at withers than at hips. There should be no slackness nor falling away back of the withers. Back should be only slightly arched at loin; loins well developed; flanks only slightly tucked. Ribs well sprung, with no falling away back of the shoulders. Ribs close together and intercostal muscles well developed; back ribs deep. Chest deep from withers to brisket, and wide from front to back ribs, and broad as viewed facing the dog.

Tail.—Short, straight, set on low, thicker where it joins the body. Should not reach below the hocks; should not be carried above the level of the back.

Legs.—Should be big boned. Forelegs straight with strong and upright pasterns, but without the stiltedness of the foxterrier. The elbows should not turn outward. Thighs, thick and wide; upper thighs, long, with muscle well developed, but without "loading." Hocks well let down. Hindlegs should turn neither in nor out as viewed from behind and carried back. Hind pasterns, short and upright.

Feet.—Compact, with the toes well arched; resembling those of the cat. Pads thick and tough. Nails short and strong.

Coat.—Dense, short, flat, stiff to the touch and with fine gloss. Skin should fit the dog tightly.

Gait.—Springy, and swinging, without roll or pace.

Color.—Any color other than white, or any color with white markings. White not to predominate.

Faults.—Light bone, legginess; round eyes; badly placed eyes; domed skull; butterfly nose; pronounced cheekiness; dished face; lippiness; throatiness; teeth not meeting evenly; long or slack back; long, thick or "gay" tail; loose shoulders; crooked elbows; loaded shoulders or thighs; weak pasterns; big feet; splay feet; toes turning in or out; soft coat; narrow chest; ewe neck.

Disqualifications.—Deafness; wall eye; pig jaw; tail carried over the back; wholly flesh colored nose.

CAIRN TERRIERS

(Illustration facing page 497)

(By Courtesy of The Terrier Club of America)

The history of the Cairn Terrier is enhanced by the fact that the modern Cairn is an attempt to preserve in his typical form the old time working terrier of the Isle of Skye. The fancier, for a proper appreciation of the Cairn, should know what the uses and appearance of these terriers were.

Fortunately weights, engravings, measurements, descriptions of their appearance, and accounts of the use of these terriers exist. From Martin's "History of the Dog" in 1845, Capt. McDonald's description and measurements of the ideal Cairn in 1876, from Ross' "Cairn Terrier," Darley Matheson's "Terriers," and many other writers it is plain that these were working terriers, having courage, used for the bolting of otter, foxes, and other vermin from among rocks, cliffs and ledges on the wild shores of their Misty Isle.

Considerable variation in the appearance of these terriers undoubtedly existed in these early times as each breeder had his own fancies. But continued selection for a definite purpose, which is the final factor in the development of any breed, soon resulted in the production of a rather definite type. This was a terrier weighing from 14 to 16 pounds, with the bitches two pounds or so under these weights; active, game, rather longish in body, short on the leg, with short, pointed muzzle, broad head, ears short, erect, pointed, and set wide apart; large, expressive, dark eyes; with hard coat not over an inch and a half long with a soft furry undercoat—admirably suited to its purpose.

His peculiarity of form which gave him great activity, his sporting instincts and vermin killing abilities made him a useful member of the laird and crofter's households. Becoming popular with those who desired a sporting terrier up to hunting in all weather, he was taken up by the fanciers and was admitted to the English Kennel Club's Stud Book as a recognized breed—the Cairn Terrier.

The keeping of this breed to its best old working type was the ideal aimed at in breeding by the English Cairn Terrier Club on its formation. The Cairn Terrier Club of America has the same object. Both Clubs have the same ideal weight for dogs 14 pounds or a stone. The two standards with only slight differences in wording describe the same dog—the old time terrier of the Isle of Skye and the West Highlands of Scotland.

The Cairn has characteristics in common with other breeds of terriers. He should have a level back with tail set on at back level, straight front, well sloped shoulders, deep brisket, strong loins and hind quarters, compact thick pads and feet—and should move easily and freely on a loose lead with marked terrier smartness and style.

But while these points of contact with other breeds of terriers exist, there are also marked differences which are of the greatest importance to the continuation of the breeds distinctive qualities which should be understood by the breeder and the judge.

In head, the Cairn differs from all other terriers. Short and broad headed, his foreface should be little, if any, longer than the distance from stop to occiput. The muzzle should be rather pointed and not too heavy or deep. He should have a well defined stop, and a slight indentation between the eyes flattening out into his broad skull. The ears should be set wide apart, neither too far down on the side, nor too high up on the head. They should be small, short, pointed, erect, and free from long hairs. The Cairn's expression should be keen, alert, varminty and hard bitten. He should have a medium sized, dark hazel eye, distinct eyelashes, and shaggy protecting brows. He should have plenty of head furnishings which may be softer than his body coat. Lack of these spoils the characteristic appearance of the Cairn's head, which is perhaps, the most important feature of the breed. A Cairn with a good head is half through in the show ring, and without being typical in head he should be nowhere.

The height of the Cairn from the ground differs from other terriers and is important in giving to the breed its distinctive conformation which the late Mr. Glynn called "Cairnishness." His height at the top of the shoulder should be about 9½ inches, and this height should be slightly less than two-thirds his body length. He is distinctly not so low to ground, and in proportion to his size, is slightly longer in back, than the Sealyham or Scottish Terrier. He should be built like a race horse, and everything about his conformation should give the definite impression of great activity—one of the breed's chief assets.

The Cairn's appearance is greatly enhanced by his typical coat, which should be double, a harsh outer jacket capable of protecting him in all weather and quite profuse, and a soft furry undercoat. Any color except white is permissible and dark points—muzzle, ears and tail are most desirable, and with the lighter body colors adds greatly to the breed's uniqueness. He is not a trimmed breed, only a certain amount of "tidying up" being allowable. He should always be shown in good coat and with plenty of head furnishings, for a proper coat is one of the breed's most distinctive features, and is an essential in the show ring, which judges should know.

The faults of the Cairn which are of the most importance are those which affect his distinctive breed type— lack of typical head qualities, proper conformation, and proper coat.

Head faults; long and strong forefaces; over and undershot mouths; lack of sufficient stop; too large, round tipped, too close and too high set on ears; narrow skull; and eyes which are too large, protruding, yellow, ringed or too small shoe button black eyes denoting modern Scottish Terrier blood, all are bad faults.

In conformation, he should not be either noticeably too high from or too low to ground, nor too short nor too long in back. Bad fronts, thin ferrety feet, lack of sufficient bone and substance, and any suggestion of cloddiness which hampers activity are bad.

The coat is one of the breed's most important features, and any deficiency in body coat, head furnishings or hair on the legs should be penalized.

There is one, and only one, correct size for the Cairn Terrier. He should weigh 14 pounds for dogs, 13 pounds for bitches, and should be in proper proportions to those weights. This point should be understood by all judges and dogs obviously over or undersized should be severely handicapped when competing with dogs of correct standard size.

Dogs which show marked terrier smartness and style at all times in the show ring should have an edge over those which will show only occasionally.

The modern Cairn should have the hardiness and be able to meet the performance of its old time prototype. The utility of a breed to its purpose should be the aim

BORDER TERRIER

BULLTERRIER (*White*)

of the breeder, and the basic thought in careful judging. It should not be forgotten that it is the expressed object of the Cairn Terrier Clubs, to preserve the breed in its best old working type. If the breed is to resist passing fads, the inroads of modernization, and maintain its distinctive breed identity the first consideration in judging should be given to those qualities which are unique to the Cairn.

DESCRIPTION AND STANDARD OF POINTS

(Adopted by The Cairn Terrier Club of America, 1938, and Approved by The American Kennel Club, May 10, 1938)

1. *General Appearance.*—That of an active, game, hardy, small working terrier of the short legged class; very free in its movements, strongly but not heavily built, standing well forward on its forelegs, deep in the ribs, well coupled with strong hind quarters and presenting a well proportioned build with a medium length of back, having a hard weather resisting coat; head shorter and wider than any other terrier and well furnished with hair giving a general foxy expression.

2. *Skull.*—Broad in proportion to length with a decided stop and well furnished with hair on the top of the head, which may be somewhat softer than the body coat.

3. *Muzzle.*—Strong but not too long or heavy. Teeth large—mouth neither over or undershot. Nose black.

4. *Eyes.*—Set wide apart, rather sunken, with shaggy eyebrows, medium in size, hazel or dark hazel in color, depending on body color, with a keen terrier expression.

5. *Ears.*—Small, pointed, well carried erectly, set wide apart on the side of the head. Free from long hairs.

6. *Tail.*—In proportion to head, well furnished with hair but not feathery. Carried gaily but must not curl over back. Set on at back level.

7. *Body.*—Well muscled strong active body with well sprung deep ribs, coupled to strong hind quarters with a level back of me-

dium length giving an impression of strength and activity without heaviness.

8. *Shoulders, Legs and Feet.*—A sloping shoulder, medium length of leg, good but not too heavy bone; forelegs should not be out at elbows, and be perfectly straight, but forefeet may be slightly turned out. Forefeet larger than hindfeet. Legs must be covered with hard hair. Pads should be thick and strong and dog should stand well up on its feet.

9. *Coat.*—Hard and weather resistant. Must be double coated with profuse harsh outer coat with short, soft, close furry undercoat.

10. *Color.*—May be of any color except white. Dark ears, muzzle and tail tip are desirable.

11. *Ideal Size.*—Involves the weight, the height at the withers and the length of body. Weight for bitches 13 pounds, for dogs 14 pounds. Height at the withers—bitches 9½ inches, dogs 10 inches. Length of body from 14¼ to 15 inches from the front of the chest to back of hind quarters. The dog must be of balanced proportions and appear neither leggy or too low to ground; and neither too short or too long in body. Weight and measurements are for matured dogs at two years of age. Older dogs may weigh slightly in excess and growing dogs under these weights and measurements.

12. *Condition.*—Dogs should be shown in good hard flesh, well muscled and neither too fat or thin. Should be in full good coat with plenty of head furnishings, be clean, combed, brushed and tidied up on ears, tail, feet and general outline. Should move freely and easily on a loose lead, should not cringe on being handled, should stand up on their toes and show with marked terrier characteristics.

Faults

1. *Skull.*—Too narrow in skull.

2. *Muzzle.*—Too long and heavy a foreface—mouth over or undershot.

3. *Eyes.*—Too large, prominent, yellow, ringed, are all objectionable.

BULLTERRIER *(Colored)*

BULLTERRIER *(Colored)*

CAIRN TERRIER

4. *Ears.*—Too large, round at points, set too close together, set too high on the head; heavily covered with hair.

5. *Legs and Feet.*—Too light or too heavy bone. Crooked forelegs or out at elbow. Thin ferrety feet; feet let down on the heel or too open and spread. Too high or too low on the leg.

6. *Body.*—Too short back and compact a body, hampering quickness of movement and turning ability. Too long, weedy and snaky a body giving an impression of weakness. Tail set on too low. Back not level.

7. *Coat.*—Open coats, blousy coats, too short or dead coats, lack of sufficient under-coat, lack of head furnishings, lack of hard hair on the legs. Silkiness or curliness. A slight wave permissible.

8. *Nose.*—Flesh or light colored nose.

9. *Color.*—White on chest, feet or other parts of body.

DANDIE DINMONT TERRIERS

(Illustration facing page 508)

*(By Courtesy of The Dandie Dinmont Terrier Club of
America)*

Most dog fanciers describe terriers as being composed
of straight lines and sharp angles. In the Dandie Dinmont we have a terrier that is made up of curves. His
weasel-like body was developed by careful breeding for
the purpose of going to ground for all kinds of "Varmint"
from rats to foxes. He has that which few terriers possess, dignity and reserve, combined with the love of a
real "roughhouse" when his master so desires. This
makes him an ideal companion whether for a brisk walk
over the hills or through the woods where he will be all
alert for everything that starts, or next to the fireside
where he is always near you watching your every movement with his deep bright eyes. Watch the Dandie in
the show-ring minding his own affairs with the dignity
of a Great Dane in marked contrast to the perpetual
scraps of some of the other terriers. However, when
aroused he has the grit to tackle anything of any size
and will fight to the finish, either of himself or of his
opponent. As a watch dog he is unexcelled and woebe-
tide the tramp or beggar that trespasses.

He was bred from selected specimens of the rough
native terrier of the Border hunters in the Cheviot Hills
between England and Scotland and was first recorded as
a distinct type or breed of terrier about 1700. He was
distinguished by his pre-eminence in hunting the otter and
the badger. A direct line of these dogs descended to the

farmers in the Teviotdale Hills where Sir Walter Scott in his travellings chanced upon them and made them famous in his "Guy Mannering" published in 1814. His character Dandie Dinmont, a farmer, supposed to have been a Mr. James Davidson of Hindlee near Hawick, kept and raised the immortal six terriers, "Auld Pepper, Auld Mustard, Young Pepper, Young Mustard, Little Pepper and Little Mustard." Sir Walter gives in "Guy Mannering" an excellent description of their pluck, "I had them a' regularly entered, first wi' rottens, then wi' stots or weasles, and then wi' the tods and brocks, and now they fear naething that ever cam' wi' a hairy skin on't." From the time of the popularity of "Guy Mannering" to the present day the breed has been known as "Dandie Dinmont's Terriers."

There is an excellent picture of a Dandie in the portrait of Henry, third Duke of Buccleuch, painted by Gainsborough in 1770. The present Dandie is identical to the one in this portrait. King Louis Philippe of France owned a pair of Dandies in 1845.

Today the hunting qualities of the Dandie are not so often required but his other sterling qualities make him an excellent house-dog. He is very fond of children, makes an excellent guard, and is of outstanding intelligence. He has a strong will of his own and will sometimes reluctantly obey a command with a loving look of "I'll do it but please don't make me."

The points of a Dandie are quite the opposite of the average terrier—there are no straight lines. Head, large with a full domed skull; eyes, large, full, of a very deep hazel and luminous,—the darker the better; jaw, strong, deep, and punishing; body, long, with a slightly arched roach between the center back and the tail, combined with a broad, deep, and powerful chest; front legs, short, with paws slightly outcurved for digging; hind legs, longer and not so heavy at front; tail, set low, slightly curved and carried at an angle of about 45 degrees,—the shorter and heavier the tail, the better; colors,—there are two distinct colors, pepper—blue grey to light silver with light tan or silver points and very light grey or white top-knot,—mustard—dark ochre color to cream with white points and topknot,—darker shades in each color are the more desirable; coat,—the Dandie has not a wire coat but has a rough double coat made up of hard and soft hair in the proportion of about double the amount of soft hair to that of hard. This forms a very thorough watershed. It feels crisp to the touch but does not have the harsh feel of the wire coated dog. The topknot and points of the ears are of light silky white hair which when fluffed up forms one of the characteristic features of the "Show" Dandie. In connection with this it might be added that in England and increasingly over here the Dandies are shown in their natural state with very little plucking and clipping,—just combed and brushed. A Dandie can be kept in show shape with only a daily brushing and comb-ing which eliminates the three or four expensive visits to the dog beauty parlor as is the case of many of the other terrier breeds.

Dandies fit in any life whether a rough and tumble out of doors life or the confines of a city apartment. They are an ideal size, between 18 and 24 pounds, small enough to fit a small apartment and yet a dog big in character. The Dandies are becoming increasingly popular for as all Dandie owners state, "once you own a Dandie you never like any other dog as well."

TERRIERS

DESCRIPTION AND STANDARD OF POINTS
(By Courtesy of The Dandie Dinmont Terrier Club of America)

Head.—Strongly made and large, not out of proportion to the dog's size, the muscles showing extraordinary development, more especially the maxillary. *Skull* broad between the ears, getting gradually less towards the eyes, and measuring about the same from the inner corner of the eye to back of skull as it does from ear to ear. The forehead well domed. The head is *covered* with very soft silky hair, which should not be confined to a mere topknot, and the lighter in color and silkier it is the better. The *Cheeks,* starting from the ears proportionately with the skull have a gradual taper towards the muzzle, which is deep and strongly made, and measures about three inches in length, or in proportion to skull as three is to five. The *Muzzle* is covered with hair of a little darker shade than the topknot, and of the same texture as the feather of the forelegs. The top of the muzzle is generally bare for about an inch from the back part of the nose, the bareness coming to a point towards the eye, and being about one inch broad at the nose. The nose and inside of *Mouth* black or dark colored. The *Teeth* very strong, especially the canine, which are of extraordinary size for such a small dog. The canines fit well into each other, so as to give the greatest available holding and punishing power, and the teeth are level in front, the upper ones very slightly overlapping the under ones. [Many of the finest specimens have a "swine mouth," which is very objectionable, but it is not so great an objection as the protrusion of the under jaw.]

Eyes.—Set wide apart, large, full, round, bright, expressive of great determination, intelligence and dignity; set low and prominent in front of the head; color, a rich dark hazel.

Ears.—Pendulous, set well back, wide apart, and low on the skull, hanging close to the cheek, with a very slight projection at the base, broad at the junction of the head and tapering almost to a point, the fore part of the ear tapering very little—the tapering being mostly on the back part, the fore part of the ear coming almost straight down from its junction with the head to the tip. They should harmonize in color with the body color. In the case of a Pepper dog they are covered with a soft straight brownish hair (in some cases almost black). In the case of a Mustard dog the hair should be mustard in color, a shade darker than the body, but not black. All should have a thin feather of light hair starting about two inches from the tip, and of nearly the same color and texture as the topknot, which gives the ear the appearance of a *distinct point.* The animal is often one or two years old before the feather is shown. The cartilage and skin of the ear should not be thick, but rather thin. Length of ear from three to four inches.

Neck.—Very muscular, well-developed and strong, showing great power of resistance, being well set into the shoulders.

Body.—Long, strong and flexible; ribs well sprung and round, chest well developed and let well down between the fore legs; the back rather low at the shoulder, having a slight downward curve and a corresponding arch over the loins, with a very slight gradual drop from top of loins to root of tail; both sides of backbone well supplied with muscle.

Tail.—Rather short, say from eight inches to ten inches, and covered on the upper side with wiry hair of darker color than that of the body, the hair on the under side being lighter in color and not so wiry, with nice feather about two inches long, getting shorter as it nears the tip; rather thick at the root, getting thicker for about four inches, then tapering off to a point. It should not be twisted or curled in any way, but should come up with a curve like a scimitar, the tip, when excited, being in a perpendicular line with the root of the tail. It should neither be set on too high nor too low. When not excited it is carried gaily, and a little above the level of the body.

Legs.—The forelegs short, with immense muscular development and bone, set wide apart, the chest coming well down between them. The feet well formed, *and not flat,* with very strong brown or dark-colored claws. Bandy legs and flat feet are objectionable. The hair on the forelegs and feet of a Pepper dog should be tan, varying according to the body color from a rich tan to a pale fawn; of a Mustard dog they are of a darker shade than its head, which is a creamy white. In both colors there is a nice feather, about two inches long, rather lighter in color than the hair on the fore part of the leg. The hindlegs are a little longer than the fore ones, and are set rather wide apart but not spread out in an unnatural manner, while the feet are much smaller; the thighs are well developed, and the hair of the same color and texture as the fore ones, but having no feather or dewclaws; the whole claws should be dark;

but the claws of all vary in shade according to the color of the dog's body.

Coat.—This is a very important point; the hair should be about two inches long; that from skull to root of tail, a mixture of hardish and soft hair, which gives a sort of crisp feel to the hand. The hard should not be wiry; the coat is what is termed piley or pencilled. The hair on the under part of the body is lighter in color and softer than on the top. The skin on the belly accords with the color of dog.

Color.—The color is Pepper or Mustard. The Pepper ranges from a dark bluish black to a light silvery grey, the intermediate shades being preferred, the body color coming well down the shoulder and hips, gradually merging into the leg color. The Mustards vary from a reddish brown to a pale fawn, the head being a creamy white, the legs and feet of a shade darker than the head. The claws are dark as in other colors. [Nearly all Dandie Dinmont Terriers have some white on the chest, and some have also white claws.]

Size.—The height should be from eight to eleven inches at the top of shoulder. Length from top of shoulder to root of tail should not be more than twice the dog's height, but preferably one or two inches less.

Weight.—From 14 pounds to 24 pounds; the best weight as near 18 pounds as possible. These weights are for dogs in good working condition.

The relative value of the several points in the standard are apportioned as follows:

	Points
Head	10
Eyes	10
Ears	10
Neck	5
Body	20
Tail	5
Legs and feet	10
Coat	15
Color	5
Size and weight	5
General appearance	5
Total	100

FOX TERRIERS (SMOOTH AND WIRE-HAIRED)

(Illustration facing page 509)

(By Courtesy of The American Foxterrier Club)

The Fox Terrier is perhaps the best known and most widely distributed of all pure bred dogs. You will find a Fox Terrier wherever the English language is spoken. Clubs have been formed in Belgium, France, Germany, Italy and other European countries to promote the interests of the Fox Terrier.

The Fox Terrier is an ancient breed of English origin. In 1790 Colonel Thornton's Pitch, a smooth coated white terrier with markings was recorded both in print and on canvas. It is probable that the Smooth and the Wire sprang from widely different sources. A profound student of the related breeds claims that the ancestor of the Wire was the old rough-coated black and tan working terrier of Wales, Derbyshire and Durham, and that the more important ancestors of the Smooth were the Smooth coated black and tan, the Bullterrier, the Greyhound and the Beagle.

The Smooth antedated the Wire by some fifteen or twenty years in the show ring and at first was classified among the sporting breeds, a tribute to his keen nose, remarkable eyesight and staying powers in accomplishing the work for which he was principally used, driving the fox from his hole or the drain in which he had taken refuge when too closely pursued by the hounds.

Wires were liberally crossed with Smooths in the earlier days of breeding in order to give to the Wire the predominating white pigmentation, the cleaner cut head and more classical outline of the Smooth. It is for this reason that no extended pedigree of a Wire-haired Fox Terrier will be found without many Smooth ancestors. On the other hand the Wire out-cross appears only in the pedigrees of such of the modern Smooths as descend in the T line, so called, from Dusky D'Orsay, bred by Mr. Francis Redmond in England in 1915 in a deliberate attempt, it is alleged, to improve the Smooth. It is believed that the T line now exists only in Australia.

The practice of interbreeding the Smooth with the Wire and vice-versa has been almost universally discontinued for some years.

An English writer has well described the ideal Fox Terrier in very short words, as follows:

"He should be strong and gay, with a brave, wise way with him in the fields or at home. His head should be long and lean, with much strength in front of his eyes; these should be small and dark and full of the pride of life. His ears should be small, set high on his head, and in shape like a V. His neck be long with a slight arch. The bones from which the forelegs spring should slope well back and be nice and long, these forelegs must be straight and round and thick; his hindlegs strong with good reach, and his hocks should be near the ground; his feet should be small and round, and his pads thick. He should have a deep, but not at all a broad, chest; and his ribs should spring well out, so as to make a deep but not a flat side. His back should appear straight, or with but a slight curve; and his loins should be firm and strong. His tail must spring from the top and not from the back of the dog; it should be stout and stand straight up. His coat should be smooth, and straight, and hard, and dense. He should be white, but his marks, black or tan or both, may be of all shapes and on all parts of the dog, but there must be more white than black or tan; he must not have red or blue or liver marks. A dog or bitch should weigh at least a stone (14 pounds), and a dog may have up to four more pounds, and a bitch up to two more; much more than this does not help. He should move in a way that shows his limbs are sound and straight and free; but it is hard to make this clear in ink, and if a man can find no guide to help him in this, it will be well to ask a good judge of a horse to show him. In brief, when the dog comes to you or when he goes from you, his legs should seem to be straight and free and not too far each from each, nor yet too near; one's eye must learn to judge this with care."

The original Fox terrier standard was so well drawn in 1876 by the Fox Terrier Club (England) that no change has been found necessary except the reducing of the weight of a male dog in show condition from twenty pounds to eighteen pounds.

The American Fox Terrier Club, which is the parent club in this country, adopted this standard when the Club was founded in 1885, and later enlarged upon it only to the extent of giving amplifying measurements to supplement the provisions as to weight.

DESCRIPTION AND STANDARD OF POINTS
(By Courtesy of The American Foxterrier Club)

The following shall be the standard of the fox terrier amplified in part in order that a more complete description of the fox terrier may be presented. The standard itself is set forth in ordinary type, the amplification in italics.

Head.—The skull should be flat and moderately narrow, gradually decreasing in width to the eyes. Not much "stop" should be apparent, but there should be more dip in the profile between the forehead and the top jaw than is seen in the case of a greyhound. The cheeks must not be full.

The ears should be V-shaped and small, of moderate thickness, and drooping forward close to the cheek, not hanging by the side of the head like a foxhound. *The top line of the folded ear should be well above the level of the skull.*

The jaws, upper and lower, should be strong and muscular and of fair punishing strength, but not so as in any way to resemble the greyhound or modern English terrier. There should not be much falling away below the eyes. This part of the head should, however, be moderately chiseled out, so as not to go down in a straight slope like a wedge.

The nose, towards which the muzzle must gradually taper, should be black.

It should be noticed that although the foreface should gradually taper from eye to muzzle and should tip slightly at its juncture with the forehead, it should not "dish" or fall away quickly below the eyes, where it should be full and well made up, but relieved from "wedginess" by a little delicate chiseling.

The eyes and the rims should be dark in color, *moderately* small and rather deep set, full of fire, life and intelligence and as nearly as possible circular in shape. *Anything approaching a yellow eye is most objectionable.*

The teeth should be as nearly as possible together, i.e., *the points* of the upper *(incisors)* teeth on the outside of or *slightly overlapping* the lower teeth.

There should be apparent little difference in length between the skull and foreface of a well-balanced head.

Neck.—Should be clean and muscular, without throatiness, of fair length, and gradually widening to the shoulders.

Shoulders.—Should be long and sloping, well laid back, fine at the points, and clearly cut at the withers.

Chest.—Deep and not broad.

Back.—Should be short, straight (i.e., *level*), and strong, with no appearance of slackness. *Brisket should be deep, yet not exaggerated.*

Loin.—Should be very powerful, *muscular* and very slightly arched. The foreribs should be moderately arched, the back ribs deep *and well sprung,* and the dog should be well ribbed up.

Hind Quarters.—Should be strong and muscular, quite free from droop or crouch; the thighs long and powerful; *stifles well curved and turned neither in nor out;* hocks *well bent* and near the ground *should be perfectly upright and parallel each with the other when viewed from behind,* the dog standing well up on them like a foxhound, and not straight in the stifle. *The worst possible form of hind quarters consists of a short second thigh and a straight stifle.*

Stern.—Should be set on rather high, and carried gaily, but not

DANDIE DINMONT TERRIER

FOX TERRIER *(Wire-haired)*

FOX TERRIER *(Smooth)*

over the back or curled. It should be of good strength, anything approaching a "pipe-stopper" tail being especially objectionable.

Legs.—The forelegs viewed from any direction must be straight with bone strong right down to the feet, showing little or no appearance of ankle in front, and being short and straight in pasterns. Both fore and hindlegs should be carried straight forward in traveling, the stifles not turning outward. The elbows should hang perpendicularly to the body, working free of the sides.

Feet.—Should be round, compact and not large; the soles hard and tough; the toes moderately arched, and turned neither in nor out.

Coat.—Should be smooth, flat, but hard, dense and abundant. The belly and under side of the thighs should not be bare.

Color.—White should predominate; brindle, red, or liver markings are objectionable. Otherwise this point is of little or no importance.

Symmetry, Size and Character.—The dog must present a generally gay, lively and active appearance; bone and strength in a small compass are essentials; but this must not be taken to mean that a fox terrier should be cloddy, or in any way coarse—speed and endurance must be looked to as well as power, and the symmetry of the foxhound taken as a model. The terrier, like the hound, must on no account be leggy, nor must he be too short in the leg. He should stand like a cleverly made hunter, covering a lot of ground, yet with a short back, as before stated. He will then attain the highest degree of propelling power, together with the greatest length of stride that is compatible with the length of his body. Weight is not a certain criterion of a terrier's fitness for his work—general shape, size and contour are the main points; and if a dog can gallop and stay, and follow his fox up a drain, it matters little what his weight is to a pound or so. *According to present-day requirements, a full-sized, well-balanced dog should not exceed 15½ inches at the withers—the bitch being proportionately lower—nor should the length of back from withers to root of tail exceed 12 inches, while, to maintain the relative proportions, the head should not exceed 7¼ inches or be less than 7 inches. A dog with these measurements should scale 18 pounds in show condition—a bitch weighing some 2 pounds less—with a margin of 1 pound either way.*

TERRIERS

Balance.—This may be defined as the correct proportions of a certain point, or points, when considered in relation to a certain other point or points. It is the keystone of the terrier's anatomy. The chief points for consideration are the relative proportions of skull and foreface; head and back; height at withers and length of body from shoulder-point to buttock—the ideal of proportion being reached when the last two measurements are the same. It should be added that, although the head measurements can be taken with absolute accuracy, the height at withers and length of back and coat are approximate, and are inserted for the information of breeders and exhibitors rather than as a hard and fast rule.

Movement.—Movement, or action, is the crucial test of conformation. The terrier's legs should be carried straight forward while traveling, the forelegs hanging perpendicular and swinging parallel with the sides, like the pendulum of a clock. The principal propulsive power is furnished by the hindlegs, perfection of action being found in the terrier possessing long thighs and muscular second thighs well bent at the stifles, which admit of a strong forward thrust or "snatch" of the hocks. When approaching, the forelegs should form a continuation of the straight line of the front, the feet being the same distance apart as the elbows. When stationary, it is often difficult to determine whether a dog is slightly out at shoulder, but, directly he moves, the defect—if it exists—becomes more apparent, the forefeet having a tendency to cross, "weave," or "dish." When, on the contrary, the dog is tied at the shoulder, the tendency of the feet is to move wider apart, with a sort of paddling action. When the hocks are turned in—cowhock—the stifles and feet are turned outwards, resulting in a serious loss of propulsive power. When the hocks are turned outwards the tendency of the hindfeet is to cross, resulting in an ungainly waddle.

N.B.—Old scars or injuries, the result of work or accident, should not be allowed to prejudice a terrier's chance in the show ring, unless they interfere with its movement or with its utility for work or stud.

Wire-Haired Fox Terrier

This variety of the breed should resemble the smooth sort in every respect except the coat, which should be broken. The harder and more wiry the texture of the coat is, the better. On no account should the dog look or feel woolly; and there should be no silky hair about the poll or elsewhere. The coat should not be too long, so as to give the dog a shaggy appearance, but, at the same time, it should show a marked and distinct difference all over from the smooth species.

	Points
Head and ears	15
Neck	5
Shoulders and crest	10
Back and loin	10
Hind quarters	15
Stern	5
Legs and feet	15
Coat	15
Symmetry, size and character	10
Total	100

Disqualifying Points

Nose.—White, cherry or spotted to a considerable extent with either of these colors.

Ears.—Prick, tulip or rose.

Mouth.—Much undershot, or much overshot.

IRISH TERRIERS

(Illustration facing page 514)

(By Courtesy of The Irish Terrier Club of America)

The Irish Terrier had been established in his native country and elsewhere, and truly bred, long before entering the Show Ring in 1879. His origin has been much debated, but there is indisputable evidence that he is one of the oldest of all the terrier breeds. In his beautiful red jacket, alert and trim, his piercing eyes reflecting a rare intelligence, he is a gallant picture of authentic Terrier type and character. He looks up to his master, radiant with the ardor of his love and fidelity.

The outline and conformation of this Terrier of Erin are peculiar to the breed, and differ markedly from those of any other in the Terrier group. The body is longer, proportionately, than the Fox Terrier's, for example, with a much more decided trend to racing lines, but with no lack of substance or sturdiness of bone structure; indeed, the difference in size and shape between the Irish Terrier and the Fox Terrier, has been well likened to that between Hunter and Cob. The Hunter-like raciness of build and greater freedom of action in the Irish Terrier is alien to the Fox Terrier, in which variety cobbiness is desired. Another comparison may be helpful: The similarity in outline of the Irish Terrier to the grand, old Irish Wolfhound is unmistakable; the drawing of one is almost a miniature of the other, and there are equally striking similarities of character.

The Irish Terrier is an incomparable pal, and the loyal, unyielding protector of those he loves. None is hardier or more adaptable. He is equally at home on the country estate, in the city apartment, or in camp; he thrives in the north-land or in the tropics. He is the interested playmate and protector of children, eager to join in their fun and frolic. In their service, as in his master's, he challenges whatever may menace. He is a born guardsman.

The Irish Terrier is an accomplished sportsman. In this country he will catch and kill woodchucks and other small game, and rates with any dog in hunting rabbits. He is death on vermin. A natural water dog, and not apt to be gun shy, he may be trained to retrieve in water as well as on land. Indeed, the Irish Terrier has many of the sporting gifts and talents of the Chesapeake Bay Dog, the Beagle, and Spaniel. He has hunted big game successfully in the far north and in the tropics.

The Irish Terrier scored as a War-Dog in the late World War. He was "over there," and not inconsiderably in evidence. As Messenger and Sentinel he did his bit, a fairly brilliant bit, with that incomparable spirit and utter disregard of danger for which he has always been justly famed.

The following is a brief excerpt from an article written by Lt. Col. E. H. Richardson, lately Commandant of the British War-Dog School, reviewing the Irish Terrier's services:

"I can say with decided emphasis that the Irish Terriers of the service more than did their part. Many a soldier is alive today through the effort of one of these very Terriers. Isolated with his unit in some advanced position, entirely cut off from the main body by a wall of shells, and thus prevented communicating his position or circumstance by telephone or runner so that help might follow, this messenger dog was often the only means his Officers had of carrying the dispatch which eventually would bring relief. My opinion of this breed is indeed a high one. They are highly sensi-

IRISH TERRIER

KERRY BLUE TERRIER

tive, spirited dogs of fine mettle, and those of us who respect and admire the finer qualities of mind will find them amply reflected in these terriers. They are extraordinarily intelligent, faithful, and honest, and a man who has one of them as a companion will never lack a true friend."

"It must be admitted," Col. Richardson also stated, "that many of our best War-Dogs were Irish Terriers. These little fellows were remarkably easily taught, and were tremendously keen on their work." In his comment upon the examination of dogs for enlistment, Col. Richardson testified that "the percentage of acceptances for service among the Irish Terriers was very high."

In the Show Ring the Irish Terrier's style and deportment are peculiarly his own. Alert and grim when challenged, the threatening demeanor of his challenger means nothing at all to him. His fearlessness and disregard of danger have won him the nickname of "Dare-Devil."

In fine, the Irish Terrier is a peerless pal; the playmate and protector of children; a consummate sportsman; and a War-Dog with the saving of human lives to his credit. In competition he is an impressive picture of intrepid Terrier character. He has been styled the D'Artagnan of the Show Ring.

DESCRIPTION AND STANDARD OF POINTS

(Revised and Officially Adopted by The Irish Terrier Club of America, July, 1929)

Head.—Long, but in nice proportion to the rest of the body; the skull flat, rather narrow between the ears, and narrowing slightly towards the eyes; free from wrinkle, with the stop hardly noticeable except in profile. The jaws must be strong and muscular, but not too full in the cheek, and of good punishing length. The foreface must not fall away appreciably between or below the eyes; instead, the modeling should be delicate and in contradistinction, for example, to the fullness of foreface of the Greyhound. An exaggerated foreface, which is out of proportion to the length of the skull from the occiput to the stop, disturbs the proper balance of the head, and is not desirable. Also, the head of exaggerated length usually accompanies oversize or disproportionate length of body, or both, and such conformation is not typical. On the other hand, the foreface should not be noticeably shorter than is the skull from occiput to stop. Excessive muscular development of the cheeks, or bony development of the temples, conditions which are described by the fancier as "cheeky," or "strong in head," or "thick in skull," are objectionable. The "bumpy" or "alligator" head, sometimes described as the "taneous" head, in which the skull presents two lumps of bony structure with or without indentations above the eyes, is unsightly and to be faulted. The hair on the upper and lower jaws should be similar in quality and texture to that on the body, and only of sufficient length to present an appearance of additional strength and finish to the foreface. The profuse, goat-like beard is unsightly and undesirable, and almost invariably it betokens the objectionable linty and silken hair in the coat.

Teeth.—Should be strong and even, white and sound; and neither overshot nor undershot.

Lips.—Should be close and well-fitting, almost black in color.

Nose.—Must be black.

Eyes.—Dark hazel in color; small, not prominent; full of life, fire and intelligence. The light or yellow eye is most objectionable.

Ears.—Small and V-shaped; of moderate thickness; set well on the head, and dropping forward closely to the cheek. The ear must be free of fringe, and the hair much shorter and somewhat darker in color than on the body. A "dead" ear, houndlike in appearance, must be severely penalized. It is not characteristic of the Irish Terrier. An ear which is too slightly erect is undesirable.

Neck.—Should be of fair length and gradually widening towards the shoulders; well and proudly carried, and free from throatiness. Generally there is a slight frill in the hair at each side of the neck, extending almost to the corner of the ear.

Shoulders and Chest.—Shoulders must be fine, long, and sloping well into the back. The chest should be deep and muscular, but neither full nor wide.

Back and Loin.—The body should be moderately long—neither too long nor too short. The short back, so coveted and so appealing in the Fox Terrier, is *not* characteristic of the Irish Terrier. It is objectionable. The back must be symmetrical, strong and straight, and free from an appearance of slackness or "dip" behind the shoulders. The loin strong and muscular, and slightly arched. The ribs fairly sprung, deep rather than round, with a well-ribbed back. The bitch may be slightly longer in appearance than the dog.

Hind Quarters.—Should be strong and muscular; powerful thighs; hocks near the ground; stifles moderately bent.

Stern.—Should be docked, and set on rather high, but not curled. It should be of good strength and substance; of fair length and well covered with harsh, rough hair, and free from fringe or feather. The three-quarters dock is about right.

Feet and Legs.—The feet should be strong, tolerably round, and moderately small; toes arched and turned neither out nor in, with black toe-nails. The pads should be deep, not hard, but with a pleasing velvety quality, and perfectly sound; they must be entirely free from cracks or horny excrescences. Corny feet, so-called, are to be regarded as an abominable blemish; as a taint which must be shunned. Cracked pads frequently accompany corny growths, and these conditions are more pronounced in hot and dry weather. In damp weather and in winter such pads may improve temporarily, but these imperfections inevitably reappear and the result is unsound feet, a deplorable fault which must be heavily penalized. There seems to be no permanent cure for this condition, and even if a temporary cure were possible the disease is seldom, if ever, eradicated, and undoubtedly it is transmitted in breeding. The one sure way to avoid corny and otherwise unsound feet is to avoid breeding from dogs or bitches which are not entirely free from this taint. Legs, moderately long, well set from the shoulders, perfectly straight, with plenty of bone and muscle; the elbows working clear of the sides; pasterns short, straight, and hardly noticeable. Both fore and hindlegs should move straight forward when traveling; the stifles should not turn outwards. "Cowhocks" —that is, where the hocks are turned in, and the stifles and feet turned out, are intolerable. The legs should be free from feather, and covered, like the head, with hair of similar texture to that on the body, but not so long.

Coat.—Should be dense and wiry in texture, rich in quality, having a broken appearance, but still lying fairly close to the body, the hairs growing so closely and strongly together that when parted with the fingers the skin is hardly visible; free of softness or silkiness, and not so long as to alter the outline of the body, particularly in the hind quarters. At the base of the stiff outer coat there should be a growth of finer and softer hair, differing in color, termed the undercoat. Single coats, which are without any undercoat, and wavy coats, are undesirable; the curly coat is most objectionable. On the sides of the body the coat is never as harsh as on the back and the quarters, but it should be plentiful and of good texture.

Color.—Should be whole-colored; the bright red, red wheaten, or golden red colors are preferable. A small patch of white on the chest, frequently encountered in all whole-colored breeds, is permissible but not desirable. White on any other part of the body is most objectionable.

Size and Symmetry.—The most desirable weight in show condition is 27 pounds for the dog and 25 pounds for the bitch. The height at the shoulder should be approximately 18 inches. This terrier must be active, lithe and wiry in movement, with great animation; sturdy and strong in substance and bone-structure, but at the same time free from clumsiness, for speed, power and endurance are most essential. The Irish Terrier must be neither "cobby" nor "cloddy," but should be built on lines of speed, with a graceful, racing outline.

The weights herein mentioned are ideal and serve as a guide to both breeder and judge. In the show ring, however, the informed judge readily identifies the over-sized or under-sized Irish Terrier by its conformation and general appearance. The weights named should be regarded as limit weights, as a rule, but it must be considered that a comparatively small, heavily built and "cloddy" dog —which is most undesirable, and not at all typical—may easily be of standard weight, or over it; whereas another terrier which is long in leg, lacking in substance and built somewhat upon the lines of a Whippet—also undesirable and not at all typical—may be of the exact weight, or under it; therefore, although the standard weights must be borne well in mind, weight is not the last word in judgment. It is of the greatest importance to select, in so far as possible, terriers of moderate and generally accepted size, possessing the other various necessary characteristics.

Temperament.—The Irish Terrier is game, and asks no quarter. He is of good temper, most affectionate, and absolutely loyal to mankind. Tender and forbearing with those he loves, this rugged, stout-hearted terrier will guard his master, his mistress, children in his charge, or their possessions, with unflinching courage and with utter contempt of danger or hurt. His life is one continuous and eager offering of loyal and faithful companionship, and devoted, loving service. He is ever on guard, and stands between his house and all that threatens.

Points

(Revised in July, 1929)

Head, ears and expression	20
Legs and feet	15
Neck	5
Shoulders and chest	10
Back and loin	5
Hind quarters and stern	10
Coat	15
Color	10
Size and symmetry	10
Total	100

NEGATIVE POINTS

White nails, toes and feet, minus	10
Much white on chest	10
Dark shadings on face	5
Mouth undershot or cankered	10
Coat shaggy, curly or soft	10
Uneven in color	5
Total	50

TERRIERS

Nose.—Any other color than black.

Mouth.—Much undershot or overshot.

Ears.—Cropped ears.

Color.—Any other color than red, golden red, or red wheaten. A small patch of white on the chest is permissible; otherwise parti-colored coats disqualify.

KERRY BLUE TERRIERS

(Illustration facing page 515)

(By Courtesy of The Kerry Blue Terrier Club of America)

The Kerry Blue Terrier originated in Ireland having been first noticed in the mountainous regions of the County Kerry, hence the name. They had been pure bred in this section for over one hundred years.

Gentle, lovable and extremely intelligent, he is an all-round working and utility terrier, used in Ireland and England for hunting all manner of small game and birds. Excellent retrievers, from both land and water. Are used quite successfully for herding sheep and cattle and are without a peer as a watchdog and companion for children.

The Kerry first came into the public eye when they were adopted as The National Dog of the Irish Republic. They were always considered a working and sporting terrier and no thought was given to them as a bench show dog. However, after the formation of the Republic and the adoption of the Blue as the National dog, they began to appear on the bench and met with instant favor. The first few came out at the Dublin show. The English fanciers were quick to realize their possibilities, if properly groomed, and the English kennel club provided regular classification for them. Their rise to popularity was almost instant and each show brought out an increasing number of entries.

There is more or less conjecture as to who imported the first Kerry and where they were first shown in this country. However, it appears that the first time they were exhibited at an important show was in Madison Square Garden in 1922.

For two years after their first appearance in the Westminster show they were relegated to the miscellaneous classes. It was not until 1924 that they were officially admitted by the American Kennel Club as a recognized breed and given an official championship rating. They are now given breed classification at all-breed American Kennel Club fixtures.

February, 1926, during the Westminster show, a group of fanciers met in the Waldorf-Astoria, New York City, and organized a specialty club for the protection of the breed. This club is known as the Kerry Blue Terrier Club of America Inc., and is a member club of the American Kennel Club.

To encourage and foster the pure breeding of thoroughbred Kerries was the object of the club as well as to make the breed and its qualities widely known and to assist breeders in every way possible; to publish an adopted standard, to preserve and foster the utility and sporting qualities of this terrier, with an aim towards field trials as well as bench shows, and to encourage interest in public exhibitions and safeguard the interests of the breeders and exhibitors of the Kerry Blues, and to foster the just claims of this terrier to greater public favor.

The Kerry in Ireland is fostered by the Irish Blue Terrier Club, of Dublin, organized by H. G. Fotterell, Edan Quay, Dublin. The principal variance in standard is that the Irish will not permit the trimming of coat. Dogs must be shown in the rough.

The Blue Terrier Club of England, organized by Capt. Watts Williams, care of The Kennel Club, Lon-

LAKELAND TERRIER

LHASA TERRIER

Strohmeyer & Carpenter

don, England, is the supporting organization back of the Blues for England. The English standard is with a few minor exceptions identical with the American standard. Coats must be trimmed.

The Kerry is endowed with a remarkable nose and has an instinctive trailing ability. He retrieves equally as well from water as from land and is tireless on the trail of his quarry. He has remarkable endurance and will fight unto death when in combat.

The Kerry is adaptable to all manner of farm work especially in the capacities of the average shepherd dog. He is a willing worker, is easily trained and enters into the spirit of his environs and his work in a whole-hearted manner. Game to the utmost degree, faithful to an unbelievable end, he is the most alert of all terriers. He has an instinctive air of watchful waiting and is quick to discern right from wrong. He is an indomitable foe, to wrong doers, and cannot be beaten as a watch dog and companion. In some instances he has been used in England for police work.

Owing to their high degree of intelligence they are most easily trained for all the utility purposes for which they are used.

They are of course subject to all the regular dog diseases but owing to their stalwart heart and nature, they have an abundance of resistance which enables them to withstand the most severe ravages of disease with the least percentage of mortality of perhaps any terrier in the terrier group.

The whelping hazard is reduced to a minimum in the Kerries owing to their rugged nature. Seldom do bitches have to be assisted at whelping time.

The skin of the Kerry should be kept lubricated by the occasional use of a shampoo of olive oil or Russian mineral oil. This will keep the skin in a healthy condition and will promote an abundant growth of silky coat. The coat should be brushed and combed each day in order to keep it in the proper condition and should be trimmed at regular intervals whether the dog is being exhibited or not.

With proper treatment, food and exercise the Kerry Blue terrier is very long lived and will usually retain his activeness until the end. Kerries at six and eight years of age might be taken for young dogs. They are very virile and healthy by nature and if given a chance and ordinary good treatment will live to a ripe and useful old age.

DESCRIPTION AND STANDARD OF POINTS
(By Courtesy of The Kerry Blue Terrier Club of America)

Head.—Long and strong.

Skull.—Flat, very slight stop.

Cheeks.—Clean, free from bumpiness.

Jaws.—Strong and deep, nearly level with cheeks.

Ears.—Small to medium size, of moderate thickness, carried forward, close to cheeks.

Mouth.—Strong and level teeth, dark gums and roof.

Nose.—Black, nostrils large and wide.

Eyes.—Dark to hazel, small to medium size, well placed.

Neck.—Well proportioned, well set on shoulders and moderately long.

Shoulders and Chest.—Shoulders fine and sloping to the body and well knit. Chest to be deep and of moderate width.

Legs and Feet.—Legs straight from both front and side view, with plenty of bone and muscle. Feet strong and fairly round with good depth of pad, free from cracks. Toe nails black.

KERRY BLUE TERRIERS

Hind Quarters and Stern.—Hind quarters strong and muscular, with perfect freedom of action, stifles moderately bent, hocks near to the ground. Tail put on high, of moderate length, carried gaily, but not over the back or curled.

Body.—Back strong and straight, medium in length, well coupled. Loin short and powerful, ribs fairly well sprung, deep rather than round.

Color.—Any shade of blue from light to dark, of a uniform color throughout, except for, lighter or darker parts on ears, muzzle, tail, head and feet. Shade of tan on head and legs is permissible in puppies up to the age of 18 months.

Coat.—Soft and wavy, body well covered but tidy. Head, ears and cheeks clear.

Height.—Dogs about 18 inches at the shoulder, bitches slightly less. Insist on proper measuring apparatus from show-giving clubs.

Weight.—Dogs about 33 to 38 pounds. Bitches 32 to 36 pounds.

General Appearance.—Active, hardy and wiry, with plenty of substance, indicating strength without clumsiness. Must show intelligence and gameness.

Positive Points

	Points
Head, ears, eyes and mouth	20
Neck	5
Shoulders and Chest	10
Body	10
Hind quarters and stern	10
Coat	15
Color	10
Legs and Feet	10
General appearance	10
Total	100

Negative Points

		Points
Head—Bumpy cheeks	minus	10
Mouth—Teeth undershot or very overshot	"	5
Back—Roach back or hollow back	"	5
Hind quarters—Stiff or stilted action	"	5
Coat—Hard, wiry or bristle	"	10
Ears—Rose ears	"	5
Eyes—Yellow or gooseberry eyes	"	10
Total		50

Disqualifications.—Dogs under 17 inches and over 20 inches. Bitches under 16 inches and over 19 inches. Dewclaws on hindlegs. Solid black. Tan or white markings after 18 months. Faking or dyeing.

LAKELAND TERRIERS
(Illustration facing page 522)

Among the latest additions to the dog fancy of the United States, the Lakeland terrier is one of the oldest working terrier breeds still known today. It was bred and raised and worked in the Lake districts of England long before there was a kennel club or an official stud book. The fact that it has been outstripped by many younger terrier breeds is not so much a reflection on its quality as a tribute to the scope of its working ability. The name "Lakeland," indeed, is a modern acquisition. In olden times the breed was known as the Patterdale terrier.

It is related that long before the days of the great John Peel, or before any packs of hounds were formed, the Lakeland was kept by the farmers in the mountain districts, who, at that time, would form a hunt with a couple of hounds and these terriers. Their work was to destroy the foxes found raiding the sheep folds. There was sport; but it was not sport for sport's sake alone. It was a very practical matter.

The color of these dogs did not matter to their owners. They bred principally for gameness, at first. The color was quite secondary as long as the terriers were game enough to withstand the punishment meted out by the foxes in their rocky, mountain lairs. Later came the packs of hounds, but there was not a single pack in the lake district that did not have one or two outstandingly game old terriers that had continually shown their courage with fox or otter. These were most coveted as breeding material. None of their puppies was ever destroyed. They were given out among the various friends and followers of the hunt; later to be tried and the best workers retained to carry on the traditions of the older dogs.

So great was the courage of the native Lakeland terriers that they would follow underground for tremendous distances. It is told that, in 1871, Lord Lonsdale had one terrier which crawled 23 feet under rock after an otter. In order to extricate the dog it was necessary to undertake extensive blasting operations. Finally, after three days' work, they reached the dog, and he was gotten out, none the worse for his experience. Still other dogs have been known to be locked underground for 10 or 12 days, and have been taken out alive. Others have paid the penalty.

Classes for the likeliest looking terrier, suitable for fox or otter, were judged in connection with the agricultural shows throughout the lake district about 1896, when more interest was evinced in this game old breed. They were judged by masters of hounds or other experienced hunting men. At that time, the color ranged from grizzle to blue and tan, red or wheaten, with a sprinkling of white terriers. Later these classes were divided in color; for white working terriers, and for colored working terriers. Always the working ability was taken into consideration.

The white terriers usually were found working with the otter hounds, as in many cases a dark terrier got severely mauled in the muddy waters due to the excitement of the younger hounds when the otter had been dislodged from under tree roots, and drains, and so forth.

It is believed by experienced terrier men that the

ancestors—somewhat remote—of the Lakeland terrier, are similar to the progenitors of the Border terrier. In fact, there is sound evidence that the Lakeland is an off-shoot of the breed that became known later as the Bedlington, which was closely related to the Dandie Dinmont.

About 100 years ago—in 1830, or thereabouts—these northern counties of England, Northumberland, Cumberland, and Westmoreland, had many varieties of terrier. Each was named after the small locality in which it was found in greatest numbers. Many of the old names have been lost since the breeds have gained recognition. This changing of names usually took place when specialist clubs were formed, with breeders unwilling to agree on any of the older names. And, of course, there were cases where the same dog might have been known by half a dozen different names.

Cumberland was the birthplace of the Lakeland terrier. This is a particularly beautiful country, richly studded with lakes, particularly in the southern part. The Bedlington is attributed to neighboring Northumberland County, but it is not difficult to suppose that there was certain traffic in dogs a century ago.

The first organized effort to promote the interest of this Cumberland County breed came at the Kersurck show in 1912, when a terrier club was formed. The new club made considerable headway for two years, and then came the outbreak of the World War. Naturally, all civilian activities were under a damper, and little or nothing was heard of the Lakeland terrier again until 1921.

In 1921, a meeting of fanciers was called, and they met at Whitehaven, in Cumberland. According to Thomas Hosking, who now resides in the United States and who was one of the nine fanciers who attended the meeting, the name Lakeland terrier was chosen at that meeting. The Standard was drawn up at that time, and shortly afterward the breed was made eligible for registration in the stud book of the Kennel Club (England).

The career of the Lakeland in the United States is in its infancy, but there is every reason to believe that this rugged little terrier will find many admirers. Although a worker for generations, he presents a very good appearance when sent into the ring. He has a dense, weather-resisting,—frequently black and tan— coat, strong jaws of moderate length, powerful hind quarters, and good legs and feet on a short, strong back. And despite his gameness and courage, he has a most attractive, quiet disposition.

DESCRIPTION AND STANDARD OF POINTS
(By Courtesy of The Lakeland Terrier Association, England)

Color.—Blue, blue and tan, black and tan, red, mustard, wheaten, grizzle and black. (White predominant to disqualify.)

Weight.—Dog not to exceed 17 pounds; bitch not to exceed 16 pounds.

Height.—Not to exceed 15 inches.

Head.—Moderately broad in skull, with broad, strong muzzle, not excessively long; black nose preferred but liver or flesh color not to disqualify.

Mouth.—Level.

Ears.—Small and dropped; round or V-shaped.

Eyes.—Dark or hazel; medium size; not too prominent.

Neck.—In proportion to body.

Front.—Narrow.

Forelegs.—Straight.

Feet.—Sound and not too flat.

LAKELAND TERRIERS

Back.—Moderately short and well coupled, with long, sloping hind quarters.

Coat.—Hard, dense and wiry; grooming allowed to improve general appearance, and judge in all cases to give preference to a good hard coat.

Tail.—Carried gaily; not docked too short.

General Appearance.—Smart and workmanlike.

LHASA TERRIERS

(Illustration facing page 523)

Dogs are considered the animal friend of man, and well do they, speaking generally, deserve this title. When one considers the number of breeds there are in the world, and their difference in shape and appearance, it is evident that man's efforts in breeding, etc. must have stretched over a long period of years.

The origin of dogs, no matter what breed, is always an interesting topic, but when a breed such as the Lhasa Terrier that has proof of existence for at least 800 years is brought to light, it naturally is of great interest to dog lovers.

In this age of ease in travel it would seem almost impossible that such circumstances should exist, as to preclude a full knowledge of this breed. It is nevertheless a fact that even now it is very difficult to obtain one of these dogs from the country of its origin.

The question naturally arises, "Where and what is this country?"

Beyond the northern boundary of India, where the mighty Mount Everest stands like a guardian sentinel, is the mysterious land of Tibet.

It is a country of huge mountains and deep valleys, with a climate of intense cold and great heat, a country where conditions are hard on man and beast. This is the home of the dog subject of this article, the Lhasa Terrier, known in that land as "Abso Seng Kye," ("Bark Sentinel Lion Dog"). It is small wonder, then, that these members of dogdom should be of such a hardy and vigorous constitution.

There are four breeds of dogs, native to this country:

(1) The Tibetan Terrier, a dog of true terrier type and raised more or less all over the country.

(2) The Tibetan Spaniel, a beautiful toy dog.

(3) The fierce and powerful Tibetan Mastiff.

(4) The Lhasa Terrier, which is raised in the Lama-series and villages around the sacred city of Lhasa.

Although only dealing in this article with the last-named member of the canine world, we wish to draw to the reader's attention the two common characteristics of the dogs of Tibet:

(a) The heavy coat of hair, which all have as a protection from the rigors of the climate.

(b) That each of the breeds carries its tail curled up over its back.

The huge mastiff is chained to a post outside the outer door as a guard to prevent an intruder from entering, and well are they able to do this duty.

This is a country, however, where danger threatens from within as well as without, and for this reason the Lhasa Terriers are kept as special guards inside the dwellings.

For this work these dogs are peculiarly adapted. Their wonderful intelligence, quick hearing, and finely developed instinct to detect intimates from strangers, is no doubt the result of long years of training in this respect.

They are very clean and loving companions, and most decidedly show appreciation when petted. To get the best from these dogs one must make a lot of them, and well do they respond. They should not, however, be spoiled by pampering, as they are quite hardy and very fond, like most dogs, of a good run in the open.

We have always found these dogs easily trained, and very responsive to kindness. To any one they trust they are most obedient and their beautiful dark eyes look so appealing as they wait for some mark of appreciation for their efforts.

The crude manner of breeding among the Tibetans is no doubt responsible for the fact that colors are not fixed, i.e.,—if one breeds say, a black and white dog to a honey colored bitch, you may get a brown or brown and white pup as a result.

The two original dogs brought from Asia to this country were:

A black and white male "Taikoo," and a female the color of raw silk, "Dinkie." Both are beautiful specimens of the breed, and from them are offspring in the following colors:

Black and white, Grizzle and white, Honey colored, Golden and Brown and White.

No doubt, under the influence of the more scientific western breeding these colors will become more certain.

The dogs, however, have not lost their peculiar characteristics as "watch dogs," nor have they lost their hardy natures. These two points should be always developed as they are outstanding points of merit.

It is now generally accepted that the carvings so often seen in China represent these dogs, and not real lions, and to see one of them crouched on the ground, with its long mane, certainly gives it a decided resemblance to the "King of Beasts."

Also there have been suggestions made that these dogs have a place in the religion of Tibet. Evidence, however, for this belief seems lacking. However, there is ample evidence that they have always held a high place in the estimation of the Tibetans, as historical records show that from time to time specimens have been sent from the Dalai Lama of Tibet to the rulers of China, as special gifts. This marks them definitely as having considerable value, either sentimental or intrinsic, perhaps both. Sufficient to say that early travellers in Tibet have never mentioned seeing these dogs, as they were always kept in the homes of the "mighty."

DESCRIPTION AND STANDARD OF POINTS
(Adopted by The American Kennel Club, April 9, 1935)

Character.—Gay and assertive, but chary of strangers.

Size.—Variable, but about 10 inches or 11 inches at shoulder for dogs, bitches slightly smaller.

Color.—Golden, sandy, honey, dark grizzle, slate, smoke, particolor, black, white or brown. This being the true Tibetan Lion-dog, golden or lion-like colors are preferred. Other colors in order as above. Dark tips to ears and beard are an asset.

Body Shape.—The length from point of shoulders to point of buttocks longer than height at withers, well ribbed up, strong loin, well developed quarters and thighs.

Coat.—Heavy, straight, hard, not woolly nor silky, of good length, and very dense.

Mouth and Muzzle.—Mouth level, otherwise slightly undershot preferable. Muzzle of medium length; a square muzzle is objectionable.

Head.—Heavy head furnishings with good fall over eyes, good whiskers and beard; skull narrow, falling away behind the eyes in a marked degree, not quite flat, but not domed or apple shaped; straight foreface of fair length. Nose black, about 1½ inches long, or the length from tip of nose to eye to be roughly about one-third of the total length from nose to back of skull.

LHASA TERRIERS

Eyes.—Dark brown, neither very large and full, nor very small and sunk.

Ears.—Pendant, heavily feathered.

Legs.—Forelegs straight; both fore and hindlegs heavily furnished with hair.

Feet.—Well feathered, should be round and cat-like, with good pads.

Tail and Carriage.—Well feathered, should be carried well over back in a screw, there may be a kink at the end. A low carriage of stern is a serious fault.

MANCHESTER TERRIERS

(Illustration facing page 544)

(By Courtesy of The Manchester Terrier Club of America)

The active, speedy little Manchester Terrier has had much influence in the formation of many of the present-day breeds.

Generations ago, there was a Black-and-Tan Terrier in England before the days of dog shows; less graceful in outline and coarser in type to be sure, than those of today. These early dogs did not present the fancy marks of pencilled toes and dotted brows; their tan was smutty, but nevertheless, they were sound, game and useful dogs, the most accomplished of rat killers whether in the pit or along water courses.

The Manchester district was a noted center for two "poor men's sports"—rat killing and rabbit coursing. A fancier by the name of John Hulme, with the idea of producing a dog that could be used at both contests, bred a whippet bitch to a celebrated rat killing dog, a cross-bred terrier dark brown in color. The result of this cross was very satisfactory, the dogs proved useful, and other fanciers in the neighborhood took to breeding them, and the Manchester school of terriers was launched. They advanced in popularity rapidly and soon spread over the British Isles and were brought to this country in considerable numbers. The name Manchester was dropped as being too restricted in its designation, and they were known as the Black-and-Tan Terrier until 1923, when the Manchester Terrier Club of America was formed, and the name of the breed changed back to the Manchester Terrier.

As a sagacious, intelligent pet and companion and as a house dog, no breed is superior to the well-bred Manchester Terrier. There is a sleek, breedy appearance about them that no other dog presents. Their long, clean head, keen expression, glossy coat, whip tail, and smart, wide-awake appearance always command attention. Their cleanly habits and short coats also admit them to homes that shut out their rough-haired brothers.

The Manchester Terrier, with all his refinement, has lost none of his gameness. He is still per se a vermin dog, unequaled and is capable of holding his own in a rough-and-tumble scrap with anything living, and will tackle anything his weight or twice his size.

About thirty-five years ago when the anti-cropping edict was passed in England many of the old fanciers became discouraged in trying to breed an attractive Manchester with a small button ear, and consequently many of these old breeders stopped breeding and the Manchester Terrier would have gone out of existence had it not been for a few fanciers who loved this game, little terrier, and kept the breed alive.

There were also several persons who deserve a tremendous amount of credit for keeping the Manchester Terrier alive in America and the present-day Manchester Terrier fanciers in this country should also give a vote of thanks to these old fanciers.

Up to 1923, the interest in Manchester Terriers was more or less desultory, many of the breeders did not even bother to register their dogs, but at least they kept on breeding them, which laid the foundation for the fine specimens that are being produced today.

In 1923, in an effort to again bring this fine little terrier back to the popularity it once enjoyed, a few of the fanciers who were still interested in the breed, formed the Manchester Terrier Club of America. The formation of the Club encouraged the old fanciers to keep on breeding and many new fanciers joined the ranks and started to breed these terriers. While the American-bred Manchester was easily the equal of the English-bred dog, several fanciers, in an effort to establish new blood lines, imported dogs from the British Isles.

With the impetus given the breed through the continued efforts of the Club since its formation, the Manchester has gained steadily in numbers and is continually making new friends. There are now increasing entries of this little dog at all the leading shows in the United States.

DESCRIPTION AND STANDARD OF POINTS
(By Courtesy of The Manchester Terrier Club of America)

Head.—Narrow, almost flat, with a slight indentation up the forehead, long and tight-skinned; level in mouth, with no visible cheek-muscles; slightly wedge-shaped, tapering to the nose, and well filled up under the eyes, with tight lipped jaws.

Eyes.—Small, bright, and sparkling, set moderately close together, as near black as possible; oblong in shape, slanting upwards on the outside; they should neither protrude nor sink in the skull.

Nose.—Should be perfectly black.

Ears.—Should be button, small and thin; small at the root, and set as close together as possible at the top of the head. If cropped, to a point, long, and carried erect.

Neck and Shoulders.—The neck should be slim and graceful, gradually becoming larger as it approaches the shoulders, and perfectly free from throatiness; slightly arched from the occiput. The shoulders slope off elegantly.

Chest.—Narrow between the legs, deep in the brisket.

Body.—Short, with powerful loins; ribs well sprung out behind the shoulders, the back being slightly arched at the loin, and falling again to the joining of the tail to the same height as the shoulder.

Legs.—Perfectly straight, and well under the body; strong, and of proportionate length.

Feet.—Compact, split up between the toes, and well arched, with jet-black nails; the two middle toes in the frontfeet rather longer than the others, and the hindfeet shaped like those of a cat.

Tail.—Should be moderately short, and set on where the arch of the back ends; thick where it joins the body, and gracefully tapering to a point, and not carried higher than the back.

Coat.—Close, short, and glossy; not soft.

Color.—Black-and-tan, as distinct as possible; the tan should be a rich mahogany color. A tan spot over each eye, and another on each cheek, the latter as small as possible; the lips of the upper and lower jaws should be tanned, the tan extending under the jaw to the throat, ending in the shape of the letter V; the inside of the ear is partly tanned; the forelegs tanned to the knee, with a black patch "thumb mark" between the pastern and the knee; the toes have a distinct black mark running up each, called the "pencil mark"; the tan on the hindlegs should continue from the pencilling on the feet up the inside of the legs to a little below the stifle joint, and the outside of the legs should be *perfectly black*. There should be tan under tail, and on the vent, but only of such size as to be covered by the tail. In every case the tan should meet the black abruptly.

Weight.—Fourteen to twenty-two pounds.

General Appearance.—A Terrier calculated to take his own part in the rat pit and not of the Whippet type.

NORWICH TERRIERS

(Illustration facing page 545)

Although the Norwich Terrier has just recently made his debut at the American Bench Shows, it would be inaccurate to say that the breed is a new one in the United States. Shortly after the World War, several specimens of these dogs, then known as the "Jones Terrier" in honor of one of the foremost English breeders of that day, arrived in the United States and were put in the hands of various Masters of Foxhounds. Ever since that time, a small kennel of these dogs has been maintained and kept pure-bred by the Cheshire Hunt in Philadelphia and to a lesser extent by other hunt clubs. These little dogs have proven their value going to ground and have done valuable work for the Hunts that have used them.

They love going out with the horses and notwithstanding their short legs, have no trouble keeping up. They also make excellent rabbit dogs. Game to the core, these little dogs are real "all-weather" terriers, and in every way answer the requirements of those breeders who are looking for a small wirecoated terrier, ten to fourteen pounds in weight, with good dark eyes, short legs, stocky build and above all, a dog with a dead-game, all-terrier personality. The standard calls for either an erect ear, a trifle larger than the Cairn's or a very neat and small, correctly dropped ear. The color, although usually red, also may be black and tan or grizzle. White markings are very undesirable, though not disqualifying.

This little terrier was first introduced into England in 1880, and shortly thereafter this admirable little dog became the fad with the undergraduates at Cambridge University; in fact, some people think that the breed should be known as the "Cantab" Terrier in honor of the collegiate atmosphere in which it made its bow so many years ago. It was not, however, until 1932 that this breed, by then well-established in type, was granted recognition of the English Kennel Club, The American Kennel Club following suit in 1936.

An ideal house-dog, because of his hard, close coat, which does not collect dirt nor need trimming, the Norwich, as are most terriers, is inclined to be a one-man dog, and his loyalty, once given, never swerves. The standard wisely calls for a foxy but strong muzzle, in an attempt to keep the breed from having any one exaggerated characteristic. Every effort is being made by the present fanciers of the Norwich to retain and perpetuate the breed's interesting personality and not subject it to so-called improvements. There have been many recent importations of show stock for breeding purposes and it will not be long before the public is able to see these little terriers regularly at the bench shows.

DESCRIPTION AND STANDARD OF POINTS

(By Courtesy of the Norwich Terrier Club of England. Adopted by the American Kennel Club, February 12, 1936)

Head.—Muzzle, "foxy," yet strong; length about one-third less than a measurement from the occiput to the bottom of the stop, which should be a good one and well defined. Skull wide, slightly rounded with good width between the ears. Ears, if erect, slightly larger than a Cairn's; if dropped, very neat and small, and CORRECTLY dropped.

Eyes.—Very bright, dark and keen. Full of expression.

Teeth.—Strong; rather large; closely fitting.

Jaw.—Clean, strong, tight lipped.

MANCHESTER TERRIER

NORWICH TERRIER

NORWICH TERRIERS

Neck.—Short and strong; well set on clean shoulders.

Legs.—Short; powerful; as straight as is consistent with the short legs at which we aim. Sound bone, feet round, thick pads.

Quarters.—Strong, with great powers of propulsion.

Tail.—Medium docked, carriage not excessively gay.

Weight.—10 to 14 lbs., 11 lbs. being the ideal.

Height.—10 to 12 inches at the withers (not to exceed).

Color and Coat.—Red (to include red wheaten), black and tan, or grizzle. White is undesirable but shall not disqualify. Coat as hard and wiry as possible, but lies much closer to the body than a Cairn's, and is absolutely straight. It is longer and rougher on the neck and shoulders, in winter forming almost a mane. Hair on the head, ears and muzzle, except slight eyebrows, and slight whisker, is absolutely short and smooth.

General Appearance.—A small, low, keen dog, tremendously active. A perfect demon, yet not quarrelsome, and of a lovable disposition, and with a very hardy constitution.

Faults.—Long weak back, a mouth badly over or under shot, full eye, soft expression.

Disqualifications.—Yellow eyes; soft coat, or wavy, or curly, or silky. A long narrow head; square muzzle, trimming is not desirable, and should be penalized rather than encouraged. Honorable scars from fair wear and tear shall not count against.

SCHNAUZERS (MINIATURE)

(Illustration facing page 556)

(By Courtesy of The American Miniature Schnauzer Club)

The Schnauzer is of German origin, and is said to be recognizable in pictures of the fifteenth century. However, the modern breed was probably derived from the crossing of black poodle and wolf-grey spitz with old German pinscher stock. The last named dogs were probably stocky black and tan, or fawn animals, containing some Württemberg droving blood. The Schnauzer is characterized by his stocky build, harsh, wiry coat, and fairly abundant, wiry whiskers. The mixed grey salt and pepper color, caused by a mixture of light and dark banded hairs, is peculiar to the breed, although solid black and black and tan also occur. By vocation, he was a yard and stable dog, a guard and a destroyer of vermin, and is consequently a great ratter. However, his size precluded his use in going to ground after small animals, and he is consequently wholly distinct in blood and origin from the British terriers. However, in general type and temperament he resembles this group, and is classed as a Terrier in this country, though not in Germany nor England.

The Miniature Schnauzer is derived from the Standard or Medium Schnauzer, and was produced by the selection of small specimens and their crossing with Affenpinschers (a small, black German breed). They were exhibited as a distinct breed at least as early as 1899, and have been bred for more than forty years. They resemble the

Medium variety in conformation, but vary somewhat more in color and are, as a rule, less aggressive in temperament. Crosses of the two breeds are not eligible for registration. A typical Miniature is hardy and active, intelligent, fond of children, and a good ratter. His size makes him a suitable dog for town life and small quarters, but he is equally at home in the country, and quite up to a dozen miles a day. As a rule, the Miniature is not a fighter, though he can stand up for himself when necessary, and is seldom addicted to wandering. Size varies considerably, allowing the individual owner to suit his fancy. However, a good medium size is to be preferred, in the neighborhood of 12 inches, or a bit more for males. There is no standard weight, but a grown bitch of reasonable size is likely to weigh around 12 pounds, and a dog around 15. Weight increases faster than height, so that the larger animals weigh more in proportion, and weight also depends considerably on the amount of bone. Light-boned, leggy animals are decidedly lighter than better built animals of the same inches.

The Miniature Schnauzer may be very useful as a ratter, and can guard the house and give an alarm as well as a dog of the biggest breed, but his primary vocation is as a pet. This is a position he is admirably fitted to fill, under almost any circumstances, as good health, good temperament, and an attractive appearance combine to form a most attractive personality.

Miniatures have been bred in the United States since 1925, and have gained steadily in popular favor. The American Miniature Schnauzer Club began its independent career in August 1933.

SCHNAUZERS (MINIATURE)

DESCRIPTION AND STANDARD OF POINTS

(Adopted by The American Miniature Schnauzer Club and Approved by The American Kennel Club, December 11, 1934)

The Miniature Schnauzer is a robust, active dog of the terrier type, resembling his larger cousin, the Medium Schnauzer in general appearance, and of an alert, active disposition. He should be sturdily built, nearly square in the proportion of body length to height, with plenty of bone, less racy in outline than a Fox Terrier, and without any suggestion of toyishness.

Head.—Should be strong and rectangular, diminishing slightly from the ear to the eyes, and again to the tip of the nose. The skull should be fairly broad between the ears, its width not exceeding two-thirds of its length, the forehead flat and unwrinkled, the nose straight and almost parallel to the extension of the forehead (i.e. neither dish-faced nor down-faced) with a moderate stop. The muzzle should be strong, in proportion to the skull, and should end in a moderately blunt manner, with wiry whiskers, accentuating the rectangular shape of the head. The tip of the nose should be black, the lips tight and not overlapping, with well developed fangs, healthy and pure white. The jaws should meet in a scissors bite, the upper teeth passing just outside the lower, with no space between. The eyes should be medium sized, dark brown, oval, turned forward, with the brow arched and wiry. Ears should be evenly shaped, set high and carried erect when cropped. If uncropped they should be small and V-shaped, of moderate thickness, folding forward close to the skull. Too long and narrow a skull, soft, silky whiskers and top knot, light yellow, large or protruding eyes, low set, houndy ears, under and overshot mouths are faults.

Neck.—Should be strong and slightly arched, set cleanly on the shoulders, and with the skin fitting closely at the throat. Too short and thick, long and light, or too throaty a neck is undesirable.

Fore Quarters.—Should have flat, strongly muscled, *somewhat sloping* shoulders, without the steep-set "terrier front." The forelegs should be straight and vertical when seen from all sides. The chest should be moderately broad, reaching at least to the elbows, and extending well back. The back should be strong and straight, with well developed withers. The length should equal the height at the withers. The belly should be well drawn up toward the flank, but should not give a tucked up appearance. Too narrow or too broad chest, loose shoulders or elbows, weak back, and shallow body are faults.

Hind Quarters.—Should have strongly muscled, slanting thighs, and should never appear overbuilt or higher than the shoulders. When standing naturally, the line from hip to knee should be vertical, from knee to hock should be parallel to the upper neck line, and from the hock to the ground should be vertical.

Tail.—Should be set moderately high and carried erect. It is cut down to three joints and should not be longer than one inch.

Feet.—Should be short and round, with the toes well arched (cat's paws), with dark nails and hard pads.

Coat.—Should be hard and wiry, neither smooth nor long, but giving a slightly rough appearance when seen against the grain. The outer coat should be harsh to the touch, the undercoat close and soft. It should be trimmed only enough to accentuate the body outline, and should be not less than three-quarters of an inch long, except on the ears and skull.

Size.—Should be from 10½ to 13½ inches for males and 10 to 12½ inches for females. Animals *under* or over these heights should be faulted, but no animal should be disqualified for oversize unless more than 14 inches if a male or 13 inches if a female. The ideal size approximates 12 inches, the males running slightly larger. Too small, toyish appearing dogs are not typical and should be penalized.

Color.—Should be pepper and salt or similar equal mixtures, light or dark, and including the "red pepper," pure black, and black and tan. Faults are solid colors other than black, also very light, whitish, spotted or tiger colors, but a small white spot on the breast is not a fault.

Faults.—Are as above enumerated, and also dogs too low or high legged; too heavy in head; with badly cut or carried ears; too steep or too level croup; straight shoulders; low shoulders; cowhocks; toed-in, long or spreading feet; weak pasterns; light bone; coat too long and soft or curly, and too short and smooth, or too closely trimmed; shy, savage, or highly nervous temperament.

Disqualifications.—Dogs over 14 and bitches over 13 inches; albinoes; dogs entered in contravention of state laws forbidding the exhibition of cropped dogs.

SCHNAUZERS (STANDARD)

(Illustrations facing pages 446 and 557)

(By Courtesy of The Standard Schnauzer Club of America)

Of the three varieties of Schnauzer; Miniature, Standard, and Giant, all of which are bred and registered as distinct breeds, the Medium, or Standard is the prototype.

He is a German breed of great antiquity and in the fifteenth and sixteenth centuries must have been in high favor as a household companion, for his portrait appears in many paintings of the period. Albert Dürer is known to have owned one for at least twelve years as the portrait of the same dog occurs several times in works of that artist between the years 1492 and 1504. Rembrandt painted several Schnauzers and Lucas Cranach the Elder shows one in a tapestry dated 1501, while, in the eighteenth century one appears in a canvas of the English painter Sir Joshua Reynolds. At Mechlinburg, Germany, in the Market Place there is a statue of a hunter dating from the fourteenth century, with a Schnauzer crouching at his feet which conforms very closely to the present-day Show Standard.

The general impression of the Schnauzer is that of a compact, sinewy, square-built dog, sturdy and alert, with stiff wiry coat and bristling eye-brows and whiskers. His nature combines high-spirited temperament with unusual intelligence and extreme reliability. He occupies the midway position between the large breeds and the toys.

As far as can be determined, the Schnauzer originated

in the crossing of black German Poodle and grey Wolf Spitz upon wire-haired Pinscher stock. From the Pinscher element derives the tendency to fawn-colored under-coat, and from the Wolf Spitz is inherited the typical pepper and salt coat color and its harsh wiry character. Solid black specimens of the breed, while fairly common in Germany, are still rather unusual in this country, except in Chicago and the Middle West, where several breeders have taken them up, and are endeavoring to correct the tendency shown by the blacks to revert to the soft coat of their Poodle ancestry.

The breed in America is classed as a Terrier. German breeders however regard the Schnauzer principally as a working dog. His original vocation was that of rat-catcher, yard dog, and guard. Before the War in Germany, fully ninety per-cent of the dogs used to guard the carts of farm produce in the market places, while the farmers rested themselves and their teams at the Inns, were of strong Schnauzer blood, and it was the extraordinary qualities of these striking looking dogs that led to further inquiries as to their breed, resulting in the discovery that the land of their origin holds the Schnauzer second to none for sagacity and fearlessness. Owing to these characteristics the "dogs with the human brain" (as their owners proudly call them) were much used by the Army during the war as dispatch-carriers and Red Cross aids; they are also employed in Germany in Police work.

German breeders are exceedingly anxious that the Schnauzer shall not deteriorate into a mere show dog— a fate that his rapidly rising popularity both at home and abroad may threaten. To this end most of the "Verein von Schnauzern" (Schnauzer Clubs) hold periodical Ratting Trials. Rats are placed in a large ring surrounded by wire netting, the floor of which is covered with straw or brush-wood; two or more dogs are turned in and the dog who noses out and kills the most rats in the shortest time is declared the winner. Ratting trials are also held occasionally at some of the larger Dog Shows in Germany and prove a great attraction to the public as well as a telling advertisement for the breed. Schnauzers are also proving themselves apt pupils for the Obedience and Intelligence Tests which are a feature of so many of the present-day Shows.

In this country and in England, where the breed has made rapid strides in favor, they are mainly used as personal guards and companions, especially for children for which purpose their devotion and bravery, coupled with an uncanny perception of approaching danger, renders them particularly suitable. They are good water dogs and are easily taught to retrieve; and on at least one Western sheep ranch Schnauzers have proved themselves the most efficient of various breeds tried as protection for the flocks against marauding coyotes.

Schnauzers were first exhibited in Germany as Wire-Haired Pinschers in 1879 at the Third German International Show at Hanover; they came from the Württemberg Kennels of Burger Leonburg, and a dog named "Schnauzer" won first prize. Württemberg is the cradle of many of the German breeds and one of the most important of the early Schnauzer breeders was a Württemberger, Herr Max Hartenstein of the Plavia Kennels.

A Standard was published in 1880 and the breed made rapid progress as a show dog. The first Specialty Show was held at Stuttgart in 1890 with the remarkable entry of 93 dogs. The Pinscher Club was founded at Cologne in 1895 and the Bavarian Schnauzer Club at Munich in 1907. In 1918 the Pinscher and Schnauzer Clubs united to become the official representative of the breed in the German Kennel Club. It is known as the Pinscher-Schnauzer Club and has well over 1,000 members. There are today official clubs devoted to the breed in Holland, Austria, Switzerland, Czechoslovakia, England, and America.

From a breeding point of view there are two major male lines of descent tracing back to two unregistered dogs, one the above-mentioned "Schnauzer," and another called "Seppel," while the two most famous basic bitches are "Settchen" and "Jette von Enz." "Settchen" traces back to "Schnauzer" and was bred to a dog of the "Seppel" line called "Prinz Harttmuth"; by this mating she became the dam of "Sieger Rex von Den Gunthersburg." "Rex" in turn became the Sire of "Sieger Rigo Schnauzerlust," and these two dogs, "Rex" and "Rigo," have had a greater influence upon the breed than any others in the Stud Book. "Jette von Enz" was the dam of "Rigo" and her line traces back to "Seppel." A litter-brother of "Rigo" named "Rex von Egelsee," also figures very prominently in the early breeding records; both these dogs were used extensively and with excellent results, for in-breeding. Demonstrative of the stamina and virility of Schnauzers is the fact that both "Rigo" and "Rex" were successfully serving as Studs when they were twelve years old.

Schnauzers have only become widely known in this country since the war, but one is said to have been shown at the Westminster Kennel Club Show in the miscellaneous class as early as 1899. The first recorded importation is "Fingal," brought over by Mr. Leisching of Rochester, N. Y. in 1905. "Fingal" died in 1914, at the age of 10. The Schnauzer Club of America was formed in 1925. The first Schnauzer to become an American

Champion was the Swiss bitch, "Resy Patricia," imported by Mrs. Maurice Newton, who bred from her the first American-Bred Champion, "Fracas Franconia." The first dog to make the American title was "Holm von Egelsee," who was also the first Sieger to come to this country. He was imported by Mr. William D. Goff the President of the Standard Schnauzer Club of America.

All Schnauzers in Germany have their ears cropped, but cropping in this country being governed by the separate laws of the different States, the American Schnauzer Club standard permits both the cropped and the natural ear.

DESCRIPTION AND STANDARD OF POINTS

(By Courtesy of The Standard Schnauzer Club of America)

General Impression.—The Schnauzer is a robust, sinewy, more heavy set than slender dog, of somewhat rectangular build. His nature combines high-spirited temperament with extreme reliability.

Head.—Strong and elongated, gradually narrowing from the ears to the eyes and thence towards the tip of the nose, in proportion to the size of the body. Its total length (tip of nose to occiput) should compare approximately to one-third the length of the back (withers—first dorsal vertebra—to the beginning of the tail). Upper part of the head (occiput to the base of the forehead) broad between the ears—its width should not be more than two-thirds of the length—with flat, creaseless forehead and well-muscled but not too strongly developed cheeks. Ears, small and V-shaped of moderate thickness, set well on the head and dropping forward closely to the cheek, or cropped with ears evenly cut, placed high and carried erect in excitement. Eyes medium-sized, dark, oval, turned forward, brows arched and wiry.

The powerful ferreting snout formed by the upper and lower jaw (base of forehead to the tip of nose) should be in proportion to the upper head and should end in a moderately blunt manner, with heavy stubby whiskers. Ridge of the nose straight and running almost parallel to the extension of the forehead. The tip of the nose is black and full. Lips tight and not overlapping, with strongly developed fangs, healthy and pure white.

Neck.—Not too short with skin close-fitting at the throat. Nape strong and slightly arched.

Fore Quarters.—Shoulders slanting and flat, but strongly muscled. Forelegs (upper and under arm) seen from all sides are vertical without any curve.

Chest.—Moderately broad with visible strong breast bone and reaching at least to the height of the elbow and slowly extending backwards. Back strong and straight with well-developed short thighs. The length of back equal to shoulder height (from withers vertical to floor) built squarely, belly well drawn up towards the back.

Tail.—Carried high and cut down to three joints.

Hind Quarters.—Thighs slanting and flat, but strongly muscled. Hindlegs (upper and lower thighs) at first vertical to the knee, from knee to hock in line with the extension of the upper neck line, from hock vertical to ground.

Paws.—Short, round, extremely compact paws, with close arched toes (cat's paws) dark nails and hard soles.

Hair.—Close, strong, hard and wiry, on the back seen against the grain—unruly—that is, neither short nor smooth; shorter on ears, forehead, legs and paws.

Height.—From 15¾ to 19¾ inches shoulder height. All dogs over or under height are automatically disqualified.

Color.—All pepper and salt colored or similar equal mixtures, pure black or black with tan.

	Points
Head and ears	10
Whiskers	10
Neck	5
Shoulders and crest	10
Back and loin	10
Hind quarters	15
Stern	5

MINIATURE SCHNAUZER

Head Study
MINIATURE SCHNAUZER
Showing cropped ears

SCHNAUZER *(Standard)*

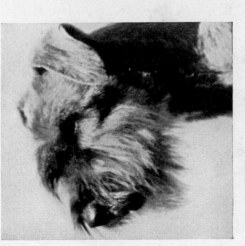

Head Study
SCHNAUZER *(Standard)*
Showing ears uncropped

SCHNAUZERS

Legs and feet 10
Coat 15
General expression 10

————

Total 100

Faults.—Too plump, or too light, low or high-legged build, too heavy around head, creased forehead, sticking-out or badly cut ears, light eye (with yellow or light-grey rings) strongly protruding cheek-bones, flabby throat skin; undershot or overshot jaw. Teeth too pointed, too small or too long, sunken or roached back, chest with barrel ribs (tubby) slanting crupper, elbows turned out, heels turned in, hindpart overbuilt, too steep, spread open toes, long and flat (hare) paws, too short, sleek, too long, soft, silky, curled, rolled, shaggy hair, all white, spotty, tigered, red and reddish colors.

Small white breast spot, or marking on the breast is not a fault.

SCOTTISH TERRIERS

(Illustration facing page 564)

(By Courtesy of The Scottish Terrier Club of America)

Most lovers of the Scottish Terrier have a deep and abiding belief that this breed is the most ancient of any of the Highland terriers; that the other breeds are only offshoots from this, the parent stem, and that the Scottie is the original, dyed-in-the-wool, simon-pure Highland Terrier. They will tell you that the Skye Terrier mentioned in early histories and chronicles was not the Skye as we know it today, but the forerunner of our favorite and very similar in type to it. They will refer you to such early writers as Jacques du Fouilloux, who published *La Venerie* in 1561, Touberville and Dr. Stevens, whose books "The Noble Art of Venerie" and "The Maison Rustique" appeared in 1570 and 1572, respectively. All of these works described an "Earth dog used in hunting the fox and the brocke," and these descriptions fit closely to what might have been the forerunner of our present-day Scottie.

In the seventeenth century, when King James VI of Scotland became James I of England, he wrote to Edinburgh to have a half dozen terriers sent to France as a present and addressed the letter to the Laird of Caldwell, naming the Earl of Montieth as having good ones. Later, the great English authority, Rawdon B. Lee, wrote as follows:

"The Scottie is the oldest variety of the canine race indigenous to Britain. . . . For generations he had been a popular dog in the Highlands where, strangely enough, he was always known as the

[559]

Skye Terrier, although he is different from the long-coated, un-sporting-like creature with which that name is now associated."

While all of this is very interesting and quite possibly true, the fact remains that it is not definite nor conclusive.

Leaving the realm of speculation and inference and coming down to history and known facts, we do know that the Scottish Terrier as we find it today has been bred in purity for over sixty years. The first show to have a class for Scottish Terriers was at Birmingham in England, in 1860. Later, a number of other shows carried this classification but the dogs shown in these classes were not Scottish Terriers, but Skyes, Dandie Dinmonts and Yorkshires.

All of the while, however, Scotchmen who saw these dogs winning as Scottish Terriers were indignant, and about 1877 they broke into print in the Live Stock Journal with a series of letters protesting this situation and discussing the points and character of the true Scottish Terrier. The discussion waxed so furious that the editors finally called a halt, with the statement, "We see no use in prolonging this discussion unless each correspondent describes the dog which he holds to be the true type." This challenge was taken up by Captain Gordon Murray, who in a letter to the "Stock Keeper" under the nom de plume of "Strathbogie," described in detail his conception of a proper Scottish Terrier. This quieted the warring factions and about 1880 J. B. Morrison was persuaded to draw up a standard. This was accepted by all parties.

The essentials of this standard have been retained in all the later standards, only minor changes having been introduced. In 1882 the Scottish Terrier Club was organized, with joint officers for England and Scotland. Later, as interest in the breed grew, the two countries organized separate clubs, although they have always worked harmoniously together. A joint committee revamped the Morrison standard and in 1933 the English Club again revised this standard. The present American standard, which follows, was adopted in 1925, Messrs. Bixby, Cadwalader and Megargee being the committee who made the revisions. In most essentials these standards are identical, the chief difference between the American and the foreign standards being in the weight requirements.

John Naylor is credited with being the first to introduce the Scottish Terrier to this country, his first importation in 1883 consisting of a dog and a bitch, "Tam Glen" and "Bonnie Belle." He showed extensively and continued importing, among his later importations being his famous dogs "Glenlyon" and "Whinstone." The first Scottish Terrier registered in America was "Dake" (3688), a brindle dog whelped September 15, 1884, bred by O. P. Chandler of Kokomo, Indiana. His sire was Naylor's "Glenlyon." This was in the American Kennel Register, published by Forest and Stream, and about the time American Kennel Club was being organized. In December, 1887, a bitch "Lassie" was registered, bred by W. H. Todd of Vermillion, Ohio. Her sire was "Glencoe," by "Imp. Whinstone" ex "Imp. Roxie." Here we find "Whinstone" figuring as a sire. Now "Whinstone" was by "Allister," who together with "Dundee" formed the two great fountain heads of the breed. "Whinstone" sired "Ch. Bellingham Baliff" which was acquired by J. J. Little, founder of the famous Newcastle Kennels. "Whinstone" therefore was the forerunner and progenitor of the Scottish Terrier in this country today.

The Newcastle Kennels flourished for many years and is still in existence, and in this way the blood of "Whinstone" through "Bellingham Baliff" was spread throughout the land.

Since those days there have been thousands of importations and many notable breeders have carried on the work. Probably very little if any of the early blood is to be found today. Nevertheless, these early dogs must take their place in history; and to that pioneer breeder and missionary of the breed, John Naylor, the great popularity of this staunch little breed today stands as an enduring monument.

DESCRIPTION AND STANDARD OF POINTS
(Courtesy of The Scottish Terrier Club of America)

Skull.—Long, of medium width, slightly domed and covered with short, hard hair. It should not be quite flat as there should be a slight stop or drop between the eyes.

Muzzle.—In proportion to the length of skull, with not too much taper toward the nose. Nose should be black and of good size. The jaws should be perfectly level and teeth square, although the nose projects somewhat over the mouth giving the impression that the upper jaw is longer than the lower.

Eyes.—Set wide apart, small and of almond shape, not round. Color to be dark brown or nearly black. To be bright, piercing and set well under the brow.

Ears.—Small, prick, set well up on the skull, rather pointed but not cut. The hair on them should be short and velvety.

Neck.—Moderately short, thick and muscular, strongly set on sloping shoulders, but not so short as to appear clumsy.

Chest.—Broad and very deep, well let down between the fore legs.

Body.—Moderately short and well ribbed up with strong loin, deep flanks and very muscular hind quarters.

Legs and Feet.—Both fore and hindlegs should be short and very heavy in bone in proportion to the size of the dog. Fore legs straight or slightly bent with elbows close to the body, as Scottish

SCOTTISH TERRIERS

Terriers should not be out at the elbows. Stifles should be well bent and legs straight from hock to heel. Thighs very muscular. Feet round and thick with strong nails, forefeet larger than the hind feet.

Tail.—Never cut and about seven inches long, carried gaily with a slight curve but not over the back.

Coat.—Rather short, about two inches, dense undercoat with outer coat intensely hard and wiry.

Size.—About ten inches high at the shoulder and weight about 18 or 20 pounds for both sexes. The correct size must take into consideration height fully as much as weight.

Color.—Steel or iron grey, brindled or grizzled, black, sandy or wheaten. White markings are objectionable and can be allowed only on the chest and that to a slight extent only.

General Appearance.—The face should wear a keen, sharp and active expression. Both head and tail should be carried well up. The dog should look very compact, well muscled and powerful, giving the impression of immense power in a small size.

Faults.—Eyes large, round or light colored. Light bone. Out at elbows. Ears round, drop, or too large. Coat soft, silky or curly. Jaw over or undershot. Over or under size.

SCALE OF POINTS

	Points
Skull	5
Muzzle	5
Eyes	5
Ears	10
Neck	5
Chest	5
Body	15
Legs and feet	10
Tail	2½
Coat	15
Size	10
Color	2½
General appearance	10
Total	100

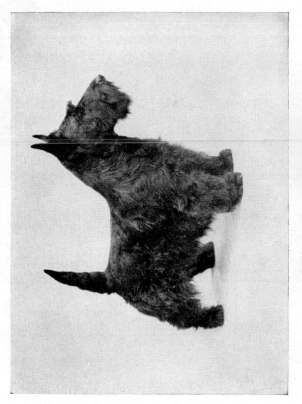

SCOTTISH TERRIER

SEALYHAM

SEALYHAM TERRIERS

(Illustration on opposite page)

(By Courtesy of The American Sealyham Terrier Club)

The Sealyham terrier derives its name from Sealyham, Haverfordwest, Wales, the estate of the late Captain John Edwardes who, between 1850 and 1891, developed from obscure ancestry a strain of dogs noted for prowess in quarrying badger, otter and fox. The requisite qualities were extreme gameness and endurance with as much substance as could be encompassed in a dog small and quick enough to dig and battle underground.

As the working ability of Sealyham terriers drew public interest, they began to take their places with other terrier breeds in prominent homes and on the show bench. Their first recorded appearance at a dog show was at Haverfordwest, Wales, in October, 1903. In January, 1908, a group of Welsh fanciers founded the Sealyham Terrier Club of Haverfordwest and at their first meeting drew up the original standard of points for the breed. The first championship show at which Sealyham terriers appeared was at the English Kennel Club Show in October, 1910. The breed was recognized on March 8, 1911, by the Kennel Club, who offered the first challenge certificates for Sealyham terriers at the Great Joint Terrier Show, London, June 10, 1911.

There are three clubs that sponsor the breed in Great Britain: the Sealyham Terrier Club of Haverfordwest, which holds an annual show in Wales; the Sealyham Terrier Breeders' Association, which holds an annual championship show near London; and the Midland Sealyham Terrier Club, which holds an annual championship show at Rugby.

The breed was recognized by the American Kennel Club in 1911, shortly after its original importation into the United States. In the comparatively few years since the American show debut of the Sealyham terrier at San Mateo, California, in September, 1911, it has become one of the most popular breeds. Great credit is due to breeders and exhibitors for having perfected the type to such an extent in this short time that it is quite a common event for a Sealyham terrier to be awarded "Best of All Breeds" at the largest shows today.

The American Sealyham Terrier Club was founded on May 15, 1913, to promote the interests of the breed in the United States and to encourage exhibition and working trials. The club offers annual trophies for competition among members throughout the country under approved judges. It holds an annual Specialty Show for American-Bred Sealyham Terriers at which numerous trophies are offered and at which its annual futurity stakes are judged. Working certificates are awarded by a committee or on recommendation of masters of foxhounds to the club. At the annual meeting of the American Sealyham Terrier Club in February, 1935, a revised standard of points was adopted. This was approved by the American Kennel Club as the official standard for Sealyham Terriers in the United States of America.

SEALYHAM TERRIERS

DESCRIPTION AND STANDARD OF POINTS

(Adopted by The American Sealyham Terrier Club, February, 1935, and Approved by The American Kennel Club, March 12, 1935)

The Sealyham should be the embodiment of power and determination, ever keen and alert, of extraordinary substance, yet free from clumsiness.

Height.—At withers about 10½ inches. Weight: 21 pounds for dogs, and 20 pounds for bitches. It should be borne in mind that size is more important than weight.

Head.—Long, broad and powerful, without coarseness. It should, however, be in perfect balance with the body, joining neck smoothly. Length of head roughly, three-quarters height at withers, or about an inch longer than neck. Breadth between ears a little less than one-half length of head.

Skull.—Very slightly domed, with a shallow indentation running down between the brows, and joining the muzzle with a moderate stop.

Cheeks.—Smoothly formed and flat, without heavy jowls.

Jaws.—Level, powerful and square. Overshot or undershot bad faults.

Teeth.—Sound, strong and white, with canines fitting closely together.

Nose.—Black, with large nostrils. White, cherry or butterfly bad faults.

Eyes.—Very dark, deeply set and fairly wide apart, of medium size, oval in shape with keen terrier expression. Light, large or protruding eye bad faults.

Ears.—Folded level with top of head, with forward edge close to cheek. Well rounded at tip, and of length to reach outer corner of eye. Thin, not leathery, and of sufficient thickness to avoid creases. Prick, tulip, rose or hound ears bad faults.

Neck.—Length slightly less than two-thirds of height of dog at withers. Muscular without coarseness, with good reach, refinement at throat, and set firmly on shoulders.

[567]

TERRIERS

Shoulders.—Well laid back and powerful, but not overmuscled. Sufficiently wide to permit freedom of action. Upright or straight shoulder placement highly undesirable.

Legs.—Forelegs strong, with good bone; and as straight as is consistent with chest being well let down between them. Down on pasterns, knuckled over, bound, and out at elbow, bad faults. Hindlegs longer than forelegs and not so heavily boned.

Feet.—Large but compact, round with thick pads, strong nails. Toes well arched and pointing straight ahead. Forefeet larger, though not quite so long as hindfeet. Thin, spread or flat feet bad faults.

Body.—Strong, short coupled and substantial, so as to permit great flexibility. Brisket deep and well let down between forelegs. Ribs well sprung.

Back.—Length from withers to set on of tail should approximate height at withers, or 10½ inches. Top line level, neither roached or swayed. Any deviations from these measurements undesirable.

Hind Quarters.—Very powerful, and protruding well behind the set on of tail. Strong second thighs, stifles well bent, and hocks well let down. Capped or cowhocks bad faults.

Tail.—Docked and carried upright. Set on far enough forward so that spine does not slope down to it.

Coat.—Weather resisting, comprised of soft, dense undercoat and hard, wiry top coat. Silky or curly coat bad fault.

Color.—All white, or with lemon, tan or badger markings on head and ears. Heavy body markings and excessive ticking should be discouraged.

Action.—Sound, strong, quick, free, true and level.

Note:—The measurements were taken with calipers.

SKYE TERRIERS

(Illustration facing page 576)

The majority of terriers have attained something of their present-day form within the last century; but the Skye terrier of nearly four centuries ago was so like the specimens of today that his description at the time almost fits the modern standard—a standard which has suffered far less change than most.

One may find mention of the Skye terrier in that historic volume called "Englishe Dogges," which was penned, strangely, by Dr. John Caius, master of Gonville and Caius College, Cambridge University, and court physician to Edward VI, Queen Mary, and Queen Elizabeth. A man of broad education—aside from the sciences —and also a great traveller and sportsman, Dr. Caius was the first man to write a book devoted solely to the dog.

Referring to the breed, he says it was "brought out of barbarous borders fro' the uttermost countryes northward," . . . "which, by reason of the length of heare, makes showe neither of face nor of body."

Thus we find the Skye terrier of today. His flowing coat is the same as the one that proved such a grand protection in the days when his only occupation was the challenging of vicious animals that otherwise might have crippled him at a single bite. Perhaps this long coat has been a handicap, for all followers of this game, old, and small working terrier have witnessed him surpassed in popularity by one after another of the newer breeds. Still they are reluctant to change him in any manner.

They, indeed, stand by the motto of the Skye Club of Scotland—"Wha Daur Meddle Wi' Me."

The breed takes its name from the chief of those north-western islands of Scotland that, as far back as he can be traced, formed his native home, and in which he was found in greatest perfection. He is the only terrier distinctively belonging to the north-western islands that is not common to the whole of Scotland.

It is believed by those who have the best practical knowledge of the Skye that he is without rival in his own peculiar domain. His followers believe that wherever there are rocks, dens, burrows, cairns, or covers to explore, or waters to take to, that his services should be called. The smallest of all the useful terrier tribe; the lowest set; the longest in body; the strongest, proportionally, in legs, feet, jaws, and chest; the most muscular in his whole frame; the best protected against weather, injury, or foes; it is claimed by his adherents that the Skye terrier has an unequalled acuteness of sight, scent, and hearing; an unrivalled alacrity of action; and indomitable pluck. In short, he is possessed of preeminent qualifications for his special work.

From the nature of Dr. Caius' allusion to him, it is evident that the Skye terrier had become known in the cities of England, especially in the royal palace. The kings and queens of England have always set the styles in that country, and as soon as the Skye had been accepted in court—evidently in the middle of the sixteenth century when Dr. Caius penned the historic work on dogs—he was soon the fashionable pet of all degrees of nobility, and after that the commoners.

No other definite terrier breed has yet existed long enough to rival the duration of the Skye's popularity, for he still was the most widely known of all the terriers down to the end of the nineteenth century. He was kept in all the English-speaking countries. Since then he has slipped quietly into the background. Yet his admirers in England and Scotland—where he has maintained his greatest foothold—are happy to point to the time when "a duchess would almost be ashamed to be seen in the park unaccompanied by her long-coated Skye."

The Skye terrier was one of the most important breeds at American bench shows before the turn of the century, and the rivalry among the leading kennels was exceptionally keen. Particular attention was paid in the judging of him that he should be two and a half times as long as the height at the shoulder, with a tail the equal in length of that same height. The average height is about nine inches. With a massive head that should measure just about half an inch less than his tail, he has a total length of some 40 inches. The dogs average 18 pounds, and the bitches 16 pounds. The coat is double, and the outer should hang down about 5½ inches.

Although the frontiers of his activities have been somewhat curtailed, the true value of the Skye terrier is evinced by the tenacious grasp which he has on those who have ever come in contact with him. Thus, entries may sometimes be small at bench shows today, but seldom does one find a major show without some specimens of this old terrier breed.

DESCRIPTION AND STANDARD OF POINTS
(By Courtesy of the "Skye" Club of Scotland)

Head.—Long, with powerful jaws and incisive teeth closing level, or upper just fitting over under.

Skull.—Wide at front of brow, narrowing between ears, and tapering gradually towards muzzle, with little falling in between or behind the eyes.

Eyes.—Hazel, medium size, close set.

Muzzle.—Always black.

Ears (Prick or Pendant).—When *prick,* not large, erect at outer edges, and slanting towards each other at inner, from peak to skull. When *pendant,* larger, hanging straight, lying flat, and close at front.

Body.—Pre-eminently long and low. Shoulders broad, chest deep, ribs well sprung and oval-shaped, giving flattish appearance to sides. Hind quarters and flank full and well developed. Back level and slightly declining from top of hip joint to shoulders. Neck long and gently crested.

Tail.—When *hanging,* upper half perpendicular, under half thrown backwards in a curve. When *raised,* a prolongation of the incline of the back, and not rising higher nor curling up.

Legs.—Short, straight, and muscular. No dewclaws. Feet large and pointing forward.

Coat (Double).—An *under,* short, close, soft and woolly. An *over,* long—average 5½ inches—hard, straight, flat and free from crisp or curl. Hair on head: shorter, softer and veiling forehead and eyes; on ears overhanging inside, falling down and mingling with side locks, not heavily, but surrounding the ear like a fringe and allowing its shape to appear. Tail also gracefully feathered.

Color (Any Variety).—Dark or light blue or grey, or fawn with black points. Shade of head and legs approximately that of body.

Average Measure.—Dog: Height, at shoulder, 9 inches; length, back of skull to root of tail, 22½ inches; length, muzzle to back of skull, 8½ inches; length, root of tail to tip joint, 9 inches; total length, 40 inches. Bitch: Half an inch lower and two and a half inches shorter than dog, all parts proportional; thus, body 21 inches, head 8, and tail 8½; total, 37½ inches.

Average Weight.—Dog, 18 pounds; bitch, 16 pounds. No dog should be over 20 pounds nor under 16 pounds; and no bitch should be over 18 pounds nor under 14 pounds.

SKYE TERRIERS

	Points
Size	15
Head	15
Ears	10
Body	15
Tail	10
Legs	10
Coat	20
Color and condition	5
Total	100

1. Over extreme weight to be handicapped 5 points per pound of excess.
2. Over or undershot mouth to disqualify.
3. Doctored ears or tail to disqualify.
4. No *extra* value for greater length of coat than 5½ inches.

STAFFORDSHIRE TERRIERS

(Illustration facing page 577)

(By Courtesy of the Staffordshire Terrier Club of America)

To correctly give the origin, and history of the Staffordshire Terrier, it is necessary to comment briefly on two other dogs; namely, the bulldog and the terrier.

Until the early part of the 19th century, the bulldog was bred with great care in England, for the purpose of baiting the bull. The then-bulldog was vastly different from our present day "Sour-Mug." Pictures that were used as late as 1870 to represent the bulldog give him the appearance of being agile, standing straighter on his legs —his front legs in particular. In some cases, he was even possessed with muzzle, and long rat-tails were not uncommon. In fact, the old bulldog of years ago, with the exception of head, looks more like our present day Staffordshire Terrier than he does the present day English Bulldog.

Some writers contend it was the white English Terrier, or the black-and-tan Terrier that was used as a cross with the bulldog to perfect the Staffordshire Terrier. It seems easier to believe that ANY game terriers, such as the Foxterriers of the early 1800's, were used in this cross, as some of the foremost authorities on dogs of that time state that the black-and-tan and the white English Terrier were none too game, but these same authorities go on to stress the gameness of the Foxterriers. It is reasonable to believe that breeders who were attempting to perfect a

[575]

dog that would combine the spirit and agility of the terrier with the courage and tenacity of the bulldog, would not use a terrier that was not game. In analyzing the three above-mentioned terriers at that time, we find that there was not a great deal of difference in body conformation, the greatest differences being in color, aggressiveness, and spirit.

In any event, it was this cross between the bulldog and the terrier that resulted in the Staffordshire Terrier, which was originally known or called "Bull-and-Terrier Dog," "Half and Half," and at times was referred to as "Pit Dog" or "Pit Bullterrier," later assuming the name in England of "Staffordshire Bullterrier." As early as 1870 these dogs began to find their way into this country and became known as "Pit Dogs," "Pit Bullterriers," later "American Bullterriers" and still later, were known as "Yankee Terriers" and were finally recognized by the American Kennel Club under the name "Staffordshire Terriers." The name "Staffordshire Bullterrier" was originally applied to this dog in England at about the time dog fighting was abolished, the people in and around Staffordshire favoring the continuance of this form of alleged sport.

Breeders in this country have developed a type many of which are a little heavier in weight than the modern Staffordshire of England. These dogs have not been primarily show dogs, but have been bred for gameness, soundness, intelligence and spirit. The weights in this country for the female are, on the average, from 35 to 45 pounds, and the average weight for the male is about from 40 to 50 pounds, while in England many specimens are approximately 10 pounds less. The excess weight that we have acquired in this country is not a result of infusion of other blood, but was obtained by selecting the

SKYE TERRIER

STAFFORDSHIRE TERRIER

larger dogs for breeding purposes, since breeders desired a bit heavier dog. While the weight may vary, it should be in proportion to size; and this dog's chief requisites should be strength unusual for his size, soundness, balance, a strong, powerful head, a well-muscled body, and courage that is proverbial.

For the sake of clarifying in the minds of even dog fanciers, the confusion that may exist concerning the difference between the all-white English Bullterrier, and the Staffordshire Terrier, it is advisable to comment briefly upon Bullterriers. The all-white English Bullterrier was introduced by Mr. James Hinks, of Birmingham, who had been experimenting for several years with the old bull-and-terrier dog, now known as Staffordshire. It is generally conceded that he used the Staffordshire, crossed with the white English terrier, and some writers contend that a dash of Pointer and Dalmatian blood was also used to help perfect the all-white Bullterrier.

In mentioning the gameness of the Staffordshire, it is not the intention to tag him as a fighting machine, or praise this characteristic. These points are discussed because they are necessary in giving the correct origin and history of the breed. The good qualities of this breed are many, and it would be difficult for anyone to overstress them. In appearance, they are very flashy looking and they attract much attention on the show bench. As to character, they exceed being dead game, but nevertheless, they should not be held in ill-repute merely because man has been taking advantage of this rare courage and using them in the pit as mere gambling tools. These dogs are one of the most docile of all breeds; with little training, are even tractable around other dogs; very intelligent, make excellent guardians, and protect their masters' property with an air of authority that counts. Around children they are absolutely safe, and easily discriminate between strangers who mean well and those who do not. They have another characteristic that is most unusual, and that is, when they are sold, or change hands, they accept their new master in a comparatively short time.

The recognition of this breed by the American Kennel Club should be accepted by supporters of all other breeds as a worthy addition to the Terrier group.

DESCRIPTION AND STANDARD OF POINTS

(Adopted by the Staffordshire Terrier Club of America and Approved by the American Kennel Club, June 10, 1936)

General Impression.—The Staffordshire Terrier should give the impression of: Great Strength for his size; a well put-together dog, muscular, but agile and graceful, keenly alive to his surroundings. He should be stocky, not long-legged or racy in outline. His courage is proverbial.

Head.—Medium length, deep through, broad skull, very pronounced cheek muscles, distinct stop; and ears are set high.

Ears.—Cropped or uncropped, the latter preferred. Uncropped ears should be short and held half rose or prick. Full drop to be penalized.

Eyes.—Dark and round, low down in skull and set far apart. No pink eyelids.

Muzzle.—Medium length, rounded on upper side to fall away abruptly below eyes. Jaws well-defined. Under jaw to be strong and have biting power. Lips close and even, no looseness. Upper teeth to meet tightly outside lower teeth in front. Nose definitely black.

Neck.—Heavy, slightly arched, tapering from shoulders to back of skull. No looseness of skin. Medium length.

Shoulders.—Strong and muscular with blades wide and sloping.

Back.—Fairly short. Slight sloping from withers to rump with gentle short slope at rump to base of tail. Loins slightly tucked.

[578]

STAFFORDSHIRE TERRIERS

Body.—Well sprung ribs, deep in rear. All ribs close together. Forelegs set rather wide apart to permit of chest development. Chest deep and broad.

Tail.—Short in comparison to size, low set, tapering to a fine point; not curled or held over back. Not docked.

Legs.—The front legs should be straight, large or round bones, pastern upright. No resemblance of bend in front. Hind quarters well-muscled, let down at hocks, turning neither in nor out. Feet of moderate size, well-arched and compact. Gait must be springy but without roll or pace.

Coat.—Short, close, stiff to the touch, and glossy.

Color.—Any color, solid, parti, or patched is permissible, but all white, more than 80 per cent white, black and tan, and liver not to be encouraged.

Size.—Height and weight should be in proportion. A height of about eighteen (18) to nineteen (19) inches at shoulders for the male and seventeen (17) to eighteen (18) inches for the female is to be considered preferable.

Faults.—Faults to be penalized are Dudley nose, light or pink eyes, tail too long or badly carried, undershot or overshot mouths.

WELSH TERRIERS

(Illustration facing page 588)

(By Courtesy of The Welsh Terrier Club of America)

Judging from the old paintings and prints of the first known terriers, the Welsh Terrier is probably the oldest of the terrier breeds for these prints show us a rough haired black and tan terrier.

In old times this black and tan wire haired terrier was more commonly known as the "Old English Terrier" or "Black and Tan Wire Haired Terrier," and as late as 1886 the English Kennel Club alloted one class for "Welsh or Old English Wire Haired Black and Tan Terriers." Even to this day the color of the Welsh is as it was a hundred years ago. In other respects also the Welsh Terrier has changed very slightly. He is, as then, a sporting dog extensively used in his native home Wales for hunting the Otter, Fox, and Badger, and possesses just that characteristic gameness that one naturally looks for in such a dog. Although game he is not quarrelsome, in fact he is one of the best mannered of terriers and probably the easiest to handle of any of the terrier breeds. As a "pal" for either Town or Country he is unexcelled and also makes an excellent watch dog, but probably his outstanding virtue is his wonderful disposition and ability to make friends. The Welsh are especially devoted and fond of children, which trait alone should recommend them as household pets.

Welsh Terriers should stand about fifteen inches and weigh about twenty pounds. Black and a rich tan in color they should be built like a cleverly made hunter, with plenty of bone and substance. Their heads should be broader than the Fox-terrier but their skull should be very flat and the eyes set fairly far apart which gives them that very intelligent, unmistakably Welsh expression so different from other terriers and so characteristic of the breed.

Welsh Terriers were first imported into this Country about forty years ago and records show that the first Welsh Terrier to be exhibited over here was Ch. Red Palm. He was shown in the miscellaneous classes as at that time there was no classification offered for the Welsh Terrier. Full classification is now offered at all shows in the country and the Welsh have become one of the most popular of the terrier breeds.

The first record of Welsh Terriers having a classification of their own in England was in 1884-85 at Carnavon where there were twenty-one entries, but even at this time it was not uncommon for dogs to be shown as Old English Terriers and also as Welsh Terriers, and as late at 1893 "Dick Turpin" a well known show dog of those days continued in this dual role. Welsh Terriers were first brought to this country by the late Mr. Prescott Lawrence in 1888. He imported a dog and a bitch "T'Other" and "Which," and showed them at the Old Madison Square Garden in the miscellaneous class. No other Welsh however were imported for some time, Ch. Red Palm making his debut over here some years later. But about 1901 classification was offered for the Welsh at Westminster and four or five dogs were shown, and from then on their popularity has steadily increased until today there is hardly a show in the United States where some of the breed are not benched.

As some writer most aptly put it "Welsh Terriers are

a wonderful Terrier, are a wonderful sport, and a wonderful friend."

DESCRIPTION AND STANDARD OF POINTS
(By Courtesy of The Welsh Terrier Club of America)

Head.—The skull should be flat, and rather wider between the ears than the Wire-haired Fox Terrier. The jaw should be powerful, clean-cut, rather deeper, and more punishing—giving the head a more masculine appearance than that usually seen on a Fox Terrier. Stop not too defined, fair length from stop to end of nose, the latter being of a black color.

Ears.—The ear should be V-shaped, small, not too thin, set on fairly high, carried forward and close to the cheek.

Eyes.—The eye should be small, not being too deeply set in or protruding out of skull, of a dark hazel color, expressive and indicating abundant pluck.

Neck.—The neck should be of moderate length and thickness, slightly arched and sloping gracefully into the shoulders.

Body.—The back should be short, and well-ribbed up, the loin strong, good depth, and moderate width of chest. The shoulders should be long, sloping, and well set back. The hind quarters should be strong, thighs muscular and of good length, with the hocks moderately straight, well let down, and fair amount of bone. The stern should be set on moderately high, but not too gaily carried.

Legs and Feet.—The legs should be straight and muscular, possessing fair amount of bone, with upright and powerful pasterns. The feet should be small, round and catlike.

Coat.—The coat should be wiry, hard, very close and abundant.

Color.—The color should be black and tan, or black grizzle and tan, free from black penciling on toes.

Size.—The height at shoulder should be 15 inches for dogs, bitches proportionately less. Twenty pounds shall be considered a fair average weight in working condition, but this may vary a pound or so either way.

TERRIERS

	Points
Head and jaws	10
Ears	5
Eyes	5
Neck and shoulders	10
Body	10
Loins and hind quarters	10
Legs and feet	10
Coat	15
Color	5
Stern	5
General appearance	15
Total	100

DISQUALIFYING POINTS

(1) Nose: white, cherry or spotted to a considerable extent with either of these colors. (2) Ears: prick, tulip or rose. (3) Undershot jaw or pig-jawed mouth. (4) Black below hocks or white to an appreciable extent.

WEST HIGHLAND WHITE TERRIERS

(Illustration facing page 589)

(By Courtesy of The West Highland White Terrier Club of America)

It is probable that the West Highland White Terrier and all the terriers of Scotland came from the same stock; the Scotties, Cairns, Dandie Dinmonts and West Highland Whites are branches from the same tree and its roots.

The West Highland White Terrier, according to notable authors and the Malcome family of Poltallock, Scotland, originated at Poltallock, and had been bred and maintained there for more than one hundred years prior to their appearance at dog shows. Col. Malcome in 1916 said that his father and grandfather both kept them. It is probable that the lineage of the Malcome dogs goes back to the time of King James I, who asked for some "earth-dogges" out of Argyleshire.

Years ago this breed was known as the Roseneath terrier also as the Poltallock terrier. The name Roseneath was taken from the Duke of Argyll's place in Dumbartonshire, Scotland.

The first show held for this breed was at Crufts in London.

Mr. Robert Goelet was the first to import the West Highlander to the United States. Mr. Goelet paid heavy money for the importation of British champions such as Kiltie of Glenmere and Rumpus of Glenmere, both grand dogs in their day. Today the breed is widely known and justly popular throughout the United States.

TERRIERS

The West Highland of today is all terrier, a large amount of Scotch spunk, determination and devotion crammed into a small body. Outdoors they are truly sporty, good hunters, speedy and cunning and have almost human intelligence. In the house they are all that can be desired in a pet; faithful, understanding and devoted yet so gay and light hearted. It is little wonder that there is such an ever increasing demand for this most lovable of little dogs.

One of the reasons the West Highland White Terrier is such a delightful little dog to own is his hardiness. They need no pampering and are in fact better without it. They love to romp and play in the snow and will follow skaters or walkers for miles across frozen lakes and harbors. They are also an easy breed to show and handle as they require very little trimming and indeed look very much better and more characteristic when in their natural state. Of course there are always a few hairs which should be pulled out just to smarten your dog up a bit but there is no prettier sight than a well kept West Highland White Terrier shown in full coat.

The West Highland's outer coat is hard and stiff and should be kept so by proper grooming and dry cleaning rather than washing. There are people who think a white dog very hard to keep clean but this is not so. The Highlander has a dry skin with none of that doggie odor and a little time spent each day with a brush and comb keeps him always in the pink of condition.

Above all things the West Highland is companionable, —they will ride for miles in a car, out walk anybody, swim with the best of you, follow behind a horse, in fact, take part in any outdoor thing that is going on, or curl up contentedly by the fire side.

While the West Highland is an active outdoor dog

and, given the opportunity, a good hunter, he seems able to adapt himself to almost any conditions and in many cases has proved the perfect city dog, adapting himself to small apartments and following his owner about the city streets in and out of traffic without a leash.

The West Highland is one of the most satisfactory dogs to breed because they always breed true. Naturally in a litter there are some pups that are better or more outstanding than others, but the whole litter will be characteristic of the breed and true Highlanders, also unlike some other breeds, are pretty from the very day they are born. Those who have raised or owned this breed are loud in praise of them and never want to be without one or more.

DESCRIPTION AND STANDARD OF POINTS

(By Courtesy of The West Highland White Terrier Club of America)

No. 1. *The General Appearance.*—Of the West Highland White Terrier is that of a small, game, hardy-looking Terrier, possessed with no small amount of self-esteem, with a varminty appearance, strongly built, deep in chest and back ribs, straight back and powerful quarters on muscular legs, and exhibiting in a marked degree a great combination of strength and activity. The coat should be about 2½ inches long, white in color, hard, with plenty of soft undercoat, and no tendency to wave or curl. The tail should be as straight as possible and carried not too gaily, and covered with hard hair, but not bushy. The skull should be not too broad, being in proportion to the terribly powerful jaws. The ears shall be as small and sharp-pointed as possible, and carried tightly up, and must be absolutely erect. The eyes of moderate size, dark hazel in color, widely placed, with a sharp, bright, intelligent expression. The muzzle should not be too long, powerful, and gradually tapering towards the nose; roof of mouth and pads of feet distinctly black in color.

TERRIERS

No. 2. *Color.*—Pure white; any other color objectionable.

No. 3. *Coat.*—Very important, and seldom seen to perfection; must be double-coated. The outer coat consists of hard hair, about 2 inches long, and free from any curl. The under coat, which resembles fur, is short, soft and close. Open coats are objectionable.

No. 4. *Size.*—Dogs to weigh from 15 to 19 pounds, and bitches from 13 to 17 pounds, and measure from 8 to 12 inches at the shoulder.

No. 5. *Skull.*—Should not be too narrow, being in proportion to his powerful jaw, not too long, slightly domed, and gradually tapering to the eyes, between which there should be a slight indentation or stop, eyebrows heavy, head and neck thickly coated with hair.

No. 6. *Eyes.*—Widely set apart, medium in size, dark hazel in color, slightly sunk in the head, sharp and intelligent, which, looking from under the heavy eyebrows give a piercing look. Full eyes and also light colored eyes are very objectionable.

No. 7. *Muzzle.*—Should be nearly equal in length to the rest of the skull, powerful and gradually tapering towards the nose, which should be fairly wide. The jaws level and powerful, the teeth square or evenly met, well set and large for the size of the dog. The nose and roof of mouth should be distinctly black in color.

No. 8. *Ears.*—Small, carried erect but never drop, and should be carried straight up, terminating in a sharp point. The hair of them should be short, smooth (velvety), and they should not be cut. The ears should be free from any fringe at the top. Round pointed, broad, and large ears are very objectionable, also ears too heavily covered with hair.

No. 9. *Neck.*—Muscular and nicely set on sloping shoulders.

No. 10. *Chest.*—Very deep, with breadth in proportion to the size of the dog.

No. 11. *Body.*—Compact, straight back, ribs deep and well arched in the upper half of rib, presenting a flattish side appearance, loins broad and strong, hind quarters strong, muscular and wide across the top.

WELSH TERRIER

WEST HIGHLAND WHITE TERRIER

WEST HIGHLAND WHITE TERRIERS

No. 12. *Legs and Feet.*—Both fore and hindlegs should be short and muscular. The shoulder blades should be comparatively broad, and well sloped backwards. The points of the shoulder blades should be closely knitted into the backbone, so that very little movement of them should be noticeable when the dog is walking. The elbow should be close into the body both when moving or standing, thus causing the foreleg to be well placed in under the shoulder. The forelegs should be straight and thickly covered with short hard hair. The hindlegs should be short and sinewy. The thighs very muscular and not too wide apart. The hocks bent and well set in under the body, so as to be fairly close to each other either when standing, walking, or trotting. The forefeet are larger than the hind ones, are round, proportionate in size, strong, thickly padded, and covered with short hard hair. The hindfeet are smaller and thickly padded. The under surface of the pads of feet should be distinctly black in color. Cowhocks detract from the general appearance. Straight or weak hocks, both kinds, are undesirable, and should be guarded against.

No. 13. *Tail.*—Five or six inches long, covered with hard hairs, no feather, as straight as possible, carried gaily but not curled over back. A long tail is objectionable.

No. 14. *Movement.*—Should be free, straight and easy all round. In front the leg should be freely extended forward by the shoulder. The hind movement should be free, strong and close. The hocks should be freely flexed and drawn close in under the body, so that when moving off on the foot the body is thrown or pushed forward with some force. Stiff, stilty movement behind is very objectionable.

ATTENTION OF JUDGES

1. Dogs should be shown strictly in the natural condition of coat.

2. That emphasis be laid on the fact that the dog is a distinct breed and not a white Scottish Terrier.

3. Any faking, such as undue plucking, blackening the nose or bleaching, or undue powdering should disqualify the dog.

TERRIERS

Scale of Points

	Value
General appearance	15
Color	7½
Coat	10
Size	7½
Skull	5
Eyes	5
Muzzle	5
Ears	5
Neck	5
Chest	5
Body	10
Legs and feet	7½
Tail	5
Movement	7½
Total value	100

Faults

No. 1. *Coat.*—Any silkiness, wave, or tendency to curl is a serious blemish, as is also an open coat, and any black, grey, or wheaten hairs.

No. 2. *Size.*—Any specimens under the minimum weight, or above the maximum weight, are objectionable.

No. 3. *Eyes.*—Full or light colored.

No. 4. *Ears.*—Round-pointed, drop, semi-erect, or large.

No. 5. *Muzzle.*—Either under or over shot, and defective teeth.

Group V—TOYS

AFFENPINSCHERS
(Illustration facing page 592)

Progenitor of the more familiar Brussels Griffon, the Affenpinscher, or "Monkey Dog," was well known on the European continent as far back as the seventeenth century. This quaint little dog's popularity during the past few years has been far over-shadowed by the Griffon, but more recently, he is enjoying a return to favor and has been recognized by the American Kennel Club by admission to the Stud Book and by being allowed a classification at shows. One may expect to see the several recent importations and their progeny at the bench shows of the future.

A game, alert, intelligent sturdy little "terrier type" of dog, the Affenpinscher is characterized by his "monkey-ish" expression, derived from a prominent chin with hair-tuft and moustache. This expression is further accentuated by his bushy eyebrows, shadowing black bordered eyelids and large piercing dark eyes which contrast strikingly with his red or grey wiry coat and the black mask which is found on many good specimens. The entire coat is stiff and wiry in texture and with his cropped ears and docked tail, he is every inch a real dog, despite his small size. The ideal Affenpinscher should be ten and a quarter inches at the shoulder and no more than seven to eight pounds in weight.

Now that these attractive little dogs are being seen at the shows, their admirers are predicting a steady rise in popular favor.

TOYS

DESCRIPTION AND STANDARD OF POINTS

(Adopted by The American Kennel Club, September 15, 1936)

As in most Toys, general appearance is one of, if not the most important single point in the Affenpinscher. Details are of secondary importance and anatomical variations are of small concern.

General Appearance.—Small, but rather sturdy in build and not delicate in any way. He carries himself with comical seriousness and he is generally quiet and a very devoted pal. He can get vehemently excited, however, when attacked and is fearless toward any aggressor.

Coat.—A very important factor. It is short and dense in certain parts and shaggy and longer in others, but should be hard and wiry. It is longer and more loose and shaggy on the legs and around the eyes, nose and chin, giving the typical monkeylike appearance from whence comes his name. The best color is black matching his eyes and fiery temperament. However, black with tan markings, red, grey and other mixtures are permissible. Very light colors and white markings are a fault.

Head.—Should be round and not too heavy, with well domed forehead.

Eyes.—Should be round, of good size, black and very brilliant.

Ears.—Rather small, set high, pointed and erect, usually clipped to a point.

Muzzle.—Must be short and rather pointed with a black nose. The upper jaw is a trifle shorter than the lower jaw while the teeth should close together, a slight undershot condition is not material. The teeth, however, should not show.

Neck.—Short and straight.

Body.—The back should be straight with its length about equal to the height at the shoulder. Chest should be reasonably deep and the body should show only a slight tuck up at the loin.

Legs.—Front legs should be straight as possible. Hind legs without much bend at the hocks and set well under the body.

Feet.—Should be round, small and compact. Turned neither in nor out, with preferably black pads and nails.

Tail.—Cut short, set and carried high.

Size.—The smaller dog, if of characteristic type, is more valuable and the shoulder height should not exceed 10¼ inches in any case.

AFFENPINSCHER

AFFENPINSCHER

CHIHUAHUA

CHIHUAHUAS

(Illustration on opposite page)

While little or nothing is known of the previous history of the Toltecs, it has been adequately established that they existed in what is now Mexico as early as the ninth century A.D., and that during their several centuries of occupancy they had a breed of dog called the Techichi. This dog was small, but not tiny, and was of a heavy-boned structure. His coat was long. Still, his most distinctive feature was his muteness.

The Techichi, regarded as indigenous to Central America, is the progenitor of the Chihuahua that now enjoys popularity throughout the United States where he has been bred to his greatest perfection. No records of the Techichi are, so far, available prior to the ninth century, but it seems quite probable that its ancestors were in the locality prior to the advent of the Maya tribes about the fifth century.

The evidence that firmly establishes the Techichi to the Toltec period is found in pictures carved on stones. These stones may be found today in the Monastery of Huejotzingo, on the highway from Mexico City to Puebla. This monastery was constructed by the Franciscan Monks around 1530 from the materials of the existing Pyramids of Cholula, built by the Toltecs. The carvings give a full head view, and a picture of an entire dog that closely approximates the Chihuahua of modern times. There also are the remains of pyramid constructions, and likewise some pointers to the early existence of the Techichi at Chichen Itza in distant Yucatan.

The Toltec civilization was centered principally around Tula, which is close to the present City of Mexico, and it is there that one finds the most abundant relics of this ancient breed. For that reason, there always has been some speculation regarding the discovery of the earliest specimens of the modern breed in the State of Chihuahua. The dogs were found, about 1850, in some old ruins close to Casas Grandes, said to be the remains of a palace built by Emperor Montezuma I.

The conclusions of K. de Blinde, a Mexican breeder and authority, who has spent years of personal investigation—traversing vast sections of the country on horseback—are that the present form of the Chihuahua evolved from the crossing of the Techichi and the small hairless dog brought from Asia, over the land bridge where now runs the Bering Strait to Alaska. This hairless dog, similar to the one found today in China, was responsible for the reduction in size.

The Aztec conquerors of the Toltecs flourished for several centuries, and just prior to the coming of Hernan Cortes the civilization was at a very high state and the wealth was prodigious. The dogs of the rich were highly regarded, and the blue colored ones were held as sacred. Paradoxical as it seems, the common people found little use for this same breed, and there are even tales that they were eaten.

The storm-like career of Cortes in Mexico during 1519–20 left little of either Aztec wealth or civilization. Practically all Montezuma's possessions were wrung from his dying hands, and it is only natural that his dogs became lost for several centuries.

While the Techichi had its principal home in Mexico there is an historic letter written by Christopher Columbus to the King of Spain that adds a curious note to the knowledge of the breed. Reporting on the seizure of the present island of Cuba, Columbus stated that he found; "A small kind of dogs, which were mute and did not bark, as usual, but were domesticated." These dogs could not have been taken to Cuba by the Aztecs, who were not a seafaring people.

Legend and history are rich in tales of the ancestors of the present Chihuahua. He is described as a popular pet, as well as a religious necessity, among the ancient Toltec tribes and later among the Aztecs. Archeologists have discovered remains of this breed in human graves in Mexico and in parts of the United States.

This phenomenon is believed due to the part the dog played in the religious and mythological life of the Aztecs. He was employed in connection with the worship of Deities; with the voyage of the soul in the underworld; and in relation to the human body. The sacrifice of a dog with a red skin, burning it to ashes with the corpse of the deceased, the sins of the human were supposed to be transferred to the dog, and the indignation of the deity thus averted. The dog also was credited with guiding the human soul through the dark and terrible regions of the underworld, fighting off the evil spirits and leading the soul of the deceased safely to its ultimate destination.

The modern Chihuahua is quite different from his early ancestors, and is regarded by its fanciers as one of the most alert and intelligent dogs in existence. Its variegated colors are an attractive feature, the breed ranging from snow white to jet black. Mexico favors the jet black with tan markings, and the black and white spotted. The United States prefers the solid colors.

American breeders have produced a diminutive type that has few comparisons, even among other breeds, for smallness, symmetry and perfection of conformation, as well as for its intelligence and alertness. Incidentally, it is a curious aspect of the Chihuahua's intelligence that it is clannish, recognizing and preferring its own kind, and, as a rule, not liking other breeds. The smooth-coated are the most numerous in the United States, and the most clannish, but the long-coated Chihuahua is rapidly increasing. It has all the characteristics of the smooth.

DESCRIPTION AND STANDARD OF POINTS
(Adopted by The Chihuahua Club of America and Approved by The American Kennel Club, August 14, 1934)

Head.—Well rounded "apple dome" skull, with molera. Cheeks and jaws lean. Nose moderately short, slightly pointed, self-colored, pink or black, depending on the color of the dog, (e.g., in moles, blues, chocolates, the noses are self-colored: in blond types, pink.)

Ears.—Large, held erect, flaring to sides at about an angle of 45 degrees and less.

Teeth.—Level.

Eyes.—Full, but not protruding, balanced, set well apart, dark, ruby, luminous.

Neck.—Slightly arched, gracefully sloping into lean shoulders, ruff or close haired about the neck. Shoulders lean, sloping into a slightly broadening support above straight forelegs that are set well under, giving free play at the elbows, with fine pasterns. Shoulders should be well up, giving balance and soundness, sloping into a level back, and never "down" or low. This also gives a "chestiness" and strength of fore quarters, yet none of the "bull-dog" chest, but plenty of brisket.

Back.—Level, slightly longer than the height. (Short back desired in males.)

Feet.—Small, toes well split up, but not spread, pads cushioned.

Is neither the "hare" nor the "cat" foot. A dainty little foot, with nails moderately long.

Hind Quarters.—Muscular, hocks well apart, but not out, well let down, firm sturdy action.

Tail.—Moderately long, (when not a natural bob, or tail-less). Carried cycle, either up or out, but not tucked under. Hair on the tail in harmony with the coat of the body, preferred furry. Bob-tails and tail-less, so-born, are not against a good dog.

Coat.—In the "smooths" should be of a soft, smooth texture, close and glossy. In dark colors, well placed over the body and neck, more scanty on the head and ears. The long-haired should have fringed ears, legs and tail with the coat on the body semi-long, soft and silken, similar to the coat of the Papillon.

Color.—Any; solid or marked or splashed.

Weight.—One to six pounds. Two to four pounds preferable. If two dogs are equally good the more diminutive is preferred.

General Appearance.—A graceful, alert, swift-moving little dog with saucy expression, compact, with terrier qualities.

Disqualification.—Cropped tail, broken down or cropped ears.

SCALE OF POINTS

	Points
Head	20
Body	20
Coat	10
Tail	5
Color	5
Legs	10
Weight	10
General appearance and action	20
Total	100

ENGLISH TOY SPANIELS

(Illustration facing page 604)

Since the whole spread of civilization has been from the East to the West, it is only natural that most of our oldest breeds of dog should trace their origin to the eastern countries. Such is the case of the English Toy Spaniels, those affectionate, intelligent, little dogs that captivated royalty, the aristocrats, and the wealthy for at least three centuries.

It has been a widespread fallacy that the Toy Spaniels made their first appearance in England during the reign of King Charles II, in the seventeenth century, for it was in honor of this sovereign that the black and tan variety took its name. Yet the Toy Spaniel had been known in England and in Scotland more than a hundred years before.

Just how long the Toy Spaniel had been known in Europe, particularly the south of Europe, before it was carried to England, must remain a matter of doubt. Yet most authorities are agreed that it goes back to Japan, and possibly China of very ancient times.

According to Leighton, the English Toy Spaniel had its origin in Japan, from where it was taken to Spain, and from thence to England. Yet the extremely short nose of the breed might very easily be evidence that it went from Spain to Japan, where it developed its present characteristics. There is a story, also, that specimens of this toy breed were brought from Japan by Captain Saris, a British naval officer, in 1613. They were presents from the Emperor of Japan—every Japanese royal present always included dogs—to King James I.

TOYS

The tale of Captain Saris seems a logical one, but it cannot be accepted as marking the debut of the Toy Spaniel into England and Scotland. The breed was known in England long before that, for Dr. Johannes Caius, the celebrated professor and the physician to Queen Elizabeth, included it in his foundational work on "Englishe Dogges." He refers to it as the "Spaniell Gentle, otherwise called the Comforter." His other references stamp it as almost the identical dog of today.

While it is difficult to associate the Toy Spaniel with the austere Elizabeth; evidence that this breed was the favorite of the warmer-hearted Mary, Queen of Scots, in the same century, is much more acceptable. The early years of Mary, during the first third of the sixteenth century, were spent in France. When she returned to Scotland as Queen, she brought specimens of the breed with her, and these dogs remained her favorites up to the time of her execution. In fact, her especial pet refused to leave her, even on the scaffold.

All Toy Spaniels up to the time of King Charles II appear to have been of the black and tan variety, later called the King Charles. This king's favorites were brought over from France by Henrietta of Orleans, and one is described as a black and white.

The development of the other varieties, the Prince Charles, which is a tricolor of white, black and tan, the Ruby, which is chestnut red, and the Blenheim, which is white and chestnut red, occurred at later times. All are identical in their characteristics, with the exception of color. For a long time they were bred without any reference to color. Often the same litter would produce dogs of several varieties. It is only in modern times that the science of color breeding set the different varieties apart.

The history of the Blenheim variety seems rather more

definite than that of the King Charles, although in some ways incompatible with other data. The development of the Blenheim, or red and white, is credited to John Churchill, the first Duke of Marlborough. Churchill, famous soldier and diplomat, was made an Earl in 1689, and became a Duke in 1702. At that time he acquired Blenheim, which has been the family seat of the Marlboroughs ever since.

It is said by Ash that the first Duke received as a present from China a pair of red and white cocker spaniels, and that these dogs were the basis of his subsequent breeding. The Chinese origin of the breed is mentioned also by Lady de Gex, who claims that during the fifteenth and sixteenth centuries there were carried from China to Italy numerous specimens of both red and white, and black and white spaniels. These dogs subsequently were crossed with cockers and springers, intensifying the sporting instincts which the Toy still retains.

The Dukes of Marlborough bred the Blenheim variety for many generations, and apparently they did so without the infusion of much outside blood—unless it were that of the cocker and other varieties of spaniel. It was said by Scott, in 1800, that the Duke of Marlborough's Blenheims were the smallest and best cockers in England. They were used very successfully for woodcock shooting. And writers of a still later period describe the dogs found at Blenheim as larger than other specimens of the red and white. Also, the Marlborough strain did not have such exaggeratedly short noses.

Regardless of the early history of the English Toy Spaniels, it seems certain that many specimens of modern times trace their origin back to various small spaniels of England. Selective breeding has reduced them down to the limits of six to twelve pounds, but it has not altogether erased their natural hunting instincts.

DESCRIPTION AND STANDARD OF POINTS
(By Courtesy of The Toy Spaniel Club of America)

Note:—Under the ruling of the American Kennel Club, passed December 16, 1902, Prince Charles, King Charles, Ruby and Blenheim Spaniels will, after January 1, 1903, be classed together as English Toy Spaniels.

Head.—Should be well domed, and in good specimens is absolutely semi-globular, sometimes even extending beyond the half-circle, and absolutely projecting over the eyes, so as nearly to meet the upturned nose.

Eyes.—The eyes are set wide apart, with the eyelids square to the line of the face—not oblique or fox-like. The eyes themselves are large and dark as possible, so as to be generally considered black, their enormous pupils, which are absolutely of that color, increasing the description.

Stop.—The "stop," or hollow between the eyes, is well marked, as in the Bull-dog, or even more so; some good specimens exhibit a hollow deep enough to bury a small marble in it.

Nose.—The nose must be short and well turned up between the eyes, and without any indication of artificial displacement afforded by a deviation to either side. The color of the end should be black, and it should be both deep and wide with open nostrils. A light colored nose is objectionable, but shall not disqualify.

Jaw.—The muzzle must be square and deep, and the lower jaw wide between the branches, leaving plenty of space for the tongue, and for the attachment of the lower lips, which should completely conceal the teeth. It should also be turned up or "finished," so as to allow of its meeting the end of the upper jaw, turned up in a similar way as above described. A protruding tongue is objectionable, but does not disqualify.

Ears.—The ears must be long, so as to approach the ground. In an average-sized dog they measure 20 inches from tip to tip, and some reach 22 inches or even a trifle more. They should be set low down on the head and hang flat to the sides of the cheeks, and be heavy feathered.

Size.—The most desirable size is from 9 pounds to 12 pounds.

Shape.—In compactness of shape these Spaniels almost rival the Pug, but the length of coat adds greatly to the apparent bulk, as the body, when the coat is wetted, looks small in comparison with that dog. Still, it ought to be decidedly "cobby," with strong stout legs, short broad back and wide chest.

Coat.—The coat should be long, silky, soft and wavy, but not curly. There should be a profuse mane, extending well down in the front of the chest. The feather should be well displayed on the ears and feet, and in the latter case so thickly as to give the appearance of being webbed. It is also carried well up the backs of the legs. In the Black and Tan the feather on the ears is very long and profuse, exceeding that of the Blenheim by an inch or more. The feather on the tail (which is cut to the length of about 1½ inches) should be silky, and from 3 to 4 inches in length, constituting a marked "flag" of a square shape, and not carried above the level of the back.

Color.—The color varies with the variety. The black and tan is a rich glossy black and deep mahogany tan; tan spots over the eyes, and the usual markings on the muzzle, chest and legs are also required. The ruby is a rich chestnut red, and is whole-colored. The presence of a few white hairs *intermixed with the black* on the chest of a Black and Tan, or *intermixed with the red* on the chest of a Ruby Spaniel, shall carry *weight against* a dog, but shall not in itself absolutely disqualify; but a white patch on the chest or white on any other part of a Black and Tan or Ruby Spaniel shall be a disqualification. The Blenheim must on no account be whole-colored, but should have a ground of pure pearly white, with bright rich chestnut or ruby red markings evenly distributed in large patches.

The ears and cheeks should be red, with a blaze of white extending from the nose up the forehead, and ending between the ears in a crescentic curve. In the center of this blaze at the top of the forehead there should be a clear "spot" of red, of the size of a sixpence. The tri-color should in part have the tan of the Black and Tan, with markings like the Blenheim in black instead of red on a pearly-white ground. The ears and under the tail should also be lined with tan. The tri-color has no "spot," that beauty being peculiarly the property of the Blenheim.

SCALE OF POINTS

King Charles, or Black and Tan. Prince Charles, White, with Black and Tan Markings. Ruby, or Red

	Points
Symmetry, condition, size and soundness of limb	20
Head	15
Stop	5
Muzzle	10
Eyes	10
Ears	15
Coat and feathering	15
Color	10
Total	**100**

Blenheim or White with Red Markings

	Points
Symmetry, condition, size and soundness of limb	15
Head	15
Stop	5
Muzzle	10
Eyes	10
Ears	10
Coat and feathering	15
Color and markings	15
Spot	5
Total	**100**

The above standard was adopted at the General Meeting of the Toy Spaniel Club of America held October 19, 1909.

ENGLISH TOY SPANIEL

GRIFFON (Brussels)

GRIFFONS (BRUSSELS)

(Illustration on opposite page)

(By Courtesy of Brussels Griffon Club of America)

The Brussels Griffon is not a dog of beauty as measured by the accepted standards but one teeming with personality, and for that reason it is not surprising that he makes lasting friends wherever he is known. He comes of neither an exalted nor an ancient lineage, yet is one of the most distinctive and unusual of all dogs. "Magnum in parvo" describes him most aptly. Although classified as a Toy Dog, there is nothing of the pampered pet in the typical Brussels Griffon, a bundle of jaunty good nature whose keynote is insouisance from his very turned up nose to the tip of his gaily carried tail. No matter what change of fortune the years may bring, he promises to remain the delightful little Belgian street urchin to the end of time.

His ancestry is interesting in that the German Affenpinscher as well as the Belgian street dog (which combined, were the true foundation from which our Griffons emanated) are both practically extinct and there is only the most meagre data available on both of these seventeenth century (or older) breeds. To all accounts, in Belgium there was a strong conformity to a distinct type in the peasants' dogs of that epoch. These dogs were nearly as large as our fox terriers but thickly built, as are most Belgian animals. Covered with a shaggy rough muddy colored coat and unlovely of feature, but intelligent and interesting of disposition, they were popularly termed "Griffons D'Ecurie," stable Griffons, and

[605]

paid their keep by killing the stable vermin. They were loyal companions and it is not uncommon to run across mention of these dogs as "chiens barbus" in the old folk songs and tales of the period, for they were to be found in nearly every household.

On the other hand, the affenspinscher, from the few old photographs available, may be said to resemble the Yorkshire terrier in many particulars, the likeness being particularly noticeable in the head properties as well as in the length of both body and leg. Doubtless it was felt that the injection of affenpinscher blood into the then Griffons would serve to further increase the ratting ability of the Belgian dogs although since we lack definite proof, this last must remain a conjecture.

At some later date, the smooth coated Chinese Pug, already established in neighboring Holland, was used as a crossing with the Griffon. This cross breeding was responsible for the two types of coat which we have even in our present-day litters.

If there was any definite rhyme or reason for adding the Ruby Spaniel to this combination, we cannot say. Suffice that this breed was also brought into the picture and is largely responsible for the interesting facial characteristics and expression which are so much a part of our present-day dog but which have made impossible for him, the work to which he was once so well suited.

And so we come to the twentieth century Brussels Griffon, a small compact dog with a harsh coat similar to that of the Irish Terrier, (or else a smooth coat traceable to the pug and termed Brabancon) with a short upturned face best described as a "speaking countenance" and a gay carriage.

The Griffon's super intelligence causes him to be sensitive and it is not at all uncommon for a young dog when in the presence of strangers, to display the same self-consciousness as does a child in its awkward teens. We must never lose sight of the fact that this is a breed which understands "English" and should always be treated accordingly. Although obedient and always easily managed, Griffons are sometimes difficult to break to the leash and this training should always be begun at a very early age. Strange as it may seem, it has been the experience of some of our leading exponents of the breed that the Brabancons display a marked stubbornness when it comes to going on a leash although in all other respects they are every bit as tractable as their rough brothers.

As a young puppy, he must be given the same intelligent care it is necessary to accord a puppy of any of the smaller breeds but the average sized Griffon becomes very sturdy as he matures and develops into a real comrade, being quite capable of holding his own on hikes and in swimming. The Griffon's ways are the more quaint and amusing because, when he acts he thinks! Therein lies the secret of his popularity.

DESCRIPTION AND STANDARD OF POINTS

General Appearance.—A toy dog, intelligent, alert, sturdy, with a thick-set short body, a smart carriage and set-up, attracting attention by an almost human expression.

Coat.—Reddish brown; a little black at the whiskers and chin is allowable. The coat should be wiry and dense. The harder and more wiry the texture of the coat is, the better. On no account should the dog look or feel woolly: and there should be no silky hair anywhere. The coat should not be too long so as to give the dog a shaggy appearance, but, at the same time it should show a marked and distinct difference all over from the smooth species.

Top Head.—Large and round, with a domed forehead and skull.

It should be covered with a wiry rough coat slightly longer around the eyes, nose, cheeks and chin thus forming a fringe.

Ears.—Small and carried semi-erect; set rather high on the head.

Eyes.—Very large, black and well open. The eyelashes long and black. Eyelids edged with black. Eyes should be set well apart and prominent.

Nose.—Very black, excessively short; its tip being set back deeply between the eyes so as to form a lay-back. The nostrils large, the stop deep.

Lips.—Edged with black; not pendulous but well brought together giving a clean finish of mouth.

Chin.—Must be undershot, prominent and large with an upward sweep.

Jaws.—The incisors of the lower jaw should protrude over the upper incisors. The lower jaw should be rather broad.

Brisket.—Good size and deep.

Ribs.—Well sprung.

Back.—Level and short.

Tail.—Set and held high: cut to the one-third.

Forelegs.—Of medium length, set moderately wide apart and on a line with the point of the shoulders, straight in bone, and well muscled; pasterns short and strong.

Hindlegs.—Set true; bent at stifles; well let down; hocks turning neither in nor out; thighs strong and well muscled.

Feet.—Round, small and compact and turned neither in nor out, toes well arched. Black pads and toe nails preferred.

Weights.—For the class of dogs and bitches of a small size, the weight should not exceed 7 pounds. For the class of dogs and bitches of a large size, that is weighing more than 7 pounds, the weight should not exceed 11 pounds for dogs and 12 pounds for bitches.

Note:—In judging, quality should be of greater importance than weight, and general balance in any Griffon should take precedence over perfection of any single feature in an otherwise inferior specimen.

Minor Faults.—Light colored or small eyes; brown nails, teeth

GRIFFONS (BRUSSELS)

or tongue showing, light colored nose, toes joined on one or more feet.

Major Faults.—Silky topknot, both teeth and tongue showing simultaneously, wry mouth, button ears, a few white hairs on chest, unsoundness.

Disqualifications.—Dudley or butterfly nose; splashes of white on coat or chest; hanging tongue; the upper jaw overshot; looseness of stifle or any other major unsoundness. Dogs limping for no matter what reason, dogs completely blind or deaf, and dogs having undergone the operation of castration cannot be shown.

SCALE OF POINTS

Head

Head (forehead and skull)	5	
Nose and stop	10	
Eyes	5	
Chin and jaws	10	
Ears	5	35

Coat

Color	12	
Texture	13	25

Body and General Conformation

Body (brisket and rib)	15	
Legs	10	
Feet	5	
General appearance (tail carriage and topline)	10	40

BRUSSELS GRIFFONS (BELGIAN AND BRABANCON)

The characteristics of the Belgian Griffon are the same as those of the *other* Brussels Griffon with this difference—that the only colors admissible are: 1. Black and reddish brown mixed, with accompanying black mask and whiskers. 2. Black. 3. Black with reddish brown markings.

[609]

TOYS

BRABANCONS.—The characteristics of the Brabancon are the same as those of the *other* Brussels Griffon with this difference—that the Brabancon has a smooth short coat like that of the Boston Terrier or English Bulldog and the only colors admissible are: 1. Reddish brown. 2. Black with reddish brown markings.

Note:—The faults and disqualifications are the same in the Belgian Griffon and in the Brabancon as they are in the *other* Brussels Griffon.

GREYHOUND (*Italian*)

JAPANESE SPANIEL

ITALIAN GREYHOUNDS

(Illustration facing page 610)

Brought to England during the early years of the seventeenth century, in the reign of Charles I, the Italian Greyhound carried with it a glorious heritage as the favorite of royalty and the privileged classes. Never a dog of great use, it had won high esteem merely because of its marvelous disposition and its small size.

There is strong evidence that the Italian Greyhound was an effete favorite in the days of ancient Pompeii; and there are numerous relics throughout Italy that point to the breed as the only known pet dog for many centuries. The old Latin motto, "Cave Canem," or "beware of the dog," is found frequently in old Roman villas. According to Leighton, this did not refer to the huge mastiff, which invariably was kept chained, but to the tiny Italian Greyhound. The motto meant that guests should take care not to hurt the tiny pet of the matron, for he might easily be crushed by a careless step.

The date, and even the general period, at which the Italian Greyhound appeared as a distinct type is not recorded in any manuscript that has come down to us. It is known only that he has existed in his present form for more than 2,000 years. His origin, of course, is not difficult to deduce, for he carries no essential characteristics other than those of the large greyhound—characteristics that have been weakened and varied, but not radically changed. It is the general belief among the accepted authorities that the breed was dwarfed, intentionally, for pet purposes, from the gazehound of the

ancients. Continual inbreeding finally led to a breed
that produced some specimens as small as five pounds.

There is a possibility that the early development of the
breed took place in Turkey, according to Dickie, but
there remains very little supporting evidence for this
conclusion. Later it became a favorite in Athens, and
by the Middle Ages it was very popular throughout all
of Southern Europe.

The type of the Italian Greyhound has not changed
greatly from the earliest times down to the present, but
like the majority of breeds it has undergone considerable
refinement. The three centuries and more that the breed
has been known in England and Scotland have brought
it to a high state of perfection. The specimens owned
by Mary Beatrice d'Easte of Modena, the Italian con-
sort of James II, and those of Anne of Denmark, con-
sort to James I, would not have done very well if taken
into the ring against the delicate little greyhounds of
Queen Victoria.

The Italian Greyhound, probably, reached its greatest
heights during the Late-Victorian period. There were
numerous big breeding kennels throughout England and
Scotland, and it was then that the breed was introduced
into the United States. It seems curious, indeed, that this
breed so designed for the warm countries and so attuned
to an even climate should have flourished so well under
the dampness and the chilly atmospheres of England
and Scotland. Still, the greatest breeder of modern
times appears to have been W. Bruce of Falkirk, Scotland. When the breed came out to America it made its
greatest early center in Pennsylvania, particularly at the
kennels of Dr. F. H. Hoyt, who bred a succession of
winners.

There are many interesting stories connected with the

Italian Greyhound. Perhaps the most curious of them all is that of King Lobengula, the black monarch of that perpetually warring South African people, the Matabele. One day while in Johannesburg, King Lobengula saw a specimen of the Italian Greyhound that was owned by Luscombe Searelle. The prancing manner of the dog so pleased the king that he made an offer for it. Mr. Searelle was reluctant to part with the dog, but finally succumbed to the pleas when the monarch promised him 200 head of cattle.

Another story is connected with Frederick the Great, King of Prussia. The king had a favorite Italian Greyhound that he carried with him wherever he went. And once, during the Seven Years' War, the tide of battle turned so quickly that Frederick found himself in a very precarious position. Dog in arms, he took refuge under the dry arch of a bridge. The dog clung to his royal master and did not utter a sound. Had the dog barked while the Austrian dragoons were passing, the fate of the king and of Prussia would have been decided right there. When this dog died, Frederick buried him with his own hands in the grounds of the palace in Berlin.

There have been certain yarns that attribute a sporting sense to the Italian Greyhound, but these all are discredited by those who have known the breed. It is solely a pet, and it has maintained that station throughout its long history.

DESCRIPTION AND STANDARD OF POINTS
(Courtesy of The Italian Greyhound Club, England)

General Appearance.—A miniature English Greyhound, more slender in all proportions, and of ideal elegance and grace in shape, symmetry and action.

[613]

TOYS

Head.—Skull, long, flat and narrow. Muzzle, very fine, nose dark, teeth level. Ears, rose shaped, placed well back, soft and delicate. Eyes, rather large, bright and full of expression.

Body.—Neck, long and gracefully arched. Shoulders, long and sloping. Chest, deep and narrow. Back, curved and drooping at the hind quarters.

Legs and Feet.—Forelegs, straight, set well under the shoulders, fine pasterns, small delicate bones. Hindlegs, hocks well let down, thighs muscular. Feet, the long "hare foot."

Tail.—Rather long, fine and with low carriage.

Coat.—Skin fine and supple, hair thin and glossy like satin.

Color.—All shades of fawn, red, mouse, blue, cream and white are recognized, black and tan terrier markings not allowed.

Action.—High stepping and free.

Size.—Two classes, one of eight pounds and under and one over eight pounds. A good small dog is preferable to an equally good large one but a good larger dog is preferable to a poor smaller one.

	Points
Skull	6
Muzzle	8
Ears	8
Eyes	5
Neck	8
Shoulders	5
Chest	5
Back	8
Forelegs	8
Hindlegs	8
Feet	8
Tail	8
Coat	4
Color	3
Action	8
Total	100

JAPANESE SPANIELS

(Illustration facing page 611)

(By Courtesy of The Japanese Spaniel Club of America)

The Japanese Spaniel or Japanese Chin is known in every part of the world and is one of the oldest of all Toy Breeds.

The general belief is that they originally came from China many centuries ago, when an Emperor of China presented the Emperor of Japan with a pair of these dogs and that they developed as they are today, under the difference in climatic conditions. Most of the old Chinese temples have images of dogs, likewise do real old pottery and old embroideries, which under close observation resemble the Japanese Spaniel. These dogs were always kept among the people of noble birth, and once in awhile one was presented to a noted person, a diplomat, or to any foreigner who had rendered some great service to Japan.

Our Commodore Perry steamed into the Harbor of Wraga in 1853 and opened the country's trade to the world. He was presented with some of these dogs, and he in turn gave Queen Victoria of England a pair. Some of them in time came to America, but no record is obtainable of their final destination in America. Soon there was thieving among the Japanese Kennels and ships took them all over the world. They poured into this country about fifty years ago. Every incoming ship from the Orient had several, with equally as many buyers. Unfortunately they were not long lived, and when the World War broke and the supply was cut off we had to use what

blood lines were left to improve and maintain our be-
loved breed. Japan too had her losses among her prized
Chins, as earthquakes played havoc among the breeders.
Since then a great many of the Japanese breeders have
taken a fancy for other breeds and the supply has dimin-
ished there.

All over the world there are, however, Japanese
Spaniels, there being breeders in England, France, Switzerland, Austria and Germany. These dogs breed so true
to type that their high quality is still maintained.

The Japanese Spaniel is not a delicate dog. His
Waterloo has been distemper, but this, we believe, has
now been eradicated by inoculation. Since this has been
his only enemy he should multiply rapidly in this country,
from now on.

Most Japanese Spaniels are Black and White,—very
black and very white,—however, there is a strain of
white with lemon or red markings, including all shades
from very pale lemon to the deepest red, and also including a brindle. Each must have nose color matching the
markings, but always a dark eye, no matter what color
the markings may be.

A Japanese Spaniel is a marvelous companion extremely bright and alert to its owner's wants. They are
very game naturally, clean by nature and an ideal pet.
They can thrive in any climate, can prosper in hot or
cold quarters, but drafty quarters are dangerous.

The Jap is a sensitive creature, his feelings are readily
hurt, and he has great likes and dislikes and never forgets friend or foe. Many times one may think his pet is
not feeling just right, while in reality someone has hurt
his feelings. These dogs are known to sulk in consequence of imaginary insults for days at a time. Treat

them with consideration and kindness and no better pal is obtainable.

There are many types in these dogs, each correct.

1. First and foremost they must have Japanese character, must look like an Oriental, be aristocratic in appearance and stylish in action, and carriage. A larger dog loses in these qualifications, therefore only a small dog is considered of show type. However, he must not be weedy in makeup.

2. Certain types carry profuse coats, others shorter and coarser coats,—either is correct, but a woolly coat is not allowed. No two dogs are just alike, but a trained eye spots a good one.

We all have our goal, our preferences, but the one that is most sought after is the type with the head that has the short turned up nose, large well placed eyes, ears V-shaped and placed correctly at the top of the head. This type usually has very fine bone and nicely shaped body. In the same litter that contains this popular type of Japanese Spaniel there will, very likely also be found one with the straight nose which probably will also have a little length. His eyes, however, must be dark and set far apart and his "cushions" should be exaggerated. In this type dog there is usually found a fine but more of the bull type of body, which is desirable, and his ears to be correct must also be V-shaped. Either type must have the same aristocratic appearance and stylish action. Color may also be mixed in the same litter, if sire or dam has other than pure Black and White blood in its veins. Frequently a Lemon and White dog produces only Black and White offspring, and it may be several generations before the colors revert again. Years ago when a Black and White parent had too much Black on the body a Lemon and White dog was used to break the color. Again the Lemon and White frequently have more profusion of coat and this blood was often used to improve the class of hair. It is far more difficult to produce a perfect Lemon and White than a Black and White.

There is nothing prettier than a Japanese Spaniel pup when it commences to get its coat. They show their good points at an early age, and many believe the old adage, "as a Japanese Spaniel looks when he is exactly six weeks of age, so he finishes." He may go off before he is eighteen months old, but he should eventually look as good, or as bad, as he did on that eventful day when his weeks numbered six.

They do not as a rule have trouble in whelping, in spite of the fact that their heads are large, and they make good mothers. It is desirable to start feeding the youngsters after the third week, especially during the day, giving the mother the babies at night.

Anyone who at any time has had the good fortune to own a Japanese Spaniel will always be the owner of one, if possible, and surely will love them forever.

DESCRIPTION AND STANDARD OF POINTS
(Courtesy of The Japanese Spaniel Club of America)

General Appearance.—That of a lively, highbred little dog with dainty appearance, smart, compact carriage and profuse coat. These dogs should be essentially stylish in movement, lifting the feet high when in action, carrying the tail (which is heavily feathered, proudly curved or plumed) over the back. In size they vary considerably, but the smaller they are the better, provided type and quality are not sacrificed. When divided by weight, classes should be under and over seven pounds.

Head.—Should be large for the size of the dog, with broad skull, rounded in front.

MALTESE

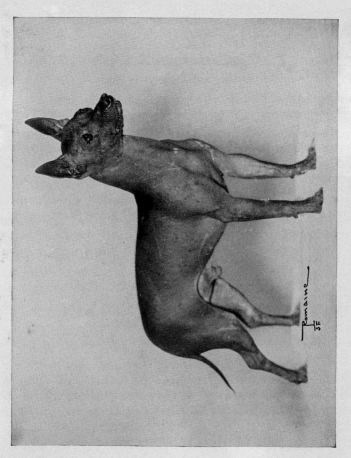

MEXICAN HAIRLESS

JAPANESE SPANIELS

Eyes.—Large, dark, lustrous, rather prominent and set wide apart.

Ears.—Small and V-shaped, nicely feathered, set wide apart and high on the head and carried slightly forward.

Nose.—Very short in the muzzle part. The end or nose proper should be wide, with open nostrils, and must be the color of the dog's markings, i.e., black in black-marked dogs, and red or deep flesh color in red or lemon-marked dogs.

Neck.—Should be short and moderately thick.

Body.—Should be squarely and compactly built, wide in chest, "cobby" in shape. The length of the dog's body should be about its height.

Tail.—Must be well twisted to either right or left from root and carried up over back and flow on opposite side; it should be profusely covered with long hair (ring tails not desirable).

Legs.—The bones of the legs should be small, giving them a slender appearance, and they should be well feathered.

Feet.—Small and shaped somewhat long; the dog stands up on its toes somewhat. If feathered, the tufts should never increase the width of the foot, but only its length a trifle.

Coat.—Profuse, long, straight, rather silky. It should be absolutely free from wave or curl, and not lie too flat, but have a tendency to stand out, especially at the neck, so as to give a thick mane or ruff, which with profuse feathering on thighs and tail gives a very showy appearance.

Color.—The dogs should be either black and white or red and white, i.e., parti-colored. The term red includes all shades of sable, brindle, lemon and orange, but the brighter and clearer the red the better. The white should be clear white, and the color, whether black or red, should be evenly distributed, patches over the body, cheek and ears.

	Points
Head and neck	10
Eyes	10
Ears	5
Muzzle	10

TOYS

Nose	5
Body	15
Tail	10
Feet and legs	5
Coat and markings	15
Action	5
Size	10
Total	**100**

MALTESE

(By Courtesy of National Maltese Dog Club)

The Maltese dog is known as *Ye Ancient "Dogge of Malta."* For more than twenty-eight centuries "The Dogge of Malta" has been an aristocrat of the canine world.

Malta has been prominent in history from the earliest times. About 1500 B.C. it was settled by the Phoenicians, but from ancient ruins of the island, we know that other Mediterranean races lived there as far back as 3500 B.C. Many writers of antiquity have dwelt in glowing terms on the fame, opulence, and magnificence of Malta.

During the Roman domination, Diodorus, Cicero, and Valerius Maximus sang the praises of the Island.

It was celebrated over all the then known earth for its proficiency in the Arts and Crafts of peace and war, and for the high civilization of its inhabitants.

It was amid these surroundings and among these people that the tiny Maltese, the "Aristocrat of the Ancient World" was developed.

And among the Ancients, this lovely little animal was held in high esteem. The Greeks erected tombs to their Maltese dogs; and, in Greek ceramic art, from the fifth century onward, innumerable paintings of Maltese appear.

On a Greek vase, dating from about 500 B.C. a beautiful Maltese dog is shown—the vase was found at Vulci, and formed a part of the Bassegio collection.

[621]

TOYS

A very fine model of a Maltese dog was dug up in the Fayum, in Egypt. It is not unlikely that this was the kind of dog worshipped by the Egyptians.

At the time of the Apostle Paul, Publius, the Roman Governor of Malta, had a tiny Maltese named Issa— this he had painted in so life-like a manner that it was difficult to tell the picture from the live dog.

When the Apostle Paul, on his way to Rome (Acts 28), was shipwrecked on Malta, Publius was the Roman Governor of the Island. To commemorate the conversion of Publius, as well as the saving of Paul's life, the body of water called "St. Paul's Bay" was named after the Apostle.

Publius possessed a tiny Maltese named Issa of which he was very fond. The epigrammatic poet Martial (Marcus Valerius Martialis, born A.D. 38 at Bilbilis, in Spain), made this attachment famous in one of his celebrated epigrams which starts as follows:

"Issa is more frolicksome than Catulla's Sparrow. Issa is purer than a dove's kiss. Issa is gentler than a maiden. Issa is more precious than Indian Jems."

The epigram ended:

"Lest the last days that she sees light should snatch her from him forever, Publius has had the picture painted——"

Besides Martial, many other ancient authors discoursed on the beauty, the intelligence and the lovable qualities of Maltese dogs, including CALLIMACHUS THE ELDER (384-322 B.C.); STRABO (63 B.C.) PLINY THE ELDER (23-79 A.D.); SAINT CLEMENT of Alexandria, in the second century, A.D.; and others equally as celebrated.

Queens of old served out of golden vases the choicest of viands to their little Maltese.

The Ancients bred the Maltese very small.

MALTESE

Dr. Caius (1570 A.D.) physician to Queen Elizabeth who wrote in Latin says:

"There is among us another kind of highbred dogs, but outside the common run of these dogs (namely) those which CALLIMACHUS called Melitei from the Island of Melita. . . .

"That kind is *very small* indeed, and chiefly sought after for the pleasure and amusement of women. The smaller the kind, the more pleasing it is; so that they may carry them in their bosoms, in their beds, and in their arms while in their carriages."

Aldrovanus, who died in 1607, wrote of the early history of the breed in Latin. Aldrovanus says he saw one sold for the equivalent of $2,000. Considering the purchasing value of a dollar in the time of Queen Elizabeth, the price paid would be equal to a sum represented by five figures at this day.

Since the time of "Good Queen Bess," the Maltese has often been mentioned. The writers all drew attention to the *small size* of the dog. In 1607 E. Topsell wrote that they were not "bigger than common ferrets."

Almost 200 years later, LINNEAUS in 1792 referred to Maltese as "being about the size of Squirrels."

Danberton in his *History Naturelle* says that Maltese were so small "that ladies carried them in their sleeves."

The fact that Maltese have for many centuries been the household pets of people of culture, wealth and fastidious taste, very likely accounts for their great intelligence, refinement, fidelity and cleanliness.

They are Spaniels, not Terriers.

For more than twenty-eight centuries, history has consistently recorded that, although tiny, the Maltese was *healthy and spirited.* These *small dogs were bred,* and reproduced *small* dogs.

[623]

TOYS

To scientifically breed dogs, the "Eugenic Laws" must be followed.

A beautiful specimen of the Maltese in the arms of an old lady is painted by W. Powell Frith, R.A., in his celebrated picture of the "RAILWAY STATION."

DESCRIPTION AND STANDARD OF POINTS
(Courtesy of National Maltese Dog Club)

General Appearance.—Intelligent, sprightly, affectionate with long straight coat hanging evenly down each side, the parting extending from nose to root of tail. Although the frame is hidden beneath a mantle of hair, the general appearance should suggest a vigorous well proportioned body.

Weight.—Not to exceed seven pounds. Smaller the better. Under three pounds ideal.

Color.—Pure white.

Coat.—Long, straight, silky but strong and of even texture throughout. No undercoat.

Head.—In proportion to size of dog—should be of fair length: the *Skull* slightly round, rather broad between the ears and moderately well defined at the temples, i.e., exhibiting a moderate amount of stop and not in one straight line from nose to occiput bone.

Muzzle.—Not lean nor snipy but delicately proportioned.

Nose.—Black.

Ears.—Drop ears set slightly low, profusely covered with long hair.

Eyes.—Very dark—not too far apart—expression alert but gentle: black eye rims give a more beautiful expression.

Legs.—Short, straight, fine boned and well feathered.

Feet.—Small with long feathering.

Body and Shape.—Back short and level. Body low to ground, deep loins.

Tail and Carriage.—Tail well feathered with long hair, gracefully carried, its end resting on the hind quarters and side.

[624]

MALTESE

MEXICAN HAIRLESS

(Illustration facing page 619)

One of the most curious and distinctive breeds, the Mexican Hairless also is one of the oldest varieties of pure-bred dog in the world. Its hairlessness long has been one of the mysteries balking the most intensive investigation of scientists. The theory has been advanced that the lack of hair has been brought about by the temperature and the climate of the country in which the breed has existed. If this is true, the process of evolution must be extremely slow—for long-coated dogs have been known to exist under similar conditions for thousands of years.

Hairless dogs exist in many other parts of the world besides Mexico, and the theory which finds most acceptance—especially among Mexican authorities—is that this breed now found in relatively large quantities in the country below the Rio Grande is a descendant of the hairless dogs of China, where two somewhat similar breeds are known.

According to Sr. Blinde, the Mexican Hairless, or Biche, was established in Mexico when the Aztecs founded the Empire of Tenochtitlan in the Valley of Mexico. This tribe of Indian conquerors had brought the dog with them from Asia, crossing over the land bridge to Alaska at what is now the Bering Strait.

Just when the Aztecs migrated from Asia is a matter of some doubt, and there even is a supposition that the migration may have been in the opposite direction. However, the more reasonable one is that the Aztecs came from Asia. Had it been the other way, the hairless dog would have undoubtedly been discovered in other parts of North America, and it would not be found so often in different parts of Asia and Africa.

The Chinese Crested bears striking resemblance to the Mexican Hairless, and there is another hairless breed in China that is not so far removed from the Mexican variety. Then there is the Rampur dog of Southern India, likewise of the same general type. Another is the African sand dog, and somewhat similar dogs are found in Turkey, and in Japan. The South American dogs, of course, are regarded as closely related to the Mexican Hairless. The identical dog is found as far south as the Peruvian lowlands.

In Mexico the hairless dog is called commonly the "Biche," and this is another bond that links it to the old Indian civilization, for the word is an Aztec one meaning "naked."

Indications are that when the Biche started its travels with the Aztecs it was a much larger dog, believed to have been about the size of a small foxterrier. Yet it always was a light-boned animal, built on racy lines that might point to a very ancient descent from the greyhounds. Quite naturally the Aztecs could not take a great many dogs with them, and consequently the inbreeding brought a reduction in size.

The old legends that still persist, today, that the Mexican Hairless is possessed of healing qualities probably had their inception back in the Aztec days. In fact, this supplies a motive for an Indian people to have preserved this breed of dog through the generations. There is little or no reason to believe these stories, aside from the fact that heat often has a curative effect in certain instances, and the skin of this dog is hot to the touch. But from that simple basis grew many widespread beliefs, and in time the ignorant were of the opinion that a person suffering from almost any disease would be cured of it if a dog of this breed were held close to the body. Specifically, one suffering from "rheumatism" could be relieved of it if the dog were placed at the feet.

The Mexican Hairless as recognized in the United States is a small, toy specimen, found in a variety of colors. Sometimes the skin is of a mottled nature, but that is less desirable. There is no hair on the body, but a slight fuzz on the top of the head, and sometimes a few hairs on the tail.

The great centers of the breed in Mexico are on the West Coast; Mazatlan, and Durango, but there also are relatively large numbers in the City of Mexico. Outside interest in the dog undoubtedly has proven a stimulus to breeders in Mexico, and the specimens of modern times are being bred to a high state of perfection.

DESCRIPTION AND STANDARD OF POINTS

The Mexican Hairless is a small, active dog, about the size of a small Fox Terrier, symmetrical and well proportioned, with rather broad chest and ribs and with slender legs.

Head.—Should be slender and skull narrow, cheeks lean, muzzle long and pointed. There should be a tuft of coarse hair on top of the skull, in the center but a bit forward, in some cases shadowing the brow.

Eyes.—Should not be too deep set but balanced and not bulging —eye rims pink or dark and the eyes themselves hazel, yellow or dark.

Neck.—Should be of good length, slender and well arched into flat shoulders and the chest rather broad, legs fairly long and slender, ribs well rounded and chest rather deep.

Back.—Should be level, rump slightly rounded.

Skin.—Smooth and soft, not wrinkled, any color, hot to touch, no hair whatever.

Muscles and sinews well developed. A nervous tremor of muscles and sinews is characteristic like that of a nervous race horse.

Feet.—Should be hare feet, nails black in dark skin or pale in pale skin dogs.

Tail.—Long, smooth tail, carried out similar to that of Manchester Terrier. A little fuzz or hair on lower half of tail permitted.

Absence of tuft on top of the head is undesirable but not a disqualification.

Cut or broken ears or tail are disqualifications, likewise a fuzz or any hair, except as above described.

PAPILLONS

(Illustration facing page 640)

(By Courtesy of The Papillon Club of America)

The Papillon is the modern development of those little dogs often seen pictured on rare old paintings or tapestries and known in the sixteenth century as "dwarf Spaniels." Rubens, Watteau, Fragonard and Boucher all depicted dogs of this breed upon their canvases. For a time, the popularity of these dwarf Spaniels was so great, it was not surprising that many of the noble ladies of the day did not consider any of their portraits complete unless one of these elegant little dogs was also pictured with them. Madame de Pompadour was the proud possessor of two, Inez and Mimi by name. Marie Antoinette was another ardent fancier, while as early as 1545 there is record of one having been sold to a lady who later ascended to the throne of Poland.

It is Spain that we have to thank for the primary rise to fame of these little dogs, though Italy, with particular reference to the city of Bologna, probably developed the largest trade. Many were sold to the court of Louis XIV, who had his choice among those brought into France. The prices ran high and the chief trader, a Bolognese named Filipponi, developed a large business, not only with the court of France, but elsewhere. An interesting fact is that, lacking our modern means of transportation, most of the dogs were transferred from one country to the other upon the backs of mules.

As time went on, a change developed in the dwarf Spaniel which gave rise to the present-day appellation of "Papillon." During the days of Louis the Great, the dwarf Spaniel possessed large, drooping ears but gradually there came into being an erect-eared type, the ears being set obliquely upon the head and so fringed as to resemble closely the wings of a butterfly, from which the present breed derives its name. The causes of this change remain largely theoretical, but whatever they may be, we are now possessed of a toy dog whose type of body and coat is about the same as that of the original dwarf Spaniel of Spain and Italy but whose ears may be either erect or drooping. Both types may, and often do appear in the same litter. In continental Europe, as well as Great Britain, the drop-eared variety is called *Epagneul Nain,* although the breed as a whole carries the nomenclature of Papillon, as it does in this country. Here both types are as yet judged together and upon an equality.

Another change which has taken place in this breed concerns color. Originally, almost all were of solid color but today white predominates as a ground color, with patches or ticking of other colors.

The Papillon is one of the hardiest of dogs. It is unnecessary to coddle them in winter; they do not suffer particularly in severe hot weather; they do not contract disease easily; they delight in country activities and are equally contented in an apartment. As ratters, these little dogs make themselves extremely useful. Too small, for the most part, to kill a rat outright, they will worry it until it is completely weary and then dispatch it quickly. The bitches usually whelp easily and give little trouble in any way when rearing puppies.

The temperament and character of the Papillon invite the respect of all dog lovers. This breed is not only extremely affectionate and without snappy or irritable tendencies, so as to commend it to women or children as a companion, but is so lively and courageous as to find itself becoming increasingly popular among boys and men.

Although this breed has been known and exhibited for many years in the United States by a privileged few, it was not until 1935 that Papillons were represented in the American Kennel Club by their own breed club, the Papillon Club of America.

DESCRIPTION AND STANDARD OF POINTS

(As Adopted by The Papillon Club of America, July, 1935, from the Standard of the Southern Counties Papillon Society, England. Approved by The American Kennel Club, August 13, 1935)

General Appearance.—A graceful little Toy Spaniel, slender and of lively and dainty action.

Varieties.—Two varieties are recognized. In one, the ears are carried upright at an oblique angle to the head, like the opened-out wings of a butterfly; in the other the ears are drop. The latter is known as Epagneul Nain.

Coat.—Short and smooth on the head, muzzle, forepart of front legs and on the back legs from the hocks downwards. Thin tufts of hair may be present between the toes and extend beyond them, but must not make the foot heavy; flat on the back and sides; abundant around neck, shoulders and breast; back part of front legs should be well-fringed, the length of fringes decreasing up to the wrist; breeches covered with long hair; tail covered with a very long, flowing plume.

Head.—Proportionate to the body and should appear small, being covered with short hair, while the remainder of the body is heavy-coated. The skull should be of medium width and slightly rounded between the ears. A fairly accentuated stop between skull and muzzle must not be too abrupt. The muzzle is abruptly thinner than the skull, getting more and more slender up to the nose;

[633]

not the wedge-shaped appearance of the Pomeranian. The muzzle should be moderately long; jaws well adjusted together. The lips must be tight and on no account pendant. The muzzle must not be flattened.

Eyes.—Rather large, round and set fairly low in the head. They should be dark in color. The expression must be lively and intelligent.

Ears.—The ears are set on at the sides in both the erect and drop, more backwards than forwards and fairly high. They must be sufficiently apart to show the slightly arched shape of the skull. In the erect variety the ears are carried obliquely like the spreading wings of a butterfly, the concha largely open and the inside entirely visible, crowned with silken hair. The ears should be large, the leather fine in texture but sufficiently strong to maintain the opened-up position while the dog is at attention or in action. The tip is rounded. In the drop variety the ears are similar except that they are carried drooping and flat against the head.

Neck.—Not short or thick, but lost in the coat.

Body.—Rather elongated; back fairly long and straight. Chest fairly deep; ribs slightly arched; stomach slightly turned up; loins moderately curving in.

Tail.—Set on fairly high and carried like a squirrel. The carriage of tail may be concealed with an abundant plume.

Shoulders.—Not too straight, very mobile and hidden by hair.

Fore Quarters.—Fine and straight, the back part covered with abundant fringes, diminishing to the wrist, the front covered with short hairs.

Thighs.—Fairly muscular, very mobile and well covered with hair.

Hind Quarters.—Slender, parallel and covered to the hocks with abundant breeches; hocks fairly high-placed and elbowed; the remainder covered with short and smooth hair.

Feet.—Thin, fairly elongated, toes close and arched, hair short, but fine tufts may appear between the toes and go beyond them provided they do not make the foot heavy.

Color.—Unicolor, of any color, provided the latter is pure, except that the tawny shades may be smutty. Two-colored, white thrown into relief by patches and ticking; the size, shape and placement of the patches being without importance; a large saddle allowable. Tri-colored, similar to the two-colored except that the white is thrown into relief by spots, patches, or by both, of two colors. In both the two-colored and the tri-colored the skull should be divided by a white blaze. The body should be as white as possible.

PEKINGESE

(Illustration facing page 641)

(By Courtesy of The Pekingese Club of America)

Fascinating, not only by reason of its Oriental background but because of its distinctive personality and beauty as well, the Pekingese justly holds a commanding place in the world of the dog. That in ancient times the original Pekingese were held sacred in China, the land of their origin, is not to be disputed as many intricately carved Foo Dog idols of varying sizes and ranging in materials from ivory to bronze and jewel studded wood, have been handed down throughout the centuries. The exact date of the origin of the breed is a debatable point, the earliest known record of its existence being traceable to the Tang Dynasty of the eighth century. However, the very oldest strains (held only by the Imperial family) were kept pure, perhaps the more so because the theft of one of these sacred dogs was always punishable by a most horrible death. That the characteristics we seek to retain and perfect today were in evidence in the earliest Pekingese is shown by three of the names by which they were designated in ancient China. Some were called Lion Dogs, evidently because of their massive fronts, heavy manes and tapering hind quarters such as required by our present-day standards. We find a second group termed Sun Dogs because of their strikingly beautiful golden red coats. Since those early days, many other darker red shades have made their appearance and have become identified with certain strains but even today we see numerous Sun Dogs at our shows. A third appellation was that of Sleeve Dog, this being given only to those diminutive specimens which were carried about in the voluminous sleeves of the members of the Imperial household. Although there is no place for even the very tiniest Pekingese in the Occidental sleeve, the little ones have found a lasting place in the heart of the fancy and there are several clubs in existence functioning solely for the improvement of the under six pound Pekingese.

The introduction of the Pekingese into the western world occurred as a result of the looting of the Imperial Palace at Peking by the British in 1860. It is a matter of history that four Pekingese were found behind some draperies in the apartments of the Aunt of the Chinese Emperor. Apparently they were the particular pets of this lady, who committed suicide on the approach of the British troops. It is said that throughout the palace the bodies of many more of these dogs were found; the Chinese having killed them rather than have them fall into the hands of the Caucasians. The four Pekingese found by the English were of different colors and a fawn and white parti-color was the one presented to Queen Victoria on the return to Great Britain. Lord Hay and the Duke of Richmond kept the remainder and bred them.

Pekingese were not exhibited in England until 1893 when Mrs. Loftus Allen exhibited one at Chester. However, the undeniable beauty and interesting history of the breed placed it in the foreground where it has since remained.

The three dogs who were outstanding in the breed's earliest development in the Occident were Ah Cum and Mimosa, termed the "pillars of the Stud Book" in England, followed by a large black and tan specimen named

PEKINGESE

"Boxer," so called because he was obtained by Major Gwynne during the Boxer uprising in 1900. Curiously enough Boxer had a docked tail and so was never exhibited. He undoubtedly did more for the breed in the early part of the century than any other Pekingese.

That the Oriental dog took quick hold of the American fancy is evidenced by the age of the Pekingese Club of America which was formed nearly a quarter of a century ago and is not only one of the oldest but also one of the largest Specialty Clubs in the United States. So much for the introduction of the Pekingese to the Occident. The transplanting of the Pekingese into Western soil has in no way changed his personality. He combines marked dignity with an exasperating stubbornness which only serves to endear him the more to his owners. He is independent and regal in every gesture and it would be the greatest of indignities to attempt to make a "lap dog" out of him. Calm and good tempered, the Pekingese employs a condescendingly cordial attitude toward the world in general but in the privacy of his family circle enjoys nothing better than a good romp. Although never on the aggressive, he fears not even the devil himself and has never been known to turn tail and run. Incidentally he has plenty of stamina, much more in fact than have a number of the larger breeds, and is very easy to care for.

Since he has been made to come down from his pedestal in Chinese Temples the Pekingese has but one purpose in life, to give understanding companionship and loyalty to his owners. It may be truly said that the Pekingese fulfills his mission to perfection in every particular.

TOYS

DESCRIPTION AND STANDARD OF POINTS

(Adopted 1935 by The Pekingese Club of America and Approved by The American Kennel Club, May 14, 1935)

Expression.—Must suggest the Chinese origin of the Pekingese in its quaintness and individuality, resemblance to the lion in directness and independence and should imply courage, boldness, self-esteem and combativeness rather than prettiness, daintiness or delicacy.

Skull.—Massive, broad, wide and flat between the ears (not dome shaped), wide between the eyes.

Nose.—Black, broad, very short and flat.

Eyes.—Large, dark, prominent, round, lustrous.

Stop.—Deep.

Ears.—Heart shaped, not set too high, leather never long enough to come below the muzzle, nor carried erect, but rather drooping, long feather.

Muzzle.—Wrinkled, very short and broad, not overshot nor pointed. Strong, broad under jaw, teeth not to show.

Shape of Body.—Heavy in front, well sprung ribs, broad chest, falling away lighter behind, lion-like. Back level. Not too long in body; allowance made for longer body in bitch.

Legs.—Short forelegs, bones of forearm bowed, firm at shoulder; hindlegs lighter but firm and well shaped.

Feet.—Flat, toes turned out, not round, should stand well up on feet, not on ankles.

Action.—Fearless, free and strong, with slight roll.

Coat, Feather and Condition.—Long, with thick undercoat, straight and flat, not curly nor wavy, rather coarse, but soft; feather on thighs, legs, tail and toes long and profuse.

Mane.—Profuse, extending beyond the shoulder blades, forming ruff or frill round the neck.

Color.—All colors are allowable. Red, fawn, black, black and tan, sable, brindle, white and parti-color well defined: black masks and spectacles around the eyes, with lines to ears are desirable.

PAPILLON

PEKINGESE

PEKINGESE

Definition of a Parti-Color Pekingese.—The coloring of a parti-colored dog must be broken on the body. No large portion of any one color should exist. White should be shown on the saddle. A dog of any solid color with white feet and chest is NOT a parti-color.

Tail.—Set high; lying well over back to either side; long, profuse, straight feather.

Size.—Being a toy dog, medium size preferred, providing type and points are not sacrificed; extreme limit 14 pounds. Anything over must disqualify.

	Points
Expression	5
Skull	10
Nose	5
Eyes	5
Stop	5
Ears	5
Muzzle	5
Shape of body	15
Legs and feet	15
Coat, feather and condition	15
Tail	5
Action	10
Total	100

Penalizations.—Protruding tongue, badly blemished eye, overshot, wry mouth.

Disqualifications.—Blindness, docked tail, cropped ears, overweight, Dudley nose.

PINSCHERS (MINIATURE)

(Illustration facing page 652)

(By Courtesy of The Miniature Pinscher Club of America, Inc.)

The Miniature Pinscher has been in existence for several centuries. Their native land is Germany, but they have been bred also in the Scandinavian Countries for a long time. The real development of the breed abroad started first in 1895 when the Pinscher Klub was formed in Germany. This Club is now called the Pinscher-Schnauzer Klub. It gave the breed its first standard.

From the time of the formation of the Pinscher Klub, the breed moved forward, both in type and popularity, but the real spurt began in 1905 and continued up to the World War. The war, of course, considerably handicapped forward progress in almost everything. After it, or beginning in 1919, the breeders and fanciers abroad again started the advancement of the Miniature Pinscher and through several importations to the United States breeding started here on a very limited and scattered scale.

There were, however, few Miniature Pinschers seen at dog shows in the United States before 1928 and the real start of the advancement of the breed began in 1929 when the Miniature Pinscher Club of America, Inc., was organized. The breed previously had been shown in the miscellaneous class in the dog shows. After the formation of the present Miniature Pinscher Club here and its acceptance as a member of the American Kennel Club, the breed became classified under the name of Miniature Pinscher, and a considerable upswing in breeding and showing became noticeable. The breed because of its small size has been put in the Toy Group. This little dog's popularity has steadily increased and as many as 34 entries of the breed often appear in dog shows. Many times there are just as many entries as of any other breed in the Toy Group.

Imported and American-bred dogs of this breed have won the Toy Group many times. One American-bred dog was awarded best in the Toy Group at the Chicago show of 1935.

Although the Miniature Pinscher is similar to a Doberman on a smaller scale, it has the nature and a way about itself suggesting a much larger dog. Therefore, it is noted as a watch dog and will bluff itself about, perhaps, in many cases better than a dog twice its size. It is a born show dog because of its attractive and smart appearance, and is noted for its active and lively temperament. Its gait is similar to that of a good hackney pony. The Miniature Pinscher is most intelligent and is often used on the stage because of its style, smartness and "pep."

For the above reasons and qualifications the breed has enjoyed the support of many socially prominent persons in Germany for a long time, and when the breed was finally introduced here a number of prominent people flocked to the fancy and to the support of it, many of them have become so attached to the Miniature Pinscher that they have established kennels of this, their favorite breed.

The owners of Miniature Pinschers will get great companionship from their pets. The close, slick coat requires

PINSCHERS (MINIATURE)

very little attention; they always look clean, and their fondness for home and master is exceptional.

If you like a small "Pinscher" with smart appearance and full of life, see them trotting around and "showing off," in some of the dog shows and you will have found what you are looking for.

DESCRIPTION AND STANDARD OF POINTS

(Adopted August, 1935, by The Miniature Pinscher Club of America, Inc., and Approved by The American Kennel Club)

General Appearance.—A miniature of the Doberman Pinscher, having on a modified scale most of its physical qualifications and specifications, viz., symmetrical proportions, sturdy though slim, pert, lively, attentive, with well distributed muscle formation and a carriage suggestive of an active and lively temperament.

General Faults.—Heavy set, coarse, poor quarters, too long or short coupled, knotty muscles, lethargic, timid or dull.

Head.—The head should be in correct proportion to the body. As viewed from the side—elongated and tapering, with only a slight drop to the muzzle, which should be parallel to the top of the skull. As viewed from the top—narrow with well fitted but not too prominent foreface. As viewed from the front—the skull appears flat, tapering forward to the muzzle. Muzzle itself strong rather than fine and delicate and in proportion to the head as a whole; cheeks and lips small, taut and closely adherent to each other. Teeth in perfect alignment and apposition.

Faults.—Too big or too small for body, too short or coarse, too long or fine or distorted, *top too broad,* foreface too prominent, skull too round or hollow with too much stop, poor teeth, *jaws undershot* or overshot.

Eyes.—Full, slightly oval, almost round, clear and bright, dark, even to a true black, set wide apart and fitted well into the sockets.

Faults.—Too round and full, too small or large, too bulging or deep-set, too close or far apart.

Ears.—Well set, and placed, firm, upstanding (or when legal, cropped short, pointed and upstanding).

[645]

Faults.—Poorly set, placed low, weak or hanging, or poorly cropped.

Nose.—Black in black and tan, red or stag red.

Faults.—Brown or spotted in black and tan, red or stag red.

Neck.—Slightly arched, and gracefully curved, blending into the shoulders, relatively short, muscular, and free from throatiness. Length from occiput to withers equal distance from nose to occiput.

Faults.—Too straight or too curved. Too thick or too thin. Too long or short, knotty muscles, loose, flabby or wrinkled skin.

Body.—Compact, wedge shaped, muscular with well sprung ribs, the base line of which is level with the points of the elbows; well knit muscular quarters set wide apart, with back level or slightly sloping towards the rear. Length of males equals height, females may be slightly longer.

Faults.—Chest too narrow or barrel shaped, quarters too wide or too close to each other, too thin or too fat, sloping rump, sway-back, roachback, wryback, hips higher or considerably lower than shoulders.

Legs and Feet.—Straight and upstanding as viewed from the front or rear with strong bone development and small joints; viewed from side—all adjacent bones should appear well angulated with well muscled stifles, short well developed hocks, well-knit flexible pasterns, strong, well-arched and closely knit toes with thick blunt nails.

Faults.—Bow or X-legs—too thick or too thin bone development, *large joints,* thin stifles, large or crooked hocks, floating knee caps, weak pasterns, spreading flat feet, feet turning in or out.

Tail.—Set high, broad, held erect and cropped 1 to 2 inches.

Faults.—Set too low, too thin, drooping, hanging or poorly cropped.

Coat.—Thick, hard, short, straight, and lustrous, closely adhering to and uniformly covering the body.

Faults.—Thin, too short, dull, upstanding, curly, dry, areas of various thickness *or bald spots.*

PINSCHERS (MINIATURE)

Color

1. Lustrous black with tan, rust-red or yellow markings on cheeks, lips, lower jaw, throat, above eyes, twin spots on chest, lower half of forelegs, inside of hindlegs and vent region. Black pencil stripes on toes. Faults—light colored or white, very dark or sooty spots,—in listed markings.

2. Solid yellow.

3. Solid red or stag-red.

4. Solid brown or brown with red or yellow markings.

5. Solid blue or blue toned with red or yellow markings.

Height.—Approximately eleven and a half inches at the shoulder or withers, with a slight variation permissible.

Faults.—Too small or too large.

Weight.—Five to ten pounds.

VALUE OF POINTS

	Points
General appearance and movement	25
Nose	5
Mouth	5
Eyes	5
Ears	5
Neck	5
Body	15
Feet	5
Color	10
Coat	15
Tail	5
Total number of points	100

POMERANIANS

(Illustration facing page 653)

(By Courtesy of The American Pomeranian Club)

The Pomeranian, acclaimed by its admirers "the most alert and ever keen of all the Toy breeds" has shown marked improvement during the past decade both in type and size and profuseness of coat, the latter perhaps the paramount feature, that is, if one is guided by the standard where this feature is allowed twenty-five points with an added ten for color.

While it is true that a Pomeranian out of coat loses a deal of its charm, one must not overlook the important fact that coat, as one old-timer expressed it "is like charity, it oft-times covers many sins," hence his strong contention that "shape and make" with marked "Pom" character, that is, right on its toes, head erect with small well placed ears, expressing marked keenness, tail well over the back and carried flat to body, and merry action —so essential in a typical Pomeranian—are of much importance.

It is claimed by some that this fashionable breed with its essential characteristics has been traced back several centuries in different countries but there is no doubt in the mind of the majority that its place of origin was Pomerania—as the name seems to imply—and its forbears the large white Spitz bred down from the Iceland and Lapland sledge-dogs. Be it as it may, the breed was not well known until 1870 when the English Kennel Club recognized the then so-called "Spitzdog." Perhaps the nearest to the original type and size of the first

"Poms" exhibited in England was the somewhat large sable dog, Ruffle, shown by Mrs. Barrett and later brought to this country by Mrs. Smythe. Pomeranians were shown in the U. S. in the miscellaneous class as far back as 1892 but regular classification with winners class was not provided for them until 1900 at the New York show. In 1911 the American Pomeranian Club, already a member of the American Kennel Club, held its first specialty show of the breed, an event that has taken place annually ever since.

The majority of the early American winners were somewhat under six pounds in weight and had type and, generally speaking, good texture of coat but they lacked the profuseness of coat in evidence today and were somewhat heavier in bone and ears. However, present-day American-breds are marked improvements on the early winners; in fact, the patient efforts of the breeders have brought them nearer and nearer to the standard of perfection so that some American-breds have been able to go abroad and gain full quota of laurels as in the case of Ch. Pall Mall His Majesty which went to Europe and on several occasions beat all the Toy breeds for the coveted "Best in show." Over here home-bred Pomeranians have become constant and in many cases successful contenders for the highest honors at all-breed shows.

The diminutive size, docility of temper and vivacity of spirit plus sturdiness and stamina characteristic of the Poms make them adorable pets and great companions and their keen sense of hearing, boldness and alertness make them wonderful watch-dogs thus adding usefulness to beauty. In the show ring they make a most exquisite picture.

To visualize what constitutes real Pom type and character one has but to peruse the Club's standard which follows and to commit to memory the accompanying photo of a very typical winner not forgetting that the general appearance of a typical Pom is that of a compact, short-coupled dog with marked activity, standing on tiny, cat-like feet, with profuse, stand-off coat, fox-like head with small, well carried ears and keen expression.

DESCRIPTION AND STANDARD OF POINTS
(By Courtesy of The American Pomeranian Club)

Appearance.—The Pomeranian in build and appearance should be a compact, short-coupled dog, well-knit in frame. His head and face should be foxlike, with small erect ears that appear sensible to every sound; he should exhibit great intelligence in his expression, docility in his disposition, and activity and buoyancy in his deportment.

Head.—The head should be somewhat foxy in outline, or wedge-shaped, the skull being slightly flat, large in proportion to the muzzle, which should finish rather fine, and be free from lippiness. The teeth should be level, and on no account undershot. The head in its profile may exhibit a little "stop," which, however, must not be too pronounced, and the hair on the head and face must be smooth or short-coated.

Eyes.—The eyes should be medium in size, rather oblique in shape, not set too wide apart, bright and dark in color, showing great intelligence and docility of temper. In a white dog, black rims around the eyes are preferable.

Ears.—The ears should be small, not set too far apart nor too low down, and carried perfectly erect, like those of a fox, and like the head, should be covered with soft, short hair.

Nose.—Should be self-colored in Browns and Blue. In all other colors, should be black.

Neck and Shoulders.—The neck, if anything, should be rather short, well set in, and lion-like, covered with a profuse mane and frill of long straight hair, sweeping from the under jaw and covering the whole of the front part of the shoulders and chest as well as the top part of the shoulders. The shoulders must be tolerably clean, and laid well back.

Body.—The back must be short, and the body compact, being well ribbed up and the barrel well rounded. The chest must be fairly deep and not too wide.

Legs.—The forelegs must be well feathered and perfectly straight, of medium length, and not such as would be termed "leggy" or "low on legs," but in length and strength in due proportion to a well-balanced frame. The hindlegs and thighs must be well feathered down to the hocks, and must be neither cow-hocked nor wide behind. They must be fine in bone and free in action. The feet should be small and compact in shape.

Tail.—The tail is a characteristic of the breed, and should be turned over the back and carried flat, being profusely covered with long spreading hair.

Coat.—Properly speaking there should be two coats, an under and an over coat; the one a soft fluffy undercoat, and the other a long, perfectly straight and glistening coat covering the whole of the body, being very abundant around the neck and forepart of the shoulders and chest, where it should form a frill of profuse, standing-off, straight hair, extending over the shoulders as previously described. The hind quarters like those of the collie, should be similarly clad with long hair or feathering from the top of the rump to the hocks. The hair on the tail must be, as previously described, profuse and spreading over the back.

Color.—The following colors are admissible: Black, brown, chocolate, red, orange, cream, orange-sable, wolf-sable, beaver, blue, white and parti-colors. The blacks, blues, browns and sables must be free from any white, and the whites must be free from lemon or any other color. A few white hairs in any of the self-colors shall not absolutely disqualify but should carry great weight against a dog. In parti-colored dogs, the colors should be evenly distributed on the body in patches. A dog with a white foot or a white chest would not be a parti-colored dog. Whole colored dogs with a white foot or feet, leg or legs, are decidedly objectionable and should be discouraged and cannot compete as whole colored specimens. In mixed classes where whole colored and parti-colored Pomeranians compete together, the preference should—if in other points they are equals—be given to the whole colored specimens.

MINIATURE PINSCHER

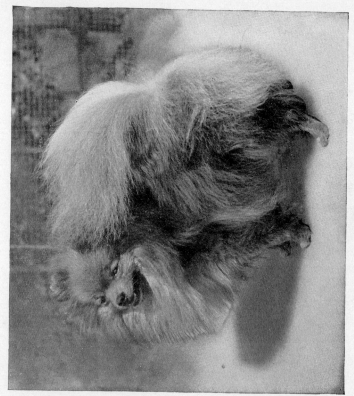

POMERANIAN

POMERANIANS

Sables must be shaded throughout with three or more colors, as uniformly as possible, with no patches of self-color. Oranges must be self-colored throughout and light shadings though not disqualifying should be discouraged.

	Points
Appearance	10
Head	5
Eyes	5
Ears	5
Nose	5
Neck and shoulders	5
Body	10
Legs	10
Tail	10
Coat	25
Color	10
Total	100

N.B.—Where classification by weight is made, the following scale, passed by the club as the most suitable division, should be adopted by Show Committees:
1. Not exceeding 7 pounds.
2. Exceeding 7 pounds.

Where classification by color is made, the following division should be adopted:
1. Black.
2. Brown or chocolate.
3. Red, orange or cream.
4. Sables.
5. Any color not mentioned above.

PUGS

(Illustration facing page 658)

(By Courtesy of The Pug Dog Club of America)

The Pug Dog is sometimes styled the "Dutch Pug" and it is taken for granted that the breed is indigenous to Holland, since, according to universal but dateless tradition, it came into initial favor in that country. It is easier, however, to attribute the origin of the Pug to China whence have come practically all of the short-faced dogs, having tightly-curled tails. It was first imported into England by traders from the Dutch East India Company and to that fact must be accorded the reason for their land of origin being attributed to the Dutch. It is most likely that the Pug shares in the claim to antiquity. Upon their importation into England they became the favored pets of the ladies of the nobility and their rise to popularity was rapid and well deserved. Their parent country, did little to exploit the breed and to two well known British fanciers must go the credit for the acclaim with which the breed was received.

Lady Willoughby de Eresby of Greenthorpe near Lincoln was one of the breed's sponsors and the dogs of her kennels were distinguished by their silver-fawn coloring. Mr. Morrison of Walham Green shares with her this honor and the dogs of his kennels were a brighter golden color. There was nothing to distinguish the two strains other than color and as they were interbred, the claim that one of the breed is now pure in either strain would be spurious. The now popular black Pug made his advent many years later and it is believed that he traces his origin to an infusion of the blood of the Japanese Pug, a breed not dissimilar to our present toy spaniels, although not so profuse in either coat or feather. The Japanese Pugs were either white or black or a mixture of those two colors and to this we may also ascribe the tendency of many Pugs to show white on the chest and feet. In addition to the all black Pug, there have appeared several all white Pugs which met with little or no favor.

The Willoughby strain was more heavily marked with black tracings than the Morrison Pugs and the interbreeding of the two strains, with some infusion of black blood, undoubtedly accounts for the loss of trace in the present-day Pug for many now show a tendency to smuttiness. Today all colors are bred together indiscriminately and the puppies will be self colored in either color with the loss of trace in these other than black as above described.

The standard was drawn originally in 1883 and has been changed considerably since that time. The breed may well be described as "Multum in parvo" for they are compact, alert, cleanly, tractable and companionable. They breed quite true to size and type and their freedom from offensive smell from breath and skin has greatly assisted their return to greater favor, for they have merited their popularity of late years since they require the minimum of care in order to be kept in good condition. They do not require the coddling of some of the other toy varieties and many have been known to willingly undertake the tasks of their larger cousins.

PUGS

DESCRIPTION AND STANDARD OF POINTS
(By Courtesy of The Pug Dog Club, England)

Symmetry.—Symmetry and general appearance, decidedly square and cobby. A lean leggy Pug and a dog with short legs and a long body are equally objectionable.

Size and Condition.—The Pug should be *multum in parvo,* but this condensation (if the word may be used) should be shown by compactness of form, well-knit proportions, and hardness of developed muscle. Weight from 14 to 18 pounds (dog or bitch) desirable.

Body.—Short and cobby, wide in chest and well-ribbed up.

Legs.—Very strong, straight, of moderate length, and well under.

Feet.—Neither so long as the foot of the hare, nor so round as that of the cat; well-split-up toes, and the nails black.

Muzzle.—Short, blunt, square, but not upfaced.

Head.—Large, massive, round—not apple-headed, with no indentation of the skull.

Eyes.—Dark in color, very large, bold and prominent, globular in shape, soft and solicitous in expression, very lustrous, and, when excited, full of fire.

Ears.—Thin, small, soft, like black velvet. There are two kinds —the "Rose" and "Button." Preference is given to the latter.

Markings.—Clearly defined. The muzzle or mask ears, moles on cheeks, thumb-mark or diamond on forehead, back-trace should be as black as possible.

Mask.—The mask should be black. The more intense and well defined it is the better.

Wrinkles.—Large and deep.

Trace.—A black line extending from the occiput to the tail.

Tail.—Curled tightly as possible over the hip. The double curl is perfection.

Coat.—Fine, smooth, soft, short and glossy, neither hard nor woolly.

[657]

TOYS

Color.—Silver or apricot-fawn. Each should be decided, to make the contrast complete between the color and the trace and the mask. Black.

POINTS

	Fawn	*Black*
Symmetry	10	10
Size	5	10
Condition	5	5
Body	10	10
Legs and feet	5	5
Head	5	5
Muzzle	10	10
Ears	5	5
Eyes	10	10
Mask	5	....
Wrinkles	5	5
Tail	10	10
Trace	5	....
Coat	5	5
Color	5	10
Total	100	100

PUG

TOY MANCHESTER TERRIER

TOY MANCHESTER TERRIERS

(Illustration on opposite page)

The toy variety of the Manchester Terrier has been known as a distinct breed for nearly a century and a half. But long before the Toy Manchester—or Toy Black and Tan, as he was known generally—became a popular favorite, the appealing type of this dog was being evolved. The two sizes carry in their veins some of the oldest blood in existence; and it is this same blood that has been crossed and recrossed to produce countless other breeds now regarded as pure-bred.

The name "Manchester" long has been regarded as somewhat misleading, for similar dogs were known in many other parts of England. The designation of the breed as the Manchester Terrier did not take place until the middle of the Victorian period, about which time the city after which it is named became a center of the breed.

The Black and Tan Terrier was one of the breeds mentioned by Dr. Caius in the famous letter concerning the dogs of England that was sent to Gesner for inclusion in his then encyclopedic work on the dogs of all nations. Dr. Caius completed his survey in 1570. His description of the breed stamps it as carrying the essential colors and the characteristics but as being more rough in coat and short on the leg.

That extensive investigator, Ash, advances a theory in making the statement that it would be interesting to know how closely the Dachshund is related to the Manchester Terrier. In substantiation of this is the description, by Whitaker in 1771, of the dog of Manchester as "a short-

[659]

legged, crooked-legged dog." While a relationship between the Dachshund and the Manchester Terrier seems somewhat fantastic, it is not an impossibility. The Dachshund's ancestor was not of such exaggerated proportions. Possibly this dog was carried to Britain during the invasions of Saxon pirates in the 4th century A.D.

The modern style of the Manchester Terriers, both large and toy, has been attributed to the infusion of some Greyhound or Whippet blood. In this manner is explained the roached back, seldom found in a terrier. Yet, if such a cross was used, it occurred prior to 1800, about which time the breed was known in its present form.

The only essential differences between the large dog—weighing about 20 pounds—and the toy—weighing less than 7 pounds—are in the size, and in the natural ear carriage. The larger specimen has semi-erect ears, while the toy has erect ears. When the ears are cropped they are identical.

Development of the Toy Manchester was a matter of chance, and then became regulated by selective breeding. The mating of two large specimens produced a litter in which all but one puppy grew to the size of the parents. This small one attracted considerable attention. As a result the breeder decided to try for more of the same size.

There have been occasions when the great popularity of the toys led to certain unscrupulous practices among breeders who sought more quickly to supply the demand. There were crosses with the Italian Greyhound and with several other similar breeds. Fortunately, these crosses were not perpetuated. The vast majority of the breeders held meticulously to the rule of mating the toys or of breeding down from the larger variety.

The toys suffered somewhat from inbreeding in the

middle of the Victorian era; this being brought about by the great demand for tininess. The weight was gotten down as low as 2½ pounds; but due to the closeness of many of the matings the tiny mites did not have the stamina of their brothers of about 4 pounds or more. For a time the breed had a reputation for being extremely delicate, and this hurt the popularity of the dog.

More sensible breeders in England and in the United States have not tried for such extreme smallness. They have been content to breed small ones of charming appearance and admirable characteristics. And it is from this blood that the present lines in both countries were developed. The return to the Toy Manchester as a favorite among the diminutive pets began about ten years ago, and today its position again is relatively strong in the world of pure bred dogs.

DESCRIPTION AND STANDARD OF POINTS

(By Courtesy of The Manchester Toy Dog Society, Manchester, England)

Head.—Long, flat, narrow, level and wedge-shaped without showing cheek muscles; well filled up under eyes, tapering tightly lipped jaws, level teeth.

Eyes.—Very small, sparkling and dark, set fairly close together, oblong in shape.

Nose.—Black.

Ears.—The carriage of the ears since cropping was abolished is a debatable point. In the large breed the drop ear is correct, but for Toys either erect or semi-erect carriage is most desirable.

Neck and Shoulders.—The neck should be fairly long and tapering from the shoulders to the head, with sloping shoulders, the neck being free from throatiness and slightly arched at the occiput.

Chest.—Narrow but deep.

Body.—Moderately short, curving upwards at the loin; ribs

well sprung, back slightly arched at the loin and falling again at the joining of the tail to the same height as the shoulders.

Legs.—Must be quite straight, set on well under the dog and of fair length.

Feet.—Should be more inclined to be cat than hare-footed.

Tail.—Moderate length and set on where arch of the back ends; thick where it joins the body, tapering to a point, and not carried higher than the back.

Coat.—Close, smooth, short and glossy.

Color.—Jet black and rich mahogany tan distributed over the body as follows: On the head the muzzle is tanned to the nose, which with the nasal bone is jet black; there is also a bright spot on each cheek and over each eye, and hair inside the ears of the same color. The forelegs tanned to the knees, with black lines (pencil marks) up each toe, and a black thumb mark in the tan above the foot; inside the hindlegs tanned, but divided with black at the back joint; tan outside the legs (breechings) is a serious defect. Under the tail should be tanned, also the vent, but only enough to be nearly covered by the tail. In all cases the black should not run into the tan or *vice versa,* but division should be well defined.

Weight.—For toys average weight 7 pounds, although there is now no restriction.

	Points
Head	20
Eyes	5
Nose	5
Ears	5
Neck and shoulders	5
Chest	5
Body	10
Legs	10
Feet	5
Tail	5
Coat	15
Color	10
Total	100

TOY POODLES

(Illustration facing page 666)

The universal esteem in which the Poodle has been held since the beginning of modern history is attested by the many variations in color and size that are found in this popular breed. Few other dogs have climbed to such high favor in so many different countries as has the Poodle. So early did he spring up in different parts of the world that there even is some doubt as to the land of his origin.

While it is concluded by all authorities that the large-sized specimens of the breed are the older varieties, there is sufficient evidence to show that the Toy Poodle was developed only a short time after the breed assumed the general type in which it is known today. This type, incidentally, has changed less than that of almost any other breed. It is a dog that has come down to us as the ancients knew it. Refinements have been effected, but there has been no change in its essential characteristics.

Those bas-reliefs, dating from the first century, that are found along the shores of the Mediterranean, portray the Poodle very much as he is seen in the twentieth century. Clipped to resemble the lion, he is not unlike some of the specimens seen at the earliest bench shows.

It is possible that in the dim past there was a link between the dog attributed to the Island of Melita—now known as the Maltese—and the Toy Poodle. Similarly, there probably was a relationship between the Poodle and the dog of Spain—the spaniel. If not from the same

[663]

progenitor, the paths of their ancestors must have crossed at some remote time.

The first concrete evidence of the existence of the Toy Poodle in England is not found until the eighteenth century, when a toy known as the "White Cuban" became exceedingly popular in England. It was a sleeve dog, and it soon became the pet of every grand lady in the country. This breed's origin was attributed to the West Indian island of Cuba, from whence it travelled to Spain, and from there to England. Queen Anne had several of these dogs in her latter years. She had first seen them about 1700 when there came to England a troupe of performing dogs known as "The Ball of Little Dogs." These Toy Poodles were exceptionally well trained, and they danced to music in almost human fashion.

The Continent had known the Toy Poodle several centuries before it came to England, and there are line drawings by the great German artist, Dürer, that definitely establish the breed in the fifteenth and sixteenth centuries. How long the dog had been known in Spain is problematical, but it was definitely the principal pet dog of the latter eighteenth century. This is known through the paintings of the famous Spanish artist, Goya. In many of his portraits of the ladies of the court may be seen excellent examples of the Toy Poodle. And France enthroned the Toy Poodle as the pampered favorite during the reign of Louis XVI, about the same period.

Considerable mystery surrounds the "White Cuban." Subsequent histories of the dog leave no conviction that this breed was indigenous to Cuba. No doubt, specimens of the poodle or the Maltese—possibly both—had been carried to the West Indies by early explorers and traders. According to Lloyd, the White Cuban was a cross between the German or French white corded poodles and the Maltese. These dogs were larger than the Maltese, and their cords trailed on the ground.

The Toy Poodle is credited with being the principal ancestor of the truffle dog of England. It is believed that the Toy Poodle was crossed with a small terrier to produce a dog that was ideal for its strange occupation. The truffle is an edible fungus that formerly was considered a great delicacy. The high prices were so attractive that the hunting of truffles became a widespread trade, especially throughout certain parts of Hampshire and Wiltshire. The difficulty of procuring truffles lay in the fact that the fungus grew underground. They had to be scented out by a dog so that the master could dig them out. The dogs had to be carefully trained, and usually they were white in color, because truffle-hunting was done at night. The sagacity and the scenting powers of the poodle were said to form a perfect complement to the terrier's ability to go to earth.

The modern history of the Toy Poodle is a straight descent from the size of the standard and miniature poodles. Standards are 15 inches or more at the shoulder; miniatures under 15 inches. The Toy must never exceed 12 pounds. The standards for all three are identical except in the matter of size. The so-called "White Cuban phase" of the breed is believed to have no influence on the present-day specimens. The dogs of the eighteenth century in England probably left few, if any, descendants.

The diminutive size of the Toy Poodle rather militates against its use in any sporting sense, but fanciers of the small dog credit it with carrying all the tendencies of the larger members of the breed. Its intelligence also is regarded as similarly high.

TOYS

DESCRIPTION AND STANDARD OF POINTS

(Adopted May, 1938 by The International Toy Poodle Club and Approved by the American Kennel Club, June 14, 1938)

General Appearance.—That of a very active, intelligent and elegant looking dog, well built and carrying himself very proudly.

Head.—Long, straight and fine, the skull not broad, with a slight peak at the back.

Muzzle.—Long (but not snipy) and strong; not full in cheek; teeth white, strong and level; gums black, lips black and not showing lippiness.

Eyes.—Almond-shaped, very dark, full of fire and intelligence.

Nose.—Black and sharp.

Ears.—The leather long and wide, low set on, hanging close to the face.

Neck.—Well proportioned and strong, to admit of the head being carried high and with dignity.

Shoulders.—Strong and muscular, sloping well to the back.

Chest.—Deep and moderately wide.

Back.—Short, strong and slightly hollowed, the loins broad and muscular, the ribs well sprung and braced up.

Feet.—Rather small, and of good shape, the toes well arched, pads thick and hard.

Legs.—Forelegs set straight from shoulder, with fine bone and muscle. Hindlegs very muscular and well bent, with the hocks well let down.

Tail.—Set on rather high, well carried, never curled or carried over back.

Coat.—Very profuse, and of good, hard texture; if corded, hanging in tight even cords; if non-corded, very thick and strong, of even length, the curls close and thick, without knots or cords.

Colors.—Any solid color.

The white, cream, apricot, or red poodle should have dark eyes, black or dark liver nose, lips and toe-nails.

The blue poodle should be of even color, and have dark eyes, lips and toe-nails.

TOY POODLE

YORKSHIRE TERRIER

TOY POODLES

All the other points of Toy Poodles should be the same as the perfect black toy poodle.

N.B.—It is strongly recommended that only one-third of the body be clipped or shaved, and that the hair on the forehead be left on.

Size.—Toy Poodle—Ten inches or under at the shoulder.

	Points
General appearance and movement	15
Head and ears	15
Neck and shoulders	10
Body, back and tail carriage	25
Color, coat and texture	15
Legs and feet	10
Bone, muscle and condition	10
Total	100

YORKSHIRE TERRIERS

(Illustration facing page 667)

The Yorkshire Terrier is notable as a breed that lays no claim to great antiquity and which attained astounding popularity within a comparatively few years after it had attained definite form. This toy breed's history is encompassed within the record of organized dogdom in the English-speaking nations, for it made its first appearance at a bench show in 1861.

The debut of the Yorkshire Terrier took place at the Leeds show, in England, but it was not exhibited under its present name. The name "Yorkshire" was not applied to this breed—in any great extent—until 1886 when it was recognized by the Kennel Club in England. According to Marples, the Leeds show of 1861 had a class for Scotch terriers in which all the specimens were of the breed now known as the Yorkshire. The term "Scotch terrier" was applied very loosely in those days. Indeed, the previous year at Birmingham, all the winners in the classes for Scotch terriers were Skyes.

The Skye terrier was definitely Scotch, but the Yorkshire was "invented" and developed in Lancashire and Yorkshire. The fact that the Yorkshire Terrier first was exhibited as a Scotch terrier gives greater basis for the belief that it is a descendant of the Skye. Considering the recent origin of the breed, it seems rather strange that there should be any doubt as to its ancestors—but breeders long have been noted for their secretiveness when developing new breeds of dogs. Apparently, they have thought principally of profits. To reveal the

[669]

crosses used in making a new breed would be only a stimulation to their competitors.

The Yorkshire Terrier became the fashionable pet of the ladies of the aristocracy and of wealthy families in the Late-Victorian era, and even before, but in its beginnings this breed belonged to the working classes. In fact, it was so closely linked to the weavers that many facetious comments were made regarding the fine texture of its extremely long and silky coat, terming it the ultimate product of the looms.

Undoubtedly the Yorkshire is closely connected to the Skye and to the Skye's exaggerated progeny, the Clydesdale or Paisley terrier. When a great number of weavers and their families migrated from Scotland to England in the middle of the nineteenth century they brought with them numerous specimens of the Skye and of the Paisley terriers. Settled in Lancashire and Yorkshire, they found themselves in a region that was quite conversant with practically all the existing breeds.

It is doubtful if many of the early Yorkshire Terriers could trace back to common ancestors, for, in a land that knew so many terriers and toy dogs, it would be unreasonable to suppose that all the breeders used the same crosses. Perhaps the one breed that was found most suitable to complement the qualities of the Skye was the old black and tan or Manchester terrier—for this coloring long has been dominant in the Yorkshire.

The other breeds credited by the majority of the old authorities with having a part in the development of the Yorkshire are the Maltese, and the Dandie Dinmont terrier. Of course, the diminutive size cannot be credited alone to crosses. It took many years before the Yorkshire was really small enough to be called a toy. The reduction in size was, most probably, due to selective breeding. Still, it is remarkable that within twenty years of its origin the breed had been dwarfed to such an extent that it was among the smallest of all varieties. At least, some specimens were very small.

The Yorkshire Terrier was introduced into the United States about 1880, and American writers of that period, such as Mason, made rather caustic comments on the fact that its type was not very well fixed. It is not difficult to imagine their perplexity as to just what kind of dog was to be the style, for show records indicate that the weights varied from 2¾ pounds to 13 pounds. In the beginning the weight is said to have been as much as 15 pounds.

Modern specimens of the Yorkshire breed true to type, and all their characteristics are well fixed. The coloring is very distinctive, being a dark steel blue from the occiput to the root of the tail, a rich, golden tan on the head, and a bright tan on the chest. It is notable, also, that puppies invariably are born black.

While a toy, and at various times a greatly pampered one, the Yorkshire is a very spirited dog. Were it not restrained, this breed would be content to engage in all the roistering activities of the larger terrier breeds— for all agree that the terrier strain in the Yorkshire cannot be denied. However, the extreme length of the Yorkshire's coat presents such a problem in care that most owners, perforce, must keep this dog in the house or under strict surveillance. Even his feet must be booted or stockinged so that in scratching he will not ruin his gloriously fine coat.

TOYS

(By Courtesy of the Yorkshire Terrier Club, England)

General Appearance.—Should be that of a long-coated Toy Terrier, the coat hanging quite straight and evenly down each side, a parting extending from the nose to the end of the tail.

The animal should be very compact and neat, the carriage being very upright, and having an important air. The general outline should convey the existence of a vigorous and well-proportioned body.

Head.—Should be rather small and flat, not too prominent or round in the skull, nor too long in the muzzle, with a perfect black nose. The fall on the head to be long, of a rich golden tan, deeper in color at the sides of the head about the ear roots, and on the muzzle where it should be very long. The hair on the chest a rich bright tan. On no account must the tan on the head extend on to the neck, nor must there be any sooty or dark hair intermingled with any of the tan.

Eyes.—Medium, dark and sparkling, having a sharp, intelligent expression, and placed so as to look directly forward. They should not be prominent, and the edge of the eyelids should be of a dark color.

Ears.—Small V-shaped, and carried semi-erect, or erect, and not far apart, covered with short hair, color to be of a very deep rich tan.

Mouth.—Perfectly even, with teeth as sound as possible. An animal having lost any teeth through accident not a fault providing the jaws are even.

Body.—Very compact, and a good loin. Level on the top of the back.

Coat.—The hair on body moderately long and perfectly straight (not wavy), glossy like silk, and of a fine silky texture. Color, a dark steel blue (not silver blue) extending from the occiput (or back of skull) to the root of tail, and on no account mingled with fawn, bronze or dark hairs.

Legs.—Quite straight, well covered with hair of a rich golden tan a few shades lighter at the ends than at the roots, not extending higher on the forelegs than the elbow, nor on the hindlegs than the stifle.

Feet.—As round as possible, and the toe-nails black.

Tail.—Cut to medium length; with plenty of hair, darker blue in color than the rest of the body, especially at the end of the tail, and carried a little higher than the level of the back.

Tan.—All tan hair should be darker at the roots than in the middle, shading to a still lighter tan at the tips.

	Points
Formation and terrier appearance	15
Color of hair on body	15
Richness of tan on head and legs	15
Quality and texture of coat	10
Quantity and length of coat	10
Head	10
Mouth	5
Legs and feet	5
Ears	5
Eyes	5
Tail (carriage of)	5
Total	100

BOSTON TERRIERS
(Illustration facing page 686)

(By Courtesy of The Boston Terrier Club of America)

The question is often asked—"How did the Boston Terrier originate?" Briefly stated it may be said to have resulted from a cross between the English bulldog and the white English terrier, and then to have been considerably inbred. Incidental peculiarities of the first dogs used as sires are partly responsible for the present type.

About fifty-nine years ago Mr. Robert C. Hooper, of Boston came into possession of a dog named Judge. This dog, which he purchased of Mr. William O'Brien of the same city, was undoubtedly imported from the other side. Judge, commonly known as Hooper's Judge, was destined to be the ancestor of almost all the true modern Boston terriers. He was a cross between an English bulldog and a white English Terrier, leaning in type rather more toward the bulldog. He was a strongly built, high-stationed dog of about thirty-two pounds weight. In color he was a dark brindle, with a white stripe in the face. His head was square and blocky, and he resembled the present Boston Terrier in that he had a nearly even mouth. Judge was bred to Burnett's Gyp (Or Kate). Gyp was a white bitch, owned by Mr. Edward Burnett, of Southboro. She was of about twenty pounds weight, had a fine three-quarter tail, and was quite low stationed. She was of stocky build, showing considerable strength in her make-up. Her head was good, being short and blocky.

From Judge and Gyp descended Wells's Eph. This

[675]

dog was of strong build, and like his dam was low stationed. His weight was about twenty-eight pounds. He was of dark brindle color, with even white markings, and, like Judge, had a nearly even mouth.

Eph was mated with Tobin's Kate. This bitch was of small size, weighing only twenty pounds. She had a fairly short head, was of golden brindle color, and had a straight three-quarter tail.

From these dogs can be traced the start of the Breed, the Boston Terrier.

In the year 1889, about thirty fanciers in Boston and nearby cities, organized what was known as the American Bull Terrier's Club. Dogs were bred and exhibited by these Fanciers as Round Heads, or Bull Terriers, and as time went on these fanciers who were interested in this breed, met with some obstacles from the Bull Terrier breeders; everything possible was done to discourage these breeders, but they would not give up after years of hard work. So in 1891, the Boston Terrier Club of America was organized, and being a Boston bred dog the name was changed from the round heads, to the Boston Terrier.

In the year 1893 occurred the most momentous event in the history of the Boston Terrier. After two years of trying to have the breed recognized, The American Kennel Club admitted the breed to recognition for registration in the Stud Book, and the Club as a member of the American Kennel Club.

Up to this time the Boston Terrier was just in its infancy. There was much hard work ahead to perfect and standardize the breed and try to breed the Boston Terriers to a more even lot.

Much progress has been accomplished in the breed since the year 1900 in the developing of different strains by scientific breeding, line breeding, and some inbreeding, that has produced some very fine dogs, with clean cut short heads, snow white markings, dark soft eyes and the happy medium body leaning more to the terrier than the bull dog.

They are not a fighting dog but always able to take care of themselves. There are few dogs, however, having the disposition of the Boston Terrier. Their kind and gentle disposition have won them the name of the American Gentleman, a name rightfully given, and as companions or house pets, they have few equals.

It is suggested to our readers that great care be taken in the selection of breeding stock, as the future of the breed lies in the careful breeding of our present generation.

DESCRIPTION AND STANDARD OF POINTS

(Adopted by The Boston Terrier Club of America and Approved by The American Kennel Club, June 14, 1932)

General Appearance.—The general appearance of the Boston Terrier should be that of a lively, highly intelligent, smooth coated, short headed, compactly built, short tailed, well balanced dog of medium station, of brindle color and evenly marked with white. The head should indicate a high degree of intelligence, and should be in proportion to the size of the dog; the body rather short and well knit, the limbs strong and neatly turned; tail short; and no feature be so prominent that the dog appears badly proportioned.

The dog should convey an impression of determination, strength and activity, with style of a high order; carriage easy and graceful.

A proportionate combination of "Color" and "Ideal Markings" is a particularly distinctive feature of a representative specimen, and a dog with a preponderence of white on body, or without the proper proportion of brindle and white on head, should possess sufficient merit otherwise to counteract its deficiencies in these respects.

The ideal "Boston Terrier Expression" as indicating "a high

degree of intelligence," is also an important characteristic of the breed.

"Color and Markings" and "Expression" should be given particular consideration in determining the relative value of "General Appearance" to other points.

Skull.—Square, flat on top, free from wrinkles; cheeks flat; brow abrupt, stop well defined.

Eyes.—Wide apart, large and round, dark in color, expression alert but kind and intelligent. The eyes should set square in the skull, and the outside corners should be on a line with the cheeks as viewed from the front.

Muzzle.—Short, square, wide and deep, and in proportion to skull; free from wrinkles; shorter in length than in width and depth, not exceeding in length approximately one-third of length of skull; width and depth carried out well to end; the muzzle from stop to end of nose on a line parallel to the top of the skull; nose black and wide, with well defined line between nostrils. The jaws broad and square, with short regular teeth. The chops of good depth but not pendulous, completely covering the teeth when mouth is closed.

Ears.—Carried erect; small and thin; situated as near corners of skull as possible.

Head Faults.—Skull "domed" or inclined; furrowed by a medial line; skull too long for breadth, or *vice versa*; stop too shallow; brow and skull too slanting. Eyes small or sunken; too prominent; light color or wall eye; showing too much white or haw. Muzzle wedge shaped or lacking depth; down faced; too much cut out below the eyes; pinched or wide nostrils; butterfly nose; protruding teeth; weak lower jaw; showing "turn up." Ears poorly carried or in size out of proportion to head.

Neck.—Of fair length, slightly arched and carrying the head gracefully; setting neatly into shoulders.

Neck Faults.—Ewe-necked; throatiness; short and thick.

Body.—Deep with good width of chest; shoulders sloping; back short; ribs deep and well sprung, carried well back to loins; loins short and muscular; rump curving slightly to set-on of tail; flank very slightly cut up. The body should appear short but not chunky.

BOSTON TERRIERS

Body Faults.—Flat sides; narrow chest; long or slack loins; roach back; sway back; too much cut up in flank.

Elbows.—Standing neither in nor out.

Forelegs.—Set moderately wide apart and on a line with the point of the shoulders; straight in bone and well muscled; pasterns short and strong.

Hindlegs.—Set true; bent at stifles; short from hocks to feet; hocks turning neither in nor out; thighs strong and well muscled.

Feet.—Round, small and compact and turned neither in nor out; toes well arched.

Leg and Feet Faults.—Loose shoulders or elbows; hindlegs too straight at stifles; hocks too prominent; long or weak pasterns; splay feet.

Tail.—Set-on low; short, fine and tapering; straight; or screw; devoid of fringe or coarse hair, and not carried above horizontal.

Tail Faults.—A long or gaily carried tail; extremely gnarled or curled against body. Note.—The preferred tail should not exceed in length approximately half the distance from set-on to hock.)

Ideal Color.—Brindle with white markings. The brindle to be evenly distributed and distinct. Black with white markings permissible but brindle with white markings preferred.

Ideal Markings.—White muzzle, even white blaze over head, collar, breast, part or whole of forelegs, and hindlegs below hocks.

Color and Markings Faults.—All white; absence of white marking; preponderance of white on body; without the proper proportion of brindle and white on head; or any variations detracting from the general appearance.

Coat.—Short, smooth, bright and fine in texture.

Coat Faults.—Long or coarse; lacking lustre.

Weight.—Not exceeding 25 pounds, divided by classes as follows: Lightweight: Under 15 pounds. Middleweight: 15 and under 20 pounds. Heavyweight: 20 and not exceeding 25 pounds.

Disqualifications.—Solid black; black and tan; liver or mouse colors. Dudley nose. Docked tail or any artificial means used to deceive the judge.

[679]

NON-SPORTING

	Points
General appearance	10
Skull	12
Eyes	5
Muzzle	12
Ears	2
Neck	3
Body	15
Elbows	4
Forelegs	5
Hindlegs	5
Feet	5
Tail	5
Color	4
Ideal Markings	10
Coat	3
Total	**100**

BULLDOGS

(Illustration facing page 687)

(By Courtesy of The Bulldog Club of America)

To the best of our knowledge the Bulldog had its origin in the British Isles. The name Bull was originally applied to this breed of dog because of its use in connection with the then popular sport of bull-baiting.

Exactly when this old English "sport" first started is hardly possible to say, but in "The Survey of Stamford" the following reference is made to its probable origin:

"William Earl Warren, Lord of this town in the reign of King John (1209), standing upon the walls of his castle at Stamford, saw two bulls fighting for a cow in the castle meadow, till all the butchers' dogs pursued one of the bulls, which was maddened by the noise and multitude, through the town. This so pleased the Earl that he gave the castle meadow where the bulls combat began, for a common to the butchers of the town after the first grass was mowed, on condition that they should find a 'mad bull' on a day six weeks before Christmas for the continuance of that sport for ever."

Anyone who has read anything about the sport of bull-baiting must have been conscious of the extreme cruelty which accompanied it. From this we can gather that the original Bulldog had, of necessity, to be a very ferocious animal. Courage must also have been a necessary attribute for a dog in such sport. Beauty and symmetry of form were in no way desirable, the appearance of the dog counting for nothing.

The extraordinary courage possessed by these dogs is hardly believable. Bred from a long line of fighting ancestors, a dog was at length arrived at of such ferocity and courage as to seem almost insensible to pain. Such was the Bulldog of the British sporting days.

Then came the year of 1835 when dog fighting as a sport became illegal in England. To all intents and purposes, therefore, the English Bulldog had outlived his usefulness, and soon his days were to be numbered. Total extinction was soon to be the sad fate of this once famous canine species. However, there were those among dog lovers who felt a deep disappointment at the passing of so fine a breed. Forthwith they set themselves the task of preserving this fine animal. They felt, however, that so ferocious a dog which had been employed in the sport of bull-fighting was no longer necessary nor desirable, but they wished to retain all the splendid qualities of the dog without its ferocity. With this idea in mind they proceeded, by superb breeding methods, to eliminate the undesirable characteristics, and to preserve and accentuate the finer qualities of these animals. This scientific breeding brought its results, namely that within a few generations the English Bulldog became one of the finest physical specimens, but minus all of its original viciousness. Now he was regarded as a dog which anyone could exhibit with pride. This is the dog which we know today. We have with us a breed of dogs of which we may be justly proud, while at the same time we must express our gratitude to those of our British "cousins" who realized sufficiently the value of the English Bull to be prompted by the desire to preserve him for posterity.

DESCRIPTION AND STANDARD OF POINTS
(By Courtesy of The Bulldog Club of America)

General Appearance, Attitude, Expression, Etc.—The perfect Bulldog must be of medium size and smooth coat; with heavy, thick-set, low-swung body, massive short-faced head, wide shoulders and sturdy limbs.

The general appearance and attitude should suggest great stability, vigor and strength.

The disposition should be equable and kind, resolute and courageous (not vicious or aggressive), and demeanor should be pacific and dignified.

These attributes should be countenanced by the expression and behavior.

Gait.—The style and carriage are peculiar, his gait being a loose-jointed, shuffling, sidewise motion, giving the characteristic "roll." The action must, however, be unrestrained, free and vigorous.

Proportion and Symmetry.—The "points" should be well distributed and bear good relation one to the other, no feature being in such prominence from either excess or lack of quality that the animal appears deformed or illy proportioned.

Influence of Sex.—In comparison of specimens of different sex, due allowance should be made in favor of the bitches, which do not bear the characteristics of the breed to the same degree of perfection and grandeur as do the dogs.

Size.—The size for mature dogs is about 50 pounds; for mature bitches about 40 pounds.

Coat.—The coat should be straight, short, flat, close, of fine texture, smooth and glossy. (No fringe, feather or curl.)

Color of Coat.—The color of coat should be uniform, pure of its kind and brilliant.

The various colors found in the breed are to be preferred in the following order:

(1) Red brindle, (2) all other brindles, (3) solid white, (4) solid red, fawn or fallow, (5) piebald, (6) inferior qualities of all the foregoing.

Note:—A perfect piebald is preferable to a muddy brindle or defective solid color.

Solid black is very undesirable, but not so objectionable if occurring to a moderate degree in piebald patches. The brindles to be perfect should have a fine, even and equal distribution of the composite colors.

In brindles and solid colors a small white patch on the chest is not considered detrimental. In piebalds the color patches should be well defined, of pure color and symmetrically distributed.

Skin.—The skin should be soft and loose, especially at the head, neck and shoulders.

Wrinkles and Dewlap.—The head and face should be covered with heavy wrinkles, and at the throat, from jaw to chest, there should be two loose pendulous folds, forming the dewlap.

Skull.—The skull should be very large, and in circumference, in front of the ears, should measure at least the height of the dog at the shoulders.

Viewed from the front, it should appear very high from the corner of the lower jaw to the apex of the skull, and also very broad and square.

Viewed at the side, the head should appear very high, and very short from the point of the nose to occiput.

The forehead should be flat (not rounded or "domed"), neither too prominent nor overhanging the face.

Cheeks.—The cheeks should be well rounded, protruding sideways and outward beyond the eyes.

Stop.—The temples or frontal bones should be very well defined, broad, square and high, causing a hollow or groove between the eyes. This indentation, or "stop," should be both broad and deep and extend up the middle of the forehead, dividing the head vertically, being traceable to the top of the skull.

Eyes and Eyelids.—The eyes, seen from the front, should be situated low down in the skull, as far from the ears as possible, and their corners should be in a straight line at right angles with the stop. They should be quite in front of the head, as wide apart as possible, provided their outer corners are within the outline of the cheeks when viewed from the front.

They should be quite round in form, of moderate size, neither sunken nor bulging, and in color should be very dark.

The lids should cover the white of the eyeball, when the dog is looking directly forward, and the lid should show no "haw."

Ears.—The ears should be set high in the head, the front inner edge of each ear joining the outline of the skull at the top back corner of skull, so as to place them as wide apart, and as high, and as far from the eyes as possible.

In size they should be small and thin. The shape termed "rose ear" is the most desirable. The "rose ear" folds inward at its back lower edge, the upper front edge curving over, outwards and backwards, showing part of the inside of the burr. (The ears should not be carried erect or "prick-eared" or "buttoned" and should never be cropped.)

Face.—The face, measured from the front of the cheek bone to the tip of the nose, should be extremely short, the muzzle being very short, broad, turned upwards and very deep from the corner of the eye to the corner of the mouth.

Nose.—The nose should be large, broad and black, its tip being set back deeply between the eyes.

The distance from bottom of stop, between the eyes, to the tip of nose should be as short as possible and not exceed the length from the tip of nose to the edge of under lip.

The nostrils should be wide, large and black, with a well-defined line between them. (The parti-color or "butterfly nose" and the flesh-color or "Dudley nose" are decidedly objectionable, but do not disqualify for competition.) Amended at a special meeting of Club, held September 5, 1914, to read: Any nose other than black is objectionable and "Dudley" or flesh-colored nose absolutely disqualified from competition.

Chops.—The chops or "flews" should be thick, broad, pendant and very deep, completely overhanging the lower jaw at each side.

They join the under lip in front and almost or quite cover the teeth, which should be scarcely noticeable when the mouth is closed.

Jaws.—The jaws should be massive, very broad, square and "undershot," the lower jaw projecting considerably in front of the upper jaw and turning up.

Teeth.—The teeth should be large and strong, with the canine teeth or tusks wide apart, and the six small teeth in front, between the canines, in an even, level row.

Neck.—The neck should be short, very thick, deep and strong and well arched at the back.

Shoulders.—The shoulders should be muscular, very heavy, wide-spread and slanting outward, giving stability and great power.

Chest.—The chest should be very broad, deep and full.

Brisket and Body.—The brisket and body should be very capacious, with full sides, well rounded ribs and very deep from the shoulders down to its lowest part, where it joins the chest.

It should be well let down between the shoulders and forelegs, giving the dog a broad, low, short-legged appearance.

The body should be well ribbed up behind with the belly tucked up and not rotund.

Back.—The back should be short and strong, very broad at the shoulders and comparatively narrow at the loins. There should be a slight fall in the back, close behind the shoulders (its lowest part), whence the spine should rise to the loins (the top of which should be higher than the top of the shoulders), thence curving again more suddenly to the tail, forming an arch (a very distinctive feature of the breed), termed "roach-back" or, more correctly, "wheel-back."

Forelegs.—The forelegs should be short, very stout, straight and muscular, set wide apart, with well developed calves, presenting a bowed outline, but the bones of the legs should not be curved or bandy, nor the feet brought too close together.

Elbows.—The elbows should be low and stand well out and loose from the body.

Hindlegs.—The hindlegs should be strong and muscular and longer than the forelegs, so as to elevate the loins above the shoulders.

Hocks should be slightly bent and well let down, so as to give length and strength from loins to hock.

The lower leg should be short, straight and strong, with the stifles turned slightly outward and away from the body. The hocks are thereby made to approach each other, and the hind feet to turn outward.

Feet.—The feet should be moderate in size, compact and firmly set. Toes compact, well split up, with high knuckles and with short stubby nails.

The front feet may be straight or slightly out-turned, but the hind feet should be pointed well outward.

Tail.—The tail may be either straight or "screwed" (but never curved or curly), and in any case must be short, hung low, with decided downward carriage, thick root and fine tip.

If straight, the tail should be cylindrical and of uniform taper.

BOSTON TERRIER

BULLDOG

BULLDOGS

If "screwed" the bends or kinks should be well defined, and they may be abrupt and even knotty, but no portion of the member should be elevated above the base or root.

		Points
Proportion and symmetry	5	
Attitude	3	
Expression	2	
Gait	3	
Size	3	
Coat	2	
Color of coat	4	
General properties		22
Skull	5	
Cheeks	2	
Stop	4	
Eyes and eyelids	3	
Ears	5	
Wrinkle	5	
Nose	6	
Chops	2	
Jaws	5	
Teeth	2	
Total, head		39
Neck	3	
Dewlap	2	
Shoulders	5	
Chest	3	
Ribs	3	
Brisket	2	
Belly	2	
Back	5	
Forelegs and elbows	4	
Hindlegs	3	
Feet	3	
Tail	4	
Total, body, legs, etc.		39
Grand Total		100

CHOW CHOWS

(Illustration facing page 702)

Due in great measure to the ruthlessness with which Chinese emperors destroyed the works of art and the literature of their predecessors, it is rather difficult to secure direct evidence which shows the undoubted antiquity of that lordly, aloof breed, the Chow Chow. Still, there was discovered, not so very long ago, a bas-relief, dating back to the Han Dynasty, about 150 B.C. that definitely places the Chow as a hunting dog in that period. While this establishes the breed as more than 2,000 years old, it is believed by many authorities that the Chow goes back much further; that it is, indeed, one of the oldest recognizable types of dog.

The theory has been advanced that the Chow originated through a crossing of the old mastiff of Tibet and the samoyede, from the northern parts of Siberia. Certainly the Chow evinces some of the characteristics of both breeds. The refutation lies in the fact that the Chow is the only breed in the world that possesses a blue-black tongue. On this score, some are of the opinion that the Chow is one of the basic breeds, and that he may have been one of the ancestors of the eskimo, the samoyede, the Norwegian elkhound, the keeshonden, and the pomeranian, all of which are of somewhat similar type.

In modern times the Chow Chow has become a fashionable pet and a guard dog, but there is plenty of evidence available in China to prove that for many centuries he was the principal sporting dog. Perhaps the most unusual, lavish kennel in all history was that maintained by one of the T'ang emperors about the seventh century A.D. It was so extensive that the emperor could not possibly have availed himself of a fraction of the facilities for sport it afforded. This kennel contained 2,500 couples of "hounds" of the Chow type, and the emperor had a staff of 10,000 huntsmen.

Apparently the Chow has been a most unusually gifted breed of dog, for his uses have run the full gamut of the work done by nearly all the recognized breeds. Even today, in China, the Chow is used as Occidentals use the setter. He is credited with great scenting powers, on being staunch to point, possessing good sense, and in being clever in his hunting tactics. He is used frequently on Mongolian pheasant, and on the francolin of Yunnan, and on both has received great praise for his speed and stamina.

Undoubtedly the Chow Chow is of far northern origin, but he has always been found in greatest numbers in the South of China, particularly in the district centering about Canton. It was from Canton that a brace was sent to England in 1780. In that region of China he is considered indigenous, and usually called merely the "black-tongue," or the "black-mouthed" dog. In the North, as in Peiping, he is called "lang kou" (wolf dog), "hsiung kou" (bear dog) or, the more sophisticated "hei she-t'ou" (black-tongued) or "Kwantung Kou," i.e. the dog of Canton.

The name "chow chow" has little basis for its origin in China, and it is believed that this euphonic expression evolved from the pidgin English term for articles brought from any part of the Oriental empire during the latter part of the eighteenth century. It meant knick-knacks or bric-a-brac, including curios such as porcelain and ivory figurines, and finally for what is today described as "mixed pickles," whether of the edible variety or not. It was far easier for the master of a sailing vessel to write "chow chow" than to describe minutely all the various items of his cargo. So, in time, it came to include the dog.

The first Occidental description of the Chow Chow was penned by the Rev. Gilbert White, Rector of Selborne, England, and this was published later in the "Natural History and Antiquities of Selborne." The brace of dogs referred to above was brought home from Canton by a young neighbor of the clergyman, on a vessel of the East India Company, in 1780. The description is a most complete one, and indicates that these dogs were not far different from the specimens of modern times.

The real start of importations of Chows into England did not begin, however, until about 1880, and the breed started toward its present popularity after Queen Victoria took an interest in it. The first specialty club of the breed was started in England in 1895. It was exhibited for the first time in the United States in 1890, when a specimen named Takya, owned by Miss A. C. Derby took a third prize in the miscellaneous class at the Westminster Kennel Club show in New York. Since 1901 the Chow Chow has made steady progress, and today it is one of America's more popular breeds.

DESCRIPTION AND STANDARD OF POINTS
(Courtesy of The Chow Chow Club)

Head.—Large and massive, with broad, flat skull, well filled under the eyes, moderate stop, proudly carried, with characteristic scowl.

Muzzle.—Short in comparison to length of skull; broad from eyes to end of nose, and of great depth. The lips should be full and overhanging.

Teeth.—Strong and level.

Nose.—Large, broad and black in color.

Tongue.—A blue-black. The inside of the mouth should be of the same color.

Eyes.—Dark, deep-set, of moderate size, and almond shaped.

Ears.—Small, pointed, stiffly carried. They should be placed wide apart, on the top of skull, and set with a slight forward tilt.

Body.—Short, compact, well ribbed up, and let down in the flank.

Neck.—Strong, full, set well on the shoulders.

Shoulders.—Muscular, slightly sloping.

Chest.—Broad, deep and muscular.

Back.—Short, straight and strong.

Loins.—Broad, deep and powerful.

Tail.—Tail set well up and carried closely to back, following line of spine at start.

Forelegs.—Perfectly straight, with heavy bone and upright pasterns.

Hindlegs.—Straight hocked, muscular and heavy boned.

Feet.—Compact, round and cat-like.

Coat.—Abundant, dense, straight and outstanding; rather coarse in texture, with a soft woolly undercoat. In the smooth-coated variety, the topcoat should be of about one and a half inches in length.

Color.—Any clear color, solid throughout, or, with lighter shadings on ruff, tail and breeching.

Size.—Chows should be massive and well proportioned.

General Appearance.—Lion-headed, scowling, compact, muscular, short-coupled, dignified, and powerful, with heavy off-standing coat.

DISQUALIFYING POINTS

Drop ears; tongue red, pink or obviously spotted. Nose spotted or distinctly other color than black, except in blue colored Chows, which may have solid blue, or slate colored noses.

DALMATIANS

(Illustration facing page 703)

(By Courtesy of The Dalmatian Club of America)

No breed has a more interesting background or a more disputed heritage than that dog from long ago, the Dalmatian. His beginning is buried so deep in the past that researchers cannot agree as to his origin. On his ancientness, and on the fact that he has come through many centuries materially unchanged, investigators are in complete concurrence.

Models, engravings, paintings and writings from antiquity have been used with fair excuse but no certainty to claim the spotted dog first appeared in Europe, Asia and Africa. Perhaps some of the divergences in opinion on the original home of the Dalmatian can be accounted for by the fact that the dog has frequently been found in bands of Romanies, and like his gypsy masters has been well known but not definitely located in any one place. Authoritative writers place him first as a positive entity in Dalmatia, a province of Austria on the Eastern shore of the coast of Venice. Though he has been accredited with a dozen nationalities and has as many native names, and is nicknamed by the English, The English Coach Dog, The Carriage Dog, the Plum Pudding Dog, The Fire House Dog and the Spotted Dick, it is from his first proved home that he takes his correct name, The Dalmatian. We find references to him as "The Dalmatian" in the middle eighteenth century. There is no question whatsoever that his lineage is as ancient and his record as straight as that of other breeds.

His activities have been as varied as his reputed ancestors. He has been the dog of war, a sentinel on the borders of Dalmatia and Croatia. He has been employed as draft dog, as shepherd. He is excellent on rats and vermin. He is well known for his heroic performances as fire apparatus follower and fire house mascot. As a sporting dog he has been used as bird dog, as trail hound, as retriever, or in packs for boar or stag hunting. His exceptionally retentive memory has made him one of the most dependable clowners in circuses or on the stage Down through the years the intelligence and willingness of the Dalmatian have found him in practically every role to which useful dogs are assigned. Most important among his talents has been his status as the original, one and only coaching dog.

The imaginative might say that his coaching days go back to an engraving of a spotted dog following an Egyptian chariot! Even the practical minded will find no end of proof, centuries old, of the Dalmatian, trimmed to the old fashion with ears entirely cropped away and padlocked brass collar, plying his natural trade as follower and guardian of the horse drawn vehicle.

He is fitted for road work physically. In his make up speed and endurance are blended to a nicety. He is gaited with beauty of motion and swiftness, and he has the strength, vitality and fortitude to keep going gaily till the journey's end. The instinct for coaching is bred in him, born in him and trained in him through the years. The Dalmatian takes to a horse, as a horse takes to him, and that is to say, like a duck to water. He may work in the old way clearing the path before the Tally Ho with dignity and determination, or following on with his ermine spottings in full view to add distinction and protection to an equipage. He may coach under the rear axle, the front axle, or, most difficult of all, under the pole between the leaders and the wheelers. Where ever he works it is with the love of the game in his heart and with the skill which has won him the title of the only recognized carriage dog in the world. His penchant for working is his most renowned characteristic but it in no way approaches his capacity for friendship. As a companion dog of splendid personality and extraordinary beauty he is unexcelled.

There is no dog more picturesque than this spotted fellow with his slick white coat gaily decorated with clearly defined round spots of jet black, or, in the liver variety, deep brown. He is unusual; he does not look like any other breed, for his markings are peculiarly his own. He is strong bodied, clean cut, colorful and distinctive. His flashy spottings are the culmination of ages of careful breeding. The onlooker cannot deny the dash and brilliance of this fine looking fellow, for he looks, every ounce of him like the thoroughbred he is.

His aristocratic bearing does not belie him, for the Dalmatian is first of all a gentleman. He is a quiet chap, and the ideal guard dog, distinguishing nicely between barking for fun or with purpose. His courtesy never fails with approved visitors, but his protective instinct is highly developed and he has the courage to defend. He will guard his master or his master's property with his life if necessary. As a watch dog he is sensible and dependable to the extent of being without a peer.

He is not everyone's dog. No casual admirer will break his polite reserve for he has a fine sense of distinction as to whom he belongs. He is first, last, and all the time, his master's or a one family dog. With children he is a perfect protector, a care-free companion with the discretion to be gentle in play and the obedience to stop on command. He is always ready for fun, and a real sport all the way through, but is neither irrepressible nor demanding, but tractable and quick to sense his master's moods. He is alert and intelligent, anxious to please. His affection is boundless. You can train a Dalmatian readily to fill your requirements, but one thing you can never teach him is loyalty and devotion—for he will teach you the real meaning of these words. For a more loyal or devoted dog than the Dalmatian never lived.

He does not mingle in every street fight but is friendly and diplomatic with other dogs, and minds his own business as long as they mind theirs. However, if affronted by a belligerent stranger he can well hold his own and can fight like a very devil and never be the first to say quit.

Fashion has not distorted the Dalmatian to make his whelping difficult. He is born pure white, develops quickly and requires no cropping, docking, stripping or artifices of any sort. He is all ready for sport or the show ring just as nature made him. He is extremely hardy, an easy keeper, suited to any climate. He requires only the minimum of care, for he is sturdy and neat and cleanly. He is happy any place from palace to stable as long as his master is with him. You must know him to appreciate him, but you will find that those who really understand and love him, have only second place left in their hearts for any dogs other than the Gentlemen from Dalmatia.

DESCRIPTION AND STANDARD OF POINTS
(Courtesy of The Dalmatian Club of America)

Head.—Should be of a fair length, the skull flat, rather broad between the ears, and moderately well defined at the temple, i.e., exhibiting a moderate amount of stop, and not in one straight line from the nose to the occiput bone, as required in a Bull Terrier. It should be entirely free from wrinkle.

Muzzle.—Should be long and powerful; the lips clean, fitting the jaws moderately close.

Eyes.—Should be set moderately well apart, and of medium size, round, bright and sparkling, with an intelligent expression, their color greatly depending on the markings of the dog. In the black-spotted variety the eyes should be dark (black or brown); in the liver-spotted variety they should be light (yellow or light brown). Wall eyes are permissible.

The rim around the eyes in the black-spotted variety should be black; in the liver-spotted variety, brown—never flesh-colored in either.

Ears.—Should be set on rather high, of moderate size, rather wide at the base and gradually tapering to a rounded point. They should be carried close to the head, be thin and fine in texture, and always spotted, the more profusely the better.

Nose.—In the black-spotted variety should always be black; in the liver-spotted variety, always brown.

Neck and Shoulders.—The neck should be fairly long, nicely arched, light and tapering, and entirely free from throatiness. The shoulders should be moderately oblique, clean and muscular, denoting speed.

Body, Back, Chest and Loins.—The chest should not be too wide, but very deep and capacious, ribs moderately well sprung, never rounded like barrel hoops (which would indicate want of speed); back powerful; loin strong, muscular, and slightly arched.

Legs and Feet.—Of great importance. The forelegs should be perfectly straight, strong and heavy in bone; elbows close to the body; feet compact, with well arched toes, and tough, elastic pads. In the hindlegs the muscles should be clean, though well defined; the hocks well let down.

Nails.—In the black-spotted variety, black and white; in the liver-spotted variety, brown and white.

Tail.—Should not be too long, strong at the insertion, and gradually tapering towards the end, free from coarseness. It should not be inserted too low down, but carried with a slight curve upwards, and never curled. It should be spotted, the more profusely the better.

Coat.—Short, hard, dense and fine, sleek and glossy in appearance, but neither woolly nor silky.

Color and Markings.—These are most important points. The ground color in both varieties should be pure white, very decided, and not intermixed. The color of the spots in the black-spotted variety should be black, the deeper and richer the black the better; in the liver-spotted variety they should be brown. The spots should not intermingle, but be as round and well defined as possible, the more distinct the better; in size they should be from that of a dime to a half dollar. The spots on the face, head, ears, legs, tail and extremities to be smaller than those on the body.

Size.—Height of dogs and bitches between 19 and 23 inches; weight, between 35 and 50 pounds.

General Appearance.—The Dalmatian should represent a strong, muscular and active dog, symmetrical in outline and free from coarseness and lumber, capable of great endurance, combined with a fair amount of speed.

	Points
Head and eyes	10
Ears	5
Neck and shoulders	10
Body, back, chest and loins	10
Legs and feet	15
Coat	5
Color and markings	30
Tail	5
Size, symmetry, etc.	10
Total	100

FRENCH BULLDOGS

(Illustration facing page 704)

(By Courtesy of The French Bulldog Club of America)

While there has been a variance of opinion as to the origin of the French Bulldog, it seems pretty well settled that one ancestor must have been the English Bulldog—probably one of the toy variety, of which there were a great number in England around eighteen hundred and sixty. These toy bulldogs, not finding favor with the English, were sent in large numbers into France. There, they were crossed with various other breeds, and finally became very popular in fashionable circles, particularly with women. It was then that they were given the name "Boule-Dog Francais," although, later on, England scoffed at the idea of applying the word "Francais" to a breed so clearly showing a strong strain of English Bulldog. At that time there was little uniformity of type and one found dogs with rose ears while others had ears of the bat variety, which has since come to be recognized as the outstanding feature of the French Bulldog.

There are two peculiarly distinctive features in French Bulldogs, not found in any other breed. Chief of these is the bat ear, as above mentioned. The well rounded form at the top of the ear is found on no other dog. The other distinction is the skull formation. The correctly formed skull should be level, or flat, between the ears, while directly above the eyes, extending almost across the forehead, the skull should be slightly curved, giving a domed appearance. Both of these features give to the French Bulldog an individuality wholly its own and add much to its unusual appearance.

[699]

The preservation of the bat ear as a distinct feature has been due to the persistent efforts of the American fanciers, since in the early days of breeding these dogs in Europe the tendency was toward the rose ear. Had this movement not been opposed by America, the breed would eventually have lost the feature that so strongly accentuates its individuality, and the result would have been almost a purely miniature English Bulldog. This controversy over type was directly responsible for the formation of the French Bulldog Club of America, the first organization in the world devoted to the breed. These ardent fanciers gave a Specialty Show in the ballroom of the Waldorf-Astoria in 1898, this being the first Specialty Show, of any breed, held in such de luxe quarters. The affair proved a sensation and it was due, no doubt, to the resulting publicity that the quaint little chaps became the rage in society. Show entries increased until the peak was reached about 1913 when there were exactly 100 French Bulldogs benched at the Westminster Kennel Club's show, and the following Specialty Shows were considerably larger.

Unquestionably the dog that did the most toward the establishment of the breed in America, was Ch. Nellcote Gamin, imported in 1904 by Mr. and Mrs. Samuel Goldenberg. With the addition of Gamin to the splendid stock already in this country, we were made independent of further importation in order to produce the finest Frenchies in the world. To Gamin belongs the credit for the greatest influence in the molding of the breed that can be attributed to any one dog. He was a famous sire, and today it is almost impossble to find a Frenchie that does not have Gamin blood.

An ideal French Bulldog should be a well balanced, compactly built, *sound* dog, having the appearance of an active, intelligent, muscular dog of heavy bone, with a smooth coat, and of medium or small stature. The weight may vary (anything up to twenty-eight pounds being permissible under the American standard), but it is generally conceded that the ideal, or most popular, size is between nineteen and twenty-two pounds.

A French Bulldog may be any color except black (meaning without trace of brindle), black and white, black and tan, liver or mouse color. Of the allowed colors no one should be preferred over the others, at least when judging in the show ring.

In expression, the sour, pugnacious expression of the English Bulldog is not desired; a French Bulldog should have a bright, alert look which gives it the appearance of always being ready for fun and frolic—as it is.

While bred principally as pets and companions, Frenchies are a remarkably intelligent breed and serve as good watchdogs. They have very affectionate dispositions, are sweet tempered, and are dependable with children. While alert and playful, they are not noisy and, as a rule, bark very little. Their size is another advantage in considering them as indoor pets, and their smooth, short coat is easily kept clean. Also, no special grooming or "fixing" is necessary for the show ring.

DESCRIPTION AND STANDARD OF POINTS
(By Courtesy of The French Bulldog Club of America)

General Appearance.—The French Bulldog should have the appearance of an active, intelligent, muscular dog, of heavy bone, smooth coat, compactly built, and of medium or small stature.

Proportion and Symmetry.—The points should be well distributed and bear good relation one to the other, no feature being in such prominence from either excess or lack of quality that the animal appears deformed or poorly proportioned.

Influence of Sex.—In comparison of specimens of different sex, due allowance should be made in favor of the bitches, which do not bear the characteristics of the breed to the same marked degree as do the dogs.

Weight.—A light weight class under 22 pounds; heavy weight class, 22 pounds, and not over 28 pounds.

Head.—The head should be large and square. The top of the skull should be flat between the ears; the forehead should not be flat but slightly rounded. The stop should be well defined causing a hollow or groove between the eyes. The muzzle should be broad, deep and well laid back; the muscles of the cheeks well developed. The nose should be extremely short; nostrils broad with well defined line between them. The nose and flews should be black. The flews should be thick and broad, hanging over the lower jaw at the sides, meeting the underlip in front and covering the teeth which should not be seen when the mouth is closed. The underjaw should be deep, square, broad, undershot and well turned up.

Eyes.—The eyes should be wide apart, set low down in the skull, as far from the ears as possible, round in form, of moderate size, neither sunken nor bulging, and in color dark. No haw and no white of the eye showing when looking forward.

Neck.—The neck should be thick and well arched, with loose skin at throat.

Ears.—The ears shall hereafter be known as the bat ear, broad at the base, elongated, with round top, set high in the head, but not too close together, and carried erect with the orifice to the front. The leather of the ear fine and soft.

Body.—The body should be short and well rounded. The chest, broad, deep and full, well ribbed with the belly tucked up. The back should be a roach back, with a slight fall close behind the shoulders. It should be strong and short, broad at the shoulders and narrowing at the loins.

Legs.—The forelegs should be short, stout, straight and muscular, set wide apart. The hindlegs should be strong and muscular, longer than the forelegs, so as to elevate the loins above the shoulders. Hocks well let down.

Feet.—The feet should be moderate in size, compact and firmly

CHOW CHOW

DALMATIAN

set. Toes compact, well split up, with high knuckles and short, stubby nails; hindfeet slightly longer than forefeet.

Tail.—The tail should be either straight or screwed (but not curly), short, hung low, thick root and fine tip; carried low in repose.

Color, Skin and Coat.—Acceptable colors are: All brindle, fawn, white, brindle and white, and any color except those which constitute disqualification. The skin should be soft and loose, especially at head and shoulders, forming wrinkles. Coat moderately fine, brilliant, short and smooth.

Disqualifications.—Other than bat ears; black and white, black and tan, liver, mouse or solid black (black means black without any trace of brindle) eyes of different color; nose other than black; hare lip; any mutilation; over 28 pounds in weight.

	Points	
Proportion and symmetry	5	
Expression	5	
Gait	4	
Color	4	
Coat	2	
Total, general properties	—	20
Skull	6	
Cheeks and chops	2	
Stop	5	
Ears	8	
Eyes	4	
Wrinkles	4	
Nose	3	
Jaws	6	
Teeth	2	
Total, head	—	40
Shoulders	5	
Back	5	
Neck	4	
Chest	3	
Ribs	4	

NON-SPORTING

Brisket	....	3
Belly	....	2
Forelegs	....	4
Hindlegs	....	3
Feet	....	3
Tail	....	4
Total, body, legs, etc.	.... ——	40
Grand total	....	100

FRENCH BULLDOG

KEESHONDEN

KEESHONDEN

(Illustration on opposite page)

It took a national political turn-over in Holland to bring the Keeshonden to wide attention in the latter part of the eighteenth century, but the breed had been one of the favorite dogs of the Dutch people for several hundred years before that. Never a hunter, and never used for any of the specialized forms of work that have characterized so many other breeds, the Keeshonden had managed by the very force of his personality to win a high place in the affections of a nation.

The events leading up to the recognition of the Keeshonden as the national dog of Holland were concerned with the social unrest that seemed to be spreading like a prairie fire throughout the world in the years immediately preceding the French Revolution. Holland was divided into two great camps, the "Prinsgezinden" or partisans of the Prince of Orange, and the "Patriotten" or Patriots.

The Patriots, consisting principally of the people of the lower and upper middle classes, were led by a man named Kees de Gyselaer, who lived in Dordrecht. Like most of his race, de Gyselaer, was a dog lover, and at the time he owned a little dog that he called "Kees." This dog gave the breed its name, for it became the symbol of the Patriots. It appeared in countless pictures and cartoons made in those days of civil strife. The men who composed the party were firmly of the opinion that their own spirit was typified in the dog. He was a dog of the people.

[705]

Histories are rather vague as to what name the Keeshonden bore prior to its adoption as a symbol by the Patriots, but it was known mainly as the barge dog. The breed had served for countless years on the rijnaken or small vessels that were found in great numbers on the Rhine River. These vessels seldom were larger than 200 tons at the time when the Keeshonden enjoyed its greatest popularity in Holland, and consequently would not accommodate a very large dog. There probably were more of this breed of dog kept as pets and watchdogs throughout the Netherlands than there were dogs on the barges. It was only natural that the dogs of the barges became better known, for they were continually moving up and down the river, coming in contact with more people.

The origin of the Keeshonden undoubtedly is Arctic, or possibly Sub-Arctic, and it is of the same strains that produced the Samoyede, the Chow Chow, the Norwegian Elkhound, the Finnish Spitz, and the Pomeranian. It seems the most closely related to the Pomeranian. Some authorities believe that the Pomeranian was produced by selective breeding of the Keeshonden.

The Keeshonden has changed little in the past two centuries, for the earliest descriptions represent it as nearly identical with the dog of today. There also are a number of old paintings and drawings that prove how well the old Keeshonden type has been preserved. A drawing, made in 1794, shows the children and the dog of a burgomaster mourning beside his tomb. The dog is a Keeshonden that probably could win at a bench show today. Other evidence is found in the paintings of that famous Dutch artist, Gan Steen.

The close linking between the Keeshonden and the Patriots in the latter part of the eighteenth century almost proved the undoing of the dog. The dog was so much in the public eye as the symbol of the Patriots that when the Prince of Orange established his party as the dominant one, few people wanted the dog that stood for the opposition. Many who owned Keeshonden disposed of them quietly; and only the most loyal maintained the breed. And then, the type of vessel used on the rivers gradually changed. Each year they seemed to get larger, until, eventually, they were quite pretentious, and had plenty of room for large dogs. This affected the popularity of the Keeshonden considerably.

The breed was at very low ebb until 1920, at which time the Baroness van Hardencroek became so interested in the old breed that she undertook an investigation to see how much of the old stock still survived. The results of this search were very surprising. Whereas the breed had passed from public attention, it was still kept in its original form by certain captains of river boats, by farmers, and by truckmen. There were many excellent specimens. Some owners even had maintained their own, crude, stud books.

The Baroness van Hardencroek began breeding Keeshonden and spreading their story throughout Europe. In some ten years she brought the breed to such a solid position that in 1933, De Raad van Beheer op Kynologisch Bebied in Nederland—te Amsterdam—accepted the standard and the points for judging the breed. Also, there was formed the Dutch Keeshond Club. Prior to this the breed had invaded England, and it made a very good impression there as early as 1925.

Very alert, and very intelligent, the Dutch called the Keeshonden the ideal companion dog. People in his native land list among his qualities the fact that he has no desire to hunt; that he would much rather remain with his master or mistress.

The whole appearance of the Keeshonden gives evidence of his alert senses. A wolf grey in color, he has a stand-off coat that looks always as if it had just been brushed and trimmed—whereas, the Keeshonden seldom needs attention. The less he is brushed and groomed, the better he appears.

DESCRIPTION AND STANDARD OF POINTS

The Keeshonden is claimed to be one of the oldest breeds of dogs in Holland, its origin, we are told, dating back to 1552. In 1879, we are informed that eight Keeshonden were entered in the German Show at Hanover thereby establishing its claim to be an old and well established breed.

Appearance.—The Keeshonden resembles the Pomeranian, but is much larger and different in color.

Characteristics.—Of the Keeshonden are faithfulness, intelligence, watchfulness, and contentment. He is hardy and able to withstand all kinds of weather. He is faithful to his master, but distrustful of strangers, and is, therefore, valuable as a watchdog. He is handsome and attractive in appearance. He has a short and sturdy body, with short pointed ears, and bushy tail. Full, straight, heavy coat which should not be curly or silky, and he should have a lion-like, bushy mane. The head, ears, and lower parts of legs should have short, close hair. He attains his prime at about 3 years of age, and usually remains in good condition until 10 to 12 years.

Head.—Should be in proportion to the body, foxlike in appearance. Seen from the top, the head is broadest at the base of skull and tapers gradually to the nose, being triangular in shape. Viewed from the side, the head shows only a slight stop. The muzzle should not be too long.

Nose.—Should be black and not too large, lips tight and not pendant and with no wrinkles at corners of mouth. Ears small, close together, triangular in shape, mounted high on head and standing erect.

KEESHONDEN

Eyes.—Medium size and slightly oval or set at slight slant or angle, and dark brown in color.

Neck.—Should be of medium length, body short as possible with straight back, slightly higher in front than in rear, and with no tendency to sway back. The ribs should be well sprung. Chest deep.

Tail.—Should be of medium length, set on high and carried in a curl to right or left over back.

Legs.—Should be of medium length, and in harmony with size of body. The front legs should be strong and straight. Hindlegs should have fairly well bent stifles. The feet should be as small as possible, round similar to cat paws and free from black thumb marks on top of same. The head, ears, and feet, outside of front legs and inside of hindlegs, should be covered with short, coarse hair; body should have full and long coat of hair.

Color.—Should be silver grey with black tipped hair; head, legs, stomach and tail of lighter shade.

Muzzle.—Should be a dark mask, but not black, and with lighter colored hair around eyes.

Height.—Of the Keeshonden is from 15 to 18 inches, measured at the top of the withers. The males, as a rule, are slightly larger than the females. Preference should be given to the larger size dogs if the general type is not sacrificed and the general symmetry is preserved. From withers to rump and from feet to top line should form a square. A real Keeshonden should have not only the proper color, but also the correct conformation and size.

Following is the scale of points for the Keeshonden:

VALUE OF POINTS

		Points
1.	Body and symmetry	25
2.	Texture, quality and quantity of coat	20
3.	Head and ears	15
4.	Color	15
5.	Tail	15
6.	Legs	5
7.	Feet	5
	Total	100

POODLES

(Illustration facing page 716)

(By Courtesy of The Poodle Club of America)

The Poodle is one of the most intelligent of the canine race, and it has within its own breed great variations of character. In fact there is something more human than canine about most Poodles and this quality makes them unique among dogs, and enchanting as companions.

The origin of the Poodle is a mystery, although it is supposed by many authorities to have originated in Germany where it is known as the Pudel or Canis Familiaris Aquatius. However, for many years it has been regarded as the national dog of France where it was commonly used as a retriever as well as a travelling circus trick dog. In France it was and is known as the Caniche which is derived from "chien canne" or duck dog. The English word Poodle is undoubtedly derived from the German Pudel, and the expression "French" Poodle was undoubtedly adopted because of the breed's great popularity in France.

As a matter of fact the unclipped Poodle of today bears a strong resemblance in type to the old Rough-haired Water Dog of England as painted by Reinagle at the beginning of the nineteenth century, and except that the Irish Water Spaniel is born with short hair on its face and tail there is little difference between this ancient Irish dog and the Poodle.

Whatever its origin the Poodle is a well established breed for as far as standards and records show it has scarcely changed at all through the centuries, and the various standards of different countries today are much alike. The Poodles of today are a trifle higher on the leg, and longer and more narrow in the head and muzzle than formerly, and if this fashion in type does not become too exaggerated, it improves the natural grace and beauty of the breed.

The aim of the Poodle breeders of America is to keep the Poodle in the niche in which the breed's versatility has rightly placed it, that of a super-companion, adaptable for any purpose, and to further these ends a Poodle must be stylish and beautiful to look at, sweet tempered and intelligent to live with, and strong enough to be used for outdoor or sporting purposes. As the Poodle is naturally hardy and easy to rear, and as there is considerable latitude in size allowed by the standard, it would seem that this aim is entirely practical and likely to survive. The larger Poodles are suitable as retrievers, watch dogs, obedience trial winners, and country companions. The smaller types and miniatures make equally attractive and intelligent pets for those who live in the city.

Poodles are divided by size only, the standard or large Poodle must be over fifteen inches at the shoulder, and the miniature must be under fifteen inches at the shoulder.

The standard demands that the colors of the Poodle be any solid or even color. The skin of some of the best whites is pigmented, that is, it is pink with silver or grey spots. The pure pink skin usually implies Albinism and succeeding generations are prone to light colored noses, light eyes and red eye rims and deafness. In England today there is an increasing demand for the so-called "silver skinned whites" which is a solid silver skin produced by a black outcross or two in the immediately preceding generations. All white and cream Poodles should have black eyes and noses, as do some apricots.

The skin of the blacks and greys is either light bluish color or matches in a lighter shade the color of the hair, the browns have light brown skin, and the apricots usually a brown skin.

The coat of the Poodle should be profuse and have a woolly body or undercoat. The top coat is either of the steel wool wiry texture, or, it should consist of thick close curls. The coat if allowed to grow indefinitely without brushing and oiled to prevent breaking will form thin cylindrical mats which when increased in length become a mass of ropelike cords, and thus the Curly Poodle becomes a Corded Poodle. Today, however, the Corded Poodle has been conceded by most breeders to be impractical to keep in condition as well as destroying the abilities of a naturally active and stylish moving animal. The Corded Poodle cannot take proper exercise because of the great length of the cords which touch the ground.

The various styles of clipping the Curly Poodle are a matter of taste, the two most seen today are the Continental where the hind quarters are bare with rosettes on the hips and hocks, and the English or saddle clip in which a short clipped blanket of hair covers the hips. The fashion of clipping the Poodle has sometimes been called artificial and detrimental to the dignity of the breed, but it is such an ancient tradition and in many ways so practical, that it is certain to continue, and one has only to know a Poodle for a brief time to realize that its great natural dignity, vitality and sportsmanship are not affected but rather enhanced by this unique and ancient style of clipping parts of the coat. Unlike other long coated dogs, the clipped feet and muzzle of the

Poodle do not carry dirt, an important factor for a house dog and pet for children.

Next to soundness and intelligence the most necessary attribute of the Poodle is style. This is produced by a natural liveliness of action, and the proportions of the length and height.

DESCRIPTION AND STANDARD OF POINTS

(As Adopted May, 1931, by The Poodle Club of America and Approved by The American Kennel Club)

General Appearance.—That of a very active, intelligent, smart, and elegant-looking dog, well built, and carrying himself proudly.

Head.—The head to be long, straight and fine. The skull slightly full and moderately peaked and slightly stopped.

Muzzle.—Long (but not snipy) and strong, not full in the cheeks, teeth white, strong and level, gums black, lips black, and not showing lippiness.

Eyes.—Oval shaped, very dark, full of fire and intelligence.

Nose.—Black and sharp.

Ears.—The leather long and wide, low set, and hanging close to the face.

Neck.—Well proportioned and strong, to admit of the head being carried high and with dignity.

Shoulders.—Strong and muscular, sloping well to the back.

Chest.—Deep and moderately wide.

Back.—Short, strong, and very slightly hollowed, the loins broad and muscular, the ribs well sprung and braced up.

Feet.—Rather small and of good oval shape, the toes well arched and close, pads thick and hard.

Legs.—The forelegs set straight from shoulders with plenty of bone and muscle. Hindlegs very muscular and well bent, with the hocks well let down. (Cowhocks a decided fault.)

Tail.—Set on rather high, well carried, never curled or carried over back.

POODLES

Coat.—For curly poodles: Very profuse, of hard texture, of even length, frizzy or curly, not at all open. For corded poodles: Very thick, hanging in tight even cords.

N.B.—Mustaches, shaving and clipping is optional. But it is strongly recommended that only one-third of the body be clipped or shaved and that the hair on the forehead be left long.

Colors.—Any solid or even color. The White, the Silver, the Blue, the Cream or Apricot, to have dark or black eyes, lips, nose and toe-nails. The Brown and the Red to have dark amber eyes, dark liver nose, lips and toe-nails.

All other points of colored Poodles should be the same as required in a black Poodle.

Sizes.—Poodles (large) to be fifteen inches or over at the shoulder.

POINTS OF THE PERFECT MINIATURE POODLE

Same as large Poodle.
Size.—Under fifteen inches at shoulders.

VALUE OF POINTS

Same as large Poodle.

So long as the dog is definitely a Miniature, diminutiveness is only the deciding factor when all other points are equal; soundness and activity are every whit as necessary in a Miniature as they are in a large Poodle, and as these traits can only be seen when the dog is in action, it is imperative that Miniatures be moved in the ring as fully and decidedly as are large Poodles.

VALUE OF POINTS

General appearance and movement	15
Head and ears	15
Eyes and expression	10
Neck and shoulders	10
Shape of body, loin, back and carriage of stern	15
Legs and feet	10
Coat, color and texture of coat	15
Bone, muscle, and condition	10
Total	100

POODLE

SCHIPPERKE

SCHIPPERKES

(Illustration on opposite page)

(By Courtesy of The Schipperke Club of America)

The Schipperke originated in the Flemish provinces of Belgium and is sometimes erroneously described as a Dutch dog, due no doubt, to popular ignorance as to the location of Flanders, a part of which extends into Northern France, and to the fact that previous to 1832 Belgium and Holland were at times united. Mr. Charles Huge, the Belgian judge, says: "The Schipperke is not derived from the Spitz or Pomeranian but is really a diminutive of the black sheepdog commonly called the 'Leauvenaar' which used to follow the wagons along our old highways in the provinces. The proof of this is that those specimens that are born with a tail carry it like the Groenendael."

About a hundred years ago some of these forty pound sheepdogs were still herding sheep in the neighborhood of Louvain and from these both the Schipperke and the Groenendael have descended. The herd dog was gradually bred larger and the Schipperke bred-down to become that "excellent and faithful" little watch dog that we know. The breed has been known for several hundred years, in fact, it may claim the first known "specialty show," as it might be called, given for any breed. In 1690 a show for the Schipperkes of the Guild workmen was held in the Grand Palace of Brussels; the men were invited to bring their dogs and the hammered brass collars which even at that time custom had ordered for the Schipperke.

The breed was called Spits or Spitske then, the name Schipperke having been given it only after the forming of the specialty club in 1888 when it was chosen as more distinctive, and, as a compliment to Mr. Renssens, known as "the father of the Schipperke," because of his efforts to gain recognition for the breed. He was the owner of a canal boat line operating between Brussels and Antwerp and had observed that there were many Schipperkes used as guards on these boats. The name is Flemish for "little Captain" and is properly pronounced "skeep-er-ker" (the last r almost silent). The name is almost always mispronounced in this country and in England, but the Schipperke Club of America obtained this correct pronunciation from the University of Ghent. Though called a canal boat dog, the Schipperke was as popular with shoemakers and other workmen, as on the canals. The "legend of the Schipperke" relates that the custom of cutting the tails arose in 1609 and tells the story of a shoemaker who, angered by the repeated thieving of his neighbor's dog, cut off his tail—thereby showing the improved appearance soon copied by others and continued to this day. There is no evidence that the breed was ever born tail-less; in fact, it seems that more dogs are born without tails now than fifty or sixty years ago. The Belgian Schipperkes Club has an amusing etching illustrating the legend "The Tail of the Schipperke."

There are few to be found in Holland at present. The canal boat dog of Holland has always been the Keeshond and Holland does not claim the Schipperke. The few Schips shown at Dutch shows are imported from Belgium. Since the war few are to be seen on the Belgian canal boats.

Being a frugal people, the Belgians have bred this

small dog to take up little room, to be exceptionally hardy and to be the keenest and most alert of watch dogs. He is often called "the best house dog"—*le meilleur chien de maison*. The breed is strongly resistant to distemper, has a coat with a close undercoat which can keep them warm even in an American winter, which is far colder than their native land, and sheds water and needs very little attention to keep in order. They have been used to hunt, due to their keen scent and at least one American, Mr. Culbertson, a well known breeder of twenty years ago, wrote that he used them with great success on 'coons and 'possums in Minnesota.

The general appearance is very distinctive, resembling no other breed very closely—a short and thick set body with a foxy head, very intelligent and keen expression, but not at all mean,—rather mischievous, the whole suggesting a dog with plenty of coat and an out-standing ruff and long culotte.

The career of the Schipperke as a fashionable pet began only in 1885 when Queen Marie Henriette, wife of Leopold II, saw a Schipperke at a Brussels show and having acquired it, made the breed fashionable. This popularity it has still retained but before this time the dog had been the companion of the lower classes. The first dog in America was supposed to have been imported in 1888 by Mr. Walter J. Comstock of Providence. A few years later Mr. Frank Dole began showing them in the miscellaneous class. There was a specialty club founded here about 1905 which died out during the war. After 1918 there was little interest until after several years of effort, by a few fanciers, the present Schipperke Club of America was founded in 1929. The Schipperke Club standard insists upon the distinctive ruff and fairly heavy body coat lest the breed degenerate into the "black

NON-SPORTING

wire haired terriers" described by Ashe's dog book as undesirable. The dog must not resemble a small black bullterrier with the tail cut off. While usually an excellent ratter the Schip is not a powerful fighter though he can hold his own with most dogs of his weight and will tackle anything in defense of his household or of his master. He is not aware of the limitations of his size— as Caesar said: "the bravest of these were the Belgians."

"Temperament" is considered important in judging this breed in France and Belgium and means what we in America would call "pep"—a Schip without this is not true to type. A judge of the breed for fifty years has expressed the opinion that the most important thing in judging is the correct silhouette: "I first look to see if the dog has the correct silhouette. If not, he is nothing and I look no further. If he has, I look into further details beginning with the bone structure."

This breed is usually long lived for a small dog, many instances of dogs living to be fifteen and sixteen years old being recorded and one dog, bred in Rothesay, Scotland, was reputed to have lived twenty-one years. They are very fond of children and in some cases have served as guards and taken the place, to some extent, of a human nurse so devoted are they to their small charges.

DESCRIPTION AND STANDARD OF POINTS

(Adopted by The Schipperke Club of America, February 12, 1935, and Approved by The American Kennel Club, March 12, 1935)

The name Schipperke is Flemish for Little Captain and is correctly pronounced Skeeper-ker (last r almost silent). This standard is an interpretation of the standard of the country of the Schipperke's origin—Belgium.

Appearance and General Characteristics.—Excellent and faithful little watchdog, suspicious of strangers. Active, agile, indefatigable, continually occupied with what is going on about him, careful of things that are given him to guard, very kind with children, knows the ways of the household; always curious to know what is going on behind any closed door or about any object that has been moved, betraying his impressions by his sharp bark and upstanding ruff, seeking the company of horses, a hunter of moles and other vermin; can be used to hunt, a good rabbit dog.

Head.—Fox-like, fairly wide, narrowing at the eyes, seen in profile slightly rounded, tapering muzzle not too elongated nor too blunt, not too much stop.

Nose.—Small and black.

Eyes.—Dark brown, small, oval rather than round, neither sunken nor prominent.

Expression.—Should have a questioning expression: sharp and lively, not mean or wild.

Ears.—Very erect, small, triangular, placed high, strong enough not to be capable of being lowered except in line with the body, nearer together at the tips than at the base when erect.

Teeth.—Meeting evenly.

Neck.—Strong and full, slightly arched, rather short.

Shoulders.—Muscular and sloping.

Chest.—Broad and deep in brisket.

Body.—Short, thick set and cobby. Broad behind the shoulders, seeming higher in front because of the ruff. Back strong, short, straight and level or slightly sloping down toward rump. Ribs well sprung.

Loins.—Muscular and well drawn up from the brisket but not to such an extent as to cause a weak and leggy appearance of the hind quarters.

Forelegs.—Straight under the body, with bone in proportion, but not coarse.

Hind Quarters.—Somewhat lighter than the foreparts, but muscular, powerful, with rump well rounded, tail-less (about an inch allowed). Hocks well let down.

Feet.—Small, round and tight (not splayed) nails straight, strong and short.

Coat.—Abundant and slightly harsh to the touch, short on the ears and on the front of legs and on the hocks, fairly short on the body, but longer around neck beginning back of the ears, and forming a ruff and jabot extending down between the front legs, also longer on rear where it forms a culotte the points turning inward. Undercoat dense and short on body, very dense around neck making ruff stand out. Culotte should be as long as the ruff.

Color.—Solid Black.

Weight.—Up to 18 pounds.

Faults.—Light eyes, large round prominent eyes, ears too long or too rounded, narrow head and elongated muzzle, too blunt muzzle, domed skull, smooth short coat with short ruff and culotte, lack of undercoat, curly or silky coat, body coat more than 3 inches long, slightly over or undershot, swayback, bullterrier shaped head, straight hocks.

Disqualifications.—Drop or semi-erect ears. Born with white, (a few white hairs are objected to but are not disqualifying). Badly over or undershot.

LIST OF POINTS IN ORDER OF IMPORTANCE

1. *General Appearance.*—A thick set lively little dog with plenty of coat and outstanding ruff and culotte. Forming an individual silhouette not closely resembling any other breed.

2. *Coat.*—Heavy ruff, standing out, undercoat on body slightly shorter, culotte long as ruff. Slightly harsh.

3. *Head.*—Fox-like with moderate stop. Teeth level.

4. *Expression.*—Keen, questioning, lively, not mean.

5. *Ears.*—Small, erect, triangular.

6. *Eyes.*—Dark brown, oval rather than round, not prominent.

7. *Body.*—Short and thick set. Back level or slightly sloping down toward rump.

8. *Chest.*—Broad and deep.

9. *Hind Quarters.*—Muscular, hocks well bent.

10. *Legs.*—Strong, but rather lightly boned, with small round feet.

11. *Shoulders.*—Muscular and sloping.

12. *Neck.*—Short, arched, rather thick.

Note:—The above in no way alters the standard but is intended as a guide, giving the points in order of merit.

[722]

GLOSSARY OF TECHNICAL TERMS
RELATING TO DOGS

COMPILED BY

VINTON P. BREESE

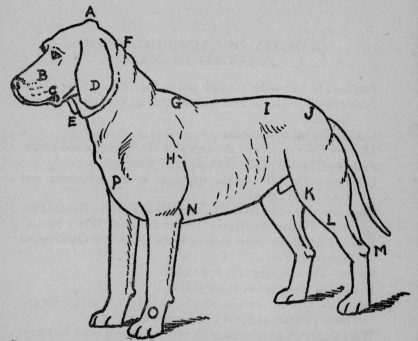

A-Occiput. B-Muzzle. C-Flews. D-Leather. E-Dewlap.
F-Crest. G-Withers. H-Shoulder. I-Loin. J-Rump. K-Stifle.
L-Second Thigh. M-Hock. N-Brisket. O-Pastern. P-Forechest.

GLOSSARY OF TECHNICAL TERMS
RELATING TO DOGS

FRILL—The hair under the neck and on the chest as in the Collie.

FEATHER—The hair or feathering on the legs as in the Setter and Spaniel.

FLAG—The tail of the Setter.

MANE—The hair around the neck as in the Pekingese and Collie.

PLUME—The tail of the Pekingese and Pomeranian.

CULOTTE—The hair on the thighs as in the Schipperke and Pomeranian; breeching.

TOPKNOT—The hair on the top of the head as in the Dandie Dinmont Terrier, Bedlington Terrier and Irish Water Spaniel.

PILE—Thick dense under coat as in the Collie and Old English Sheepdog; Piley.

STERN—The tail, especially in hounds.

BRUSH—A bushy tail as in the Collie.

DOUBLE COAT—A dense woolly under jacket and longer harsher outer covering as in the Old English Sheepdog.

WIRE COAT—A double coat with very hard dense outer hair as in the Wire Fox Terrier.

STAND-OFF COAT—A long, profuse coat with the hair standing straight out from the body as in the Pomeranian and Chow.

SMOOTH COAT—Short, hard, close fitting hair.

BRINDLE—An even and equal mixture and distribution of composite colors.

TIGER BRINDLE—The same with the darker color describing stripes.

WHEATEN—A pale yellowish or fawn color.

GRIZZLE—A bluish grey color.

MERLE—A bluish grey color often occurring with black, tan and white as in the Blue Merle Collie.

GLOSSARY OF TERMS RELATING TO DOGS

TRI-COLOR—Black, tan and white.

HARLEQUIN—Patched and spotted, particularly relating to the black markings and white field in the Harlequin Great Dane.

PIED—Large patches of two or more colors, piebald, parti-colored.

PARTI-COLORED—Variegated in two or more colors.

SABLE—Outer coat shaded with black over a lighter under color as in the Sable Collie.

HOUND-MARKED—Black, tan and white.

PENCILLING—The black marks or stripes dividing the tan on the toes of the Manchester Terrier.

THUMB MARKS—The round black spots on the tan pasterns of the Manchester Terrier.

BREECHING—The tan-colored hair on the inside and back thighs of the Manchester Terrier. Also relates to a profusion of hair on the thighs; culotte.

TRACE—The dark stripe down the back of the Pug.

FOUL COLOR—Any color not characteristic of a breed as mouse marking in a Harlequin Great Dane or black in a Bulldog.

LAYBACK—Receding nose as in the Bulldog and accompanied by undershot jaws.

UPSWEEP—Upturning underjaw as in the Bulldog.

Frog Face.

FROG FACE—Extending nose and receding jaw, usually overshot, especially relating to short-faced breeds.

GLOSSARY OF TERMS RELATING TO DOGS

Overshot.

OVERSHOT—The upper jaw protruding beyond the lower jaw; overhung, pig jaw.

Undershot.

UNDERSHOT—The opposite of overshot; underhung.

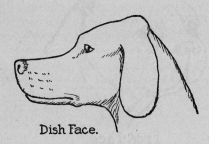

Dish Face.

DISH FACE—The nose turned up and the face hollowed out before the eyes.

[727]

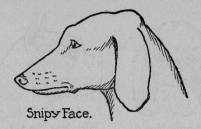

Snipy Face.

SNIPY—A too sharply pointed, narrow or weak muzzle.

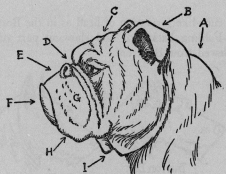

A-Crest. B-Rose Ear. C-Wrinkle.
D-Stop. E-Layback. F-Upsweep.
G-Cushion. H-Flews. I-Dewlap.

CUSHION—Fullness of the foreface or top lips as in the Bulldog.

FLEWS—The lips, especially referring to the more pendulous lipped breeds as the Bulldog and Bloodhound.

CHOPS—Same as flews also relating to the foreface of the Bulldog.

SHELFY—A flat underjaw, especially relating to a Bulldog lacking upsweep.

DEWLAP—The loose skin under the throat.

THROATY—An excess of loose skin under the throat.

LEATHER—The ears, especially in Foxhounds.

CHEEKY—Pronounced development of cheeks as in the Bulldog.

OCCIPUT—The bony bump on the top skull between the ears; pronounced in Setters, Pointers and Hounds.

BURR—The irregular inside formation of the ear.

STOP—The step from the top skull to the foreface.

Apple Head.   **Blocky Head.**

APPLE HEAD—A domed or round skull, pronounced in the Toy Spaniel.

BLOCKY—A cube-like formation of head as in the Boston Terrier.

ROSE EAR—Folding backward and showing part of the inside when viewed from the front.

Button Ear.   **Prick Ear.**

BUTTON EAR—Folding forward close to the skull and pointing toward the eye as in the Fox Terrier.

PRICK EAR—Carried stiffly erect.

TULIP EAR—Carried erect with slight forward curvature.

Semi Prick Ear.

SEMI-PRICK EAR—Carried erect with the tips folding forward and downward as in the Collie.

[729]

GLOSSARY OF TERMS RELATING TO DOGS

WRINKLE—Loose folding skin over the skull and around the fore-face as in the Bulldog and Bloodhound.

BROKEN-UP FACE—Refers particularly to the face of the Bull-dog, Toy Spaniel and Pekingese and includes receding nose, projecting jaw, deep stop and wrinkle.

MASK—The dark colored muzzle particularly of the Pug and Mastiff.

FURROW—The indentation down the center of the top skull from occiput to stop; pronounced in the Bulldog.

WALL EYE—A blue or blue mottled eye frequently found in Blue Merle Collies; watch eye.

HAW—The red membrane inside the lower eyelid; pronounced in the Bloodhound and Saint Bernard.

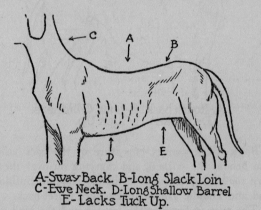

A-Sway Back. B-Long Slack Loin
C-Ewe Neck. D-Long Shallow Barrel
E-Lacks Tuck Up.

SWAY BACK—Showing a concave curvature from the withers to the hips.

EWE NECK—Showing a concave curvature of the top line of neck.

[730]

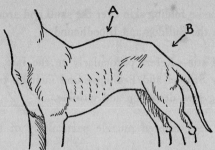

A-Camel Back. B-Goose Rump.

CAMEL BACK—The opposite of sway back.
GOOSE RUMP—Falling off too abruptly from the top of the hips backward.

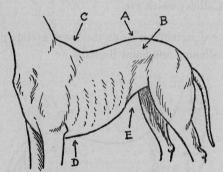

A-Roach Back. B-Loin. C-Withers.
D-Brisket. E-Tuck Up.

ROACH BACK—The convex curvature of the back rising gently from behind the withers and carrying on over the loins and down the hind quarters as in the Greyhound, Bulldog, Dachshund and Dandie Dinmont Terrier; wheel-back.
LOINS—The portion between the last rib and the hind quarters.
WITHERS—The point at the top of the shoulder blades where the neck joins the body.
BRISKET—The chest between and just back of the forelegs.
TUCK-UP—The belly tucked up under the loins as in the Greyhound; small waisted.

[731]

Ring Tail.   Sickle Tail.

RING TAIL—Describing almost or a complete circle.

SICKLE TAIL—Describing a semicircle.

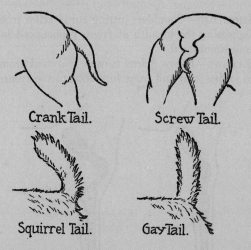

Crank Tail.   Screw Tail.

Squirrel Tail.   Gay Tail.

CRANK TAIL—Short, resembling a crank handle in shape and also found in the Bulldog; crook tail.

SCREW TAIL—Short, kinky, knotty tail frequently found in the Bulldog and Boston Terrier.

SQUIRREL TAIL—Curving forward over the back.

GAY TAIL—Carried erect.

WHIP TAIL—Stiffly straight, pronounced in the Pointer.

TWIST—The curled tail of the Pug.

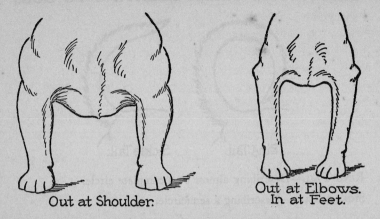

Out at Shoulder.

Out at Elbows.
In at Feet.

OUT AT SHOULDER—Shoulders jutting out in relief from the body and increasing the breadth of front, pronounced in the Bulldog; out-shouldered.

OUT AT ELBOWS—Elbow joints turning outward from the body due to faulty joint and front formation; loose-fronted.

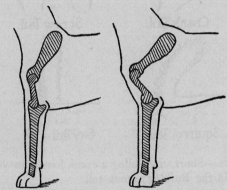

Straight Shoulder   Sloping Shoulder.

STRAIGHT SHOULDER—Lacking sufficient angulation of the bony structure instead of oblique formation; not laid back; up-shouldered.

SLOPING SHOULDER—Angulated obliquely and laid back.

IN SHOULDERED—Narrow fronted, forelegs too close together.

[733]

GLOSSARY OF TERMS RELATING TO DOGS

FLAT SIDED—Flat ribs.

SPRING—Rounded or well sprung ribs.

BEEFY—Big, beefy hind quarters.

CLOSE-COUPLED—Short in loins and back.

HEIGHT—The vertical measurement from ground to withers or top of shoulder-blades.

CLODDY—Low, thick-set stature.

COBBY—Compact build.

RACY—Elongated in legs and body and slight in build as the Whippet and Greyhound.

RANGY—Elongated but indicating more substance than racy.

REACHY—Forefeet and hindfeet far apart, covering considerable area; long neck as in the Greyhound.

CORKY—Compact and active.

SHELLY—Lacking bone and substance; shallow narrow body.

FRONT—The fore part of the chest and forelegs.

Fiddle Front.

FIDDLE FRONT—Crooked or bandy forelegs; a combination of out at elbows, in at pasterns, out at feet or bent bone.

PASTERN—The foreleg from knee joint to foot.

DOWN IN PASTERN—The pastern showing a pronounced angle and letting down the forelegs proper near to the ground.

ERECT PASTERN—Showing no angle at the knee joint.

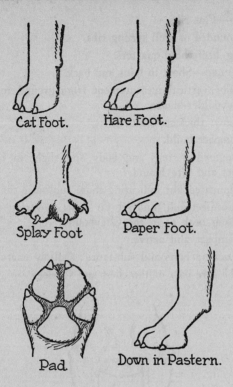

Cat Foot. Hare Foot.

Splay Foot Paper Foot.

Pad Down in Pastern.

PAD—The under portion of the feet.

CAT-FOOT—Short, round, deep and compact like that of a cat.

HARE-FOOT—Long, deep and close-toed like that of a hare.

SPLAY-FOOT—Spreading, open toes.

PAPER-FOOT—Pads too thin.

STIFLE—The upper or thigh joint of the hindleg.

SECOND THIGH—The muscular development between the stifle joint and the hock.

HOCK—The lower joint of the hindleg.

[735]

COWHOCK—Hocks turned inward like those of a cow.

STRAIGHT HOCKS—Erect, lacking bend or angulation.

HOCKY—Used to designate faulty hocks.

DEWCLAWS—Superfluous claw inside the hindleg just above the foot.

TIMBER—Bone.

LUMBER—Superfluous flesh.

BOSSY—Over development of shoulder muscles.

ANGULATION—The angles of the bony structure at the joints.

ARTICULATION—The joints or junctures of the bones.

CHARACTER—A combination of points of appearance and disposition contributing to the whole and distinctive of the particular breed of dog.

EXPRESSION—A combination of color, size and placement of eye together with countenance distinctive of the particular breed of dog.

VARMINT EXPRESSION—Rather small, dark, beady eyes showing no haw nor white, set about horizontal as in the Fox Terrier and having a keen piercing look.

ALMOND EYE—Rather a small three-cornered or slit-shaped eye set obliquely with the outer corners pointing toward the ears particularly in the Bull Terrier.

DUDLEY NOSE—A flesh-colored or yellowish nose usually accompanied by light eyes; a disqualification in some breeds.

CREST—The upper arched part of the neck, particularly in the Bulldog.

UP FACE—The entire muzzle tilting upward as in the Bulldog.

DOWN FACE—The entire muzzle tilting downward.

BUTTERFLY-NOSE—A parti-colored nose.

BAT-EAR—Ears rounded at the tip and shaped like those of a bat and held erect.

SPREAD—The width between the forelegs as in the Bulldog.

INDEX

INDEX

INDEX

INDEX

INDEX

INDEX

[743]

INDEX

INDEX

[745]

INDEX

INDEX

INDEX

INDEX

Boots. Oct 29./39

Boots . 5/27/40
Boots 11/29/40.
Boots 7/14/41
Boots 7/24/43
Boots 1/1/46